THE BALTIC WORLD
1772–1993

THE BALTIC WORLD 1772–1993

Europe's Northern Periphery in an Age of Change

David Kirby

Longman
London and New York

Longman Group Limited
Longman House, Burnt Mill
Harlow, Essex CM20 2JE, England
and Associated Companies throughout the world.

Published in the United States of America
by Longman Publishing, New York

First published 1995

ISBN 0 582 00408 X CSD
ISBN 0 582 00409 8 PPR

British Library Cataloguing-in-Publication Data

A catalogue record for this book is
available from the British Library

Library of Congress Cataloging-in-Publication Data

Kirby, D.G.
The Baltic World 1772–1993 : Europe's northern periphery in an age of change / David Kirby.
p. cm.
Includes bibliographical references and index.
ISBN 0-582-00408-X (CSD) : £16.99 (est.). -- ISBN 0-582-00409-8 (PPR) : £42.00 (est.)
1. Baltic States--History. I. Title.
DK502.7.K57 1995
947'.407--dc20 94-22617
CIP
AC

Set by 7B in 10/12pt Bembo
Produced by Longman Singapore Publishers (Pte) Ltd.
Printed in Singapore

Contents

List of Maps

INTRODUCTION

Northern Europe, Eastern Europe: Some Historical and Contemporary Perspectives

When I began work on the first of my two volumes charting the history of the Baltic region, the first breezes of change were just beginning to eddy through the fug of forty-odd years of communist misrule in eastern Europe. I completed that volume as the breezes increased to gale force, sweeping away outmoded regimes and shaking to its foundations the seemingly solid edifice of the Soviet Union. As I began writing my second volume in 1991, the Soviet empire itself collapsed, releasing once more into the world of sovereign, independent nations the three Baltic states which had been absorbed into that empire some five decades earlier. No historian can afford to be indifferent to the happenings of his or her own times, and the unfolding of events over the past few years will clearly be reflected in these pages. This introductory essay was originally intended to be a link between my first and second volumes; now, I feel that it should also seek to present some kind of historical perspective of an earlier imperial experience which might be useful in the understanding of contemporary developments. Moralists and optimists might like to believe that history teaches us lessons, though I fear only cynics can draw any joy from that particular adage. Historians feel obliged to make some sort of sense of the past, although if they are wise they will refrain from drawing too many conclusions. But one conclusion cannot be avoided at the present moment: the old terminology of 'eastern' and 'western' Europe is no longer adequate and may indeed hinder future efforts to reshape or redefine a wider European community. In this volume, I hope to examine the prospects for a more balanced regional perspective, pointing up the affinities and shared experiences as well as indicating the obvious differences and connections elsewhere of an area all too often relegated to an ill-defined 'periphery' or – more commonly – split into the political, Cold War categories of 'east' and 'west'.

Definitions are made difficult by the lack of any generally accepted term for the region lying between 21° and 90° longitude and north of 55° latitude. This was not always the case: indeed, this was the precise territorial definition of 'the North' in Daniel Ernst Wagner's nine-volume Nordic history, published between 1778 and 1789. The 'Northern tours' undertaken by gentlemen of leisure usually embraced Poland and Russia, as well as the Scandinavian lands. Journals with the prefatorial adjective '*Nordische*' appeared from Hamburg to St Petersburg (the 'Palmyra of the North'). German patriots such as Ernst Mauritz Arndt and Theodor Körner hailed the Russian forces which swept the Grand Army across Europe as deliverers from the North, and the historian Ranke elevated both Karl XII of Sweden and Peter the Great of Russia to the pantheon of 'Nordic heroes'.[1] This notion of northern Europe derived from antiquity; the septentrional regions were those beyond the boundaries of the western and eastern empires. Hans Lemberg has argued that philological and ethnographical research was partly responsible for the narrowing of the term 'Nordic' to be synonymous with the Scandinavian lands, and for the greater emphasis upon a Slavonic eastern Europe, though clearly, political nationalism considerably hardened these new contours.

This separation of northern from eastern was not, however, to be achieved easily. As the Baltic German writer Julius Eckardt observed in 1869, it left 'a dividing-line between the territories of the Western and Slavic-Eastern peoples, running along the 43° of longitude, a narrow strip of land inhabited by a mixture of peoples of the most diverse kinds . . . a world of its own, whose highly peculiar circumstances are as little known in the western half of Europe as they are in the eastern.'[2] Along this strip of territory, taken into the Russian empire between 1721 and 1809, there existed what Eckardt called an unequal dualism of ruling and subject races, in three distinctive cultural areas: Swedish, German and Polish–Lithuanian. In all three regions, the aristocratic upholders of these cultural traditions were separated from

1. Lemberg H 1985 Zur Entstehung des Osteuropabegriffs im 19. Jahrhundert. Vom 'Norden' zum 'Osten' Europa *Jahrbücher für Geschichte Osteuropas* **33**: 48–91. It may be added that until reorganisation after the Second World War, the British Foreign Office included Russia and Poland in its Northern Department.

2. Eckardt J 1869 *Die baltischen Provinzen Russlands*, Leipzig (reprint edition, Hanover 1971), p. 1.

their spiritual and moral hinterlands. As a dedicated publicist of the cause of one of these cultural aristocracies, Eckardt was especially incensed to discover that whereas the Swedes in Finland and the Poles in Lithuania found an immediate rapport in their spiritual homelands, the Baltic Germans were little more than the whipping-boys for the liberal German press. His collection of essays was in fact part of the cannonade of polemic gunfire which echoed across the dividing-line he had described. Not only were Moscow nationalists such as Yuri Samarin and Mikhail Katkov pressing the historical and cultural claims of Russia in the western borderlands: the protagonists of the indigenous peoples were also beginning to raise their voices. One year before Eckardt's book was published in Leipzig, the Estonian nationalist C. R. Jakobson had proclaimed the coming of Christianity (enforced at the point of the sword by the German knights) as an 'unhappy year' for his people, the beginning of a time of darkness. In St Petersburg, a small group of Latvian intellectuals challenged many of the assumptions of the Baltic German ruling elite in the columns of their short-lived newspaper, *Pēterburgas Avīzes*. And Y. S. Yrjö-Koskinen's Finnish-language textbook on the history of the Finnish people, published in 1869, provoked a leading Finnish–Swedish intellectual to vent his scorn at what he called 'a bold attempt to reconstruct Swedish history to the benefit of one of its provinces', a rejection of the prevailing notion of the civilising mission of Sweden in the eastern periphery.[3]

The revendications and claims of the age of nationalism were to echo across a vast area of Europe which had come under Russian control in the space of less than a century. What early eighteenth-century diplomats had termed the 'balance of the North' was no more. Sweden, the dominant Baltic power in the seventeenth century, was now confined to the Scandinavian peninsula, having taken Norway in 1814 as compensation for the loss of Finland in 1809. The Polish–Lithuanian commonwealth had ceased to exist, its lands, which had extended from the Pomeranian coast to the steppes of the Ukraine, partitioned between Prussia, Austria and Russia. The memory, traditions and images of that commonwealth (*rzeczpospolita*) remained, however, sustained in exile and encouraged by the rapid

3. Jakobson C 1870 *Kolm isamaa kõnet Tartus Wainemuine seltsis*, St Petersburg, pp. 1–29. Estlander C 1905 *Från flydda tider. Uppsatser, skildringar och tal*, Helsingfors, pp. 31–59, for the review of Yrjö-Koskinen's *Oppikirja Suomen kansan historiasta*. The best general overview of these polemics is the introductory chapter by Edward Thaden in Thaden E (ed.) *Russification in the Baltic Provinces and Finland*, 1855–1914, Princeton, NJ, pp. 15–108.

political fluctuations in revolutionary Europe. The destruction of Poland also put an end to any hopes of reforming and revitalising the one state in eastern Europe not ruled by an absolutist or autocratic monarch, and enabled the partitioning powers to fortify themselves against the winds of political change blowing from the west in the era of the French revolution.[4]

Imperial Russia, the principal territorial beneficiary of the partitions, granted a wide measure of autonomy in the grand duchy of Finland (gained from Sweden in 1809) and in the kingdom of Poland (created at the Vienna Congress in 1815). This policy owed less to Alexander I's supposed enthusiasm for constitutionalist experiments than to a desire to ensure peace on the western frontier by confirming the privileges of local ruling elites, much as the landowning aristocracy of the Baltic provinces of Livland, Estland and Ösel continued to enjoy their privileges and to exercise local control according to the terms of their capitulations to Peter the Great in 1710–11. Imperial policy was not without its critics in Russia, nor was it entirely conciliatory. In the former Polish lands, where revolts broke out in 1830 and again in 1863, coercion and the imposition of Russian rule became the order of the day. In Finland and the Baltic provinces, however, the perceived benevolence of the ruler was rewarded with gratitude and loyalty on the part of the ruling elites, for whom the empire also offered an opportunity for social and career advancement. Not until the latter years of the reign of Alexander II (1855–81) in the case of the Baltic provinces, or the reign of Alexander III (1881–94) in the case of Finland, did the relationship begin to turn sour.[5]

No longer a great power in the North, having lost the last of its non-Scandinavian territories during the Napoleonic wars, Sweden had nonetheless to contend with its own nationality problem. The demands of the Norwegians for independent statehood were finally resolved peaceably in 1905, the year of the first Russian revolution. The national conflict in the duchies of Slesvig and Holstein, which assumed serious proportions during the 1840s, had a decisive impact

4. The German historian Michael Müller argues that the subsequent ideological and political division of Europe into a predominantly liberal west and a neo-absolutist east can also be seen as a consequence of the partitions of Poland. Müller M 1984 *Die Teilungen Polens 1772: 1793: 1795*, Munich, pp. 8–9. See also Venturi F *The end of the Old Regime in Europe 1768–1776. The first crisis*, Princeton, NJ, pp. 172–234.

5. See Thaden E 1984 *Russia's Western Borderlands, 1710–1870*, Princeton, NJ. The future republic of Estonia included the historic Baltic provinces of Estland, Ösel and northern Livland: southern Livland and Kurland were included in the republic of Latvia.

on the constitutional and political history of the kingdom of Denmark. Although the future of the duchies was not resolved so easily or amicably as was the dissolution of the union between Sweden and Norway, the Danish government behaved with commendable restraint on the two occasions when the opportunity for territorial readjustment presented itself, after the two world wars of this century. There developed a strong sense of Scandinavian solidarity, even though the bolder vision of the Scandinavists of the mid-nineteenth century remained unfulfilled. The relatively tranquil constitutional and political development of the three northern kingdoms and the impressive economic, cultural and social achievements made during the first half of this century have immeasurably strengthened the 'Scandinavian' image.

The former possessions of the Swedish crown in the eastern Baltic have been fated to pass through stormier seas during the last hundred years. Of the states which emerged on the western frontiers of Soviet Russia in the collapse of empires at the end of the first world war, it was Finland which had the most fully-developed and coherent form of state and national identity. In the long run, it was that which united the Finns as they ensured that the scars of the civil war which erupted at a time of revolutionary upheaval, political uncertainty and social misery would heal, not fester. The eastern marchlands of the Swedish realm which passed under imperial Russian rule in 1809 brought with them firmly-rooted notions of fundamental law, which the emperor saw fit to encourage. Unlike the narrow particularism of the Baltic German provinces, with which the native nationalist movements could never identify, the grand duchy's inheritance from Swedish times proved to be the bedrock of the future Finnish state. The Latvians and Estonians had no experience of embryonic statehood; they rejected almost everything associated with the hateful dominance of the Baltic Germans; and they were also caught up far more intensely than were the Finns in the waves of revolution and war between 1905 and 1918. The Lithuanian nationalists found to their chagrin that the revendications of their Polish counterparts did not diminish, and were, moreover, backed up by military force. The occupation of Vilna by Polish forces in 1920 soured relations between Poland and Lithuania: the occupation of Memel by Lithuanian troops in 1923 may have done something to restore the injured pride of Lithuanian nationalists, but it also stored up more trouble for the future.

In the newly independent Baltic states and Finland, the formerly dominant elites became minorities – as Finlanders, playing an active and fully integrated role in the life of the nation in Finland, but as upholders of Germanness, remaining aloof and distrusted in Latvia and Estonia. The former 'peasant peoples' who now controlled their own destiny in the nation-state not only had to cope with the indifference of the wider world to their continued existence; they were also beset by internal anxieties and threats. The civil war of 1918 split Finnish society asunder. It cast into doubt all the assumptions of a poor but loyal and God-fearing people upon which the 'nationalist idyll' had been based. Democracy survived nevertheless in Finland, and the nation as a whole resisted Soviet aggression in 1939, confounding the fond hopes of the invaders that the oppressed workers would rise up and welcome them. Finland emerged from the maelstrom of war with its sovereign independence intact by virtue of gallant military resistance, and an element of good fortune which enabled the republic to wriggle free of the potentially deadly embrace of alliance with Germany in 1944. The Baltic states were not so fortunate. It is highly unlikely that they could have preserved their independence by resisting Russian demands in 1939. Quite simply, they were too small, too disunited and too near the cruel partners of the Nazi–Soviet pact. They also suffered from their designation as 'Baltic states'. Finland was able to align itself with the Scandinavian countries, and that orientation did produce palpable advantages, during the war and afterwards. The part played by neutral Sweden during the 1940s may not always be acknowledged by its neighbours who suffered the hardships of war and occupation, but it was crucial, nevertheless. The Baltic states, however, remained outside the Nordic ambit, their collective designation masking serious differences of foreign policy orientation and security policy.[6] With no firm links to the wider world, only illusions, they were swallowed into the maw of the Soviet Union, from which they were to emerge some fifty years later.

The restoration of the independence of the Baltic states is a remarkable event in the history of international relations, and offers some hope for the creation of a new regional identity in north-eastern Europe. To date, the three republics have acquitted themselves creditably in the difficult task of maintaining stability whilst at the same time attempting to cast off the shrouds of the past. Not the least of their problems has been the lack of strong foundations upon which to build a new order. States which survive and last are invariably the

6. As is made clear in the essay by Edgar Anderson: The Baltic entente: phantom or reality? in: Vardys V, Misiunas R (eds) 1978 *The Baltic States in Peace and War 1917–1945*, University Park (Penn.) and London, pp. 126–35. See also Hiden J and Salmon P 1991 *The Baltic nations and Europe*, London, pp. 59ff.

creation of strong, well-developed societies. The experience of the lands which came under Russian rule during the eighteenth century was one in which the state was excessively coercive, authoritarian and bureaucratic, and did not provide the necessary stimulus of participatory political activity. There was little or no tradition or experience of fully representative institutions, free and open access to law courts, and above all, of an independent arena in which public opinion could flourish.

It may be argued that this was largely a consequence of re-feudalisation in the sixteenth and seventeenth centuries, and of the devasting effects of war and depopulation. It may also be noted that the towns which were able to band together as the Hanseatic League to protect their commercial interests failed to produce a sustained challenge to the absolutist pretensions of the state as did the towns of the Netherlands in the sixteenth century. Above all, however, the nature of settlement and colonisation of a region on the periphery of an altogether more populous, diverse and dynamic European heartland has played an important part. The colonisers subjugated the autochtonous peoples, albeit in different ways. Those whom nineteenth-century progressives regarded as peoples without a history have indeed had to come to terms with a history not of their making, with customs, traditions and institutional structures they do not always relish, and usually in crisis circumstances. That they have survived and been able to pursue national ambitions is a tribute to their sense of purpose and tenacity; but the deleterious legacy of the colonisers and imperial rulers who have exercised power and control without in any meaningful way involving society at large has been a serious hindrance to their efforts.

The local hegemony of the colonisers acquired an overlay of Imperial Russian rule from the eighteenth century onwards. However, measures intended to bring the western borderlands more firmly under Imperial Russian control were rarely consistent or coordinated. They were often implemented without the necessary resources such as properly-qualified and well-motivated teachers or judges, they were open to abuse at the lowest level and to criticism at the highest. In the end, they succeeded merely in alienating those representatives of the indigenous majority who might otherwise have been reasonably well-disposed towards moves to undermine the powers of the entrenched local elites.

Assimilationist tendencies were by no means confined to the western borderlands of the Russian empire. The small Danish minority in the northern part of the Prussian province of Schleswig-Holstein fought vigorously to preserve their distinctive identity within the German Empire; a much larger Polish population strenuously resisted the determined efforts of successive Prussian and Imperial German ministers to bolster the German presence in West Prussia and Posen. If there is a difference between the national conflicts in the Russian and German empires, however, it might be that in the latter there were more opportunities for the expression of public opinion, which allowed opponents of the existing order to adopt and utilise a range of strategies – legalistic, parliamentary, organisational. With the partial exception of the Finns, who could rely upon their own internal traditions and organisations (though they too were basically unable to carry the fight into the Empire at large), the peoples of the western borderland of the Russian Empire had very little purchase upon their oppressor. There was no national parliament until 1905 in which opposition might be voiced, no widely-read national liberal newspapers in which oppressed minorities might gain a hearing. Imperial Russia was too weak or inept to sweep aside local institutions and replace them with those created by Alexander II's reforms (such as the local assemblies, or *zemstvo*); but the local institutions were often quite inadequate as forums for popular opinion and incapable of producing necessary changes and reforms. The only effective means of challenging the regime was by revolution. Again, the Finns were exceptionally lucky, for their 1905 was peaceful and produced the most democratic (on paper, at least) single-chamber legislature in the world to replace the outmoded four-estate Diet. 1905 in the Baltic provinces ended in a peasant jacquerie and bloody repression. The revolution of 1917 was more successful in destroying the regime, though its consequences were to reverberate for much longer.

The oppressive nature of the Russian state and its seeming inability to embark upon a consistent path of reform without ultimately deviating into coercion and repression has engaged the attention of countless scholars and analysts. It is not my purpose to join this discussion, save only to remark upon what I perceive to be at the heart of the problem with the relationship between that state and the western borderlands, namely that the Russian state itself is inherently unwieldy, potentially unstable and in the last analysis, lacking any truly symbiotic relationship to the societies over which it has spread its control. The peoples of the Baltic states do have traditions of independent organisation and institutions, and a belief in their national destiny which survived the worst impositions of Soviet rule. They may not have the same degree of experience of democracy as their Scandinavian neighbours, but they are better positioned and better equipped to acquire that experience than are the peoples of the massive rump of the Russian state. It is Russia which continues to be the unpredictable element in the Baltic, a region in which it has wielded a powerful influence for the past two hundred years, and will in all likelihood continue to do so. One can only hope that a more democratic Russia will be able to make a more positive and constructive contribution in the Baltic region than its predecessors.

As my previous volume was dominated by Sweden, the great power in the Baltic region for much of that period, so will this be dominated by the Russian and Soviet empires, albeit seen from a peripheral perspective. That periphery will stretch beyond the Gulf of Bothnia to include the Scandinavian kingdoms (though Norway will once more have to occupy a very marginal position), and will also take in the northern margins of another empire, created by Prussian force of arms in 1871.

The book is divided into two parts. The first covers a period in which the Russian empire dominated the Baltic region – a century of major territorial changes, and considerable technological advances, both of which greatly affected the lives of all Europeans. The second part deals with the collapse of empires and the emergence of new national states in the aftermath of the First World War, and their subsequent fate as Russian hegemonic claims in the region were revived by the Soviet Union during and after the Second World War. The less dramatic course of Swedish and Danish history runs as an integral element throughout the book. Rather than cover ground already trodden by a wide range of surveys and more detailed mongraphs in English, I have preferred to explore areas and aspects for which the English reader is less well served. Place names in Part One are given in Swedish (for Finland) and German (for the Baltic provinces and the Prussian lands); in Part Two, they are given as far as possible in the appropriate national language: thus, Reval becomes Tallinn, Helsingfors becomes Helsinki, and so on. Both variants are given in the index. I have exercised the judgement of Solomon over the duchies, using the Danish Slesvig and the German Holstein (but referring to the single province created by the Prussian state as Schleswig-Holstein).

The publishers would like to thank the Trustees of the Tenth Duke of Northumberland deceased for granting permission to publish copyright material.

PART ONE

The Age of Empire

CHAPTER ONE

Sturm und Drang: The Baltic in an Age of Revolution, 1772–1815

STORMCLOUDS

The long series of wars which had been fought in Europe and overseas in the middle of the eighteenth century had cruelly exposed the military and financial weaknesses of many governments. The wars were followed by a period of considerable political turmoil, the beginnings of the age of democratic revolution according to R. R. Palmer, and of the 'first crisis' of the old regime according to Franco Venturi. Indeed, Venturi believes that 'the first links of the long chain' of reforms, revolutions, rebellions and repressions which brought about the collapse of the old regime are to be sought not in the capitals of the West or the heartland of Europe, but on the margins of the continent.[1] This bold assertion is open to dispute. As this and subsequent chapters will attempt to show, the 'old regimes' of northern Europe proved quite adept at surviving and adapting, and it is the degree of continuity rather than of change which is often the more striking feature of nineteenth-century Swedish (and more especially, Finnish) or Danish history. It was possible for systems of government to adapt because there was always present in the Scandinavian lands that element of social and political consensus which

1. Palmer R 1959 *The age of the democratic revolution: 1 The challenge*, Princeton, NJ. Venturi F 1989 *The end of the old regime in Europe 1768–1776. The first crisis*, Princeton, NJ, p. ix. This is a translation by R. Burr Litchfield of the third volume of Venturi's *Settecento riformatore*, which was published in 1979. Developments in Northern Europe in the 1760s are treated in Chapters 13 and 14 of my previous volume, *Northern Europe in the early modern period: The Baltic world 1492–1772*, London, 1990.

enabled reforms to be carried through in a manner which built upon the traditions and laws of the past, and which was strong enough to steer the state through sudden crisis. This consensus was noticeably lacking in the doomed Polish-Lithuanian commonwealth and in the expanding Russian empire, and it was not very evident either within the shifting boundaries of the kingdom of Prussia.

Of the northern kingdoms, it was the Prussia of Frederick the Great which seemed most aptly to exemplify the well-ordered, enlightened absolutist state in the pre-revolutionary era; and yet within a generation the edifice had been shattered by military defeat. The collapse of the Frederician state was primarily the result of weaknesses in the military system upon which it had been founded, but it also revealed for all to see the brittleness of an authoritarian system which rested on coercion, and not consensus. The monarchical absolutism laid down in the Danish Royal Law of 1665 proved to be more resilient, surviving the embarrassment of a mentally incapable (and cuckolded) king, Christian VII (1766–1808), the bombardment of Copenhagen by the British Royal Navy in 1807, and the loss of Norway in 1814. Absolutism in Denmark was formally brought to an end not by revolution, but by tacit agreement, in 1848. From 1784, when the sixteen-year old Crown Prince Frederik managed to overthrow the conservative regime which had prevailed since the downfall of the Struensee faction in 1772, the system was run by enlightened members of distinguished families, whose reforming enthusiasm helped transform Danish rural society.

The period of reform stretched over thirty years: the educational reform of 1814, which introduced compulsory schooling for children from the age of seven until confirmation, had been in the making since 1789, whilst the Great Land Commission set up in 1786 was not finally wound up until 1816. The main measures which emancipated the peasantry of Denmark were nevertheless set in train during the initial period of reform. The law of 1787 guaranteed the rights of tenants on private estates and forbade their landlords to inflict cruel punishments. One year later, the decree of 1733 binding peasants to the land (*Stavnsbaand*) was rescinded and a new system of recruiting for the army adopted. Further legislation established the principle of life tenancies and stipulated that the amount and nature of labour services should be fixed, with government mediation if agreement could not be reached. Enclosure of the land proceeded rapidly, and by 1837 only one per cent of agricultural land was still held in common. This also meant the end of the old, informal village government, which was replaced by the commune and its elected officials; and the new social and economic distinctions between prosperous freehold farmers and the impoverished rural proletariat were subtly revealed in the provisions of the 1803 poor law.[2]

The reforms were by no means universally welcomed. Count A. P. Bernstorff encountered tough opposition from the more conservative members of the Great Land Commission, and had to rely more than once on the support of the crown prince to push measures through. The peasants who, like the travelling companion of the narrator of C. Olufsen's poem *Resen* (The Journey, 1791), were full of talk about liberty 'and the times we live in', aroused great alarm amongst the landowners. A hundred and three such gentlemen from Jutland in 1790 warned the crown prince of the growing insolence of the peasantry and their diminishing lack of respect for authority, with a not too subtle allusion to what was going on in France.[3] Although the government made it clear that it would not tolerate stiff-necked opposition from the landowners, it was not prepared to concede reforms which would have done away with the landlord's right to exercise discipline over his tenants, nor did it favour the abolition of labour services. Bernstorff's approach to land reform in the duchies of Slesvig and Holstein (where the first moves towards change had been taken in the 1760s) was cautious, and it was not until several years after his death that serfdom here was finally abolished (1805).

The more humane and enlightened attitude towards the peasantry which began to spread amongst the landowning classes in Denmark and the duchies helped create a favourable climate for reform, though Bernstorff and the reform-minded members of the numerous commissions also had to perform a balancing act between the competing demands of social justice, property rights and the needs of the state.[4] In spite of, or perhaps because of the reforms, the principles of absolutism laid down in the latter half of the seventeenth century remained undisturbed. There were no demands for a revival of the estates-general in Denmark, still less any talk of constituent or

2. Details of these reforms are given in Hovde B 1943 *The Scandinavian countries 1720–1865* 2 vols, Ithaca NY, vol. 1 and Barton A 1986 *Scandinavia in the revolutionary era 1760–1815*, Minneapolis. The social and economic consequences of the reforms will be considered in more detail in Chapter 2.

3. Bjørn C 1981 *Bonde-Herremand-Konge. Bonde i 1700-tallets Danmark*, Copenhagen, pp. 33, 151.

4. Mary Wollstonecraft, who spent four months in Scandinavia in 1795, was of the opinion that Bernstorff was 'more anxious not to do wrong, that is to avoid blame, than desirous of doing good'. Wollstonecraft M 1796 *Letters written during a short residence in Sweden, Norway and Denmark*, London, p. 228.

legislative assemblies and foreign visitors were struck by the fierce loyalty and patriotism of the Danes they encountered and the paradox of the liberal atmosphere of enlightened reform existing under the canopy of absolutism.[5]

The outward benevolent calm of Denmark was in sharp contrast to the mood of disillusionment and discontent which descended upon Sweden in the 1780s. Gustav III's bloodless coup in 1772 had been generally welcomed as a necessary corrective to party strife which had threatened to get out of hand and drag the country down to the same level as Poland. Gustav himself declared that he had nobly refrained from exercising absolute authority. The Form of Government which was issued shortly after the coup dutifully spelled out the rights of the State Council (*Riksrådet*) to be consulted, and of the four estates of the Diet (*Riksdag*) to consent to taxation and the waging of an offensive war: but it was apparent that the balance had swung decisively towards royal power, prompting a number of contemporaries from Catherine II of Russia to the Abbé Raynal to believe it opened up the way to despotism.[6]

Although inclined to confuse the important and the trivial – trying to deal at the same time with Catherine II's conquest of the Crimea and the actress Siri Brahe's dresses and giving orders concerning matters of state and dinners in the same breath, as one adviser unkindly revealed after the king's death – Gustav nevertheless played an active role in the affairs of state, and a number of important reforms and investigations were set in motion. The currency was placed on a more secure footing, something was done about civil servants' pay, and the gradual relaxation of tariffs and restrictions on trade begun in the 1760s was continued. Torture was abolished and the number of capital offences was reduced. Religious toleration for non-Lutheran Christians was introduced to encourage immigration, against the objections of the estate of clergy and at least one peasant who complained that 'we can never consent to this, for then the country would be swarming with rogues and gypsies and other riff-raff, who

5. As did Mary Wollstonecraft, though her observations were largely confined to Norway. A Scot, stranded in Denmark shortly after the British bombardment of Copenhagen, found the Danes (not surprisingly) very touchy on patriotic matters: McDonald J 1810 *Travels through Denmark and part of Sweden during the winter and spring of the year 1809*, London, p. 23 *passim*. See also Venturi 1989, pp. 235–78, and the chapter on Denmark by Ole Feldbæk in Dann O and Dinwiddy J 1988 *Nationalism in the age of the French Revolution*, London, pp. 87–100.

6. Barton 1986, pp. 82–4. Venturi 1989, pp. 325–39, for foreign reactions.

are the greatest nuisance for the common folk'.[7] The law on the freedom of the press was however more restrictive than that of 1766, and a number of measures to promote agriculture – especially the creation of a crown monopoly over distillation – were widely unpopular.

The peasants may have grumbled about that monopoly, which was in fact abandoned in 1786, and the restrictions upon their landholdings, but they remained loyal to the king. It was in the ranks of the nobility that the spirit of opposition revived, surfacing in the *Riksdag* of 1778. Press censorship and Gustav's own somewhat erratic character kept the rumour mills busy in the capital. In the eastern provinces of Finland, twice overrun and occupied by Russian forces in the space of seventy years, there was talk of Gustav III having agreed to hand over Finland to Catherine II of Russia in return for assistance in wresting Norway from Denmark. Although the local authorities tried to play down the extent of this disaffection, it is clear that there was a small core of malcontents who were at least considering the alternative of seeking independent status for Finland in preference to Russian subjugation. At the heart of these conspirations was the redoubtable figure of Göran Magnus Sprengtporten. This ardent supporter of the royal coup in 1772 had broken with the king in 1778, and entered Russian service in 1786. Before his departure, however, he had presented a plan for the separation of Finland from Sweden to the Russian ambassador to The Hague, and had also drafted a constitution for Finland. There were no stirring phrases about the rights of man in Sprengtporten's draft, which was basically a reiteration of the ideals of Swedish aristocratic constitutionalism. The one novel feature, perhaps drawn from Sprengtporten's abortive involvement in Dutch affairs, was that the Finnish republic was to be a federal union, with each province having its own four-estate annual assembly and electing a congress. Congress (which in its composition resembled the Secret Committee of the *Riksdag* during the Age of Liberty) was to be responsible to the national parliament and was to appoint life-term ministers to the State Council.

'That Sprengtporten in truth worked for Finnish independence I know from his own mouth', Professor Henrik Porthan, a leading luminary of intellectual life in the Finnish university town of Åbo,

7. Cited in Hennings B 1957 *Gustav III*, Stockholm, p. 70. Not even copious amounts of food and drink supplied by the secretary of the peasants' estate, assisted by the poet and avowed friend of Bacchus, C. M. Bellman, could entirely win over the suspicious *allmoge*.

later remarked; 'but I believe that with the exception of a few madcap adventurers, he found no adherents'. J. A. Ehrenström, a former close associate of Sprengtporten, considered his support was limited to army officers with whom he had served for a number of years in the isolated frontier region of Savo in eastern Finland.[8] The chancery-president, Gustav Filip Creutz, was inclined to discount the possibility of Sprengtporten winning over the king's brother Carl to his cause, but he was aware that growing discontent in Finland as a result of new impositions and the way in which the land redistribution (*storskiftet*) was being carried out might cause unrest and encourage the Russians to intervene. The king himself appears to have believed that the situation in Finland was much better than that painted by the rumour-mongers, though he did act quickly in response to this warning, ordering suspension of the land redistribution on 25 April 1784.[9]

The rumour that Gustav III intended to abandon Finland in favour of compensation in Norway was not entirely groundless. The king had indeed long toyed with the idea of seizing Norway, and tried to take advantage of the Russian plans to annex the Crimea in 1783 to persuade Catherine II to back him. Catherine preferred to maintain an alliance of the three northern powers to counter Bourbon France, and her success in the Crimea a year later obliged Gustav to abandon his idea. It was his meeting in Fredrikshamn with the empress which had sparked off the rumours that Finland was about to be handed over to the Russians. The defence instructions of 1785, which would have abandoned much of the eastern frontier region in the event of a Russian attack, angered officers with estates in the region, though the instructions were rescinded by the king two years later. The renewal of the Russo-Turkish war in 1787 prompted Gustav to push forward the idea of an alliance including Denmark directed against Russia. Count Bernstorff did not however succumb to the personal charm of the Swedish king, who paid him a surprise visit in Copenhagen, nor was Gustav any more successful in securing an alliance and subsidies

8. Grotenfelt K 1911 H. G. Porthanin mielipide 1788–1790 vuosien sodasta *Historiallinen Arkisto* **22**: 1. Cederberg A 1932 Johan Albert Ehrenströmin kirjallista jäämistöä vuosilta 1787–1789 *Historiallinen Arkisto* **39**: 119, 121. An unknown Swedish contemporary dismissed Sprengtporten's influence altogether: Alanen A 1964 *Suomen historia kustavilaisella ajalla*, Porvoo-Helsinki, p. 386.

9. v Törne P 1936 'Oron' i Finland 1783–1784 *Historisk Tidskrift för Finland* **21**: 142–72. Lesch B 1938 Stämningar och strävanden i Finland vid tiden inför Gustav IIIs italienska resa *Skrifter utgivna av Svenska Litteratursällskapet i Finland* **265:** 338–45. In general, Swedish-speaking Finnish historians have tended to downplay the scope and extent of separatism in Finland: see Lesch B 1941 *Jan Anders Jägerhorn* Skrifter utgivna av Svenska Litteraturssällskapet i Finland **288**: 95–153.

from the British. By March 1788, he had decided to go it alone and an exchange of shots on the frontier in June provided the excuse to launch an attack on Russia.

The time for an attack on Russia was not unpropitious, since the bulk of Catherine's forces were tied up in the war against the Turks. However, the Russian fleet destined for the Mediterranean had not yet left the Baltic, and this proved decisive. The king's military plan had hinged upon Sweden obtaining naval superiority in the Gulf of Finland; but although the Swedes obtained a slight advantage in the naval battle off Hogland on 17 July, they were not able to compel the Russians to retire to Kronstadt. The advance of the army on the fortified town of Fredrikshamn was suddenly abandoned, and the main forces of the army withdrew to the village of Liikkala. There now followed an extraordinary sequence of events. Even before the war had begun, there had been rumours of secret negotiations between Sprengtporten and his sympathisers in the Finnish army. According to one eye-witness, the whole war enterprise was perceived as a desperate gamble by the king to restore his wavering authority; to frustrate this endeavour, the commanders of the armed forces would refuse to cross the frontier and would get rid of the king with Russian assistance.[10] The ignominious retreat of the army and news of further naval setbacks seem to have driven the king to the edge of despair. He contemplated abdication, and eagerly sought to make peace with Russia. Gustav's pathetic attempts to extricate himself from a disastrous war may have persuaded some officers to go along with the proposal to address an appeal from the army to the empress Catherine, though the moving spirits behind this idea were primarily animated by dislike of Gustav III and a desire either to restore the pre-1772 system or to secure a separate status for Finland. The note drafted in the camp at Liikkala on 9 August was breathtaking in its political naivety. The commander and six leading officers of the Finnish forces who signed

10. Ekman C 1900 Dagbok förd under kriget i Finland 1788–1790 *Skrifter utgivna av Svenska Litteratursällskapet i Finland* **44**: 15–16. Ekman, born in Sweden, was attached to the Åbo infantry regiment. His diary offers a compelling day-by-day account of events, seen from a royalist perspective. On 29 July, ten days after the river Kymi frontier had been crossed, he reflected (p. 28): 'There is a strange mood in the corps; the step taken by the king is regarded as highly illegal, his noble favourites are seen as traitors whose blood should flow, the Russian should be appealed to for assistance in dethroning the king, Finland should be independent, all this for the felicity and honour of the nation, for thereby the whole world would see that the Swede knows how to guard his rights.' This mood seems to have been all-pervasive, and those who held a contrary opinion could only look to divine intervention to get them out of their difficulties.

the note claimed that they had only realised before the walls of Fredrikshamn that the invasion was 'in conflict with the rights of the nation' (i.e. in breach of the 1772 constitution, which required the consent of the estates for an offensive war). Indicating that the blame for the war lay with the king's favourites and advisers, they suggested to the empress that the best guarantee of peace would be the restoration of the Swedish-Russian frontier of 1721. Finally, the highly unreliable Major Anders Jägerhorn, who had played a leading role in the composition of the note, was entrusted with the task of conveying it to the empress.

Not surprisingly, the Imperial State Council was reluctant to consider these proposals seriously, though it realised the usefulness of keeping the Swedish-Finnish army in a state of mutiny. The reply – which Catherine was careful not to sign – sought to play upon Finnish separatist feelings. It suggested that a representative assembly of the Finnish nation should empower delegates to negotiate. Nothing was said about the restoration of territory. Finnish troops were urged to withdraw beyond the frontier, but since it was unlikely that the king would follow suit, the reply continued, it might be necessary for Russian forces to invade Finland. Fervent assurances of the benevolence and goodwill of the empress towards the Finnish nation did little to assuage the conspirators, who had in the meantime formed a confederation in Anjala in response to the king's demand that all officers of the Finnish army sign an oath to fight to the last man to defend the realm against its enemies.[11] A number of the leading confederates now began to try and disengage themselves, whilst others sought to win over the king's brother. All ideas of Finnish independence, noted an officer in his diary on 25 August, were now abandoned, and the confederates began pressing for a *Riksdag* as a way out of the impasse.[12]

The idea of Finnish independence was well and truly buried in the army, though in truth it had probably never carried much weight beyond a small circle of officers. It was the policies of the king, not

11. Alanen 1964, pp. 370–96. Lesch 1941, pp. 189–226. Odhner C 1905 *Sveriges politiska historia under konung Gustaf III:s regering*, Stockholm, vol. 3:1, pp. 134–60. The statement drafted by the Anjala confederates, and signed by 113 officers, sought to justify the peace initiative on the grounds that an offensive war had been undertaken without the consent of the Swedish estates, in breach of the 1772 constitution, but promised nevertheless that, in the event of the empress not agreeing to an honourable peace, the signatories would fight to the death to defend the fatherland.

12. Ekman 1900, p. 66. Odhner 1905, pp. 159–60.

the separatist wishes of a few Finnish gentlemen, which had caused unrest and discontent. The situation in eastern Finland remained tense, however. Rumours and pamphlets continued to circulate after the king's departure for Sweden at the end of August. Jägerhorn was active in arranging numerous secret meetings along the frontier, and a memorial supposedly signed by thirty-three Finnish noblemen proposed an independent Finland under Russian protection. In November 1788, the king felt secure enough to order the arrest of the leading conspirators (one of whom was eventually executed).[13] The royal proclamation issued to the Finnish people in December urged them to ponder the sad fate of other borderlands of Russia (Kurland, Poland and the Crimea) and of their former fellow-countrymen, whom an unhappy peace (in 1721 and again in 1743) had consigned to the enemy. Such allusions were probably unnecessary. The activities of the noble malcontents found few sympathisers amongst the non-noble estates. In spite of inadequate clothing and equipment – Professor Porthan recalled seeing troops begging on the streets of Åbo for socks and scarves to keep them warm in the winter of 1789 – the land forces in Finland succeeded in repelling Russian attacks in 1789. At sea, the Swedish fleet obtained a significant success at Svensksund on 7 July 1790, enabling Gustav to make an honourable peace at Värälä. The 1743 frontier remained unchanged, but there was no clause in the peace treaty entitling Russia to interfere in Swedish affairs as the would-be guarantor of the constitution, as had been the case in the peace of Nystad in 1721.

It cannot be said that the events of 1788 reflect much credit either on the king or upon his aristocratic opponents. The military incompetence of the king was more than matched by the clumsy politicking of his officer corps, who made themselves vulnerable by choosing to negotiate separately with the Russians, entrusting an ill-concocted, highly circumlocutory note to a born intriguer whose own motives are still unclear. Whether Jägerhorn did or did not pursue the Sprengtportian ideal of Finnish independence in his talks in Russia during August 1788 is, in any event, of secondary importance. The fact is that his advent offered the hard-pressed empress a golden opportunity to weaken her enemy: and as Bruno Lesch pointedly reminded Finnish nationalist historians in 1941, the idea of an

13. Odhner 1905, pp. 259–60, 269–71. Lesch 1941, pp. 260–92, 345–88, 405–17. One member of the Finnish delegation to St Petersburg in 1809 described Jägerhorn as a born project-maker – an apt description.

independent Finland was Russian in origin.[14] Catherine II's letter to Sprengtporten on 6 September 1788, in which she urged the necessity of the convention of the Finnish estates under Russian protection, was a direct echo of the Empress Elizabeth's manifesto of 1742. In 1742, the Finnish estates not only had to come to terms with renewed Russian occupation; they were also uncertain about the succession to the childless King Fredrik I. Neither circumstance obtained in 1788. Catherine's encouragement of Finnish separatism simply sowed confusion in the ranks of the confederates, whilst her incitement of the Danes to join in the war enabled Gustav to appeal to Swedish patriotism and confound his enemies.[15]

Gustav was thus able to turn near-disaster into personal triumph over his enemies in 1789. The estates were summoned to meet early in the new year. When the nobility objected to the king's proposal to set up a secret committee drawn from all four estates 'to consider and agree upon the means and ways which are to be adopted in the present circumstances of the realm for the preservation of the security, existence and independence of the realm', Gustav began urging the peasants to demand privileges for the non-noble estates. At a session of all four estates on 17 February 1789, the king launched into a fierce tirade against the nobility and forced them to leave the chamber. A non-noble committee was then set up to consider an act of union which had already been drafted by the king and his advisers. The resulting Act of Union and Security further strengthened the king's powers. He alone had full powers to govern and defend the realm, conduct foreign policy, declare war, and appoint to office; the estates were only permitted to deliberate upon matters proposed by the king. All subjects were guaranteed the same rights under the protection of the law and the act acknowledged the incontestable right of the Swedish people to discuss and agree to financial subsidies to the state. The right to buy and own land was given to all estates; the nobility retained

14. Lesch 1941, p. 100. Finnish nationalist historians have sometimes gone to absurd lengths to discern a burgeoning national spirit. Einar Juva, for example, was moved to declare that 'one would like to believe that even the vague sentences of the Liikkala note contain a reference to Finnish independence – without all its signatories having meant it.' Juva E 1947 *Suomen tie Uudestakaupungista Haminaan 1721–1809*, Helsinki, p. 197.

15. The Danish invasion of southern Sweden was halted by the energetic diplomacy of the British minister Hugh Elliot, who threatened Prussian and British intervention on Sweden's behalf. Jägerskiöld O 1957 *Den svenska utrikespolitikens historia II:2 1721–1792*, Stockholm, pp. 322–4. For details of Elizabeth's manifesto of 1742, see my previous volume, pp. 328–9.

only their ancient privilege of allodial possession. Crown peasants were also permitted once more to buy up the freehold of their farms.

The non-noble estates may have been happy to accept such concessions in return for an augmentation of the king's power, but they refused to swallow the creation of a committee of 112 members, 28 from each estate, which was intended to deliberate over the king's proposals regarding the management of finances, and was to vote by head, not by estate. The acknowledgement of the right of the Swedish *people* to consent to taxation also implied that the king might in future seek to bypass the estates – even to the extent of reviving the sixteenth-century practice of raising money from provincial assemblies, according to the Swedish constitutional historian Fredrik Lagerroth. As was the case with the constitution of 1772, the Act of Union of 1789 seemed to confirm the legal and political rights of citizens, whilst at the same time implying a significant augmentation of royal power. [16]

The Act of Union, with its implicitly anti-noble provisions, stands in sharp contrast to the explicit delineation of the duties and rights of each estate in the Prussian General Code of 1791, and Catherine II's charters to the nobility and to the towns, which were intended to introduce into the Russian empire some of the rights and obligations which had long existed elsewhere in Europe. Seen within the context of social developments in Sweden, however, the Act of Union symbolically acknowledged the shift from estate-bound privilege towards a class-based society. In a country which did not have to liberate the majority of its inhabitants from the fetters of servitude, this transformation was possible. South of the Baltic, where serfdom still prevailed, it was far less likely. In the Baltic provinces of the Russian empire, where the local nobility and burghers jealously guarded their rights of self-government, Catherine II's attempts to introduce reforms were resented as an unwarranted and unnecessary imposition. Although allowing a modicum of relief for the peasantry – above all, they obtained access to justice in disputes with their noble landlords and even served as assessors in the lower courts – the reforms did nothing to challenge the entrenched land-owning dominance of the Baltic German *Ritterschaften*. Indeed, in order to soften their resistance to the provincial reform introduced in 1783, Catherine had granted them allodial rights to their land. The abolition of the organs of

16. Lagerroth F 1945 *Nordens frihetsarv*, Stockholm, p. 78. Palmer 1959, vol. 1, pp. 312–13 prints an English-language version of the 1789 Act of Union. The Gustavian constitution was superseded in Sweden after 1809, but it is noteworthy that the Finnish estates continued to regard the acts of 1772 and 1789 as fundamental laws inherited by the Grand Duchy until the very end of Russian rule.

Ritterschaft rule was certainly a serious blow, though it is worth remembering that Karl XI had also attempted to weaken Baltic German self-government a century earlier. War and the subsequent peace settlement had nullified Karl XI's efforts to impose absolutist rule over the provinces; Catherine's reforms were done away with in 1796 by her successor. In both instances, the period of enforced reform was too brief to permit any fundamental changes, and the restoration of the old order merely served to reinforce the local elite's belief in the immutable virtues of their privileged position.

THE REVOLUTIONARY NINETIES

The Baltic nobility protested loud and long against what they perceived to be the violation of their privileges by Catherine II, and even appealed to Sweden as a signatory of the treaty of Nystad which had finally transferred the provinces to Russian rule. However, a Swedish spy advised Gustav III in 1788 that it would be unwise to reckon on any support from the disaffected nobility in the event of a Swedish landing in the provinces. 'Far from being able to produce a Washington, who with sword in hand would make so bold as to urge his countrymen to defend their violated rights,' he reported, 'I doubt even if there is one of them who with the courage of a Franklin would dare to carry their appeal for help to a foreign throne. They are like bound sacrificial beasts, who already feel the knife at their throats'. Profoundly mistrustful of the peasants, still simmering over the increased burdens imposed by the poll-tax, the Baltic nobility preferred 'cold egoism' to 'warm patriotism'.[17]

The attacks upon the privileges of the landowning and office-holding aristocracy being made by the adherents of enlightened reform opened up a debate which was intensified by the outbreak of revolution in Paris in 1789. The events in France were eagerly followed and debated in a wide variety of circles. On the whole,

17. Cederberg A (ed.) 1932 Johan Albert Ehrenströmin kirjallista jäämistöä vuosilta 1787–1789 *Historiallinen Arkisto* **39**: 77f. One of Catherine's closest advisers, Count Johann Jakob Sievers, believed however that the nobles and burghers were loyal, but the peasantry – who had recently caused disturbances over the poll-tax – were likely to cause mischief. Brückner A 1869 Die Ostseeprovinzen während des Krieges 1788–1790 *Baltische Monatshefte* **18**: 235–8. Catherine's reforms are considered in detail in: Madariaga I de 1981 *Russia in the age of Catherine the Great*, London, pp. 292–324 and Thaden E 1984 *Russia's western borderlands, 1710–1870*, Princeton, NJ, pp. 18–31. For the impact of the municipal reforms in the Baltic, see also my previous volume, p. 396.

however, enthusiasm for the French revolution in Scandinavia was more evident in polite salons than at the work-bench or the plough. Most admirers of Danton and Robespierre in Denmark were careful to declare their loyalty to the Danish monarchy, and out-and-out republicans such as Malte Conrad Bruun were very much the exception. Opponents of Gustav III hailed the revolution, but had no intention of emulating the French example. The assassination of the king at the masked ball in 1792 was an act of revenge by a disgruntled clique of nobles, not a blow for the liberty of the people.

Of much more immediate significance for northern Europe than the happenings in Paris was the final dismemberment of Poland in 1793 and 1795. Not only did this enable Russia to consolidate the westwards expansion of early decades, and Prussia to lay the foundations of the nineteenth-century great power; it also bound the three partitioning powers together into an unholy alliance to ensure that their victim did not revive. At the last, the Polish nobility had showed signs of pulling together to reform their country. The May 1791 constitution offered the promise of stronger, more effective government under a hereditary monarchy: but it came too late to be effective. The outbreak of the Russo-Turkish war in 1787 had seemed to offer the Poles an opportunity to free themselves from Russian control and to embark upon a programme of reform. When Catherine II turned down the proposal of an alliance in return for allowing an increase in the size of the Polish army and some measures of reform, the Poles allied in March 1790 with Prussia. The king of Prussia's promises to use his good offices (and if need be, provide military support) to prevent foreign (i.e. Russian) intervention in Poland barely concealed his own territorial desires. The British prime minister William Pitt seems to have thought that the transfer of Thorn and the port of Danzig to Prussia would have diminished Britain's dependence upon Russia for its naval stores. King Stanisław ruefully observed in September 1790 that Poland might have signed a commercial treaty with Britain 'which would have diverted to Poland the British millions which are now harvested every year by Russia', had not the Diet (*Sejm*) passed an act of non-cession forbidding the alienation of any part of the territory of the commonwealth; but it is hard to imagine how the transferrance of Poland's principal port to Prussia (which the king was apparently prepared to do) would have improved his country's commercial fortunes.[18]

18 Łojek J 1975 The international crisis of 1791: Poland between the Triple Alliance and Russia *East Central Europe* **II/1**: 22. de Madariaga 1981, pp. 402–20.

An Anglo-Prussian assault on Russia was however very much a possibility in the spring of 1791. The British cabinet agreed on 21–22 March to inform Frederick William II of their intention to send thirty to forty ships of the line to the Baltic and a squadron to the Black Sea: Frederick William ordered the mobilisation of 88,000 troops on the Livonian frontier. Catherine was, however, more than a match for her opponents. She was able to keep Sweden out of the projected anti-Russian coalition, and her minister in London adroitly mobilised the Whig press and opposition against Pitt. The cabinet hastily abandoned its bellicose plans at the end of March, leaving an angry king of Prussia and a relieved empress of Russia to settle their differences in a new partition of Poland. The ending of the war with Turkey in 1791 and the fact that Prussia and Austria were becoming increasingly preoccupied with quenching the revolutionary flames in the West enabled Catherine to turn her attentions to her erstwhile protectorate. Opponents of the king and the Patriotic party who formed the confederation of Targowica helped provide the excuse for Russian military intervention in 1792. Frederick William II refused to come to the aid of the Poles, on the grounds that by introducing the constitution of May 1791, they had rendered the conditions of the 1790 treaty null and void. Resistance to the invader was undermined by King Stanisław's willingness to negotiate and by his acceptance of the confederation in July. Prussia and Russia nevertheless claimed to detect the pernicious doctrines of Jacobinism at large in the commonwealth, and signed the second partition treaty in January 1793.

According to Catherine the Great's biographer Isabella de Madariaga, 'Jacobin' Poland was made to pay for the continuation of the war against Jacobin France.[19] If the ageing empress were indeed so fearful of the spread of revolutionary doctrine, she certainly exacted a heavy price for protecting the Poles from its malign influence. By trampling on the constitution of 1791 and destroying all prospects of internal reform, reducing Poland to little more than a Russian province, Catherine may indeed have given 'Jacobinism' a new lease of life in Poland. The insurrection led by General Tadeusz Kościuszko in 1794 served to reinforce Catherine's conviction that revolutionary fires on her doorstep had to be extinguished. Russian and Prussian military intervention crushed the revolt and the third partition of

19. de Madariaga 1981, p. 436. See also Lord R 1915 *The Second Partition of Poland* Cambridge, Mass. Müller M 1984 *Die Teilungen Polens 1772 – 1793 – 1795*, Munich, pp. 56–87. There will be an analysis of the effects and consequences of the partitions for Poland and her neighbours in Chapter Three.

1795, in which all three eastern powers participated, finally expunged Poland from the map.

The reforms set in motion in 1788–91, and the proclamations of liberty and peasant emancipation issued by Kościuszko bequeathed to future generations a legacy which is perhaps a less than accurate reflection of the true state of affairs in the *rzeczpospolita.* As a contemporary surveyor of the European political scene pointed out, Poland was one of the weakest states in Europe because of 'the oppression of the tradespeople in the towns, and the slavery of the peasantry'. It is hard to see how last-minute constitutional reforms or revolutionary proclamations could have materially altered such a situation. The same commentator also noted: 'the Russian government cannot, with propriety, be called despotic, as many provinces of Russia enjoy particular privileges, and as the present sovereign has promulgated a code of laws, which must naturally limit the absolute power of the monarch', and yet even Catherine's reforms failed to transform Russia into a balanced, well-functioning corporate society.[20] That Poland was cast in the role of unfortunate victim and Russia, above all, as the arch-villain, cannot conceal the social deficiencies – a servile, ignorant peasantry, the absence of a thriving commercial class and the lack of an educated, self-conscious professional elite – which were common to both countries.

Catherine's fear of Jacobinism was no doubt exaggerated, but there were signs of unrest along the shores of the Baltic. There were complaints about the steeply rising cost of food, and numerous observers noted with alarm the growing disparity between impoverished and famished workers and farmers growing fat on profits. A correspondent in the *Neue Monatsschrift von und für Mecklenburg* in 1795 calculated that a labourer with three or four children would need to spend all his earnings on bread-grain alone, and Professor C. J. Kraus of Königsberg concluded that the price of grain had risen incomparably more than the average cost of labour during the last decade of the eighteenth century. Later studies have merely confirmed these conclusions.[21] Northern German landowners insisted on their right to export grain freely, and were usually backed up by the ruler,

20. Zimmermann E 1787 *A Political Survey of the Present State of Europe, in Sixteen Tables*, London, pp. 9–10, 84.

21. Schildhauer J 1959 Gesellen und Tagelöhnverhebung in den mecklenburgischen Städten vom 1790 bis 1800 *Zeitschrift für Geschichts-wissenschaften* **7**: 1258. Spading K 1967 Volksbewegungen in den Städten Schwedisch-Pommerns um die Wende vom 18. zum 19. Jahrhunderts *Jahrbuch für Regionalgeschichte* **2**: 87–112. Abel W 1980 *Agricultural fluctuations in Europe from the thirteenth to the twentieth centuries*, London, pp. 197–203.

since grain exports yielded revenue. High prices and shortages led to protest and occasional violence. Protesters in the Swedish Pomeranian port of Barth prevented ships laden with corn from leaving the harbour in April 1795. After lengthy negotiations, the magistrates agreed to enforce a lowering of prices, but discontent continued to simmer throughout the summer and a 300 strong contingent of troops was called in to arrest the leaders of the protest movement. There were similar disturbances in 1800 in Wolgast, whose magistrates had hitherto avoided trouble by renting out land for grain cultivation and by persuading merchants to sell grain at reasonable prices to the poorer inhabitants, and there were riots in Rostock and Güstrow.

Economic distress fuelled these disturbances, though the language of revolution occasionally percolated through. Discontented farmhands on Rügen voiced their intention in 1797 of following the French example by making a start with the bailiff; radical-minded citizens and students from Greifswald to Uppsala called themselves Jacobins, wore red ribbons in their hats and planted liberty trees. The distant glow of the Bastille fires also flickered in Kurland, although events in Poland had rather more to do with the creation of the burghers' association (*Bürgerliche Union*) in 1790. 'The mood of the estates towards each other was one of deep, albeit concealed hatred', according to a contemporary pamphlet, *Die pohlnischen Conföderirten in Curland*, 'and although the burgher publicly paid the nobleman the honour of a "my lord", at the same moment he heartily wished him to the devil. The new French system, as a consequence of this mood, attracted many supporters, and here and there one heard a "*ça ira!*" or "from the Rhine, from the Rhine, our noble brothers call, freedom lives!" amongst the champagne bottles.'[22] The burghers of the towns of Kurland, long denied any say in the affairs of the duchy, responded to the conversion of the Polish *Sejm* into a confederation to which representatives of the towns were invited by forming their own Union and presenting their demands to Duke Peter in July 1790. The burghers demanded the right to participate in the Kurland Diet (*Landtag*), to buy noble estates and to appointment to all offices, as well as protection of trade. The artisans presented their own demands

22. Cited in Bosse H 1983 Zunftgeist oder Revolution? Die Mitauer Müllerunruhen im Lichte des Geselleausstände des 18. Jahrhunderts *Zeitschrift für Geschichte Osteuropas* **32**: 563, and Donnert E 1978 Gesellschaftspolitisches Denken und soziale Bewegungen in Kurland im Wirkungsbereich der amerikanischen und französischen Revolution *Zeitschrift für Slawistik* **23**: 199. See also Donnert E 1992 *Kurland im Ideenbereich der Französischen Revolution* Schriftenreihe der Internationalen Forschungsstelle "Demokratische Bewegungen in Mitteleuropa 1770–1850" **5**, Frankfurt am Main.

for the right to share in the government of the towns, and in September 1790 broke away from the Union to form their own, the *Künstler und Professionisten.*

This split gave the nobility an opportunity to play off the two sides against each other. *Ritterschaft* deputies in Warsaw insinuated that the Union was merely a cabal whose members – mostly foreigners – approved of revolutionary events in France. The Union disavowed any revolutionary intentions, and cast aspersions in turn on the artisans. This conflict soon became entangled with a complicated dispute involving the outraged honour of a master miller. A rumour that the duke intended to abolish all gild privileges provoked a revolt in December 1792. Revolutionary slogans were heard, a tree of liberty planted, but the main demand of the apprentices was for the duke to pay the costs incurred during the dispute. The duke responded by ordering troops to open fire, and fourteen insurgents were killed. Although the Kurland peasant failed to respond to the blandishments of those whom the author of *Die pohlnischen Conföderirten* darkly suggested were more than willing to interpret the newspapers to him over a glass of brandywine, Duke Peter took the precaution of having a battalion ready to deal with unrest and issued a patent in German and Latvian in May 1794 threatening imprisonment for any caught spreading French revolutionary doctrines. The duke had some reason to be worried, for the Jacobins appeared to be in control in Vilna and Kościuszko himself was appealing to the Kurland peasantry to join his revolt. The threat of insurrection persuaded Duke Peter to seek Russian protection, a course already pursued by his leading nobles. At the end of 1795, the *Landtag*, having obtained assurances guaranteeing the rights and privileges of the nobility, invited Catherine to become overlord in place of the ex-king of Poland. Duke Peter Biron was persuaded to abdicate, the memory of his unfortunate line being preserved for posterity in a passing reference by his English namesake.

By the late 1790s, the ardour of many early enthusiasts had begun to cool. The Swedish poet Frans Michael Franzén, who visited Paris in 1795, recorded in his travel journal the lack of enthusiasm he encountered, and his own bitter disillusionment, which compelled him to toss his cockade into the sea on the crossing from France to England. Like a ship on fire, the century was passing away, a terrible beauty casting its lustre and fearsome images on the night-dark shore; in vain did humanity look to see it carrying peace towards truth and liberty; only ruins marked out its course. The powerful imagery of Franzén's poem on the philosophy of the eighteenth century reflects the disappointment of many, though it also reveals in its later stanzas that the faith in enlightenment and reason was not undimmed.[23] In the end, the heat of revolution was too far away to distort or destroy the rather calm and homely rationality which had flourished in the northern kingdoms for more than half a century. It remained to be seen, however, how the recently-partitioned Polish lands and the territories as yet untouched by emancipatory reform would stand up to the impact of the revolutionary armies which had begun to break out eastwards across the Rhine and into the Low Countries in the mid-1790s.

THE SPREAD OF WAR

'Since the days of Peter the Great, and Charles XII, the Baltic has made no figure in the History of the World, nor (till of late) have any events occurred there, that tended to influence the Politics of the South of Europe', declared a pamphlet published in Berlin in 1800, 'It was reserved for the French Revolution to shake the foundations of European Politics, and the Northern Powers are now compelled to make the hazardous attempt, and to show how far they are capable of displaying their former valour, or of resuming that rank in the History of Nations which they once maintained'.[24] The northern powers were suddenly brought to the forefront of the European stage at the end of the eighteenth century because of events at sea – most notably, Admiral Nelson's crushing victory over the French fleet at Aboukir Bay in 1798. The 1790s were prosperous years for Danish and Swedish merchantmen, who plied the oceans from the Caribbean islands to the Levant. The belligerent powers were often heavily dependent on neutral vessels for vital supplies; the British government, for example, was even prepared to suspend the Navigation Act in 1799 in order to allow foreign vessels to carry vital naval stores to British ports, and neutral shipping also imported grain into Britain. The warring powers could, however, make difficulties for the neutral states in order to deny supplies to their enemies. Thus, the French Directory's order of 29 Nivôse An VI (18 January 1798) declared that cargo alone determined a ship's nationality; hence any vessel carrying

23. Franzén's poem and extracts from his travel journal are cited by Manninen J 1989 Frans Michael Franzén och den franska revolutionen *Historisk Tidskrift för Finland* **74**: 30–64.

24. *The Sound and the Baltic . . . Translated from a German pamphlet, published in Berlin, April 1800*, London, 1801, p. vi.

British cargo was a lawful prize. As a result of this order, ninety-one Danish and Norwegian vessels were seized by French privateers in the first five months of 1798. Attempts by the Danish government to reach agreement with the Directory proved fruitless, and relations were eventually broken off.

Nelson's victory at Aboukir Bay tilted the balance decisively in Britain's favour in the Mediterranean; and, as the Directory started to take steps to modify its policy towards neutral shipping, the British began to tighten theirs. Many Norwegian timber merchants were hard hit by the Royal Navy's blockade of Dutch ports in 1799. One hundred and fifty-nine Danish vessels were seized and taken into British ports between 1799 and 1801, and many cases still remained to be resolved in the prize courts after the signing of the Peace of Amiens in 1802. The neutrals' response to marauders was to implement a convoy system. Although the Royal Navy was at first inclined to allow Swedish and Danish convoys to pass unhindered, there were clashes. A Swedish vessel, the *Maria*, was deemed a lawful prize by the courts in July 1799 on the grounds that it had resisted a Royal Naval demand that it be searched. In December 1799, a Danish frigate opened fire on a British search party off Gibraltar, and seven months later, the frigate *Freya*, having fired the first shot, was obliged to strike colours and was escorted into Deal harbour. This was interpreted in London as a deliberate attempt to spark off a crisis, and the experienced diplomat Lord Whitworth was despatched to Copenhagen to persuade the Danish government either to abandon its convoy instructions or to allow convoys to be searched. The situation was made more delicate from a British point of view by the sudden and rapid deterioration in relations with Russia, and it was to prevent the Danes seeking succour from the Emperor Paul that Whitworth resorted to a naval demonstration off Copenhagen to press his point. Christian Bernstorff was amenable to agreement, but crown prince Frederik's insistence on Danish prestige being respected delayed agreement until the end of August 1800.

Although the Danes promised to suspend all convoys until negotiations on the whole question of visitation and search of neutral shipping had resulted in agreement, Bernstorff made it clear to the Russians that the *principle* of the convoy system had not been abandoned. The Emperor Paul, now totally at odds with Britain, proposed reviving the League of Armed Neutrality, first created in 1780. The Danes had gone along with Catherine II's League rather reluctantly, since they were well aware that its main purpose was to further Russian interests, and that Denmark was, moreover, in the front line should the British decide to mount an assault against the League's members. Denmark's adherence to the League formed in 1800 was to reveal that very vulnerability which had persuaded A. P. Bernstorff to keep open the channels of communication with London in 1780. As Ole Feldbæk remarks, 'the prospective members of the Armed Neutrality had divergent and to a certain extent irreconcilable goals for a joint neutral action'.[25] Sweden hoped to exploit the Anglo-Danish conflict to regain exemption from payment of the Sound dues, relinquished in 1720, and the suggestion that Norway be transferred to Sweden, with Denmark receiving compensation in northern Germany, was once more raised in St Petersburg by Gustav IV Adolf. The mentally unstable ruler of Russia, enraged by British interference in what he regarded as his own domain, the island of Malta, sought to push his partners into a more aggressive stance than the Danes, at least, were prepared to take.

The formation of the League of Armed Neutrality effectively closed the Baltic to British trade, depriving the Royal Navy of vital naval stores. Three-quarters of the grain imported into Britain came from the Baltic, and the sudden loss of supply at a time of poor harvests and rising prices was a matter of concern for the government. The Grenville administration chose to confront the League, hoping to frighten the Swedes and Danes into abandoning it. Swedish and Danish colonies in the West Indies were seized and an embargo placed on the shipping of the League's members. The mysterious expulsion from Russia of the Danish minister Niels Rosenkrantz and the withdrawal of the Russian minister to Copenhagen did little to calm Danish nerves. Nevertheless, in spite of growing doubts about Russian and Swedish policies, the Danish Council of State seems deliberately to have opted for war with Britain as the lesser of two evils.[26] Admiral Sir Hyde Parker's fleet passed through the Sound at the end of March, having suffered no damage from the Danish guns at Kronborg, and engaged the Danish fleet off Copenhagen at 10.30 a.m. on 2 April. By 3.00 p.m., the action had ended, with both sides having suffered heavy casualties. However, whilst the British fleet emerged relatively unscathed, the Danes lost one ship and had twelve captured. An armistice was arranged on 9 April, though neither Bernstorff nor the crown prince were prepared to accept Parker's demands for Denmark

25. Feldbæk O 1980 *Denmark and the armed neutrality 1800–1801. Small-power policy in a world war* Institut for Økonomisk Historie Publikation no.**16**, Copenhagen, p. 77.

26. Feldbæk 1980, p. 137. For a rather more critical assessment of Danish policy in 1801, see Linvald A 1923 *Kronprins Frederik og hans Regering 1797–1807*, Copenhagen (1979 reprint edition) vol. 1, pp. 144–50.

to abandon the Armed Neutrality, fearing that this would provoke an attack by their erstwhile allies. Eventually, it was settled that Denmark would suspend membership of the League for the duration of the armistice, an arrangement for which Parker was much criticised in London. The Swedish fleet was too late to be of any assistance to the Danes, and prudently withdrew to the safety of Karlskrona harbour. Admiral Parker was recalled at the beginning of May, leaving Nelson in command of the fleet. Nelson, whose boldness in battle had been matched by the unequivocal manner in which he forced the Danes to agree to a ceasefire, paid a brief 'friendly' visit to Reval (a sentiment not shared by the new emperor) before leaving his command on grounds of ill-health.

The League of Armed Neutrality was brought to an end, not by British naval action, but by the assassination of Paul I, a fortnight before the battle of Copenhagen. Neither Sweden nor Denmark was involved in the negotiations between Russia and Britain which effectively terminated the League. Bereft of support, Bernstorff was forced to abandon the Danish position on the inviolability of neutral convoys. As a consolation, the seized Danish colonies were returned by the British. Sweden had already acceded to the terms of the Anglo-Russian agreement. After having twice sought unsuccessfully to renew the old alliance with France in the 1790s and again in 1803, Sweden gravitated towards Russia and Britain on the resumption of hostilities. Gustav IV Adolf's personal dislike of Bonaparte had assumed pathological proportions during his year-long sojourn in Germany (1803–04), but his agreements with Russia and Britain in 1804–05 were designed largely to protect Sweden's remaining north German possessions of Stralsund and Hither Pomerania. In October 1805, Gustav IV Adolf agreed to enter the coalition with a force of 12,000 men, financed by a monthly British subsidy. His activities as commander of the allied forces in northern Germany were largely confined to keeping a watchful eye on Prussia. In December 1805, Frederick William III suddenly concluded an agreement with France which allowed him to occupy Hanover. In April 1806, Prussian troops marched into the adjoining tiny duchy of Lauenburg, driving out a token Swedish force. The Swedish king retaliated with a naval blockade of the Prussian ports, thereby frustrating allied hopes of detaching Prussia from the French camp. Gustav IV Adolf's one positive achievement during his lengthy stay in Pomerania was to declare null and void all the rights and privileges of the Pomeranian estates when they dared to protest to the imperial court about his attempts to raise a conscript army. The final dissolution of the Holy Roman Empire enabled the king to introduce the Swedish constitution and Swedish law, abolishing serfdom in the process. Thus, at the last, administrative swedification was carried out in one of the territories acquired, but never absorbed into the realm during Sweden's age of greatness.[27]

The northern kingdoms were once more caught up in the spreading European conflict. At first, the renewal of war had brought fat profits to the merchant marines of Sweden and Denmark: the Danish College of Commerce could declare with some satisfaction that 'the year 1805 can with good reason be described as one of the most propitious in the annals of Denmark's trade'.[28] But 1805 marked a turning point. With the British commanding the seas and Napoleon the continent, economic warfare once again became a crucial element of the struggle. The tightening of the British blockade of the continent in 1807 revived the old conflict with Denmark over the rights of neutrals. The new British foreign secretary George Canning was in no mood to bear with complaints about the 'frequency and frivolity' with which Danish vessels were being seized, and despatched an emissary with a fleet to demand that the Danish navy place itself under British command. Negotiations broke down, and 30,000 British troops were put ashore on the island of Sjælland. Having defeated the militia and caused much destruction of the capital by intensive naval bombardment, the expeditionary force departed with most of the Danish fleet in tow.

FROM TILSIT TO EIDSVOLL

The uncompromising and brutal manner in which the British acted in the 'Copenhagen business' was undoubtedly meant as a response and a warning in the immediate aftermath of the signing of the peace of Tilsit. Like the treaty of Brest-Litovsk a century later, this agreement was to be overshadowed by a subsequent general peace treaty in which western European interests prevailed: and yet both had far-reaching consequences for the continent of Europe. Prussia had already lost most of her territories to the west of the Elbe as a result of the

27. On the relationship between Sweden and its peripheral territories, see my first volume, pp. 222–7. For an interesting contemporary account of the last days of Swedish rule in Pomerania, see Arndt E 1817 *Geschichte der Veränderung der bauerlichen und herrschaftlichen Verhältnisse in den vormaligen Schwedischen Pommern und Rügen vom Jahr 1806 bis zum Jahr 1816*, Berlin.

28. Cited by Linvald 1923, vol. 1, p. 173.

ill-judged campaign against Napoleon which came to grief on the fields of Jena and Auerstädt in October 1806. The royal court was forced to spend the winter of 1806–07 in East Prussia, crammed for much of the time into the small town of Memel on the easternmost extremity of the duchy. From Berlin, Napoleon issued the decree establishing the Continental System, a kind of blockade in reverse designed to prevent British goods entering the continent; and he also devised a scheme for the occupation of Prussia to persuade his enemies to a general peace. Frederick William III found the French terms too onerous, and concluded with Alexander I a convention in April 1807, which proclaimed the intention of the two rulers to liberate Germany from French oppression. Sweden was also brought into the alliance, and given promises of subsidies and troops to reinforce Stralsund by the British.

All these plans were blown apart on the battlefield of Friedland on 14 June 1807. Within a fortnight, the Russian tsar was holding secret discussions with the French emperor on a barge moored on the banks of the river Niemen in the small East Prussian town of Tilsit. The outcome of their discussions was a peace treaty with secret clauses, designed to force Napoleon's remaining enemies to submit. Although he abandoned his erstwhile Prussian ally, Alexander was unwilling to take on the task of administering Prussia's Polish territories. Napoleon had therefore to indulge in a fourth partition of Poland. The Duchy of Warsaw, given a French constitution and an hereditary Saxon duke, was a landlocked state fashioned out of territories acquired by Prussia in the earlier partitions. It did not survive the downfall of Napoleon, and was grievously exploited by its effective masters, who carefully avoided all mention of 'Poland' in erecting the new duchy. Nevertheless, the hope of independence once more was kindled in the hearts of thousands of Polish patriots.

The constitution of the Duchy of Warsaw also overturned the principle of estates by declaring all citizens equal, and it abolished serfdom. This caused much confusion, but it had blown a clear breach through the constricting walls of noble privilege which had so enervated the independent state. In defeat, the Kingdom of Prussia also turned to reform. A southern German who wrote of his experiences of the siege of Danzig in the spring of 1807 summed up what he described as the bitter lesson learnt by the Prussians, who had rested on their laurels since the days of the Seven Years' War. The brutal and uncultured military had been allowed to rule the roost: 'a miserable *von* is still, even in our times, worth more than talent, knowledge and education . . . What a wretched state of affairs in our times! in our times, when it is above all the third estate which by virtue of its wealth (*Wohlhabenheit*) is in a position to give its children a better and a finer education than the petty rural nobility, whose sons become officers and eventually generals, but can hardly write their names legibly . . .'[29]

The Prussian reforms were the work of well-educated and enlightened servants of the state, anxious to wrest control of affairs from the hands of decrepit generals living off the dregs of Frederician glory. It is worth remembering that the state in which these reforms were first implemented had in fact become far more 'Prussian' as a result of Jena and Tilsit. The October 1807 decree abolishing serfdom was initially confined to East Prussia, and Karl Wilhelm von Humboldt's planned educational reform was first put into practice in Königsberg, the seat of government in 1808-09. East Prussia had to bear the burden of the French occupation, and pay a sizeable proportion of the 120 million francs war indemnity imposed on the kingdom by the peace treaty signed in Paris in 1808. The fulcrum of the Kingdom of Prussia had moved significantly eastwards during the reign of Frederick the Great; and although that germanophobe monarch held the East Prussians in low esteem, he was even more contemptuous of the Holy Roman Empire, from which he sought to detach his kingdom. The events of 1806–07 once more raised the whole question of Prussia's role and place in Germany, and the fundamental ambivalence of a kingdom straddling two worlds (and probably seeking to be a fully-integrated member of neither) was to continue into the postwar decades.

The secret articles of the Tilsit treaty between France and Russia clearly placed the onus of persuading the British government to seek peace with Napoleon upon the Russians. Alexander's ministers were unable to persuade the Portland ministry to agree to peace terms, and the tsar himself declared war on Britain before the deadline decreed in the secret articles, affecting outrage at the British treatment of the Danes. The failure of Russian mediation in London also put pressure on Sweden, since article five of the treaty declared that if Sweden refused to close its ports to British vessels, break off relations and declare war on Britain, it would be treated as an enemy. Gustav IV Adolf, whose hatred of Napoleon had grown even greater after the loss of his north German lands, proved insensible to diplomatic persuasion. At the beginning of 1808, Russia declared war on Sweden, and the Finnish frontier was crossed on 21 February.

29. *Danzig. Eine Skizze in Briefe: geschrieben vor, während und nach der Verlagerung im Jahr 1807*, Amsterdam and Hamburg, 1808, p. 195.

Gustav IV Adolf was not entirely friendless, for the British had promised a monthly subsidy of £100,000, and an expeditionary force commanded by Sir John Moore set sail for Göteborg in May. The Spanish troops sent to Denmark to join forces with the Danes in an invasion of Skåne mutinied on hearing of the revolt in Spain, and 9,000 were eventually shipped off by the Royal Navy to join their compatriots fighting a guerrilla war against the French. The war in Finland was, however, an utter disaster for Sweden. The main army commanded by General Klingspor beat a steady retreat before the advancing Russian forces, and had reached the Ostrobothnian town of Gamla Karleby by the end of March. The military successes at Siikajoki and Revolax at the end of April were not enough to offset the loss of the fortress of Sveaborg, surrendered without a fight at the beginning of May. Russian forces occupied the Åland islands, and there were fears that the Swedish mainland would be attacked. Having failed completely to establish any sort of understanding with the king (who at one stage ordered him under house-arrest), Sir John Moore and his expeditionary force left Göteborg and set sail for Spain. The British subsidies covered only 40 per cent of Swedish military expenditure: by July, all hitherto requisitioned sources had been exhausted and supplies to the army had to be cut by half. As the financial crisis deepened, relations between the king and his servants worsened. John Fiott, a Cambridge University student travelling through Sweden at this time, noted the growing dissatisfaction and discontent: 'the war with France was always an unpopular measure and the losses in Pomerania and in Finland are considered as the consequences of it: but the king is inflexible and would never listen to such a thing as peace with Buonaparte; although the rest of the Nation desire it'.[30]

Fiott was, however, careful to make a distinction between general criticism and the mood of determination to resist the Russian invasion, and his account of peasant resistance to the invader in Finland and the Åland islands accords well with other evidence. As in 1788, it was the peasants in Finland who showed the greatest willingness to fight, whilst the upper classes contemplated submission to Russian rule. There was little confidence in Sweden's ability to defend Finland successfully. The hasty and shameful capitulation at Sveaborg probably helped tip the balance. Jakob Tengström, the bishop of Åbo, expected little of Gustav IV Adolf's planned expeditionary force or of possible British help. The Finnish army was abandoned to its misery and in

30. John Fiott to Lord Percy, 20 June 1808 (Stockholm): Duke of Northumberland papers, Alnwick: Correspondence 1807–1809. British Museum, microfilm no. 33.

such a situation the bishop thought it his duty to do what he could to soften the misfortunes of war. So did many others, and the road towards union with Russia had been well trodden long before the Finnish estates finally convened in the town of Borgå in March 1809. 'We separated from Sweden', was the judgement of Carl Johan Walleen, in a letter to Tengström in 1814, 'because that country with the most extraordinary *lâcheté* abandoned us to our fate'.[31]

The brief period of military success enjoyed by Klingspor's forces in the summer of 1808 was not sufficient to dislodge the Russians. By the end of the year, the Finnish army had been compelled to evacuate Ostrobothnia and withdraw west of the Kemi river according to the terms of an armistice signed on 19 November. Concerned about the international situation and anxious to pacify Finland as quickly as possible, Alexander I may have been persuaded to shift from his initial declared intention of incorporating Finland into Russia as a conquered territory towards a more accommodating approach. Orders were issued by the military governor Friedrich von Buxhoevden in June–July 1808 for the election of a deputation of members of the estates. This deputation presented a memorial to the tsar in St Petersburg, asking for a general meeting of the estates of the land 'to obtain the nation's voice in those matters which concern the wellbeing of all and the common good'.[32] On 1 February, Alexander issued the order for the estates to convene in the small town of Borgå for a general *Lantdag* (provincial diet) on 22 March 1809.

Less than a fortnight before the ceremonial opening of the assembly by the emperor himself, 'a most remarkable revolution took place' in Stockholm. On 7 March, the Western Army under the command of Lt.Col. Georg Adlersparre abandoned its position on the Norwegian frontier and began marching on the capital. The king did not learn of this revolt until 12 March, and his plans to go south and join forces he believed loyal to him were forestalled by a group of military and civilian officals, already deeply alienated by the king's conduct of the war and his refusal to heed their advice. On 13 March, Gustav IV Adolf was placed under arrest by a group led by General C. J. Adlercreutz. His uncle Carl assumed the regency, a provisional

31. The citations are from: Bonsdorff C von 1918 Opinioner och stämningar i Finland 1808–1814 *Skrifter utgivna av Svenska Litteratursällskapet i Finland* **141**, the most comprehensive study of public mood in Finland during these critical times. For Klingspor's intructions, and the course of the war in 1808, see: Schybergson M 1903 *Finlands historia*, Helsingfors, vol. 2, pp. 296ff. and the massive study by Osmonsalo E 1948 *Suomen valloitus 1808*, Porvoo-Helsinki.

32. Schybergson 1903, vol. 2, p. 345.

government was formed, and a *Riksdag* summoned for May. The young John Fiott, clearly somewhat discomfited to find himself in such a bloodless revolution ('one is much inclined to enquire, as the lady did when the town was taken by storm, and the troops were plundering, "When the ravishing fun will begin?" '), reported to his noble friend on 1 April:

> It is curious to see and hear the same people who a few weeks ago were silent obedient to the commands of a despotic monarch, now talking in the wildest and most revolutionary and outrageous terms which they call Liberty, Many complaining that he was not killed at first, that he is suffered still to live, some wishing to confine him for life, others to send him out of the country, etc, etc, in the most ungracious terms.[33]

The deposed king was ultimately suffered to go into exile, where his eccentricities led him into a downward spiral of personal hardship and loneliness. His uncle was rewarded for a life of malicious intrigue with the title of King Carl XIII. On 18 July, the estates elected as crown prince Adlersparre's candidate for the succession, the Danish prince Christian August. His sudden death in May 1810 gave rise to rumours that he had been murdered. Suspicion fell – quite erroneously – upon Count Hans Axel von Fersen, the organiser of the flight of Louis XVI and Marie Antoinette, which had ended in Varennes in 1791. At the funeral of the crown prince, a mob which appears to have been incited by high-placed officials hacked Fersen to death as troops looked on.[34]

The sudden death of the crown prince increased tensions in Sweden. Already, old Gustavians were hatching plots and the king himself was involved in a plot to alter the new constitution and restore Gustav IV Adolf's son Gustav to the succession. There were worries of possible Danish intervention, in spite of King Frederik VI's declared willingness to respect the new Swedish constitution. It was a twenty-nine-year-old lieutenant, acting on behalf of a group of younger officers looking to restore Sweden's eclipsed military glory,

33. John Fiott to Lord Percy, 1 April 1809 (Stockholm): Microfilm 311, British Museum. Fiott's concluding remark that 'this arises from the faults of their education, their ignorance of real liberty, and from the errors of their constitution' is what one might expect from a student of St John's college, Cambridge. British Museum microfilm no. 311. This letter is published by kind permission of the Trustees of Tenth Duke of Northumberland deceased.

34. There is a full biography of Fersen by Barton H Arnold 1975 *Count Hans Axel von Fersen: Aristocrat in an age of revolution*, Boston. On the succession question, see also Barton H Arnold 1970 The Swedish succession crises of 1809 and 1810, and the question of Scandinavian Union, *Scandinavian Studies* **42**: 309–33.

who first approached Jean-Baptiste Bernadotte, Marshal of France, whose political star had waned during the years of the Empire. Bernadotte expressed interest in the offer of the Swedish crown. Napoleon, who had initially favoured the king of Denmark, raised no objections. The Secret Committee of the *Riksdag* abandoned the candidature of Frederik Christian, the brother of the deceased Christian August). On 21 August 1810, the four estates unanimously elected Bernadotte crown prince. The forty-seven-year-old Gascon, who never learnt to speak Swedish, adopted the name Carl Johan, and succeeded to the throne on the death of Carl XIII in 1818.

The de facto separation of the Finnish provinces from Sweden which had occurred in 1808 was formally acknowledged in the peace of Fredrikshamn, concluded in September 1809. The loss of Finland laid bare the deficiencies of the Swedish state. Gustav IV Adolf had paid the price for his blundering inadequacies, but there was a desperate need for something which might salvage the pride of the nation. There can be no doubt that the French marshal was elected in the hopes that he, and his erstwhile master, would help Sweden gain revenge on Russia. But even before his own candidature had been mooted, Bernadotte had let it be known that Russia should seek to ensure that the Swedish throne was occupied by someone capable of keeping the peace on a vital frontier in the event of war between the tsar and France or Austria. He also informed Russian diplomats in Paris before his departure for Sweden of his intentions of forging good relations with the tsar. In his first address to the estates in November 1810, Carl Johan declared that peace was the only honourable goal of an enlightened government, unwittingly echoing the sentiment of the poet Esias Tegnér's revised epic poem *Svea*, that Finland would have to be rewon within Sweden's own frontiers. The experienced soldier soon realised that Sweden's military resources were unequal to the task of reconquering Finland, and he took up the alternative which previous kings of Sweden had toyed with – the acquisition of Norway.[35] Napoleon made it clear in 1811 that he did not support such an idea, and although in March 1812 he guaranteed support for the restoration of Finland to Sweden if Carl Johan would attack Russia, his offer was rejected.

The ultimate outcome of Carl Johan's policy of acquiring Norway has perhaps tended to obscure the fact that he was walking a difficult

35. Holmberg N 1933 Från Svea till Frithiofs saga *Scandia* **6**: 208–11. Johnson S 1985 1812 års politik *Scandia* **51**: 100ff. Tommila P 1962 *La Finlande dans la politique européenne en 1809–1815* Studia Historica 3, Helsinki, pp. 134–42.

tightrope as the crisis in Europe developed. Not only had he to take heed of domestic opinion (though he was not afraid to have dissentient voices silenced, when necessary); he was also all too conscious of the sudden shifts of political alignments, which had left many European states stranded and at the mercy of predators. Agreement was reached with Russia in the spring of 1812. Both sides guaranteed each other's territorial integrity; Russia was to furnish military assistance to Carl Johan to enable him to take Norway; thereafter, both sides would cooperate in Germany against France. The agreement was to come into force as soon as one or other party declared war on France. However, neither side activated the terms of the agreement when the Grande Armée invaded Russia in June 1812. Carl Johan was wary of breaking openly with France, and Alexander I was primarily concerned with the defence of Russia. The two rulers met in Åbo in August 1812, at a critical stage of the war – news of the surrender of Smolensk was broken during the meeting – and agreed upon a revision of the spring alliance. Alexander was sufficiently emboldened by the renewal of the accord to withdraw troops from Finland – which had been earmarked for the joint Swedish-Russian descent upon Sjælland – for use on the Riga front. During the autumn, he attempted to persuade Denmark to detach itself from the French camp; but, with the Grande Armée now in full retreat, the tsar juggled the terms of the original alliance agreement. Denmark was to be compensated with territory in northern Germany, and Norway was to be ceded to Sweden, no longer as a *precondition*, but as a reward for furnishing military assistance in Europe. Carl Johan for his part was quite prepared to spoil his ally's game by revealing to Denmark the full terms of the agreement, and in October 1812 he contemplated offering military assistance to Alexander in return for Finland as a security for Norway.

By the end of the year, the tattered remnants of the mighty Grande Armée had crossed the Niemen, and were limping westwards.

The huge casualty figures of the campaign – of the 1,700 men of the Schwerin contingent who went to Moscow, 1,500 perished, for example, and a mere 20,000 of the 100,000 Poles returned – added to the misery of the years of French occupation. The loss of the British grain market badly affected landowners across northern Germany. By 1810, three-quarters of the estates indebted to the East Prussian credit institutions were under sequestration, whilst these *Landschaften* themselves were short of credit for further loans to hard-pressed landlords. The heaths of Mecklenburg were infested with robber bands, and the coves and small harbours everywhere attracted smugglers. In the once-prosperous hinterland of the port of Memel, badly affected by Napoleon's Continental System and the exactions of new Russian landlords, the misery was so bad that one Lithuanian nobleman predicted there would soon be no alternative but to go out and buy a rope to hang himself.

Any hopes of liberation under Napoleon that the Poles might have had were soon dashed. The *Sejm* which met in Warsaw at the end of June 1812 and declared itself to be a general confederation of the kingdom of Poland was little more than a puppet of the French-appointed council of ministers. Concern was voiced in Warsaw at the creation of a separate provisional government for Lithuania, but on 14 July this government acceded to the confederation and thereby preserved the dualistic notion of the Polish-Lithuanian state. In practice, the government was little more than a French device to ensure supplies for the army. The peasants welcomed Napoleon as a deliverer, and there were numerous instances of refusal to perform labour services and of uprisings against landlords. On 7 July, however, Napoleon hastened to assure the landowners that he had no intention of freeing the peasants, who were ordered to return to their homes and to obey their masters. The pillaging and indiscipline of the Grande Armée were resented by peasants and townspeople alike. Nine regiments of troops were raised by conscription, and the peasants on whom this burden fell were markedly unresponsive to government appeals to their patriotism and assurances that they would serve only six, as opposed to the twenty-five years of service imposed by the Russians.

The city of Vilna was an important staging post between the Grande Armée and the West, and was the headquarters of Napoleon's minister of foreign affairs, the duke of Bassano. Virtually bereft of supplies, the inhabitants fled the city; by November, over a quarter of the dwellings had been abandoned. 'The sight of devastation saddened our eyes,' wrote a member of the emperor's entourage in Lithuania, 'the fine harvests spoiled, the ancient trees chopped down, the hamlets, entire villages built of wood and thatched with straw, devastated, thrown down, almost entirely reduced to oblivion'.[36]

Efforts to detach the Prussian forces from the French were set in motion almost as soon as news was received of the evacuation of Moscow. Cut off from the French forces he was supposed to be covering, and with no clear instructions from Berlin, General Yorck concluded a convention with the Russian commander Diebitsch at Tauroggen on 30 December 1812, effectively withdrawing the

36. Cited in Dundulis B 1940 *Napoléon et la Lithuanie en 1812,* Paris, p. 116.

Prussian forces from the war. In March 1813, Frederick William declared war on France, and joined the swelling coalition of forces against Napoleon. Even Frederik VI of Denmark was beginning to be persuaded by his foreign minister Niels Rosenkrantz of the advisability of leaving the French alliance and seeking support from Britain. The Austrian foreign minister Prince Metternich appeared to support Denmark's retention of Norway, and Russia once more sought to soften the conditions for a Danish entry into the coalition. Although he managed in March 1813 to secure British backing for his claim to Norway, and the rights to the conquered French island of Guadeloupe, the favourable circumstances of 1812 in which Carl Johan had been able to obtain Russian support no longer obtained. He therefore had little alternative but to postpone his plans for Norway and join in the continental war.[37]

Carl Johan accepted the offer of the allies to command the Army of the North, but was reluctant to participate in the final stages of the war, preferring to act as intermediary in the hopes of being chosen to rule France after Napoleon's fall. After the battle of Leipzig (16-19 October 1813), he determined finally to settle matters with Denmark, which had concluded a new treaty of alliance with France in June. Lübeck was occupied on 5 December, the Danes defeated two days later at Bornhöft, and peace finally signed in Kiel in January 1814. Frederik VI agreed to join the anti-French coalition, for which he was to be rewarded with Swedish Pomerania and the island of Rügen. In return, he was to cede Norway as a kingdom, united with that of Sweden (his negotiators were careful not to reveal to their Swedish counterparts that Greenland, Iceland and the Færoes had belonged to the medieval kingdom of Norway). The exchange was to take place as soon as four fortresses in south-east Norway were handed over to the Swedes.

Carl Johan's willingness to contemplate a union of two kingdoms may be seen as a conciliatory gesture, much as Alexander I had sought to win over the Finnish estates by offering to maintain and uphold their privileges and by creating a separate administration. But many Norwegians were not disposed to accept the terms of the treaty; whilst the senescent king Carl XIII remained inactive and his successor was tied up in European affairs, there developed a powerful national resistance in Norway. Aided and abetted by King Frederik VI's representative prince Christian Frederik – whom they elected king on

37. Tommila 1962, p. 394. Guadeloupe was in fact restored to France by the terms of the Peace of Paris, with Britain agreeing to pay compensation of 24 million francs to Sweden.

17 May 1814 – 112 delegates assembled in a national assembly at Eidsvoll, drafted a constitution and proclaimed Norway's independence. Carl Johan marshalled an army on the frontier, but both sides preferred negotiations to a prolonged war. After a fortnight's hostilities, an armistice was concluded, together with a convention, at Moss. The convention provided for the calling of a special Norwegian parliament (*Storting*) to establish the terms of the union. Christian Frederik quietly abandoned his throne, though he was to become a king once more in 1839, this time as Christian VIII of Denmark. Carl Johan indicated his willingness to accept the Eidsvoll constitution; and the Storting 'unanimously elected and acknowledged' Carl XIII as king of Norway on 14 November 1814. There were still unresolved issues to be settled at the Vienna congress. Carl Johan accused the Danes of aiding and abetting the Norwegians, thereby breaching the treaty of Kiel, and refused to hand over Pomerania. Lord Castlereagh, the British foreign minister, was initially sympathetic to the Danish position, but by March 1815 was beginning to back away. The only consolation Denmark obtained was the tiny duchy of Lauenburg, whilst Swedish Pomerania and the island of Rügen went to Prussia.

The manner in which the union of Norway and Sweden was concluded was to give rise to endless disputes in later years. As the Swedish historian Sten Carlsson observes, this was a consequence of the fact that the principal actors in 1814 were more concerned with immediate advantage than with the legalistic consequences.[38] The same may also be said of the settlement of 1809 which Alexander I graciously bestowed upon Finland. Both unions were concluded at a time of considerable international tension. Alexander I sought to win over the relatively quiescent and undemanding Finnish estates with fair words and promises, Carl Johan preferred to conciliate and appease the rather more determined Norwegians. But what happened in 1809 and 1814 was not merely a simple transfer of territories, blessed by favourable internal settlements for the regions so transferred. The decades of warfare had shaken loose many long-established connections and opened up new vistas: and, whilst it would be premature to speak of an awakening of national consciousness, there was undoubtedly a positive willingness to seize new opportunities. Neither in Norway nor in Finland was there any serious popular support for a return to the

38. Carlsson S, Rosén J (eds) 1968 *Carl Johanstiden och den borgerliga liberalismen 1809–65*. Stockholm *(Den svenska historien*, vol. 8), p. 78. There is a good summary in English of the events of 1814 in Derry T 1973 *A History of Modern Norway 1814–1872*, Oxford, pp. 1–16.

old connection, nor was there to be the same degree of enthusiasm for Scandinavism in these countries as there was in Denmark and Sweden. In a number of significant respects, these hitherto neglected peripheral regions were beginning to come into their own, to discover and cherish a sense of their own worth and importance.

CHAPTER TWO

The Baltic in 1800

LAND AND PEOPLE: IMAGES AND REALITY

To educated eighteenth-century Europeans, the most striking feature of the northern periphery of their continent was its climate. It had long been held that climate shaped the character and culture of a people; the Roman historian Tacitus was largely responsible for the persistent belief that the long, cold hyperborean winters had made northern Europeans into rude, hardy folk, with few civilised pretensions. Around the middle of the eighteenth century, however, this image of the North began to change. The 'clear blue skies' of Voltaire's History of Charles the Twelfth, first published in 1731, started to cloud over, and the robust warrior race was overcome with an introspective melancholia. The writings of that great arbiter of Romantic taste, Madame de Staël, are full of assertions that melancholy ('*ce sentiment fécond en ouvrage de génie*') belonged almost exclusively to the perpetually gloomy and misty climate of the North. Another influential French literary critic, Jean François de la Harpe, described the North as 'a remote and dismal region where the mountain mists, the monotonous sound of the sea, and the soughing of the wind among the crags, inspire the mind with a contemplative sadness which becomes habitual.'[1]

This changing image owes much to a work written by a young Swiss teacher of French and published in Copenhagen in 1755 –

1. Staël, Madame de 1820 *De la Littérature. (Œuvres complètes)* 16 vols, Paris, vol. 4, pp. 253, 259. La Harpe J F de 1805 *Lycée, ou, cours de la littérature*, Paris, vol. 3, p. 217.

Paul-Henri Mallet's *Introduction à l'histoire du Dannemarc.* In his account of the origins of the Scandinavian peoples, Mallet had been influenced by Simon Pelloutier's *Histoire des Celtes* (1740), which had endeavoured to show that most of the peoples of Europe were descended from the Celts. The subsequent translation into German (1764–66) and English (1770, with an introduction by Bishop Percy) of Mallet's history of Denmark coincided with the enormous enthusiasm for the mythology and poetry of the ancient Celts which had been aroused with the publication of the purported poems of Ossian by James McPherson. Mallet's subsequent translation of ancient Norse poems were also of seminal influence. Celtic and Norse thus became inextricably mixed together – Gibbon called Edda the sacred book of the ancient Celts, and Chatterton's Druids were worshippers of Thor – and all were cast into the gloomy mists and wild desolation so beloved of the Romantic soul.[2]

Horrid crags, mournful skies and 'the mythological ideas of the inhabitants of the North' which constantly conjured up 'ghosts and phantoms' (Madame de Staël again) or inspired 'emotions of the sublime' provided unlimited inspiration for the poet.[3] The average traveller in northern Europe was somewhat more prosaic, and still inclined towards the classical view of the influence of climate on character. Although rather too many of their published accounts reveal more about their own prejudices than the lands they visited, travellers' tales can often provide graphic descriptions of great value to late twentieth-century readers seeking to visualise a world bereft of most of the things, such as street lighting, underground sewers, breakdown services, instant communication systems, which we take for granted.

We should also remember the true sense of novelty, of venturing into the unknown, which made travellers' accounts so popular with the reading public. Those who ventured to outlandish places (and northern Europe was still considered a bit off the map) were not always quite sure what to expect. Those who travelled in the winter-time clearly expected the worst, and clad themselves appropriately.

2. On this changing image of the North, see: Castrén G 1910 *Norden i den franska litteraturen*, Helsingfors; Farley F 1903 *Scandinavian influences in the English Romantic movement* (Harvard Studies and Notes in Philology and Literature, vol. 9), Boston; and Texte J 1895 *Jean-Jacques Rousseau et les origines du cosmopolitanisme littéraire*, Paris.

3. Staël, Madame de 1968 *Ten years' exile*, Fontwell, Sussex, p. 430. A reviewer of J. Acerbi's *Travels through Sweden, Finland and Lapland to the North Cape in the Years 1798 and 1799* averred that nature in the North 'takes on a bolder outline, and assumes those features of savage grandeur which inspire emotions of the sublime'. *Monthly Review* **39** (1802): p. 226.

Foreign travellers were often surprised to discover that winter was a time of great activity, when travel across the frozen landscape was relatively easy. The journey from Reval to St Petersburg could be accomplished by horse-drawn sledge in less than two days, for example, and well-to-do families in the Baltic provinces, accompanied by their servants, regularly travelled in convoys of sledges to visit their friends and relatives in the countryside.

Winter travel was by no means without its hazards. After a stormy crossing of the open sea from Sweden to the Åland islands in December 1799, Edward Clarke experienced an equally nasty crossing of the ice to get to the Finnish mainland. A sudden wind could spell disaster on the frozen sea, forcing huge blocks of ice to rear and ride up as tall as a two-storey house and rending the surface asunder, much as an earthquake on land. The weeks of thaw also claimed many victims, plunged into icy waters as paths across the ice proved too weak to bear their weight.

The wildernesses of northern Europe were rarely traversed, even by the most intrepid traveller. Most preferred the relative security of the highroad, even if jolted unconscionably in unsprung carts or stagecoaches. The Swedish conveyancing system, whereby peasants were obliged to provide horses and drivers at wayside posting-houses, was generally praised. One young man claimed to have made 206 miles in forty hours on the road from Jönköping to Stockholm. He noted that the roads were 'uncommon good', and that horses were changed regularly every Swedish mile (approximately six English miles), which took them about an hour to travel. But in general, travel by road was slow and uncomfortable. It took George Borrow thirteen hours to cover the thirty miles between Hamburg and Lübeck in 1833 on ill-paved roads, whilst another English traveller in the 1820s thought four miles an hour would be good going on Danish roads. The first real advance towards catering for the growing numbers of tourists who required speed and comfort was at sea. In 1827, a steamship line between London and St Petersburg was inaugurated. The *George IV* could carry up to one hundred passengers, and the journey lasted some nine or ten days. A contemporary traveller estimated that for sixty guineas, one might enjoy a six-weeks' holiday, spending one week each in St Petersburg and Moscow. To undertake the same journey by road would take at least seven weeks, and the expenses of posting alone would be three times as much as the cost of a berth on board ship. By the end of the 1830s, scores of steamships were plying the sea routes and the inland waterways, carrying summer visitors to the new spas and bathing resorts, allowing country cousins a chance to visit relatives and to do some shopping in the big city. A number of these vessels were English-built, such as the fourteen horse-power *Caledonia* which had formerly plied between London and Margate, but which carried William John Monson from Copenhagen to Kiel in the 1820s (as Monson smugly noted, the Danish government had 'engaged from necessity a Scotchman to superintend the works, a manifest confession of the incapacity of the Continent to rival us in these discoveries').[4]

With the exception of Norway and the Swedish uplands, there was little in the way of spectacular scenery to detain the traveller. Vast tracts of heath and moorland, interminable rocks and forests, scattered farmsteads with an occasional cluster of wooden huts and very infrequently a small town were what the voyager could expect to see. The largest city in the Baltic area was St Petersburg (191,000 inhabitants in 1787), the capital of a vast empire of 20 million people, scattered thinly over more than one million square miles. Only four other cities – Danzig, Königsberg, Stockholm and Copenhagen – had more than 50,000 inhabitants. In the relatively populous provinces of East and West Prussia lived one and a half million people, a population density of sixty-seven per square mile. The Kingdom of Sweden, which stretched from the Kattegat to the Kymi river in eastern Finland, was ten times bigger than these two provinces but had only twice the population: the Kingdom of Denmark-Norway had even fewer inhabitants than Sweden (2.2 million), and a population density of twelve per square mile.[5]

Travellers in Scandinavia were frequently surprised at the contrast between the external appearance of peasant huts and their well-scrubbed interiors; and although many wondered whether they would find a dinner at all in the middle of nowhere, they usually were supplied with eggs, smoked meat, salted fish and rye bread, at modest prices. A Swedish pastor on mission to the fell Lapps, Per Læstadius, once had occasion to dance attendance on a party of French tourists eager to feast on Lappish delicacies such as the marrowbones of reindeers. They were served up a dish of salmon trout by a Lapp, who

4. The traveller through Sweden in 1808 was John Fiott, whose letters to Lord Percy are in the Duke of Northumberland's archives, Alnwick. The calculations of the costs of travel to Russia are in: Granville A 1828 *St Petersburgh. A journal of travels to and from that capital* 2 vols, London, vol.1, pp. 455–7. The undated travel diary of William John Monson (1796–1862) is in the Lincolnshire Archive Office, MON 15/B/10. There is a superb description of a steamboat journey on Lake Mälaren in the novel by Jonas Love Almqvist, *Det går an* (1839).

5. The statistics are taken from Zimmermann E 1787 *A political survey of the present state of Europe, in sixteen tables*, London, pp. 6–7, 28, 136.

> had not quite found the best way of stimulating his guests' appetite, for, as they were about to eat, he unfastened his blouse and squashed between his thumbnails a quantity of lice which he discovered there. The foreign gentlemen saw that he was fiddling with something, but did not understand what it was, and so asked me what he was doing, and I enlightened them without more ado. They shook their heads and wondered; but no less did the Lapp wonder, for he could not understand how something so natural could so upset someone, but he stopped doing it nevertheless.[6]

Læstadius' little anecdote not only reveals the sharp contrast between figures from a more refined world and the rude peasantry; it also indicates a certain wry sympathy of the clergyman for his fellow-countrymen, put upon by outsiders whose notions of primitive simplicity were culled from books and not real life. The pleasures of a *partie de campagne* were not unknown amongst the leisured classes of northern Europe: one of the best-known songs of the late eighteenth-century Swedish poet Carl Mikael Bellman describes the delights of an alfresco meal, where red wine is drunk and snipe, eggs and olives consumed. Trips *ins Grüne* were much in vogue amongst town-dwellers, though to the rather jaundiced eye of a German observer, they were less than idyllic:

> I myself once was a member of such a party. Our abode was a wretched, blackened, unfloored peasant hut, from which the inhabitants were absent during the harvest, lit only by an open door and a window hole, in which there was neither chair nor table or benches. At night, everyone slept in the barn, which was also blackened and smoky, like sheep in pens. There everyone piled in together, big and small, old and young, married and single persons of both sexes, with few concessions to modesty. Furthermore we were horribly bitten and tormented by mosquitoes, fleas, flies, crickets and other insects. Nevertheless, everyone was in raptures over the delights of the place . . .[7]

One of the most noteworthy occurrences of the eighteenth century had been the extension westwards of the frontiers of Russia. Russia continued to fascinate western Europeans, many of whom (like their descendants two centuries later) were apt to assume that those who fell under the sceptre of its emperor had been irrevocably changed by that experience. The fact that a peace treaty had placed Lutheran Finns living on the eastern bank of the river Kymi under Russian rule a

6. *Journal af P Læstadius för första året af hans tjenstgöring såsom missionaire i Lappmarken* 2 vols, Stockholm 1831, vol. 1, p. 460.

7. Petri J 1809 *Neuestes Gemählde von Lief-und Ehstland unter Katharina II und Alexander I* Leipzig, vol. 1, p. 331.

mere thirty years earlier clearly counted for little with Sir Nathaniel Wraxall, who crossed the frontier from the Finnish side in 1774. According to Wraxall,

> Here every thing announced a different people from those I had just quitted. The features, the complexion, the manners, the dress of the inhabitants were all Muscovite: and a thousand leagues could not have made a more striking alteration than a few miles had done. It . . . plainly evinces how strongly the character of the individuals which compose society is tinged and formed by the government, policy and religion of the nation.

The more observant Archdeacon Coxe noted, however, that the inhabitants of the region enjoyed considerable privileges and possessed a different religion, which caused him to wonder how far these circumstances rendered them more enlightened than the Russians.[8]

In the autumn of 1809, the remaining Finnish provinces were lost to Sweden for ever when they were transferred to Russian rule after a disastrous war. Although the Emperor Alexander I had flattered his new subjects by summoning the estates earlier in the year and proclaiming the elevation of their country to the ranks of nations, the peace treaty listed only the individual provinces and made no mention of Finland. Mme. de Stäel, who passed rapidly through the country in September 1812, was at a loss to discover any centre of activity in this frozen northern province; a Russian cavalry officer on campaign here in 1809 felt Europe edging away the more he penetrated into the wild and gloomy interior. Later travellers professed to find in Finland an almost antediluvian simplicity, far removed from the turmoil of revolution and civil strife.

An altogether different Finland existed behind this idyllic image. A French observer noted as early as 1812 that Russia, hitherto lacking a merchant marine, had acquired a considerable asset in Finland, with ports from Helsingfors to Uleåborg, extensive shipyards and large numbers of vessels.[9] Peasant boats from the western seaboard had long

8. Wraxall N 1775 *Cursory remarks made in a tour through some of the northern parts of Europe* London, pp. 198–9. Wraxall's book went through two editions in a year, and was also published in Dublin in 1776. Edward Clarke, who crossed the frontier in 1800, was also much struck by the evident inferiority, both in looks and condition, of the Russian Finlanders in comparison with the Swedish. Coxe W 1784 *Travels into Russia, Poland, Sweden and Denmark* 3 vols, London, vol. 3, p. 76. Swinton A 1792 *Travels into Norway, Denmark, and Russia in the years 1788, 1789, 1790 and 1791*, London, p. 484.

9. Staël, Madame de 1968, p. 428. Kiparsky V 1945 *Suomi Venäjän kirjallisuudessa*, Helsinki, p. 41. Catteau-Calleville J 1812 *Tableau de la mer baltique* 2 vols, Paris, vol. 2, pp. 248–9.

supplied Stockholm with a wide range of foodstuffs and articles. The freeing of trade in 1766 had brought considerable prosperity to the towns of Ostrobothnia, whose merchants had played an important and active part in the burghers' estate of the *Riksdag*. Many had business interests and connections in Sweden (as indeed did most of the Finnish aristocracy). Finland's absorption into the Russian empire opened up new possibilities for trade, which the Ostrobothnian peasant-traders and shipowning merchants were quick to exploit.

Beyond the business of buying tar barrels or timber, there were few contacts between this predominantly Swedish-speaking coastal area and the Finnish-speaking inhabitants of the densely forested hinterland. The eastern frontier had been gradually eroded by war during the eighteenth century, and the territory (Old Finland) which Alexander I reunited with the rest of the Grand Duchy in 1811 bore the marks of decades of Russian rule. The extensive donation of crown lands to imperial favourites threatened to reduce the unfortunate peasants on these lands to the servile status of their Russian counterparts. Secondary schools in the region were modelled on German pedagogic methods, and were designed primarily to produce bureaucrats for the service of the state. The language of instruction was German, which was also widely spoken by the mercantile and educated classes in the one big town, Viborg. There was considerable tension when the 'damned Swedes' from the other side of the old frontier started to demand uniformity on their terms after the reunification of Old Finland with the rest of the Grand Duchy.[10]

South-eastern Finland had also been greatly influenced by the growth of St Petersburg, whose population had rocketed to 386,285 in 1818 and was over half a million by mid-century (in comparison, Stockholm had 65,474 inhabitants in 1810, and the largest Finnish town, Åbo, a mere 10,224). Peasants from as far afield as northern Savo brought their butter, horses, chickens, pigs, geese, fresh and salted fish for sale in the capital: by the 1830s in many parishes of the Karelian isthmus, well over half the total earned income came from carrying goods to St Petersburg. Thousands of Finns migrated to the city in search of work. They tended to find jobs in the skilled trades and industry, and were well represented amongst the goldsmiths, clockmakers and bookbinders. More than half of the chimney-sweeps

10. The Finnish historian Matti Klinge has written extensively on this subject in his collections of essays *Bernadotten ja Leninin välissä*, Porvoo 1975, and *Kaksi Suomea*, Helsinki 1982. See also Teperi J 1965 *Vanhan Suomen suomalaisuusliike* Historiallisia tutkimuksia **69**, Helsinki.

in the capital in 1869 were from Finland, a large proportion from the parish of Parikkala, from which the founder of one of the largest firms of chimney cleaners had come in the 1830s. Immigrants also poured into the city from Ingria, the Baltic provinces and especially the Russian hinterland. Not all prospered, and many saw the dark side of life in the capital. 'Winter beggars' from the impoverished regions of eastern Finland were not an uncommon sight on the wide prospects and streets, nor were girls dismissed from domestic service or fleeing to the city from domestic tyranny, and forced to earn a crust by prostitution. The artist Robert Ker Porter, who visited St Petersburg at the beginning of the nineteenth century, also witnessed 'great numbers of hale, stout women, who have newly become mothers' driven 'in droves like milch cows' from the villages of Ingria and the Karelian isthmus to breast-feed the foundlings at the hospital.[11]

No other town in the Baltic area could match St Petersburg's growth rate; indeed, stagnation and regression were more common. Danzig was no longer the queen of the Baltic, its trade and population sadly reduced by the ravages of war and the policies of rival rulers. Göteborg, Sweden's second largest town with 17,000 inhabitants in 1800, enjoyed an unprecedented boom during the Napoleonic wars, but its fortunes took a knock in the immediate postwar years. Monson, who arrived in the town after a four-day crossing on the packet boat from Harwich some time in the 1820s found the quays deserted and grass growing high over the pavement, and an almost complete lack of shops in the town. The disappearance of the herring shoals which had brought prosperity to Sweden's west coast at the end of the previous century, the final winding-up of the East India Company in 1813 and the decline in exports of iron to Britain all contributed to this slump, which reduced the number of vessels visiting the port from an annual average of over 1,400 between 1811 and 1815 to half that number between 1815 and 1820.

The population of Stockholm, the Swedish capital, rose only marginally between 1800 and 1820, in contrast to that of Göteborg and the country as a whole. There were several reasons for this relative stagnation. The towns along the Gulf of Bothnia no longer had to

11. Cited in Engman M 1990 Hittebarnets värld i 1700– och 1800–talets Europa – Findelhuset i S:t Petersburg *Historisk Tidskrift för Finland* **75**: 420. See also Engman M 1983 *S:t Petersburg och Finland. Migration och influens 1703–1917* Bidrag till kännedom av Finlands natur och folk **130**, Helsingfors. Amburger E 1980 *Ingermanland. Eine junge Provinz Russlands im Wirkungsbereiche der Residenz und Weltstadt St.Petersburg-Leningrad* Beiträge zur Geschichte Osteuropas **13:1/2**, Cologne, vol. 1 has details of the economic and social importance of the capital for the surrounding district of Ingria.

direct their trade through the capital after 1766; Stockholm had also to face competition from Göteborg; and the reduction of state support for the city's manufactories reduced the numbers of workers from 7,500 in 1765 to 3,200 in 1815. In common with other large European cities, early nineteenth-century Stockholm also had a high infant mortality rate (one in three babies died before they reached their first birthday) and a high number of illegitimate births (half of these babies died in infancy).

Somewhat larger than the Swedish capital was Copenhagen, with a population in 1800 of around 100,000. The city was ravaged by a disastrous fire in 1797, and suffered extensive damage ten years later from the bombardment unleashed by the British fleet. New building regulations intended to lessen the risk of fire were frequently flouted or ignored; crammed tight within the ramparts, surrounded by fetid, stinking canals, the citizenry were ready victims of waterborne diseases such as cholera and typhoid which ravaged the cities of early nineteenth-century Europe. Copenhagen had acquired a reputation as a city of leisure and pleasure long before Georg Carstensen opened his Tivoli and Vauxhall gardens on meadowland outside the ramparts in 1843. According to Jean-Pierre Catteau, writing in 1802, there were at least twenty clubs in the city, offering amusement and recreation for all classes, whilst a Finnish visitor three years earlier had observed the Sunday parade in the royal garden of people 'of all classes, ages, nations and habits, old men wearing bag-wigs, half-naked nymphs and respectable matrons with nothing uncovered but the tips of their noses . . .'[12]

The combined population of the three Baltic provinces in 1800 was around one million. The great majority were unfree peasants, speaking Estonian in the northernmost province Estland and in northern Livland, and Latvian in southern Livland and the duchy of Kurland, which became part of the Russian empire as a result of the third partition of Poland in 1795. Further west along the Baltic coast, in mixed-language areas such as Pomerania and Slesvig, the percentage of German-speakers was steadily increasing. This did not occur in the Baltic provinces. Here, German was confined to the exclusivist landowning nobility (*Ritterschaften*) and the educated and commercial classes; the unfree peasantry spoke their own tongue and abandoned it

12. Catteau J-P 1802 *Tableau des États danois, envisagés sous les rapports du mécanisme social* 3 vols. Paris, vol. 3, p. 91. These clubs however fell into disfavour and were dissolved in the 1820s: Hovde B 1943 *The Scandinavian countries 1720–1865* 2 vols Ithaca, NY, vol. 2, p. 762. The Finnish traveller was Carl Böcker, whose notes (*Hvarjehanda allehanda (1799)*) are to be found in file E ö I 10, University of Helsinki library.

only if they were lucky enough to climb out of servitude into the ranks of the petty craftsmen or professionals. There were small groups of Swedish speakers on the islands off the north-west coast of Estland, remnants of the Livs around the bay of Riga, whilst on the wilder eastern borders a rich and often confusing mixture of linguistic groups and cultures was to be found. Riga, with some 27,000 inhabitants in 1800, was predominantly German, though there were also large communities of Russian Old Believers and Jews in the city. The first reliable census of 1867 showed that 42.8 per cent of the 102,590 inhabitants were German, 25.1 per cent Russian, 23.5 per cent Latvian and 5.1 per cent Jewish. There were sizeable Jewish communities in the small towns of Kurland, and an even greater number in the adjoining Lithuanian lands annexed to Russia. Russia in fact inherited a 'Jewish question' with the partitions of Poland, a question which successive emperors failed to resolve, or even to understand.[13]

Small provincial towns, with their low wooden houses and dusty streets, offered little to delay the traveller. Most were like the small town on the banks of the river Aa, memorably described by the Baltic German writer Julius Eckardt, where the main political excitement was provided by the early temperance movement and the establishment of a seminary for schoolteachers, where respectable citizens dozed over the staid columns of *Das Inland* or the *Augsburger Allgemeine*, spending their summer leisure time in the skittle alley and their long winter evenings over cards and glasses of punch. Local centres of administration such as Mitau, Reval and Arensburg could, however, offer a rather broader range of facilities and entertainments. During Balthasar von Campenhausen's period of residency as vice-governor (1783–97) on the island of Ösel, the town of Arensburg acquired street lighting, a library and reading circle and a gentleman's club; there was even talk of starting a journal to be called *Der nordische Mischmasch*. The fashion for seaside bathing in the early nineteenth century brought steamship parties to the spa facilities specially built for their delectation in towns such as Arensburg, Hapsal and Helsingfors. More lively still were the major towns strung along the southern Baltic coastline from Riga to Lübeck. One local patriot averred in 1805 that Riga society during the winter season was comparable to the best Germany could offer, and he only regretted that an excess of card-playing prevented these brilliant circles of polite society becoming the most delightful in northern Europe. Another writer offered a

13. Klier J 1986 *Russia gathers her Jews. The origins of the 'Jewish question' in Russia 1772–1825*, DeKalb, Illinois.

somewhat more down-to-earth description of polite company everywhere: when general talk about the weather, of the newspapers, of one's neighbours, of purchases for the household was exhausted, then the cards were produced and finally, all sat down round a well-laden table, where complaints about bad hands and compliments on the exquisite dishes being consumed continued to flow unabated. This southern German writer, who landed up in Danzig just before it was besieged by the French in 1807, was also critical of the natives' artistic taste and values, claiming that they preferred a good joint to a work of art, and he felt that the local youth might find better employment than spending their evenings learning about horses, tobacco and ladies of the night in low clubs. He did however praise the new theatre, erected at a cost of 30,000 thaler to replace the ruinous wooden building compared by an earlier visitor to a stables.[14]

The theatre was indeed the great symbol of a town's cultural life. Like Danzig, Riga also acquired a new theatre in 1780. Built on the initiative of Otto von Vietinghoff, it could seat five hundred, and had a clubroom on the second floor. The stage was in use four days of the week, with balls and concerts every fortnight. Four or five new performances were staged each month, including a major and a minor opera, by a company of thirty-three actors, six dancers and twenty-four musicians. In Denmark, there was a veritable theatre mania at the beginning of the nineteenth century. One contemporary recorded that every small place between Aalborg and Skanderborg had its theatre, some for the nobility, some for the schoolchildren and even some for farmhands and dairymaids. The most popular playwright on the repertoire was undoubtedly August Kotzebue, who was for a time director of the theatre in Reval, and who turned out plays by the dozen. One of the undoubted hits of its day was Carl Maria von Weber's opera *Der Freischütz*, performed in all the major theatres of northern Europe within a year of its Berlin premiere. When it was staged in St Petersburg in 1824, it proved almost impossible to get tickets, though it was performed twice weekly. Artistes going to the Russian capital often gave recitals and concerts en route, sometimes performing in an unheated theatre in the dead of winter; it was so cold in the Mitau theatre that the breath of the famous virtuoso

14. *Fragmente aus den Briefen eines Reisenden aus Liefland* s.l., 1795, pp. 4–5. *Danzig. Eine Skizze in Briefe; geschrieben vor, während und nach der Verlagerung im Jahre 1807*, Amsterdam and Hamburg, 1808, pp. 46–7, 63, 114–15. Feyerabend K 1798 *Kosmopolitische Wanderungen durch Preussen, Liefland, Kurland, Litthauen*, 2 vols Germanien, vol. 1, p. 127. See also the memoirs of Johanna Schopenhauer 1847 *Youthful Life and Pictures of Travel*, 2 vols London.

H. W. Ernst reportedly froze to his violin. Such visits were plainly welcomed and patronised by the public; at other times, however, they probably had to endure sopranos screeching like owls in *La Muette de Portici*, or prompters bellowing loud enough to be heard on the market-place. On the other hand, actors often had to make do with inadequate dressing rooms and primitive stages (often in tobacco warehouses or even cattle-byres in the smaller towns) and compete with the rustling of sweet and cake wrappings as the audience sustained themselves during the performance before going off to the nearby *Conditorei* to consume vast amounts of grog, punch and *Glühwein*.[15]

ESTATES AND CLASSES

Although the pressures of economic and social change were beginning to reshape the social order, the corporate structures which had evolved over centuries – the gilds, magistracies, estates and orders – remained essentially intact. Enlightened reformers might look forward to the day when the fortunes of society could be guided by a self-confident middle class, but that day was still far off. Closed corporations continued to run the affairs of the cramped, dirty, old-fashioned cities of the Baltic much as they had done for centuries. In Prussia, urban government was reformed in 1808; but in the ancient Hanseatic towns along the southern shores of the Baltic, the old system continued. In Lübeck, a city of 24,000 inhabitants in 1835, power was exercised by a self-recruiting senate of four burghermasters and sixteen councillors; in Riga, where a similar system of government survived until 1877, the patriciate of wealthy merchants, members of the gild of St Mary's, numbered less than a thousand and citizenship was confined to a tiny fraction of the city's growing population.

15. The multi-volumed *Theatergeschichte Europas* by H Kindermann, offers a general introduction to the history of the theatre; I have also drawn on: Bosse H 1989 The establishment of the German theater in eighteenth-century Riga *Journal of Baltic Studies* **20**: 207–222; Hirn S 1970 *Teater i Viborg 1743–1870*, Helsingfors; the first volume of the memoirs of Schauman A 1892 *Från sex årtionden i Finland*, Helsingfors. For the visit of Ernst, and the general state of the theatre in the Baltic provinces in the 1840s, see the columns of *Das Inland* (1847), pp. 132, 413. The sweetmeat eaters were heard in the theatre in Königsberg by Karl Rosenkranz, a philosophy don at the university, whose two-volume *Königsberger Skizzen* was published in Danzig in 1842. According to Rosenkranz, the fourth largest city in the kingdom was isolated, and likely to be more so as the new steamer service between Lübeck and St Petersburg came into operation. Berliners looked down on the city as a cultural desert, poorly lit and badly paved.

As the volume of trade across the oceans of the world began rapidly to expand, the Baltic was in danger of becoming a stagnant backwater. The revival of the grain trade at the end of the eighteenth century was killed by the agricultural depression which set in after the Napoleonic war: the annual average volume of wheat and rye exported via Danzig and Elbing in the early 1820s was less than one-seventh of that exported in the boom years at the beginning of the century. Other products of the Polish and Russian hinterlands still managed to find markets in the West. Boards, deals and planks were shipped in vast quantities from Memel to supply the shipwrights and house builders of Britain. With the thaw came the flotillas of crudely-built rafts, crewed by wild *dzimken* in sheepskins, carrying cargoes of flax and hemp downriver to the ports of Riga, Memel and Königsberg. J. C. Petri, writing in 1809, claimed that in a good year, as many as a thousand of these rafts were moored on the banks of the Düna, each carrying a cargo worth 8,000–10,000 thaler. This riverborne trade continued to flourish until the advent of the railways.[16] A review of the foreign trade of the Livonian ports in 1847 concluded that there had been a relative decline since the golden years of the late eighteenth century; but what is more striking is the fact that the type of goods imported had changed very little since the middle ages. Salt constituted one-fifth of the 5 million roubles' worth of Riga's imports in 1845, followed in importance by sugar (997,000 roubles), herrings (548,000) and wine (410,000). Manufactured goods accounted for only 394,000 roubles. There were few manufacturing industries in the city even twenty years later; only two steam-powered sawmills, two cork factories and a linen mill employed more than one hundred workers.

Alongside the commercial *Bürgertum* was to be found the growing number of educated, professional people, academics, clergymen, lawyers and doctors, often in the forefront of movements for reform. However, although occasionally called an 'estate' (e.g. the *Literatenstand* of the Baltic provinces) or regarded as persons of quality (*ståndspersoner* in Sweden and Finland), such people did not easily fit into the established categories, and their political activities were still largely confined to the pages of journals, to coffee-houses and assembly rooms. To their number may also be added well-established entrepreneurs such as the Swedish ironmasters, and the standard-bearers of economic change – surveyors, land agents, engineers and the early industrialists.

16. Petri J 1809, vol. 2, pp. 178, 233. Schopenhauer J 1847, vol. 1, pp. 53–65. There is a good description of these rafts and the *dzimken* in the short story *Die Reise nach Tilsit* by Hermann Sudermann, published in 1917.

Throughout the Baltic region, it was the nobility which remained the dominant social and political class, in spite of attacks by reformers and revolutionaries and the encroachments of commoners on their status and position. Commoners were busily buying up gentlemen's estates on the southern shores of the Baltic, especially during the agricultural boom years of the late eighteenth century, when land prices often quintupled within fifty years and estates – as it was rumoured in Königsberg – could change hands two or three times during the course of a dinner. The agricultural depression of the early nineteenth century also forced many impoverished Junkers to sell up. In Denmark, the old nobility had long ceased to occupy an important position as landowners; the typical estate owner was more likely to be a more recently ennobled proprietor or even a hard-headed farmer of commoner stock. Non-noble possession of *frälsejord*, land originally owned by the Swedish nobility and endowed with tax privileges, rose sharply during the reign of Gustav III. This trend was given official sanction in 1789, when the Act of Union permitted the purchase and acquisition of noble land (with the exception of allodial demesnes) for all estates. By 1809, over a quarter of all *frälsejord* in Sweden was in non-noble hands; by 1825, this had risen to over one-third. The Swedish nobility had long claimed the right to occupy the highest offices of state, but here too, they were losing ground. The formal abolition of noble prerogatives within the administration in 1809 actually had little immediate effect until the 1820s, when the first non-noble member of State Council was appointed. The proportion of high offices held by commoners rose from just over half in 1820 to over two-thirds in 1865, on the eve of the reform which transformed the four-estate *Riksdag* into a bicameral legislature. The fact that the four estates survived so long, and that noblemen continued to serve as prime ministers and foreign secretaries until the twentieth century, should however serve as a reminder of the continuing social and political importance of the Swedish aristocracy.

The gentry of the eastern provinces of Gustav III's kingdom were fewer in number, and their means more modest than those of their counterparts in Sweden proper. Few, if any Finnish gentlemen could afford to live off the incomes of their estates, and they were compelled, as one contemporary put it, 'to strive and jostle for office with the young men of other estates'.[17] The transfer of Finland from Swedish to Russian rule in 1809 opened up new career opportunities

17. Cited in Wirilander K 1982 *Herrskapsfolk. Ståndspersoner i Finland 1721–1870* Nordiska museets handlingar **98**, Stockholm, p. 171.

at home and in the empire at large. During the nineteenth century, aristocrats began to fill posts at all levels in the Grand Duchy: one-fifth of Finland's postmasters and land surveyors in 1840 were noblemen, for example. Several unfortunates failed even to reach the middling ranks of the salariat: the Finnish calendar of the nobility for 1872 recorded a blue-blooded cobbler and a crofter of gentle birth. By and large, however, the aristocracy maintained a presence far in excess of their size as a social group within the upper echelons of the bureaucracy in Finland throughout the first half of the nineteenth century. In 1818, six of the eighteen members of the Finnish government, or Senate were non-noble, but by 1850, the proportion had declined to four out of seventeen. The proportion of non-noble holders of high office also declined over the same period from 60 to 54 per cent. Even though there was a steady increase in the share of non-noble holders of high office thereafter, noblemen still occupied thirty per cent of these posts in 1890, when they constituted a mere 0.1 per cent of the population at large.

The possession of land still carried with it many of the privileges appertaining to the nobility. East Prussian landowners retained the right to hold their own courts until 1848, and to exercise police powers on their estates until 1872. Private courts (*Birkeret*) were abolished in Denmark in 1849, and tax privileges a year later, though demesne land remained exempt from payment of the tithe and the landowners still had the responsibility for collecting their tenant farmers' taxes. Large landowners were also automatically members of the parish assemblies (*Sogneforstandskaber*) and were given special representation in the provincial assemblies established in the 1830s.

The nobility of the Baltic provinces of Estland, Livland and Kurland, with their jealously-guarded matriculation rolls, provincial assemblies (*Landtage*) and effective control of provincial and local government, were, however, in a class of their own, maintaining many of their antiquated privileges until the collapse of the Russian Empire. The reforming Empress Catherine II had attempted to break down this wall of privileges which so effectively limited the powers of the central authority. The 1775 statute for the administration of the provinces of Russia was implemented in Livland and Estland (renamed Reval and Riga provinces) in 1782–83; the charters to the towns and to the nobility, both of which undercut the exclusivity of the burghers and *Ritterschaften*, were introduced in 1785, and the principal institutions of noble self-government were abolished one year later. Imperial institutions were also introduced into Kurland upon its annexation in 1795. One year later, the empress was dead and her successor Paul restored Estland, Livland and Kurland as special provinces of the empire governed according to their ancient rights and privileges.[18] At the apex of their elaborate system of local self-government stood the provincial *Landtag*, which elected an executive council (*Landratscollegium* in Estland and Livland, *Ritterschaftskomité* in Kurland) and appointed noble officers to supervise justice, law and order and ecclesiastical affairs. Possessors of estates who were not matriculated noblemen were kept strictly on the margins, allowed to vote on matters of taxation (and not until 1866 was that right conceded in Estland) but having precious little else to say or do. Not without reason did the German traveller J. G. Kohl describe the Baltic nobility as 'independent kings'.[19]

REFORMING THE 'COMMON PEOPLE'

The era of the French revolution was also one of major land reform throughout Europe. East of the Elbe this process was conducted on terms less than favourable to the peasantry. The Prussian emancipation edict of 9 October 1807 laid the basis for a free market in land and labour, and ended hereditary bondage for the peasantry as from Martinmas 1810. However, it did not distinguish between the personal and purely tenurial obligations of the peasant, and it allowed estate owners to absorb plots of land to which the peasant farmer could show no hereditary claim. In these circumstances, the landowners were able to take advantage of the ambiguities of the edict, in spite of later attempts by the government to prevent peasant lands being absorbed wholescale into noble estates. Only those peasants who performed labour service with a team of draught animals and who could prove the validity of their family's tenancy from a specified date were 'regulated', according to an edict of 1816. An ordinance in 1821 decreed that regulated peasants were to retain all their land and they could buy their freedom from obligatory service on payment of a sum

18. Madariaga I de 1981 *Russia in the age of Catherine the Great*, London, pp. 316–24. Thaden E 1984 *Russia's western borderlands 1710–1870*, Princeton, NJ, pp. 18–31, 51.

19. Kohl J 1841 *Die deutsch-russischen Ostseeprovinzen* 2 vols, Dresden/Leipzig, vol. 1, p. 34. For details of the institutions of Baltic German autonomy, see Haltzel M 1977 *Der Abbau der deutschen ständischen Selbstverwaltung in den Ostseeprovinzen Russlands 1855– 1905* Marburger Ostforschungen **37**, Marburg, pp. 6–8, and the contribution on the Baltic Germans by the same author in: Thaden E. (ed.) 1981 *Russification in the Baltic provinces and Finland, 1855–1914*, Princeton, NJ, pp. 113–14.

calculated at twenty-five times the annual value of such services. The sum calculated was based on the high grain prices of the early nineteenth century, and many peasants, already struggling at the onset of the depression and not entitled to obtain cheap loans from the nobles' *Landschaft* credit institutions, were unable to pay and had to settle for an annual rent or the loss of their lands. Even so, peasants with hereditary status probably fared better than those without such protection, who were obliged to surrender up to half of the land they leased to the landowner as the price of emancipation, and who were still obliged to perform compulsory labour services. The most reliable estimate suggests that the peasantry lost something like one million hectares of land in the kingdom as a whole; in East Prussia, the proportion of peasant farmers declined from over one-third of the rural population in 1805 to a quarter in 1867.

Personal emancipation did not greatly alter the circumstances of the Estonian and Latvian peasantry, either. '*Land mein, Zeit dein*' (the land is mine, yours is the time) was the brutally succinct summation of the land reforms of 1816–19 in the Baltic provinces. Not only did the peasant have no legal title to the land he farmed, he was forbidden to leave agriculture, and even movement from one estate to another was severely restricted. The landowner still had the right to administer physical chastisement to those working on his lands, and he exercised judicial and police control over those on his estates. Although the ideas of modern, commercial farming were beginning slowly to influence the landowners, according to a leading Estonian agrarian historian, the peasantry still remain locked in the old order. They took little interest in the issues of freedom and ownership, but continued to fight against exploitation of their labour services, and to look to the monarch for a truly just redistribution of the land.[20]

In Denmark, where reforms began in the 1780s, the outcome was rather different in the lands to the east of the river Elbe. Here, the peasantry had always had a legal existence, and they occupied and farmed as tenants something like nine-tenths of the total acreage under cultivation. The reformers of the Great Land Commission (active between 1786 and 1806) were conscious of the need for a free and prosperous peasant-farmer class, and to this end, they sought not only to regulate the relationship of tenant and landlord more precisely, but to allow tenants to buy up the freehold of their land. Between 1780 and 1820, two-thirds of the leasehold farms in Denmark were

20. Kahk J 1993 *Talude päriseksostmise aegu*, Tallinn, pp. 13–16.

converted to freehold. This process was most advanced on the Jutland peninsula, and it was not until the 1830s that the decisive shift from tenancy to freehold ownership took place on the more fertile island of Sjælland. Much of the land was enclosed during the same period; the hedging, ditching and draining of the fields and the stone or brick farmsteads which the newly-independent farmers built beyond the narrow confines of the old pre-enclosure village created the landscape of much of present-day Denmark.

There were also more mouths to feed in this changing rural world. Between 1700 and 1785, there had been a 50 per cent increase in the population of Denmark; numbers more than doubled in the next eighty-five years (from 840,000 in 1785 to 1,785,000 in 1870). In spite of a modest degree of urban growth, three out of four Danes still continued to live, work and die in the countryside, and farming was their main source of livelihood; 44 per cent of the population in 1870 was engaged in agriculture, one per cent more than in 1787. There were considerable differences of wealth and status within the rural community, further increased by the pressure on land. Parcellisation was common as a means of helping defray the cost of purchasing the freehold on the whole farm. The estimated 55,000 farmsteads of 1805 had increased by 10,000 thirty years later, largely as a result of division, but the number of cottages had jumped from some 57,000 to 90,000, of which over a quarter were without land. The smallholdings attached to these cottages varied greatly in size. On the sparsely-populated Jutland peninsula, for example, where the cottagers (*Husmænd*) were usually freeholders, their holdings were often quite extensive. On the more fertile and more densely-populated islands, tied cottages (*Lejehus*), with a plot of land to feed the occupants and their families, were more common. The colonies of smallholders which grew up on the margins of villages provided a labour force for the local farmers, though they also developed specialist trades, such as clog-making in the wooded region around Silkeborg. The relationship between the cottager and the new class of yeoman-farmers (*Gaardmænd*) was often a tense one. The legislation of 1807 left the two parties to a contract to determine the obligations of the *Husmænd*, but said nothing about the rights of the farmer to chastise his labourers with physical force – a right denied the estate owner over his tenants since 1791. Farmers were also admitted to the ranks of persons deemed suitable to administer local government, a privilege denied to the cottager.

The consequences for the countryside of population growth were felt elsewhere, too. In Finland, where the population doubled between

1750 and 1810, and doubled again in the next fifty years, the proportion of landless rural habitants rose from 35 per cent in 1754 to 52 per cent in 1875. The rural population of Sweden grew by 1.3 million between 1800 and 1870, but two-thirds of that increase occurred amongst the poorer classes, the crofters, cottagers and landless labourers. At the bottom of the rural social order were the *statare*, farmhands (as a rule, married) on an annual or six-monthly contract, for which they received a tied cottage and an agreed wage, much of it paid in kind. Around 40,000 in 1805, their numbers had trebled to 128,000 by 1870. In some areas such as the relatively fertile plains of Skåne, the pressure on land forced many small peasant farmers into the ranks of the landless. The new breed of landowner, the non-noble *possessionater*, preferred when they could to convert their crofters into simple *statare*, and incurred a great deal of criticism for so doing.

A. I. Arsenyev, who had been a member of the 1804 Livonian land reform commission, maintained that the peasant lands of that province were cultivated by a mere 20,000–30,000 families, leaving over 300,000 people without land. In his opinion, the peasant farmer treated his landless labourers worse than the estate-owner, and there is certainly evidence of farmers in the northern half of the province concluding agreements amongst themselves in the 1840s to keep wages down. The emancipation of the peasantry had not resolved the question of land ownership, and the peasant-farmer still had to carry out a number of obligations in order to be able to farm the land he occupied but did not own. Folk poetry portrayed the owner of the manor (*mõisa, muiža*) as a foreign invader who had seized the land, driving the indigenous people into subservience. According to the folklorist Friedrich Reinhold Kreutzwald, the peasants believed that they had forcibly been deprived of their land by the Germans, and that they would have to use violence as well to regain it.

The poverty and degradation of the peasantry in the Baltic provinces was widely commented on. The German traveller J. G. Kohl was of the opinion that many a savage in his wigwam enjoyed more confort than did the Estonian peasants in their ill-constructed huts, in which humans slept, worked, ate, gave birth and were ill in the company of bleating lambs, grunting pigs and barking dogs. Mihkel Martna's recollections of his childhood in an Estonian village in the 1860s confirm this grim picture of overcrowding, dirt and disease. The daily diet was bread and salted Baltic herring, washed down with milk. Butter was the only thing that could be sold, and was therefore never consumed by the peasant household. If anyone made meat broth in the summer, news soon got around, for this was a sign of wealth: all the salted meat had been used up well before that time. Springtime for the gentry was a time of joy, lamented a Latvian poet in 1832, but for the peasant, it was a time of hunger.[21]

Emancipation brought little improvement to the lot of the peasant in the lands east of the Elbe. The agricultural expert William Jacob found much evidence of poor agricultural equipment and methods in East Prussia, where:

> The working class of the inhabitants, amounting in the maritime provinces to upwards of a million, including both those who work for daily wages and those who cultivate their own little portions of land, cannot be compared to any class of persons in England. This large description of the inhabitants live in dwellings provided with few conveniences, on the lowest and coarsest food; potatoes, or rye or buck wheat, are their chief, and frequently their only food; linen, from the flax of their own growth, and wool, spun by their own hands, both coarse and both worn as long as they will hold together, furnish their dress; whilst an earthen pot that will bear fire, forms one of the most valuable articles of their furniture. They are warmed more by the abundance of fuel than the shelter of their draughty houses. Honey and chicory serve as substitutes for sugar and coffee, but are often sold to meet tax demands. Though the price of whiskey is low, yet the farm produce is still lower; and neither that, nor the bad beer which is commonly brewed, can be afforded by the peasantry as a usual drink.[22]

Further north, in the fells or the dense forests along the Swedish-Norwegian border, in the hinterland of eastern Finland, or on the countless small coastal islands, families scratched a meagre existence from the soil, feeding on what they could catch as much as what they could grow. Occasionally, even the most inured traveller was upset by

21. Kohl J 1841, vol. 2, pp. 202–4. Martna M 1914 *Külast. Mälestused ja tähelepanekud Eesti külaelu arenemisest pärast 1860-id aastaid*, Tallinn, pp. 26–34, 55. Kahk J 1969 *Die Krise der feudalen Landwirtschaft in Estland*, Tallinn, p. 159, citing the Latvian poem. Woltmann J 1833 *Beschriebung einer reise nach St Petersburg, Stockholm und Kopenhagen*, Hamburg, p. 39 also notes that the Latvians call spring *baddu laiks*, 'the time of hunger'.

22. Jacob W 1826 *Report on the trade in foreign corn and on the agriculture of northern Europe*, London, pp. 50–1. It should, however, be remembered that Jacob was writing during a period of severe agricultural depression. There were areas where the farmers were industrious and wealthy, such as the delta of the Vistula, where descendants of the Mennonite refugees impressed visitors with their excellent cheeses and dairy products and their solid brick-built farmhouses, and there is evidence that peasant farmers were beginning to switch to cash crops such as flax – with some success – by the 1820s and 1830s, as the depression was beginning to lift.

the misery of the poverty they witnessed, such as that of the family encountered by Edward Clarke at Christmas time on a remote Åland island, wracked with smallpox and subsisting on salted herring, or the inhabitants of tumbledown huts up in the fells of Mora, on the Swedish–Norwegian border, who had nothing to offer a visiting Danish pastor but sour milk in a wooden scoop (they had a marvellous view, however). Visiting the same area in the 1850s, the Swede Carl Säve found that rye bread was regarded as a delicacy: the natives were satisfied if they could eat a bread made of one-third barley, one-third oats and one-third pea flour 'which gives the bread such a harsh and bitter taste that, unless it is chewed thoroughly and at length, not one single mouthful can be persuaded to slide down the gullet of a southern Swede'.[23]

The poverty of the landless was a major topic of debate during the first decades of the nineteenth century. Conservatives tended to attack the plutocratic, grasping new men and to idealise those who farmed in the good old-fashioned way with their own and their children's labour, supported by unmarried farmhands, whom they fed and lodged. Liberals believed that abolition of restrictions on the freedom of labour and employment was the best means of tackling the problem of pauperism. Books written for a peasant readership, such as *The Swedish peasant, portrayed in his improved and degenerated state, by tales from the lives of two brothers, one of whom was a model and the other a blot on his estate* (1831) served an evident didactic and moral purpose: but what was lacking were workable practical solutions to the problems of poverty.

One of the most hotly-debated problems was the excessive consumption of alcohol. In most of northern Europe – where the temperance movement began to take root in the 1830s and 1840s – the poor man's favoured tipple was the fiery brandywine rather than the foaming tankard.[24] Since distillation consumed great quantities of grain, unrestricted production was regarded as unwise by many economists. This was particularly the case in Sweden after the loss of

23. Levander L 1944 *Våmhusfjärdingen* Folklivsskildringar utgiven av Kungl. Gustav Adolfs Academien **4**, Stockholm, p. 22, 191. 'Between what is poverty in England, and absolute destitution, there are many steps', observed a Scottish writer in the 1830s. 'Poverty here, in Sweden, means absolute destitution.' Laing S 1839 *A Tour in Sweden in 1838*, London, p. 150.

24. These two terms were used by E. von Rechenberg-Linten, a Kurlander who claimed that the peasantry of his native province were more sober than those further north because they preferred beer (and were more 'civilised' because they got on better with their landlords). See Rechenberg-Linten's contribution to the debate on drunkenness in the periodical *Das Inland* (1847), p. 334.

its major grain-supplying territories in 1721. In the middle of the eighteenth century, it was calculated that Sweden spent as much on imported grain which was then turned into spirits as it did on all other imported goods. Various ways of curbing or controlling production were tried, including a complete ban on distillation between 1756 and 1760; but all failed in the face of determined peasant opposition. In 1800, farmers were granted limited rights to distil for their own domestic needs. Ten years later, the right to produce spirituous liquor was conceded to virtually all sections of society by the *Riksdag*. In 1855, home distilling was legally restricted, though per capita consumption of alcohol had begun to fall before then.

The Grand Duchy of Finland continued to operate the more restrictive system brought into force in 1800. Improvements in equipment and techniques in the 1820s prompted measures to control output, and fines for drunkenness were increased. The ready availability of strong liquor at peasant weddings and dances was seen as a potent source of violence, though it has been argued that the sudden rise in the homicide rate in southern Ostrobothnia between the 1780s and 1830s was more likely a consequence of social tensions and a weakening of official sanctions against violent crime than of drunken, knife-wielding peasants yielding to their inherently aggressive tendencies.[25] In the Baltic provinces, where the right to distil and sell alcohol was a noble privilege, it would seem that output actually declined as a result of competition from cheaper Russian spirits, and many landowners turned to other possible sources of income, such as flax-growing and sheep-rearing. However, using new and more efficient equipment and mixing potatoes with grain, landowners were able to increase production significantly from the 1840s. The number of rural inns in Livland doubled between 1823 and 1840 (when there was one per two hundred inhabitants) and sales of brandywine to Russia also rose. Beef cattle for the St Petersburg market were fattened on the draff; in the 1840s, over twenty thousand beasts from north-eastern Estland were supplied annually to the city, a trade which was largely in peasant hands. The beneficial uses to which the waste product of distillation could be put was one of the arguments raised against those who sought to curb production; rising land prices and high interest rates were adduced as another obstacle to landowners

25. Ylikangas H 1976 *Puukkojunkkareitten esiinmarssi. Väkivalta-rikollisuus Etelä-Pohjanmaalla 1790–1825*, Helsinki. A brief résumé of the arguments advanced in this fascinating study is provided in Ylikangas H 1976 Major fluctuations in crimes of violence in Finland *Scandinavian Journal of History* **1**: 91–5.

cutting production, which in Livland absorbed as much as one-fifth of the total grain yield.[26]

To regulate and control the changing rural world, new institutions had to be created. In order to avoid errors and upsets to the civil and economic order, as the 1819 peasant ordinance for Kurland put it, the peasantry had to be released gradually into liberty. The peasant communes (*Bauerngemeinde*) which were established in all three Baltic provinces were carefully supervised by the estate owners; but in comparison with other parts of the Russian empire, the Estonian and Latvian peasantry were able to exercise a considerable degree of influence over their own affairs. The increased use of Latvian and Estonian in documents and minute-books made the standardisation of language a matter of some urgency. This was, however, no easy matter, in spite of the enthusiasm of enlightened clergymen such as Otto Wilhelm Masing and Karl Watson, who published newspapers in Estonian and Latvian during the 1820s, and the appearance of the first swallows of modern Estonian and Latvian literature, Kristjan Jaak Peterson (1801–22) and the blind poet, Indrikis (1783–1828). Languages, like constitutions, have specific social and political implications and functions: and both, in the early decades of the nineteenth century, had still to be freed from the moorings of a paternalistic and intensely conservative society.

The emancipated Estonian and Latvian peasantry were confined to the management of their communal affairs: local government remained in the hands of the Baltic German landowners. In Sweden and Finland, where the peasantry had always constituted a distinct estate, it was from the ranks of the farmers that the members of the parish assembly, commissions and boards were largely drawn, though the clergy continued to play a central supervisory role.[27] But even though they constituted a kind of village elite, controlling the lives of the less fortunate members of the community in a variety of ways, the peasant-farmers still remained separated from the higher echelons of the social order. Indeed, considerable efforts were made to maintain this distinction. Although increasingly committed to the provision of

26. Details of the production and sale of alcohol in the Baltic provinces are to be found in Konks J 1973 *Pärisorjustest kapitalismi läveni* Tartu riikliku ülikooli toimetised **316**, Tartu, pp. 55–61, and Kahk J 1969 *Die Krise der feudalen Landwirtschaft in Estland,* Tallinn. See also the contribution by Mangelheim von Qvalen in *Das Inland* (1847), pp. 65–7.

27. For an interesting comparative overview of institutional change in the countryside, see Jansson T 1987 *Agrarsamhällets förändring och landskommunal organisation* Studia Historica Upsaliensia **146**, Uppsala.

general elementary education, the authorities were careful to ensure that a little learning for the children of the common folk did not become a dangerous thing. The sons of Danish elementary schoolmasters, like the sons of peasants, millers and innkeepers were liable for conscription unless they chose to follow in their fathers' footsteps. Prussian seminary graduates were obliged to serve a reduced term in the ranks, unlike the gymnasium teachers, whose privileged status was confirmed by their exemption from military service. In order to avoid the risk of would-be rural schoolmasters acquiring airs and graces which might set them apart from their charges (and set a bad example), teacher-training seminaries were often located in the countryside, and their pedagogical programmes tailored to the severely practical purpose of drumming the basics of the alphabet, multiplication tables and the catechism into unwilling country children. The regulations of an elementary school founded in the southern Finnish parish of Sippola in 1858, for example, specifically decreed that its main purpose was to teach children to be God-fearing, to love and honour their peasant estate and their fatherland: the rough homespun of their fathers was not to be rejected through careless pride.[28]

The assault on serfdom had been led by members of the educated classes at the end of the eighteenth century; it was the selfsame people who sought to respond to the implications of peasant emancipation when that was achieved. In the Baltic provinces, several attempts were made to produce suitable literature in Estonian and Latvian, and a group of local worthies in the small town of Arensburg on the island of Ösel even launched an Estonian Society in 1817, with the declared intention of correcting and improving the language. Johann Heinrich Rosenplänter's semi-annual journal, *Beiträge zur genauern Kenntniss der ehstnischen Sprache*, read largely by fellow-clergymen who ministered to the Estonians in the Baltic provinces, attempted for almost twenty years to grapple with the problems of communication. The fundamental dilemma was expressed thus by Rosenplänter in the eleventh volume (1818): 'The Germans wish to educate [*bilden*] the Estonians. That is fine and worthy; but education only comes from teaching, teaching only through language. If however the teachers

28. Hellgren K 1957 *Sippolan historia*, Myllykoski, p. 496. LaVopa A 1980 *Prussian schoolteachers. Profession and office 1763–1848*, Chapel Hill, NC, pp. 54–77 shows how the controlled experiment of seminaries in Prussia failed to prevent discontent amongst the graduates. On the elementary school in Estland, see Speer H 1936 *Das Bauernschulwesen im Gouvernement Estland vom Ende des 18. Jahrhunderts bis zur Russifierung*, Tartu, and Andresen L 1991 *Eesti rahvakooli vanem ajalugu*, Tallinn.

speak the language but poorly, how can the task of education be successfully accomplished?' The debate aroused by this question continued until the journal ceased publication, with no satisfactory conclusion ever being reached.[29]

Those who sought to raise up the peasantry had to face a number of difficulties, not least the peasants' own lack of self-esteem. The legacy of servitude had left a deep mark, which was not easily erased. Most observers made a sharp distinction between those recently emancipated from serfdom and the 'free' peasantry of Norway, Sweden and Finland. Archdeacon Coxe commented favourably on the free status of the Norwegian peasant compared with his enslaved Danish counterpart in the 1780s. A pastor from Hamburg travelling through the Baltic provinces and Scandinavia in the early 1830s was struck by the contrast between the easy and self-confident behaviour of the Swedes and the self-abasement of the Latvian peasantry. He believed that it was premature to speak of the latter as 'free peasants', since their circumstances were so miserable. The well-known German traveller J. G. Kohl found that the peasantry were regarded with contempt, especially by uneducated Baltic Germans. The inquisitive foreigner was invariably told that the Latvians were deceitful thieves, that they could only be controlled by a good whipping or with a bottle of schnapps. As for the Estonians, they did not even have a name for themselves, and referred to the country in which they lived simply as '*meie maa*', our country.[30]

One of the toughest problems faced by those seeking a better understanding of the peasants' tongue was frequently the downright indifference of the peasants themselves. Ambitious people of humble origin shed their Low German or Danish speech as they climbed the social ladder, or abandoned what they regarded as their clumsy peasant dialect in order to assimilate into the predominantly German- or Swedish-speaking culture of the urban centres of the eastern Baltic. In Finland, with its free peasantry and relatively few large landowners, a significant section of the swedified ruling elite was in the course of time able to establish its credentials for national leadership by playing

29. *Beiträge zur genauern Kenntniss der ehstnischen Sprache*, Pernau 1818, vol. 11, p. xii. The journal appeared between 1813 and 1832. Significant contributions to the debate include an article in volume 12 (1818) by Otto Masing, and a lengthy disquisition on the origins of Estonian by Heinrich von Jannau in volume 19 (1828). For a recent overview of Rosenplänter's journal, see Scholz F 1990 *Die Literaturen des Baltikums. Ihre Entstehung und Entwicklung* Abhandlungen der Rheinisch-Westfälischen Akademie der Wissenschaften **80**, Opladen, pp. 113–17.

30. Woltmann J 1833, p. 40. Kohl J 1841, vol. 2, pp. 35–44, 190.

an active, even decisive role in the development of Finnish-language nationalism. In a word, there was not the kind of racial gulf dividing those who spoke Swedish from those who spoke Finnish as there was between the German-speaking ruling class and the servile peasantry of the Baltic provinces. This bitter historical relationship of 'Germans' and 'non-Germans' was a major obstacle to painless assimilation, and proved to be too great a barrier for mutual understanding; the enthusiastic optimism which pervades the pages of Rosenplänter's little journal was too fragile to last.

It would, however, be unwise to read the pages of this journal through the lenses of latter-day nationalism, for the contributors were looking primarily for means, not ends. The same may be observed elsewhere in Europe. Concern for the low cultural level of the common people by no means implied that reformers wished to overthrow the existing social order, or create a new political programme. What they were seeking, by and large, was a society in which all could realise their potential to the best of their ability and within the limits set by God, nature and the social order. The most ardent champions of the language of the peasantry were often socially conservative. Only one of the seven speakers who gave their views on the subject of 'the germanisation of the Latvians' in a debate organised in 1819 in the Kurland capital of Mitau was prepared to argue that, with the recent emancipation of the peasantry, language alone separated Latvians from Germans. He urged the Latvians to forget their history and abandon their language – which offered them little – and to assimilate with the Germans. The other speakers all believed that a free peasantry could best raise its own moral and cultural standards by the use of its own God-given language. Language was not considered as a means of social advancement: as one speaker pointed out, 'the peasant is by nature shaped for mechanical work, and he must not be tempted away from his plough and his scythe'.[31]

The contrast between the Estonian and Latvian peasantry and the German upper class was particularly marked; but there were quite palpable differences between the rude commoners and polite classes in unilingual communities as well. In the words of one Danish contemporary, 'their dress, chiefly consisting of heavy, coarse material often crudely cut and stitched, did little to elevate the peasant estate . . . and they were additionally separated from those who lived in the towns, or on gentlemen's estates or who occupied a post in the civil

31. The talks are printed as: Sieben Vorträge über Germanisierung der Letten *Baltische Monatsschrifte* **59**: (1905), pp. 61–71.

service by virtue of their lesser education, language, habits and manners'.[32] For much of the nineteenth century, peasants still bore the onerous obligations and duties of a previous age, such as the provision of horses for travellers or eligibility for military service. 'With regard to the people who belong to the peasant estate', wrote the Dane Jakob Mandix in 1813, 'our laws contain such provisions which not only impose upon these people, or a significant number of them, burdens from which other citizens of the state are exempt, but also which seem to assume that they, taken as a whole, constitute a less independent and a less enlightened class than the rest of the citizens of the state.'[33] It was perhaps as much this continuing legacy of the past as it was the differences of speech, manners or dress which continued to divide the farmer from the 'quality'; though equally, it served in the long run to make him the spokesman for the rural community at large.

One indication of what might be regarded as a form of rural protest against established authority was the religious revivalism which grew out of earlier Pietist traditions. In Denmark, the first clash between the rationalist Lutheran church and the people occurred at the end of the eighteenth century, when the church attempted to replace the much-loved hymnal of Bishop Kingo and Pontoppidan's catechism with modern texts. There was intense and prolonged resistance to these measures in eastern Jutland, where the peasants refused to allow their children to attend schools where the new books were used. Eventually the government gave way, and permitted these 'sturdy Jutes' to run their own schools. Their resistance to change was grounded in a deep conservatism, and the movement as such never attempted to proselyte, unlike the 'awakened' brethren on the island of Fyn in the 1820s and 1830s or the followers of Hans Nielsen Hauge in Norway. During the first half of the nineteenth century, numerous revivalist or 'awakened' movements spread amongst the people of northern Europe. They were characterised by intensely emotional meetings, in which communal prayer and singing played an important part, and by a high degree of lay involvement. In some instances, nobles and peasants came together in conventicles, as on the Pomeranian estates of the von Below brothers, though the relationship remained a paternalistic one beyond a shared spiritual experience.

Rather more egalitarian were the Moravian or Herrnhut brethren, so named after the estate of their eighteenth-century spiritual leader,

32. Cited in Bjørn C (ed.) 1988 *Det danske landbrugs historie 1810–1914*, Odense, p. 100.

33. Cited in Jensen H 1931 *Den danske Stænderforsamlingers historie* 2 vols, Copenhagen, vol. 1, p. 25.

Count Nikolaus Zinzendorf. In the Baltic provinces, where membership of the brethren doubled from 31,554 in 1818 to 66,330 in 1839, the peasantry were actively encouraged to play an active role by the 'German workers' sent out from Herrnhut. Although trained in theology, these workers had no special privileges or position of authority, and often earned their living by practising a trade. They succeeded in winning the confidence and releasing the deep religious emotions of the Estonian and Latvian peasantry in a way that the official church could not. The clergy were all too easily identified with the hated Baltic German landowner, as many pastors themselves admitted. The 'awakened' movements not only provided a valuable emotional release for those condemned to a harsh and bitter existence on this earth; it also offered the opportunity to gain confidence and learn leadership skills. 'The Brethren communities here form without a doubt the aristocracy of the people, their word counts everywhere, and the decisions made by the people are very much dependent upon what they say', commented Pastor Jannau in 1856, and others in the Baltic provinces noted the correlation between active participation in the brethren and leadership of peasant communal institutions. Leaders of 'awakened' communities in Denmark also played a prominent role in the politicisation of the peasantry during the 1840s.[34]

The increased attention paid to the peasantry, by poets and politicians alike, was significant. Previous generations had regarded the peasant as little more than a slovenly, uncouth boor fitted only for the company of his animals, whom he much resembled. Such attitudes persisted, but were being gradually edged out by a new respect and even admiration for the sturdy countryman. The importance of good farming practice and of the dissemination of knowledge to all who tilled the soil had been emphasised not only in countless tomes, but through agricultural societies, schools and institutions, and practical reforms. The Pietist movement in its various forms strove to improve the moral and spiritual welfare of the peasant. The enormous enthusiasm for folk poetry placed the life of the common people in the spotlight, albeit in somewhat romantic colours. The very poverty of the Finnish peasantry became a positive virtue for the poet Johan Ludvig Runeberg, whose *Bonden Paavo* responded to spring floods by

34. Philipp G 1974 *Die Wirksamkeit der Herrnhuter Brüdergemeinde unter den Esten und Letten zur Zeit der Bauernbefreiung* Forschungen zur internationalen Sozial-und Wirtschaftsgeschichte **5**, Cologne, p. 337. On the awakened movements in Denmark, see Lindhardt P 1959 *Vækkelse og kirkelige retninger*, Copenhagen, and the same author's general history of the church in Scandinavia, published in 1983, *Kirchengeschichte Skandinaviens* Göttingen, pp. 74–125.

digging more ditches to drain his poor land and by commanding his wife to mix ground bark with the rye bread-flour. The second verse of Runeberg's poem *Vårt land*, which was to become the Finnish national anthem, unequivocally declares that: 'Our land is poor, so shall remain/ for those who crave for gold'.[35] As a result, a new image of the peasant began to emerge: pious, endowed with natural wisdom, frugal and hard-working, and content with his lot.

The consequences of what we might term the re-evaluation of the humble countryman will form a major theme in this book, and it might therefore be helpful at this stage briefly to indicate some of the ways in which contemporaries were obliged to think anew about those who dwelt and toiled on the land. Firstly, since they constituted the great majority of the population, they were of interest to the state as taxpayers, recruits for the army, even as providers of involuntary labour for the repair of roads and bridges. This, of course, had always been so: but the keen interest in the land as the primary source of a nation's wealth which had been so much a feature of eighteenth-century thought had undoubtedly cast the cloddish peasant of yore in a new and more favourable light (as indeed did the effusions of poets, publicists and even politicians). Secondly, the uncertainties of the times, when the age-old problems of social unrest acquired new and menacing dimensions in the fallout from the French revolution and when the territorial configurations of states as large as Prussia could change with alarming rapidity (or simply collapse, as in the case of Poland), forced rulers to review and even revise their strategies of control. Amongst the options which were considered and even employed were the inculcation of loyalty and patriotism through education, the elevation of the self-esteem and the feeding of the self-interest of the peasant. Thirdly, as the administrators of the state sought to shake loose the constricting coils of provincial and corporate particularism, the outmoded world of rank and privilege which nevertheless still shaped the lives of most Europeans, they not infrequently saw the peasantry as a means of breaking through the obstacles. But how precisely this was to be achieved was rarely apparent, and it is the constant confusion of 'feudal' and 'modern', particularist corporatism and bureaucratic centralism, subject and citizen, *Land* and *Nation*, which makes reaching firm conclusions so difficult.

35. Pipping H 1942 Den fattiga Finland *Skrifter utgivna av Svenska Litteratursällskapet i Finland* **289**: 143–62. Elias Lönnrot, the other great Finnish image-maker, took a far less romantic view than Runeberg of the causes and effects of poverty in the Finnish hinterland. See for example his letter of 12 June 1833 to L. I. Ahlstubbe in Lönnrot E 1990 *Valitut teokset*, Helsinki, vol. 4, pp. 17–22.

CHAPTER THREE

States and Unions: 1815 to the Revolutions of 1848

CONSTITUTIONS OF DIVERSE KINDS

When the long era of European war came to an end in 1815, the political map of the continent had already been considerably altered, and it was to be redrawn once more at the Congress of Vienna. The Russian empire had pushed its frontiers some ten degrees westwards, acquiring in the process a mixture of peoples of widely different cultural, religious and ethnic backgrounds. The kingdom of Prussia, which at one stage had seemed destined to become a half-Slavic state east of the Elbe, now stretched from the Rhine to the Niemen, having acquired Swedish Pomerania, sizeable portions of Saxony and lands on the Rhine and in Westphalia in the peace negotiations. The Polish-Lithuanian commonwealth, which even after the first partition of 1772 was seven times larger than Prussia, had disappeared completely. Parts of this vast territory were subsequently carved out to form duchies or even a kingdom; but always under the sceptre of foreign rulers. Sweden lost territory in the Baltic, and became a more 'Scandinavian' power through the union with Norway, separated from Denmark at the treaty of Kiel in January 1814.

Before the revolution, Germany had been a myriad of tiny states, such as Eutin, a few miles south-west of Lübeck. Wearing a varnished tin cross to signify the church militant, the red-uniformed guards spent as much of their time defending the prince-bishop's aviary from marauding town cats as in keeping a watchful eye out for the revolutionary French armies.[1] The Holy Roman Empire disappeared for ever in 1806; the Confederation of the Rhine set up in its stead was a short-lived French protectorate; and at the peace talks in 1815, the much-reduced number of German states were organised into a confederation (*Bund*), under the presidency of Austria.

These territorial changes necessitated new political arrangements; indeed, rulers of member-states were obliged by Article 13 of the act establishing the confederation to provide a constitution (*Verfassung*) for their lands. However, the provincial mentality, the attachment to region, patrimonial rights and the traditional class structure of the estates did not disappear with the demise of the Holy Roman Empire. As late as 1848, a Scottish writer could remark that 'the Prussian subjects are not a nation, but a lot of fourteen millions of people torn from other nationalities in 1816 (sic), and held together in the shape of a nation, only by functionary government, civil and military duties, and discipline'.[2] This verdict would have found support amongst many of the king of Prussia's more traditional-minded subjects. The assemblage of widely differing provinces which constituted Prussia could never become a nation, argued the ultra-conservative Friedrich von der Marwitz; to try and fuse them together would be 'to rob them of their individuality and to create a dead carcass out of a living body'.[3] Karl August von Hardenberg, chancellor of Prussia between 1810 and 1822, failed to undermine the particularist opposition of the landowners through the medium of an assembly of notables, and later, a provisional national assembly. The Prussian nobility insisted on the preservation of the *Verfassung des Landes*, which they took to mean not only the royal guarantees given to provincial estates during preceding centuries and embodied in provincial law, but also the entire structure of social relations and the authority of the landowning nobility over

1. Laing S 1850 *Observations on the Social and Political State of the European People in 1848 and 1849*, London, p. 503. Laing had visited Eutin as a young man whilst studying German in the nearby town of Kiel. As he noted, the prince's court at Eutin at the end of the eighteenth century attracted all the literary figures of the day. Not all these small states disappeared in the reconstruction of Germany between 1806 and 1815. Lauenburg, Denmark's consolation prize in 1815, had fewer than 40,000 inhabitants, who had to support a full complement of officials, including a forest- and huntmaster, two senior foresters, and a complement of fifteen other foresters, all clad in uniform.

2. *Ibid.*, p. 188. See also Simon W 1953 Variations of nationalism during the great reform period in Prussia *American Historical Review* **59**: 309–21. Winkler-Seraphim B 1955/6 Das Verhältnis der preussischen Ostprovinzen, insbesondere Ostpreussens zum Deutschen Bund im 19 Jahrhunderts *Zeitschrift für Ostforschung* **4**: 321–50 and **5**: 1–33.

3. Cited by Berdahl R 1988 *The politics of the Prussian nobility. The development of a conservative ideology 1770–1848,* Princeton, NJ, p. 132.

their subjects, the peasantry. Frederick William III promised in 1815 to issue a written constitution and establish consultative representative bodies at the provincial and national level. In the eastern provinces of the kingdom there was little enthusiasm amongst the landowning nobility for a national Diet, and the rising tide of reaction in Europe effectively killed hopes of one being established in the foreseeable future.

The term '*Verfassung*' was in fact capable of more than one interpretation. Article 13 of the act establishing the German Confederation qualified this noun with the adjective '*landständische*', a word dear to the hearts of those devoted to provincial laws and customs and the corporate social order of the estates (*Stände*). The demise of the Holy Roman Empire in 1806 had afforded an opportunity to the rulers of individual German states to try and impose their authority and override particularist rights and privileges. In this, they were seldom completely successful. King Gustav IV Adolf of Sweden had declared the Pomeranian *Landesverfassung* null and void in 1806 and had already begun to remodel his last German possession on Swedish lines when the tide of war washed over his lands, ultimately casting the Pomeranians into the lap of the king of Prussia (who confirmed their ancient rights and privileges). The dukes of Mecklenburg also attempted to take advantage of the end of the Holy Roman Empire to assert their sovereignty. Duke Friedrich Franz laid a proposition before the estates in Rostock in 1808, declaring that he intended to issue a constitution for the whole land and claiming that Article 26 of the act establishing the Confederation of the Rhine gave him full and unlimited powers of sovereignty. Challenged by the estates, he began to give way, and ultimately settled for an extraordinary contribution to relieve his financial distress. Friedrich Franz quietly abandoned his claim to be 'sovereign prince' after the congress of Vienna, where both dukes were elevated to the rank of *Grossherzog* with the title of 'royal highness'. The Federal Diet in Frankfurt was petitioned in 1817 to take up the question of constitutional reform in Mecklenburg, but nothing came of this. The noble landowners, some 280 in number in 1840, clung tenaciously to their claim to fill the offices of state and resisted attempts to change the antiquated constitutional order right up to the revolution of 1848.

The rulers of Mecklenburg and Pomerania had never been strong enough to impose their will upon the indigenous *Ritterschaft*. From the time of the great elector Frederick William (1640–88) onwards, the rights and privileges of the nobility of the Prussian lands had been effectively limited to their own estates. They were, nevertheless, still able to mount an effective resistance to the plans of the great reformers, Stein and Hardenberg, partly as a result of the revival of local assemblies in the aftermath of the catastrophe of Prussia's defeat at the battle of Jena, but also because the reformers themselves had no intention of upsetting the social order. Faced with determined resistance, Stein and Hardenberg diluted their programme, or quietly abandoned measures such as the Gendarmerie Edict of 1812, which would have undercut the authority and power of the nobility at a local level. For the reformers, administration (*Verwaltung*) was ultimately more important than any constitution (*Verfassung*). Stein toyed with the idea of a quorum of elected officials and Hardenberg's state council established in 1817 was intended to be the highest advisory body in the state, a kind of parliament of officials, which would eventually act as a counterweight to the provincial diets created by royal edict in 1823.[4] Good government and effective central control were a higher priority than any form of national representation to kings and statesmen haunted by the frightful spectre of the French example. In this respect, the conservative provincial estates, even if they cavilled at the demands of the central authority, were a safer bet.

Nowhere was provincial particularism more solidly entrenched than in the Baltic provinces of Estland, Livland and Kurland, where the nobility jealously guarded their rights and privileges. In the words of the Baltic German historian Reinhold Wittram: '*Ständische* thinking permeated all aspects of life and was an expression of the powerful historical principles upon which the social order of this colonial land rested.'[5] The position of the Baltic German nobility was much stronger than that of their Prussian counterparts. The administration of the provinces was in their hands, and they could claim (as they frequently did) that their rights and privileges had been solemnly guaranteed by successive rulers since 1561. Catherine II's attempt to subordinate the provinces to the centre had been abandoned by her successor. In the 1820s, governor-general marquis Filippo Paulucci encountered tough resistance when he attempted to break through the

4. Berdahl 1988, pp. 189–202. Berdahl follows closely the arguments advanced in Koselleck R 1967 *Preussen zwischen Reform und Revolution*, Stuttgart. There is a good brief summary of the 'Janus-faced' character of the post-1815 Prussian state in: Nipperdey T 1983 *Deutsche Geschichte 1800–1866*, Munich, pp. 331–7.

5. Wittram R 1949 *Drei Generationen. Deutschland-Livland-Russland 1830–1914,* Göttingen, p. 27. Even the renowned German liberals Carl Rotteck and Carl Welcker accepted that 'the *Stände* form the skeletal structure of society' in their 1843 *Staatslexikon.* Cited by Berdahl 1988, p. 221.

dense web of interlocking local institutions. The zeal of the marquis for improving the postal services irritated the Livonian gentry, on whom the increased costs would fall, and for whom changes in the service was a matter of decision for the *Landtag*, and not the governor-general. Paulucci's proposals for changing the constitution of the local courts also caused anger; the nobility objected to what they perceived as an attempt to make the court systems of the three provinces uniform, and they disliked the idea of introducing burghers on to the panel of assessors. In other respects, however, Paulucci sheltered the native nobility from interference from the ministries in St Petersburg, and he was in no way hostile to the privileges and rights claimed by the Baltic *Ritterschaft*. Although several highly-placed persons in the Imperial Russian administration entertained notions of curbing the autonomy of the Baltic Germans, they had little success in persuading Nicholas I to back their schemes.[6]

On the northern shores of the Baltic, territorial changes and political convulsions produced rather different and contrasting results. The charter granted by Alexander I to the Finnish estates meeting at Borgå in March 1809 followed the established pattern of agreements between ruler and the representatives of the land. The emperor confirmed and promised to maintain the religion of the land, and the rights and privileges of the estates in particular and the inhabitants in general; but his charter did not define or specify the 'constitution' upon which these rights rested. The autonomous status of Finland was given true substance as a result of the vigour and persuasiveness of Count Gustav Mauritz Armfelt, an experienced statesman who returned to his Finnish estates in 1811. Armfelt was recruited by the emperor as a man with useful diplomatic contacts, and he was also made chairman of a reformed Committee for Finnish Affairs, which was to prepare for submission to the emperor all legislation concerning the civil administration of Finland. Armfelt had succeeded in persuading the emperor to accept his proposal that all members of the committee should be inhabitants of Finland, and before his death in

6. Baltic German historians are fond of citing Nicholas I's assurance to the leader of the Kurland nobility, Baron Hahn, that 'The gentlemen can rest assured that no hair of their head will be touched nor will any right be taken away, I am just as good a Baltic provincial (*Ostseeprovinzialer*) as you.' Cited in Tobien A von 1925 *Die livländische Ritterschaft in ihrem Verhältnis zum Zarismus und russischen Nationalismus*, Riga, vol. 1, p. 80. See also the articles by R Baron Stäel von Holstein, published in the *Baltische Monatshefte* **51** (1901): Zur Geschichte der livländischen Privilegien, pp. 1–30, 81–98, and Die Gefährdung des Landesrechte durch den Marquis Paulucci, pp. 241–78, 355–94.

1814 he had been instrumental in building up the somewhat sketchy government council created in 1809 into a fully-equipped central administration. Renamed in 1816 the Imperial Senate, with members appointed by the emperor from amongst his Finnish subjects, it was divided into two sections: *Justitie*, which administered the courts system and acted as the supreme court, and *Ekonomie*, consisting of eight departments, which functioned as the civil administration of the land. The Committee for Finnish Affairs was wound up in 1826 at the instigation of governor-general Count Arseny Zakrevsky and replaced by a non-advisory State-Secretariat for Finnish Affairs: but the internal administration of Finland remained separate from that of the empire, and in spite of his formal position as chairman of the Senate, the governor-general was unable to exert much influence.

Alexander I had been primarily concerned to ensure the loyalty of his new subjects in 1809. In a letter to governor-general Count Fabian Steinheil in 1810, he emphasised that he had given the Finnish people a political existence 'so that they would not consider themselves conquered by Russia, but joined to it by their own self-evident interests'. He was not minded to indulge in constitution-making; the draft proposal submitted in 1819 by the Committee for Finnish Affairs, which provided for regular meetings of the estates and an extension of their powers, including a measure of control over the bureaucracy, was never taken up. On the whole, however, Alexander's new subjects responded positively to the settlement, taking full advantage of the benefits of attachment to a powerful empire and suffering relatively few disadvantages as a result of separation from Sweden. The estates were not summoned again until 1863, but the government of the country remained in the hands of native-born bureaucrats, and the privileged status of the Grand Duchy was no more disturbed by the over-zealous attentions of Zakrevsky as were the rights of the Baltic provinces upset by his contemporary, Paulucci.[7]

Alexander had convened the Finnish estates and presented them with his charter before Sweden formally ceded the Finnish provinces to Russia at the treaty of Fredrikshamn in September 1809. The cession of Norway to Sweden had already been agreed in Kiel (14

7. Kirby D (ed.) 1975 *Finland and Russia 1808–1920: From autonomy to independence. A selection of documents*, London, p. 25, for Alexander's letter. See also Thaden E 1984 *Russia's western borderlands, 1710–1870*, Princeton, NJ, pp. 81–113. and Schybergson M 1904 *Historiska Studier*, Stockholm, pp. 150–293, for essays on Speransky and Zakrevsky.

January 1814) before leading elements of Norwegian society, abetted by the stattholder, Prince Christian Frederik, took the first steps that were to lead to the convention of a national assembly in April. On 17 May, the delegates at Eidsvoll voted unanimously to approve a constitution and a monarchy under Christian Frederik. The prospect of military defeat and the lack of external support for an independent Norway persuaded the Norwegians to accept union with Sweden. Bernadotte, for his part, was willing to accept the Eidsvoll constitution, mindful that constitutions could always be changed, but perhaps also aware of the advantages to a parvenu prince of having another kingdom to which he might retreat should the Swedish throne be once more shaken. On 4 November 1814, a special *Storting* unanimously elected and acknowledged Carl XIII of Sweden as king of Norway (though a majority of the members preferred to state that he was elected).[8] Like so much else in this union of two kingdoms, the dates soon acquired a significance of their own. The commemorative celebration of 17 May by Norwegian students and burghers in 1824 incensed Carl Johan, who remembered that not only had the constitution been declared that day, but a member of the house of Oldenburg had been elected king of an independent Norway. In Swedish eyes, 4 November was the proper date for celebration. As a result of this conflict, which was blown up out of all proportion by the overreaction of the king, two stattholders were disgraced, and the post was eventually allowed to fall into disuse. As we shall see, Russian governors-general in Finland and the Baltic provinces had relatively few resources to hand, and often little support from St Petersburg, in their attempts to bring these outposts of empire into line; but after 1829, the Swedish crown did not even have its own representative in Norway.

The Norwegians regarded their constitution as a 'palladium of liberty and the foundation of their national dignity', reported Crown Prince Oscar to his father in April 1824. Samuel Laing found the Norwegians a 'free and happy people living under a liberal constitution', which was 'but a superstructure of a building of which the foundations had been laid and the lower walls constructed, eight centuries before'.[9] The Norwegian constitution was not only an inspiration and a model for liberals in absolutist Denmark, but also in

8. Derry T 1973 *A history of modern Norway 1814–1972*, Oxford, pp. 2–16.

9. The crown prince's letter is cited in Söderhjelm A, Palmstierna C-F 1944 *Oscar I*, Stockholm, p. 131. Laing S 1836 *Journal of a Residence in Norway during the Years 1834, 1835, and 1836*, London, p. vi, 479.

Sweden. At first sight this seems strange, for the Swedes had secured their own constitution in 1809. The estates had, moreover, insisted on this as a priority before the question of succession to the deposed Gustav IV Adolf was resolved. In the preamble to the Form of Government Act which was dated on 6 June 1809, the estates also made it perfectly clear that they had acted as representatives of the Swedish people in rescinding previous fundamental laws and ordaining a new constitution. Yet within three years, Carl Johan was contemplating replacing it with a new form of government more suited to the interests of the ruler; the Regency Act of 1810 and the Act of Union with Norway were both passed by extraordinary sessions of the *Riksdag*, in breach of the constitutional stipulation that only ordinary sessions had such authority; and several of those responsible for producing the constitution cast around for reasons why it had failed to live up to expectations.

Undoubtedly, the Swedish constitution was conceived of in a hurry, and the members of the constitutional committee of the estates were working under pressure, though it might also be argued that the Norwegians in 1814 had to work in similar circumstances. There was, however, a much sharper division of opinion in Sweden, and far more factions, than was the case in Norway. Gustavian malcontents plotted a new coup with Duke Carl, whilst at the other extreme, the 'democratising shriekers' of the Riddarhus suspected that the government intended foisting upon them an Act of Security (Gustav III's 1772 constitution) clad in a new coat, and levelled the same accusation at the estates' fifteen-man constitutional committee.

This committee, whose moving spirit was the erstwhile radical Hans Järta, was mindful of the need to preserve continuity and avoid previous pitfalls. However much the committee was or was not influenced by the ideas of Montesquieu or foreign examples, the balance it sought to achieve was derived from Swedish experience. Executive power was to reside with the king, who was to appoint the nine members of the State Council. The king shared legislative authority with the *Riksdag*, each having the power of veto over the other. The approval of three estates was required to pass a law, and all four had to consent to constitutional amendments, in two consecutive sessions. The estates alone were to decide on matters of taxation, thereby exercising an 'ancient right' of the Swedish people. The *Riksdag* also controlled the bank of Sweden and the national debt office. Six standing committees were to be set up, and these became the effective centres of power, unitary forces within the cumbersome structure of the four-estate *Riksdag*, each estate deputing an equal number of members for each committee. In 1823, the committees adopted the principle of voting by head, an early breach of the tradition of voting by estate. The constitutional committee could instruct the judicial ombudsman to impeach a minister for violation of the constitution, or to ask for a negligent minister to be dismissed. Although the choice of ministers was the king's prerogative, each was made individually responsible for countersigning all executive acts, and they were to refuse their signature and resign office if they believed any act was contrary to the constitution. The judiciary was independent and separate (the king was given two votes in the High Court, but they were never used); and although it could declare laws inconsistent with the constitution, it had no authority to overrule the estates on constitutional legislation.

The peasants' estate had wanted some readjustment of the balance of privileges and obligations, and had refused to sign the constitutional document until their grievances were met. The entire estate was summoned to the palace on 27 June to be given a stiff lecture by the new king and his council of state. They then 'freely and voluntarily' agreed to their speaker signing the document in their name. In order to appease the peasantry, the last remnants of noble exclusivity in regard to land ownership were surrendered, but the tax differential between 'noble' (*frälse*) and non-noble land remained.[10]

In certain respects, particularly with regard to the definition of executive power, the Swedish constitution of 1809 did not markedly differ from that adopted by the Norwegians five years later. The most striking contrast is to be found in the assignment of legislative power. The Eidsvoll constitution declared unequivocally that this was exercised by the *Storting* as the representative national assembly of the people. The king was allowed only a suspensive veto; a bill passed by three consecutive sessions of the *Storting* was to become law even if the king disapproved. The Norwegian constitution also proclaimed full liberty of the press, forbade any future creation of noble titles, and protected the ancient peasant freehold rights of *Odels-* and *Åsetesrett.* The freedom of the press enshrined in the Swedish constitution was curbed in 1812, an unconstitutional measure which the estates nonetheless accepted for fear that Bernadotte might quit the country if his wish were not obeyed. The government was empowered to ban periodical publications deemed a danger to public security, and Carl Johan saw to it that journals which overstepped the line were punished.

10. For details of the events of 1809, see the collection of articles edited by Björklund S 1965 *Kring 1809. Om regeringsformens tillkomst*, Stockholm.

The Norwegian *Storting* divided after elections into two sub-chambers; no special provisions were made on the basis of class or estate. The Swedish *Riksdag* remained an assembly of four estates until 1866; and although the nobility no longer had any presumptive claim on the high offices of state, in practice they continued to fill these posts for several decades. The 1809 constitution, in other words, failed to adjust the balance of social forces, though in truth that was clearly not the intention of those charged with the task of drawing up the document. The Norwegian constitution also contained a fair measure of inconsistencies and weak points, but these imperfections were lessened by the far more important symbolic role which the constitution came to have, as the expression of national independence and unity. The experience of union with Sweden only served to strengthen this feeling, a sentiment not reciprocated on the eastern side of the frontier, where neither 4 November nor even the (uncertain) anniversary of the signing of the constitution aroused much public enthusiasm.

The Polish-Lithuanian lands had experienced a bewildering variety of rulers and political systems since they were partitioned between Prussia, Russia and Austria in the last quarter of the eighteenth century. After the first partition in 1772, Frederick the Great had ordered his officials to put his newly annexed provinces on a 'Prussian footing' as soon as possible. The Prussian administrative system was introduced, the Protestant church placed under the Berlin consistory and pro-Prussians placed in office in the Catholic hierarchy. The Polish gentry, many of whom preferred to reside in Warsaw, were not permitted to hold county assemblies; Polish landowners had to pay a higher rate of land tax than Germans. These harsh measures were relaxed by his successor, though a creeping Germanisation through settlement continued. Frederick William III promised the Polish inhabitants of the Grand Duchy of Posen, created in 1815 as a result of the Vienna peace settlement, that he would respect their nationality, and for fifteen years, he kept his word. Polish was accepted as an official language, and Poles participated actively in the running of local and provincial affairs.

In some respects, Alexander I offered an even more generous settlement, for he was willing to resurrect a Polish kingdom and give it a considerable measure of autonomy. The favoured status given to the Kingdom of Poland (or 'Congress Poland') did not extend to other parts of the former Polish-Lithuanian commonwealth now under Russian rule. Plans for a Grand Duchy of Lithuania with an autonomous status modelled on that of Finland had been drawn up in

1812, but Alexander hesitated, no doubt aware of opposition from Russian landowners in the annexed lands and the mutterings of conservatives such as the historian N. M. Karamzin, who disliked the Finnish settlement and claimed Lithuania as ancient Russian territory, and the project was soon abandoned.[11] The Kingdom of Poland was given a constitution drawn up by Prince Adam Czartoryski, who had long been pressing the case for a separate Polish state united to Russia through the person of the emperor as hereditary king. The kingdom was to have its own government, appointed by the king-emperor, its own civil service, judiciary and army, and a two-chamber assembly, the *Sejm*. The *Code Napoléon*, freedom of the press, religious toleration and the personal liberty of the subject were formally guaranteed.

The 1815 constitution seemed to hold out better prospects of future political development for the Kingdom of Poland than did the emperor's old-fashioned affirmation of the rights and privileges of the estates for the Grand Duchy of Finland; and yet within fifteen years, revolt had broken out in the Polish lands and Czartoryski's vision of unity was irredeemably shattered, the prince himself going into exile. Nicholas I, shaken by the experience of an army officers' revolt in St Petersburg at the beginning of his reign, ruthlessly pursued the Polish secret societies and sought to cow the opposition in the *Sejm*. The Polish insurrection which broke out in November 1830 was so badly mismanaged that the old leaders of the country had to step into the breach as a provisional government and enter into negotiations with St Petersburg. The chief Polish negotiator was instructed to seek the extension of the 1815 constitution to all former lands of the Polish commonwealth under Russian rule, whose inhabitants were also to elect delegates to a general *Sejm*. The king-emperor was also to declare an amnesty and withdraw his troops from the kingdom.

Nicholas contented himself with calling upon the Poles to return to their former loyalty, but his deposition by the *Sejm* in January 1831 left him no option but war. The revolt also spread into Lithuania. Promises of eventual emancipation failed to win over the Lithuanian peasantry outside the region of Samogitia, where the petty nobility were able to make common cause with peasants oppressed by the exactions of absentee Russian landlords. By May, the insurrection had

11. Dundulis B 1940 *Napoléon et la Lithuanie en 1812*, Paris, p. 60ff. Kukiel M 1955 *Czartoryski and European unity 1770–1861*, Princeton, NJ, p. 97, suggests that the project had to be abandoned because leading Lithuanian magnates were unwilling to break the historic Polish-Lithuanian union. See also Zawadzki W 1993 *A man of honour. Adam Czartoryski as a statesman of Russia and Poland 1795–1831*, Oxford, pp. 202–4.

been quelled in Lithuania, and the Polish rebels finally surrendered five months later.

The relatively harmonious state of affairs in the Grand Duchy of Posen also began to break down in the 1820s. The local gentry (*szlachta*) wanted Polish to be the language of instruction for Poles in the higher classes of the grammar schools, and they sought in vain to have a university established in Poznań. In a word, they distrusted the velvet-gloved attempt to make their children into good Prussians by directing them to German-language secondary schools and German universities. The tide was already beginning to turn before the revolt in the Kingdom of Poland (in which Prussian Poles played little part). A new provincial president, Eduard Flottwell, pursued the kind of anti-Polish policies favoured by Frederick the Great. German became the exclusive language of internal administration. Landlord-appointed rural police were replaced by German district commissioners, who combined police duties with surveillance of the nationalist movement. German peasant colonisation was encouraged and Flottwell tried to create a Junker class by selling to Germans parcels of royal demesne land and estates bought with state funds from bankrupt Polish nobles. A more benign policy was followed after Flottwell's departure in 1841; but the Poles still remained hostile to any idea of integration, repulsing the call of the German liberal deputies in the provincial diet of 1841 to join them in demanding an all-Prussian parliament. Two years later, they had shifted their ground and were willing to support this call in return for liberal backing for their linguistic rights. This newly-minted alliance was not, however, long to survive the first weeks of the 1848 revolution.

In the end, the memories and traditions of the past were too strong, and the basis for mutual understanding and cooperation too weak for the Catholic Poles to live amicably within Prussia or Russia. The Lutheran ruling elite in Finland, accustomed to service and obedience to higher authority, and with no deep or particularist sense of national tradition were soon won over by the generosity of the emperor. In the immediate aftermath of occupation and separation from Sweden, many complained of the lack of public spirit and patriotic sentiment, but there was little enthusiasm for a return to a country which had so badly let them down, and there was also growing recognition that Finland now possessed advantages 'whereby we, considered as a separate people, Finns, undeniably possess more liberty and independence than formerly under Swedish governance'.[12] This was

12. C. J. Walleen to Bishop Tengström, 21 January 1814: Bonsdorff C von 1918 Opinion och stämningar i Finland 1808–1814 *Skrifter utgivna av Svenska Litteratursällskapet i Finland* **141**, p. 55.

also true of Norway after separation from Denmark; but the Norwegians could justifiably claim that they had achieved this through their own efforts. Union for the Norwegians did not bring the kind of advantages that the Finns were able to secure from their attachment to a major European power – the opportunity to rise high in Imperial service, new markets, and ultimately, the forging of a sense of nationhood. Sweden offered few career opportunities, and little attraction for the mercantile classes of the Norwegian coastal towns, whose trade was directed across the North Sea and Atlantic, whilst the Norwegians had already begun to revive their sense of national identity and to rediscover their historical past as a nation.

In the Kingdom of Denmark, the absolutist regime established by Frederik III after 1660 remained in force until 1848. In many respects, however, Denmark was a model of the liberal state, with a relaxed press censorship, religious toleration and an enlightened administration committed to wide-ranging social and economic reforms.[13] The unitary state (*Helstat*) of Denmark included Norway (until 1814), Iceland, Greenland, the Færoes, and the duchies of Slesvig, Holstein and Lauenburg as well as Denmark proper. The two duchies of Slesvig and Holstein were a bewildering patchwork of fiefs and enclaves, and there were wide variations of local forms of government from the freeholding Frisian-speaking peasantry behind their dykes on the west coast to the feudal fiefs of the south, all of which caused problems for the *Helstat* pretensions of the king of Denmark. The linguistic frontier had retreated steadily northwards over the years, and although a Danish national consciousness had begun to make itself felt north of the Kongeå (the river frontier separating Slesvig from Jutland), the Danish language in Slesvig suffered from benign neglect.

After the dissolution of the Holy Roman Empire in 1806, the Duchy of Holstein was declared to be incorporated into the Kingdom of Denmark, but in 1815, Frederik VI abandoned this *Helstat* policy and as duke of Holstein allowed the duchy to enter the German

13. Jensen H 1931 *De danske Stænderforsamlingers Historie 1830–1848*, Copenhagen, vol. 1, pp. 1–35, offers a fine summary of what an earlier Danish historian, V. Falbe-Hansen, called the 'model state of peaceful liberalism'. The Scottish traveller Samuel Laing thought the paradox of liberal institutions within an absolutist state could be explained by the existence of the democratic institution of a collegial government which did not draw its members exclusively from one class, as in Britain. Laing was, however, highly critical of 'the host of functionaries who must be employed where a government attempts to do everything, and regulates and provides in matters which a people can best manage for themselves'. Laing S 1839 *A Tour of Sweden in 1838*, London, p. 14.

Confederation. This obliged him to provide his Holstein subjects with a constitution; and it gave the Holstein nobility and their professorial aides in the University of Kiel an opportunity to reconsider their historic rights (and revive their complaints about their demesne lands being taxed). Frederik VI was able to procrastinate over the introduction of the constitution until the outbreak of revolution in France in 1830, when the Austrian president of the confederation, supported by Metternich, urged him to introduce a constitution as soon as possible in order to avert trouble. The king's confidant J. P. Höpp was sent to the duchy to investigate, and reported back that there was no support for a constitution; but his fellow-passenger on the steamship to Kiel, a minor civil servant called Uwe Jens Lornsen, was to change all that. In his pamphlet '*Über das Verfassungswerk in Schleswigholstein*', Lornsen demanded the introduction of a Norwegian-style constitution for the two duchies, united with Denmark in a personal union. Lornsen's ideas were rejected by the conservative *Ritterschaft* of Holstein, but the stir they caused alarmed the authorities, and may have finally persuaded the king of the necessity of resolving the constitutional issue. This he did by seeking to appease all his subjects: in January 1831, two royal rescripts ordered the setting-up of assemblies of the estates (*Stænderforsamlinger*), one for each of the duchies, one for Jutland, and one for the islands.

These assemblies were clearly modelled on the the *Provinziallandtage* which had been set up in Prussia in the 1820s. They were intended to reflect the prevailing social order (though by founding the franchise on property, the basic principles underpinning the notion of estates were weakened). In Prussia, the landowners dominated the county assemblies (*Kreistage*), and filled the all-important local office of *Landrat*. Large landowners had less say in Danish local affairs, though they were expected to sit on school boards and poor law commissions, and they still enjoyed certain tax advantages and residual rights to nominate persons for appointment to clerical livings and patrimonial courts. The nobility played a far less significant role in Danish public life than did the Junker in Prussia. Whereas the rulers of Prussia had pressed the landed gentry into service in their military-bureaucratic state, Frederik III and his successors had preferred to create their own functionary class. By the end of the eighteenth century, the Danish civil service was overwhelmingly non-noble in composition, and two-fifths of the large estates of the land had passed into the hands of rich bourgeois proprietors. Only in the armed forces and the highest offices of state did the nobility manage to preserve something like its traditional dominance.

In the provincial assemblies in the eastern lands of the Kingdom of Prussia, the landowning aristocracy had as many representatives as the other two estates put together. Controlled by conservatives, their deliberations were confined mostly to issues which affected landed interests. The outcome was rather different in Denmark. Since the reforms had made virtually all the inhabitants of the *Helstat* into peasants, it was argued, the peasantry should therefore be proportionately represented in the *Stænderforsamlinger.* The assembly for the islands (which included Iceland and the Færoes) had ten nominated members, and sixty elected (twelve from Copenhagen, eleven from the other towns, seventeen big landowners and twenty farmers). Similar proportions applied in the other three assemblies. The vote was confined to owners of land and property of a certain value, and in the kingdom, to tenant-farmers over the age of twenty-five. In the duchies, over 4,000 urban property-owners and 12,000 landowners and farmers, just over two per cent of the population, were given the vote. About one in forty of the inhabitants of the kingdom, or some 26,000 landowners and farmers, and 6,000 urban property-owners were enfranchised.[14]

The peasant deputies who appeared at the first assemblies in 1836 were often shy and nervous – 'dumb as perch' according to one of the town representatives – and apologetic in voicing their opinions and requests. The coming together of different social classes inspired the poet and clergyman N. F. S. Grundtvig, a loyal upholder of the absolutist monarchy, to press ahead with his plans for folk high schools, intended to provide humble people with an education for life. Two years after the first assemblies, the liberal bourgeoisie and the peasantry symbolically came together to commemorate the fiftieth anniversary of the abolition of the *Stavnsbaand.* At this Bellevue meeting, the young Orla Lehmann launched his peasant programme, which stressed the value of a freeholding peasantry for farming and the fatherland. Lehmann saw the resolution of the land question in terms of state intervention to compel landowners to give up their privileges and to allow peasant farmers full and unrestricted rights of ownership.

The liberal-peasant alliance thus forged was to have momentous consequences in subsequent decades; but the peasant-farmers were not entirely without experience of public affairs. The abolition of the *Stavnsbaand*, which released the peasantry from the obligation to reside in their home district unless they had the permission of their lord to

14. Bjørn C 1990 *Fra reaktion til grundlov 1800–1850* Gyldendals og Politikens Danmarkshistorie **10**, Copenhagen, pp. 188ff.

depart, had necessitated measures to deal with vagrants and paupers. The provisions for administering the poor law of 1803 and the school ordinances of 1806 and 1814 created commissions based upon the *Sogne*, an area which usually embraced several pastorates. These commissions were chosen by the county governor (*Amtmand*) from amongst the wealthier peasant-farmers, and were generally presided over by a local clergyman. The creation of *Sogne* councils in 1841 further expanded the arena in which the enfranchised rural population (albeit still a minority) could participate; and the role of the awakened movements in training skilled debaters and organisers must not be forgotten. Within a very short time, the shy peasants of 1836 were to become a formidable and independent political force.

GOVERNMENT AND SOCIETY, 1830–1848

The provincial assemblies in Denmark and the duchies were from the beginning much livelier arenas of debate than their Prussian counterparts. They came into being as the Danish economy was beginning to recover from the agricultural depression of the post-Napoleonic years. The relative prosperity of Danish agriculture and trade in the 1840s created a mood of self-confidence and optimism, which enhanced the chances of reform. The relatively liberal press laws in Denmark permitted the existence of reform-minded newspapers such as *Fædrelandet*, and the rumbustious satirical journal, *Corsaren*, on whose front cover boldly sailed the pirate ship, tricolour at the masthead and trailing a pennant bearing the revolutionary legend '*Ça ira!*'. *Fædrelandet* (founded in 1834) drew upon the well-established tradition of petitioning by drafting a programme of liberal reforms in 1835, which electors were urged to press upon their representatives for presentation at the assemblies. The government also presented a long list of reforms, of which the most important were fiscal, and the first assemblies deliberated at length over customs and excise, the freeing of trade and the national budget.

Although the assemblies were consultative, and had no legislative powers, they were able to shape and influence government thinking and policy, discussing a number of important measures such as communal self-government for the towns and new and more liberal customs regulations, which were later implemented. The liberal T. Algreen-Ussing argued the case for a united assembly in Denmark on the eve of the second session of meetings in 1838, and his demand was endorsed by the estates of Jutland (which met in Viborg) and of the islands (which met at Roskilde). Great hopes were entertained of Christian VIII, who ascended the throne in 1839, and he received an address from a student meeting organised by Orla Lehmann, calling for a constitution in Denmark similar to that of Norway. As Prince Christian Frederik, stattholder of Norway, the new Danish king had of course played a significant role in the creation of that constitution, but age, caution and the warning words of Tsar Nicholas and Prince Metternich (both of whom he had met in Central Europe in 1838) had served to erode any liberal sentiments he might once have had. The liberal tide continued to rise, however, undeterred by clumsy attempts to silence leading figures with fines and prison sentences. The introduction of parish councils in 1841 saw the beginnings of rural associations, open to all members of the community, and inspired J. A. Hansen, a cobbler, and Rasmus Sørensen, an elementary schoolteacher, both experienced 'awakened' campaigners against the rationalist church leadership, to found *Almuevennen* (the 'Common People's Friend').

Almuevennen has been called 'the first "class-political" newspaper in Denmark . . . its connection with constitutionalist liberalism in no way deterred it from pursuing its main objective; to rouse and mobilise the peasantry to energetic action in the interests of their *Stand*'.[15] A constant stream of articles attacked the injustices to which the peasantry continued to be subjected, such as *Hoveri* (labour services), the tithe, and inequalities in taxation between privileged estate lands and non-privileged peasant lands. In 1844, Sørensen devoted himself full time to agitation, tramping from village to village and urging the rural population to bombard the *Stænderforsamlinger* with petitions. The government attempted to put a stop to this by banning meetings held without police permission; but within six months, this ban had been lifted by the king. Two days after the lifting of this ban, liberal constitutionalism and the peasant movement came together formally when the Society of Friends of the Peasant (*Bondevennernes Selskab*) was founded on the initiative of a teacher from Holbæk county, Asmund Gleerup.

No such broad-based popular movement developed in Prussia, in spite of promising developments in the 1840s. The four questions posed to the provincial diet in Danzig in 1841 by the Königsberg doctor Johann Jacoby sold like hot cakes in Berlin, and made Jacoby the hero of the hour. In 1841–42, the *Königsberger Zeitung* moved into

15. Jensen H 1934, vol. 2, p. 503.

the liberal camp, provoking the king to call it the *Hurenschwester* (the sister-whore) of the radical *Rheinische Zeitung* of Moses Hess. In its columns, the case for the constitutionally-guaranteed participation of the citizenry in the affairs of state – Jacoby's own answer to his first question – was vigorously propagated until pressure from the censor obliged the editor to choose less contentious copy. The high-water mark of the liberal-democratic movement was the founding in 1844 of the *Bürgergesellschaft* to bring together citizens of different occupations and from different walks of life to combat the problems of pauperism. Within a month, it had 700 members, mostly artisans. Banned by the authorities in April, its members took to meeting on Sundays in a beer-garden outside the town to listen to talks on popular representation and the necessity of a people's militia. Jacoby had denounced the selfishness and cowardice of the so-called educated classes in a letter to a friend in 1843, and pinned his faith in the working class – the 'true people': but in spite of the popularity of the Böttcherhöfchen meetings, which attracted thousands, no lasting alliance was made between the liberal democrats and the working classes, still less the peasantry.[16]

The proponents of change in Denmark on the other hand were well-organised and had secured support in all sections of society, from cottagers to landed proprietors. It was nevertheless the convoluted problem of the duchies which ultimately brought about the introduction of a constitutional monarchy in Denmark. What had appeared as little more than a puff of smoke from the steamer *Frederik VI* which had carried Lornsen and Höpp to Kiel in 1830 had become a dense, choking cloud of nationalist invective by 1848. Professor Christian Paulsen raised the ethnic issue for the first time in his book *Über Volksthümlichkeit und Staatsrecht der Herzogthums Schleswig* (1832). Paulsen asserted that Slesvig had since ancient times been a part of Denmark, and he demanded that Danish be used as a language of administration and justice where it was taught and employed in church, i.e. in the predominantly Danish-speaking northern districts. At first, there was little opposition to what seemed a perfectly reasonable demand. The cause was taken up across the Kongeå and amongst the farmers and townspeople of northern Slesvig, where the first Danish-language nationalist newspaper, *Dannevirke*, made its appearance in 1838.

16. Silberner E 1976 *Johann Jacoby. Politiker und Mensch*, Bonn-Bad Godesberg, pp. 79–87, 114ff. Orr W 1977 Königsberg und die Revolution von 1848 *Zeitschrift für Ostforschung* **26**: 271–306.

For the Danish-speaking rural population of northern Slesvig, the specific issue of language was probably of less importance than their hostility towards German-speaking officialdom, but it served as a means for voicing their demands. The petition which the farmer Nis Lorenzen laid before the Slesvig assembly in 1836, calling for Danish to replace German as the language of administration and the judicial process in areas where Danish was the language used in church, was buried in committee, though the main demands were taken up in Christian VIII's rescript of 1840. Lorenzen and his adviser Professor Christian Flor were more clearly in sympathy with the monarchist-conservative ideals of the poet, clergyman and inspirer of the folk high school movement in Denmark, N. F. S. Grundtvig than with liberalism. In his first statement on the folk high school idea, *Den danske Fiir-Kløver* (1836), Grundtvig had declared king, people, fatherland and mother tongue to be the four leaves of the Danish clover. It was this ideal, which sought liberty for great and small, rather than liberalism, which wanted the lesser to share power with the great, which would save Denmark and Slesvig, according to Christian Flor. When *Dannevirke* asked rhetorically in May 1841: 'Who can withstand the united will of the king and people?', it was reflecting the widely-held belief of the peasantry in Slesvig that the king would intervene to save them from the machinations of 'the great'.[17]

In a speech on 28 May 1842, the flamboyant Danish liberal leader Orla Lehmann declared the river Eider on the southern frontier of the Duchy of Slesvig to be Denmark's natural frontier. Lehmann's speech echoed liberal suspicions of Christian VIII's policy of upholding the unitary state with the support of conservative elements in the duchies, and anxieties that Denmark might be sucked into a general European war as a result of the king's commitments as a member of the German Confederation. Danish as well as duchy troops were inspected in September 1841 as part of the plans to mobilise the forces of the confederation in the event of war over the Near Eastern crisis, and suggestions had been made in Germany that Denmark be included in the confederation to provide it with a naval force. The growing tensions left less room for the adherents of the cause of the united and indivisible duchies. The Kiel lawyer Theodor Olshausen argued as early as 1839 for the abandonment of Slesvig and the historic formula of eternal indivisibility; Holstein should set its hopes on Article 13 of

17. Schultz Hansen H 1990 Den danske bevægelse i Sønderjylland ca. 1830–1850 *Historie* **18**; 386. Feldbæk O (ed.) 1991 *Dansk identitetshistorie*, Copenhagen, vol. 2, pp. 350–78. Rerup L 1982 *Slesvig og Holsten efter 1830*, Copenhagen, pp. 78ff.

the Act of Confederation. The hostility of the majority of the Slesvig estates to Christian VIII's language rescript prompted the Haderslev merchant P. Hiort Lorenzen to break with Schleswig-Holsteinism and to cause a scandal at the 1842 session by insisting on speaking Danish and refusing to withdraw when asked to do so by the president of the assembly. Hiort Lorenzen complained to the king, and publicised his case in *Fædrelandet.* Outraged liberals petitioned the king to defend the Danish language in Slesvig; the king and his advisers were at a loss as to how to proceed, and issued contradictory orders and advice.

The events of 1842 placed the national question firmly at the forefront of the Danish liberals' agenda and sparked off a genuinely popular movement in the duchies. Singing clubs became centres for the Schleswig-Holsteiners; the anthem '*Schleswig-Holstein, meerumschlungen, Deutsche Sitte hohe Wacht*' was sung by a mass demonstration sporting the blue-white-red colours of the united duchies outside the assembly hall in Schleswig in 1844. Danish nationalists organised the Slesvig Association, and began staging mass rallies on the hill of Skamlingsbank. On the first occasion, Hiort Lorenzen was presented with a silver drinking horn inscribed with the historic words from the records of the 1842 assembly, 'He continued speaking Danish'.

Added to the language and the constitutional conflicts was the complicated question of the succession. This had been tirelessly kept in the public eye by the duke of Augustenburg, whose dynastic claim to the duchies was based on the argument that the Danish Royal Law – which permitted succession via the female line – was not valid in Slesvig. The Danish liberals, mindful of Christian's age and the childless state of his heir, the corpulent Crown Prince Frederik, were also beginning to take an interest in the question. Algreen-Ussing proposed in the 1844 Roskilde assembly that the king declare the validity of the rights of succession as laid down by the Royal Law throughout *all* his territories, and this received majority backing. This provoked a storm of protest in Itzehoe, the seat of the Holstein assembly. The king of Denmark was reminded that he was merely duke of Holstein, and should the succession pass to the female line, that tie would be broken. A three-point protestation of the rights of the duchies was proclaimed: that they were independent states, indissolubly united, and acknowledging only the agnatic succession.

After much discussion, and against the advice of some of his ministers, Christian VIII issued an Open Letter on 8 July 1846, in which he declared that, whilst the succession as laid down in the Royal Law obtained in Slesvig and Lauenburg, the same could not be said of certain parts of Holstein. Instead of calming the situation, the

Open Letter made it much worse. The German-dominated Slesvig estates elected an uncompromising radical as their president, and voted to accept the three-point Holstein protestation. Orla Lehmann seized upon the terms of the Open Letter to press the case for a constitutional Eider Danish state, urging Christian VIII to convene a constituent assembly of delegates from Slesvig, Jutland and the islands, and to negotiate with Holstein and Lauenburg once the question of the succession had been resolved as to how these two members of the German Confederation might wish to be associated with Denmark. This was rejected by a majority of delegates in the Roskilde assembly; and although officials and even the king himself were beginning to acknowledge in private that a constitution would have to be introduced, they still clung to the idea of the *Helstat.* This belief still persisted into the heady, dangerous days of March 1848, as the new king, Frederik VII, was buffeted by the squalls and tempests of the Eider Danes and Schleswig-Holsteiners and his conservative advisers desperately strove to hold the wheel of state steady as Denmark entered the unknown waters of constitutionalism.[18]

The liberal opposition found the going rather more difficult in Sweden, though it had gained ground by the end of Carl XIV Johan's reign. The first breakthrough occurred in the 1840–41 *Riksdag,* where an alliance of moderate landowners, intellectuals, merchants and peasants from western Sweden managed to trim down expenditure on the bureaucracy and the armed forces, and to strengthen the position and authority of the State Council by insisting on a proper departmental structure of government. The dominance of the landowning classes in local government was also weakened by the 1843 reform, which gave the vote to lessees and non-farming rural residents by basing the franchise on taxation (the number of votes held being in proportion to taxes paid) as well as the land register. The power of the church was also diminished, for the new executive parish councils (*sockennämnder*) were to elect their chairmen, rather than the parish priest being automatically confirmed in that post, as had hitherto been the case.[19]

18. The crisis of 1848 will be considered in the next chapter; but for an eye-witness (though biassed) account of the formation of March ministry and the attempts to preserve the *Helstat,* see: Breve fra Geheimeraad P.G.Bang til Provst H.K.With paa Bornholm *Historisk Tidsskrift* **3:VI** (1867–9), pp. 105–34.

19. The Swedish *socken* remained essentially the same as the medieval parish; the Danish *Sogn,* as already indicated, was based on the district covered by the poor law and school boards, and embraced several church parishes. For a useful comparative overview of local government in northern Europe, see Jansson T 1987 *Agrarsamhällets förändring och landskommunal oganisation. En konturteckning av 1800-talets Norden* Studia Historia Upsaliensia **146**, Uppsala.

The local government reform was the first serious breach of the four-estates system which the 1810 *Riksdag* ordinance had confirmed. The two estates which proved to be the most resistant to change were also the least represenitive; in 1866, the nobility and clergy together constituted a mere 0.7 per cent of the population. The estate of burghers, elected by 2 per cent of the population, tended to be dominated by the magistracy and wealthy merchants; the artisans, who constituted the majority of those entitled to vote, were poorly represented. The most representative section of the nation was the peasantry. Adult male peasants entitled to vote constituted 7 per cent of the population. Although by comparison with other European countries possessed of an extensive franchise in 1809, Sweden's system of representation, based on a social and economic order which was rapidly changing, was becoming antiquated and inadequate by mid-century.

This much was recognised by Oscar I, who succeeded his father in 1844. The author of a widely-read book on prison reform, an advocate of the reorganisation of elementary education and the poor laws, Oscar confided to the editor of a liberal newspaper on his accession that resistance to change, even amongst the aristocracy, must give way. But, although dyed-in-the-wool conservatives muttered about a Swedish Louis-Philippe who consorted with liberal journalists, Oscar proved to be more concerned with social and humanitarian reforms than constitutional change. In the freer atmosphere of Oscar's early reign, the press and party politics flourished. On 20 February 1848, a number of liberal *Riksdag* members founded the Society of Friends of Reform to add momentum to the stalled question of changing the system of representation, and three weeks later, the king authorised the constitutional committee of the *Riksdag* to work out a new proposition for franchise reform. On the night of 18 March, as the royal family and the governor of Stockholm were admiring Jenny Lind's performance in *Der Freischütz*, rioting broke out in the capital, and continued the following day, when troops were ordered to fire on the crowds massed outside the Riddarhus. The principal cause of the riots was the widespread fear of unemployment as a result of lower import duties on manufactured goods amongst the workers and apprentices of the town. Shaken by these events and disillusioned by the less than enthusiastic response to social reforms he had helped sponsor, Oscar dismissed the unfortunate governor, appointed a more conservative ministry, and gradually abandoned hope of introducing fundamental changes into the system of parliamentary representation.

EUROPE'S POLICEMAN

The struggle for constitutional reform in northern Europe did not take place in an empty theatre; the watchful eye of the Emperor and Autocrat of all the Russias was constantly upon the performers. Denmark was heavily dependent on Russia during the post-Vienna period, even seeking Russian advice before concluding a trade treaty with Brazil. Carl Johan's foreign policy was founded upon his alliance with Russia, and he was not averse to using this, and the threat of Russian intervention, to stifle opposition. Above all he feared an Anglo-Russian conflict which would oblige Sweden to choose between the two, and which might also have exacerbated the conflict between the popular anti-Russian tendency and his own dynastic interests.[20] His declaration of Swedish neutrality in the event of war during the crisis which followed Russia's signing of the highly favourable treaty with the Ottoman empire in 1833 pleased neither side and angered the Swedish liberals, who were also incensed at the presence of an official representative at the unveiling in St Petersburg of a statue of Alexander I.

The delicacy of Sweden's position was well-illustrated by the plan to establish a free port at Slite on the island of Gotland. This plan acquired significance with the opening in 1832 of the Göta canal, linking the Baltic and the North Sea, and the creation of the German Customs Union in 1834. Britain was attracted to the proposition, partly because the Customs Union raised barriers to the continental transit trade to Russia, but also because the route was seen as cheaper, since it avoided the Sound and the dues levied by Denmark, and safer. The British minister to Stockholm believed that Slite, just sixteen hours' sailing time from the Baltic terminal of the canal at Söderköping, could become a second Heligoland, 'paying off the Prussians for driving our commerce out of Germany with their confounded system of reunions'.[21] When the Slite company asked the Swedish government for bonding and transit rights, however, the Russians protested about the dangers of the port being used for widescale smuggling of goods into Russia. Tsar Nicholas took up this matter with Carl Johan during his visit to Stockholm in 1838 (a visit that coincided with riots in the capital, prompted by the imprisonment

20. Such were the observations of Russian diplomats stationed in Stockholm during Carl Johan's later years. Palmstierna C 1932 *Sverige, Ryssland och England 1833–1855*, Stockholm, p. 8.

21. Cited in Palmstierna 1932, p. 173.

of the writer M. J. Crusenstolpe for seditious utterances). Carl Johan advised his ministers to drop the plan, for political as well as commercial reasons, shortly afterwards. During the king's absence in Norway, Crown Prince Oscar took up the issue; once more, Russian pressure was brought to bear. Although the *Riksdag* passed the bill authorising the establishment of the Slite company in 1840, the government did little to facilitate trade and the port did not prosper.

The rising chorus of Scandinavist sentiments, strongly tinged with russophobia, was also a matter for frequent intervention by Russian ministers from the late 1830s. Not even an article in an obscure southern Swedish provincial newspaper, welcoming the first number of *Nordisk Ugeskrift* (1837) as a step on the road to closer Nordic cooperation and eventual union which could lead to an active, united and anti-Russian foreign policy, escaped the attention of St Petersburg. Ministers in Copenhagen and Stockholm were instructed to draw the attention of the respective governments to this dangerous tendency. Russian pressure obliged the Danish government to bring charges against the Danish student leader Carl Ploug for using incautious language in a speech to a Scandinavist meeting in Kalmar in 1843. Carl Johan and his successor, mindful of Russian opinion, tried to place obstacles in the way of Swedish students wishing to attend similar Scandinavist rallies, and Oscar I intervened to prevent the nomination of the Finnish poet J. L. Runeberg to the Swedish Academy on the grounds that this would cause offence to the emperor.

The hand of the autocrat, of course, rested more heavily upon his own lands. A trickle of Finnish dissidents who fell into disfavour for their views made their way to Sweden. Aware of anti-Russian sentiment in Sweden, the authorities in Finland took all possible steps to isolate the Grand Duchy from the outside world. The postal services to Sweden were cut off for long periods, imported foreign newspapers such as the liberal Swedish *Aftonbladet* were carefully scrutinised by the censor and if necessary, confiscated, and the native press was fed with official communiqués charting the progress of Russian armies against Napoleon in 1812–14 and against the Polish rebels in 1831. The church was also used by the authorities to enforce obedience and loyalty. The proclamations read out from the pulpit on special prayer days were intended to contrast the benefits enjoyed by the Finnish people under the sceptre of the emperor-grand duke with their former situation. In December 1831, for example, the proclamation warned of those who sought to sow mistrust between ruler and people and condemned those who attempted to take the power of authority into their own hands – a clear reference to the recent events in Poland.[22]

Finland's old ties with Sweden had already begun to shrink in a number of ways. Finns lost the right to export agricultural produce duty-free to Sweden in 1817; as a consequence of this, and of Sweden's growing self-sufficiency in grain, Finnish traders began to look to the markets of the empire. The 1835 decree permitting the establishment of Finnish commercial agents in St Petersburg, Riga and Reval is an indication of the growing volume of trade, much of it carried in small peasant boats from Ostrobothnia and the skerries. By the mid–1840s, something like 40 per cent of Finland's trade was with Russia. Sweden's share had declined from around a half in the early 1820s to a mere 10 per cent. Swedish money was also finally withdrawn from circulation in 1840, and the rouble decreed the only medium of exchange. The capital was moved eastwards from Åbo to Helsingfors in 1812 on the advice of leading Finnish officials, and the university was transferred there sixteen years later after fire had devastated Åbo. By 1840, the population of the new capital had risen to over 16,000, and although most lived in wooden one-storey houses scattered over the rocky promontory, they could be justly proud of Carl Engel's fine neo-classical buildings which graced the administrative and cultural centre of the city.

On hearing news of the Polish revolt, the Finnish state-secretary in St Petersburg, R. H. Rehbinder, had predicted gloomily that the autonomy of the Grand Duchy was now under threat; but the principal danger to the country in 1830–31 came from the cholera epidemic, and not from Russian repression.[23] Congress Poland and the

22. Paasivirta J 1981 *Finland and Europe. The period of autonomy and the international crises 1808–1914*, London, pp. 25–35, 53–8. There is an interesting and unusual example of a sermon preached in Estonian to a congregation on the island of Ösel in 1810 in *Beiträge zur genauern Kenntniss der ehstnischen Sprache* (Erstes Heft, 1813), pp. 92ff. Pastor Frey painted a favourable contrast between the warring nations of Europe and the peace and tranquillity enjoyed by the inhabitants of the island, under the benevolent rule of the emperor, guaranteed by the Capitulations signed a hundred years before. The sermon was illustrated with references to the family and the Scriptures, on the theme of 'a house divided cannot stand'; and the pastor even managed to justify the high price of salt by ascribing this to the need to defend the realm: as parents defend their children, so does the emperor defend his subjects.

23. Paasivirta 1981, p. 54. A contemporary traveller through Finland felt that a correspondent in a St Petersburg newspaper who had lauded the Finns as thoroughly loyal to Russia during the Polish uprising was only partially correct; the old attachment to Sweden still remained. He also dismissed claims by Riga newspapers that the youth of Kurland were willing to serve their emperor in the wars against the Turk as a patriotic lie: the woods were full of draft-dodgers, and many others mutilated themselves in order to avoid conscription. Woltmann J 1833 *Beschreibung einer Reise nach St. Petersburg, Stockholm und Kopenhagen*, Hamburg, pp. 54–5, 198.

Lithuanian lands were dealt with severely. Over 5,000 noble estates were confiscated. Civil servants were dismissed from their posts, army officers and troops were transported to the Russian hinterland, along with thousands of civilians. Ten thousand Poles emigrated, to continue the cause in exile. The Organic Statute of 1832 retained the shell of the constitution of 1815 (though doing away with the Polish army), but Congress Poland was in fact under martial law until 1856 and ruled with an iron hand by Field Marshal I. F. Paskevich. The very names Lithuania and Belorussia were officially abolished in 1840: the provinces (*gubernii*) of Minsk, Grodno and Kovno were placed under the military governor of Vilna. Large numbers of petty *szlachta* in the western provinces were reclassified as state peasants or burghers. Provincial governors were ordered to fill administrative posts with non-natives as much as possible.

In this endeavour they were largely unsuccessful, simply because native administrators were more knowledgeable of local circumstances, languages, customs and institutions than outsiders. The repression in Poland and the western provinces was brutal, and the uprooting and attempted destruction of local laws, institutions and even culture was far more intense than was to be the case in the Baltic provinces and Finland later in the century; but the final result was failure, just as the Prussians failed to extirpate Polishness from Posen. The reasons for this will be examined in more detail later, as will the strategies pursued by successive rulers and administrators in the borderlands. At this stage, it is worth recalling that the Russian empire, which expanded not only into eastern Europe but to the Caucasus and into the Muslim khanates of central Asia, lacked most of the resources regarded as essential for the efficient and proper running of the state by contemporaries in western Europe. True, western-style institutions had been introduced, and reforms intended to bring Russia into line with western models were discussed and sometimes carried out. But there remained an enormous gulf between the good intentions of the reformers and the reality of the empire; the masses of illiterate and impoverished peasants, the absence of a prosperous and self-confident commercial middle class, and indeed of any social elements or institutions which might have challenged the power and authority of the autocracy, or at the very least forced it into a dialogue. In this vast and constantly-expanding empire, with its poor system of communications, ill-paid and often poorly educated officials, exposed to the temptations of bribery and not infrequently seeking solace in the bottle, sought to enforce the decrees and mandates emanating from St Petersburg. Their task in the western borderlands was even more difficult. Not only were they often unfamiliar with the language, customs and culture, they were also few in number and surrounded by native lawyers, administrators and their loquacious supporters in the press, universities, clubs, churches, assemblies and diets, all firmly convinced of the superiority and sanctity of their laws and institutions.

With the exception of Poland, the Vilna and Kiev military districts – and even here, Russian administrators warned of the dangers of excessive centralisation – the western borderlands during the reign of Nicholas I suffered few rude intrusions into their affairs. The one instance of fairly intensive social and religious disruption which occurred in the 1840s was not planned, and in fact revealed the inadequacies of the Orthodox church when faced with a new challenge. In 1841, rumours began to circulate amongst the peasantry of Livland that cheap land was available in the south of Russia. Burdened with heavy and unregulated labour services, and plagued by bad harvests, many peasants trudged to Riga to seek more information, in spite of official attempts to quash the rumours. Harassed by officialdom, the peasants turned to the Orthodox bishop in Riga, who received them sympathetically. On this occasion, governor-general Baron Karl Magnus von der Pahlen and the *Ritterschaft* worked closely with the minister of the interior A. G. Stroganov and the head of the notorious third department of the emperor's own chancery, General A. K. Benckendorff (a Baltic German), to nip any potential conversion movement in the bud. The bishop was forbidden to receive peasant petitions by the emperor, and eventually removed from his post; the peasant unrest was quelled in the winter of 1841–42 with the assistance of military courts and whippings for those found guilty.

This was not the end of the matter, however. Benckendorff's replacement, Count A. F. Orlov, was much more sympathetic to the cause of Orthodoxy in the Baltic provinces. St Petersburg refused to back von der Pahlen's efforts to prevent conversions to Orthodoxy in 1845, and his replacement, General E. A. Golovin, was given instructions to permit conversions on genuine religious grounds. Orthodox priests appear to have echoed the authorities in discountenancing hopes of material benefits, though expressions of sympathy with the plight of the peasants may have weakened the impact of this message. Golovin warned of the destabilising effects of mass conversion, and managed to persuade the Emperor Nicholas to decree a six-month period for reflection before the potential convert could be received into the church, to ensure he was moved by religious conviction and not merely a misguided belief that land and liberty would follow. Although tacitly admitting that distress might lie behind the conversions, the emperor also pointedly remarked that not a single Lutheran Finnish peasant had converted to Orthodoxy, and stated publicly what many in the Baltic German community would admit in private: the pastorate was firmly associated in the minds of the Estonians and Latvians with the landowning nobility.[24]

The conversion movement died away in 1849, as the peasantry began to realise that no improvement in their circumstances was likely to occur; but according to the statistics collected by the Orthodox bishop in Riga, 65,683 Estonians and 40,397 Latvians had become members of the Greek-Russian church between 1845 and 1848. Although some steps had been taken after 1841 to prepare priests for the Baltic provinces, Orthodoxy was not equipped to deal with this flood of converts, many of whom believed it was possible to belong to both the Lutheran and the Orthodox church. The law of 1832, which had ended the autonomy of the Lutheran church in the Baltic provinces and placed it under the administrative control of the ministry of the interior and the judicial authority of the ruling senate in St Petersburg, also forbade Lutheran clergymen to minister in any way to a member of the Orthodox church without special permission. Many who became disillusioned with their new faith were thus left in limbo, and their fate became something of a cause célèbre for evangelical Protestants in Europe, as well as one of the most contentious issues in Baltic-Russian relations. The mass conversions of the 1840s were essentially a protest against the exactions of the landowners at a time of great distress. As such, they revealed how deep a gulf existed between the landed classes (which included the clergy) and the peasantry, and posed a dilemma both for the imperial authorities and the Baltic German landowners, both conservative and committed to preserving the social status quo and yet increasingly at odds over who was to exercise the authority that would guarantee the maintenance of that order.[25]

Although the privileged status of Finland and the three Baltic provinces was preserved in all essentials during the reign of Nicholas I, the slow process of codification of the laws begun by Mikhail Speransky and the erection of an imperial superstructure of

24. Thaden 1984, pp. 177–80. Philipp G 1974 *Die Wirksamkeit der Herrnhuter Brüdergemeinde unter den Esten und Letten zur Zeit der Bauernbefreiung* Forschungen zur internationalen Sozial- und Wirtschaftsgeschichte **5**, Cologne, p. 183, for examples of Baltic German self-doubt about the relationship of the pastor and his flock. Tobien 1925, vol. 1, p. 177 claimed that the conversion movement was 'a well-laid plan, consciously pursued by government circles in St Petersburg since the 1830s'.

25. Chapter on the Baltic Germans by M Haltzel in: Thaden E, (ed.) 1981 *Russification in the Baltic Provinces and Finland 1855–1914*, Princeton, NJ, pp. 122–3.

government and administration were to have consequences in these borderlands. The replacement of the provincial criminal law code in the Baltic provinces with the first edition of the Russian law code in 1832 was the first step towards the integration of administrative and judicial procedures in the Empire, and as such rather more significant than the confirmation of the local laws (*Provinzialrecht*) of the Baltic provinces in 1845. The Finns reacted rather sharply at first to the codification, which one of Speransky's successors in the second department, D. N. Bludov, bluntly declared was intended to create the necessary link between the legislation of the empire as a whole and that of the Grand Duchy. However, they soon saw an opportunity to clarify the question of what precisely did constitute the fundamental laws of Finland, and to obtain imperial ratification of those laws. To this end, a draft constitution, based essentially upon the Gustavian fundamental laws of 1772 and 1789, was drawn up in 1841. Bludov rejected this on the grounds that a uniform administrative and legal system could not tolerate separate laws, a view with which the governor-general, Prince Alexander Menshikov and the emperor concurred. But if the Finns were unsuccessful in obtaining a clear confirmation of a written constitution, they did manage to persuade Menshikov to argue for the postponement of the integrative measures proposed by the codification committee, on the grounds that it would be most unwise to upset the loyalty and gratitude of the Finns towards their new ruler.[26]

Finnish bureaucrats were prone on occasion to indulge in morbid speculation as to what might happen when less benevolent rulers occupied the imperial throne. Nevertheless, even the formidable Lars Gabriel von Haartman, for almost two decades the leader of the Finnish Senate, admitted in 1854 that Finland was 'less Russian' than it had been in 1820. The nation honoured the monarch and was unquestionably loyal, thought von Haartman, but the age-old barrier between Finland and Russia was likely to remain. Complete assimilation of two nations so different in language, religion, political traditions and social organisation was impossible, as well as unnecessary since great empires flourished by favouring separate nationalities: only weak countries and revolutionary governments sought to level everything. The aristocratic bureaucrats who ran Finland's affairs were

26. On the codification of the laws, and the consequences for the western borderlands, see: Raeff M 1969 *Michael Speransky. Statesman of Imperial Russia 1772–1839* (revised edition), The Hague, pp. 320–46. Haltzel 1981, pp. 118–19. Jussila O 1967 *Suomen perustuslait venäläisten ja suomalaisten tulkintojen mukaan 1808–1863* Historiallisia Tutkimuksia **77**, Helsinki, pp. 186–211.

in fact remarkably successful in heading off plans to tie the Grand Duchy more closely to the Empire, and although distrusted by the intelligentsia in Helsingfors (who were in turn regarded with some contempt by grandees such as Alexander Armfelt, minister state-secretary from 1841 to 1876), they laid the basis for Finland's subsequent vigorous national development during the reign of Alexander II.[27]

Baltic Germans were also fond of worrying about the future, though perhaps with more reason. J. F. Wittram, a Hanoverian who came to teach in the Baltic provinces in the 1830s, noted in his correspondence the anxieties felt about the growing influence of Orthodoxy and the threat of russification hanging over the educational system. The measures proposed in the 1830s by the minister of education Sergey Uvarov for increasing the amount of Russian taught in secondary schools and for appointing qualified Russians to posts in the Baltic educational system had only limited success, however, though the administration of education was removed from the university and placed in the hands of the school district curator. Determined resistance by the nobility also frustrated Uvarov's plan to have elementary education placed under the control of his ministry. Although nominally under the ministry of the interior, the elementary educational system was largely run by the local clergy and *Ritterschaften*. In Livland, the emancipation edict of 1819 had decreed that each peasant commune should have its own school. In Kurland, one school was to be provided per thousand inhabitants. Estland was less well provided for, and it was not until the 1840s that serious steps were taken here to improve the situation. The nobility was somewhat keener on providing village schools than the clergy, for whom religious education in the environs of the home was sufficient; but although anxious to improve the 'uneducated, brutal estate', the landowners also feared they might create a half-educated intelligentsia which would not be satisfied with farm labour.[28]

A Finnish commentator noted in 1850 that there were more elementary schools in the Baltic provinces than in Finland, and that the peasantry there had the advantage over their Finnish brethren in that the business of the commune had to be written up in Estonian or

27. Krusius-Ahrenberg L 1934 *Der Durchbruch des Nationalismus und Liberalismus im politischen Leben Finnlands 1856–1863* Annales Academiae Scientiarum Fennicae **33**, Helsinki, pp. 17–18. Thaden 1984, pp. 211–13.

28. Speer H 1936 *Das Bauernschulwesen im Gouvernement Estland vom Ende des 18. Jahrhunderts bis zur Russifizierung,* Tartu, pp. 171ff.

Latvian, in accordance with the peasant statutes. The poem with which he ended his article, however, subtly pointed up a rather more striking contrast:

Kai, mis ma sul üttelen:	Hark to what I tell you:
Kolm olli surma suvveel;	Thrice came death in the summer;
Üks olli kurri kolemine	The first a bitter death
Toine tautsi tappemine	The second a pestilential death
Kolmas voera vottemine.	The third taken by a stranger.
Voeras vottis ommas orjas	The stranger took us as his slaves
Sulgus sundija sullases	Chaining us to thralldom
Käni omma käskijallas	Binding us to do his will
Vellekese, mis ma laulan?	Little brother, what shall I sing?
Laulo om ikkene halleda!	Sad the song of bondage!
Orja polveke vägga rasseda!	Harsh the aeons of slavery! [29]

The memory of centuries of servitude and the hatred of the arrogant stranger who had imposed that yoke made it highly unlikely that the Estonians and Latvians would wish to stand shoulder-to-shoulder with the Baltic Germans in defending Est- Liv- and Kurland against the attacks of russifiers. The first thrusts at the privileges of the provinces made by Uvarov in the 1830s had provoked the rector of Dorpat university, Karl Christian Ulmann, into a vigorous defence of the historic foundations of *Deutschtum* in the Baltic. The conservative Ulmann bound together language and religion as the essence of the national identity (*Volkstümlichkeit*) of the Baltic Germans. Liberals of a later generation were to play down the religious element, and sought to bring the quasi-feudal dominance of the *Ritterschaften* to an end, but they were at one with the conservatives in defending the rights and privileges of the Baltic provinces (*Landesprivilegien*) from the attacks of the Panslavists.[30]

National sentiment was to add a new and often confusing dimension to political life in nineteenth-century Europe. As we have seen, the essentially dynastic concept of the Danish *Helstat* was on its

29. S. E(lmgren) 1850 Estnisk poesi *Litteraturbladet för Allmänna Bildning*, pp. 209–14. The poem had been published that year in *Ehstnische Volkslieder*.

30. Garve H 1978 *Konfession und Nationalität. Ein Beitrag zum Verhältnis von Kirche und Gesellschaft in Livland im 19. Jahrhundert* Wissenschaftliche Beiträge zur Geschichte und Landskunde Ostmitteleuropas **110**, Marburg, pp. 80–92. See also the articles written by the leading liberal Georg Berkholtz in 1864 (*Baltische Monatshefte* **9**: 377–84, 474–86), in which he declares that in stormy weather (i.e. the attacks of the Panslavists), the Baltic Germans, like travellers, draw their cloak (of privileges) ever tighter round them; only when the sun of liberty and enlightenment (*Bildung*) shines upon the Russians will the Germans have less reason and desire to draw the cloak of their *Eigentümlichkeit* around them.

last legs on the eve of the revolutionary year of 1848, weakened not only by a constitutionalist movement which the reforms of the enlightened absolutist monarchy had indirectly helped to launch, but by a curious and explosive mixture of old-style *ständisch* mentality and an as yet imprecise but emotionally powerful linguistic-cultural nationalism. This volatile element proved too much for principled, moderate liberalism as well; and although conservatives such as Bismarck showed themselves more adept at handling it, they too could be caught out by its unpredictability.

CHAPTER FOUR

The Era of Nationalism

POINTS OF COLLISION

As the life of Christian VIII of Denmark slowly slipped away during the early days of January 1848, the first flickers of revolutionary lightning were beginning to flash across the European horizon. In the dying monarch's own lands, political agitation was rife. His Open Letter of 1846 had inflamed opinion in the duchies, and made them virtually ungovernable. By the end of 1847, the king and his ministers had tacitly acknowledged that a constitution would have to be introduced, although they continued to remain faithful to the principles of the unitary state. So did the new king, Frederik VII, but he was under strong pressure from the Danish national liberals to grant a constitution for Denmark and Slesvig; Holstein was to have its own legislative assembly, army and control of its own finances.

The constitutional rescript issued by the new king on 28 January 1848 proposed the establishment of a united diet, with limited powers, alongside the four provincial assemblies. The drafters of this rescript had few illusions that it would be acceptable either to the national liberals in Denmark or to the estates in the duchies, and any remaining hopes of a solution in the spirit of the January rescript were shattered by the spread of revolution throughout the German lands in March. On 18 March 1848, as troops were firing on demonstrators in the streets of Berlin, deputies of the estates of Slesvig and Holstein met in Rendsburg and drafted a five-point programme calling for a constitution and a separate army for the duchies and Slesvig's inclusion in the German Confederation. The national liberals in Copenhagen had already demanded the incorporation of Slesvig into a constitutional Danish state, and were staging mass meetings to put pressure on the government. On 21 March, the king announced that his ministers had resigned. After a flurry of negotiations, a new ministry including leading national liberals was formed and accepted by Frederik VII, who now acknowledged himself to be a constitutional monarch. Fruitless talks were held with a deputation from the Rendsburg meeting. The reply drafted by Orla Lehmann, now a government minister, would have allowed Holstein to become an independent German state with its own constitution. Slesvig and Denmark were however to be constitutionally united.

Against a background of international tension, revolution and war in the duchies, the national constituent assembly (*Rigsforsamling*) was elected and convened in the summer of 1848. One-quarter of its members were nominated by the crown. The rest were to be chosen by an electorate of male householders over the age of thirty, and not dependent on poor relief, though only one-third of those entitled to actually registered to vote. The peasant movement (*Bondevenner*) fared better on the islands than on the Jutland peninsula, where the conservatives did reasonably well. The conservatives and the deputies of the centre collaborated effectively to obtain majorities on the committees charged with considering the constitutional draft prepared by the national liberal D. G. Monrad, and were able to stifle the left's proposals for a unicameral legislature elected by universal male suffrage. The final bill was approved by 119 votes to 4 on 25 May 1849, and received the royal assent on 5 June. It provided for a division of powers, with a constitutional monarchy and guaranteed civil rights. The *Rigsdag* was to consist of two houses, a *Folketing* of 100 members, elected directly every four years, and a *Landsting* of 51 members, elected every eight years by indirect ballot of all entitled to vote (male householders over the age of thirty). Eligibility for election to the *Landsting* was confined to males over forty with a substantial income, and this chamber was in future years to become the bastion of conservative property-owners, facing a liberal-dominated *Folketing*.

Almost two centuries of absolutism was thus brought to an end peaceably, at a time when the hopes of liberals elsewhere in Europe were being dashed on the rocks of reaction. In truth, the Danish crown had long ceased to function as a despotic force, and constitutional reform enjoyed genuinely popular support. The atmosphere during the March days was tense, certainly. A nervous bishop prayed that God would give the government wisdom and steadfastness against the 'Parisian fury', and Orla Lehmann, the liberals' rising hope (and a young man with a high opinion of himself), worried whether 'the miasma of communism, which had spread throughout Europe, would . . . find a fertile soil in the cottar class'. There was, however, little likelihood of the sort of civil strife feared by conservatives; and indeed the rapid escalation of the conflict over the duchies soon distracted attention southwards.[1]

The duke of Augustenburg had already attempted to place himself at the head of the Schleswig-Holstein movement, and on 21 March travelled to Berlin to seek the support of the Prussian king. He returned to discover that a provisional government had been set up in Kiel. The members of that government defended their actions on the grounds that their overlord was no longer free, but had been forced by a popular uprising in Copenhagen to dismiss his advisers and adopt the Eider programme of the national liberals. It was a clever ruse, for it won over the civil service and the German-speaking population, and gained the fortress of Rendsburg. The revolt spread northwards; most of the towns of Slesvig recognised the authority of the Kiel government. Augustenburg's brother, the prince of Nør, had only around three thousand troops and an assortment of volunteers (including Werner Siemens, a young Prussian artillery officer who upset the Danish blockade of Kiel harbour by setting off electrically-charged mines). The Danish forces in northern Slesvig numbered 11,000, and this superior force won the day when the two sides met in battle at Bov, outside Flensburg, on 9 April. Three days later, the German Confederation recognised the provisional government and sent a division to join General Wrangel's Prussian troops already in Holstein. Wrangel defeated the Danes in battle, and crossed the Jutland frontier on 2 May.

In these straitened circumstances, the March ministry turned to the European powers for assistance. Frederik VII also made a personal appeal to Oscar I. Worried about possible Russian reactions, Oscar declared in the State Council on 27 April that Swedish intervention in Danish affairs would be a 'quixotic' gesture; and yet, four days later, he came out for armed assistance. The secret committee of the *Riksdag* and the State Council agreed unanimously, and on 4 May, an offer of

1. Meyer P 1985–7 Regering og rigsdag 1849–1866 *Historie* **16**: 206–7. Bishop Fogtmann's letter of 4 March 1848 to his fellow-conservative, Bishop J P Mynster, is in: Bagge P et al. (eds), 1958 *Danske politiske breve*, Copenhagen, vol. 4, p. 108. Orla Lehmann was in Italy with his convalescent wife when the revolutionary wave began, and had to hasten back via France and Belgium. He castigated the radical liberals in Denmark as 'communist fanatics who condemn us and everything else but universal suffrage'. (Letter to his wife, 17 March 1848, *ibid.*, p. 129).

15,000 Swedish troops for the defence of Jutland and the islands was made. Why Oscar changed his mind remains something of a mystery. It was by no means sure that Russia would view favourably a Swedish military intervention, nor was it certain that public opinion was unanimously behind Swedish involvement. Liberals as well as conservatives had their reservations about the increased tax burden which would be required to cover the costs of the military expedition, and worried about the consequences for Swedish trade of open conflict with Prussia. Liberals also suspected that the king wished to undermine the movement for political reform at home by engaging in a military adventure abroad.[2]

The possibility of a Scandinavian alliance or even union did, however, impel Russia to put pressure on Prussia to withdraw from Jutland. Wrangel's troops were in fact pulled back at the end of May, though Slesvig remained under Prussian military control. At a meeting of Danish and Swedish ministers in Malmö on 9 June, the Danish foreign minister tried in vain to persuade the Swedes to allow their troops to be used in active operations. The Swedes acknowledged that Denmark could not accept Prussia's terms for an armistice as long as Slesvig remained under occupation, but they were only prepared to give more than moral support if Russia was willing to lend force to the Danish demand for an evacuation of Slesvig by Wrangel's troops. On 23 June, the British foreign minister, Lord Palmerston set out his proposals for an armistice and eventual peace settlement. Slesvig could either be divided on national lines, or the duchies could be united administratively, but without the incorporation of Slesvig into the German Confederation. Neither option was favoured in Denmark, where it was decided to negotiate a straightforward military truce in Malmö. The Swedes put pressure on Denmark to abandon its demand to administer Slesvig, and the final agreement reached at the end of August – after having been initially rejected by the Kiel government and Wrangel, on behalf of the confederation – proposed the setting up of a five-man joint committee to administer the duchies. After a second round of fighting in the spring of 1849 and another uneasy

2. Oscar's motives are discussed in Holmberg Å 1946 *Skandinavismen i Sverige vid 1800-talets mitt (1843–1863)*, Göteborg, pp. 130–58. Danstrup J 1944 Den politiske Skandinavisme i Perioden 1830–1850 *Scandia* **16**: 257ff. The most recent, and comprehensive study of political Scandinavism in this period is by Becker-Christensen H 1981 *Skandinaviske drømmer og politiske realiteter 1830–1850* Arusia – Historiske skrifter 1, Århus. The diplomatic ramifications of the Slesvig-Holstein conflict are covered in Steefel L 1932 *The Schleswig-Holstein question*, Harvard, and Sandiford K 1975 *Great Britain and the Schleswig-Holstein question 1848–1864: A study in diplomacy, politics and public opinion*, Toronto.

truce, Prussia and the confederation concluded a simple peace treaty with Denmark in 1850, effectively abandoning the rebels to their fate.

The settlement ultimately devised for the duchies owed not a little to the wishes of the powers, and did little to resolve the conflict. The right of succession in the duchies via the female line was upheld by the powers, and the duke of Augustenburg was obliged to renounce his claim. The powers guaranteed the Danish *Helstat*, but recognised the separate status of Holstein as a member of the German Confederation. Neither this London Agreement of 1852 nor the publicly proclaimed Danish policy of reconciliation in the duchies inspired much confidence.[3] The national liberals, and Frederik VII himself, distrusted the designated heir to the throne, Christian of Glücksburg, and the possibility of a united Scandinavia under the Bernadotte dynasty was once more canvassed.

The failure to reach a satisfactory constitutional settlement meant that the duchies continued to be administered according to pre-1848 principles. The royal commissary in Slesvig, F. F. Tillisch, purged the civil service and replaced those dismissed with loyal, but often incompetent Danes. The police were authorised to confiscate publications deemed seditious, which in practice meant anything critical of the absolutist regime which still obtained south of the Kongeå. According to the British minister to Copenhagen, the danicisation policy doggedly pursued by August Regenburg, director of education and ecclesiastical affairs in Slesvig, merely caused hostility and distrust instead of bringing the people closer to Denmark.[4]

On the eastern flank of the Kingdom of Prussia, another national conflict excited the attention of the delegates assembled in Frankfurt and Berlin during the revolution of 1848. A Polish National Committee was set up in Posznań and an army of 10,000 Poles recruited in preparation for the anticipated war of liberation against Russia. When this crusade did not materialise, the Germans, who had initially supported an independent Poland, began to grow cool. In April-May, the Polish legionaries in Posznań were forced to disarm by Prussian troops. Containment and suppression of Polish rights became the order of the day for Prussian bureaucrats in the *Provinz Posen* which replaced the Grand Duchy in Frederick William IV's dictated constitution of December 1848.

3. Sandiford 1975, pp. 28–33. The Prussian ambassador to London, Christian von Bunsen, described the agreement as a 'declaration of bankruptcy'.

4. Rerup L 1982 *Slesvig og Holsten efter 1830*, Copenhagen, p. 150. Bracker A 1972–3 Die dänische Sprachpolitik 1850–1864 und die Bevölkerung Mittelschleswigs *Zeitschrift für Schleswig-Holsteinische Geschichte* **97, 98**.

Delegates from the eastern provinces of Prussia were amongst the most vociferous opponents of Polish claims to national self-determination in the Frankfurt parliament. Sympathy for the Poles rose and fell according to how near or far away one was from them, in the words of Eduard Jordan.[5] The proposals for Polish autonomy made by the radical liberal Johann Jacoby were particularly disliked, and may have contributed to his defeat in the May elections to the Frankfurt parliament. The East Prussians were especially worried about the threat of Russian invasion; it was said that spring was about to come from the Neva, not the Seine, so green was the eastern frontier (green being the colour of the Russian army uniforms). The countryside was swept by rumours, of plots to dethrone the king or to force Catholic Poles to convert to Protestantism. In areas where the land reforms had caused social dislocation and distress, there were widespread attacks on officials and landlords, and refusals to pay taxes. The citizens' militia (*Bürgerwehr*), originally the proud symbol of popular liberty, had to be used by the authorities to restore law and order. In the summer of 1848, the conservatives began to rally. By the autumn, the conservative *Preussenverein*, with 3,000 members, was the largest political organisation in Königsberg. The liberals were still strong enough to demonstrate in November against the prorogation of the National Assembly, and organised a moderately successful boycott of the elections under the three-class system of franchise in July 1849; but the high tide of liberalism was now ebbing. Relations between the Democratic Club and the Workers' Union were often poor, and amongst the labouring masses, liberalism never managed to strike root.[6]

The revolution galvanised liberal forces in Mecklenburg, whose two dukes had managed to put off their obligation to provide a constitution for their subjects for over thirty years. Both politely declined to receive any more petitions for reform, but the rising tide of revolution elsewhere in Germany obliged them to proclaim the freedom of the press and to call an extraordinary *Landtag*. The news from Berlin heightened tension; on 24 March, the *Rostocker Zeitung* urged Mecklenburgers to follow the Berliners' example, and become Germans, not slaves. The dukes and the *Ritterschaft* expressed their

5. Winkler-Seraphim B 1956 Das Verhältnis der preussischen Ostprovinzen, insbesonders Ostpreussens, zum Deutschen Bund im 19. Jahrhundert *Zeitschrift für Ostforschung* **5**: 13.

6. On the failure of liberalism in East Prussia, see Orr W 1977 Königsberg und die Revolution von 1848 *Zeitschrift für Ostforschung* **26**: 271–306, and Orr W 1980 East Prussia and the revolution of 1848 *Central European History* **13**: 303–331.

readiness to concede a constitutional order, and a constituent assembly finally convened in October. Composed of all sections of society, and dominated by the liberals, it debated a wide range of topics, hitherto rarely aired in this antediluvian rural backwater. The final draft constitution produced in spring 1849 endorsed the principle of popular sovereignty and proclaimed the end of nobility. In its passage through the assembly, however, this radical draft was considerably amended. Noble titles and orders were restored, the right of veto was granted to the rulers, and a restricted franchise was introduced. The constitutional law passed by a majority of 55 to 34 in August 1849 provided for a 60 member chamber, 40 of whose members were to be directly elected, the rest selected by specific propertied groups. It proved impossible to enforce. Duke Georg and a considerable section of the *Ritterschaft* refused to accept it, and were able, by appealing to the confederation's arbitration procedure and the king of Prussia, to compel Duke Friedrich Franz to abandon his ministers and the constitution. All that remained of the brief era of reform was a new ecclesiastical commission and a reformed structure of government (though the old collegial form of government remained in operation in the Strelitz section of the joint duchy until 1909).[7]

The reaction of Nicholas I to the revolutionary events in Europe was to prepare for war and to raise the shutters against the gale. Troops were massed on the western frontiers of the empire and directly intervened in Wallachia and Hungary. The postal service and passenger traffic between Sweden and Finland was suspended, and the frontier closed, when it was feared that the revolutionary wave might wash against the northern walls of the empire. The authorities in Finland had already taken steps to curb what they regarded as a dangerously political tendency in the hitherto largely cultural fennophile movement. The Swedish-language newspaper *Saima* published by the Hegelian philosopher and man of letters, Johan Vilhelm Snellman, was suppressed in 1846, the Finnish-language *Kanava* a year later. In order to ensure that the 'lower orders' remained uncontaminated by pernicious foreign doctrines, entry permits were only to be granted to foreign workmen and apprentices if their prospective employers could give guarantees of the reliability of their beliefs and behaviour. Students at the university in Helsingfors were placed under strict surveillance, and the authorities saw to it that

7. Vitense O 1920 *Geschichte von Mecklenburg*, Gotha, pp. 451ff. on the 1848 revolution in Mecklenburg.

Snellman – whom they considered a dangerous communist agitator – was passed over for appointment to a post in the university in 1848.[8]

Finnish involvement in the Scandinavist movement of the 1840s was minimal, though the wresting of Finland from the grip of the Russian despot was a popular cause amongst Swedish student activists. The future of Finland came under the spotlight in the mid-1850s, during the Crimean War. Although the major theatre of war was the Crimean peninsula, British and French naval forces cruised the Baltic in 1854 and 1855. The attacks on the Ostrobothnian trading ports launched by Admiral Plumridge's squadron in the summer of 1854 did little to further the British cause, either militarily or politically. The bombardment of the Sveaborg fortress off Helsingfors the following year provided spectacular entertainment for the citizenry, but had no further consequences.

The one episode of the campaign which did have political repercussions was the capture of the fortress of Bomarsund in August 1854. The building of this fortress on the Åland islands had caused alarm in Sweden, and the demilitarisation of the islands in the final peace settlement was advantageous to Sweden's security.[9] During the spring and summer of 1854, it looked as if Sweden might be persuaded to enter the war on the allied side. The joint declaration of neutrality issued by the Danish and Swedish governments favoured the allies, who were freely able to use Scandinavian ports. Oscar I conducted secret negotiations with British and French representatives, but his terms for participation were too high, and he was unwilling to risk entering a war without considerable allied military backing and guaranteed support for the reconquest of Finland. When it was proposed that Swedish forces should occupy the Åland islands after the fall of Bomarsund, Oscar declined the offer. There was a renewed flurry of diplomatic activity in the autumn of 1855, resulting in an allied agreement to guarantee the territory of Sweden-Norway, and further talks on the possible entry of Sweden into the war. The sudden cessation of hostilities came as a blow to Oscar, who attempted in vain to press Sweden's claims to the Åland islands or for the demilitarisation of the Finnish coastline west of the Sveaborg fortress.

8. Paasivirta J 1981 *Finland and Europe 1809–1914*, London, pp. 72–86, and Johansson R 1930 Skandinavismen i Finland *Skrifter utgivna av Svenska Litteratursällskapet i Finland* **214**: 222–9, for the consequences of the 1848 revolutions in Finland.

9. On the naval campaigns, see Greenhill B and Giffard A 1988 *The British assault on Finland 1854–1855*, London. For the impact of the war in the Baltic region, see Paasivirta 1981, pp. 87–105, and Anderson E 1974 The Crimean War in the Baltic area *Journal of Baltic Studies* **5**: 339–61.

Having broken with the pro-Russian policy of his father, Oscar I now took up the idea of Scandinavian dynastic union. Leading Scandinavists were carefully cultivated, the student delegation from Denmark was wined and dined in the royal palace in Stockholm, and the king's agents worked sedulously to spread unionist propaganda in London and Paris. There was a good deal of optimism in court circles, encouraged no doubt by good dinners and friendly words from Frederik VII and Napoleon III's cousin, Prince Jérôme, who cruised the Scandinavian coastline in the summer of 1856 and had several meetings with the Swedish Crown Prince Carl Johan and prominent Scandinavists.

The euphoric mood was broken in February-March 1857, when Oscar's offer of an alliance, and 16,000 troops to defend Denmark to the Eider frontier, was turned down by the Danish government on the grounds that it excluded Holstein. This had in fact been foreseen by King Oscar's conservative foreign minister and the Swedish representative in Copenhagen, both of whom felt that the king was basing his policy upon false assumptions. The majority of Danes, and the newly-appointed Scheele government, were not willing to abandon Christian of Glücksburg, surrender Holstein and enter a union under the Bernadotte dynasty. Swedish liberals distrusted the king's motives; conservatives such as the cabinet secretary C. F. Palmstierna expressed their reservations concerning the king's propensity to conduct foreign affairs without consulting the government. The displeasure of the estates feared by Palmstierna in January 1857 soon surfaced. A proposal to amend the constitution to make it obligatory for the king to listen to the members of the State Council before deciding upon negotiations and alliances with foreign powers, and forbidding him to become ruler of a foreign state without the consent of the *Riksdag*, won considerable support and was a powerful rebuff to royal ambitions. Carl Johan, who assumed the regency in September 1857, was no longer as keen on dynastic union as he had been the previous summer, and he declined a request by the new Danish government to resume talks on the Swedish alliance proposals.

The policies pursued by Carl XV Johan as king (1859–72) did much to diminish the prospects of a Scandinavian union. Handsome and dashing, but at bottom a shallow and indecisive man (as the memoirs of his contemporaries clearly show), he lacked the caution and finesse of his father. His attempt to appease the Norwegians by abolishing the office of stattholder ended in disaster. The endorsement of this proposal in 1859 by the *Storting* angered the Swedish estates, which declared that such matters could only be settled in the context of a general revision of the act of union. The Swedish government threatened to resign unless the king vetoed the *Storting* bill; unable to find ministers more amenable to his designs, Carl Johan gave way, thereby deeply offending the Norwegians. This brief crisis was a turning-point in several respects. It marked the ascendancy in government circles of the justice minister, Louis de Geer, the man who was to steer through parliamentary reform some six years later, and was a decisive setback for personal monarchical power in Sweden. It was also a defeat for the pro-Norwegian Scandinavists; Swedish nationalism, voiced in the columns of the new and aggressive newspaper *Nya Dagligt Allehanda*, was now in the ascendancy. Finally, and perhaps most importantly, it was a blow from which the Swedish-Norwegian union did not recover. The proposals made for extended constitutional, diplomatic and military cooperation by the second Union Committee (1865–67) were overwhelmingly rejected by the *Storting* in 1871.[10]

The prospect of Sweden becoming actively involved in the process of reshaping Europe, which many contemporaries believed was now at hand, was given encouragement by the king. He gave his backing to the voluntary sharpshooter movement started in 1860 (in spite of its Garibaldian leanings), and made a good deal of noise in support of the Polish revolt in 1863. Meetings between the kings of Sweden and Denmark as conflict flared once more in the duchies seemed to presage a revival of plans for an alliance and dynastic union. Public opinion in Sweden was, however, markedly cool towards any idea of alliance, as the king himself well knew.

The relationship between the duchies and Denmark had not been resolved by any of the attempts to create or impose a common constitution. The estates in Slesvig and Holstein appealed in 1860 to the German states to intervene and help them regain their sorely oppressed rights and liberties; the Eider-Danish *Dannevirke* association gathered 71,000 signatures, including those of nearly all the members of the *Rigsdag*, for an address calling for the constitutional union of Slesvig and Denmark as an indivisible and independent state. When the British foreign minister Lord Russell, who like his predecessors had wrestled unavailingly with the problem, proposed in September 1862 that Denmark and the three duchies should each have their own

10. Holmberg 1946, pp. 328–57. Derry T 1973 *A history of modern Norway 1814–1972*, Oxford, pp. 87–94. Elvander N 1961 Från liberal skandinavism till konservativ nationalism i Sverige *Scandia* **27**: 366–86.

separate representation and no common constitution, deep gloom descended upon the Danish government, which feared they were about to share the fate of Poland. The effect of Russell's Gotha despatch, though supported by other European powers, was to draw Sweden and Denmark closer together. At the beginning of 1863, the national liberals Monrad and Lehmann renewed the call for a Nordic defensive alliance. Although his ministers were decidedly unenthusiastic, Carl XV Johan responded positively. Frederik VII and his ministry, stiffened by assurances of support and sensing that the Polish revolt might either distract attention or be the signal for the great reshaping of Europe under Napoleon III's aegis, took the first step towards realising the Eider Danish state on 30 March 1863, when a separate constitution was imposed upon Holstein.

On 22 July, shortly after the German Confederation demanded the withdrawal of this March Patent on pain of a federal execution (i.e. military intervention) in Holstein, the two kings met at Skodsborg, on the island of Sjælland. According to the Swedish minister to Copenhagen, Count Henning Hamilton, Carl Johan, offered a defensive alliance backed by Napoleon III, advised the Danish government to reject the demand of the confederation, but not to resist the entry of troops into Holstein, and promised 20,000 troops for the defence of Slesvig. Other evidence, however, suggests that Carl Johan made the complete severance of Holstein from the rest of the realm a condition for Swedish military aid. His foreign minister Carl Manderström was prepared to see how far Britain and France would support the idea of a defensive alliance, but even that more modest objective was overruled by his colleagues in government.[11]

The situation came to a head at the end of 1863. In November, a common constitution for Denmark and Slesvig was approved by the council of state, in the absence of the German-speaking members from the duchies. Two days later, Frederik VII died. He was succeeded by Christian of Glücksburg, in accordance with the terms of the London Agreement. Pressed by the foreign powers to withhold his signature, but facing the prospect of a major government crisis and revolutionary unrest at home if he did, Christian IX approved the new constitution, which was to come into force on New Year's Day 1864. The son of the duke of Augustenburg promptly proclaimed himself Friedrich VIII of Schleswig-Holstein, and sought the backing of the confederation

11. Holmberg Å 1946/7 Skandinavismens kris. Alliansfrågan våren och sommaren 1863 *Scandia* **17**: 137–211. See also the interesting diary entries of one of Carl Johan's closest associates: Dardel F von 1912 *Minnen*, Stockholm, vol. 2, pp. 52–4, 58–9, 89.

Diet. The small German states backed the Augustenburg claim, and overruled an Austrian-Prussian proposal to occupy Slesvig if Denmark refused to withdraw the November constitution.

The latter proposal was part of the strategy adopted by the king of Prussia's chief minister, Count Otto von Bismarck. Bismarck reasoned that the powers would be unlikely to countenance an invasion of Slesvig in support of the dubious Augustenburg claim but could be appeased by a policy of strict adherence to the terms of the London Agreement. As Bismarck made clear in his response to the pleas of the Prussian minister to Paris to support the Augustenburg claim and so prevent Napoleon III allying with the small German states, he was not willing to align Prussia with professors and their armchair democracy (*Vereinsdemokratie*). For Bismarck, the constellation of forces in Europe was far more important than the fate of the duchies.[12]

Bismarck revealed his annexationist intentions at a meeting of the Prussian State Council on 3 February, three days after Austrian and Prussian forces had crossed the Eider river into Slesvig. Napoleon III was willing to support annexation in order to cause a rift between Prussia and Austria. Russia, anxious to revive the anti-French coalition and in no state to engage in war, deemed the duchies expendable. Without the support of either power, the British government felt unable to intervene actively on Denmark's behalf. The outnumbered Danish forces rapidly abandoned the Dannevirke line of fortifications; Kolding fell on 18 February, and the loss of the fortress of Dybbøl two months later forced Denmark to the negotiating table. Bismarck was able to exploit the divisions and mutual mistrust of the powers, and was unwittingly abetted by Danish intransigence. The London conference failed to come up with an acceptable solution, and the war was resumed. Facing further military disaster, Christian IX dismissed the Monrad ministry and appointed the conservative Bluhme to negotiate a new truce.

The final peace treaty was signed in Vienna on 30 October 1864. Denmark surrendered the duchies to joint Austro-Prussian control, after a minor rectification of the frontier to compensate Denmark for the loss of enclaves in western Slesvig. The Augustenburg claim, although widely supported in the duchies themselves, was opposed by a small but influential group of conservative landowners and the German national-liberal *Nationalverein*, whose agents in the duchies

12. Linstow P 1978 Bismarck, Europa og Slesvig-Holsten 1862–1866 *Historisk Tidsskrift* **78**: 415.

were already busily working in the Prussian interest: it was ultimately declared invalid by Bismarck's lawyers.

The joint administration was ended in 1865 by an agreement giving Prussia administrative control of Slesvig and Austria control of Holstein (though Prussia retained the important naval base at Kiel). One year later, Prussia crushed Austria on the battlefield of Sadowa (Königgrätz). Austria surrendered to Prussia all its claims to the duchies; but Article 5 of the peace of Prague which concluded the Austro-Prussian war also made provision for the inhabitants of northern Slesvig to be reunited with Denmark should they express such a wish in a free plebiscite. This provision, included at the insistence of Napoleon III, was declared no longer valid by Austria and Prussia in 1879; but the Prussian government had already made it clear that it had no intention of allowing a free vote. The two duchies were made into one province (Provinz Schleswig-Holstein), into which the tiny Duchy of Lauenburg, sold by Denmark to Prussia, was incorporated in 1876. The old patchwork of medieval liberties, sokes and bailiwicks was swept away and replaced by Prussian-style rural counties, and a flood of Prussian decrees and laws drowned the last remnants of the duchies' ancient privileges.

THE POLITICS OF NATIONHOOD

The suddenness with which the national question flared up in Slesvig-Holstein, and its effects upon Danish and German liberalism, is a vivid example of the unsettling and often unpredictable force of nationalistic sentiments and ideas. Here, an ancient and well-established regional identity was assaulted by conflicting nationalisms sponsored by forces external to the duchies. Divisions often occurred along the line of existing antagonisms: farmers resentful of the demands of German-speaking officials, workers in the shipyards of Åbenrå at odds with their employers, peasants on the island of Als who were in frequent conflict with the duke of Augustenburg. The failure to push through much-needed administrative and judicial reforms as a result of the conflict also increased tension and indirectly affected attitudes.

There was, however, a strong sense of local identity and resentment at the excessive interference of outsiders. The young poet Theodor Storm disliked the demagogic tones of the speakers at the 1844 Frisian festival, for example, and his fellow-marshlanders still retained a strong loyalty to the monarchical ideas of the *Helstat*. The *Helstat* ideal did not lack supporters; what it did not have was a clear sense of direction.[13] Attachment to regional rights and liberties and the preservation of the old order was under attack from centralisers and modernisers all over northern Europe. In Slesvig and Holstein, the pressure came from several directions – the rival dynastic claimants, Danish and German national liberalism. Those who endeavoured to preserve the special status and rights of the duchies, such as the landowners and farmers of the Haderslev area (many of them Danish speakers) who had formed the *Schleswig-Holsteinische Patriotische Verein* in 1844, or who tried to rally the inhabitants of the area to the third force of 'national colourlessness' in 1848, were swept aside. Local sentiment in the duchies was still strong, and there is little evidence to suggest that the language question was a divisive factor before the authorities made it so. To local ears, the tiny locomotives struggling with the incline on the light railway system of eastern Slesvig continued to puff in Danish '*hjælp mæ dog*' and whistle in Low German '*ek schiit di watt*' on the downward slope. It was the policies of administrators such as August Regenburg in the 1850s and the Prussian provincial *Oberpräsident* Ernst Matthias von Köller in the late 1890s which placed strains upon the everyday bilingualism of central Slesvig and the towns in the northern part of the duchy.[14]

The unification of Germany under Prussian leadership, proclaimed as the ultimate fulfilment of the national will by a powerful phalanx of historians, politicians and publicists, has tended to push older forms of identity to the margins reserved for historical failures. The historiographical legitimacy of the settlement of 1871, laid down by Heinrich von Treitschke and his followers, has also glossed over the many things which divided Germans, over and above particular territorial or dynastic loyalties. The misfortunes of the north German Tony Buddenbrook, disastrously married to the Bavarian hop-dealer Permaneder and quite unable to accommodate to the outlandish tongue and customs of the Catholic south, were probably not untypical. Differences in everyday language and religious practices and habits could also frustrate the efforts of those seeking to promote a

13. Schultz Hansen H 1990 Den danske bevægelse i Sønderjylland ca. 1830–1850 *Historie* **18**: 353–95, offers a useful overview of the historiography and debates of recent years on this subject. See also the contribution by A Pontoppidan Thyssen in: Mitchison R 1980 *The roots of nationalism. Studies in Northern Europe*, Edinburgh, pp. 37–45.

14. Rerup 1982, p. 242. Schultz Hansen 1990, p. 384 sees the demand raised in the late 1830s for the use of Danish in judicial and administrative matters as 'simply a necessity if the farmers were to participate in local government'.

popular national unity. The old-fashioned beliefs of the Low German-speaking farmers of the eastern provinces of the Kingdom of Prussia did not accord easily with the rationalism of the established church, any more than did those of the 'strong Jutes' who fought a protracted battle against church and state in Denmark to have their children taught according to their own fundamentalist convictions. Low German, the language of the common people across northern Germany, differed from High German in its syntax and grammar as well as vocabulary. Undoubtedly, the development of communications, the elimination of barriers to trade and commercial activity, the work of political and cultural associations, and the less easily-measured influence of mass-circulation family journals such as *Gartenlaube* fostered a spirit of German identity; but it was the state which gave form and structure to that identity. The German fatherland was defined on the battlefields of Sadowa and Sedan and in the conference chambers of Vienna, Prague and Versailles. It was rather more of a coercive device to ensure the hegemony of the ruling order in Prussia than a glorious culmination of the national ideal.

In the course of the eighteenth century, the notion that national affinity was determined solely by loyalty to a patrimonial ruler had been supplemented, and even replaced, by sentiments of attachment to a country and its people. The gradual emergence of 'the people' from subjugation to the control and jurisdiction of a landowning class and the growing awareness of the need to provide a basic education for their children gave an added dimension to an enlightened patriotism, which endeavoured to foster and promote the well-being of these newly-minted citizens. Typical of this rationalist and utilitarian patriotism is the draft school ordinance prepared by the Danish School Commission in 1799, which declared that the purpose of an education was to make the children of the peasantry into 'good and upright people in accordance with the teachings of the Evangelium and sound reason, imparting unto them such skills and knowledge that they may thereby be able to become happy people and useful citizens in the state'. In addition to religion, reading, writing and arithmetic, pupils in schools with trained teachers should have the opportunity to learn something of the history and geography of the fatherland, natural history and natural sciences. This draft soon ran into opposition from conservatives in the privy council, who insisted that peasants' children should learn only what was needful for their allotted station in life. The final edict of 1814 which established an elementary school system for Denmark, made no mention of sound reason or of happiness, and confined instruction to religion and the three Rs (though reading primers were to give children some idea of the history and geography of their fatherland and knowledge which might be useful in their daily occupation).[15]

During the turmoil of the Napoleonic wars, the importance of education as a means of inculcating patriotic values was taken up by numerous publicists. Laurits Engeltoft's *Tanker om Nationalopdragelsen* (Thoughts on National Education, 1808), which envisaged state-sponsored education, a citizen's catechism, national songs and a patriotic festival at which young people would swear their citizen's oath and be admitted into civic society, echoed the ideas expressed by Fichte, Arndt and Niethammer in Germany, and several of his proposals were in fact taken up. The inculcation of patriotic ideals and values nevertheless lagged a good way behind the teaching of morality, obedience to authority and fear of God. Not until the 1830s did Danish reading primers contain extracts of national history, taken from Ove Malling's textbook (also used in grammar schools) which reinforced the image of the unitary state and its monarchs. The first major historical work to shift the focus from monarchs to the people was C. F. Allen's *Haandbog i Fædrelandets historie* (1840). Allen's book proved more popular than Grundtvig's conservative vision of a partnership of king and people (*Mundsmag af Danmarks Krønike*, 1842) and was an inspiration for other writers producing textbooks for the elementary school pupil.

The reinterpretation of the past in terms of people and fatherland, rather than the deeds of kings, was an important element in the liberals' campaign for a Danish national state. The *Selskabet for Trykkefriheds rette Brug* (The Society for the Proper Use of Press Freedom), founded in 1835, actively encouraged the publication of cheap or subsidised books which could be used in the battle to revive Danishness in northern Slesvig. Far more popular than any of the scholarly historians, as C. F. Allen himself admitted, was the historical novelist B. S. Ingemann, whose works were much in demand at the popular libraries set up in northern Slesvig in the 1840s and 1850s. This 'literary nationalism', as Lorenz Rerup has called it, differed from the patriotism of enlightened reformists in that it clearly set 'the people' at the centre of the stage. The calling of the provincial estates in the 1830s added a political dimension.[16]

15. Feldbæk O (ed.) 1991 *Dansk identitetshistorie*, Copenhagen, vol. 2, pp. 266–8. Significantly, gymnastic and military exercises were added to the curriculum.

16. Feldbæk (ed.) 1991, p. 344. The novels of Ingemann were originally written for adults, as the literary critic Georg Brandes wickedly observed in 1869, but the sound common sense of the nation had allowed them to sink to their natural readership – children aged between ten and twelve.

There was yet another dimension, or more properly, a protective layer: Scandinavism. Literary Scandinavism could trace its roots back to the revival of interest in the ancient Nordic past and folk-poetry of the late eighteenth century, but it began to assume firmer shape in the 1820s, thanks in part to regular steamship crossings between the Swedish mainland and Copenhagen. In a ceremony at the Swedish university of Lund in 1829, the Swedish bishop and bard, Esias Tegnér, crowned with a laurel wreath the leading Danish poet of the day, Adam Oehlenschläger and solemnly proclaimed the age of division to be a thing of the past. The journal *Brage og Idun* (1839–42), although largely a Danish venture, succeeded in attracting attention amongst the educated classes throughout Scandinavia. Scandinavian unity was a popular theme in literature, from H. C. Andersen's '*Vi er et Folk, vi kaldes Skandinaver*' (1839) to the lesser-known C. W. Törnegren's *Öresund* (1837), which had Svea offering the hand of friendship to Dana, a handshake which resounded:

Från Beltens våg till Lapplands fjäll.
Hell Skandinavien, trefaldt hell,
Förenadt, starkt och fritt!

From the Belt's waves to Lapland's fells.
Hail Scandinavia, threefold hail,
United, strong and free![17]

Political Scandinavism drew its early inspiration from Germany. The idea of a customs union for the Nordic lands was enthusiastically endorsed by the young Orla Lehmann in the late 1830s, for example. In an anonymous article published in Germany in 1838, Lehmann also raised the possibility of a new Kalmar Union, with a Norwegian-style constitution and a Swedish monarch, should the male line of the ruling house of Oldenburg die out. Such ideas were for the time being little more than straws in the wind, though Christian VIII's rejection of demands for a constitution modelled on that of Norway gave an added edge to liberalism in Denmark, particularly in student circles.

Student Scandinavism in the early 1840s was very much a Danish-Swedish affair. It found little resonance in Norway or Finland, nor did it have many adherents outside the universities and intellectual circles. Although anti-Russian sentiments publicly voiced by Danish Scandinavists such as Frederik Barfod and Carl Ploug were welcomed

17. Cited in Johansson 1930, pp. 230–1.

by Swedish liberals, there was no concrete political issue to serve as a stimulant for political Scandinavism in Sweden, as there was in Denmark. Danish liberals looked to a Scandinavian alliance and possible union for security and support against an increasingly aggressive German nationalism. On the whole, they did not pursue economic union. Viggo Rothe, secretary of the Danish Federation of Industry, advocated in 1843 a free trade zone, on the grounds that the Danish corn export boom was reaching its limits, and Danish industry would have to take up the strain in the near future; but his book was poorly received. Swedes were worried about Danish dominance of a possible customs union; the countries were rivals in the British market; and Norwegian interests were also markedly different from those of their partner in the Union, Sweden.

Towards the end of the decade, however, the fortunes of Scandinavism seemed to be improving. Oscar I appeared to be sympathetic, and after the visit of the Danish crown prince, Frederik, to Stockholm in 1847, there was talk of verbal assurances of Swedish assistance in the event of war over the duchies. A section of the liberals in Denmark and Sweden was prepared to temporise over reform. It was not liberty, but nationality, which was now relevant, argued C. F. Allen; let us fight the Prussians first, then deal with 'our own Prussians at home', as the Swedish Scandinavist O. P. Sturzen-Becker wrote to his friend Carl Ploug.[18] But there was also a party which thought like the leader of *Bondevenner*, Rasmus Sørensen, that 'liberty was the main thing', or were critical of *Fædrelandet* for 'damaging the cause of nationality by pushing liberty into the background'.[19] Swedish liberal adherents of Scandinavism were attracted more by its cultural and fraternal appeal and its anti-Russian edge. They did not relish conflict with Germany, an important market for Sweden and in 1848 the great hope of European liberalism, particularly as they suspected the designs of Russia and Oscar I's own ambitions. The seeming alignment of the royal family with liberal Scandinavism could not mask the fundamental differences between the two. Liberals continued to associate the question of internal and

18. Allen to Laurids Skau, 6 March 1848, in *Danske politiske brev*, vol. 4, p. 121. Sturzen-Becker to Ploug, undated, 1848, cited in Holmberg 1946, p. 167.

19. According to one who was present at the first Casino meeting in 1848, Sørensen 'spoke a little against the cause in that he thought liberty was the main thing'. *Danske politiske brev*, vol. 4, p. 127, and pp. 128–30 for Lehmann's account of the meetings at the Casino and the Hippodrome, where 'the opponents' demanded universal suffrage. The criticism of *Fædrelandet* was expressed by a Jutland radical, Bernhard Rée. *Ibid.*, pp. 125–6.

constitutional reform with the idea of union, which they preferred to see as a coming together of peoples with a common heritage, rather than a mere dynastic arrangement. As the editor of *Aftonbladet* put it in June 1858: 'We are firm opponents of a dynastic connection pure and simple, whose beneficiary, by not making concessions to popular liberty in Sweden, has given no guarantee that he will preserve the liberty which prevails in the other two states.'[20] The great reshaping of Europe widely anticipated in the early 1860s, and the example of Italian unification, caused a revival of hopes of a Scandinavian union: but it was Bismarck, not Napoleon, who redrew the map. Instead of soldiers, Sweden sent woollen stockings to Denmark in 1864; and instead of cutting a figure on the European stage, Carl XV Johan had to bow before his prime minister's ultimatum in 1860 and consent to parliamentary reform, enacted five years later.[21]

It was Finland, rather than Slesvig, which occupied the minds of Swedish liberal Scandinavists, and when the long-awaited war between the western powers and Russia broke out in 1854, it seemed as if the moment for the reconquest of Finland had dawned. With the exception of certain conservatives in military circles, who were rather more aware of the difficulties, and in spite of differences over whether or not Finland should be part of a Nordic federation or simply reincorporated into Sweden, it was widely assumed in 1854 that it was only a matter of time before Sweden (and Denmark) joined the allies. This did not happen, and it also became obvious that neither the Norwegians or Danes, nor even the Finns, were very keen on the idea. The destruction wrought by Admiral Plumridge's ships on the coast of Ostrobothnia and the seizure by the British of almost half of the sizeable Finnish merchant fleet was a sharp reminder to the Finnish people of the cost of war, and this episode if anything strengthened feelings of loyalty towards the tsar-grand duke. Leading figures such as the journalist and poet Zachris Topelius publicly proclaimed this loyalty and privately supported preservation of the status quo as the least evil.

The debate on Finland gave a sharper political profile to what might best be termed cultural fennophilia (or in contemporary

20. Holmberg 1946, p. 324, and p. 273 for similar comments from the tireless Scandinavist O. P. Sturzen-Becker in 1856. Oscar had been suspected in liberal circles of planning to use the prospect of war and lavish allied subsidies to buy off the press and muzzle the opposition during the early weeks of 1856: see Lidman T 1979 *Adlig partipolitik vid 1800-talets mitt*, Stockholm.

21. The comment on woollen stockings was made by Dardel in January 1864: Dardel 1912, vol. 2, p. 73.

parlance, *fennomani*). In his pamphlet, *Fennomani och Skandinavism* (1855), the émigré poet Emil von Qvanten advocated the liberation of Finland, but acknowledged that his compatriots had grown accustomed during the years of separation from Sweden 'to the shadow, if not of freedom, then of a kind of independence and unity' which would make reunion as a mere province impossible.[22] Allusions to a Finnish national consciousness struck a sour note in liberal as well as conservative Swedish circles. An anonymous reviewer of von Qvanten's pamphlet in the conservative *Svenska Tidningen* held that fennophilia was anti-Swedish, whilst the liberal August Sohlman declared that:

> To seek to build hopes of a genuine Finnish culture on the basis of the *Kalevala* and the other Finnish folksongs . . . is a poetical heresy . . . the Finns, in a transport of delight over this attention and fame have completely overstated the real importance of this cycle of poems by seeking to read into them evidence of an ancient high degree of culture amongst the Finns as well as a definite basis for the development of their own Finnish nationality.[23]

The belief that the Finnish race lacked an inner life-force or conspicuous urge towards civilisation, and that only the Swedish cultural inheritance could sustain Finland against Russian pressure was a reflection of a general attitude amongst liberal-minded western Europeans towards the so-called 'historyless peoples'. We find the German traveller J. G. Kohl voicing similar views about the Latvians' and Estonians' lack of energy needful for a true national consciousness in 1841, for example.[24] Baltic Germans and Swedish-speaking opponents of political *fennomani* were also fond of referring to their civilising mission and the superiority of their cultural inheritance. The sense of inferiority thereby created was not the least of the problems which faced those who sought to raise awareness of a separate and distinct national identity amongst the Finnish-speakers, Estonians and Latvians.

The foundations of a language-based identity were carefully laid down by philologists who studied the origins and development of language; morphologists and lexicographers who refined and

22. Cited in Kirby D (ed.) 1975 *Finland and Russia 1808–1920. From autonomy to independence*, London, p. 44.

23. Kirby D (ed.) 1975, pp. 45–6, citing Sohlman's reply to von Qvanten.

24. Kohl J 1841 *Die deutsch-russischen Ostseeprovinzen*, Dresden/Leipzig, vol. 2, pp. 35, 190.

standardised it; and learned societies which sponsored scientific investigation and research, and published the findings. The folk poems collected by Elias Lönnrot on his five great expeditions through Karelia formed the basis of the *Kalevala*, the first edition of which was published by the Finnish Literature Society in 1835. Four years later, a lecture given to the Estonian Learned Society in Dorpat by Friedrich Robert Faehlmann (like Lönnrot, a man of humble origins and a doctor) raised the possibility of creating a similar poetic epic around the legendary figure of *Kalevipoeg*. The task was taken over and completed by yet another physician, Friedrich Reinhold Kreutzwald, the author of numerous stories and articles for an Estonian readership. Kreutzwald presented his first draft version of *Kalevipoeg* to the Estonian Learned Society in 1854, and it was published in a German and Estonian version between 1857 and 1861. It proved more difficult to compile a similar epic from existing folk poetry of the Latvian and Lithuanian peoples. Józef Kraszewski's Romantic verse epic *Anafielas* (1840–45), although written in Polish, drew upon Lithuanian folk poetry and mythology; the first part, *Witolorauda* (Witold's lament), was translated into Lithuanian in 1881. The need for a work which would glorify a mythical national past and elevate the oppressed Latvian people to a position of moral superiority over their German oppressors was met by the autodidact and poet Andrejs Pumpurs, whose *Lāčplēsis* (The Bear-slayer) appeared in 1888.

Those who strove to realise these epic works were acutely conscious of their role as 'national awakeners'. Elias Lönnrot did not hesitate to claim for example that posterity would value the results of their labours as highly as the Gothic peoples cherished their Edda, or the Greeks and Romans their Homer and Hesiod.[25] It is, however, a moot point whether their works had any immediate impact upon the deep ranks of the people, however much they have subsequently influenced the cultural and intellectual life of the peoples of the eastern Baltic. It was in fact to an educated public that these epics were primarily addressed. The initial 'national awakening' was essentially a debate conducted in learned societies, journals, newspapers and in middle-class drawing rooms, usually in Swedish or German. The Finnish Literature Society in Viborg, founded in 1845 was unusual in

25. A comparison made by Elias Lönnrot, the compiler of the *Kalevala*, in a letter to Professor Linsén in 1834. Lönnrot E 1980 *Matkat 1828–1844*, Espoo, p. 168. For details of folk poetry epics in the Baltic region, see Scholtz F 1990 *Die Literaturen des Baltikums. Ihre Entstehung und Entwicklung*, Opladen, pp. 264–88.

conducting its proceedings in Finnish and in striving to defend the interests of the common people: the Finnish Literature Society in Helsingfors, the Estonian Learned Society in Dorpat and the Latvian Literary Society in Riga were exclusive clubs for the *literati*, however worthy their aims.

From the middle of the century, however, there was a greater commitment to the active use of the native languages, especially amongst students. In Finland, summer vacations in Finnish-speaking peasant households were a popular way for young men from Swedish-speaking homes to learn the language. From the late 1840s, groups of students solemnly committed themselves to speaking and promoting Finnish. A decade or so later, small groups of young men of peasant origin studying at the universities in Dorpat and St Petersburg began to refer to themselves as 'Latvians', and set about reinterpreting their past. The Germans were portrayed not as masters, but as usurpers in a land historically belonging to the Latvians. The peasantry were to be persuaded to abandon their traditional acceptance of subordination, and to be weaned away from the notion that Latvian literature was and should be confined to devotional works.

Criticism of the Baltic Germans was expressed in the columns of the short-lived *Pēterburgas avīzes* (1862–65), and links were established with the Slavophiles by one of the newspaper's founders, Krišjānis Valdemārs. Already under fire from the Slavophiles and stung by the critical review of agarian conditions in Kurland published in 1860 by Andrejs Spāģis, a Latvian studying in Germany, the Baltic Germans muttered darkly about 'fanatical nationalists' in St Petersburg and elsewhere consorting with dangerous revolutionaries. In fact, as Juris Alunāns admitted in 1861, the Latvians found the ideas of their Polish and Russian fellow-students in St Petersburg too advanced. The first generation of activists stood between two worlds, their ideas a mixture of old-fashioned peasant values adapted to new horizons. Valdemārs, for example, saw economic progress as the means of advancement for the Latvian people, and was actively involved in promoting sea-trading ventures. Atis Kronvalds was more aware of the dangers of a loss or dilution of the language and culture if increased social mobility was not accompanied by an effective elementary education in Latvian. He urged the Baltic Germans to recognise that they had common interests with the Latvians, and the general thrust of his work, *Nationale Bestrebungen* (1872) was towards a strengthening of the autonomous character of the Baltic provinces. Valdemārs, on the other hand, saw the future interests of the Latvian people lying with the empire at large, and could see only benefits from learning Russian and supporting the efforts of the imperial government to supplant Baltic German institutions in the provinces.[26]

Amongst the Estonians, a similar division of opinion occurred. The moderates laid more stress on cultural activities, and looked to collaborate with the Baltic Germans. The radicals wished to weaken the influence of the ruling elite, and to this end were prepared to welcome measures designed to strengthen imperial Russian authority at the expense of the Baltic Germans. Relations between the two wings became increasingly strained, with fateful consequences. During the 1860s, the moderates held centre stage. An elementary schoolteacher, Johann Voldemar Jannsen, had founded an Estonian-language newspaper (*Perno Postimees*) in 1857, and had used its columns to foster a spirit of self-awareness amongst the Estonians. In 1864, he moved to Dorpat, a centre of Estonian intellectual life, and edited the newspaper *Eesti Postimees*, with the assistance of his daughter, the poet Lydia Koidula. Jannsen also worked closely with Jakob Hurt, a graduate in theology from the university in Dorpat, and both clashed with the anti-clerical radical, Carl Robert Jakobson, and his ally in St Petersburg, Johann Köler, a professor at the Academy of Fine Arts. Neither Jakobson nor Köler felt there was any reason to stage a song festival in 1869 to commemorate the emancipation of the peasantry; they objected in particular to the involvement of Baltic German pastors in the planning of the festival, which drew its inspiration from similar gatherings of choirs in northern Germany. Bitter infighting eventually led to the closure of the Society of Estonian Literati in 1893, and undermined the attempt to found a secondary Estonian-language school.[27]

For many Estonians, Finland offered inspiration and example. Visiting Finland in 1871, Jacobson was greatly impressed by the 'truly patriotic spirit' he found there, and saddened by the enormous difference between the status of the free Finnish peasantry and that of

26. Plakans A 1974 Peasants, intellectuals and nationalism in the Russian Baltic provinces 1820–1890 *Journal of Modern History* **46**: 445–75, and the same author's chapter in Thaden E (ed.) 1981 *Russification in the Baltic provinces and Finland 1855–1914*, Bloomington, Ill., pp. 207–26. Walters M 1923 *Lettland. Seine Entwicklung zu Staat und die baltischen Fragen*, Rome, pp. 279–80, 305–10.

27. Raun T 1987 *Estonia and the Estonians*, Stanford, pp. 62–5, 74–5, and the same author's contribution to Thaden E (ed.) 1981, pp. 292–305. The bitterness and animosity which moved Jacobson can be gleaned from his correspondence with Lydia Koidula, Johann Köler and J Adamson, published in *Eesti Kirjandus* between 1911 and 1914: the Baltic Germans are 'blood-enemies', whose rear ends are slavishly attended to by Jannsen (letter to Adamson, 23 October 1871, *Eesti Kirjandus* **8** (1913): pp. 313–14.). See also Laaman 1964 *Eesti iseseisvuse sünd*, Stockholm, pp. 13–20.

the Estonians, still under the German yoke.[28] Finns were less encouraged by what they found on the other side of the Gulf. Paying a short visit to Reval in 1864, a leading Finnish nationalist found nothing but indifference and neglect of Estonian in the town, though he noted things were better in Dorpat, where Jannsen was claiming 2,000 subscribers for his newly-started *Eesti Postimees*. Comparing the Finnish and Estonian national movements at the very end of Alexander II's reign, Axel August Granfelt felt that, although less had been achieved in Estonia, the people were more supportive of the movement than was the case in Finland. He also pointed out that whereas a significant section of the educated class in Finland had championed the cause of the people and identified themselves with the Finnish national movement, the educated class in the Baltic provinces regarded itself as German and separate from the mass of the people.[29] A discussion between a Finnish tourist and a Baltic German student on board a steamer in the autumn of 1885 also indicates something of this crucial difference. Reluctant to accept that serfdom had not existed in Finland and surprised to learn of the Grand Duchy's privileged autonomy, the student went on to claim 'that "we too have privileges", which Peter the Great, etc., etc., to which I pointed out that in Finland, the entire "*Volk*" support "their privileges", "all have an interest in them", but not in Estonia, where they are therefore lacking any foundation and for that reason "undermined". This explanation, as well as my saying that the nobility in Estonia had oppressed the people, seemingly struck this toffee-nosed student as a bit odd, for soon afterwards, he toddled off . . .'[30]

The first decade of Alexander II's reign was crucial for Russia's western borderlands; the first real test of the ability of the empire and its constituent parts to face up to the problems of dealing with the modern world of improved communications, social mobility and

28. C Jacobson to J Adamson, 19 May 1871, in *Eesti Kirjandus* **8** (1913), pp. 309–10. Kruus H 1939 C R Jacobson ja Suomi *Jäämereltä Emäjoen rannoille*, Helsinki, pp. 183–92. Kruus argues that this visit made Jacobson even more hostile towards the Germans and moderates such as Jannsen, who could find nothing better to say of Finland than 'peace, peace!' 'We all want peace, but a peace as between equals and not as between the butcher and the bull', as Jacobson wrote to Adamson in August 1871 (*Eesti Kirjandus* **8** (1913): p. 312).

29. Koskinen Y 1904–6 *Kansallisia ja yhteiskunnallisia kirjoituksia* Suomalaisen Kirjallisuuden Seuran toimituksia **108**, Helsinki, vol. 2, pp. 219–20. Granfelt A 1881 Kansallisesta liikkeestä Virossa *Valvoja* **1**: 393. Granfelt was a leading figure of the later Finnish national movement, and was one of the initiators of a meeting in March 1881 to promote closer contacts with the Estonians.

30. A Heikel to J Hurt, 17/29 September 1885, Suomalaisen Kirjallisuuden Seuran Kirjekokoelma 385 (archives of the Finnish Literature Society).

public opinion. What happened, or even what was said in one part of the tsar-autocrat's vast domains could have repercussions elsewhere. Thus, when the rector of Helsingfors university publicly expressed the hope in September 1856 that the Finnish people would in future have more dealings with their ruler via the estates (i.e. a veiled call for the estates to be convened), he angered Scandinavists in Sweden who felt that he was trying to reinforce the bonds of loyalty between Finns and the emperor, but he also alarmed officialdom. Both governor-general Berg and minister state-secretary Alexander Armfelt feared that such demands would spread to Poland; Alexander II, although prepared to relax controls in Poland, had pointedly warned the Poles not to entertain daydreams when he visited Warsaw in May 1856.

Within three years, a greater degree of public discussion of reform was being allowed and even encouraged, and the empire entered the 1860s in a general spirit of optimism. The restoration of some of the autonomous status of the pre-1831 Kingdom of Poland in March 1861 was interpreted in Finland as a sign of hope that the estates there would soon be convened. Foreign ambassadors in St Petersburg, however, noted the rising tide of Panslavism. Count Wedel Jarlsberg reported to the Swedish foreign minister in August 1860 that although the emperor valued highly the loyalty of the Finns, their constitutional privileges and rights were a thorn in the flesh of the Russian nationalists. The emperor himself told a Finnish senator that in view of the unrest over peasant emancipation in Russia and the tense situation in Poland, he could not give the order to convene the Finnish estates, though in April 1861 he did order the selection of a committee of 48 members, 12 from each estate, to discuss financial reforms and prepare recommendations for the emperor. This was seen in liberal circles as a means of circumventing the convening of the estates, and attempts, including the first sizeable political demonstration in the Grand Duchy's history, were made to commit the emperor to call a *Lantdag* in the near future. At the end of the year, Alexander let it be known that the *Lantdag* would be summoned as soon as the committee had finished its work.

The committee met in January 1862, and made several recommendations and requests, including the more general use of Finnish in the courts and in the administration, the introduction of a Finnish currency, and the abolition of the censorship. Its proposals were favourably received by the emperor and liberal opinion in Russia, though the nationalists grouped around the Slavophile newspaper *Moskovskie Vedomosti* were less impressed. At the same time, moves were afoot to institute reforms in the Baltic provinces. The four-point plan laid before the Livonian *Landtag* in 1862 by Woldemar von Bock called for a supreme court for the provinces, recognition of the right of all burghers in Livland to own noble estates, the restoration of the right of representation at the *Landtag* for the smaller towns, and for a united *Landtag* of the three provinces. The meeting was attended by delegates from Estland and Kurland, and in his opening speech, the *Landmarschall* stressed the necessity of meeting change by consolidation; but the only concession the Livonian nobility was prepared to make was to relinquish its exclusive right to own manorial land. A further fourteen reform proposals were rejected by the *Landtag* between 1864 and 1880.

Under criticism from outside and within for failing to resolve the question of peasant emancipation, alarmed by the violence of the peasant uprisings in northern Livland in 1858, and worried about the plans of centralisers in St Petersburg, the Baltic Germans tended to draw their cloak more tightly about them. They complained that the Russian nationalists were less hostile towards the revolutionary pretensions of the Poles than they were towards the loyal designs of Baltic particularism; they were irritated that the Estonians and Latvians persisted in heeding the 'siren song of an independent cultural existence' when common interests and the gradual abolition of restrictions on property-owning, etc. ought surely to bring them closer to their fellow-compatriots; and they were saddened to discover that whilst the 'sea-girt lands' of Slesvig-Holstein had become a sacred cause in Germany, the inhabitants of the lands betwixt the Narowa and Niemen were virtually ignored, or treated as whipping-boys, by German liberals.[31] The petition submitted to the 1864 Livonian *Landtag* by the town of Wenden, asking for representation for the towns and the *literati*, is typical of the narrow, corporate mentality in the provinces: burghers and nobles united would hold high the banner of the *Landesverfassung* and this coming together of 'all vital elements' would not only enrich German cultural life and strengthen the constitutional position of the Baltic provinces, but provide 'the only effective protective force' against the intrusions of an alien nationality

31. On plans for reform, see Stäel von Holstein R 1906 Livländische Erinnerungen aus den Jahre 1855–1862 *Baltische Monatsschrift* **62**: 1–24, 65–91, and his 1907 article series, Reformbewegungen in der 60er Jahren des vorigen Jahrhunderts *Baltische Monatsschrift* **63**: 66–76, 111–30. *Baltische Monatsschrift* is the best mirror of Baltic German attitudes in the 1860s. See: Wir und die Anderen (**7** (1863): 457–65): Zur Nationalitätenfrage (**9** (1864): 568–75). On German neglect of the Baltic provinces, see Eckhardt J 1869 *Die baltischen Provinzen Russlands*, Leipzig, pp. 2–3.

and foreign ways.[32] Liberals might inveigh against the antiquated, feudal institutions of the provinces as the main obstacle to reform and progress; but faced with the attacks of Russian nationalism, they too tended to rally to the outmoded but identifiable institutions of Baltic Germanness.

There was in the end too little common ground upon which Germans and the 'nationals' could meet, in spite of tendencies on both sides which did lead to a degree of collaboration. Although willing to work with benevolent pastors in staging song festivals, it was unlikely that Estonians or Latvians would stand fast in defence of the *Landeskirche* which was so intimately associated with the Baltic Germans, for example. They might still kiss the cuffs of the clergyman in greeting and address him as '*gnädige Kirchenherr*', but they regarded him as one of the German masters.

The Catholic church provided an effective rallying-point for the Lithuanian peasantry, as a symbol of resistance to outside oppression. Inspired by the enlightened intellectual atmosphere of the university of Vilna, the clergy and nobility of Samogitia had been in the forefront of the 'Lithuanian movement' during the 1820s. Prince Józef Giedroyć, bishop of Samogitia, had the New Testament translated into the Samogitian dialect of Lithuanian, founded schools and encouraged the development of the written language and vernacular. The uprising of 1830–31 brought these promising developments to an abrupt end. The university was closed, the seminary for priests transferred to St Petersburg, and Giedoryć was placed under surveillance. The work of developing peasant education was carried on by his successor, Motiejus Valančius, who also ran a highly successful temperance movement in the late 1850s. Valančius disapproved of peasant involvement in the uprising of 1863–64, and was prepared to cooperate with a policy of teaching Russian alongside Lithuanian in Catholic schools. However, closure of church schools and the ban on the publication of Lithuanian books in the Latin alphabet turned him into a fierce opponent of russification. He called upon Lithuanians to boycott Russian schools, to teach their children from old books printed in the Latin alphabet and to respond in Lithuanian to questions asked in Russian. Large quantities of books printed in the East Prussian towns of Tilsit, Ragnit and Memel were smuggled over the frontier. Measures taken by officialdom against the Catholic church provoked a fierce response

32. Cited in Wittram R 1954 *Das Nationale als europäisches Problem*, Göttingen, p. 155. A somewhat more critical approach to the presumptions and pretensions of the Baltic Germans is to be found in: Pistohlkors G von 1978 *Ritterschaftliche Reformpolitik zwischen Russifizierung und Revolution* Göttinger Bausteine zur Geschichtswissenschaft **48**, Göttingen, pp. 19ff.

amongst the people. Crowds tried to prevent the closure of church buildings, and blood was shed at Kražiai in 1893, when the troops opened fire on protesters.[33]

Catholicism could not in the long run, however, serve as a source of support and inspiration for a secular nationalism. Its hierarchy was too closely wedded to the Polish vision, and too conservative in its social and political views: as in Ireland, the generation of nationalists at the turn of the century found themselves increasingly at odds with the church. That this should matter is in itself an indication of the importance of Catholicism in Lithuanian and Irish life. The Lutheran church in Finland and the Baltic provinces was conspicuous more for its subservience to higher secular authority and its singular inability to provide moral leadership or spiritual solace. Those who sought comfort in the dark night of the soul had to look elsewhere to find it, to the 'awakening' movements on the margins of the official church.

Although language and ethnicity were beginning by the 1860s to assume greater importance with the spread of education, and the creation of a fully functional cultural basis (newspapers, theatres, popular and 'highbrow' literature, clubs, etc.), it had also proved possible in Finland (and to a degree, in the Lithuanian lands) to foster a patriotism which was not predicated solely upon monolinguistic pretensions. A Frenchman neatly brought together the two most famous examples when he compared Adam Mickiewicz to Johan Ludvig Runeberg; both sang the praises of their fatherland, albeit in their own language. There were clear differences, of course; the patriotism of Mickiewicz or the historian Joachim Lelewel was inspired by commitment to the cause of Poland's past greatness, whereas the poet Runeberg or the more openly fennophile Zachris Topelius were seeking to blend deep love of the fatherland and its people with loyalty towards the ruler and obedience to God. In this regard, Finnish patriotism was a good deal less dangerous in Russian eyes, as the pointedly favourable treatment bestowed upon the Grand Duchy by the Emperor Alexander II in 1863 was doubtless meant to demonstrate.[34]

33. On the attitude of Estonians and Latvians towards the church, see Philipp G 1974 *Die Wirksamkeit der Herrnhuter Brüdergemeinde unter den Esten und Letten zur Zeit der Bauernbefreiung*, Cologne, pp. 174, 182–3. On the Catholic church in Lithuania, Čeginskas K 1958/9 Die Russifizierung und ihre Folge in Litauen *Commentationes Baltica* **6/7**: 30–48.

34. The different strands of thinking in pre-1863 Lithuania are drawn out by Alesandravičius E 1992 Political goals of Lithuanians 1863–1918 *Journal of Baltic Studies* **23**: 227–31. See also Davies N 1981 *God's playground. A history of Poland*, Oxford, vol. 2, pp. 366–8, and Thaden E 1984 *Russia's western borderlands, 1710–1870*, Princeton, NJ, pp. 231–42.

The Swedish-speaking intelligentsia in Finland sought to discover the Finnish people and to make them worthy of nationhood. In this – and in the willingness of many of them consciously to set aside their 'Swedish' for a 'Finnish' cultural milieu – they differed from well-meaning Baltic German pastors such as Otto Masing or Karl Watson, and from the tenacious defenders of the Catholic faith in Samogitia. As early as 1860 Axel Freudenthal, an early proponent of Finnish-Swedishness, commented upon the 'quite exceptional phenomenon' of a nationality fighting against itself, and warned Swedish speakers in Finland against committing 'national suicide' through their eager advocacy of the cause of Finnishness.[35] The convening of the estates in 1863 ushered in an era of major reform which considerably strengthened the institutional autonomy of the Grand Duchy and enhanced the national self-confidence of its inhabitants. The anguish caused during the struggle over the language question in the 1870s and 1880s was to some extent eased by the economic growth of these years and the concomitant creation of new jobs and professions. There was still a considerable imbalance between Swedish and Finnish in a number of crucial areas, such as secondary education, though the gap was rapidly closing by the end of the century. Politically as well as economically, Finland lagged some way behind the Scandinavian countries. Ideologically, Finnish nationalists such as Yrjö Koskinen sought to distance the country from its Swedish past. But in all essentials (with the possible exception of the Karelian isthmus, under Russian rule since 1721 and closely linked to the economy of the Russian metropolis), Finland remained much closer to the Scandinavian than to the Slavic-Russian world.

The flutterings of Scandinavism during the crisis of 1863, the emergence of a 'Swedish' party in the 1860s and the somewhat optimistic constitutional demands of the liberal *Helsingfors Dagblad* raised the spectre of Finnish 'separatism' in certain circles in St Petersburg; but it was for the Baltic Germans and the contumacious Poles that the Russian nationalists reserved most of their ire.[36] The revival of the national Diet provided the Finnish people as a whole, in spite of the antiquated system of representation, with a forum for debate. The peasantry of the Baltic provinces, unable to voice their

35. Kirby (ed.) 1975, pp. 46–7.

36. Kirby (ed.) 1975, pp. 50–1, 54–5, for the programme of *Helsingfors Dagblad* and the reaction of Governor-General Rokassovsky to 'separatist' proposals. See also Krusius-Ahrenberg L 1954 "Dagbladsseparatismen" år 1863 och den begynnande panslavismen *Skrifter utgivna av Svenska Litteratursällskapet i Finland* **346**: 170–214.

demands in any national forum, their fate left to the Baltic German masters to decide in their exclusive *Landtage*, resorted to petitioning the tsar as they had done in the 1840s and were to do again in 1881.[37]

It is perhaps as well to remember that the land question was and remained a major issue in Russia's western borderlands (although it assumed different dimensions north and south of the Gulf of Finland). The inability of the state to alleviate the problems of land hunger and lack of employment opportunities (which were, if anything, made to seem more acute by the jerky and uneven progress of industrialisation, and which were highlighted by a press willing to take up such issues and present them to a growing readership) had a powerful effect on the course of nationalist politics. The nationalist movements of the western borderlands could not afford to neglect the land question, since the 'people' to whom they appealed were part of the rural economy. The complexities of this question, and the growing gap between farmers and the landless, meant, however, that remedies or solutions which would or could satisfy all the 'people' were unlikely to be propounded by those who were perhaps more concerned with general principles than specific issues. The nationalist awakening in the sixties and seventies broadened out into organisational activity in the Baltic provinces and Finland. The recruitment of members into clubs and associations thus created an interaction between the ideals of the national awakening and the specific interests of those recruited, and this in turn influenced the political direction of the movement, even leading to splits and divisions. This was more apparent in the case of Finland, where it was possible to engage in party politics within a quasi-parliamentary framework, than it was in the Baltic provinces, where the autochthonous national movements had no such opportunities; but even here, mass involvement produced factions, political infighting and struggles for power.

It is difficult to arrive at firm conclusions as to who or what constituted the nationalist movement, and this is true as much for Finland, with its wealth of statistical material, as it is for the territories from which the very name of Lithuania was expunged after 1863, for the spread of associations or the growth of a national-minded press tells us in the end little about mental attitudes or perceptions of

37. Kruus H 1934 *Eesti rahvusliku ärkamise algupäevilt. Palevkirjade-aktsioonid 1860-ndail aastail*, Tartu, pp. 3ff. maintains that this was a renewal of the 'foreign policy orientation' of the peasantry. Brutus L and Loone L 1958 *Põhisjooni majandusliku mõtte ajaloost Eestis XIX sajandil*, Tallinn, pp. 147ff. argues that it was not simply confined to the tenant-farmers, as Kruus suggested, but involved all the peasantry, and the petitions contained much more clearly articulated ideas than hitherto.

identity.[38] Social status, economic hardship (or well-being), religious affiliation, even where and how an individual lived, all played a part in shaping responses to outside influences.[39] We know, for example, that rural adherents of nationalist organisations tended to come from the more prosperous farming class. Poor farmers and the landless labourers were less evident in such movements, partly because they simply could neither afford the time nor the money to be able to participate in the manner deemed suitable: but one ought not to rule out the possibility that there were substantial numbers who were as keen to sing patriotic songs as their neighbour, but were effectively prevented from joining the choir or glee club for want of a decent suit of clothes or even a pair of shoes.

The relationship between religious revivalist movements and the national awakening is by no means easily defined. Involvement in revivalism frequently brought the laity into conflict with established authority – the state as well as the local parson – and it also forged new links between classes and across the sexual divide. This may have helped prepare the ground for later nationalist movements, as some historians have claimed; but others have pointed to conflicts over education and questions of morality between secular nationalists and revivalists, and have stressed the function of nationalist associations in leading people from a fundamentally religious to a secular world view.[40] The search for the kingdom of God and the quest for modernity and national unity, in the end, lead down very different roads; and if the latter endeavour was fast gaining ground in a more evidently materialistic world, the former still directed the spiritual, moral and intellectual life of the people as they entered the last three decades of the nineteenth century.

38. Some of this statistical evidence is presented in Hroch M 1984 *Social preconditions of national revival in Europe*, Cambridge. See also Liikanen I 1988 'Light to our people'. Educational organisation and the mobilisation of fennomania in the 1870s *Scandinavian Journal of History* **13**: 421–38.

39. Memoirs and reminiscences can often throw a great deal of light on how attitudes were shaped. A good example is the memoirs of Martna M 1914 *Külast. Mäletused ja tähelepanekud Eesti külaelu arenemisest pärast 60-id aastaid*, Tallinn. There is also an interesting, if uneven, series of edited recollections of veterans of the Finnish labour movement, published since the 1960s. Since such evidence cannot be quantified, and may be seen as overly subjective and partial, it is usually ignored by historians who are of a precisely scientific persuasion.

40. Granfelt A 1881, p. 393. Numminen J 1961 *Suomen nuorisoliikkeen historia I Vuodet 1881–1905*, Helsinki, pp. 55–6 argues that revivalism 'without a doubt' cleared the path for the national movement in Southern Ostrobothnia. There is a thoughtful discussion of the relationship of revivalism and the national awakening in Finland by Markku Heikkilä and Juha Seppo in Alapuro R et al 1987 *Kansa liikkeessä*, pp. 70–85.

CHAPTER FIVE

Society in an Era of Change

LANDSCAPES

From J. L. Runeberg's Bonden Paavo on the cold, inhospitable heathlands of Saarijärvi to Theodor Storm's Deichgraf Hauke Haien on the Frisian marshlands of the North Sea, the man with his simple tools and his own strength, rooting up stumps and boulders, digging ditches or building embankments, is a familiar figure in nineteenth-century northern European literature. Relentless population pressure pushed the margins of cultivation into the wilderness. Primeval boglands, moors, heaths and woods disappeared under the axe, the mattock and the flames; their water-logged soils were drained, their boulders wrenched out one by one and piled high in the small fields so painfully created. In the province of East Prussia, roughly one-third of the total land area in 1802 was cultivated, and another third was waste land. Sixty years later, half of the land was under cultivation, whilst the moors and marshes had been reduced to a mere thirteen per cent. Within fifty years of the foundation of the Danish Heath Society (*Hedesselskabet*) in 1866, the amount of heathland in Jutland had been reduced by half, and 4,000 square kilometres of new farming land had been acquired. The members of the society may have been inspired ideologically by the exhortations of its founding spirit, Enrico Dalgas, to regain what had been lost by Denmark to Prussia by making inroads into the heathlands, but it was the coming of the railways which made such ventures profitable.

In the well-established areas of arable cultivation, enclosures helped break up the traditional village structures as farmhouses were built in proximity to the fields. The fields themselves were marked off, and the land marled, manured, ditched and drained. New and more efficient Scottish ploughs bit deeper into the soil, clod-crushers and iron-toothed harrows broke up the earth into a finer tilth, seed-drills sowed the seed more efficiently than broadcasting by hand, and the corn harvest (now producing yields far in excess of the meagre achievements of the sixteenth and seventeenth centuries) was processed by steam-powered threshing machines. Prices of factory-produced machinery began to fall as output increased; and the increase in real income enjoyed by successful farmers in the middle decades of the century made ploughs, seed-drills and threshing machines cheaper still. Success transformed farming from a traditional way of life into a business; and the repercussions were immense.

By no means all who farmed the land prospered, however. Many, if not most, of those who broke new ground on the margins of cultivation did so out of dire necessity; the tumbledown shacks clustered on the fringes of heathland or the forest, with their pitiful inhabitants eking out a miserable existence, were a common sight, from the sandy moraines of Prussia and Pomerania right up into Lapland. Within a single parish could be found prosperous farmers practising the latest methods and a growing number of impoverished smallholders scratching a living from the land as their ancestors had done, supplementing their income in whatever way they could. The extensive surveys conducted in Prussia during the 1840s clearly revealed what modern research has tended to confirm, that the worst instances of rural poverty tended to be found in remote, isolated areas bereft of work opportunities. The poorest people in the Memel district were those living furthest away from the town, which not only provided work for the nearby cottars and labourers, but also manure for their plots of land. In the forested regions of Prussian Lithuania, those living near the woods and rivers could always find work as foresters or on the log-floats; but those who had little possibility of such extra earnings, living on a small and inadequate patch of land carved out of the village meadows or pastureland during the enclosures, lived with their families in 'the direst need'.[1]

1. Langerke A von 1849 *Die ländliche Arbeiterfrage*, Berlin, p. 77. This book was based on reports to a questionnaire sent out by the Royal Rural Economy Collegium to 168 districts of Prussia, and offers a wealth of detail on wages, working conditions – as well as an insight into the mentality of the would-be reformers. On the connection of work opportunities (or the lack of them) and poverty, see: Söderberg J 1982 Causes of poverty in Sweden in the nineteenth century *Journal of European Economic History* **11**: 369–402, and O. Löfgren's study of the rural proletariat in a southern Swedish parish in: Åkerman S et al. (eds) 1978 *Chance and change. Social and economic studies in historical demography in the Baltic area*, Odense, pp. 95–106.

Peasant farmers were generally criticised for a deep-rooted conservatism and resistance to change: but lack of capital or of easy access to credit, insecurity of tenure and the burden of innumerable obligations and payments no doubt increased their unwillingness to contemplate costly or risky new ventures. Peasants in the Baltic provinces were loath to abandon their simple hook plough, which they could make themselves with a little help from the local smith, and purchase a fancy new one, when they knew it would immediately be commandeered for the use of the landlord to whom they owed labour service (*Frondienst*). The obligations of labour service on the estate also meant that the peasants' own land was not ploughed at the right time. The loss of common land frequently meant that the small peasant farmer had not enough pasture or grazing land for his livestock; this seems to have been a particular problem in Prussia and Pomerania. There was in consequence an inadequate supply of manure for his fields, a situation made worse by his attachment to the three-field system of crop rotation long since abandoned by the large estate-owners. Lacking tools and draught animals, and reluctant to borrow these from the farmers in return for additional labour, the Jutland cottar (*Husmand*) or the Finnish crofter (*torppari*) rarely rose above the levels of self-sufficiency. 'Bread in the house and fodder for a cow' may well have been a comfortable cliché to fall back on, but it was also an indirect expression of the constraints upon the efficiency of the smallholder almost everywhere in Europe.[2]

One should not, however, judge the peasant farmer solely by the standards of the rationalising, improving big landowner, with his leys of clover, nine-course crop rotation, expensive machinery and pedigree herds. In much of northern Europe, peasants had learnt over centuries to be adept at survival in times of adversity or on marginal land – and it must not be forgotten that this part of Europe is not favoured with fertile, warm soil and a long growing season. They were quick to turn their hand to anything which might supplement their income. Peasants from Dalarna in their distinctive costumes sold their baskets and wickerware as far afield as Finland and Russia; large

2. For an incisive and critical view of peasant farming in the Baltic provinces, see: Der Proletariarer-Charakter der bäuerlichen Ackerbau-Industrie in Liv- und Estland *Baltische Monatschrift* **2** (1860): 99–133. Langerke A von 1849 *Schilderungen der baltischen und westfälischen Landwirtschaft*, Berlin, 2 vols, gives a detailed account of farming in Pomerania, and advances a number of reasons for the shortcomings of peasant husbandry. Schissler H 1978 *Preussische Agrargesellschaft im Wandel* Kritische Studien zur Geschichtswissenschaft **33**, Göttingen, p. 150ff. has a clear and well-argued analysis of the effects of the land reforms on the peasantry of Prussia. On Danish agriculture, see Bjørn C (ed.) 1988 *Det danske landbrugs historie 1810–1914*, Odense.

quantities of grouse trapped on the fells of Lapland were shipped off annually from Narvik to the London wholesale markets; Finns from the stony, thin soils of northern Savo tramped to St Petersburg with their butter, fish and game, causing the citizenry of the local town of Kuopio to complain of the high prices they had to pay in consequence. Pressure on available land extended the frontiers of settlement and cultivation. Outsiders found it hard to believe that people actually wanted to settle in the high fells of Lapland, where nothing seemed to grow; but there were excellent upland pastures and water meadows in the river valleys, and plentiful game and fish. The inhabitants practised a natural economy, trekking over the passes into Norway and trading their butter, meat and game for tools, coffee, salt and flour at Mo i Rana. They even managed to make habitable houses from the stunted and twisted dwarf birches, stopping up the gaps with reindeer moss.

Farming north of 60° was less affected by rationalisation and innovation than were the more fertile regions of arable cultivation. 'The fir in our forests is the poor bread-tree, which nature gives us for our nourishment', declared A. W. Liljenstrand in his inaugural lecture as professor of national economy at the university of Helsingfors; only man's own back-breaking efforts and intelligence 'allowed us to maintain a place amongst civilised people here, on the edge of the eternal snows'. In eastern Finland, where the traditional burn-beat method of cultivation was no longer able adequately to provide sustenance for an ever-increasing population, the basic unit of the large family began to break up, and there was a massive increase in the numbers of landless. Arvo Soininen has concluded that by mid-century, Finnish agriculture was in serious crisis, no longer capable of satisfying demand for cereals. Crop failures in the 1860s led to catastrophe in 1867–68, a famine in which it has been estimated that as many as 100,000 people perished. Much of Sweden and the Baltic provinces was similarly afflicted.[3]

Within two decades, increased world demand for timber had transformed the fir into 'green gold'. Exports of boards and deals from Sweden quintupled between 1850 and 1870, and timber products

3. Liljenstrand A 1857 Om näringarnas framtid i Finland *Litteraturblad för allmänna bildning* **11**: 268. On Finnish agriculture, see: Soininen A 1974 *Vanha maataloutemme* Historiallisia tutkimuksia **96**, Helsinki. On the famine of 1867–78, Turpeinen O 1986 *Nälkä vai tauti tappoi? Kauhunvuodet 1866–1868* Historiallisia tutkimuksia **136**, Helsinki: Nelson M 1988 *Bitter bread. The famine in Norrbotten 1867–1868* Studia Historica Upsaliensia **153**, Uppsala. Häkkinen A (ed.) 1992 *Just a sack of potatoes? Crisis experiences in European societies, past and present* Studia Historica **44**, Helsinki.

made up 43 per cent of the total value of exports in the 1870s. In Finland, the volume of marketed roundwood increased sevenfold between 1870 and 1910. The volume of wood pulp produced by both countries rose steeply from the 1890s, with the development of the sulphite cooking process and the seemingly insatiable world demand for newsprint and paper.

Industry in Sweden and Finland was primarily located in the countryside, by the main watercourses and in the mining areas. As elsewhere, communications were vastly improved by the advent of the railways, but in neither country was the network fully completed before the end of the century, and many settlements remained miles away from the nearest railhead. Unending forests, outcrops of granite and gneiss, lakes and rivers, 'the mighty stillness and loneliness of Nature' (to quote the Swedish Touring Club's 1898 *Guide to Sweden*) were what the traveller expected to find north of the sixtieth parallel. But even in the wilderness, too far for the casual eye to see, changes were taking place. In some instances, they could be dramatic. The wholesale purchase of farms in Småland by timber companies eager to satisfy the demands of the matchstick industry in nearby Jönköping created what the ethnographer Åke Campbell called a 'ruined' landscape, in which the farmers became employees of the timber companies, their fields and farms were neglected, their buildings used for stabling horses and storage of machinery, and their woods were cut down. Exploitation replaced self-sufficiency, resources were no longer carefully husbanded and protected (the removal of the last restrictions upon cutting down the forests and setting up sawmills by watercourses was an essential prerequisite of the timber boom in the latter half of the century); jealously guarded skills and traditions were pushed aside by professionally trained engineers and patented devices, the local ironmasters by company directors, and the native workforce by a proletariat.[4]

In spite of the unprecedented increase in population throughout the Baltic region, the proportion of town to country dwellers did not significantly alter between 1800 and 1870. The big cities continued to expand, although not always at an even pace (partly as a result of high mortality rates). Stockholm and Copenhagen each had some 200,000 inhabitants in the 1880s, and Königsberg, Danzig and Riga each had topped the 100,000 mark. The one really big city in the Baltic was St Petersburg, with almost 900,000 inhabitants in 1881. Behind the imposing public buildings of these cities lay an unplanned and often

4. Campbell Å 1936 *Kulturlandskapet*, Stockholm.

unsightly jumble of dwellings; it was not until the last decades of the nineteenth century that the infrastructure and residential quarters of the modern city began to take shape. The new Finnish capital city of Helsingfors was for decades little more than a collection of wooden houses and buildings, whose inhabitants lived in much the same fashion as country people, baking their own bread, salting and pickling their own preserves, and keeping a couple of cows in the outhouse. The keeping of pigs within the town walls of Lübeck was banned by the city fathers in 1844, but pigs were still driven nightly along the largely unpaved town streets. Visitors commented on the great number of medieval houses in the old Hanseatic towns. Not all were so romantically inclined as a visitor to the first North German music festival, held in Lübeck in 1839, who compared the town to a jolly, venerable greybeard; many also commented on the overcrowding, filthy streets and pestilential odours of decay.

The throwing down of the old fortifications and ramparts which occurred in cities such as Copenhagen and Riga from the 1850s onwards allowed for unhindered expansion and provided new recreational amenities, though the chief beneficiaries were the prosperous middle classes who moved en masse to the pleasant new villas springing up in the suburbs. The unhygienic, overcrowded living quarters at the centre of the city and the lack of a proper water supply or sewage system were the main reasons for periodic outbreaks of cholera and typhoid. More effective municipal government as a result of suffrage and other reforms seemed to offer the prospect of improvement, though ambitions often had to be trimmed in the face of financial constraint or determined opposition. The Livonian *Landtag* had to finance the construction of the gas and water works of Riga in the 1860s in order to get round the refusal of the imperial authorities to allow the town magistracy to raise the money to pay for these works. Even after the municipal reforms of 1877, the ministry of the interior still refused to sanction a buy-out by the new city council. In 1852, the liberal-controlled town council (*Borgerrepræsentation*) of Copenhagen voted to carry out an extensive programme of laying down sewers, water-pipes and gas mains at a cost of three and a half million rigsdaler, to be raised by public loan. The conservative government and the city magistracy (which remained virtually unaffected by the reforms of 1839–40) opposed such a plan, even after cholera claimed 5,000 lives in 1853. A more sympathetic government eventually approved a watered-down version, gave the *Borgerre-præsentation* more powers and streamlined the municipal administration. This enabled the burghermaster in charge of the so-called second section to overhaul and modernise the city's fiscal system, replacing the occupational levy with an income tax, and getting round the problem of assessment by estimating incomes and publishing these estimates in what was to become an annual best-seller.

Before the introduction of effective city government, able to raise the money needed to undertake major construction work of hospitals, asylums and other institutions, private philanthropy had borne much of the burden of coping with the poor, the sick and needy. Those who qualified could obtain relief from gild funds. Abandoned infants were taken care of (if they survived) in the foundling hospitals, orphans, the deaf, dumb and blind, fallen women and old soldiers could seek a home in charitable institutions. The *Literärisch-praktische Bürgerverbindung* founded in Riga in 1802 opened a further education institute for apprentices in 1817, a school for orphans in 1836, an institute for the deaf and dumb (1839) and for the blind (1872). It also had substantial funds to assist those in service who had fallen ill or who were in need during their old age. Private initiatives were also launched to clean up and beautify city streets and squares, or to erect statues and memorials to deserving public figures.[5] Municipal authorities in subsequent decades were to take over many of these private activities, which were often limited in scope and lacked central coordination, and were actively involved in replanning and providing a multiplicity of services for the growing urban areas under their control.

LIFESTYLES

The commercial exploitation of the vast forests of Norrland and of the Finnish hinterland from the 1870s onwards provided work opportunities and a welcome injection of capital for the farmers who owned the land; but it also caused considerable disruption of the traditional social order and customs. Large numbers of Värmlanders with their superior forestry skills came to the remote villages of Dalarna, bringing with them food hitherto regarded as an unobtainable luxury by the locals – rye bread, American bacon, peas and wheat flour. The flow of money to the region went into home improvements. The old box bed was thrown out, followed by the wooden benches, the corner cupboard by the door and the fixed

5. Hovde B 1943 *The Scandinavian countries 1720–1865*, Ithaca, NY, vol. 2, pp. 707–36, provides the most detailed and entertaining account in English of developments in Scandinavia.

shelves over doors and windows. The village carpenter replaced them with sofas, beds and chiffoniers in the 'Gustavian' style. Doors and windows were widened, and the outside walls painted red. Boots, essential for working on the log floats, came into use in the 1870s, at the same time as the oil lamp made its appearance.

Similar changes in life-style had begun to take place even earlier in the more fertile southern Baltic farming regions. Traditional dress was amongst the first things to vanish. Young maidens on the island of Rügen were forsaking the black bonnets with their white hoods (long since abandoned in the towns) by the end of the Napoleonic wars. Everywhere, trousers replaced knee-breeches, and coats and jackets of more fashionable cut were worn by the young men in preference to home-spun. On the north German plains and in Denmark, houses built of brick and stone, with proper foundations, wooden floors, stoves and chimneys, distinguished the prosperous farmer from the poorer members of the rural community in their sooty and often verminous timber-built cottages. Red- or yellow-painted wooden houses were an indication of status and prosperity in Sweden and Finland, although the chimneyless hovel was still to be found in the remoter parishes even at the beginning of the twentieth century. More substantial farmhouses, with several well-furnished rooms and neatly laid-out gardens instead of untidy dung-heaps, marked the emergence of a prosperous class of peasant farmers in the Baltic provinces from the 1860s onwards.

The wish of country people for the good things in life was hindered by restrictions upon trade in rural areas, which were only gradually removed between the 1840s and 1870s. Concern over increasing pauperism during the first half of the century prompted a flood of moralising about the pernicious effects of wasteful consumption, and there were even attempts to enforce controls. Lyngby parish council in southern Sweden passed a series of regulations in 1817, prohibiting the wearing of blue or green clothing (unless made of native cloth), excessive coffee drinking, smoking and dancing. Fines were levied upon offenders, the proceeds being used to reward parishioners who distinguished themselves by their patriotism and Christian virtue. Consumption of tea and coffee seems to have excited almost as much disapprobation as the peasants' well-known predilection for strong drink. Attempts to curb or prevent the drinking of coffee in the late eighteenth-century had failed; and as prices fell with the entry of cheaper Brazilian blends into the market, coffee-drinking spread to all levels of society, as a Finnish peasant poem written in 1839 makes clear:

Nyt on tehty teelusikat,	And now teaspoons,
Kupit kaunihit kuwatut,	Finely painted cups
Retakannut kanssa wielä,	Even copper pots,
Tungettu joka tupahan.	Have made their way into every home.
Tällä juomalla jalolla	With this noble drink
Moni tuhlawi talonsa;	Many have ruined their house;
Wiepi wiimeisen kopekan,	Taken the last copeck,
Kulettawi kauppiaalle,	Spending it with the merchant,
Miehen welkahan wetäwi.	Dragging the man into debt.[6]

This poem reveals the inbred caution of a man living in a land on the margins of subsistence, where crop failures actually caused a major famine almost thirty years later; but it also shows that coffee-drinking implied considerable changes in patterns of consumption and spending and promoted new eating habits and rituals. The coffee table, according to Bishop Olesen of Ribe, was the third sacrament for the southern Jutes, and as the author of a study of this ritual observes, it was no coincidence that the increased use of cast-iron stoves in the 1850s and 1860s corresponded with an upsurge in the publication of cookbooks offering mouth-watering recipes for cakes and pastries.[7] Coffee-drinking implied sugar, cream, fine pastries, porcelain cups and side-plates; it presupposed that the guests would sit upon chairs at a table covered with a fine cloth; it was, in a word, part of a civilising process (even if many still preferred to slurp their coffee out of a saucer, with a lump of sugar between their teeth). The withdrawal from a rough-and-ready communal life was also reflected within the home; the new-style farmhouse had private rooms for family use, furnished, carpeted and curtained. Servants and animals now had to accommodate themselves in outbuildings. For the poor, privacy was unknown; the household slept on the floor and ate from the same wooden bowl, sometimes without benefit of table or benches. A bed of one's own, individual plates, knives and forks, utensils made of copper, pewter and porcelain instead of wood – these were not only evident signs of modest well-being, but also a departure from a scratchy, quarrelsome, snotty-nosed and rheumy-eyed existence and an

6. *Kahwiruno taikka Wirsi kahwista katsottu Runo ruoasta hywästä,* written by Petteri Makkonen, a farmer from Kerimäki in eastern Finland, and published with comments by Elias Lönnrot in his newspaper *Mehiläinen* in May 1839. *Elias Lönnrot. Valitut teokset 2* Suomen Kirjallisuuden Seura **531**, (1990): pp. 453–6.

7. Adriansen I 1979 Kaffebordet – sønderjydernes tredie sakramente *Folk og Kultur,* p. 8. On the spread of coffee-drinking in the duchies, see also Sievers K 1970 *Volkskultur und Aufklärung im Spiegel der Schleswig-Holsteinische Provinzialberichte* Quellen und Forschungen der Geschichte Schleswig-Holsteins **58**, Neumünster, p. 97.

entry into the world of comforts, gentility and privacy.[8]

Reading habits also reflect this transition. Religious and devotional literature declined considerably as a percentage of works published – from over half of the titles in Estonian published between 1800 and 1850, for example, to just over a quarter between 1850 and 1900. Readers in the latter half of the century not only had a much wider choice of literature, they could also subscribe to an ever-growing range of newspapers and journals. The thirteen newspapers published in Finland in 1850 had increased to fifty-four some thirty years later, for example, with the Finnish-language press tripling in size during the 1870s. Symbolic of the growth of secular literature, in several ways, were the illustrated journals for family reading. Stylishly produced and lavishly illustrated, aggressively promoted and sold through chains of agents, magazines such as the German *Gartenlaube* and *Leserkränzchen* (translated and marketed in Sweden as *Familjevännen*) were widely copied and achieved high circulation figures. Although these journals eschewed political and religious controversy, and sought to amuse, enlighten and edify within the moral conventions of the day, they did also seek to influence ideas and opinion, even if only to persuade their readers that all things French were to be abhorred as decadent and immoral. The 'family' frequently depicted on the front covers of these journals was not the same as that of the older tradition, to which writers of moral tales such as the Skåne landowner Carl Adam von Nolcken or the Baltic German Count Peter von Mannteuffel referred. The extended household gathered by the stove on winter evenings, each performing some task necessary for the domestic economy, with the paterfamilias reading aloud a suitably uplifting passage – an image projected in von Nolcken's *Läsning för allmogen* (Readings for the common people, 1855) – belongs to the old Lutheran tradition of the family. The atmosphere conjured up by mass-circulation journals, of everyday domestic comfort, emotional warmth, the presence of small children, and the exclusion of the outside world is that of the modern family.[9]

8. Christiansen P 1978 Peasant adaptation to bourgeois culture? *Ethnologica Scandinavica*, pp. 98–151, argues that, far from renouncing their peasantist heritage, prosperous farmers imitated urban lifestyles as a means of redefining their self-image in a rural context. For a perceptive and sympathetic study of social change in an isolated rural community, see: Moritz P 1990 *Fjällfolk. Livsformer och kulturprocesser i Tärna socken under 1800- och 1900-talen* Acta Ethnologica Umensia **2**, Umeå.

9. Johannesson E 1980 *Den läsande familjen. Familjetidskriften i Sverige 1850–1880* Nordiska muséets handlingar **96**, Stockholm, discusses the spread and impact of 'family reading', and has much to say about the changing concept of the family as well.

The extension of the private sphere, with all its attendant comforts, is the hallmark of the bourgeois world (memorably portrayed in Thomas Mann's novel, *Buddenbrooks*, or on the screen, in Ingmar Bergman's *Fanny and Alexander*). Family life became more immediate and intimate, the patriarch became the paterfamilias, domesticity and consumerism replaced the self-sufficient, productive household. Cheap mass-produced fashions offered choice instead of serviceable home-made last-a-lifetime clothes and furniture. The mass-circulation family journal provided instruction and entertainment (and bourgeois values), and the oil-lamp enabled the family to read it in comfort round the table, in cottage or mansion. Mail-order catalogues and a nationwide postal service made it possible for even the remotest settlements to obtain the same commodities as their city cousins – coffee sets, bicycles, carbide lamps, toothbrushes and soap, some of the items ordered from the mail-order firm of Åhlén & Holm by the inhabitants of Tärna, high up in the Swedish fells at the beginning of this century.

The slow, halting disintegration of old communities and communal values as a consequence of economic change allowed (or obliged) citizens (no longer subjects!) to choose new liaisons – to marry for love if they could afford it, to couple and procreate in defiance of respectable opinion if they could not; to praise the Lord in a new fashion, and to abjure the ways of the ungodly (who might include neighbours, fellow-workers or parsons); and to travel, take work, buy and sell, live and die with minimal obstruction or assistance from the state. Choice and individuality were reflected in the diversity of children's names. The religious delved into the Old Testament, the patriotic scanned the pages of the ancient myths and sagas to find appropriate names for their offspring. Choice is at the heart of C. J. L. Almquist's celebrated novel, *Det går an* (1839). Sara Videbeck, striving to keep going the business her drunken, brutal father almost ruined, prefers a free love relationship with Albert to a marriage which will mean everything she has becomes his property. Choice is more crudely expressed by the Lithuanian peasant Ansas in Hermann Sudermann's *Die Reise nach Tilsit* (1917), when his wife doubts whether they will be admitted in their country clothes to a grand military concert clearly intended for German burghers: it doesn't matter if you speak German or Lithuanian, as long as you can pay the entrance money.

These two examples suggest that choice was often rather more fictitious than real. There were many psychological, as well as practical obstacles to social advancement. Those who made it usually sought to obscure or forget their humble origins. When a Latvian pastor taking up a living in 1881 publicly declared his origins and his wish to speak Latvian at home, he dumbfounded his parishioners. Just a few years previously, Hermann von Samson had resolutely fought liberal attempts to include representatives of the autochthonous peoples in the Livonian *Landtag* and had publicly voiced his doubts whether gentlemen could sit in the same room as hay-thieves. Desperately seeking to hide the tell-tale signs of peasant or 'national' origins, but never fully acquiring the social graces or linguistic polish of the upper classes to which they aspired, many lived in the curious in-between world of the *Halbdeutsche*, the butt of jokes and gibes on both sides of the language barrier, as in the following Baltic German poem, *Die Oberpahl'sche Freundschaft*:

"Was Teiwel" ruft' ich, "tu ast Rum!
Wo ast tu's mugglirt?
Und trinkst kar Krog! tas ist nicht tumm!
Tu pist kanz siwlischirt!"

Er sagt' "Ich öhrt tas Krieg, tas war,
Für Siwlischation;
Nu tenkt' ich immer in und er:
Was ist tas für Person?"

"The Devil" cried I, "thass rum, my lad!
Where you smuggled that from, eh?
And drinking grog! That ain't half bad!
Civ'lished, thass what you are!

'E said, "I 'ear the war's abaht
Civil-iz-ay-shun;
But somehow, I can't make aht
'Oo the 'ell's that person?"[10]

Sara Videbeck's bold assertion of the virtues of love without binding ties aroused a storm in Sweden; but in reality, Sara would have been a quite exceptional woman (and Albert an unusually tolerant man) had she flouted the conventions in such a manner. The

10. In an earlier encounter, the two settle down to a bowl of punch, but come to blows over cards: the 'friend from Oberpahl', accused of cheating, assaults the narrator and throws him out of the house. In the continuation, dated 1857, the narrator has returned from Reval, worried about the possibility of bombardment, and re-encounters his old friend – who mixes another bowl of punch. The poem was written by a customs official, Johann Jakob Malm, and is printed in: Grotthuus J von 1894 *Das baltische Dichterbuch*, Reval, pp. 230ff.

1734 Swedish law code placed unmarried women under the guardianship of their fathers or nearest male relatives. Married women were under the guardianship of their husbands. Only widows could act on their own account as regards their person or property. Most trades and professions were closed to women, and the few that were open to them were subject to controls. Education and training for women was virtually unknown. Ladies from genteel homes passed their days in sewing, visiting and doing good deeds. There was little mixing of the sexes; the men preferred their wives and daughters to sit at home and serve their needs. 'The place of women is inferior to that of men, and it is the common belief amongst the womenfolk as well as the menfolk that a woman without a man cannot maintain a farmstead, and that women are dependants of the men', commented the farmer Eljas Raussi in his account of life in an eastern Finnish parish in the 1840s. The drudgery of women servants was described in horrific detail by the Swedish national economists, Bishop C. A. Agardh and C. Ljungberg, in 1854. Their report concluded: 'In short, woman in the North is the household beast of burden and the slave of man. We are so used to it that it does not arouse our shame.'[11]

The protection men sought to exercise over the female sex became somewhat flimsy when it came to the consequences of heterosexual intercourse. The rising numbers of children born out of wedlock, particularly in the towns, was accompanied by a chorus of disapprobation of which the unfortunate mothers – invariably poor and with few resources – bore the brunt. The rate of illegitimate births varied considerably from region to region: high on the island of Fyn, but low in the parts of southern Jutland which were strongly influenced by religious revivalism, for example. Jonas Frykman has argued that high rates of extramarital fertility in Sweden tended to occur in areas with a high degree of social stratification, where there was a large landless population, such as Skåne and the Mälare valley. Anna-Sofie Kälvemark has pointed out that a significant proportion of children borne out of wedlock in such areas were subsequently legitimised by the mother's marriage, which was not the case in areas with a low rate of illegitimate births. Such areas tended to be dominated by small peasant households, with relatively few landless workers, and they were also strongly influenced by religious movements, which may have strengthened already existing social

11. Raussi E 1966 *Virolahden kansanelämää 1840-luvulla* Suomalaisen Kirjallisuuden Seuran toimituksia **280**, Helsinki, p. 313. Hovde 1943, vol. 2, pp. 681–2. See also Qvist G 1960 *Kvinnofrågan i Sverige 1809–1846* Kvinnohistoriskt arkiv **2**, Göteborg.

controls and sanctions against extramarital intercourse. Diminished opportunities for marriage and the weakening of the widespread rural northern European institution of *nattfrieri (yöjalka, ehal' käimine)*, where the young men of the village spent the night with their intended, may also have increased the rates of illegitimate births. Frykman has for example suggested that the massive influx of lumberjacks and navvies during the boom years at the end of the nineteenth century destroyed the degree of control hitherto exercised by local youth in Norrland. Parents were subsequently unwilling to accept as suitors men from outside the area, and preferred their daughters to give birth to bastards. The contemporary observer of Finnish peasant life, Eljas Raussi, also thought that the refusal of parents to consent to marriages was one reason for the increase in the number of extramarital births, another being the seduction of young virgins by lusty farmhands 'whose circumstances prevent marriage'.[12]

Another consequence of sexual intercourse, and a scourge of nineteenth-century Europe, was venereal disease. The response of the authorities was to ensure closely-regulated treatment, which made up somewhat for the imperfections of the cure. In general, despite measures taken to safeguard public health, many doctors felt themselves to be little more than sanitary officials, fighting against blind ignorance and superstition with inadequate resources. They themselves were largely ignorant of the causes of the most deadly contagious diseases of the day, until the 1880s and Robert Koch's discovery of the tuberculosis and cholera bacilli. The general public remained distrustful of all advances of medical science. For many years, large numbers of Finns refused to believe that typhoid fever was contagious, dismissing the notion as an invention of the upper classes. When an outbreak of cholera was detected in Åbo in 1866, the locals claimed that the raising of a timing device at the observatory the day before had been a signal by the 'gentry' to unleash the disease.[13]

12. Raussi 1966, p. 276. Frykman J 1975 Sexual intercourse and social norms: a study of illegitimate births in Sweden 1831–1933 *Ethnologica Scandinavica*, pp. 111–50. Kälvemark A-S 1978 Hotet mot familjen. Den ogifta modern i Sverige i historiska perspektiv *Historisk Tidskrift* **98**: 83–101.

13. Bonsdorff B v 1975 *The history of medicine in Finland 1808–1918*, Helsinki, pp. 80–2. See also the articles by Dr Holst, a country doctor in Livonia, in *Baltische Monatsschrift* **13** (1866): pp. 500–15, and **15** (1867), pp. 469–78, for a revealing glimpse of the mental attitudes of a mid-century physician.

BELIEFS

The history of Protestantism in northern Europe during the nineteenth century is one of great paradox. Waves of deeply spiritual, often intensely emotional religiosity crashed against the stern breakwaters of the established church at the same time as an undercurrent of withdrawal from religious observance began to gain strength. The assault on the coldly rationalist Lutheran state-church came from many quarters and was at its most intense during the first half of the century. Thereafter, political changes which stripped the church of many of its secular powers and the shift within the church itself towards a more evangelical direction helped transform the official, orthodox and sometimes repressive church into one more responsive to the religious needs of the people. Although 'free' churches did establish themselves, they failed to attract significant numbers. By adopting a broader profile and a looser structure, the Lutheran church in the Nordic lands was able to retain the loyalty of the great majority of believers. In the Baltic provinces, the *Landeskirche* was under threat from those who wished to weaken the privileged status of the Baltic Germans; and although the great majority of Estonians and Latvians remained within the evangelical Lutheran tradition, they could not embrace wholeheartedly the pretensions and precepts of their quondam masters.

External impulses have always shaped the history of the church on the northern European periphery. Germany continued to provide theological inspiration – sometimes a heady brew for young men hitherto constrained by provincial dullness and a repressively old-fashioned, state-backed orthodoxy, imbibing the ideas of David Friedrich Strauss or the philosopher Ludvig Feuerbach for the first time. It was Britain, rather than Germany, however, that provided organisational inspiration. Bible societies and evangelical organisations were modelled on British examples. A two-year sojourn in England gave N. F. S. Grundtvig a taste for a more broad-based tolerant church, and other Scandinavian visitors came to England to learn about the Bell-Lancaster monitor system, Sunday schools and the tractarian movement. There were also English and Scottish evangelicals at work in Scandinavia, such as the Methodist preacher George Scott, and the industrialist Samuel Owen, both active in the Stockholm area in the 1820s.

Radical new ideas may have offered ammunition for young men eager to snipe at old-fashioned and authoritarian priests (the dark and brooding existentialism of that eccentric and detached observer of life, the anti-Hegelian Søren Kierkegaard, had to await a later age for proper appreciation); but the church was convulsed far more profoundly by the demand for a return to the Bible made by the 'awakeners'.[14] In some respects, this was a reflection of the general move to educate and raise up the mass of the people. Religion and morality featured prominently in elementary school curricula, and the lack of both amongst the poor was constantly alluded to as one of the main reasons for their wretched situation. The work of Bible societies in producing cheap copies of the Old and New Testaments, and the assiduous efforts of native and foreign writers of religious tracts and homilies, reaped its reward; wills and inventories show a significant increase in the household stock of religious and devotional literature from the 1820s onwards. On the other hand, there are unmistakable signs of a steady decline in domestic religious observance amongst the better-off sections of the community.

The clergy themselves worried about the breakdown of patriarchal values and discipline. 'Most of the educated classes do not come to church, neither do most of the poor; either they are prevented by their lord and master, or they have no decent clothing', lamented the priest in charge of a congregation of 10,000 in Prussian Masuria.[15] A Livonian clergyman raised a storm in 1862 when he declared that the educated and a large proportion of the 'nationals' were indifferent to religion; many Baltic German clergymen privately admitted that a deep gulf separated them from their peasant congregations. There was much discussion of the growing shortage of suitable candidates for the priesthood, and of the poor quality of those ordained, a reflection of a more critical attitude towards a church no longer able to rest somnolently and securely in the bosom of a state which tolerated no deviation from the orthodox path.

Religious revivalism in the early nineteenth century was heavily influenced by lay people. A number of the movements were inspired and led by clergymen, such as Henrik Renqvist in eastern Finland and Lars Levi Læstadius in northern Sweden, but they were carried

14. For a general overview of the Scandinavian churches, see: Lindhardt P 1983 *Kirchengeschichte Skandinaviens*, Göttingen, pp. 74–125. On the Baltic provinces, Wittram R (ed.) 1956 *Baltische Kirchengeschichte*, Göttingen, pp. 166–242. Juva M 1950 *Suomen sivistyneistö uskonnollisen vapaamielisyyden murroksessa 1848–1869* Suomen Kirkkohistoriallisen Seuran toimituksia **51**, Helsinki, suggests that ecclesiastical reform was a victory for conservatism rather than for liberalism, but concludes that the church retained support amongst the educated classes by virtue of the fact that moderate liberals and progressive churchmen had stood together in the fight to win reform.

15. Cited in Hubatsch W 1968 *Geschichte der Evangelischen Kirche Ostpreussens*, Göttingen, vol. 1, p. 358.

forward by the enthusiasm of the lay 'awakened'. This intensely active involvement 'from below' frequently led to conflict with the authorities, and there were a number of prosecutions during the early decades of the nineteenth century. Clergymen who were suspected of deviating from the true Word were frequently subjected to interrogation, and sometimes humiliation, by the 'awakened'. Edvard Rhén, in charge of 1,300 souls in the remote northern Swedish parish of Arvidsjaur, had to fight hard to win over his congregation, who had been strongly influenced by the fundamentalist *nyläsare*, or 'new readers'. Rhén was often accused of not preaching in accordance with Luther's word, but he managed to turn the tables on his opponents by using Luther's own texts – including his letter concerning those who secretly creep in holes and corners and falsely preach – against them. In the 1850s, a number of *läsare* in the northern parish of Orsa were prosecuted for illegal cohabitation after they had been denied a church marriage because of their refusal to take communion celebrated by a (in their eyes) 'godless' priest. The 'readers' of Orsa not only conducted their own marriage ceremonies, they also set up their own schools, like the sturdy Jutes in Denmark.

The sociological roots of these 'awakened' movements have been much discussed. It is generally agreed that the social changes brought about by the land reforms, the breakup of the old communities and the great increase in population were a major stimulus, but there is some disagreement about who were most affected, how and why. Poul Lindhardt has argued that peasant farmers, given increased self-confidence by the acquisition of their own land, were foremost in the early 'awakened' movements in Denmark, whilst H. P. Clausen believes it was the poorest elements of society who were most drawn to revivalism. The multi-volume project on the 'awakened' movements in Denmark presents a mixture, with farmers in Jutland, and the lowest social classes on Sjælland being the most prominent adherents, whilst research covering the islands of Fyn, Ærø and Langeland in the 1830s found recruits being drawn from all sections of society.[16] Religious revivalism continued to enjoy the support and patronage of noble families such as the von Belows and von Thaddens in Prussia, or the von Stackelbergs in Estland. Swedish nobles were numbered

16. The 'awakened' movements in Denmark are exhaustively covered in the volumes edited by A Pontoppidan Thyssen (*Vækkelsens frembrud i Danmark i første halvdel af det 19. århundrede* Copenhagen, 1960–). See also Lindhardt P 1959 *Vækkelse og kirkelige retninger* revised edition, Copenhagen, and Balle-Petersen M 1977 Guds folk i Danmark. Nogle synpunkter på studiet af religiøse grupper *Folk og kultur*, pp. 78–126.

amongst the *läsare*, and many were actively involved in the *Evangeliska fosterlandsstiftelsen*, the principal neo-evangelical organisation in the country. The Baptists, who had broken with their evangelical partners in the 1850s, appealed far more to the lower classes, and were more receptive to radical social ideas. The role of women in the early revivalist movements in Finland has been emphasised by Irma Sulkunen. Although she believes women's involvement perpetuated rather than challenged the traditional role-division of the old social order, she highlights what is perhaps the most profound aspect of 'awakening', that it was 'a personal resolution, and one which radically altered the nature of human relationships'.[17]

That choice could divide families and communities, but it could also create new bonds, transcending old boundaries – familial, social and regional. 'Awakening' could lead to conflict between parents and children. An 'awakened' daughter was often seen as having lost her value in the marriage market, for example. The 'awakened' tended to withdraw from traditional festivities and institutions; some even gave up occupations deemed unsuitable, such as playing the fiddle at village dances. Girls had to decide whether wearing crinolines was consonant with Christianity; ungodly boys, angered by what they saw as the unwarrantable machinations of the 'holy ones', jeered and pelted mud at girls who no longer appeared to want to have anything to do with them. Christen Hansen of Vejstrup was torn between following tradition or his conscience when it came to celebrating births in the family:

> My wife and family said: 'Do like other people', the holy brethren say 'If you do not receive the godly congregation, we have misjudged you' and my own heart said: only receive those who want to be present to give thanks to Our Lord. What did I do then? Of course, the worst of all things, I wanted to please both parties. My father issued invitations as before for a feast in celebration of the child's birth, whilst I invited the holy brethren to a godly meeting . . .

The outcome was predictable. When the godly entered the parlour 'singing hymns from Brorson's hymn-book, reading from Luther's sermons, praising and praying, it was noticeable that the other guests became exasperated and began to drink and swear even more, and

17. Sulkunen's observations are in her chapter on the woman's movement in: Engman M, Kirby D (eds) 1989 *Finland. People – nation – state*, London, pp. 182–5. See also: Sulkunen I 1983 Väckelsrörelserna som ett förskede i organiseringens historia *Historisk Tidskrift för Finland* **68**: 1–14. On Sweden, see: Gustafsson B 1963 *Svensk kyrkohistoria*, Stockholm.

some of them went home angry, and neither of the two sides could feel themselves free or at ease.'[18]

The 'awakened' set themselves apart from their neighbours in a variety of ways, most notably in their form and manner of worship. 'To become a Christian, you have to separate from other folk, hardly speaking, eating or sleeping with them, dress in skirted jackets, rush through your work and spend night after night singing the *Verses of Sion*, reading the *Crying Voice* or other such books', was a common lament amongst the people in north-eastern Finland, according to Elias Lönnrot, writing in the mid-1830s.[19] Each group had its own special language and terminology; some, like the Finnish Pietists alluded to above, had their own distinctive dress. Some, though not all, waged war on the demon drink. The followers of Lars Levi Læstadius in the far north perceived drunkenness as a sin, but were indifferent towards the early, American-inspired temperance movement in Sweden, which regarded excessive drinking primarily as a social evil. The Finnish lay revivalist Paavo Ruotsalainen not only enjoyed a tipple himself, but accused the 'awakened' clergyman Henrik Renqvist – who proclaimed total abstinence – of hypocrisy. Some, though not all, were strict sabbatarians. On the Skagen peninsula, the refusal of 'awakened' fishermen to fish on Sundays caused bad blood, since it breached traditional community habits. Many members of the *Indre Mission* in Denmark refused to deliver milk on Sundays, and in some districts, sabbatarians even built their own dairies which were closed on Sundays. Danish religious movements also created their own infrastructure, right down to sports clubs and insurance companies. In north-west Sjælland, boys from a Grundtvigian home were enrolled in the local shooting club as soon as they had been confirmed, and it was a commonplace that wherever there was a dairy chimney, there would be a Grundtvigian congregation house. The meeting houses were the pride and joy of the Herrnhut brethren in the Baltic provinces, a place where they could be at ease amongst their own, and could give vent to their pent-up emotions in prayer and singing. Suspicious landowners believed they fostered rebelliousness amongst the peasantry; it was claimed that the revolt against the poll tax in 1784 had raged most fiercely in areas where the brethren were strongest (although the Herrnhuters were also accused of standing aside by those

18. Cited in Balle-Petersen 1977, pp. 88–9.

19. Lönnrot printed this lament in his newspaper *Mehiläinen* in May 1836 with an assurance that 'these and other such statements about the changing times are from the mouth of the people, gathered in the wilds, and are not to be taken as mere empty words'.

who did participate in the revolt). When an Estonian assistant in the brethren was identified amongst the rebels at Waiwara in 1858, that was enough for the local landowner to accuse the local meeting house of planning the unrest.

The content of the 'awakened' message was not particularly new; indeed, the 'awakened' frequently displayed a hostility towards new prayer-books or hymnals and were fiercely attached to what they held to be the pure, unadulterated word of the gospels or of Martin Luther. Nor can it be said that the 'awakened' movements consciously strove to realise social ideals or to bring about change. The better life was in the next world – or the state of Utah, to which Mormon missionaries sought to guide willing converts with the help of loans to buy tickets. Where some historians see revivalism as the first spiritual movement in the modern sense to win broad support amongst the rural population, others find insufficient evidence to qualify it as a mass-based associational phenomenon. Undoubtedly there are elements of protest to be found in the myriad of conventicles and gatherings which flourished across the length and breadth of Protestant northern Europe; but just as it has proved difficult to trace connections between eighteenth-century Pietism and nineteenth-century revivalism, so it has not been easy to establish firm links between 'awakened' movements and later secular phenomena, such as 'backwoods communism'. There is indeed a danger in over-emphasising the societal or quasi-political aspects at the expense of what was after all an intense and deeply religious experience.[20]

What was new about the 'awakened' movements was the shift of emphasis. The community of believers, and not the church, was to determine the norms of Christian life, and individual conscience, not

20. See Pontoppidan Thyssen's introduction to the first volume of *Vækkelsens frembrud i Danmark*, v. Religious revivalism is regarded as the first genuinely popular movement by Lundkvist S 1976 *Folkrörelserna i det svenska samhället 1850–1920* Studia Historica Upsaliensia **85**, Uppsala, p. 26, and by Skovmand R 1951 *De folkelige bevægelser i Danmark* Copenhagen, pp. 15–16. Neither Jansson T 1985 *Adertonhundatalets associationer* Studia Historica Upsaliensia **139**, Uppsala, nor Stenius H 1987 *Frivilligt jämlikt samfällt. Föreningsväsendets utveckling i Finland fram till 1900-talets början* Skrifter utgivna av Svenska Litteraturssällskapet i Finland **545**, Helsingfors, pay much attention to revivalism, which Stenius discounts as a mass movement on the grounds of a lack of strong, formal organisation and its intimate association with the official state church. Sulkunen 1983, pp. 2, 6–7. Suolinna K 1975 Herätysliikkeet sosiaalisena liikkeenä *Uskonnollinen liike* (J Pentikäinen, ed.), Helsinki, pp. 28–56. Suolinna sees revivalism in terms of the conflict between centre and periphery, which was essentially a clash of value systems, and the emphasis upon equality, she believes, also served the aim of integration. This seems to me an excessively 'secular' interpretation of a deeply spiritual phenomenon.

external higher authority, was to be the sole guide to belief and the religious life. Given the very formidable battery of sanctions which the authorities could deploy against the dissident, it is rather surprising that there was so little active religious persecution. Groups of 'awakened' were prosecuted in the 1820s and 1830s, and a few leaders were briefly imprisoned, but there was nowhere a determined campaign to put down or root out deviation from orthodoxy. The conventicle laws, on which most prosecutions were based, were abolished in Norway in 1842, in Sweden in 1858. Sweden also lagged behind its union partner in granting religious freedom in 1860, fifteen years after a similar measure in Norway. (Those leaving the church had to enter one approved by the state, or to form one with the state's permission.) Dissenters were not permitted to leave the church in Finland until 1889, though legislation in 1869 did away with most of the irksome restrictions of the seventeenth-century church law. Religious freedom was guaranteed in the July 1849 constitution in Denmark, and one of the principal grievances of the 'awakened', the obligation to worship only in the church of their parish (*Sognebaand*), was abolished in 1855.

The abolition of controls upon religious uniformity established by absolutist monarchs enabled a wide variety of religious strands to work together in a broad-based institutional church made more responsive to the demands and wishes of its active members. The battle to reform the church had been largely fought and won inside it. Even those most critical of the priesthood and its practices, such as the followers of Læstadius, recognised the value of the church as an institution and preferred to remain within it. Conflict between priest and congregation still went on. A. E. Granfelt, who became vicar of Forssa in southern Finland in 1855, and remained there for over forty years, gradually became reconciled to the evangelicals in his parish who in his early years had trekked many miles to hear 'one of theirs' rather than attend his services, but in his declining years was again plagued by lay preachers who challenged his interpretations of the gospel and tried unsuccessfully to take over control of the local meeting house. There were fierce, though usually short-lived battles between churchmen and sectarians; but as Paavo Kortekangas points out, by responding to challenges with new methods and practices, the church was shifting from the traditional notion of a homogenous and uniform religious culture to one of a community of believers who had to be catered for beyond the framework of divine service and the sacraments.[21]

21. Kortekangas P 1965 *Kirkko ja uskonnollinen elämä teollistuvassa yhteiskunnassa. Tutkimus Tampereesta 1855–1905*, Helsinki, pp. 170–2.

Religious imagery and the conventions of religious observance, however formal, shaped the mental world of early nineteenth-century men and women; by the end of the century, this was far less the case. It is not easy to say why people cease to believe (or, less dramatically, imperceptibly slip into indifference). Undoubtedly, the loosening of coercive bonds assisted the process of secularisation, though this relaxation may, of course, have been brought about as much by that very process as through the pressures for a more responsive and vital church for believers. The freedom to choose for believers, which was an implicit element of church reform, also permitted people not to believe, or formally to observe the rites of the church. And it might be argued that greater material prosperity made this world a rather pleasanter and more appealing place than it had been formerly. The acquisition of worldly goods has always been inimical to religious devotion.

Greater freedom to choose, and a broader and more accessible range of choices to make, were basic prerequisites for the development of new forms of social activity. In many instances, of course, these arose out of religious communities or were directly inspired by religious ideals: charitable organisations and a whole range of social welfare institutions are obvious examples. Such organisations were, however, very much directed 'from above'; and the same may also be said to apply to the temperance movements which enjoyed considerable, albeit brief, success in the 1830s and 1840s. The Swedish Temperance Society (*Svenska nykterhetssällskapet*) claimed 100,000 members in 1845, but 'membership' was largely confined to signing the pledge, and the leadership of the movement was largely in the hands of the clergy and the upper classes. Within less than a decade, the movement had faded away. In the Baltic provinces, the efforts of local clergymen to set up temperance societies amongst the peasantry were frustrated by the authorities, fearful of unrest. Officialdom was also suspicious of attempts to approach the people in Finland, and noticeably tightened controls upon the press and public activities in 1848–50.[22]

22. Jansson 1985, pp. 143–64. Wittram H 1982 Vom Kampf gegen das soziale Elend in den baltischen Provinzen *Zeitschrift für Ostforschung* **31**: 530–40. Stenius 1987, pp. 31–2 suggests that the popular movements which developed in Sweden were more hostile towards officialdom than was the case in Finland. A contemporary Scottish observer took a rather sceptical view of the Swedish temperance movement: 'The Swedish gentry adopt the fashionable subjects – without considering that infant schools and temperance societies . . . are inapplicable in a thinly peopled country . . . people could not meet to be sober, without a vexatious loss of time, and a fatigue which would almost excuse their getting drunk'. Laing S 1839 *A tour in Sweden in 1838*, London, p. 136.

Patriotic zeal had for many decades inspired the creation of societies for the promotion and improvement of the common good. From the 1830s onwards, however, there was a shift away from the material to the spiritual. Not only were the peasants to be taught the virtues of clover leys and crop rotation: they were also to be morally, spiritually and intellectually uplifted, to take their place in the nation. In Denmark, the constitutional and national ferment of the 1830s and 1840s facilitated the emergence of a genuine peasant activism in politics, at a rather more intense level than was the case either in Sweden or even Norway. After the three years' war (1848–50), the Society of Friends of the Peasant (*Bondevennernes Selskab*) was able to put pressure on the government to provide funds for the establishment of people's high schools north of the Kongeå. A number were set up in the 1850s, some inspired by Grundtvig's Christian-democratic ethos, others more straightforwardly seeking to elevate the peasants' self-confidence and self-esteem and to provide future leadership, and the idea spread to the other Scandinavian countries in subsequent decades.

In the Baltic provinces and Finland the peasantry had not only to be raised up as a class; they were the raw material out of which the nation was to be forged. The 'awakening' of the people was initially sponsored by Swedish- or German-speaking cultural enthusiasts, who formed literary or learned societies, collected folk materials and published papers and proceedings. The authorities in general viewed such worthy activities with benevolence, even granting scholarships for study and research. From mid-century, however, a different and sharper note began to make itself heard. In Finland, the indefatigable J. V. Snellman sought to add a political edge to cultural fennomania. Temporarily muzzled during the revolutionary years of the late 1840s, he was to become in the 1860s the leading spokesman of an aggressively linguistic nationalism which demanded equal rights for Finnish and pressed for the establishment of secondary Finnish-language schools. This prompted a reaction amongst Swedish-speakers, though the subsequent 'language conflict' was conducted in a civilised manner through the columns of the press, rather than on the streets.

Many, if not most, of the first generation of Finnish-language nationalists came from a Swedish-speaking milieu, inspired by the work of cultural fennomania. A similar switch of loyalties was impossible for the Baltic Germans, no longer certain of an assured place in the imperial system, but separated politically, socially and psychologically from the Estonians and Latvians. It was from the ranks of the people that the first generation of Estonian and Latvian nationalists arose in the reign of Alexander II, and one of their first tasks was to combat the ingrained feelings of inferiority and servility of their fellows and to create an awareness of and pride in belonging to the nation. They were influenced far more than were the Finnish nationalists by events in Russia, where many of them studied or worked. This circumstance, and the deep hostility felt towards the German elite, gave Estonian and Latvian nationalism a rather more radical and uncompromising edge than was the case in Finland, an autonomous duchy which remained almost blissfully isolated from the deep turmoil of Russian revolutionary politics.

The bringing together of large numbers of people was of course vital for nationalist movements. Song festivals and vast open-air meetings had played an important part in shaping opinion and attitudes in the Slesvig-Holstein question, as had student festivals in the Scandinavian university towns in the development of Scandinavism. Rallies and gatherings continued to serve a useful purpose – witness the massive singing festivals of the Estonian and Latvian national movements – but the relaxation of official controls which was noticeable everywhere after the fading of the spectre of revolution in the 1850s, and the development of better communications offered an opportunity for a much wider range of organisational activities. Over 100,000 Danes in 1883 pledged themselves to raise money for defence improvements by voluntary self-taxation, and substantial sums were raised in subsequent years. On the eve of the First World War, national-minded Swedes raised over seventeen million kronor to fund the building of the so-called F-boat, after the liberal government of Karl Staaff had suspended work on the vessel. The Estonians campaigned and raised money for years for a secondary school in which Estonian would be the language of instruction; the Finns, facing fewer obstacles from officialdom, were rather more successful in similar campaigns in the 1870s.

A more diverse pattern of permanent organisations was also utilised to carry forward the national ethos (and, as many historians would now claim, introduce the people to the values of a secular world). Blows to national pride often produced a number of quasi-militaristic fencing or rifle clubs, as did the inspiring example of foreign hero-liberators such as Garibaldi. Voluntary fire brigades brought together men of different social classes to sweat and swear together over the pumps and hoses. As the Finnish newspaper *Åbo Underrättelser* declared in 1868, the voluntary fire brigades were the only democratic institutions in the country 'and the beautiful idea of equality and common defence against a common enemy, which constitutes their base, should not be allowed to give way to caste differences and gild mentality'.[23] The second wave of the temperance movement, which got under way in the 1870s, was quite different in its organisation and objectives from the first, offering a wide range of activities, lobbying effectively for controls on the sale of alcohol in Norway, Sweden and Finland, even offering low-cost housing schemes for members. Deprived of their leading role in local government and elementary education by the reforms of the 1860s and 1870s, the clergy were no longer considered indispensable initiators and leaders. There was often antagonism and hostility between clergy and aggressively secular mass movements. In a curious way, however, such movements took over some of the 'civilising mission' of the Protestant church, drawing the rural population away from simple, unorganised pastimes and rough rustic pleasures. The Finnish newspaper which in 1882 scolded the young people in the countryside for playing on the swings on a Sunday afternoon and disturbing respectable citizens' nightly repose with their bawdy songs was echoing the strictures of the Lutheran priest Jacobus Finno exactly three centuries earlier. Then, the clergy had been concerned to bring within the fold of the church a still largely pagan people. At the end of the nineteenth century, youth clubs, sewing groups and a branch of the temperance movement were seen as the most efficacious ways of bringing the people out of darkness into the light of progress and national awareness.[24]

WORK

Many of the habits and attitudes of the old order remained, however, and survived long after the formal abolition of restrictions and controls upon occupation, domicile or ownership of property during the middle decades of the nineteenth century. It proved easier for women to acquire equal rights of inheritance and the gradual abolition of male guardianship than to obtain entry into the male domain of work and the professions. Only 83,000 of the 446,000 adult women in Denmark

23. Stenius 1987, p. 251.

24. Huuhtanen T 1978 *Ypäjän historia*, Loimaa, pp. 117–24 describes this process in one Finnish village in the 1890s. Sulkunen I 1986 *Raittius kansalaisuskontona* Historiallisia Tutkimuksia **134**, Helsinki, argues that the ideology of the later temperance movement functioned as a 'civic religion' for the working class; sobriety and civilised behaviour were certainly held aloft by the organised labour movement which took off in Finland after 1905; to that extent, it was treading in the footsteps of the earlier mass movements.

in 1870 earned a living outside service, and most of these were seamstresses and day labourers. After heated debates in the *Riksdag*, women were employed as telegraphists by the Swedish post office from the 1860s onwards, but for many years afterwards, any female employee who married was deemed automatically to have forfeited her job. As late as 1883, a woman in Denmark had her application for the post of translator in the ministry of the interior turned down on the grounds that she was married and therefore a minor (even though the law no longer recognised this distinction).

Those with no property, or fixed abode, or regular employment were also subjected to irritating or degrading controls upon their lives. Farm bailiffs continued to wield their cudgels against their underlings, and tyrannical farmers indulged their whims amongst their farmhands and dairymaids, confident that the law and tradition sanctioned such behaviour. Pehr Thomasson, himself the son of a peasant and a prodigious writer of popular literature in mid-nineteenth century Sweden, did not shrink from drawing comparisons between the slaves of the American South and the Swedish rural proletariat, describing an auction of the poor in *En arbetares lefnadsöden eller slaflifvet i Sverige* (A worker's fate, or slave life in Sweden, 1859) and ending with the emigration of his principal character, who reflects upon his homeland at the end of the book:

> I don't understand how it can be, but there must be something wrong with a government in a country where so little is done for the upbringing of the children of the poor; where young people can be maltreated at whim until they are eighteen; where one cannot worship God with one's friends without being watched over, but one can booze and swear as much as one likes; where the child cannot be the heir to its parents, where the law is implemented according to estate and property . . . where the thief is well looked after, and the honest worker allowed to die of want and hunger in the poor-house.[25]

Employers assumed the role of the traditional patriarch, providing welfare services for their employees but preventing them from subscribing to socialist newspapers or organising independently. Under the system of 'legal protection' (originally designed in the previous century to ensure a supply of farm labour and to prevent vagrancy), which was done away with from the mid-1860s onwards, workers in Sweden and Finland who left their employment without authorisation could be classified as vagrants. This was initially advantageous to the

25. Cited in Furuland L 1962 *Statare i litteraturen*, Stockholm, p. 154.

factory owner, who could thus be fairly certain of a regular workforce that could be trained, though controls upon the free movement of labour became a hindrance to expansion from mid-century onwards, and were gradually abolished. Workers might now be free to change jobs, or to move from one town to another, but they were still regarded as dependants of their employers. In Finland they were specifically disbarred from voting in local elections on these grounds. In the workplace, they lacked the most elementary forms of protection against dangerous machinery or exploitation by those in charge. Sexual harassment of female workers and rude or abusive behaviour by foremen or chargehands was a constant source of tension, often leading to walk-outs and strikes. Out of work, they had few resources and little hope of obtaining relief from a state whose guardians believed firmly that such matters fell into the private and not the public domain. The dividing-line between the middle classes and the proletariat was everywhere; on the trains and trams, in the public bath-houses, inns and eating-places, the waiting-room of the police-station, in hospitals and in the graveyard.[26]

Work in the factory and life in the town might have been dangerous and degrading, but it was probably preferable to the drudgery and poverty of rural life. Wages were generally higher, and there were fewer irksome restrictions upon the worker. Many factories provided cheap housing, medical care, education and welfare facilities, and workers were often placed on short time rather than laid off in times of trade depression. For women in particular, the factory could offer a means of achieving an independence unheard of in rural areas, in spite of low pay and the limited prospects of further occupational or social advancement.[27]

There were rather few truly industrial conurbations in northern Europe. The rapid growth of the timber-processing industry occurred in rural areas such as Norrland in Sweden and the Kymi valley in Finland. Only in four towns – Eskilstuna, Borås, Södertalje and Norrköping – did factory workers make up more than one-fifth of the population in turn-of-the-century Sweden. At the same time, a mere

26. See Sven-Erik Åström's chapter on the formation of an urban society in Rosén R et al 1956 *Helsingfors stads historia*, Helsingfors, vol. 4:2, p. 46, and the pioneering study of the emergence of a working-class in that city by Waris H 1932–4 *Työläisyhteiskunnan syntyminen Helsingin Pitkänsillan pohjoispuolella* 2 vols, Helsinki.

27. Haapala P 1986 *Tehtaan valossa. Teollistuminen ja työväestön muodostuminen Tampereella 1820–1920* Historiallisia Tutkimuksia **133**, Helsinki, offers an original interpretation of the evolution of the industrial working class in the textile and engineering town of Tampere.

10 per cent of the entire population of Finland earned its living from industry and construction.

Studies of the artisanate in Denmark and Sweden suggest that they enjoyed a considerable degree of protection, or at least sympathy, from the local authorities, and, as in other countries, were able to adapt rather well to the freeing of trades and occupations from 1846 onwards. Those making consumer goods such as bakers or tailors prospered, as did workers in the construction industry. Artisans also became wholesale or retail traders, or were able to use their skills within mechanised industrial processes. Improved communications often had a more immediate and dramatic impact on the local economy than the freeing of restrictions on trade and occupations. The opening in 1861 of the British-financed and constructed rail link between Riga and Dünaburg (which connected to St Petersburg and Warsaw) dealt a severe blow to riverborne traffic. The number of barges (*Strusen*) laden with flax and hemp which made their way annually down the Düna to Riga fell from over 1,000 in the 1850s to only 300 in the late 1860s. Abolition of the duties paid by shipping passing through the Sound, reduction of customs duties and tariffs and railway construction helped Denmark to break free of the dominance of Hamburg. Industrial communities sprang up alongside railway lines: the location in the 1860s of a steel works at Sandviken on the Gävle-Dala line transformed a deserted gravel ridge into a settlement of over 6,000 inhabitants within forty years. Above all, the railways gave access and opportunity. The Copenhagen hairdresser who was offering his services twice weekly to the citizens of Roskilde within months of the opening of the railway between the capital and this provincial town was without doubt not the only one to travel in search of business.

In the decades before the outbreak of the First World War, the Baltic provinces became one of the most advanced industrial regions of the Russian empire. This had momentous consequences for the towns, especially those with a concentration of industries, such as Narva, Reval and Riga, where the growth of the working class also affected the ethnic composition of the population. Riga's economy in 1861 was still contained within the parameters of the medieval Hanseatic town, and it was to all intents and purposes a German town with sizeable Russian and Latvian minorities. Trade and commerce were supervised by the gilds, which also shared political power with the city magistracy. Exports continued to exceed imports; only half of the ships arriving at the port between 1866 and 1870 were carrying goods – the remainder were in ballast. Riga's principal export commodities remained essentially the same as in former centuries, and there was some resistance to efforts to abandon entirely the restrictive quality controls on flax and hemp.

The coming of the railways marked a significant change. Riga's trade suffered something of a setback during the 1880s, but there was a major upsurge of economic activity in the last decade of the century which carried it into the industrial era. The factory workforce quadrupled between 1874 and 1900. The textile industry was no longer the major employer; engineering workshops, sawmilling, rubber and chemical factories dominated the eastern quarters of the city. Between 1867 and 1897, the population of the city more than doubled, from 102,590 to 269,001. Latvian speakers now constituted 41 per cent, as against 23 per cent of the inhabitants in 1867, and were beginning to establish themselves as shopkeepers, foremen and charge hands, and in the professions. The Baltic Germans' share of the population had declined from 42 to 25 per cent, though they still maintained a strong grip on the levers of commerce and industry. Of 37 firms with an annual turnover of half-a-million roubles or more in 1900, 31 were owned by Baltic Germans, who also controlled the three big banks in the city. Baltic German entrepreneurs also played an active role elsewhere in the Russian empire, and had close links with the stock exchange and banking circles in St Petersburg. One of the largest enterprises in the city, the Russia Baltic Wagon Company, originally established by a Reich German firm, was taken over in 1900 by a consortium of Riga and St Petersburg industrialists. Trade and industry brought the old Hanse city into ever closer contact with the rest of the empire, 'enfeebling the feeling for life's ideals' in the eyes of those who struggled to maintain Baltic German exclusivity against the encroachment of the outside world, but also creating opportunities for those seeking professional advancement or a business fortune.[28]

St Petersburg was also a major industrial city, attracting large numbers from the countryside to its engineering works and textile mills; but even more were employed in service and (during the summer months) in the construction industry. The Russian capital was a huge sieve of humankind, a city of comers and goers. Great numbers of peasants flooded into the city in summer to work on building sites; equally large numbers (many engaged in seasonal work such as

28. The quotation is from Julius Eckardt's memoirs, cited in Henriksson A 1983 *The tsar's most loyal Germans*, Boulder, p. 81. In addition to this detailed study, there is much information on Riga's development in: Lenz W 1954 *Die Entwicklung Rigas zur Grossstadt* Marburger Ostforschungen **2**, Kitzingen. On developments in Estonia, see Pullat R 1972 *Eesti linnad ja linlased*, Tallinn.

tailoring) left to work in the fields. In spite of its 'peasant' character, however, the city did contain a growing number of experienced, skilled factory workers, and a flourishing artisanal sector, which was to play an important role in the development of the labour movement.[29]

Slowly, work ceased to be determined by the seasons and the weather, limited or curtailed by technological inadequacies, and performed by a labour force subject to a multiplicity of regulations. As the land reforms had transformed the rural scene, so did the rise of mechanised industrial production erode the old contours of corporate society. Remnants of the old structure still survived; mental attitudes were also slow to change, especially where ancient privileges and rights were threatened. Rural workers continued to receive much of their income in the form of lodgings, food or grazing land; the absence of shops, inns or commercial amusements in the sparsely-populated countryside meant that their few pennies tended to remain in their pockets or purses. Workers on the railways, in the foundries, mills and factories, on building sites and in workshops, on the other hand, were generally paid a money wage from which they were expected to provide for themselves and their dependants. The living standards of working-class wage earners were by no means always as rosy as those of the millgirl who got her wages from the big house on Friday and was able to buy sugar and syrup, coffee and cakes on Saturday in order to give her young man a treat on Sunday: but the *possibilities* which lay before the wage-earner in a town full of shops and places of entertainment were not even available to the farmhand in remote up-country districts.[30]

Writing on the eve of the great famine which afflicted Finland in the late 1860s, a Finnish patriot lamented the fact that 'honest poverty' was no longer feared or respected by many of his compatriots, who preferred to idle their time away enjoying fine wines and the latest fashions. His exhortations to remember that Finland had been made fit for cultivation by blood, sweat and hunger were no doubt apt in the context, but in vain as a remedy. The future, as the more prescient J. V. Snellman well knew, lay in the production of manufactured

29. McKean R 1990 *St. Petersburg between the revolutions. Workers and revolutionaries, June 1907–February 1917*, New Haven and London, pp. 14–29.

30. The poem about the millgirl is quoted in Haapala 1986, p. 40. The simple country hick bowled over by the wonders of urban consumerism is a common character in late nineteenth-century literature. Eventually, the mail order catalogue provided some consolation, though for the very poor, it remained a fairytale book, as H F Spak discovered when investigating the circumstances of the rural proletariat in Sweden in the early twentieth century: Furuland 1962, p. 199.

goods and trade, not honest, back-breaking toil to produce a meagre crop of rye or oats.[31] It is the unbound Prometheus of mechanised mass production which has transformed the world, for better or for ill: and the millgirl who bought ribbons to adorn her hair, or the farmer's boy who bought a pair of factory-made boots or an umbrella (all the rage in rural Sweden at the end of the century) were innocent participators in the greatest revolution of the modern age – the consumer revolution.

31. M(eurman) A 1866 Warallisuus ja yleinen talous Suomessa *Kirjallinen Kuukauslehti*, p. 103. For Snellman's views, see Myllyntaus T 1991 *Electrifying Finland. The transfer of a new technology into a late industrialisng economy* Helsinki, pp. 60–1.

CHAPTER SIX

The Age of Imperialism, 1871–1905

THREATENED PERIPHERIES

Reflecting on the progress made by nationalist movements at the end of a long career spent advancing the cause of Finnishness, Johan Vilhelm Snellman observed sadly that:

> many dangers threaten the nationality of small nations. Experience shows that free institutions do not lessen the injustice and violence of ruling nations. Look at the English in Ireland, the Germans in Posen, and in Slesvig. In Alsace-Lorraine, they have proceeded more gently, but the goal is still the same; assimilation, pitiless assimilation.[1]

That day of reckoning had not yet come to Finland, though Snellman clearly believed it would not be long delayed. Snellman was correct in his gloomy prognostication; the harmonious image of loyal subjects ruled over by local bureaucrats under the benevolent sceptre of the emperor-grand duke was fading, and the strident notes of Russian national self-assertiveness were beginning to sound more powerful and ominous. The ground upon which it had been possible for decades to co-exist amicably was rapidly shrinking, and the differences and conflicting interests which had hitherto lain dormant or had been masked by bureaucratic lethargy or guile now began to

1. The article appeared in *Morgonbladet* on 31 December 1880. The Finnish translation is in Snellman J 1930 *Kootut teokset*, Porvoo, vol. 7, p. 543.

emerge. But the reasons for the attacks on regional self-rule and the policies adopted by the imperial powers were by no means consistent or even coherent, any more than were the responses of those living in the regions under attack.[2]

The adoption and enforcement of measures designed to produce a degree of uniformity and a closer liaison between central authority and the regions invariably encountered opposition and resentment, even when there was general support for the national ideals that central power claimed to represent and uphold. That Prussia was the only power capable of uniting Germany was widely accepted amongst Protestant north Germans, especially businessmen and entrepreneurs. But a willingness to accept German unification under Prussian leadership was one thing; facing up to the consequences, such as increased defence burdens and higher taxes, was quite another. The pretensions of local princelings invariably did not accord with Bismarck's designs, and loyalties to these petty potentates were still anything but residual. As the *Oldenburger Zeitung* put it on the occasion of the visit of King Wilhelm of Prussia to the Grand Duchy in June 1869, the Oldenburgers had acknowledged the creation of a North German Federation 'more as the result of judicious reflection than as an emotional matter. . . . We are by conviction national, but by inclination particularist'.[3]

In the duchies of Slesvig, Holstein and Lauenburg, centuries of particularism were swept into oblivion by the Prussian state; the Provinz Schleswig-Holstein retained few traces of the ancient judicial and administrative institutions. With the ideals of the *Helstat* now irredeemably shattered, the aristocracy transferred their allegiance to their new monarch. The anti-Prussian sentiments of the German-speaking population as a whole, however, helped turn Schleswig-Holstein into one of the bastions of oppositional progressive liberalism in the Reich. German nationalism was given a sharper edge here than in other small north German states drawn into the Reich by the

2. Or the understanding of the outside world: Jules Verne's novel *Un drame en Livonie*, published in 1904, says more about the author's anti-German prejudices (and the Franco-Russian alliance) than it does about the true state of affairs in Livland. For an interesting study of the way in which other considerations coloured the attitude of the British towards Finland, see Maude G 1973 The Finnish question in British political life, 1899–1914 *Turun Historiallinen Arkisto* **28**: 325–44.

3. Cited in Schwarz P 1979 *Nationale und soziale Bewegung in Oldenburg im Jahrzehnt vor der Reichsgründung*, Oldenburg, p. 70.

continuing problem of the Danish minority in the northern parishes. It was from the ranks of the lesser officials that demands for a hard-line policy emanated, according to Oswald Hauser; at the highest level, the traditions of patriarchal even-handedness still acted as a moderating influence, and foreign policy considerations could also play a part. The perceived need for better relations with the Scandinavian countries after 1905 led to a relaxation of the German government's position with regard to the descendants of those who had opted for Danish nationality so as to avoid conscription into the Prussian armed forces, for example. Such gestures merely angered the German nationalists, whilst failing to appease the Danish minority, which – with ample support from across the border – had developed a unity and sense of purpose in the face of the assimilationist policies of the Prussian state authorities.

The circumstances of that minority were in several respects unpropitious. Danish as a spoken language had been steadily losing ground in Slesvig for decades, and was essentially confined to the rural areas in the northern half of the duchy. The loss of thousands of young men, who moved across the frontier into Denmark rather than be conscripted into the Prussian army, and the high level of emigration from the region in general further reduced numbers: population increase in North Slesvig between 1867 and 1910 was a mere 8 per cent, compared with 63 per cent in Prussia and 51 per cent in Denmark. Representatives of the Danish minority elected to the Prussian *Landtag* were prevented from taking their seats because they refused to take the oath of loyalty. Schools in the towns were rapidly germanised. Rødding folk high school moved north across the border to Askov, but others were closed. Six hours' teaching a week in German were stipulated for schools in Danish-speaking rural districts in 1871. Seven years later, German was given equal status with Danish, and in 1888 made the sole language of instruction with exceptions made for the teaching of religious knowledge and introductory courses for children without the language.

This onslaught of germanisation and the dashing of lingering hopes that the Prussian state might be persuaded to agree to hold a plebiscite in North Slesvig united the Danish minority as nothing else had done. An impressive network of clubs and associations was set up to coordinate and direct educational, cultural and political activities. The school association, founded in 1892, sponsored the further education of over 6,000 youngsters at Danish secondary or folk high schools before the outbreak of war in 1914. During the same period, some fifty assembly halls had been built by the electoral association, of which H. P. Hanssen was the leading spirit. *Fyrretyve Fortællinger af*

Fædrelandets Historie, patriotic tales written by A. D. Jørgensen and financed by the founder of the Carlsberg brewery, ran through six impressions and 46,000 copies, mostly for distribution in North Slesvig via the language association. The non-participatory policies of the 1870s were gradually abandoned; more and more young men stayed and performed their military service, and the elected representatives of the Danish minority dropped their opposition to swearing the oath of loyalty, thus assuring them of a forum in the Prussian *Landtag*.

The Danish minority had need of a spokesman of Hanssen's calibre to meet the challenge of German officialdom. The most notorious of these officials was the Pomeranian Junker who served as *Oberpräsident* of the province between 1898 and 1901, Ernst Matthias von Köller. With the full backing of the Emperor Wilhelm II ('In my house, I have the right to defend my rights and to chuck out any blackguard (*Schubjack*)' is a typical example of the Kaiser's attitude), Köller expelled Danish citizens deemed to be politically active in the province and threatened further expulsions if the sending of young people to study in Denmark did not cease.

Köller's hard-line policy was abandoned soon after his departure for Alsace-Lorraine, partly in order to repair relations with Denmark, but more importantly, because it had exacerbated the general shortage of labour in the region and pushed up wage levels. The economic dimension is crucial in any understanding of the success of the Danish minority in holding out against official pressures. The relative stagnation of the urban economy in North Slesvig deprived German nationalism of a dynamic base; although there were pro-German associations such as the *Deutsche Verein für das nördliche Schleswig*, they were never able to match the rural-based Danish movement, which rested upon a solid base of prosperous farmers. According to one Danish activist, over three-quarters of the farms of North Slesvig in 1893 were owned by Danish-minded farmers. Their position was not, however, completely secure. Many were elderly, their farming methods often old-fashioned and ill-suited to cope with the agricultural depression, and migration had also taken its toll. Here, as in the eastern provinces, German officialdom promoted attempts to buy up land for redistribution to German settlers. The Danes, like the Poles, responded with organisations to provide funds for struggling farmers and even to buy up farms which were resold on favourable terms to young Danish-minded farmers. A measure which would have given the German state the right to pre-emptive purchase in 'nationally threatened' areas was abandoned on the outbreak of war, when Danish-minded farmers still owned as much land as they had twenty-five years earlier.[4]

Prussian officialdom met with equally tenacious and resourceful resistance from the far more numerous Polish population of the eastern provinces. The policies of the Prussian government, endorsed by the *Landtag* in the 1870s, were intended to bring to heel a people described by Bismarck as subjects at twenty-four hours' notice, ready at any time to revolt. Hundreds of Catholic priests who refused to submit to government controls in accordance with the laws of 1872 were deprived of their posts, and many were jailed. A series of decrees in 1873–74 made German the language of instruction in all schools in the province of Posen; Polish was to be used only for religious instruction and to teach young children German. In 1879, German was made the sole permissible language in public administration and in the courts. Bismarck's successor as Prussian minister-president and German chancellor, Count Caprivi, adopted a milder attitude towards the Poles; this merely served to enrage German nationalist opinion. After hearing the ex-chancellor denounce Caprivi's policies, a group of Junkers from the eastern provinces founded an association for the advancement of the German cause in the eastern marches, known from 1899 as the *Ostmarkenverein* (its supporters were known more popularly as the *Hakatisten*, after the initials of the three principal leaders). With 48,000 members by 1913, the *Ostmarkenverein* exercised considerable influence in German politics, though it frequently clashed with rival nationalist organisations such as the Farmers' League (whom the *Hakatisten* accused of employing cheap Polish labour in the eastern marches) and it annoyed the more traditional-minded conservatives.[5]

As in North Slesvig, economic circumstances helped shape the contours and outcome of the conflict; it was the inability of German landowners in the eastern marches to stem the flight from the land to the cities and factories of the west that ultimately weakened the German cause. The efforts of the colonisation commission, which could claim in 1908 to have settled almost 14,000 German colonists and their families, did little to alter the situation. The real beneficiaries

4. Hauser O 1960 *Preussische Staatsräson und nationale Gedanke* Quellen und Forschungen zur Geschichte Schleswig-Holsteins **42**, Neumünster; Hauser O 1961 Obrigkeitsstaat und demokratische Prinzip im Nationalitätenkampf. Preussen in Nordschleswig *Historische Zeitschrift* **192**: 318–61; Rerup L 1982 *Slesvig og Holsten efter 1830*, Copenhagen, are amongst the most recent works on Prussian policy and the Danish minority's reaction.

5. Hagen W 1980 *Germans, Poles and Jews. The nationality conflict in the Prussian east, 1772–1914*, Chicago, p. 267, concludes that germanisation in the eastern provinces was not simply the consequence of lobbying by the *Ostmarkenverein*, 'but flowed from the heart of Prussian monarchical conservatism as Bismarck and his allies had refashioned it'.

in the eastern provinces after 1890 were the peasant farmers, able to obtain reasonable credit from cooperatives and banks in order to obtain the farm machinery and artificial fertilisers which revolutionised farming in the region, and to sell their produce at good prices in a booming market. The large estate-owners were tempted to sell up to liquidate the debts incurred during the years of agricultural depression; the percentage of land farmed in units of more than 100 hectares declined from 58.5 per cent in 1882 to 40 per cent in 1907. There was little change in the proportions of German and Polish farmers, which would suggest that the numbers of farms created for Poles by their self-help organisations kept pace with the activities of the colonisation commission. Poles also moved into the commercial sector, as the traditionally dominant Jewish entrepreneurs sold up or migrated westward.

The policies of the Prussian state antagonised the Polish population and provided welcome grist to the mills of politicians. The national democratic movement of Roman Dmowski began to make headway in Posen, overturning the clerical-conservative monopoly of Polish seats in the 1903 *Reichstag* elections and capturing control of the gymnastics movement *Sokół,* and the Polish trade unions. The school strike movement launched in 1901 as a protest against German-language teaching involved thousands in a new style of activist politics, for which the cautious Catholic hierarchy and its supporters were poorly suited. A sense of Polish pride even spread to the Masurian and Kashubian minorities in the province of Prussia. The Polish reaction, nevertheless, was also tempered by awareness of greater oppression across the eastern frontier; the fear of a Russian invasion was as great amongst Poles as it was amongst Germans in the eastern provinces, and the Polish deputies in the *Reichstag* voted without hesitation for war credits on the outbreak of hostilities in August 1914. The more openly insurrectionist Polish Socialist Party (PPS) enjoyed little support amongst the Poles in Prussia, where clerical conservatism retained a powerful influence to the end.

The Lithuanian minority on the easternmost frontier of Prussia was also affected by government educational policies, though the natural processes of linguistic assimilation had been at work here for decades. Lacking natural leadership or traditions of independence, divided from their fellows across the frontier by religion and custom, this rapidly dwindling linguistic minority (from 118,000 in 1890 down to 94,000 twenty years later) nevertheless provided invaluable assistance for the Lithuanian cause. The Lithuanian seminary of the university of Königsberg was founded in 1718 to provide language teaching for pastors intending to work in Lithuanian-speaking parishes. Its director in the early decades of the nineteenth century, Professor Ludwig Rhesa, was a seminal figure in the development of the literary language, and his work was carried on by his pupil, Friedrich Kurschat. The first Lithuanian-language newspapers were published in Prussia in the 1850s, and a Lithuanian Literary Society was founded in Tilsit in 1879. Prussian printing presses enabled the Lithuanians in the Russian empire to combat the ban on literature in the Latin script, imposed after the 1863 uprising; thousands of books, and for a brief period, the nationalist newspaper *Aušra*, were smuggled across the frontier.

The paradox of inspiration and support emanating from a community which was itself in the process of being assimilated, and which never became a centre of the national movement, may partly be explained by the fact that Lithuanian identity in Prussia was essentially linguistic, not historical. The language and customs of a small minority on the remote eastern frontier were not regarded as a major threat to the Prussian state, particularly as the Protestant Lithuanians were loyal subjects with no separatist tendencies. A sense of national identity based on claims of language and ethnicity rather than on historical antecedents developed more vigorously amongst exiles and emigrants in the United States and elsewhere than in the *gubernii* of Kovno and Vilna. The experience of emigration to a strange land tended to strengthen linguistic affinities and identity and weaken the sense of a common historical fate which had emotionally bound many Lithuanians to the cause of Polish nationhood. Similarly, young Lithuanians who fell under the spell of radical new ideas during their years of study in the universities of the empire or in western Europe often broke with the church and the polonophile leadership of the Catholic hierarchy. Jonas Basanavičius, who claimed to have been influenced during his student days in Moscow by the Latvian nationalist leader Krišjānis Valdemārs, sought to replace the polonophile vision of the past by emphasising the glories of the pagan medieval Lithuanian state in the pages of *Aušra*. This earned him the enmity of the church hierarchy, who smelt the whiff of Orthodoxy or godlessness in anything that challenged their authority. The vital role of the Catholic church in the resistance to imperial Russian policies was, however, something which the secular nationalists could not ignore, however much they disliked the polonophile inclinations of the hierarchy. The towns, with their polonised middle and upper classes and large Jewish populations, were infertile ground for the Lithuanian nationalist movement, though it did establish itself in the grammar schools of a number of towns in Samogitia and in the seminary for elementary schoolteachers at Veiveriai in the Suwałki region.

The Russian authorities had tried to detach the peasantry from the Polish landlords by a generous measure of emancipation in 1863. Weakened numerically by deportations and exile, the Polish landowners nevertheless retained control of most of the large estates in Kovno and Vilna *gubernii*; and although a prosperous class of independent Lithuanian farmers began slowly to emerge, the persecution of their faith linked the two groups together. The cyrillisation of the Lithuanian printed word, intended as a first step on the way to restoring the Lithuanians to the fold of Russian Orthodoxy from which they had supposedly been seduced by Polish Papists three hundred or so years before, symbolised that persecution. Far from winning back the Lithuanians, it made them cling more fiercely to their church, and probably generated an active unwillingness to have anything to do with things Russian. Given the fraught state of affairs in the Lithuanian lands after 1864, it is unlikely that the Russians would have considered a more moderate or conciliatory policy which might have persuaded the Lithuanians to view more favourably the 'Russian' option. The economic backwardness of the region, moreover, precluded the kind of everyday contact which might have favoured natural or pragmatic assimilation. Ironically, the one section of the population of which a significant element wished to become assimilated Russians were denied this wish at almost every turn, and were beaten and discriminated against for being what they were. The Jews added another dimension to what Lev Rosenberg emphatically categorised as the 'purely historical-political concept' of Lithuania, constituting almost half of the urban population of the *gubernii* of Kovno, Vilna and Grodno according to the census of 1897, with their own intensely rich yet separate cultural life.[6]

As we have seen, the first generation of Estonian and Latvian nationalists was favourably disposed towards a greater integration of their people into the mainstream of imperial Russia, partly for economic reasons, but principally in order to destroy Baltic German hegemony. The Estonian radicals were largely responsible for drafting the mass petition of 1881 which called for further land reforms in the peasants' favour; the introduction of *zemstvo* institutions into the provinces, with equal representation for Estonians and Baltic Germans;

6. Rosenberg L 1918 *Die Juden in Litauen*, Berlin, p. 17. See also Frankel J 1981 *Prophecy and politics. Socialism, nationalism and the Russian Jews, 1862–1917*, New York/Cambridge on Jewish assimilationist hopes.

the removal of elementary education from the control of the Baltic German landowners and greater emphasis on the teaching of Russian in the schools; the introduction of Russian police and judicial institutions and the appointment by central government of justices of the peace. Great things were expected of N. M. Manasein's senatorial inspection tour of Kurland and Estland in 1882–83, and the senator was bombarded with petitions based on the demands of the 1881 programme. A significant part of his brief was to enquire into what progress had been made towards implementing reforms set in motion already in the 1860s, and his extensive report constituted the point of departure for the policies pursued in the reign of Alexander III.[7]

The measures implemented over the next decade certainly weakened the grip of the Baltic German landowning class, but did little to improve efficiency, partiality or good government. Many of the justices appointed by central government were incompetent, ignorant of local conditions, or simply corrupt. Deprived of control over the elementary education system, the Baltic Germans closed the teacher-training seminaries and refused to be drawn back into cooperation by the administration, which privately admitted it was unlikely to be able to maintain the standards achieved by the voluntary system established by the *Ritterschaften*. Teachers unable to acquire the necessary proficiency in Russian lost their jobs. In Livland, school attendance figures declined from 117,568 in 1886 to 93,241 in 1904, whilst the number of elementary schools was reduced by 123 over the same period. A new wave of conversions in the 1880s and immigration from the Russian lands substantially increased the size of the Orthodox community, which was now much better organised and supported. The Lutheran church was restricted in its activities and placed under closer governmental supervision. Unable to bridge the gap separating it from the indigenous peoples and with its underpinnings of exclusivity, autonomy and privilege grievously eroded, the church was ill-adapted to respond to change and entered an acute crisis at the end of the century.[8]

7. For the context and scope of Manasein's inspection, see: Thaden E (ed.) 1981 *Russification in the Baltic provinces and Finland, 1855–1914*, Princeton, NJ, pp. 56–67, 153–4, 229–34.

8. The Estonian writer Friedebert Tuglas, recalling his own childhood, claimed that parents wanted their children to learn the language of the empire in order to better themselves, but that very few got beyond even the basics. Tuglas F 1960 *Mälestused*, Tallinn, pp. 68–71. On the travails of the church, see: Garve H 1978 *Konfession und Nationalität. Ein Beitrag zum Verhältnis von Kirche und Gesellschaft in Livland im 19. Jahrhundert* Wissenschaftliche Beiträge zur Geschichte und Landeskunde Ost-Mitteleuropas **110**, Marburg. Thaden (ed.) 1981, pp. 161–7.

The structures of local particularism and social exclusivity of the Baltic provinces were weakened as much by economic change and the consequent regional and social mobility as by the efforts of the Russian authorities. Behind the polemical outpourings of the *literati* and the grim motto of '*ausharren*', sticking it out, the ranks were beginning to break. Many Riga Germans prospered as a result of the industrial expansion of the city, which brought them into close contact with business and professional circles elsewhere in the empire. The Germans in the city also proved rather adept at getting round the irksome obligation to use Russian on all official business, and were able to maintain political control of the municipality by judicious alliances across national lines. A considerable portion of the aristocracy had 'russified' branches. In only thirty of the 104 matriculated noble families of Estland was there no marriage with a Russian between 1860 and 1914, and in some leading families such as the Benckendorffs and Knorrings, over half of the marriages during this period were mixed. The tradition of service in the empire was also strong amongst the nobility, creating conflicts of loyalty and tension when the pressure to demolish the particularist institutions of the Baltic provinces was at its height. It was the intelligentsia who suffered most from the policies of the imperial government, which obliged them to use Russian and observe Russian practices. Within a year of the introduction of the reforms to the judiciary and legal system in 1889, only one of the twenty-seven judges assigned to the Riga district court was German, for example, and the voluntary or forced closure of German-language secondary schools and the russification of the university of Dorpat put a number of teachers out of work. The ranks of the clergy were diluted by the appointment of non-Germans, who constituted one-third of the ministry in Livland by 1904, and who were beginning to raise demands for a people's church, separated from the *Herrenkirche* of the German minority. There was a steady stream of emigrants to Germany from the 1860s onwards; over seventy professorial chairs in the Reich were filled by Baltic Germans in 1914.[9]

Imperial Germany, however, offered little encouragement or inspiration to the Baltic Germans, who were distrustful of Bismarckian ambitions and alarmed by the rise of socialism in the Reich. Battered

9. Henriksson A 1983 *The tsar's most loyal Germans*, Boulder, p. 45 *passim*. Schlingensiepen G 1959 *Der Strukturwandel des Baltischen Adels in der Zeit vor dem ersten Weltkrieg* Wissenschaftliche Beiträge zur Geschichte und Landeskunde Ost-Mitteleuropas **41**, Marburg.

and hurt as they were by the policies of a regime they had faithfully served for decades, they nevertheless remained loyal to the tsar as the upholder of a conservative order and tradition to which they were wedded. The doors to the inner councils of the empire were never closed to them; and in the aftermath of revolution in 1905–06, their value as stout defenders of the conservative order was again recognised by tsarism. Although the noble corporations gave up their exclusive right to own the large estates (*Rittergüter*) in the 1860s, they still retained considerable privileges to the very end of empire, and possessed by far the greatest share of the agricultural land in all three provinces.[10] Baltic Germans were heavily involved in the commercial life of the provinces. The three big banks in Riga were all founded and managed by local Germans, and they invested extensively throughout the empire. Riga Germans put up the initial capital for railway construction and procured foreign investment; they were active promoters of the Riga Steamship Company and financed the expanding industries of the city, such as sawmilling, tobacco- and food-processing. Of thirty-seven Riga firms with an annual turnover of more than half-a-million roubles in 1900, thirty-one were German-owned. Germans also continued to dominate the top echelons of public life and the professions, and were able to maintain control of many municipal governments up to the end of empire.

For the Estonians and Latvians, the reforms instituted by imperial rescript were a mixed blessing. Some doors opened, certainly: significant numbers of Latvians and Estonians found employment in state service, and the concessions made by the *Ritterschaften* (commutation of labour rents and sale of land to the peasants) helped create an independent farm-owning peasantry. Estonians and Latvians were also drawn into the expanding local economy as industrial workers, small shopkeepers, or white-collar workers. But many felt obliged to move elsewhere in search of job opportunities or career advancement. Andrejs Pumpurs complained in 1903 that, without a fatherland or national rights, poor, often unemployed, the young Latvian had to seek work in Russia, and a year later, the Riga Latvian

10. Fifty-eight per cent of agricultural land in the newly-independent state of Estonia, 48 per cent in Latvia, according to: Rauch G von 1970 *The Baltic States. The years of independence*, London, p. 87. Different perspectives on the status and role of the Baltic Germans are offered by: Rothfels H 1944 The Baltic provinces: some historical aspects and perspectives *Journal of Central European Affairs* **4**: 117–46. Kroeger G 1968 Zur Situation der baltischen Deutschen um die Jahrhundertwende *Zeitschrift für Ostforschung* **17**: 601–32. Pistohlkors G von 1972 Führende Schicht oder nationale Minderheit? *Zeitschrift für Ostforschung* **21**: 601–18.

Association claimed that over a quarter of a million Latvian speakers had left the provinces since 1860.[11] Many farmers who bought the title to their land struggled with repayments; fewer than 10 per cent of Estonian farmers were free of debts at the end of the century, and many were forced to sell up and join the growing ranks of the landless.

In the three-cornered struggle – central authority vs. traditional elite minority vs. aspiring autochthonous majority – there emerged no clear winner, nor any clearly-defined concept or vision of a future order for the Baltic provinces, beyond the abortive schemes of the 1860s for reform and the idea of a redivision of the three historic provinces along ethnic lines. The self-government accorded to Finland by Alexander I, on the other hand, was considerably extended during the reign of Alexander II. The four-estate *Lantdag* met regularly after 1863. The leading spokesman of Finnish nationalism, J. V. Snellman, was appointed to the Senate, and was largely instrumental in carrying through the reform of 1865–66, which gave Finland its own currency and bank. The structure of local government was remodelled in 1865, following the Swedish example (though without the regional tier of representation, the *Landsting*, which was being created in Sweden at this time). Separated from its local administrative functions, the church also lost directive control over education in 1869, when a new church law was passed and a central board of education created. The *Lantdag* of 1877–78 abolished the last restrictions on freedom of occupation and introduced equal rights of inheritance for men and women. It also created a Finnish army of 5,600 men selected by lottery; those not called to the colours for the three-year period were obliged to undergo summer-time training as a reserve force.

The most contentious issue in Finnish political life during the period was the language question. The emperor issued an edict in 1863 which obliged officials and the courts henceforth to accept documents and papers in Finnish; within twenty years, all functionaries were to use Finnish in their written communications with speakers of that language. For the Finnish nationalist movement, growing in numbers and confidence, this was merely the first stage on the road to the total replacement of Swedish as the language of the nation. The principal arena of conflict over the next two decades was education, as

11. Walters M 1923 *Lettland. Seine Entwicklung zum Staat und die baltischen Fragen*, Rome, p. 265. Plakans A 1974 Peasants, intellectuals and nationalism in the Russian Baltic provinces *Journal of Modern History* **46**: 445–75, estimates that 40–50 per cent of qualified Latvians were obliged to emigrate in search of work between 1860 and 1900.

the Finnish nationalists fought to establish provision for teaching in Finnish at secondary-school level. By 1886, when a second imperial edict ordered the Senate to make regulations to bring about the equal status of the two languages in all official business, the battle was beginning to turn in favour of the majority party. Whereas only three secondary schools had Finnish as the language of instruction in the mid-1870s, eighteen of the fifty-one state schools and fourteen of the forty-three private schools a decade later were Finnish-language. Two-thirds of the matriculated students in the academic year 1905–06 were Finnish speakers, as against only a quarter a generation earlier, whilst the balance between the two languages in the numbers of secondary schools was beginning to approximate to the proportions in the population as a whole.[12]

It is worth noting that the use of Russian remained largely confined to the channels of communication between Finland and St Petersburg. In comparison with the Baltic provinces, let alone the other western borderlands of the Russian empire, the limited degree of Russian involvement in the affairs of Finland (or Finnish participation in the affairs of the empire) seems remarkable. As Johannes Gripenberg, a member of the committee for Finnish affairs in St Petersburg, observed in 1889:

> It would seem as if Russian statesmen have only just woken up to the fact that they are now faced with a quite new and remarkable phenomenon which has grown and matured silently whilst their predecessors were either sleeping the sleep of indifference or were looking the other way. They are surprised and annoyed to see that small embryonic state which Alexander at the stormy dawn of the century hastily created 'somewhere the other side of Viborg' now grown into an autonomous state within the course of three-quarters of a century, and possessing all the attributes of such a state in more or less fully developed order.[13]

The 'February manifesto' issued by Nicholas II ten years later, which enunciated the principle that local laws were subordinate to general imperial laws, was seen as a bolt from out of the blue by Finnish public opinion. It had been evident for some time, however,

12. Kiuasmaa K 1982 *Oppikoulu 1880–1980*, Oulu, pp. 21–97. It was the children of the urban middle classes who filled the school benches of the *lyceum/lyseo* or *realskola/reaalikoulu*; farmers tended to send their children to local private co-educational schools. On the campaign for Finnish-language secondary schools, see: Rommi P 1973 Fennomannien 'liikekannallepano' 1870-luvulla *Turun Historiallinen Arkisto* **28**: 253–89.

13. Cited in: Kirby D 1975 *Finland and Russia 1808–1920*, London, pp. 70–1.

that the hitherto benign relationship was about to change to the detriment of Finland's constitutional situation, as perceived on the Finnish side. There had been extensive skirmishing in print on this issue during the reign of Alexander III. The constitutional arguments advanced by Finnish campaigners such as Leo Mechelin and J. R. Danielson-Kalmari may have been less than watertight, but they did serve to provide a strong line of defence which could unite Finns across the language divide once the 'era of oppression' arrived.[14]

The personification of Russian oppression in Finnish eyes was the governor-general Nikolay Ivanovich Bobrikov, appointed in 1898 and sent to an untimely grave in 1904 by the bullets fired by a patriotic upper-class Finn (who then turned his pistol upon himself). Tuomo Polvinen's biography of Bobrikov reveals him to have been a corrupt, elderly military bureaucrat who had been passed over in the career stakes, but still entertained hopes of higher things: an unimaginative man, wrestling with inadequate resources (even having to type his own letters for lack of qualified staff), baffled by the Finns, and increasingly at odds with his main rival in St Petersburg, V. K. Plehve.[15] The disbanding of most of the Finnish army from 1901 and the proposed conscription of Finns into the imperial Russian forces gave the Finnish opposition an ideal issue on which it could fight. Fewer than half of those called up appeared before the draft boards in the spring of 1902. Although the number of absentees fell in the subsequent drafts of 1903 and 1904, the military conscription decree was suspended in March 1905, and eventually replaced by an annual financial levy as the Finnish contribution to imperial defences. Whereas the 1900 decree ordering the gradual introduction of Russian as the principal language of state in the Finnish administration had no immediate impact on the population, the drafting of young men for service anywhere in the empire did. The 1901 military service law affected others besides the draftees. Clergymen were required to read the law from the pulpit to their congregations, and doctors and clerks

14. The historiography and background of the February manifesto is crisply and concisely dealt with by: Jussila O 1984 The historical background of the February manifesto of 1899 *Journal of Baltic Studies* **15**: 141–7. In the same issue, see also: Schweitzer R The Baltic parallel: reality or historical myth? The influence of the tsarist government's experience in the Baltic provinces on its Finnish policy, pp. 195–215. The first 'era of oppression' (*sortokausi/ofärdsår*), another as yet hardly challenged creation of Finnish national history, covers the period 1899–1905.

15. Von Plehve was minister state-secretary for Finland (1899–1904) and minister of the interior from 1902 until he too was blown to smithereens by assassins. Polvinen T 1984 *Valtakunta ja rajamaa – N. I. Bobrikov Suomen kenraalikuvernöörina 1898–1904*, Porvoo.

were obliged to serve on draft boards. Opinion over the law was divided in Finland. The more conservative elements of the Finnish nationalist movement counselled compliance with the wishes of higher authority (with whom certain elements believed it was still possible to negotiate) and voiced their suspicions of the constitutionalist opposition, in which a section of the Finnish party was deemed to have become a mere appendage of 'the most intransigent Vikings' of the Swedish party. That opposition, which created a national organisation for the promotion of a campaign of passive resistance, was also internally divided, and a falange of younger activists broke away in 1903–04 to form closer ties with the Russian revolutionary movement and to engage in direct action against agents of the oppression.[16]

It is clear that the policies embarked upon by imperial officials in Russia and Germany were inspired at least in part by a wish to impose uniformity and a greater degree of central control over peripheral regions. They also reflected a rising spirit of nationalism which was no longer tolerant of regional particularism. National minorities had to be made into 'good and willing' citizens, as the minister of the interior told the Poles in the Prussian chamber of deputies in 1904 (or more bluntly, in the words of the conservative Count Westarp, 'the Poles are Prussian citizens (*Staatsangehörige*), and since they are Prussian citizens, they are also German citizens. . . . They do not have the right to speak of a special Polish nationality').[17] The rule of the German nobility in the Baltic provinces was a 'complete anomaly, of a kind which had never existed in Europe' according to K. P. Pobedonostsev, procurator of the Russian Synod, echoing a view commonly expressed by an earlier generation of Panslavists.[18]

Nevertheless, there were wide inconsistencies in these policies, usually carried out by one particular ministry or group with little coordination or adherence to a generally applicable line of conduct. Not infrequently the principal local representative of central authority adopted an ambivalent or even critical attitude towards the policies he was required to carry out. Oswald Hauser has suggested that even the infamous von Köller was more moderate than is generally thought,

16. Kirby 1975, pp. 76–102, for a selection of documents illustrating various aspects of this period, and Kirby D 1979 *Finland in the twentieth century*, London, pp. 25–9 for a brief summary and analysis of events. See also: Huxley S 1990 *Constitutional insurgency in Finland* Studia Historica **38**, Helsinki. The consequences of the 'era of oppression' will be examined in more detail in Chapter eight.

17. Hauser 1960, p. 177, and Hauser O 1961, p. 342.

18. See: Eine Unterredung mit Konstantin Pobjedenosjew im Jahre 1885 *Baltische Monatsschrift* **59** (1905): p. 159, and Thaden (ed.) 1981, pp. 34–8, 124–33.

and was under considerable pressure from the Kaiser and local German opinion to adopt much tougher policies. M. A. Zinov'ev, governor of Livland at the height of the imperial onslaught on local institutions (1885–95), complained in his first report to Alexander III that for two hundred years the Baltic German nobility had been able to use their influence in the highest circles to maintain their privileged self-government; but he himself was susceptible to persuasion. In 1889–90, he abandoned the idea of depriving the Livonian *Landtag* and its council of their powers in communal affairs (including taxation) after discussions with the leaders of the nobility and intervention by the ministry of war, which preferred recruitment in a strategically vital area to remain under noble control. Characterised as an unspeakably inconsiderate and brutal artillery general by the Baltic German historian Alexander von Tobien, Zinov'ev nevertheless came to respect the administrative abilities of the Livonian nobility, and modified his attitudes during his ten-year governorship.[19] Other feared agents of imperial power defended the status quo when they deemed it necessary. F. L. Heiden, governor-general of Finland between 1881 and 1897, opposed the minister of war's plans for reforms of the Finnish army; and recent research has shown that even the despised superannuated military men who filled the offices of the Finnish Senate after 1909 stoutly resisted attempts by the ministry of war and imperial state council to make Finland contribute more to imperial defence costs.[20]

In many respects, the reforms introduced in tsarist Russia were long overdue, but they were in no way democratic. The reform of municipal government in the 1870s, for example, finally broke down the walls of corporate burgher privilege in the Baltic provinces; but the suffrage was limited to around five per cent of the total urban population, and further reduced in 1892 (though the three separate categories of voters disappeared). The aspirations of the linguistic (and overwhelmingly plebeian) majority in Finland and in the Baltic provinces were encouraged, and to a degree advanced; but in times of crisis, the regime turned to its natural allies and supporters – the Baltic Germans, and the conservative elements in Finland who had kept lines of communication open to St Petersburg throughout the 'era of oppression'. The Russian impact on the western borderlands was considerable, certainly. The idyllic provincial tranquillity of the early

19. Tobien A von 1925 *Die livländische Ritterschaft in ihrem Verhältnis zum Zarismus und russischen Nationalismus* Riga, vol. 1, pp. 154–68.

20. Luntinen P 1984 *Sotilasmiljoonat* Historiallisia Tutkimuksia **125**, Helsinki, p. 160f.

nineteenth century, in which the Russian presence was barely perceptible, passed away for ever; but its demise owed at least as much to steam-power and industry as it did to the efforts of administrative russifiers.

The conflicts in the western borderlands also arose because the original agreements between ruler and estates were no longer adequate. They acquired immense symbolic and mythical value – in the case of Finland, it may be argued that the perceived implications of the 1809 Borgå settlement provided one of the foundation-stones of the future nation-state – but it was impossible to maintain a functioning relationship on this narrow and outmoded basis. This much was recognised by most reasonable persons; but since issues of legitimacy and competence were intimately attached to these agreements, all efforts to redefine the relationship sooner or later became ensnared in arguments about what had or had not been conceded by Peter the Great or Alexander I. Russian bureaucrats were less disposed to wrangle endlessly about fundamental laws and ancient privileges, but they were equally hampered by the inadequacies of an autocratic system of government. That system was only likely to be changed by revolution, a prospect which neither the bureaucrats nor their moderate opponents welcomed.

THE BREAK-UP OF THE UNION

Revolution finally shattered the bonds which held together the Russian and the German empires. The union between Sweden and Norway was ended without bloodshed or internal convulsions in 1905. Although a relatively evenly balanced union of equal partners, it was also based upon agreements which in time proved inadequate. Held together by the dynasty, it began to come apart when the national parliaments began to assert their claims to determine the structure and shape of the union: the emergence of parties, deeply divided over issues deemed vital to the national interest, such as defence and tariff reform, also narrowed the margin for compromise. A good deal had already been lost before Oscar II succeeded to the thrones of Norway and Sweden in 1872. One of the last acts of his brother had been to veto a bill, with the approval of the conservative Norwegian prime minister Frederik Stang, which would have allowed ministers to participate in *Storting* debates but not vote. This 'Inclusion Bill' raised a number of fundamental constitutional issues, which its promoter Johan Sverdrup continued to raise over the next decade. In 1880, a majority of the *Storting* demanded that the ministry promulgate the Inclusion Bill, which had already been passed four times. Ministers were impeached and sentenced to loss of office for improperly using the royal veto; and in 1884, Oscar II was finally obliged to concede the principle of ministerial responsibility to the *Storting* and appoint Sverdrup, as leader of the left (*Venstre*) majority, to the office of prime minister.

The rising tide of nationalism affected Sweden as well as Norway. Bjørnstjerne Bjørnson's demand for the Norwegian people to be the master in Norway was echoed across the border by the cry of 'Sweden for the Swedes', uttered by those fearful of the consequences of foreign competition at a time of agricultural crisis and industrial uncertainty. At the same time, the reformed *Riksdag* was attempting to secure greater control over defence and foreign affairs, and succeeded in 1885 in adopting a constitutional amendment designed to shift responsibility for the conduct of foreign affairs away from the king's ministerial council of the Union to the Swedish cabinet. The representation of the cabinet in the ministerial council was enlarged to three, and the Norwegians (who had first been invited to send a representative in 1835) were offered parity, on condition that the foreign minister, although acting on behalf of both countries, was Swedish.

The Norwegians had long resented the fact that the conduct of foreign affairs for the two kingdoms was effectively in Swedish hands. The proposal of the Swedish government served only to irritate them further. Sverdrup was unable to secure a compromise which would have assuaged Norwegian pride, and his political star faded. The compromise arrangement arrived at by his successor, which sought to leave the nationality of the foreign minister undefined, was rejected by the *Storting* majority. The formation of a new government of the radical left, headed by Johannes Steen, brought the two countries once more on to a collision course. Steen's tactic was to press for the creation of a separate Norwegian consular service. Oscar II was caught between two fires, for his Swedish ministers threatened to resign if he sanctioned the Norwegian proposals, and the Steen government did resign when he did not. The 'brotherly hand' offered by the Swedish foreign minister in 1893, conceding that his post might be held by either nationality if the Norwegians agreed to abandon their unilateral stance and enter into joint negotiations on the consular question, was rejected by the radical left in Norway.

Steen's declaration that his party would seek to break the union if the rights of the *Storting* on the consular issue were not acknowledged raised the temperature several degrees, and the crisis reached a climax in the summer of 1895. Spurred on by intense lobbying by nationalist organisations and politicians, the *Riksdag* voted increased military credits and demanded a revision of the statutes of the union. The new foreign minister Count Ludwig Douglas was known to favour armed intervention if necessary, a policy urged upon the king by Kaiser Wilhelm II, whose visit to Stockholm at the height of the crisis did little to calm nerves. However, Oscar II showed a much greater propensity for compromise than his more militant advisers, who included Crown Prince Gustav. His long-serving prime minister Erik Boström was able to control and neutralise the intransigents of the first chamber of the *Riksdag*. Lacking a strong defence force, or even the desire to provide adequate provision for one, and bereft of international support, the radical left in Norway backed down and agreed to negotiations on the consular issue.

Outright confrontation had been narrowly avoided, but the third union committee was unable to reach any consensus over the issues which divided the two partners. The removal of the union symbol from the flag of the Norwegian merchant marine, a law which Oscar II was obliged to promulgate in December 1898 after the bill had passed the required three times through the *Storting*, was a further irritant to the nationalist right in Sweden. Count Douglas blocked notification of this change through diplomatic channels and attempted – in vain – to persuade Germany and Austria-Hungary to condemn Norwegian separatism and proclaim the necessity of the union. In this way, Douglas hoped to create a government crisis in which Steen would have to resign, thus permitting the reform of the Norwegian constitution along conservative lines.[21]

Curiously, the final break-up of the union came at a time when it seemed at last as if agreement on outstanding issues could be reached. Douglas's successor Alfred Lagerheim was noticeably more conciliatory on the consular question, and there did appear to be grounds upon which a negotiated agreement could be reached. This was not to be. Lagerheim was forced out of office by the intransigent Swedish nationalists in November 1904. Prime minister Boström insisted on a more rigorous control of consuls than the Norwegians were prepared to accept, and though his government was prepared to make some concessions, outraged Norwegian opinion did not permit the coalition

21. The ideas of Count Douglas and other right-wing activists are discussed in: Hadenius S 1964 *Fosterländsk unionspolitik. Majoritetspartiet, regeringen och unionsfrågan 1888–1899* Studia Historica Upsaliensia **13**, Uppsala.

government in Christiania to discuss these. A new Norwegian ministry headed by the shipping magnate Christian Michelsen chose confrontation rather than continued negotiation. In May 1905, a consular law was passed by the *Storting*. Oscar II refused to sanction it, and the Norwegian ministers thereupon resigned, refusing to countersign the royal veto. On 7 June, the *Storting* unanimously approved a resolution authorising the Michelsen cabinet to exercise provisional powers as the government of Norway, in which, it was held, constitutional monarchy had ceased to operate by virtue of the king's admitted inability to provide the country with a new government.

This revolutionary breach of the union was softened by an apologetic address to Oscar II, and a formal invitation to allow a prince of his house to accept election as king of Norway. A fortnight later, the Swedish government proposed recognition of the separation and sought full powers to negotiate a final settlement. The *Riksdag* insisted on the Norwegians holding either fresh elections or a plebiscite to demonstrate popular support for separation, and for negotiations to be held without reference to the unilateral action of 7 June.

The final break-up of the union occurred at a time of heightened international tension, which none of the major European powers wished to exacerbate still further by a prolonged crisis in the north. Sweden's request for non-recognition of Norway until the end of the union had been formally negotiated was acceded to. Although Wilhelm II took up the candidature of Christian IX's youngest son Valdemar (an uncle of Tsar Nicholas II) in preference to his grandson Carl (a brother-in-law of King Edward VII) and attempted to bind the Russian emperor to a grandiose alliance aimed at excluding Britain from the Baltic, he was unable to persuade his ministers to back him, and had lamely to fall into line in accepting Carl's candidature. Sweden also had to bring pressure to bear on Denmark to withold permission for Carl's candidature should the *Storting* go ahead and elect him before Oscar had formally abdicated as king of Norway. This finally persuaded the Norwegians to negotiate, after a massive plebiscitary vote in favour of ending the union. Three weeks of talks in Karlstad finally resolved the outstanding issues of which Norwegian fortifications were to be razed and the extent of the neutral zone between the two countries; all future disputes were to be referred to arbitration at The Hague. Oscar renounced the throne on 26 October; a second plebiscite declared solidly in favour of a monarchy, and prince Carl of Denmark accepted the invitation, taking the title of Haakon VII.

The relatively swift and peaceful termination of the union was helped by the attitude of the great powers, which left both sides with no alternative but to negotiate a settlement; but essentially it occurred because there was no significant body of opinion in Sweden willing to fight to maintain the connection. The momentum towards separation had steadily gathered pace in Norway from the time of Carl XV Johan, and it was the Norwegians who set the agenda in a conflict in which the Swedish people as a whole were never fully engaged, and which the Swedish ruling class had neither the will nor the heart to pursue to the bitter end. The more belligerent forces of the Great Swedish nationalism of the 1890s failed to coalesce. Leading figures on the right, such as Rudolf Kjellén and Harald Hjärne publicly doubted the wisdom of continuing the union, and those who urged a more aggressive policy towards Norway were either increasingly marginalised by Boström or shifted their ground, like Crown Prince Gustav. The preservation of what had been essentially a dynastic rather than a state union was less important than the consequences of its disappearance, augmented by an irrational, but powerful russophobia which gripped Sweden in the last years of the nineteenth century. The advances made by Finnish-language nationalism in the 1880s were widely seen as part of a Russian plot, and energetic measures were taken to swedify the Finnish-speaking frontier areas in Norrbotten and to curb the migration of Finns into northern Norway. There was considerable opposition from the nationalists to the northwards extension of the railway network to the Norwegian coast and the Finnish frontier (ironically, Russians also opposed the northern extension of the Finnish railway network: on both sides, strategic considerations were uppermost). The measures undertaken by Bobrikov, which included the banishing of leading figures of the constitutionalist resistance (who promptly established themselves in Stockholm) further fuelled anxieties; and whilst Pontus Fahlbeck welcomed the end of the union as once more allowing Sweden to have a foreign policy of its own, the veteran liberal Adolf Hedin feared it would mean that Sweden would be compelled to cover its weakness and isolation by seeking a great power alliance.[22]

22. The break-up of the union can most conveniently be followed in: Lindgren R 1959 *Norway-Sweden. Union, disunion and Scandinavian integration*, Princeton. Lindberg F 1958 *Den svenska utrikespolitikens historia* ***III:4****. 1872–1914*, Stockholm, deals comprehensively with a variety of aspects of Swedish foreign policy thinking during this period.

REACTION AND REFORM

The union question also had a significant bearing on domestic politics. The more ardently nationalistic protectionists sent out bellicose signals of their eagerness to defend Swedish interests within the union, but the consequences of the higher tariffs on imported grain, pushed through in the late 1880s, were interpreted by their free trade opponents as an encouragement to socialist agitators amongst the working class. The prospect of conflict with Norway and the fear of Russia gave added urgency to the need to bring Sweden's antiquated defence system up to date. This, however, could only be achieved at the cost of much bargaining and compromise. The peasants who constituted the backbone of the Farmers' Party (*Lantmannapartiet*) in the *Riksdag* insisted on the abolition of the land taxes (which bore more heavily upon the owners of unprivileged 'non-noble' land) as the price for reform of the seventeenth-century system of recruitment and maintenance of Sweden's armed forces on the land (*indelningsverk*).

In 1873, the *Riksdag* agreed in principle to resolve both issues simultaneously, a decision which proved extremely difficult to realise. A compromise reform was achieved in 1885, with agreement to reduce the burden of the land taxes by 30 per cent and transfer to the state the same percentage of the costs of maintaining the *indelningsverk*. Determined opposition by the intransigent wing of the Farmers' Party obliged the government to settle for forty-two rather than forty-eight days as the period of training for conscripts.[23] The compromise of 1873 was finally realised in 1892, when Erik Boström managed to drive through a package of measures increasing the period of training from forty-two to ninety days, with the state taking over the costs of running the recruitment system and agreeing to the final elimination of the land taxes over a period of twelve years. The increased costs were to be met by income and property taxes. Increased public unease about Sweden's vulnerability to attack eased the passage of Boström's reform, and ensured the replacement of the *indelningsverk* in 1901 with universal conscription for a period of 240 days.

The modernisation of Sweden's defence capability was an integral part of the process of detaching the country from the outmoded legacy of static agrarian self-sufficiency, and as such was enmeshed with the

23. Nevéus T 1965 *Ett betryggande försvar. Värnplikten och arméorganisationen i svensk politik 1880–1885* Studia Historica Upsaliensia **20**, Uppsala. On the origins and working of the *indelningsverk*, see Kirby D 1990 *Northern Europe in the early modern period*, p. 222.

whole question of taxation and representation – as the tireless fighter for democracy, Adolf Hedin, constantly reminded his opponents. The reform of the *Riksdag* set in train by Louis de Geer in 1861 and finally realised five years later produced something less than the powerful legislature envisaged in Hedin's programme for the short-lived Liberal Party in 1867, though it was a symbolic break with the social structure of the old order. The four estates were replaced by two chambers. The first (*Första Kammaren*) was to be elected by the newly-created provincial assemblies (*Landsting*) and the magistracy of large cities for a nine-year period. Members had to be over thirty-five years of age and of considerable financial standing: it has been calculated that there were only around 6,000 men in Sweden who fulfilled these requirements. This, together with the indirect nature of the franchise and the graded scale of votes permitted according to property and wealth made the first chamber a bastion of the upper classes. The elections of 1867 returned 125 members, of whom 78 were noblemen; and although a few small businessmen, wealthier farmers or professional men gained election over the years, large landowners and the upper echelons of the bureaucracy continued to dominate the first chamber for decades.

The second chamber (*Andra Kammaren*) was elected for a three-year period by men over the age of twenty-one who disposed of a certain taxable property or income. Farmers constituted the largest single group of voters, but the less restrictive qualification level permitted a wider variety of social groups entry into the chamber. With an electorate of no more than five per cent of the total population, or just over one-fifth of all adult males (and until the late 1880s, fewer than a quarter of the enfranchised actually bothered to vote), the second chamber nevertheless assumed the character of a popular forum increasingly at odds with the conservative, exclusivist first chamber.

A similar situation obtained in Denmark after the loss of the duchies. The conservatives were able to push through a new constitution in July 1866 which significantly restricted the electorate of the upper chamber (*Landsting*), and allowed the king the right to nominate 12 of its 66 members. The Danish farmers, however, had a much higher political profile than their Swedish counterparts. Proud of their history and traditions of political struggle, committed to the restoration of the 'people's constitution' of June 1849 and the principle of parliamentary government, the largely rural forces of the left (*Venstre*) dominated the lower chamber (*Folketing*) from 1872. Alarmed by the rise of socialism, and enraged by the radical new ideas advanced in his lectures by the literary critic, Georg Brandes, the conservatives rejected the very notion of uneducated farmers in their stiff collars and sombre broadcloth suits taking the place of the upper-class 'excellencies' whom it was the king's pleasure to appoint as his ministers. This sharp antagonism, vividly portrayed in the stories of Henrik Pontoppidan, fuelled the conflict which erupted in 1877.

Denied entry into government, the opposition pinned its hopes on the provisions of the 1866 constitution which brought financial matters before the scrutiny of the *Folketing* and decreed that taxes should not be collected before the finance bill had been passed. The conservatives took comfort in the interpretation placed upon the constitution by Professor Henning Matzen, who claimed that the king had the right to issue a provisional budget in the absence of the *Rigsdag*, and were invigorated by the stout assertion of this position by J. B. S. Estrup, the head of the government from 1875 to 1894. The 1866 constitution had not made clear what should happen in the event of conflict between the two chambers. Estrup believed the two were duty-bound to act together, and if not, government should act to ensure that the state continued to function.

The occasion to test this arose in April 1877. Unable to secure the agreement of the *Folketing* majority to his budget proposals, Estrup had the *Rigsdag* prorogued and a provisional finance bill proclaimed. By confronting his opponents in this way, Estrup was able to expose their internal divisions. In 1876, he had persuaded the king to dissolve the *Folketing* in the hopes of exposing *Venstre*'s defence proposals to the electorate, but in fact, the tables had been turned, and his opponents had accused him of seeking to provide an expensive land fortification defence system for Copenhagen whilst ignoring the defences of the rest of the country. *Venstre*'s mandate had jumped from 54 to 79 seats, and Estrup could not be sure even of the wholehearted support of the right (*Højre*). Three years later, the united left had divided, and notwithstanding the patient obduracy of their leaders or the loyalty of their supporters, the forces of *Venstre* were slowly exhausted in the face of Estrup's continued use of provisional legislation. A crisis point appeared to have been reached in 1885. Christian IX adhered to the conservatives' position: that he could not dismiss the Estrup ministry as a condition of the budget being approved without ceding his constitutional right. In order to curb the activities of the rifle associations being set up by the left, provisional legislation was introduced, and teachers were forbidden to join rifle clubs by express orders of the ministry of education. Police powers were strengthened, and the *Rigsdag* yet again dismissed. In the countryside, the 'blue men' of the new gendarmerie symbolised the hateful regime of the man whom not even bullets fired at almost point-blank range could kill.[24]

J. B. S. Estrup was something of an oddity in his own times. A man devoted to simple, anti-democratic principle, with no clearly thought-out line of policy other than the defence of order and the constitutional right of the sovereign to appoint ministers, he was a remote figure, uncommitted to party. His refusal to countenance tax reform effectively destroyed any hope of reaching accommodation with elements of *Venstre* over his budget proposals in 1875–77. The spiralling costs of the fortification works around Copenhagen ate up the reserves accumulated during the period of retrenchment before 1885. By 1890, half of the state's expenditure was being spent on defence. Naval circles made it plain that they believed the money could be more effectively spent on ships, and the self-taxing defence movement launched in 1883 was no longer able to keep pace. In the country as well as in the cramped temporary accommodation of the *Rigsdag* (the Christianborg palace having been destroyed by fire in 1884), new alliances were slowly forming to press for reforms. Farmers came together to press the government to take the farming interest more seriously. The campaign to protect the reputation of Danish butter on the British market by imposing strict controls on the manufacture of margarine, launched by the radical *Venstre* politician Viggo Hørup in November 1887, cut right across party lines. The agrarian association set up in response to the crisis which hit farming in the mid-nineties demanded tax reforms, cuts in 'unproductive' state expenditure and a political truce to enable reforms to save farming. Professor Matzen talked of social reforms as a way of halting the progress of socialism, and urged moderates of the left and right to unite on this.

The electoral success of a socialist in a rural constituency, where rival *Venstre* candidates had split the vote, encouraged the moderate *Venstre* leader Frede Bojsen to take this suggestion seriously, and to seek accommodation with the government. The increased duty on beer was attacked by the radicals as a tax on the working man, and the provision of sickness benefits this was meant to finance was also criticised as smacking of charity; but the passing of legislation encouraged hopes of a compromise. The death of the obdurate leader of the main *Venstre* grouping, Chresten Berg, in 1891, the dismissal

24. A nineteen-year old printer attempted unsuccessfully to assassinate Estrup in October 1885. On this period, see Fink T 1986 *Estruptidens politiske historie 1875–1894* 2 vols, Odense. The tense mood is captured (albeit in a very partisan manner) in Henrik Pontoppidan's collection of short stories, *Skyer*, published in 1890.

from government of the equally uncompromising (though highly compromised) Jacob Scavenius, and the defeat of the radical Viggo Hørup in the 1892 elections by the moderate *Venstre* candidate P. A. Alberti, backed by the votes of the right, seemed to offer scope for further moves to break the political deadlock.[25]

Negotiations between the moderate *Venstre* leaders and the government eventually produced compromise. *Venstre* had to accept the fortifications and to grant the monies needed to maintain them, though they were able to obtain cuts in military expenditure. The *Rigsdag* was to issue a ruling on how conflicts over the finance bill were to be resolved in future, and a declaration was to be made that defence spending was to uphold Danish neutrality. Estrup finally resigned in August 1894. The coalition of moderates and *Højre* which had made the compromise suffered a setback in the *Folketing* elections the following year. The various oppositional strands of the left came together as *Venstrereformpartiet*, with a programme calling for tax reform, reductions in military expenditure, and provision of smallholdings for cottars. On this last point, left and right were able to agree in 1899, when a state fund was established to provide cheap loans for those seeking to buy a smallholding.

After the 1901 *Folketing* elections, in which *Højre* was reduced to eight seats, Christian IX finally agreed to change the system, and asked a relative outsider, Professor J. H. Deuntzer, to form a *Venstre* government. Although dependent on the support of a group of free conservatives in addition to the *Venstre* minority in the *Landsting*, the new ministry was able to push through several important reforms. The old land and property taxes were replaced by a property tax based on market value, and a progressive income tax was also introduced. Congregational councils were established in 1903, with the responsibility for dealing with the practical affairs of the church and with a say in appointments of clergy, a long-standing demand of the Grundvigian wing of *Venstre*. The school system was given an organic uniformity with the creation of the *mellemskole*, or middle school. It was, however, the defence question which brought down the government, and once more split the left. The ministry collapsed in January 1905 after the minister of war was forced to resign as a result of persistent attacks by the radicals. Backed by a majority of

25. Scavenius had survived the persistent and aggressively public revelations that he had frequented a house of ill-repute made by a member of a group which made it its business to remonstrate with those who used the services of prostitutes; his fall from grace was occasioned by the disorderly state of his private finances. P. A. Alberti was to cause an even more spectacular financial scandal some two decades later.

Venstrereformpartiet, J. C. Christensen formed a new ministry. Eight rebels left the party, eventually linking up with the members of the radical club in Copenhagen to form *Radikale Venstre*. Notwithstanding its open commitment to a minimal defence force and neutrality, the radicals were in the long run to prove as divided over the defence issue as their predecessors in *Venstre*.[26]

These protracted struggles can be misleading, for it was at the municipal and communal, rather than the national level that the cutting edge of reform was at work, and it may be argued that it was a growing realisation that the state had to be brought into line with these developments which ultimately made redundant the outmoded obstinacies of the old-order conservatives (and perhaps the posturings of old-style peasant politicians such as Chresten Berg in Denmark, or the Rundbäcks in Sweden). Similarly, organised interest groups were pressing for change, and calling for a more active involvement on the part of the state. This in itself implied a significant shift of attitude. When the Swedish free trader Robert Themptander countered the demands for tariff reform in the 1880s by declaring that the state should not interfere in the productive process, he was reiterating a still prevalent view that it was not the duty of the public sector to regulate the private. This rather doctrinaire liberal view was at times difficult to maintain; anxieties about rising levels of poverty, or mass emigration, prompted calls for a more active state involvement. In the 1869 *Riksdag* debate on emigration, speaker after speaker complained of the increased burden placed on the poor relief system by those who emigrated, leaving behind dependants or debts; but all pulled up short of advocating compulsory means of curbing emigration, since that would be to curtail personal freedom. Almost forty years later, the Swedish government proposed a grant to assist the activities of the national association against emigration, deeming it to be a 'state interest of the first order'. This aroused opposition in the *Riksdag*, though it was the deep-rooted mistrust of excessive officialdom rather than the defence of personal freedom which was the guiding sentiment.

By the end of the century, a more positive attitude towards the state as a regulating force in society was evident, on the right as well as the left, and the scope of central government and administration was

26. Kaarsted T 1958 *Hvad skal det nytte? De radikale og forsvaret 1894–1914*, Århus. The title of Kaarsted's book refers to a famous speech made by Viggo Hørup in 1883 to justify his opposition to the Copenhagen fortifications. *Hvad skal det nytte?* (roughly: what's the good of it?) became a rallying-call for all good radicals in future generations.

extending considerably. Farmers in Denmark and Sweden lobbied successfully for the creation of a separate ministry of agriculture; entrepreneurs were able to obtain subsidies to enable them to compete in international markets; government commissions investigated a range of social and economic problems, ranging from child labour to workers' housing conditions. There was still considerable resistance to the idea of active state involvement in labour relations, and a reluctance to create yet more bureaucrats to handle social problems; citizens were expected voluntarily to declare their income for tax assessment, and charitable and voluntary institutions still played a central role in the provision of welfare. The state no longer confined itself to 'public' affairs, even though its involvement in the 'private' sphere was still largely determined by pragmatic rather than purely ideological considerations.[27]

Political groups still coalesced around issues, rather than represented specific interests. Issues could inspire considerable organisational activity; the protectionists in Sweden during the 1880s created a very effective electoral organisation, though no fully-fledged political party emerged from this. The suffrage movement which emerged a decade later had an extensive national organisation, with paid officials and publicists, and it conducted a very effective extra-parliamentary campaign, in which liberals and social democrats collaborated. Out of the movement emerged a tighter, more centralised organisation, but by 1907, this Liberal National Association (*Frisinnade Landsföreningen*) had been obliged to restructure itself to give the local branches more say. The constitutional crisis in Denmark in some respects helped preserve entrenched attitudes: reverence for the June 1849 constitution, attachment to Grundtvigian ideals, dogged anti-militarism, the three main strands within *Venstre*, and a commitment to positive defence measures and the maintenance of royal prerogative on the right. There was a constant tension in the ranks of *Venstre* between the puritanical peasant wing and the adherents of the 'modern breakthrough'. There was a world of difference between the sober religiosity of the Jutland peasantry, and their leaders in the *Venstre* party, and the anti-clerical modernism and cosmopolitan free thinking advanced in the columns of *Politiken* by Viggo Hørup, Georg and Edvard Brandes.

Newspapers and journals played a crucial role in the shaping of political attitudes; even royal personages penned (anonymous) articles

27. Kilander S 1991 *Den nya staten och den gamla. En studie i ideologisk förändring* Studia Historica Upsaliensia **164**, Uppsala.

for publication in their favoured organs. In the German and Russian empires, a war of words accompanied (and at times urged on) the assimilationist moves of the authorities. *Moskovskie Vedomosti* was the principal organ of the Russian nationalists, and its pronouncements provoked sharp responses from the Finnish and Baltic German press. The intellectual contributors to the journal *Przegląd Poznański* refuted the assertions of the German nationalist *Kreuzzeitung*. It was in the columns of the press that new ideas and policies were advanced and debated; the idea of Finnish neutrality in the event of a war between Russia and Britain was first put forward in the pages of *Helsingfors Dagblad*, for example. It was deemed vital to have an outlet in print. Ado Grenzstein conceived of *Olevik* in 1881 as a vehicle for weaning the Estonian peasant readership away from the 'firebrands and madcaps' who edited *Sakala*, the newspaper founded by C. R. Jacobson after he had been eased out of the list of favoured contributors to the more conservative *Eesti Postimees*.[28] Having lost his job as editor of *Nya Pressen* when that paper was banned by Bobrikov, the larger-than-life Finnish adventurer Konni Zilliacus started up an exile press in Stockholm, and became deeply involved in the smuggling of his own material and illegal Russian revolutionary newspapers via the many inlets and channels of the Finnish coastline.[29]

Great importance was also attached to international publicity. Carl Schirren, Woldemar von Bock and Julius Eckardt laboured tirelessly in Germany to refute the attacks of Yuri Samarin and the Slavophiles on Baltic German privilege. The Finns organised international addresses and protests against the February 1899 manifesto, lobbied politicians, academics and journalists, and paid 500 guineas to an Ulster journalist to state their case in a book entitled *Finland and the Tsars*. The debate on Russian policy towards Finland even spilled over into the columns of the European press, with the Russian minister of the interior defending his government's actions against the attacks of the British journalist W. T. Stead.

In the last quarter of the nineteenth century, a new political force began to make its presence felt – social democracy. The German social

28. On *Sakala* and *Olevik*, see the articles by: Kruus H 1957 *Eesti ajaloost XIX sajandi teisel poolel*, Tallinn, pp. 138–211.

29. Zilliacus was also involved in gun-running. For the glorious fiasco of the voyage of the *John Grafton* and other episodes, see the highly entertaining study by: Futrell M 1963 *The Northern underground. Episodes of Russian revolutionary transport and communications through Scandinavia and Finland 1863–1917*, London, and Zilliacus K 1919 *Från ofärdstid och oroliga år*, Helsingfors.

democrats managed to win one-fifth of the votes cast (on an admittedly low poll) in Königsberg as early as 1874, and began to make significant inroads in the province of Schleswig-Holstein from the 1890s. The German Social Democratic Party (SPD) was to become an inspiration and a model for the rest of northern Europe. The first to organise a social democratic party were the Danes, many of whom had come into contact with socialist ideas whilst working in Germany after serving their apprenticeship. After a brave beginning in the shadow of the Paris Commune of 1871 had come to grief in 1872, when police broke up a workers' demonstration and arrested the leaders Louis Pio, Harald Brix and Poul Geleff, the Danish Social Democratic Workers' Party was founded in 1876. Shortly afterwards, two of the early leaders emigrated to America and membership was hit badly by a trade depression. There was a slow recovery in the 1880s, and two socialists were elected to the *Folketing* in 1884. The party collaborated informally with *Venstre* in elections and the campaign against the Estrup government, and there was considerable support from *Venstre*'s rural supporters for the workers in the industrial dispute which affected the engineering industry in 1885. Trade unionists were strongly represented in the Danish labour movement from the outset, and a national organisation (*Det samvirkende Fagforbund*) came into being in 1898. A major industrial conflict in 1899 was finally resolved in the so-called September agreement, which established procedures for future disputes and provisions for arbitration. By 1910, over half of the Danish workforce were members of a trade union, which compared favourably with fewer than one in four in Britain or the other Scandinavian countries.

Trade unionism in Finland remained very much in the shadow of the Social Democratic Party, which took off spectacularly after the revolution of 1905. Founded only in 1899 (ten years after the Swedish Social Democratic Workers' Party) and adopting the 'social democratic' label and the orthodox Marxist preamble of the SPD's 1891 Erfurt programme in 1903, the party played only a modest and subsidiary role in the politics of the Bobrikov era. Many of the provincial leaders urged support for the passive resistance; the orthodox Marxists in the capital refused to take sides in what they believed to be a bourgeois conflict. Interestingly, the Finnish social democrats were legally tolerated and suffered rather less at the hands of the tsarist authorities than did the more outspoken advocates of constitutionalism. Their comrades elsewhere in the Russian empire, who were also rather less isolated from the main currents of European socialist thought, were not so fortunate.

The Finnish labour movement, like its Swedish, Danish and German counterparts, grew out of an earlier tradition of liberal concern for the moral and educational improvement of the working classes; its members were also emphatically of 'the people' whose support the nationalists relied on. Up until the revolution of 1905, members of the social-reformist wing of the Finnish nationalist movement continued to play an active role in many provincial workers' associations. Finnish nationalism, and social democracy in its turn, was excessively 'state-centred'; both sought to capture and utilise for their own ends the structures of the embryonic state; neither paid too much attention to the struggle against tsarism elsewhere in the empire.[30]

The more radical elements of the nationalist movements and the socialists in the other western borderlands could not so easily focus their attention solely upon their own territorial patch, primarily because they lacked constitutional traditions and institutions which they could call their own. The Russian revolutionary movement learnt to use Finland as a safe haven and a base for operations after 1905, but otherwise, its activities were confined to the troops and sailors stationed there. There was no such invisible barrier south of the Gulf of Finland, where there were not only large numbers of Russian workers, but also political movements influenced by and intimately connected to the constellation of radicals of the revolutionary movement in the Russian cities. Common to all the political movements on the left in late-imperial Russia was the great importance attached to ideas. Often imperfectly understood and misinterpreted in the columns of the small-circulation journals which were eagerly devoured by the members of study circles, ideas nevertheless offered a hope of emancipation from the stultifying atmosphere of political repression and the stuffy airless salons of the self-contented bourgeoisie. The kind of movement which came into being in Finland, in which the workers proudly posed outside the headquarters they had built with their own hands and where they could fulfil their cultural, social and political aspirations on their own terms, simply did not and could not exist elsewhere in the empire. Discipline, respectability and a watchful preparedness were the key features of social democracy in Finland, and indeed in the other countries of northern Europe where mass, legally tolerated labour movements developed. Smuggled newspapers, fighting groups and agitation amongst the troops were not part of the tradition;

30. For further discussion of the 'state-centredness' of Finnish nationalism and social democracy, see: Alapuro R 1988 *State and revolution in Finland*, Los Angeles.

and ideas were more often buried in committees and carefully framed in resolutions than they were flung around in heated debate by workers and students, crammed into tiny candle-lit rooms.

The city of Vilna was a true microcosm of this world of feverish activity and discussion. The census of 1897 revealed that 41 per cent of the city's inhabitants were Jewish. Most of these were poor: almost one in four Jews in the city received assistance from the poor relief agency Maôt-Chitim in 1898. The pressures of the modern urban world had frayed traditional Jewish community values. Vilna was a centre of the Haskalah movement, which helped provide a bridge to the modern secular world; many of the early socialists had been strongly influenced by the Haskalah. They had also grown up in an atmosphere of hardening discrimination, but had been brought into close contact with Russian ideas from their schooldays onwards. As the Jewish socialist movement developed in Vilna, the tensions between the desire for assimilation and the wish to fight for Jewish interests grew. The intense debate in the mid-nineties was also influenced by the split in Polish socialism. Józef Piłsudski, leader of the national-minded Polish Socialist Party (PPS), criticised the assimilationist tendencies of the Jewish workers' circles, and urged them to join his party in fighting tsarism. The shift from propaganda to agitation in order to win over the masses gave Yiddish a more central role. The separate Jewish labour organisation advocated by Martov in 1895 was formally created two years later with the creation of the General Jewish Workers' Union in Russia and Poland, commonly known as the Bund. Unlike the PPS and the Lithuanian social democrats, the Bund wished to work within the ranks of Russian social democracy, and it was well represented at the 1898 founding congress of the Russian Social Democratic Workers' Party in Minsk. This proved to be a somewhat unsatisfactory relationship. Furthermore, the Bund found itself frequently at odds with the other socialist groupings of Poland and Lithuania, and it also had to face the direct and indirect challenge of Zionism.

The 'national question' could not simply be ignored by facile utterances about workers' inherent internationalism: for Jewish socialists, it was immensely more complex and painful than it was for their Polish or Russian comrades. The fourth congress of the Bund in 1901 embraced the notion of a future national autonomy, but thought it would only be premature, and likely to obscure class consciousness, in the present circumstances; in vain did Mark Liber argue that national agitation could only raise class consciousness and would not lead to isolation. For many Jews, socialism was a means of escaping from their past into a modern, secular world. It offered a universalist vision of emancipation, whilst at the same time it was a means of fighting back against oppression, whether the oppressor was a Jewish brush-factory owner or a Black Hundred agent of tsarism.[31]

The fire in which Latvian social democracy was forged was not so intense, though the furnaces were stoked by an equally rich mixture of fuels. Riga was a metropolis in its own right, a city of almost half-a-million inhabitants in 1913, with an industrial workforce of almost 100,000. It was the home of a new generation of young intellectuals, writers and artists, members of the 'New Current' who rejected the conservative and inward-looking values of the older generation of nationalists, and embraced socialist and progessive ideas, which they expounded in the columns of *Dienas Lapa*. In 1897, the authorities struck, closing the newspaper, arresting its editorial board and a number of other activists. A number were deported or fled abroad, and a Latvian Social Democratic Union was founded in western Europe in 1903. This grouping advocated national autonomy for the territory currently inhabited by Latvians. The Latvian Social Democratic Party which came into being in 1904 adopted a strictly internationalist stance, and placed class solidarity within the empire above nationalism. By the outbreak of revolution in October 1905, the socialists had begun to create an effective network of circles and districts, and had a membership of around 18,000, roughly the same as the Finnish Social Democratic Party. It was able to join forces with the Bund in January 1905 to bring out on strike some 50,000–60,000 workers in Riga, and it helped sustain a rising campaign of political unrest in the countryside of Kurland and southern Livland throughout the summer of that year. Humiliated in the Far East, the Russian empire stood on the brink of revolution. Within a dozen years, the old order would totally collapse, and the new forces which as yet were still blanketed by two layers of that order, the imperial and the local, would emerge, blinking in the dusty light over the ruins.

31. Tobias H 1972 *The Jewish Bund in Russia. From its origins to 1905*, Stanford. Sabaliūnas L 1990 *Lithuanian social democracy in perspective 1893–1914*, Durham/London, pp. 15–40.

CHAPTER SEVEN
Fin-de-siècle

THE CITY

> Never have I felt happier and prouder to be from a city than when I returned from the countryside as a child one autumn evening and saw the lights glowing round the quays. Now, I thought, now those poor devils back there in the country will have to stay indoors or trudge about in the dark and the dirt.
> – But it's true, he added, they do have a quite different firmament in the countryside to what we have here. Here, the stars are eclipsed in competition with the street lighting. And that is a pity.
> – The stars, said Markel, are no good to light us on our nightly wanderings. It's sad how much they have lost all practical meaning. Earlier, they regulated our entire lives; and if you open a cheap almanac, you'd think they still do. It would be hard to find a more striking example of the persistence of tradition than that; something which is still the most popular piece of folk literature, filled with precise information on things no-one bothers about any more. [1]

In this sliver of conversation, recorded by the eponymous narrator of Hjalmar Söderberg's novel *Doktor Glas*, is reflected in miniature an urban bourgeois view of the world – secular, rational, sceptical, but tinged with an edge of nostalgia. Sitting with his slightly dissolute companions outside the Grand Hotel in Stockholm, overlooking the harbour, on a fine summer's evening, the melancholic narrator feels the need to have people around him, strangers with whom he is not obliged to talk. Glas is emphatically of the bourgeois world of cigars

1. Söderberg Hj 1974 *Doktor Glas* Stockholm, pp. 59–60. The novel was first published in 1905.

and whisky-toddies, though he looks askance at it. He is of the generation of doubters, who no longer have the massive assurances of a steadfast faith.

The early memory of the welcoming glow of street lighting is a vivid reminder of the sense of security created by the late nineteenth-century city with its piped amenities safely, silently and efficiently functioning beneath paved streets patrolled by the upholders of law and order, and flanked with shops, restaurants, cafés, and imposing public and private buildings. Most of the bigger European cities had illuminated their main thoroughfares with gas-lamps from mid-century onwards, and a number of northern European cities had their own municipal electrical undertakings by 1900; but many small country towns still relied on paraffin lamps, and rural areas continued to sleep under the thick blanket of darkness, in which none but the unfortunate country doctor, stray travellers and those determined on a bit of company ventured forth.[2] Small country towns were deficient in other services and facilities. Only Reval and Narva of the towns of Estland had piped water supplies and sewage-disposal systems by 1910, for example. It is unlikely that small, dusty towns such as Wesenberg, with its fifteen kilometres of streets lit by fifty-eight paraffin lamps, would provide much in the way of diversion to the visitor, or employment for the town's thirty-five cabbies and carriers. Late-Victorian tourists such as the redoubtable Mrs Tweedie complained of the lack of decent accommodation in Finland, and even the Swedish Touring Club felt obliged to warn travellers in 1898 that 'the accommodation and appointments [in the provinces] are frequently not up to the mark nor in respect of cleanliness are they all that could be desired, though prices rule fairly high'.[3]

2. Myllyntaus T 1991 *Electrifying Finland* London/Helsinki, pp. 21ff. offers much fascinating information and insight into the rapid development of electricity as a source of energy in Finland. There is a good description of the hazards of night-time visiting in the countryside in book one, chapter seven of Martin Andersen Nexø's novel, *Pelle Eroberen* (Pelle the Conqueror). Obliged to sit huddled up on a primitive peasant cart in the wind and rain for hour after hour, trailing through the deepest mire at a snail's pace, shaken by every jolt, stiff, battered, soaked to the skin, the rural doctor returns home in the small hours and counts himself lucky if he escapes with a cold, acording to the writer of: Die landärtzlichen Verhältnisse Livlands *Baltische Monatsschrift* **10** (1864): p. 75.

3. *The Swedish Touring Club's guide to Sweden* London, 1898, p. xxiii. Tourists were, however, reassured that the so-called common people were as a rule quiet and respectable in behaviour. Mrs Alec Tweedie's *Through Finland in carts*, published in 1897, enjoyed considerable sales. For further arcane details concerning the street-lighting and cab-drivers of Estonian towns on the eve of the First World War, see the table in Pullat R 1972 *Eesti linnad ja linlased*, Tallinn, pp. 98–9.

The visual impact of the big city captured the imagination of artists and writers, though by no means all were uncritical admirers of city life. The lure of long summer days in the countryside continued to have a powerful appeal. Martin Birck, the young man of Söderberg's novel for whom the glow of the street lamps is so welcoming, also longs in the winter for the green grass of summer and wild strawberries in the woods. The city could also appear threatening and alien, with its vast medley of comers and goers, an endless, anonymous stream of people on the pavements (as in Edvard Munch's 1892 painting, *Evening on Karl Johan street*). Those who drew their cultural and emotional inspirations from a rural, peasantist tradition were often ambivalent about the attractions of a city which in so many ways was obviously 'foreign'. In spite of the considerable inroads made by the first sizeable generation of city-based Finnish, Estonian and Latvian intelligentsia, with their journals, theatres, publishing houses, even their own contribution to the street scene, ranging from shop signs to architectural motifs, there was often a frisson of unease and anxiety, especially when the word 'culture' cropped up. The Finnish writer Juhani Aho wrote with a mixture of pride and irony of the fine new buildings in Helsingfors, which could bear comparison with those of other cities in the world, and the cultivated manners and fashions which were visibly Parisian in inspiration:

> But sometimes one feels so insecure . . . It is as if, in spite of everything, one is not really at home, as if there were more foreign folk than one's own kith and kin around one. . . . And that is why one has that constant longing to be away from here, to be able to see the native turf, hear a language which whispers like a forest brook and to see faces without foreign features. One longs for the heart of the country.[4]

The dramatic change in the appearance of the cities owed a lot to new building techniques and materials, but even more to the energetic and ambitious endeavours of the municipal authorities. The destruction of the medieval wall around the old city enabled the municipality of Riga to transform an asphyxiating, fetid girdle into a ring of parks, gardens and wide boulevards. The services of a modern city were gradually extended into the outlying suburbs; sixteen publicly-owned steam ferries linked the city with the Mitau suburb across the Düna river, electrification of the privately-owned trolley

4. Aho J 1953 *Maan sydämeen* (*Kootut teokset*), Helsinki, vol. 4, pp. 50–1. Aho's short story neatly illustrates the highly ambivalent attitude of Finnish-language nationalism towards the culture of the city.

system in 1901 heralded the quintupling of the length of track over the next thirteen years. Cheap workmen's fares made easier the journey to work from the working-class Moscow district, whilst the middle classes settled in the pioneering garden suburb of Keiserwald at the end of the trolley line. The city council was hampered in its task by the refusal of the imperial government to permit fiscal reform, and had to rely on loans from local banks to finance the building of a new quay on the right bank of the Düna and measures to regulate the flow of the river around the turn of the century. As with other big cities in the Russian empire, municipal enterprises also provided an important source of revenue, even enabling Riga to pay the interest on its debt and to embark on new public works projects.[5]

The number of city dwellers in Imperial Russia jumped from around 9 million in the mid-nineteenth century to 25 million on the eve of the First World War. The population of Riga quintupled in less than fifty years, and was approaching the half-a-million mark in 1914. In one year alone, 1913, the number of inhabitants of St Petersburg increased by 107,000, twice the average annual increase recorded over the period 1890–1914. The number of town-dwellers in Finland rose from 174,300 (8.5 per cent of the total population) in 1880 to 432,200 (14.7 per cent) in 1910: Helsingfors had grown from an idyllic jumble of wooden houses scattered around the more substantial buildings of the administrative centre into a city of more than 100,000 inhabitants. There was significant migration to the towns in the Scandinavian countries as well. The urban population of Sweden rose from 539,649 in 1870 to 1,485,840 (around 25 per cent of the total population) in 1913. On the eve of war, two in five Danes lived in a town, though only the capital, with 560,000 inhabitants, exceeded the 100,000 mark. Other cities around the Baltic which had surpassed that mark by 1914 included Stockholm (382,000), Göteborg (178,000), Stettin (236,000), Königsberg (246,000), Kiel (211,000), Danzig (170,000) and Lübeck (116,000).

The urban population explosion placed even greater strains on already inadequate infrastructures. The demand for housing in Swedish towns was so great in the 1870s that old buildings had to be commandeered and tents erected as temporary accommodation in Stockholm, whilst in Göteborg, homeless families were housed in an old fort. Around the outskirts of the cities were ramshackle shanty

5. Much valuable information on the city in imperial Russia is provided in: Hamm M (ed.) 1986 *The city in late imperial Russia*, Bloomington, Ill., pp. 43–78 (James Bater on St Petersburg), and pp. 177–208 (Anders Henriksson on Riga).

towns, lacking basic amenities; ringing the city centre were grossly overcrowded quarters, such as Södermalm and Vasastaden in Stockholm, where there was an average of three or four dwellers per room, or the district 'north of the long bridge' in Helsingfors, where single-roomed accommodation was the norm. When wages failed to keep pace with rent increases, working-class families were often compelled to put up with even more cramped conditions and take in one or two young men who could help reduce the rent bill.[6]

The city fathers came in for a good deal of criticism then (and later) for their timid and ineffective planning and housing policies, and their inability to curb speculation. At the same time, influenced by the garden city movement in England and similar developments elsewhere in central Europe, but also drawing upon domestic and rural notions of 'a house of one's own', companies were being set up to build suburban cottages and villas for home owners. Although the municipalities took over a great many functions, others remained primarily the duty or obligation of the private citizen: the 1752 general ordinance which made the citizens of Königsberg responsible for keeping the streets of the city clean remained in force until 1899, for example. The provision of a clean supply of drinking water frequently caused headaches for the city authorities. Reval's water supply laid on under contract by the Riga firm of Weir & Co. in the mid-1860s was immediately found to be inadequate, but the system was greatly extended in the 1880s and 1890s. The water was piped from a nearby lake, and acquired a muddy taste in stormy or windy weather. It was also periodically affected by algae. Whilst the council debated the options, the demand for water increased; at the outbreak of war in 1914, a commission set up at the order of the commander of the naval defences concluded that the water supply was still unsuitable. Similar problems were encountered in Riga, where parts of the city remained without adequate water supply or sewage disposal, and the slight rise at the end of the century in what had since the 1870s been a declining death rate showed that much still had to be done in the field of public health.

The annual incidence of deaths per thousand inhabitants showed a tendency to decline in all cities; from 26.1 in 1876–80 to 13.6 in 1911–15 in Helsingfors, 20.0 in the 1860s down to 13.0 in the 1910s in Copenhagen. Improvements in public hygiene and better medical

6. Waris H 1973 *Työläisyhteiskunnan syntyminen Helsingin Pitkänsillan pohjoispuolelle* (original edition 1932–4), Helsinki, pp. 158–88. In 1900, there were lodgers in almost half the working-class dwellings in this part of Helsingfors.

care and treatment greatly reduced the numbers of deaths from infectious diseases. Scourges such as the ague, which had carried off 4,200 persons in Denmark as late as 1831, had been virtually eradicated by 1914. Other killer diseases such as diphtheria and measles had been brought under control with the help of better medicines and provision of hospital treatment. Tuberculosis was still prevalent, but was being treated in sanatoria, and associations to combat the disease carried out valuable educational work in areas particularly badly afflicted, such as the coastal districts of Ostrobothnia. An exception to the general picture was St Petersburg, described in 1909 by the British consul as the city with one of the highest death rates from infectious diseases in Europe – largely due to the contaminated water supply taken from the Neva river.

The medical profession had acquired a level of competence and public acknowledgment hitherto unknown, though wise men and quacks still practised and patent medicines such as Dr Popp's stomach powders enjoyed good sales. Hospitals were no longer feared as the last resort of the poor, and medical care was carried to the wider public by the provision of dispensaries, lying-in hospitals, inoculation and vaccination campaigns, and above all by the provisions for public hygiene made by local authorities. Sound health was there for all who cared to take heed and could afford it. Observing the prohibitions against spitting as he stepped on board, a man might take a ride on a tram to a professionally qualified dentist who would rid him of his toothache with the minimum of discomfort (though had he just finished reading Thomas Mann's *Buddenbrooks,* first published in 1901, he might have viewed the encounter with some trepidation). He could be reasonably assured that the water with which he rinsed his mouth had been filtered and purified in the town's waterworks; and he might have recourse to a wide variety of patent medicines (several opiate-based) sold in the city's pharmacies and dispensaries to relieve the after-effects of the treatment.

Such a man, however, would have belonged to the better-off classes, who could afford dental treatment, and who were invariably taller, heavier, and healthier than the members of the underclass. The incidence of infectious diseases, infant mortality rates and the overall death rate were all higher in working-class areas of the city than in the more salubrious quarters of the bourgeoisie. The unequal struggle for existence began at conception. The number of illegitimate births was much higher in working-class districts (twice as high 'north of the bridge' than in the better-off areas of Helsingfors, for example), and there were usually more mouths to feed in a working-class family than in those of the middle classes. The diet of these families was monotonous – rye bread, salted herrings, sour milk, fat bacon – and lacking in essential nutrients and vitamins. A 1906 survey of the health of elementary schoolchildren in Helsingfors (almost all from working-class families) found that one in ten was seriously undernourished, and a further 18.3 per cent were in need of extra nutrition. Damp, ill-ventilated workrooms, dangerous machinery and materials and the sheer strain of hard physical labour for twelve or more hours a day increased the likelihood of illness, maiming and premature death. The incidence of deaths from tuberculosis recorded in Tammerfors between 1889 and 1898 was 4.4 per thousand for the city's population as a whole, but 12 per thousand for artisans and their assistants, and 10 per thousand for shop assistants; both occupational groups worked in crowded, confined spaces where the bacillus was most deadly. A survey carried out by the trade unions in St Petersburg in 1912 revealed a lack of adequate ventilation, dampness, poor lighting and high temperatures in the majority of installations visited. In certain occupations, such as bootmaking and tailoring, workers rarely survived their fortieth birthday. Recorded industrial accidents in the St Petersburg *guberniya* shot up from 7,865 in 1909 to 14,288 in 1913, with a particularly high rate in the metalworking industry. There was a significant increase in the number of sickness and disability funds to which the workers themselves contributed, but they were a meagre protection against crippling injury or the more insidious loss of physical strength with the onset of old age.

The worker secured little rest and relief at home, and precious little solace in brandywine and schnapps, which undermined his health and threatened ruination to his family. The rents demanded for two- or three-roomed flats were usually too expensive for a working-class family to afford; and the cosy images of domesticity portrayed in advertisements and purveyed in the many journals devoted to house and home accorded ill with the reality of life for poor families, forced to move as many as three times in a year with their minimal amounts of furniture and bedding. A 1909 survey of working-class housing in Tammerfors commented laconically that rats played a very noticeable part in domestic life and concluded that a large section of the town's population lived in conditions not only dangerous to themselves but to the town in general.

Conditions were, if anything, even worse in the rural areas. Writers such as Jeppe Aakjær in Denmark or the Estonian writer Eduard Vilde, or campaigning journalists such as Isidor Kjellberg in Sweden revealed the darker side of life in the countryside. Working conditions and wages were generally poor. The eight-hour day introduced in Swedish factories in 1919 was not extended to the countryside, where the first regulations on working hours were brought in as late as 1936. Skilled factory workers could often earn two or three times as much as a farm labourer. Frequently obliged to move in search of employment, compelled to set his children to work at an early age, the farm labourer had little time and few resources for anything other than the basics of life. Malnourished and disease-ridden, his children started to resemble him from an early age, with their round-shouldered, sunken-headed posture. Isolated from the community, with few toys or books other than the treasured mail-order catalogue, the *statare* and his family existed in what one Swedish researcher of the 1920s described as a 'deep spiritual stagnation'.[7]

It was, however, the sheer concentration of the underfed masses in the cities which most pricked the bourgeois conscience and fuelled unease. State or communal assistance for the unemployed, sick and aged was still minimal, and there was considerable opposition to the whole idea of providing welfare benefits out of tax revenue. Nevertheless, the rapid growth of the proletariat threatened to overwhelm the already strained resources of private philanthropy. The likely consequences caused much anxiety in bourgeois circles. Outlining a plan for more effective central coordination of poor relief to a general meeting of the Literary and Practical Society of Riga in 1866, Alfred Hillner emphasised that 'poor relief [is not] merely a noble passion or a pietistic hobby of the so-called "devout" people, but it is the concern of the whole of human society, for it should be a fight of love, of wisdom and of discipline against the enemy, which, drawing together the individual elements of poverty and demoralisation into a compact force of disastrous dimensions, bears already in its very name – proletariat – a declaration of war against all that is good and orderly in human society'. The seeds of such a proletariat existed in Riga and would undoubtedly send up the weeds unless prompt and effective measures were taken to counter this pernicious prospect. Similar dire warnings and urgent cries for action were voiced in other northern European cities.[8]

7. Furuland L 1962 *Statarna i litteraturen*, Stockholm, p. 203. Dybdahl 1971 *De nye klasser 1870–1913* Gyldendals og Politikens Danmarkshistorie vol. 12, Copenhagen, p. 268, for the comments of a doctor in mid-Jutland on the health of over a thousand children of farm labourers that he had examined in 1906–67.

8. Vortrag über die Centralisation der Armenpflege Riga's *Baltische Monatsschrift* **14** (1866), p. 407. See for example Yrjö-Koskinen Y 1874 Työväen seikka *Kirjallinen Kuukauslehti* pp.1–9.

Although the steady advances made by the labour movement by the turn of the century seemed to confirm the worst bourgeois fears of an independently organised proletariat, it is possible to discern a strong integrationist current beneath the aggressive rhetoric of class struggle. It is now clear that the labour movement – where it was legally tolerated, at least – did not arise simply and solely as a response to proletarian class consciousness, but was part of a general pattern of associational activity which brought citizens together locally and nationally, opening up new perspectives and even career opportunities. Those who formed the core of the labour movement were not from the ragged, demoralised masses – the 'proletariat' of the popular imagination – but were respectable, sober and serious-minded skilled workers and artisans. It is tempting to argue that where repression was the order of the day, the possibilities for integration via participation in a whole range of decision-making processes (in parliament or local council, on the shop-floor, in consumers' cooperatives, even in workers' debating or glee clubs) was that much less; but even so, any perusal of the demands made in the 1905 Russian revolution would suggest that the strongly-expressed desire to be accorded full civic rights reflected a wish to be full and active members of society. The violence so feared by the respectable bourgeoisie was more often than not ignited by occurrences such as a sudden lockout, an eviction, or on occasion the clumsy overreaction of the police, and was invariably condemned by the labour leadership as counterproductive. Discipline was as essential for the organised labour movement as it was in the eyes of those who sought to raise the standards of the working classes.

In the western borderlands of the Russian empire, class also had an ethnic dimension. The rapid growth of the cities there significantly changed their ethnic and social composition, sometimes quite rapidly. Estonian speakers constituted only one-third of the inhabitants of Reval in 1820, when the city's population was less than 13,000. By 1913, the city's population had grown to 116,132, of whom over two-thirds were Estonian, just over 10 per cent German, and 11 per cent Russian. A massive influx of workers from the Russian hinterland during the war years tripled the numbers of Russian inhabitants in the city, no doubt adding to the city's housing problems. By the beginning of the twentieth century, a prosperous Estonian middle class was beginning to emerge; by 1912, Estonians constituted 42 per cent of the moderately wealthy property owners in the city.

The Germans were much more numerous and more powerfully entrenched in Riga, but here too, a Latvian middle class was beginning to take shape, with its own business and social networks.

How extensive was the blurring of the language and ethnic divisions at an everyday level is hard to determine, though the existence of sharply defined and strongly endogamous communities (Old Believers, Orthodox Jews) and the strong traditions of exclusivity reinforced by patterns of social activity and behaviour (i.e. patronising 'German' or 'Latvian' shops, services, institutions) would tend to suggest there was rather little.

Elsewhere, where language was not entirely class-exclusive, there does appear to have been a considerable degree of bilingualism. Heikki Waris concluded in the early 1930s that, at a time when the language question was top of the political agenda in Finland, it hardly existed in the working-class quarters 'north of the long bridge': 'here they worked together, lived in the same room, got married across the language divide, learnt to understand and even to speak each other's language tolerably well'. A survey published in 1920 concluded that bilingualism had increased over the past twenty years in the towns of Finland, and was far more common where there was a sizeable minority linguistic group. In the ten towns surveyed, with a total population of 437,600, almost one in three claimed to be bilingual, and the proportion rose by several per cent when the under-fifteens were omitted. In Helsingfors, with roughly the same number of Swedish- and Finnish-speakers around the turn of the century, and a sizeable Russian presence in the form of soldiers and sailors, the true street urchin (*stadin kundi*) spoke an intricate slang composed of elements of all three languages.[9]

LEISURE AND MORALITY

For the vast majority of adults, leisure was at best a luxury, at worst the bitter mockery of enforced idleness caused by unemployment. Hours of work were long, particularly on the land, and the opportunities for enjoying leisure were restricted. The Swedish farmhands portrayed by Martin Andersen Nexø rarely manage to get a break from their labours on the big farm on Bornholm during the

9. Waris 1973, p. 101. Tudeer A 1922 Kaksikielisyys Suomen kaupungeissa *Valvoja*, pp. 201–10. Paunonen H 1989 Från Sörkka till kulturspråk. Iakttagelser om Helsingforsslangen som språklig och sociokulturell företeelse *Historisk Tidskrift för Finland* **74**: 585–622. The poet Czesław Miłosz gives a fine portrait of the multilayered cultural and ethnic milieu of early twentieth-century Vilna in his book *Beginning with my streets*, London, 1992.

summer months, and when they do, they spend the time drinking brandywine or testing each other in games of strength. Card-playing, drinking and visiting the girls were pretty much the sum total of entertainments available in Mihkel Martna's rural Estonian childhood, a situation which was probably little different in other country villages of northern Europe. Country dances and music-making of the kind lovingly described in Carl Nielsen's reminiscences of his childhood on the island of Fyn were often frowned on by the stricter religious movements, and by the upholders of order and morality for their rowdiness and occasional boozy violence. Those who endorsed the notion of greater free time for the working man, from the bourgeois philanthropist to the labour leaders, with their demand for eight hours' labour, eight hours' rest and eight hours' leisure, were also anxious that this free time should be spent in earnest self-improvement. Backsliders who got drunk or went to bourgeois dances were obliged to apologise to their comrades in rural Finnish workers' associations, the records of which resemble nothing so much as a constant duel with the sins of the world, especially the demon drink. There were many who kicked against the pricks, as in this instance, recorded by an indignant female contributor to the handwritten newspaper (tellingly entitled *Paheiden piiska*, or the scourge of vices!) of the Kiuruvesi branch of the social democratic youth league in 1920:

> Should not working people provide an example to others in obeying the law [on prohibition] which they themselves have demanded? But with deep astonishment and sorrow, it must be admitted that this is not so. Often one can see actual members, even leading figures, of the workers' association and even of the youth league actually appearing drunk in public places . . .[10]

The fight against alcohol abuse played a key role in this broad civilising process, and it is not without significance that there was a particularly close relationship between the temperance and labour movements in all the Scandinavian countries. Although the Danish socialists differed over the consumption of beer, and contested the emphasis on individual accountability, they agreed with the Danish temperance association about the evils of brandywine and other spirituous liquors, which were to be had very cheaply in the country.

10. *Paheiden piiska*, 31/3/1920: this splendid piece of grass-roots literature is to be found in the collections of the People's Archives (*Kansanarkisto*) in Helsinki. See also Kirby D 1988 New wine in old vessels? The Finnish socialist workers' party 1919–1923 *Slavonic and East European Review* **66**: 426–45.

Workers should take the pledge for their own sake as well as for the sake of example, argued the social democrat A. C. Meyer, who went on to paint the inestimable economic, cultural and social benefits which would accrue. Influenced in the 1870s by American example, the temperance movement in Scandinavia grew rapidly; 22,000 Danes had joined the ranks by 1885, and 114,000, or 6.8 per cent of the population, by 1913. Sixty-four per cent of the members of the Second Chamber of the *Riksdag* between 1911 and 1917 were active supporters of temperance, whilst in 1908 over half the rural communes in Sweden responded positively to a request for a local vote on the sale of spirits, and 1,016 out of the 1,342 favoured prohibition. An unoffical national poll on total prohibition in 1909–10 recorded a 56 per cent vote in favour (though as state and local revenue from taxes on distillation and sales was very high, such a step would have had calamitous consequences without wholescale fiscal reform, at a time of considerable conflict over expenditure). The pressure exerted by the temperance movements in the Nordic countries resulted in a significant tightening-up of the laws governing the production and sale of spirituous liquors, and in the case of Finland, led to a rather disastrous period of prohibition in the 1920s.

Combating the evils of drink was merely one aspect of the temperance movement. It has been argued that it provided a means of passing from the norms and values of a patriarchal, church-bound rural society to those of a modern secular society, and it played an important role in the raising of national consciousness and self-esteem. This much was explicitly, if rather intemperately admitted by a leading Finnish advocate of prohibition in a parliamentary debate in 1921, when he accused representatives of the Swedish People's Party of seeking to improve the Swedish 'coastal race' with alcohol, whilst 'we intend to improve the Finnish race with sobriety and the prohibition law'.[11] On a more mundane level, temperance associations could sponsor housing projects, sports clubs, even build dairies. In the factory town of Silkeborg in central Jutland, the local association was able to open its own premises within five years of its foundation, offering meat soup at 50 øre a portion in its restaurant, accommodation and stabling for travellers, and a billiard room for the use of the public. Regular dances were also held as a further inducement to forsake the pubs, but the committee of management had some problems with modern fashions (and perhaps the habits of the clientele), for the rules adopted in 1911 stated categorically that: 'No-one may dance wearing

11. *Valtiopäivät 1921: Pöytäkirjat I*, Helsinki 1922, p. 192.

outdoor garments or headgear or with a cigar in the mouth or hand, similarly it is forbidden to dance with the wrong – left – foot forward'.[12]

The opportunities for hard-working citizens to pay their money and have a good time were rather more limited in northern European cities than in a great metropolis like London or Paris. There were occasional visits by the circus or the travelling fair, with its tightrope walkers and jugglers, and in the summertime, the populace could visit the Tivoli gardens, or admire the flora and fauna in the city's parks or zoo. In the long dark months of winter, there was rather less to do. The better-off classes could drink punch (or if they were more fashionable, whisky) or dine on oysters or veal in one of the city's fashionable restaurants, such as Blanch's café in Stockholm or Otto Schwarz' café on the Riga boulevards. In the 1890s, a typical Swedish evening repast, the *Sexa*, wine, a half-bottle of punch and coffee was likely to cost between four and five kronor. The average daily wage of an industrial worker at this time was 2:50 kronor, of a male farmworker, 1:40 kronor, and the working classes had to make do with rougher fare at cheap eating-houses or in their own cramped living quarters.

There were few music halls; and the Swedish Touring Club predicted in 1898 that varieties were unlikely to thrive any longer after the sale of punch on their premises had been declared illegal 'and the public are not content with beer alone'.[13] Professional, commercialised sport was as yet in its infancy, though ice skating was popular, and skiing for recreation was beginning to catch on. There was a wide selection of newspapers available. Riga at the turn of the century could boast fourteen German, six Russian and four Latvian newspapers and journals; the number of Estonian newspapers and periodicals published rose from twenty-seven in 1900 to eighty-eight in 1914, peaking at over 100 in the immediate aftermath of the relaxation of controls in 1905. Danes at the turn of the century had a choice of 206 newspapers, mostly small local journals. In addition to national, local and party political newspapers, there was a growing range of technical, professional and educational periodicals, whilst the illustrated family journals continued to enjoy huge circulation figures – Carl Aller's *Illustreret Familiejournal*, founded in 1877, was printing 260,000 copies

12. Poulsen P 1985 Afholdsbevægelse som disciplineringsagent *Fortid og Nutid* **32**: 171. It was probably the tango or the one-step which had earned the disapproval of the management.

13. *The Swedish Touring Club's Guide to Sweden*, London 1898, p. xxvi.

weekly in 1901, one for every other household in Denmark. This was also the golden age of the satirical journal – *Blæksprutten, Ravn, Söndags-Nisse, Kurikka, Fyren, Meie Mats* – and of talented cartoonists such as the Swede Albert Engström or the Estonian K. A. Hindrey. The American strip cartoon, syndicated throughout Europe, also began to make its appearance, the violent antics of the Katzenjammer Kids stirring up clouds of furious denunciation in the more sober-minded press.

The theatre throve in the larger towns. It was a point of pride and honour for the different linguistic communities in the cities of Russia's western borderlands to have their own theatre building and permanent company. The *Estonia* theatre, designed by the Finnish architects Lindgren and Lönn (1909–13), was rivalled by Bubyor and Vassiliev's German theatre (1910) in Reval. The city fathers of Riga helped subsidise the construction of a Russian (1902) and a Latvian (1908) theatre, to join the city's German theatre, built by the *Landtag* in 1863; there were also several variety and summer theatres in the suburbs. The stage was a popular diversion, and there were many enthusiastic amateur groups attached to the larger youth clubs or workers' associations. An even greater attraction was the cinema. The number of kinematograph theatres mushroomed in the years immediately before the outbreak of war. Moderate-sized towns could boast three or four theatres, offering a mixture of live entertainment and short films. The *Rekord* theatre in Reval, for example, tempted potential patrons with a chanteuse performing comical and satirical songs, a wisecracking comedian, a xylophonist and an Italian opera singer before the famous detective John Grey in a three-part drama flickered upon the silver screen. The popularity of Charlie Chaplin presaged the future conquest of the world by the American entertainments industry, but sharp entrepreneurs such as the Danish fairground showman Ole Olsen or the young Swedish bookkeeper Gustaf Björkman, able production managers and a talented range of directors such as Victor Sjöström and Mauritz Stiller laid the foundations of a successful domestic film industry.

Entertainment pure and simple was rather frowned upon by the tireless men and women who were so deeply involved in associational activities. A fairly sharp distinction was made between athletic exercise which was morally and physically uplifting (and beneficial to the nation) and that which was competitive and merely entertaining. The state actively supported the shooting clubs set up in Denmark in the 1860s; the ministry of war subsidised a handbook on gymnastics which was distributed gratis to these clubs in 1869; and even though *Venstre* supporters captured the central committee of the movement in 1885, they were careful to keep a couple of conservatives on the board to ensure that state subsidies continued. The movement – already divided over the kind of gymnastic exercises it should adopt, with progressives favouring the Swedish drill and the conservatives the more lively Danish model – split in two after a demonstration by clubs in the Vejle district on the release of the jailed *Venstre* leader Chresten Berg, but was reunited in 1893. Throughout this period, however, subsidies continued to be granted to both wings, though not to dissident bodies, nor indeed to other sporting organisations such as the Danish Athletics Association, which were deemed to promote individual competition. The link between gymnastics and nationalism has a long history, stretching back to the *Turnerbünde* of the Napoleonic era through to the *Sokoł* movement in the Polish lands of eastern Prussia at the turn of the century. The purpose of athletic exercise, it was argued, was not to win, or even to enjoy oneself in a reasonably sociable manner, but to become strong and disciplined, in harmony with one's fellows. The labour movement took up this ethos, though its male sporting heroes excelled in wrestling and weightlifting rather than gymnastics, fencing or shooting.

As we have seen, the relatively small size of the potential public, and the isolated situation of the northern European cities tended to place them on the outer fringes of the European concert or theatre tour, and their talented artists, like the singers Jenny Lind and Aino Ackté, became part of the same pattern of fleeting visits once they were established on the international stage. The longing for the heart of the country, or for the sighing of the wind through the firs, was in the end not enough for a composer of genius such as Sibelius; he needed audiences in Berlin and London for a reputation, much as painters such as Edvard Munch or Pekka Halonen needed to study and mix in artistic circles in Paris to learn techniques and make themselves known.

The need to be in close touch with the mainstream of European cultural developments was not without its problems. In certain cases, it could blur or destroy an artist's native originality. In many more, it led to a clash of values which went rather deeper than the reactions of an offended public or incensed critics to an exhibition of paintings or the performance of a new string quartet. Isolation had something to do with this, as did the streak of puritanism which marked so much of the nineteenth-century religious revival in northern Europe, but on the whole, it was not the inhabitants of Jutland fishing villages or the black-coated fundamentalists of Ostrobothnia who took part in cultural debate. At the heart of the feuding was the relationship of art and the artist to the national identity being forged by the myriad of organisations. The strong emphasis on the collective, uniting experience of active participation – especially noticeable in the vast music festivals staged with increasing frequency from the 1860s onwards – tended towards a certain narrowness of vision, an indifference or even hostility to that which did not fit, or did not belong. Andrejs Pumpurs' advice to his people not to think, say, do or sing what other people did, but to be faithful to their own roots and to act on their own behalf was echoed across Europe, wherever the frail plant of the native tradition appeared to be threatened by external cultural currents. Having invested much time and effort in creating an image of the people for the people's edification and enlightenment, the intellectual and cultural elites were often hostile to those who challenged or defied that image. Writing after the shattering experience of the civil war of 1918, for example, the Finnish critic Ilmari Havu praised the third-rate peasant writer Pietari Päivärinta for confirming and representing the idealist image of the people inherited from Runeberg and Topelius by the national movement, a pleasing image which Aleksis Kivi 'had dared to undermine'. In his own lifetime, Kivi's raw-boned portraits of peasant life had aroused fierce criticism, and he had decidedly not been one of the inner circle of favoured writers.[14]

The furious arguments which erupted in the mid-1880s over sexual morality, in which the old conventions and attitudes upheld by church, state and the better sort seemed to be challenged by an alliance of progressive artists, freethinkers and social reformers, revealed a state of social turmoil and exposed men, perhaps for the first time, to a contemplation of inner lusts and desires which was distinctly at odds with their conventional notions of womanhood and femininity. It also had wider ramifications. When in November 1871 Georg Brandes began his series of lectures at the university of Copenhagen on the main currents of modern European literature, he was attacked for supposedly endorsing 'what the men of the International call 'free love', i.e. in plain Danish: promiscuous copulation'.[15] The use of the term '*Internationale-Mændene*' was clearly intended to conjure up the

14. Havu I 1922 Pietari Päivärinta ja talonpoikainen leima suomalaisessa sivistyksessä *Valvoja*, pp. 152–5. See also Alhoniemi P 1972 *Idylli särkyy* Suomalaisen Kirjallisuuden Seuran toimituksia **305**, Helsinki.

15. By C. Rosenberg in the journal *Hjemdal*, 1872: cited in: Bredsdorff E 1973 *Den store nordiske krig om seksualmoralen*, Copenhagen, p. 27.

frightening bogey of the recently-crushed Paris Commune, and Danish readers needed no reminding that sparks from that conflagration had landed in their own backyard and were being vigorously fanned by Louis Pio and his companions. The distinction between 'European' and 'Danish' was later made by one of the leaders of *Venstre*, Sophus Høgsbro, to separate the anti-clerical radicals from the Grundtvigian-peasantist wing which he himself represented; and although the Copenhagen radicals remained within the camp of the opposition to Estrup, this distinction continued to set them apart from the solid nativism of mainstream *Venstre*.

A number of preliminary salvoes were fired by lesser writers before Henrik Ibsen's *Et dukkehjem* (A Doll's House, 1879) launched a major debate on the conventions of bourgeois marriage. Bjørnsterne Bjørnson, who had been an advocate of 'free love' before 1882, weighed in with *En handske* (A Glove, 1883), in which he advocated sexual abstinence before marriage for men as well as for women. This led to a breach of relations with August Strindberg, whose 1884 collection of short stories on married life (*Giftas)* brought upon him a charge of blasphemy. Even more sensational developments were taking place in Norway, where a tale of Bohemian life in the capital incurred the wrath of the authorities and caused its author to flee the country, to be followed by the banning of the painter Christian Krohg's novel about prostitution and police corruption. A debate on the moral issues involved organised by the liberal Uppsala students' organisation *Verdandi* in 1887 caused a scandal, with the organisers of the meeting hauled before the rector of the university and the wife of Professor Holmgren being shunned in polite society for not having left the hall when one speaker launched into an assault upon the Christian religion.

Much of the debate centred upon hypocritical sexual behaviour, and there was much vigorous campaigning for the removal of police controls over prostitution, which, the abolitionists claimed, merely encouraged and sanctioned the sale of human bodies for immoral purposes. Doctors, on the whole, were in favour of retaining regular medical inspection under police supervision in order to control the spread of venereal disease. Given the high incidence of reported cases – 5,000–6,000 cases of gonorrhoea and up to 2,000 cases of syphilis annually in Copenhagen in the 1890s, for example (in 1960, there were 4,542 cases of gonorrhoea and a mere 140 of syphilis in the city, with its much larger population) – and the pressures on hospital space, their attitude is understandable. Their laudable desire to curb the spread of sexually transmitted diseases did not, however, extend to an open endorsement of prophylactics. On the subject of sexual behaviour, they were as prone to moralise as the layman. The medical officer of the Danish city of Aarhus, for example, attributed the decline of the birthrate in the town in part to the fact that 'the public, informed by the advertisements in the Copenhagen yellow press, are obtaining for themselves: 'prophylactic or safety sponges', or 'protectors' for women, and for men, 'prophylactic condoms', and it has come to my knowledge that a not insignificant trade in these articles is being plied in the town'.[16]

Whilst it would be interesting to know who used such devices and in what circumstances, we are still snared by the great veil of ignorance which was firmly kept in place over the subject of sex. Pornography was probably only for the discreet and well-to-do. The crudely sensational covers of cheap paperbacks 'for men only' concealed pages of turgid and highly unilluminating prose.[17] In his surgery, Söderberg's Dr Glas is brought face-to-face with the harsh reality which underlay the fanciful notions of romantic love purveyed by the writers of cheap fiction and endorsed (though in more subtle ways) by writers of quality; the haggard women who cannot face another pregnancy, the tearful girls who have paid the price for surrendering their virtue. He himself commits murder in order to rid a young wife of the loathsome attentions of her elderly clergyman husband; and yet at the same time, he too is haunted by visions of romantic love.

Portrayal of the harsher realities of life caused turmoil and furore in the ranks of the better sort, though it is unlikely that the stormy waters spilled over into the 'deep ranks' (a popular term amongst the intellectuals) of the people. Those who wrote books which offended their peers were unlikely to enjoy massive sales amongst the populace. Georg Brandes reckoned on selling no more than 1,500 copies of his books, whilst a sale of 10,000 copies for a novel in Denmark was deemed a great success. Only 3,000 copies of the revised edition of *Giftas* were printed in 1885, and the impression was only sold out in 1900. Writers might hope to reach a wider audience through the many illustrated magazines and journals which did enjoy high

16. Cited in Dybdahl 1971, p. 289. To judge from advertisements in the press, at least, it would seem that condoms were intended for use in encounters with ladies of the night, and not for family planning.

17. Dybdahl 1971, pp. 347–58 is good on penny-dreadfuls and the not-so-naughty kiosk literature. Max Engman has also discovered a hand-written guide to eligible young ladies which circulated amongst the Finnish cadet corps in the late nineteenth century, though manners, upbringing and the fear of punishment if caught *in flagrante* make this a fairly innocent document. Engman M 1990 Finlands Tärnor – ett stycke manshistoria *Historisk Tidskrift för Finland* **75**: 264–97.

circulation figures, but their short stories were part of a general package of entertainment and enlightenment. The labour movement strove to bring high culture to its members by including stories by writers such as Zola and Anatole France, and tasteful reproductions of Rodin nudes, in the annual album; but to judge by the records of workers' libraries, the members preferred escapist or sensationalist literature to a serious read.

The civilising process was an integral part of the work of societies for the propagation of popular education such as the Finnish *Kansanvalistusseura* or the Finnish-Swedish *Svenska Folkskolans Vänner.* Such societies often enjoyed remarkable success; for example, within five years of being allowed to function freely, there were almost a hundred Estonian societies for popular education, with 20,000 members, supporting a range of kindergartens, schools, libraries and adult education courses. The civilising message was carried abroad by the seamen's missions, whose pastors strove manfully to winkle the sailors out of the clutches of the crimps, and to the very frontiers of the land, by Swedes amongst the Finns and Lapps of the north, by Finns on and across the border into deepest Karelia, by Latvians in backward, Catholic Latgale.

Women's leagues, farmers', workers' and youth associations, all created a sense of belonging and self-confidence, epitomised in the countless club rooms and assembly halls erected by the members. In certain respects, these organisations maintained a degree of continuity – staging festivals on traditional feast days, for example – but they also introduced new customs and habits. By the turn of the century, the Estonian bagpipes were virtually unknown to the younger generation, and the simple rustic dances at the village inn at which these pipes were often the only accompaniment had become a thing of the past. Like much else, dancing had become an organised affair, usually staged in conjunction with a choral performance or a play. The village fiddler was also on his way out, replaced by semi-professional musicians playing expensive factory-made instruments such as the hugely popular accordion. The traditional repertoires of choral societies were also changing. Instead of a handful of well-remembered sacred melodies, the rank-and-file member of a choral society was now expected to to be able to read music and to perform secular works by modern composers.[18]

18. See the contributions by Ellen Karu and Igor Tõnurist in: Viires A (ed.) 1985 *Eesti külaelu arengujooni*, Tallinn, pp. 58–109.

The elementary schools and their teachers inculcated not only the basic skills needed to help run these activities, but also discipline and good manners. As the Finnish novelist Väinö Linna noted drily in his 1950s novel *Täällä Pohjantähden alla* (Here under the North star), the handkerchief in the pocket of the schoolchildren on parade was a visible sign of Finnish culture. Martin Andersen Nexø's farmhand Lasse reminds his son Pelle, about to start school, that he has a pocket handkerchief and shouldn't use his fingers, because that is frowned upon. The fact that Lasse also says that if nobody is looking, Pelle can of course save on wear and tear raises the question of how receptive were those whom the national-cultural elite and their humbler minions in the schools sought to civilise. Conservatives had been shaking their heads for years over the foolishness of trying to raise up the ploughboy; the experiences of the first two decades of the twentieth century prompted many more to agonise over the worthiness of 'the people' in the national scheme of things.

Those who worried about the way things were going in the world spoke a great deal about falling moral standards and irreligiosity. The decline in religious observance was indeed particularly marked from the last decades of the nineteenth century, when measured in terms of church attendance or frequency of communion, though this was but one aspect of a more complicated picture. The loosening of the bonds between church and state had in several respects liberated the community of believers and revitalised Christian beliefs; but these beliefs were shared by fewer and fewer people. The churches did concern themselves rather more than hitherto with social questions, and there were significant new developments in pastoral work and lay involvement; but their adherents still tended to claim a close affinity between church, people and nation. The 'Young church' movement in Sweden strove for a religiously motivated people's church which would make the Swedish nation a people of God; socially aware and active in the promotion of social welfare, its adherents were also strongly nationalistic and enthusiastically supported the campaign to finance the F-boat armoured vessels in the immediate prewar years. Everyone would no doubt agree, argued a leading Finnish nationalist in 1889, that it was religion and the state church which upheld the national existence against the threat from the east; the morality of the people is founded entirely upon religion, and would vanish with its demise, claimed another participant in this debate. *Aamulehti*, an ardent champion of the Finnish national cause, fulminated in 1883 against the 'cultural nihilists' of the Swedish-minded party who would undermine the people's faith by abolishing religious instruction in schools; over three decades later, a succession of lay speakers at the general church assembly defended the proposal to increase the number of hours of religious instruction with stout assertions that this was the people's devout desire, in spite of all the efforts of the 'educated' classes and their godless allies in the labour movement to destroy this.[19]

THE TWILIGHT OF THE OLD ORDER?

The mood of resignation and pessimism was not peculiar to the Baltic region; it was a general fin-de-siècle phenomenon. The sense of living on borrowed time appeals very strongly to our own feelings of nostalgia about the pre-1914 world. We can admire the gaiety and bonhomie of Hugo Birger's 1886 painting of the Scandinavian artists' lunch at the café Ledoyen in Paris, or we can feel uncomfortable at the sight of manacled prisoners on the island of Sakhalin, photographed by the Dane Holger Rosenberg at the beginning of this century; but since we cannot smell or taste the past, we lack a vital, material dimension. Nostalgia, like the paintbrush or camera, is selective and prefers to idealise; it might be less receptive to the fug of tobacco on heavy clothing and drapery, or the smell of cockroaches and stale sweat.

This contrast between an idealised or imagined world and the mundane, everyday course of life may also be applied to the order of society a century ago. The old corporate order had split apart and disintegrated because it could no longer accommodate or contain the tide of expansion. In abolishing and abandoning the regulations and structures of the well-ordered eighteenth-century state, governments were acknowledging the momentum and scale of change, and allowing the initiative for the wellbeing of the commonweal to pass to the private sphere. The state by no means abdicated all its responsibilities. It played a key role in the financing of communications, and provided the legislative framework in which modern commerce and industry could properly function; it also defended and promoted national interests abroad, and it was the strains of bearing the cost of national

19. Juva M 1960 *Valtionkirkosta kansankirkoksi* Suomen Kirkko-historiallisen Seuran Tomituksia **61**, Helsinki, p. 271. Kortekangas P 1965 *Kirkko ja uskonnollinen elämä teollistuvassa yhteiskunnassa. Tutkimus Tampereesta 1855–1905*, Helsinki, p. 138. *Suomen Evankelisen-luterilaisen kirkon VIII:n yleisen kirkolliskokouksen pöytäkirja*, Turku, 1918, pp. 96–9, 544, 552, 555, for instances of the differing attitudes of the church leadership and the laity.

defence which prompted debate on the state's role as internal protector of those whom it sought to defend externally. Officialdom was also a palpable reality, in Denmark as much as in imperial Russia, though the *Amtmand* was rather less oppressive and certainly less corrupt than the *chinovnik*. But the established bastions of state authority were being outflanked by new innovatory forces. The balance between the exercise of state authority and the circulation of ideas and initiatives in society at large is always a delicate one, and harmony between the two is rare. Where the state would not or could not allow the free flow of ideas and action, as in Russia and to a certain extent in Germany, frustrations built up and there was always the likelihood of internal conflict. The blockage to the legislative system in Denmark during the Estrup ministry caused similar frustrations, which went further than the two entrenched political camps, as the initiatives taken by the farmers' lobby in the 1890s would seem to suggest.

The inadequacies of the patriarchal, patrimonial order with its narrow, static vision of the world may have been decently buried by the legislators, but many of the attitudes survived. The desire to protect and to restrict – a universal human characteristic – was certainly carried over from the age of the gilds and the estates into that of the free market in goods and services. The glittering trappings of aristocracy continued to have a powerful allure, and aristocrats themselves still managed to occupy top positions in government, the army, even in business. Rank and precedence were important, even though the scaffolding which had held up the edifice had been removed. Monarchy was still regarded as the natural form of government, as the Norwegians demonstrated in 1905, voting four to one in favour of having a king, rather than a republic. Rulers claimed the right to appoint and dismiss their own ministers, and to play an active role in politics. The injunctions of Martin Luther to obey higher authority were not lightly set aside in lands with strong traditions of loyal obedience, as the anguished debate over resistance in Finland during the early years of this century revealed. There was, in other words, a certain hesitancy and trepidation, as well as a sense of pride and exhilaration, about the present moment and an excessive reliance on the inheritance of the past; a past which was also stylised and romanticised, whether by the admirers of Karl XII in Sweden or the creative artists and writers in the Baltic provinces who delved into the realms of mythology for inspiration. The Danish radicals who cast doubt on the existence of God or the merits of Grundtvig, and who struck a doughty blow against hallowed tradition by refusing to adopt the honorary title of 'excellency' when appointed to government, or the 'dark masses' of the people aroused from their servility and lethargy by socialist schoolteachers (whose pernicious influence, so the Baltic German establishment believed, the policies of imperial authorities had somehow advanced), both in their different ways produced a counter-reaction which stressed order, discipline and loyalty to established institutions.

Around the edges of the closely-printed political columns of the daily press and beyond the loudly-voiced concerns of public men, however, life tended to follow its own directions. Tradition-conscious young scions of the Baltic German nobility boasted that they would thrash anyone who tried to explain to them the workings of the telephone. Historians have devoted a great deal of time to the thoughts and actions of such people, the Dellinghausens and the Samson-Himmelstjernas, and rather little to those who did take an interest in telephones; yet who can doubt which set of people have had more impact on the modern world? The way we live now has been shaped, more than we realise, by the young men, often with little formal education and often stuck in dead-end jobs in sleepy provincial towns, who eagerly read the available literature, built their own dynamos or ran the first picture-show in town, or who realised that the motor omnibus had a future.

Life in the provinces – and indeed, in the city suburbs – took its cue from high society, often to the point of parody, as in Hjalmar Bergman's sharply observed scenes of life in the imaginary Swedish town of Wadköping; but people did have other concerns, other aspirations, even other loyalties. Thousands from the scores of run-down dusty towns and villages between the Vistula and the Düna, and from the forests and stony fields of Scandinavia chose to follow their dreams of a different life by travelling westward across the Atlantic. Many thousands more took the less dramatic step, often out of necessity, of moving to the cities, or into the wilderness, northwards to the Arctic coast or into the depths of Russia. This vast movement of peoples no longer held in check by irksome restrictions binding them to a place of birth, work or worship was in itself a potential challenge to those who sought to redefine the state in terms of nation, rather than as the patrimony of a ruler. There was much concern in nationalist circles in Sweden in the early twentieth century about the outflow of emigrants to the New World and the influx of Jewish peddlers, Russian saw-sharpeners, Galician farmworkers and Finnish lumberjacks, for example. The German press wrote angrily about the unchecked influx of Russian immigrants and Polish seasonal workers, whilst the government and pressure groups strove to eliminate non-German elements in the eastern borderlands, from which large numbers of predominantly German-speaking migrants continued to move westward in search of better prospects. Communities heavily affected by the consequences of out-migration, such as the Jews, were also obliged to redefine their loyalties, aspirations, even beliefs. The first stirrings of national consciousness were even felt amongst linguistic minorities in which a separate sense of identity had hitherto been barely discernible, such as the Kashubians in West Prussia.

The context in which the above-mentioned developments were taking place is of course vital. Sweden and Denmark had had to adjust to the loss of territory, but neither had to absorb peoples of different religion, language and culture, or to cope with the kind of problems of empire with which Berlin and St Petersburg had to wrestle. Their peripheral position, the absence of large centres of population, long-established traditions of obedience to higher authority and accessibility to the administration, legislature and courts enabled them to avoid the more upsetting forms of social and political turmoil which beset central and eastern Europe. An honest and accountable bureaucracy, constructive and free debate of issues of national concern, educational systems which, in spite of their defects, were amongst the best in Europe, and a peasantry which participated actively in all aspects of national life were some of the features which set the Scandinavian countries apart from the closed and autocratic Russian empire.

Attached to that empire was the curious anomaly of the Grand Duchy of Finland, which resembled the Scandinavian countries in many ways. Finland's embryonic statehood grew from the institutional inheritance of 1809 and the impetus to use this actively and constructively in the reign of Alexander II; a sense of nationhood flowed as much from this as from the efforts to displace Swedish as the dominant cultural and administrative language. An ethnic Lithuanian national movement, on the other hand, had to contend with the powerful emotive appeal of the glorious, crushed past of the Polish-Lithuanian commonwealth, sustained to a very large extent by the Catholic clergy, as well as with the repressive measures of the imperial Russian authorities. The Jewish population in the Lithuanian lands also had its own concerns and aspirations. The legacy of serfdom hung heavily upon the Lithuanian, Latvian and Estonian national movements; but whereas the Lithuanians could derive some comfort from their historic past, the indigenous peoples of the Baltic provinces could see only the yoke of alien rule. A ruling elite which obstinately refused to become a nation, the Baltic Germans offered little by way of positive example for emulation. Their institutions were outmoded, and their ethos of service and devotion to the maintenance of the status quo could not serve as a rallying-point for conservative opinion across the national divide since it was so obviously predicated upon the preservation of German privilege.

The state was patently a good deal more brutal in its exercise of authority in the Russian empire than elsewhere, though some parts of the empire bore the brunt more severely than others, and there was an overall lack of consistency of oppression. Jews were treated far more harshly than other communities, but individual Jews could and did prosper and suffer relatively little discrimination. The use of Cossacks to break up a demonstration on the streets of Helsingfors in 1902 shocked Finnish public opinion, but was a very mild affair in comparison with the shooting of unarmed demonstrators on the streets of St Petersburg, Riga, Reval and other cities in the empire during 1905. Finns were dismissed from their posts or sent into exile (and after 1910, were imprisoned) for refusing to comply with measures deemed to be in breach of the Finnish constitution, but others were able to keep lines of communication open to influential figures in St Petersburg. There was always a degree of flexibility (or inconsistency) amongst the ruling circles, in Berlin as well as St Petersburg, which encouraged the advocates of working with the system, like J. R. Danielson-Kalmari in Finland, or H. P. Hanssen in Slesvig, and weakened the cause of stiff, uncompromising resistance.

Seen from a purely political perspective, the ambitions and aspirations of the autochthonous national movements in the borderlands of the Rusian empire were inextricably caught up in the tussle between a centralising power and the peripheral privileged elites. On the other hand, business was done, properties bought and sold, public space shared and jointly developed by the different communities. The organisation of specific interest groups – employers' federations, trades unions, chambers of commerce, householders' leagues, and so on – which proceeded apace here, and indeed throughout northern Europe from the turn of the century, suggests at least that there were concerns other than those highlighted by national struggles. By turning our attention to such developments, we may also acquire a new perspective on the complexities of national identity, which is as much about choice of partner, doctor or contractor, friends and social affiliations as it is about the symbols of nationhood devised and purveyed by those who make it their business to propagate such things.

CHAPTER EIGHT

The End of Empire: Russia in Revolution, 1905–1917

1905

On the second day of the new year of 1905, the Russian naval base of Port Arthur surrendered to the Japanese, almost a year after the outbreak of hostilities between the two countries. Two months later, the Russian land forces in Manchuria suffered defeat in the three-week battle of Mukden. Worse was to come; the Baltic fleet, which had set sail from Libau in October 1904, was virtually destroyed by the Japanese in May 1905. The Russian government immediately began making overtures for peace, and the war was brought to an end by the Treaty of Portsmouth in September 1905.

Against this background of military failure, the Russian empire was beginning to boil over internally. The forces of political opposition had begun to gather and articulate demands, and the hard-pressed regime was obliged to make concessions. A decree issued in December 1904 relaxed the censorship throughout the empire and promised a measure of religious toleration; in May of that year, the forty-year ban on the use of the Latin alphabet for Lithuanian literature was lifted; and the Finnish estates, convened at the end of the year, were able quietly to bury the 1901 military service law by offering to pay instead an annual sum towards imperial defences. There was a good deal of cooperation and consultation between the various oppositional parties within the empire, ranging from the smuggling of illegal literature and arms to the staging of conferences to draw up a programme for the transformation of Russia into a democratic republic.[1] But the one event which unleashed a fury of mass action and set Russia well and truly on the path to revolution was the cold-blooded shooting of hundreds of unarmed demonstrators in St Petersburg on 22 January 1905. 'Bloody Sunday' triggered a wave of massive demonstrations and strikes throughout the empire. In Riga, over 50,000 workers responded to the strike call issued by the Bund and the Latvian social democrats, and there were heavy casualties when demonstrators clashed with police and troops. In Kovno, where not only the factories and workshops but also the city's tram system and shops were closed down, crowds ignored the attempts of the governor to incite a pogrom. Jewish and non-Jewish workers also displayed solidarity in demonstrations in Vilna.

The unrest continued throughout the spring and summer, spreading into the countryside. To counter rural discontent, the government in February allowed the peasants the right to petition the council of ministers. The Estonian press encouraged the peasantry to take up this offer by printing model petitions. Jaan Tõnisson's moderate *Postimees* laid emphasis upon educational reforms and civil rights, and argued that the Estonian population should be united in one province, with all classes of society having the right to participate in the running of its affairs, at communal, municipal and provincial level. The more radical Reval newspaper *Teataja* wanted a democratically-elected assembly and the reform of provincial institutions on the same principles. The social democratic *Uudised* called for a democratically-elected all-Russian parliament, and wide autonomy for the peoples of the empire. Both *Teataja* and *Uudised* demanded land reforms in favour of the peasant farmer, though the latter envisaged nationalisation of the land as the ultimate objective.

The rural proletariat in the Baltic provinces was also organising itself. In the late summer of 1905, some 800 delegates convened and elected an executive to prepare for a national congress of Estonian farm workers in November. In Kurland, 30,000 farmhands went on strike in July, and managed to win pay rises and a shorter working day. The conflict on the land was particularly bitter and protracted in this province and in southern Livland, and a virtual state of war existed by the end of the summer, with groups of peasants attacking and

1. On this pre-revolutionary period, see: Akashi Motojir 1988 *Rakka Ryūsui, Colonel Akashi's report on his secret cooperation with the Russian revolutionary parties during the Russo-Japanese war* Studia Historica **31**, Helsinki, which also contains a lengthy article by Antti Kujala on the Paris and Geneva conferences of the opposition parties of the empire.

burning manor houses and fighting pitched battles with the forces hastily assembled by the local Baltic German nobility. The nobility bombarded St Petersburg with requests for effective measures to be taken to combat the unrest. In June, for example, referring to recent disorders in the Wenden district, they demanded aggressive action (i.e., the use of firearms) against all gatherings under the red flag; peasant communes which had countenanced secret meetings or disorder, or had done nothing to ensure the arrest of ringleaders, would have to bear the costs of quartering troops. It was also to be made known that any cyclist who failed to halt and prove his identity would be handed over to the authorities for punishment. There were strikes on large estates in the Lithuanian lands, and unrest on the land in Finland, where there were numerous instances of leasehold crofters refusing to perform boon work.

Throughout the empire, the press defied the modified censorship, reporting on the strikes and disorders and pressing the case for thoroughgoing reform of a corrupt and rotten system. The festering boil burst in October. Lacking the will or the means to combat the revolutionary strikes which were spreading throughout the empire, the tsar issued a manifesto on 30 October, promising full civil rights and a liberal franchise for the election of a parliament (*Duma*) which was given the right to approve all legislation.[2] This action was insufficient to stem the rising tide of unrest. The principal cities of the Baltic provinces and the Polish-Lithuanian lands had been plunged into revolution on 25–26 October. The Finns were much slower to join in, and did so on their own terms. The strike on the railways in Russia was already four days old before traffic on the stretch of line from the Finland Station in St Petersburg to the Finnish border was brought to a halt. The Finnish labour movement agreed on 30 October to join forces with the constitutionalists in setting up an eight-man coordinating committee and organising the national strike, though reserving the right to withdraw if joint action was impossible. The labour delegates supported the constitutionalists' demand for the dismissal of compromised officials and the Senate, but rejected the convention of the *Lantdag* in favour of a constituent assembly elected by universal suffrage.

2. For the text of the manifesto, and an extensive survey of the events leading up to it, see Ascher A 1988 *The revolution of 1905*, Stanford, p. 229 *passim*. To avoid confusion, dates of events in the Russian empire will be given according to the Gregorian (new-style) calendar, which was thirteen days ahead of the old-style Julian calendar; hence for all other Europeans, the February revolution occurred in March, and the October revolution in November 1917.

This difference of opinion was soon to drive a wedge between the two sides, but on the whole, the strike was a patriotic demonstration supported by workers and bourgeoisie alike. Order was maintained by volunteer national guards. The soldiers stationed in the country kept a low profile, though rumours of troop movements added a slight edge of tension to what was a remarkably peaceable week, in comparison to what was happening across the Gulf of Finland, where troops had fired on a demonstration in the New Market in Reval on 29 October, killing 60 people and wounding 200. On Wednesday 1 November, the Finnish constitutionalists, having secured the resignation of the Senate and believing that the situation in St Petersburg was returning to normal, argued for a termination of the strike in order not to provoke a reaction from the Russian side. It was their draft for the restoration of the constitutional order which the governor-general agreed to transmit to St Petersburg, not the demand of the labour movement for the convention of a national assembly, and it was this draft which formed the basis of the tsar's manifesto, brought back from St Petersburg by a Finnish delegation on 4 November. The central strike committee went ahead with the rather meaningless election of a provisional government by the citizens of Helsingfors, and brought the strike to an end two days later.[3]

'The struggle begun by the workers of these past few grand days was at first completely national and patriotic', declared Yrjö Mäkelin, a Finnish social democrat with pronounced nationalist proclivities, 'but now it is changing, through force of circumstance, into a class struggle.'[4] Even allowing for Mäkelin's own sense of frustration (he was the principal author of the scheme to elect a provisional government), there is a ring of truth in his words, borne out by the evidence of strike committee reports and the minutes of workers' meetings. The experience of the strike week gave workers a sense of their own power, and of their own interests. It drew large numbers into the Finnish Social Democratic Party. Membership rose from around 16,500 at the end of 1904 to 45,298 a year later, and reached a peak of nearly 100,000 in 1906.

Emboldened by this flood of support, the Social Democratic Party sought to raise the political stakes. The next struggle would be against

3. Documents covering the strike week are printed in: Kirby D (ed.) 1975 *Finland and Russia 1808–1920*, London, pp. 105–17. The most detailed account is by a contemporary: Roos S 1906 *Nationalstrejken i Finland*, Helsingfors 2 vols, though see also Kujala A 1989 *Vallankumous ja kansallinen itsemääräämisoikeus* Historiallisia Tutkimuksia **152**, Helsinki.

4. *Kansan Lehti*, 11 November 1905: Kirby 1975, p. 117.

bourgeois privilege, proclaimed the central strike committee on 6 November at a mass meeting in Helsingfors. The workers were to be prepared to renew the strike to ensure their demands were met, and the party created an organisational structure to deal with that eventuality. Privately, however, party leaders worried that the situation might slip out of their control. In February 1906, the party council finally ruled out strike action as a means of applying pressure for suffrage reform, since it was believed such a tactic without corresponding action in Russia would be doomed to failure. This decision was, however, blurred by the party council's policy of continuing publicly to prepare for strike action, and by the inflammatory language of the socialist press. The national guards which had been set up at the beginning of the strike had soon split into a workers' Red guard and a bourgeois White guard, and an open clash between units of these two bodies on the streets of Helsingfors had been narrowly avoided at the end of the strike. During the spring of 1906, there was a spate of robberies and thefts of dynamite, in which elements of the Red guard were involved. Contacts were also made with Russian revolutionary groups, and the Finnish Red guard leadership was involved in plans for a military uprising. As it turned out, the revolt began prematurely at the end of July on the island fortification of Sveaborg. The Red guards actively supported the uprising, and threatened at one stage that the city of Helsingfors would be bombarded from the island if the party council continued to refuse to sanction a general strike. As the mutiny collapsed on 2 August, an armed detachment of White guards attempted to prevent gangs of workers and Red guards shutting down the tramway power system, and a scuffle broke out. Shots were fired and troops and police had to restore order. Party leaders who tried to persuade the workers to return to work were shouted down, and although the unrest subsided, a legacy and a myth had been created which was to dog the Social Democratic Party once again in 1917.[5]

The Finnish Social Democratic Party maintained a careful distance between itself and the revolutionary movement in the rest of the empire. Intimate involvement with the Russian revolutionaries could endanger Finland's special status, in the view of party leaders, whose principal objective in 1906 was to ensure the transformation of the outmoded four-estate *Lantdag* into a modern, unicameral legislature

5. Kujala 1989, p. 155 *passim*. There is also a brief account of the unrest of 1906 and the Sveaborg uprising in my unpublished (1971) London Ph.D. thesis, *The Finnish Social Democratic Party 1903–1918*, pp. 60–80.

elected on the basis of universal suffrage. Once this objective had been attained, with remarkably little disagreement amongst the non-socialist members of the four estates which had been convened to debate the proposals for reform, the Finnish Social Democratic Party could focus its class rhetoric on electioneering, not on renewal of a mass strike which it well knew would not succeed. Socialists elsewhere in the empire were not so fortunate, for although a fairly generous measure of suffrage was conceded for the elections to the first *Duma*, there was widespread mistrust of the tsar's promises of civil liberties, which were belied by the presence of troops on the streets and the armed suppression of workers' organisations.

The epicentre of the revolution in the Baltic provinces was the Latvian countryside, where democratically elected executive committees replaced the peasant communes, and exercised considerable powers. Local administrative functions were also taken over by democratically-elected officials in many parts of the Lithuanian lands. It has been argued that the organisational structure adopted by the Latvian social democrats was pivotal to the party's expansion into the countryside and its revolutionary activities. Other explanations for the revolutionary temper of the peasantry of Kurland and southern Livland range from a decline of religiosity and respect for elders to friction with the Baltic Germans (the largest number of estates destroyed were located in districts with relatively high proportions of Baltic German residents, for example).[6] Northern Livland was less troubled by disturbances. The main outbreak of looting and burning in Estland occurred in December, when, angered by the imposition of martial law which had prevented the meeting in Reval of a congress of delegates of rural communes, bands of workers and peasants went on the rampage in the surrounding countryside and destroyed some 100 estates within a week. The peasant fury in the Baltic provinces, where almost 600 estates suffered damage totalling over 12 million roubles, was ruthlessly suppressed in the winter of 1905–6. Hundreds were

6. See the report to the third *Duma* on the unrest, printed as: Pribaltiyskiy kray v 1905 godu *Krasnyi Arkhiv* **11/12** (1925): p. 275. On the Latvian social democrats' impact on the countryside, see the article by A Puļķis in: Ezergailis A, Pistohlkors G von, (eds) 1982 *Die baltischen Provinzen Russlands zwischen den Revolutionen von 1905 und 1917* Quellen und Studien zur Baltischen Geschichte **4**, Cologne, pp. 115–24. Raun T 1984 The revolution of 1905 in the Baltic provinces and Finland *Slavic Review* **43**: 453–67. A Reich German observer noted in 1916 that the reason why the native element in Kurland, unlike that of Prussia, had not been assimilated lay in the 'determined exclusivity which the German lord maintains against the Latvian underlings': Marquart B 1916 *Die landwirtschaftlichen Verhältnisse Kurlands*, Berlin, vol. 1, pp. 120–1.

killed or executed, many more were forced to flee or were sent into exile.[7]

Amongst the Latvians, it was social democracy which dominated the scene and set the political agenda. Estonian social democracy was much weaker. Here, it was the disparate strands of nationalist opinion which predominated. The moderates around the newspaper *Postimees* came together to form the Estonian Progressive People's Party in November, and shortly afterwards, convened an all-Estonian congress in Dorpat. Although the method of selection was intended to favour the moderate cause, the radicals gained the upper hand in the initial stages, and the congress thereupon split into two meetings, both of which produced resolutions. Both favoured national autonomy, though the radicals looked to the revolutionary overthrowal of tsarism as the necessary precondition, whilst the moderates pinned their faith in the existing government to call a constituent assembly for Estonia. The moderates also spelled out in detail their proposals for self-government for Estonia, which was to be created through the administrative union of Estland and the Estonian districts of Livland. The radicals' resolutions dwelt more upon the methods of continuing the revolutionary struggle and advocated settlement of the land question by expropriation of the large estates, abolition of all noble privileges and hindrances to peasant freedoms. Jaan Tõnisson, the leading spokesman of the moderate wing, rejected the continuance of the revolutionary struggle advocated by the left, but also spurned overtures by the Baltic Germans.[8]

The question of national autonomy was also raised at the congress of delegates of the executive committees in Riga at the beginning of December 1905, but the social democrats managed to deflect this into discussion of the convention of an All-Russian constituent assembly which would determine the scope of Latvian self-government. A two-day national congress held at the same time in Vilna also demanded autonomy for the Lithuanian lands. The significance of these demands lies not in their immediate practicability – for the main emphasis at the time was upon revolutionary seizure of power in a highly volatile situation – but as a marker for the future. The concept

7. For two differing contemporary accounts, see: Ames E (ed.) 1907 *The revolution in the Baltic provinces of Russia*, London, and: Pribaltiyskiy kray v 1905 godu *Krasnyi Arkhiv* **11/12** (1925): pp. 263–88.

8. Raun T 1987 *Estonia and the Estonians*, Stanford, p. 84–5. Jürisson M 1908 *Punaset vuodet Virossa 1905, 1906 ja 1907*, Helsinki, p. 158 *passim*. Karjahärm T 1975 Reformide küsimus Eestis 1905 aastal *Revolutsioonist revolutsioonini 1905–1940* (Arumäe H, (ed.)), Tallinn, pp. 23–42.

of autonomy was much discussed, but without a clearly defined context, it was hard to relate to reality. The Lithuanian social democrats had, for example, endorsed in 1896 the idea of an independent democratic federal republic which would have included Poland, Lithuania, Belorussia, the Ukraine and – presumably for reasons of linguistic affinity – Latvia.[9] In January 1905, the party central committee issued a manifesto which visualised the creation of a democratic Lithuanian state with its own parliament (*Seimas*) and government within a federation (which by now seems to have included Russia). There was opposition to the nationalist tendencies within the party, which surfaced after the 1905 revolution. Critics of the nationalist tendency argued that the rather utopian position adopted by the party in 1896 now had to be redefined in the light of the revolutionary events of 1905. At a nine-day congress in Kraków in 1907, the autonomists – whose primary concern was the establishment of a democratic Russian republic in which Lithuania would have autonomous status – won the day over the federalists.[10]

The rather confused debate within the Lithuanian Social Democratic Party reflects the multifaceted background of the Polish-Lithuanian historical legacy, the pull of the Russian revolutionary movement, and the diverse influences of contemporary socialist movements – the nationalist socialists of Piłsudski's PPS, the anti-nationalists of the SDKPiL (Social Democracy of the Kingdom of Poland and Lithuania), and the cultural autonomists of the Bund. Latvian social democracy was more resolutely anti-national. It was committed to a democratic Russian state in which there should be a wide measure of local self-government for the different provinces; party ideologues such as Pēteris Stučka frequently voiced their preference for proletarian solidarity over bourgeois nationalism. Nevertheless, the ideas on national autonomy advanced by the Austrian Marxists Karl Renner and Otto Bauer were taken up in Latvian socialist circles. On the eve of the First World War, Margers Skujenieks argued the case for national cultural autonomy, claiming that russification was harmful to the cultural development of the

9. Sabaliūnas L 1990 *Lithuanian social democracy in perspective 1893–1914*, Durham and London, p. 37. The idea of a federal state based on the old Polish-Lithuanian commonwealth was an old one, and had been raised, for example, in the 1863 rebellion. Alesandravičius E 1992 Political goals of Lithuania 1863–1918 *Journal of Baltic Studies* **23**: 230.

10. Sabaliūnas 1990, pp. 35–40, 50, 118–27. For a somewhat different picture, which draws on Lithuanian communist writings, Page S 1959 *The formation of the Baltic States*, Cambridge, Mass., pp. 6–8.

Latvian working class: all workers belonging to small and politically oppressed peoples had perforce to be nationalists. Mikelis Valters, who had been one of the founding members of the small Latvian Social Democratic Union which had come out for self-rule and a constituent national assembly for Latvia in December 1905, advocated at around the same time a peasant-worker alliance to defend national and democratic rights. These ideas did not please the internationalists, who placed class solidarity before nationalism; but in spite of their negative attitude, the Latvian social democrats, by pressing for radical democratic reforms which would have shattered the grip of the Germans and the Russian bureaucracy, were 'the only ones who indicated a political course which might offer the possibility for further development of the national culture'.[11]

The revolution shook the established order profoundly. The Swedish-speaking upper-class element in Finland accepted with good grace the abolition of the four estates, which had given them a disproportionate say in the affairs of the nation, and were able within a short space of time to weld together a highly effective minority Swedish People's Party, with almost 50,000 members in the autumn of 1906. The Baltic Germans were less adaptable, although proposals for reform were discussed. The project laid before a conference of representatives of all the *Ritterschaften* in May 1905 and later presented to the ministry of the interior envisaged a restructuring of local government, with a series of assemblies elected on a three-class system which would have ensured the Baltic German minority control at all levels. This proposal, which was endorsed by all the provincial diets, was overtaken by events. The restoration of order and the protection of property was the main concern of the Baltic German leadership, and to this end they sought military assistance through their friends in high places in the capital, and demanded the restoration of the governor-generalship for the three Baltic provinces. This last request was conceded in December 1905. An imperial rescript created a temporary governor-generalship, with an advisory Baltic Council composed of two delegates from each of the four provincial diets, Reval, Riga and Mitau and eight delegates from the rural communes of the Estland, Livland, Kurland and Ösel. This council laboured for over a year to devise an acceptable scheme of reform for the

11. Alksnis I 1983 *Den marxistiska publicistiken i Lettland 1912–1914* Bibliotheca Historica Lundensis **52**, Lund, p. 150. Alksnis also analyses in detail Skujeniek's book *Nacionālais jautājums Latvijā* (St Petersburg, 1914). There is a brief but useful overview of Latvian social democracy up to 1905 by Detlef Henning in: Loit A (ed.) 1990 *The Baltic countries 1900–1914* Studia Baltica Stockholmiensia **5**:1, Stockholm, pp. 167–75.

provinces; but the one project sent to the ministry of the interior, which envisaged representation for all tax-payers at the local and provincial level in Livland, was simply shelved. Talks between Baltic German leaders and representatives of the Estonians failed to arrive at any lasting agreement. The experiences of 1905–6 made it highly unlikely than any common accord could be found. Max von Sivers, writing to the historian Theodor Schiemann in April 1906, complained of feeling like a powerless stranger coming back to his estate at Roemershof, watched by his smirking servants, and he admitted later that year that the landowners could not hope to hold out without the backing of the imperial government. Without that support 'like Californian desperadoes, we would be able to hold out at the most only a few months'.[12]

The Lutheran church also suffered a severe loss of prestige and authority. Church buildings were targets for popular demonstrations in Livland and Kurland, and clergymen seem to have been especially singled out for ill treatment in 1905–6. The authority of the church in Finland was badly dented during the Bobrikov era, when its doctrine of obedience to higher authority went against the grain of patriotic sentiment, and the abolition of the four estates in 1906–7 was a further blow. Since its bitterest opponents were the most enthusiastic supporters of democracy, many clergymen held a rather jaundiced view of parliamentarianism, and the Finnish clergy as a whole remained firmly anchored on the conservative right of the political spectrum for many decades. The Catholic church in the Lithuanian lands had been in the forefront of the educational battle against the russifiers, and the majority of private Lithuanian schools permitted by the authorities after 1905 were controlled by Catholic societies. As in other Catholic countries, however, there was a strong streak of anti-clericalism in the secular teaching profession. The Lithuanian teachers' union was organised under the wing of the democratic party, which inherited many of the secularist, radical-liberal traditions of the *Varpas* group, and which proclaimed as its ultimate goal a free and independent Lithuania. In the Baltic provinces, elementary schoolteachers tended to align themselves with social democracy, and many fell victim to the punitive expeditions sent in to restore order in

12. Pistohlkors G von 1972 Führende Schichte oder nationale Minderheit? *Zeitschrift für Geschichte Osteuropas* **21**, pp. 606–7. On the Baltic Germans in 1905–7, see Pistohlkors G von 1978 *Ritterschaftliche Reformpolitik zwischen Russifizierung und Revolution* Göttinger Bausteine zur Geschichts-wissenschaft **48**, Göttingen, and Tobien A von 1925 *Die livländische Ritterschaft in ihrem Verhältnis zum Tsarismus und russischen Nationalismus*, Riga, vol. 1, pp. 442–54.

1906. Their supposedly malign influence over the young was seen by the Baltic Germans as a contributory factor in the outbreak of violence and terror of 1905.[13]

Although the banners upon which they were inscribed often bore the bullet-holes of the forces of repression, the revolutionary slogans of the left had undoubtedly won the day in 1905, and continued to have an immense appeal. On the whole, support for the bourgeois nationalist parties was largely confined to the thin strata of the native intelligentsia and middle class. Lively and original ideas were advanced, certainly, but they were limited to small circles such as the Young Estonia group. The Finnish Agrarian Union formed after the parliamentary reform of 1906 remained a regional farmers' party for the next decade. *Lidums*, the newspaper of the Latvian Peasant Union, added a new voice to political debate after 1914, and the Union itself claimed 20,000 members in 1917, but its political effectiveness was limited. Social democracy in the Russian empire was given no opportunity to establish itself as a legal, mass movement like the SPD in Germany, but no other political movement capable of attracting mass support emerged during the last days of the empire. In Finland, largely untouched by the tsarist reaction until 1908–9, the Social Democratic Party won 80 of the 200 seats in the first parliamentary elections of March 1907 and maintained that dominant position in subsequent elections.

Social democracy's popularity owed little to Marxist ideology or declared policies, which were in any case often contradictory and unclear in certain crucial areas, such as the land and national questions. Its success lay rather in its ability to strike a resonant chord amongst people living in wretched and miserable conditions, in which vibrant visions of a radical and total transformation were far more attractive than cautious promises offered by remote gentlemen in smart town clothes. Its uncompromising message, often couched in evangelical tones, echoed the hostility of the poor and deprived towards those evidently better situated than themselves, and offered a hope for the future.[14]

The momentous days of October–November 1905 seemed to suggest that such hopes could be realised by revolutionary action; and

13. See for example Gustav Seesemann's article, Die Revolution und die Jugend in Hunnius C, Wittrock V (eds) 1908 *Heimatstimmen. Ein baltisches Jahrbuch* vol. 3, Reval, pp. 78–95.

14. The quasi-religious language and appeal of social democracy has been commented upon by several writers. See Soikkanen H 1961 *Sosialismin tulo Suomeen*, Porvoo-Helsinki, pp. 295ff. Alksnis 1983, pp. 79ff.

the possibility of a second chance, though momentarily dashed, was ever-present in an empire which was living on borrowed time. Notwithstanding the changes which did occur and the brief moments of political vigour of the immediate post-revolutionary years, the empire lacked the power and ability to regain the confidence of huge and diverse sections of its inhabitants. Few of those living on its western borderlands privately imagined that their departure would be so sudden, and none publicly advocated independent statehood. The established order had nevertheless been challenged, notions of ethnic-territorial unity had been advanced, plans for radical reform of the structure of government had been adumbrated and the replacement of non-representative bodies by democratically-elected institutions demanded – and in the case of Finland, achieved. If not the dress rehearsal for 1917, 1905 certainly gave the players a good opportunity to learn and practise their parts.

THE ROAD TO WAR

Whilst the Russian empire was wracked with internal disorder, the union between Sweden and Norway was being peaceably dissolved. With the attention of the great powers distracted by war in the Far East and the growing Moroccan crisis, Sweden and Norway had been able to effect their divorce with relatively little outside interference. Nonetheless, the balance of forces in northern Europe was significantly affected by the breakup of the union, and as a result of the naval disaster which befell the Russian Baltic fleet at Tsushima Bay. The Baltic area attracted the attention of British foreign policy-makers in a manner that had not been seen since the early eighteenth century. The British war plans of 1907 assigned a significant role to the Baltic as a possible theatre of offensive war operations against Germany, whose naval pretensions were viewed with great suspicion by Sir John Fisher, first sea lord at the admiralty from 1904 to 1910. Fisher had already dispatched the Channel fleet to carry out manoeuvres in the Baltic in the summer of 1905 as a veiled warning to the Kaiser not to contemplate too active involvement in the Scandinavian crisis, an action repeated in succeeding years. The British were also perturbed at the prospect of a divided Scandinavia falling easy prey to German or Russian designs, and these fears were increased in 1907 when the Russian foreign minister A. P. Izvolsky proposed to the British and French governments the rescinding of the clauses of the 1856 Paris peace treaty which prohibited the fortification of the Åland islands. Izvolsky was also working secretly towards a Russo-German agreement, to which Sweden and Denmark would also be attached, designed to exclude non-Baltic powers from influence in the area. The spectre of a renewed form of the Armed Neutrality of the late eighteenth century alarmed the French even more than the British, and there was a rapid cooling of the Franco-Russian entente, which was an added complication to the already over-intricate game Izvolsky was playing.

Although alarmed by the Russian demand for the abrogation of the Åland island clauses, the Swedes were also annoyed with the British for failing to persuade the Norwegians to accept Sweden as one of the guarantors of Norway's territorial integrity. Without such a status, the Swedes believed the guarantee treaty could only be directed against them, and would leave them with a potentially troublesome neighbour. The British, on the other hand, did not favour a guarantee of Norwegian neutrality which might prevent them making a pre-emptive strike against Norway in the event of Germany seizing Denmark and threatening to close off the Baltic to British shipping. Sweden was attracted to the idea of a Russo-German agreement on the Baltic, and elements of the government (and the king) were even prepared to agree to a revision of the Åland islands convention after a tripartite treaty guaranteeing the status quo in the Baltic had been signed. The Swedish minister to St Petersburg spoke out strongly against this, however, arguing that, in spite of Izvolsky's assurances to the contrary, the Russians did intend to fortify the islands. The issue was taken up by the press and the liberal opposition. Swedish public opinion was clearly opposed to any concessions over the Åland islands, and the government beat a retreat on the issue. The final agreement, signed by Denmark, Germany, Russia and Sweden, guaranteed the status quo in the Baltic; no mention was made of the Åland islands convention, though the door was left ajar by a clause acknowledging the free exercise of the rights of sovereignty of the contracting parties within their respective territories.[15]

Izvolsky had been thrown off course by the Germans' desire to extend the scope of the agreement to cover the North Sea. This

15. These negotiations are examined in detail in: Lindberg F 1958 *Scandinavia in great power politics 1905–1908*, Stockholm, and Luntinen P 1975 *The Baltic question 1903–1908* Suomalaisen tiedeakatemian toimituksia **B 195**, Helsinki. See also Sweet D 1970 The Baltic in British diplomacy before the first world war *Historical Journal* **13**: 451–90.

agreement also skated over the vital question of defining precisely where the North Sea ended and the Baltic Sea began – a matter of some importance in regard to access to the Baltic. It was also rendered largely nugatory by developments on other fronts. The Danes were anxious to assure the Germans of their willingness to repel any British attempt on the seaward defences, as the 1909 defence plans with their provisions for a powerful defence of Copenhagen from the sea sought to demonstrate. The fact that Germany so effectively controlled the Sound and the Belts further weakened support for Fisher's ideas of an active naval strategy in the Baltic. The decision of the committee of imperial defence to commit British forces to the defence of France in the event of war with Germany meant that the Royal Navy in such circumstances would not enter the Baltic until Germany had been defeated. Britain and France provided financial and material assistance towards the rebuilding of a Russian Baltic fleet. The Russians also embarked on a revised defensive operational plan, significantly taking into their calculations the possibility of a Swedish attack. This had consequences for Finland, whose inhabitants were generally regarded as untrustworthy by Russian military officials; measures taken after 1908 to curb Finnish autonomy were without doubt partly motivated by the anxieties of the army command.

Fear of Russian intentions, luridly portrayed by the publicist Sven Hedin in his 'warning words' of 1912 and 1914, continued unabated in Sweden and cast its light upon the heated debate over defence. In truth, there was not a great difference between the liberals and conservatives on this issue, as a careful scrutiny of the public utterances of the liberal leader and prime minister from 1911, Karl Staaff, makes clear. What was at issue was who governed Sweden. Gustav V's personal antipathy towards Staaff led the king into intrigues with right-wing politicans. The mass demonstration of peasants organised at the beginning of 1914 was intended primarily to express general concern about the defence issue, and was not deliberately anti-government. The speech which the king delivered to the demonstrators on 6 February, however, was confrontational, an open challenge to the principles of the government's defence policy, and it prompted Staaff's resignation.[16]

16. The speech was largely the work of Sven Hedin; Gustav V had disregarded advice to tone down some of the more openly partisan passages. See Wichman K 1967 *Gustaf V, Karl Staaff och striden om vårt försvar 1901–1914*, Stockholm, pp. 145–81. Brusewitz A 1951 *Kungamakt, herremakt, folkmakt. Författningskampen i Sverige (1906–1918)*, Stockholm, pp. 59–79.

This constitutional crisis – the repercussions of which will be considered later – underlined once again the close and often uneasy relationship between matters of national security and domestic politics. By intimating that the introduction of social reforms such as provision of old age pensions would mean cuts in defence spending, Staaff had linked the two together, and entered into an area which the king still thought of as pre-eminently his own. Hence the defence of 'my' army by Gustav V and the king's wholehearted identification with the demands of the army experts on controversial issues such as the period of training.

Gustav V's sensitivity on the question of defence was comparable to that of Christian IX of Denmark some years earlier, when the radicals had formed their first government. Even though *Radikale Venstre* toned down its anti-militarism considerably once in office, suspicions still lurked in court and conservative circles. Both monarchs continued to demand and play an active role in the conduct of foreign policy, though neither was as foolhardy or troublesome to his officials as was Kaiser Wilhelm II. The conduct of foreign policy did not significantly change either in post-1905 Russia; the minister was still responsible directly to the tsar, who could alone authorise discussions of policy issues by the council of ministers. Nevertheless, a certain amount of information was conveyed to the *Duma* by informal briefing sessions, and the press discussed issues with relative freedom during Izvolsky's period of ascendancy. His inept handling of the Bosnian crisis in 1908–09 led not only to his downfall, but to a general hardening of mood, especially with regard to Austria. In the heavy atmosphere of international tension, the more strident note of nationalism appealed to many moderates as well as conservatives.

WAR AND REVOLUTION

The invasion of East Prussia by the First Russian Army in mid-August 1914 was something of a surprise to the Germans, who had not expected the Russians to be in a position to gather their unwieldy forces so speedily. The unfortunate commander of the German Eighth Army and his chief of staff were relieved of their command and replaced by Generals Hindenburg and Ludendorff. Within a week, the Russian advance had been shattered at the four-day battle of Tannenberg. A second German victory around the Masurian lakes drove the Russians out of East Prussia. A major German offensive in the summer of 1915 pushed the front as far as the river Düna (Dvina), where the northern front was to remain for the next two years.

At the outbreak of war, the three northern kingdoms moved quickly to declare their neutrality, and continued to consult at regular intervals thereafter. Their relations with the belligerents were primarily determined by their economic value to either side. As the war intensified, the neutrals came under pressure to curb or suspend exports of commodities to one or other of the warring countries. Neutral shipping also suffered heavy losses, particularly during the period of unrestricted German U-boat warfare in 1917. The economies of the Scandinavian countries were also affected by the war. Certain export industries were badly hit by the disruptions of trade routes, others – such as the Danish canning industry – were able to reap high profits. In general, real wages did not keep pace with the rise in the cost of living, forced sharply upwards by shortages and price inflation in 1917–18. Although far from experiencing the miseries of the German working class during the dreadful 'turnip winter' of 1916–17, Scandinavians did face serious shortages of fuel and basic items of diet, which led to outbreaks of unrest in the spring of 1917.[17]

Given the disaffection of substantial numbers of the tsar's subjects, and the outbreak on the very eve of war of a general strike in the capital, St Petersburg, the expressions of loyalty ostentatiously proclaimed by representatives of the minorities and the general mood of enthusiasm for the war effort may seem surprising.[18] It should, however, be remembered that the Russian empire was not the only country with serious internal conflicts; trouble was simmering in Ireland, the French and German governments had devised elaborate plans to contain socialist anti-war activities (which in the event they did not need to put into force), and the national question was largely responsible for the confrontation between Austria and Serbia which led to war in the first place. Nowhere did the coming together of ranks in the face of a perceived external danger survive the first withering blast of casualty figures, or the hollow mockery of the call for common sacrifices in the service of the fatherland.

17. Studies of Scandinavia during the first world war include: Riste O 1965 *The neutral ally. Norway's relations with belligerent powers during the first world war*, Oslo. Koblik S 1972 *Sweden, the neutral victor*, Stockholm. Kaarsted T 1974 *Storbritannien og Danmark 1914–1920*, Odense.

18. The common view that a truly revolutionary situation obtained in Russia on the eve of war has been contested by McKean R 1990 *St Petersburg between the revolutions. Workers and revolutionaries June 1907–February 1917*, New Haven, Conn./London, pp. 297–317.

With its backward economy, inadequate communications system and poor military command, Russia was less able to bear the strain of modern warfare than its western allies or the Central Powers. Vital industrial and commercial regions lay directly in the path of the German advance, and were, moreover, inhabited by non-Russian peoples with their own aspirations. This latter aspect was to play an important part in Germany's war aims. Finns, Poles and Ukrainians were to be encouraged to rise up and throw off the Russian yoke, and considerable sums of money were devoted to supporting insurrectionary and revolutionary tendencies.[19] The promise of a unified self-governing Poland under Imperial Russian rule and subsequent efforts by Russian politicians to devise a satisfactory solution to the Polish question did little to overcome decades of mistrust and hostility; it was the German occupation of the Polish heartlands from 1915 and subsequent advances eastward that proved decisive. As long as the war lasted, Russia was in no position to determine the fate of the national minorities of the western borderlands. These minorities established representations in the Entente countries and sought the sympathy and support of American politicians and public opinion; but their immediate fate depended upon Germany.

As the war progressed, German annexationist aims were adumbrated by politicians and public figures, and debated in official circles. By April 1916, Chancellor Bethmann-Hollweg was ready to include 60,000 square kilometres of Lithuania and Kurland as part of the 'rectification' of frontiers to be demanded of Russia, and a conference of the Kaiser's military and political advisers a year later included these areas in the territories to be ceded to Germany at a future peace settlement. The 'Germanness' of the Baltic provinces was also emphasised in the right-wing press. The liberation of Poland was not a sufficient reward for German sacrifice, declared Theodor Schiemann in November 1915: the Baltic Sea had once more to become a German sea, as it had been until the mid-sixteenth century. What to do with 'liberated' Poland was a question which much exercised the minds of the ministers of the Central Powers, subject as they were to constant and conflicting pressures from all sides. In November 1916, the German and Austrian emperors announced their intention to recreate an independent Kingdom of Poland, though no details of how this was to be constituted were provided. For the Lithuanians, this was a

19. Fischer F 1959 Deutsche Kriegsziele, Revolutionierung und Separatfrieden im Osten 1914–1918 *Historisch Zeitschrift* **188**: 249–310. Zetterberg S 1978 *Die Liga der Fremdvölker Russlands 1916–1918* Studia Historica **8**, Helsinki, for details of German policy.

blow, the more so as they were well aware that they were heavily outnumbered by powerful Polish lobbyists in Berlin and Vienna. Attempts to obtain more than a sympathetic hearing in high circles had borne little fruit. Bethmann-Hollweg was reluctant to encourage a Lithuanian movement which might seek to detach parts of East Prussia, and which would go against German plans of erecting a Polish barrier against Russia, and in discussions with the Habsburg foreign minister in August 1916, the German chancellor had consigned the Vilna region to a future Polish state. Jewish leaders, who had generally welcomed the German occupation as a deliverance from the anti-semitic policies of the Russian authorities and the excesses of the soldiery, soon found that the war brought unprecedented hardship. Thousands fled the devastated Lithuanian lands to Warsaw, which now became the main centre of Zionism.[20]

Like the Poles, the Lithuanians were divided by the front, and the various groups which were formed during the war lacked coordination and were prone to fall out with one another. Relatively far removed from the front (though with sizeable army detachments stationed in the country, and most of the big ships of the Baltic fleet anchored in the harbour at Helsingfors), the Finns were also excused military service in the Imperial Russian army, paying instead an annual contribution to defence. A small number of professional army and naval officers and a few hundred volunteers served in the Russian army. Some 2,000 Finns went illegally to Germany for military training. As the 27th Royal Prussian *Jäger* battalion, they saw action on the eastern front in 1916, and members of this force were to play a role in subsequent events in Finland in 1918. A coterie of Finnish activists based in Stockholm coordinated these efforts, and had extensive connections with pro-German Swedish activists, representatives of other national minorities, and even individual members of the Finnish Social Democratic Party. These activists were operating on the margins, but with mainstream political life in Finland rendered virtually impotent by the measures of the imperial authorities, they were able to play a not insignificant role for the future of the Finnish state.

Theodor Schiemann, professor of East European history at the university of Berlin and highly esteemed as an adviser by the Kaiser, was a moving spirit on the council (*Baltischer Vertrauensrat*) set up by

20. Germany's war aims were exhaustively, if controversially revealed by: Fischer F 1964 *Griff nach der Weltmacht. Der Kriegszielpolitik des kaiserlichen Deutschland 1914–1918*, Düsseldorf. See also: Linde G 1965 *Die deutsche Politik in Litauen im ersten Weltkrieg*, Wiesbaden, pp. 20–7, 72–89. Laaman E 1964 *Eesti iseseisvuse sünd*, Stockholm, pp. 68–75.

Baltic German exiles in Germany. This council vigorously propagated the case for German protection and possible colonisation and annexation of the Baltic provinces. The *Ritterschaften* also attempted in the winter of 1916–17 to establish contact with Germany via Stockholm. No longer assured of the unconditional loyalty of the Baltic Germans, the Imperial Russian government was nevertheless reluctant to concede the right to form national units within the army to the Latvians and Estonians. The contribution of Latvian volunteers to the defence of Mitau in the summer of 1915 helped overcome resistance, and eight regular battalions of Latvian riflemen were eventually organised. The Estonians were less successful in pressing their claims, however, and units of Estonian troops were not set up until after the February revolution.

St Petersburg, or Petrograd, the renamed capital of the Russian empire, was once more the epicentre of revolution in 1917. The city's industrial labour force increased from 242,600 at the beginning of 1914 to 382,628 on 1 January 1917, and the population of the city as a whole rose by over 300,000 in the same short period. A substantial number of these newcomers were refugees from the war zones, though the great majority were peasants seeking employment. Although the demand for labour tended to outstrip supply, workers derived little benefit from this advantageous situation. Working hours were long, working conditions primitive and dangerous, and wages failed to keep pace with the sharply rising cost of living. There were shortages of essential foodstuffs from early 1915 onwards, and the situation was particularly acute in the winter of 1916–17. It was the lack of bread in working-class districts which provided the spark to light the dry tinder of revolution, in a city whose military garrison sided with the insurgents at the crucial moment. Within little more than a week, the tsar had abdicated and a provisional government headed by a liberal landowner, prince Georgey L'vov, had been set up by the *Duma* committee. Its authority was immediately challenged by a Council (Soviet) of Workers' Deputies set up a few days earlier; this duality of power was to persist until a second revolution in October/November swept away the enfeebled provisional government in favour of the Leninist idea of Soviet rule.[21]

21. McKean 1990, pp. 318ff. for details of Petrograd during the war, and the first days of the February revolution. The revolution in Petrograd has been extensively studied: see Hasegawa T 1981 *The February revolution: Petrograd 1917*, Seattle, and Mandel D 1983 *The Petrograd workers and the fall of the Old Regime. From the February revolution to the July days*, London. For the October revolution, see Rabinowitch A 1976 *The Bolsheviks come to power. The revolution of 1917 in Petrograd*, New York.

The revolution soon spread to the Baltic region. Several unpopular officers were summarily dispatched by soldiers and sailors, who followed the example of Petrograd and formed their own Soviets, usually led by trusted junior officers or NCOs. Hated representatives of the old regime were either dismissed and imprisoned or simply melted away. Crowds of troops and workers, all wearing the red ribbon of liberty, demonstrated and fraternised in the streets in an atmosphere of general euphoria. The political parties were taken aback by the rapidity of events, and it was some time before their leaders were able to return from imprisonment or exile and establish their authority.

For the peoples of the western borderlands, the revolution opened up the possibility of radically altering their position within the former empire. At the same time, price inflation, food shortages and the prospect of mass unemployment as war orders dried up, or as factories were evacuated from the danger zone, exacerbated social tensions and provided fertile ground for the revolutionary parties to cultivate. In the early weeks of the revolution, the rearranging of the administrative order occupied centre stage. The representatives of peoples living under German occupation had the most difficult task in this regard, though a national council for Lithuania, already planned on the eve of the revolution, was set up in Petrograd on 26 March. This elected a twelve-man temporary administrative committee, to which other nationalities were invited to send representatives. A Diet (*Seimas*) attended by 336 delegates met in Petrograd at the end of May, and called for the creation of an independent Lithuanian state. The socialists voiced their opposition to this demand on the grounds that independence under existing conditions would simply mean subjection to Germany, and they pressed the case for Lithuania to be a part of a federal, democratic Russia.

The fair words of the Russian provisional government were not backed up by concessions, and the Petrograd Lithuanians gradually looked towards the Lithuanian Council (*Taryba*) set up at a delegate conference convened with the consent of the German military authorities in Vilna in September. The *Taryba* consisted of twenty members and was intended to act as a provisional government. Two socialists were included, and places were offered to representatives of other nationalities, but not taken up. Although recognised by Lithuanian organisations abroad, the *Taryba* was suspected in other circles of being a puppet of the German occupying forces, a stigma which was to have repercussions in the troubled months ahead.[22]

22. Senn A 1959 *The emergence of modern Lithuania*, New York, offers the best

Meetings of delegates for the various provinces of the Baltic were held throughout the spring, and councils designed to take over administrative functions were elected. In this respect, the Estonians had far more success than the Latvians. The provisional government authorised the unification of the Estonian territories in mid-April, after a large-scale demonstration by Estonians in the capital had reinforced the decision taken by a general conference of delegates held in Dorpat to demand the creation of a new administration for an autonomous Estonia. The mayor of Reval, Jaan Poska, was appointed government commissar for the newly united territory, with an elected assembly (*Maapäev*) to assist him. Elections to the *Maapäev* were held in rural districts on 5 June, in spite of Bolshevik efforts to have them postponed. The weakness of the Bolsheviks in the countryside at this time is reflected in the fact that they obtained only one seat, though as urban representatives were added to the assembly in the autumn, their presence was increased.[23]

The temporary provincial council elected in March by a delegate conference of Latvian inhabitants of southern Livland was recognised by the provisional government but challenged by the Latvian left, which had been busily creating Soviets in the towns and countryside. A rival provincial council was set up by a congress of landless peasants meeting in Wolmar a month later. The two councils merged in May, but the non-socialists finally left in the autumn, having failed to push through measures to prepare the way for a national parliament (*Saeima*). The Latvian socialists quickly established a dominant position throughout the unoccupied territories, and although supporting the demand for territorial unity of ethnographic Latvian areas, they did not conceive of a separate status for Latvia outside a democratic Russian republic. The Russian provisional government was also noticeably less favourable to Latvian demands for administrative unification than it had been at an early stage of the revolution with regard to a similar request from the Estonians. It opposed the demand of the provincial council elected at Rositten in May for the incorporation of the Latgale district into a future Latvia (no doubt influenced by the demands of a

account in English of these developments. See also Linde 1965, pp. 69ff. and Colliander B 1935 *Die Beziehungen zwischen Litauen und Deutschland während der Okkupation 1915–1918*, Åbo, pp. 119ff. Various Polish organisations were also actively lobbying for Lithuania to be part of a future Poland.

23. In addition to the general works already cited, see the article on the Estonian *Maapäev* by Olavi Arens in Vardys V and Misiunas R (eds) 1978 *The Baltic states in peace and war 1917–1945*, University Park, Penn., pp. 19–30.

later Russian-dominated assembly which wanted the district to remain part of the *guberniya* of Vitebsk), and it also opposed attempts to reorganise education along national lines in the Baltic provinces.[24]

The initial willingness of the provisional government to make concessions to local aspirations soon turned to reluctance and outright obstruction, as the ministers reasserted the sovereign rights of the All-Russian constituent assembly finally to determine the future relationship of the former empire and its constituent parts. The Finnish social democrats, who had reluctantly agreed at the end of March to enter into a coalition government with representatives of Finland's non-socialist parties, gradually formed closer relations with the revolutionary parties and the Petrograd Soviet in their efforts to secure greater autonomy for Finland. The first all-Russian congress of Soviets passed a resolution on 3 July, urging the provisional government to concede full internal sovereignty to the Finnish parliament (*Eduskunta*). Only foreign affairs and military matters were to remain outside the legislative and administrative competence of the *Eduskunta*. The Finnish socialists, carefully omitting the reference to the final solution of the Finnish question lying within the competence of the All-Russian constituent assembly, incorporated the three points of the resolution into a short enabling bill, which the *Eduskunta* passed with the required two-thirds majority on 18 July. This act would in effect have transferred supreme authority to a parliament in which the social democrats had an absolute majority of 103 of the 200 seats. It was more an instrument for the exercise of power (as its popular title, *maktlag/valtalaki*, clearly indicates) than a declaration of independence, although the Social Democratic Party had clearly opted in June for an internationally guaranteed independent Finnish state. The Russian provisional government, temporarily strengthened after the crushing of a Bolshevik-inspired uprising in Kronstadt and the capital, was able to ignore the law and order the dissolution of the Finnish parliament at the end of July.[25]

The situation in the Baltic area was a particularly difficult one for the provisional government. Not only were the various nationalities demanding an increasing degree of self-rule, but the troops and

24. Ezergailis A 1974 *The 1917 revolution in Latvia* East European Monographs **8**, Boulder, Colorado, concentrates on the role of the Latvian Bolsheviks. For a succinct overview, Rauch G von 1974 *The Baltic states. The years of independence 1917–1940*, London. There is useful material in Walters M 1923 *Lettland. Seine Entwicklung zum Staat und die baltischen Fragen*, Rome.

25. The best study in English of the events in Finland is: Upton A 1980 *The Finnish revolution 1917–1918*, Minneapolis, Minnesota.

particularly the sailors of the Baltic fleet were passing under the influence and control of the Bolsheviks. By the end of September, the government had virtually no authority in the area: it was the orders of the Bolshevik-dominated regional Soviets which were obeyed. In Finland, with its own separate institutions, the Soviets were confined to the military units and played no part in Finland's internal affairs beyond the occasional (and generally unwelcome) outburst of fraternal assistance to striking workers. In the nascent states of Estonia and Latvia, however, the situation was rather different. Soviets in Estonia were largely confined to the towns, but in Latvia, with its much stronger socialist traditions, they were established in the countryside as well. The Latvian riflemen also constituted a significant political force, and the executive committee of their Soviet fell under Bolshevik control by the end of May. The Riga Soviet was also effectively in the hands of the Latvian Bolsheviks from the spring of 1917, and it controlled the city until it fell to the Germans at the beginning of September. The final tier in the complex structure of Soviets in Latvia was the creation of an executive committee (*Iskolat*) at a congress of delegates from the workers', soldiers' and landless peasants' Soviets on 11 August. This too appears to have been dominated by the Bolshevik wing of Latvian social democracy. In municipal and provincial elections staged just after the fall of Riga, the Bolsheviks were triumphant, and could count on a majority of the representatives returned to the provincial assembly for southern Livland. The left was less successful in Estonia, though the Bolsheviks began to make rapid gains in the large towns, and polled over a third of the vote in local elections held in September.

The deteriorating living standards of large sections of the population undoubtedly aided the Bolsheviks, with their bold, simple demands and a cadre of enthusiastic activists who strove tirelessly to take advantage of any opportunity. As a party of intransigent opposition, untainted by association with government, their denunciation of the war began to appeal to many once the initial fervour of revolutionary patriotism had begun to wear off. In the turmoil and confusion of front-line Latvia, the local Bolsheviks by their determination and organisational ability may well have stood in favourable contrast to the industrialists hastily closing down and evacuating their factories or the farmers suspected of hoarding foodstuffs. The Latvian social democrats had already established themselves as a powerful force before the revolution, and had forged close links with the Russian Bolsheviks. The Latvian bourgeoisie, on the other hand, remained politically weak and divided, and attempts to create political organisations in 1917 yielded few positive results. Estonia, by contrast, was further removed from the front line, and the university town of Dorpat was an important centre of bourgeois liberal activity, drawing upon the decades of national awakening which had flourished more richly in the south than the north. Social democracy had not managed to establish itself so firmly here as in Latvia, and although several leading Estonian Bolsheviks emerged during the course of the revolution, the party was strongest where there were significant numbers of Russian troops or workers, i.e. in the northern industrial centres of Reval and Narva.

The Finnish Social Democratic Party had established a dominant position after the 1905 revolution. Winning 376,030 votes in the 1916 parliamentary elections (and 444,670 in the more fiercely contested elections of October 1917), and with hundreds of wooden meeting halls across the country in which party members could gather for social evenings and political discussions, the party epitomised a kind of moral earnestness more familiar in the Protestant lands of north-western Europe than in the rest of the empire to which Finland was attached. The radical and uncompromising tone employed by the party press and leading politicians masked the party's fundamental commitment to achieving change by parliamentary means, but it helped sustain the spirits of the rank-and-file, who responded in equally uncompromising language in their frequent denunciations of the misdeeds of the oppressive bourgeoisie. Having challenged the provisional government and lost, the social democratic leadership found the political initiative slipping away in the autumn to the bourgeois parties who began to coalesce around a programme calling for Finnish independence and the restoration of law and order. The socialist members of government gradually withdrew: the party tried and failed to reconvene the dissolved *Eduskunta*, and then lost its absolute majority of seats in the October 1917 elections (although still remaining the largest single party with 93 seats).

Party and trade union leaders were coming under growing pressure to take decisive steps to ameliorate the condition of the working population, and in October 1917, some of the demands were presented in the form of an ultimatum to parliament, with the threat of a general strike if they were not met. The setting up of workers' guards was also sanctioned by the party, in spite of misgivings born of the previous experiences of 1905–06. The speaker of the *Eduskunta* refused to table the demands, and the threatened general strike erupted on 13 November, less than a week after the Bolshevik seizure of power in Petrograd. Much of southern Finland was effectively under the control of the workers' Red guards, but the planned revolution which had been alluded to by Finnish socialist leaders in talks with local Russian Bolsheviks on 8 November did not materialise. In a fraught all-night session of the *Eduskunta* on 15–16 November, the social democrats, with Agrarian Union support, managed to push through immediate promulgation of an eight-hour act and a reform of local government. This was sufficient to persuade the moderate majority of the revolutionary strike committee to call off the strike, a measure fiercely opposed by the Red guards. The ending of the strike virtually split the movement in two. The Red guards busied themselves with preparations for an armed showdown, obtaining arms from disaffected troop units and promises of sizeable deliveries from Petrograd. The party leadership, unable to reach any sort of working arrangement with the new bourgeois government determined to restore law and order and unwilling to abandon its followers, was driven to attempt a seizure of power at the end of January 1918.[26]

Social unrest was by no means confined to the lands of the former Russian empire. Price inflation and food shortages led to threats of strike action and prompted a flurry of negotiations and compromise measures in the neutral Scandinavian countries. Radical socialists looked to the Russian revolution for inspiration, though only in Norway did they succeed in winning control of the labour movement. In the second half of April, Sweden witnessed a number of strikes and demonstrations, calling for reform of the food rationing system. Soldiers marched in the streets to protest about their rations. Forays were made into the countryside by gangs of workers looking for hidden grain or potato stores, and troops had to be called in to restore order on the island of Seskarö after bread had been seized from the stores of local bakers and distributed to the populace. There was talk in right-wing circles of setting up a paramilitary guard to maintain order, which left-wing socialists threatened to match with their own workers' Red guards. The Social Democratic Party leadership responded to the tense situation by setting up a workers' committee to coordinate action. Although the trade union leadership, mindful of the disastrous consequences for their membership figures of the 1909 general strike, firmly opposed any repetition in 1917, party representatives on the workers' committee, worried about losing control of the situation to the syndicalists and left socialists, seem to have

26. Upton 1980, pp. 138ff. for the general strike and drift into civil war, and Kirby D 1975 *Finland and Russia 1808–1920*, London, pp. 189–223 for a selection of documents illustrating events. The ensuing civil war will be dealt with in the next chapter.

favoured some sort of mass action. The situation in Sweden remained tense throughout the summer, but the authority of the veteran party leader Hjalmar Branting was not seriously challenged; with the powerful trade union leaders behind him, Branting was able to keep the labour movement on the path of moderation.

Although affected by the war, Sweden was not being dragged down by it, as was the beleaguered provisional government, trying desperately to keep together a disintegrating Russian empire. The resignation of Karl Staaff's liberal ministry in 1914, and the constant rumours of pro-German intrigues in and around the court kept alive the question of who governed Sweden. The shaking of the foundations of imperial power in Europe was undoubtedly a powerful factor in persuading Gustav V to accept the liberal Nils Edén as prime minister in October 1917, after elections to the second chamber in which the conservative representation slumped from 86 to 57 seats. The king's acknowledgment of Edén's proposition 'that as long as we were the king's advisers no others should come between him and us' marked the end of the monarch's personal power and the final breakthrough for parliamentary democracy in Sweden. Constitutional reform in Sweden was a central plank in the social democratic platform, and it was vigorously upheld by Branting, a man of undisputed authority who had been at the head of the socialist movement for thirty years.[27] The moderating influence of socialist leaders such as Branting, and the Dane Thorvald Stauning, may well have had a part to play in shaping the contours of the Swedish and Danish labour movements, though their moderation and their unchallenged leadership may also have reflected existing tendencies. In both countries, trade unionism was relatively strong and well-established and some headway had been made towards the creation of an effective framework of industrial relations. The social democratic parties had long worked informally with the radical-liberals for constitutional and other reforms, and were noticeably pragmatic on sensitive issues such as entry into government. Thorvald Stauning became a minister without portfolio in 1916, whilst the Swedish social democrats entered government under Edén's premiership in October 1917, but both parties had tacitly acknowledged the necessity of such an action before 1914.

27. Edén's memoirs, cited in Brusewitz A 1951 *Kungamakt, herremakt, folkmakt. Författningskampen i Sverige (1906–1918)*, Stockholm, p. 113. Branting's great authority probably diminished the chances of the left socialists in establishing a strong foothold; one of the leading left socialists, Zeth Höglund, was later to write Branting's biography.

By contrast, the Finnish labour movement, although numerically impressive, was relatively young and inexperienced. Party politics as such in Finland dated only from the parliamentary reform of 1906, and there was no liberal bourgeois party with which the social democrats could make common cause. The class-conscious isolationism of the party, in a way, reflected its political impotence in circumstances in which parliament did not function, and also its political loneliness. The revolution of 1905 had not only swelled the ranks of the party, but had also created a tradition of direct action, which was to be revived once more in 1917. Trade unionism remained weak, poorly funded and organised, and Finnish employers were noticeably more reluctant than their Scandinavian counterparts to enter into collective bargaining arrangements. The powerful labour leadership in Sweden was able to control and channel economic grievances in the spring of 1917; the Finnish labour leaders spent much of their time exhorting workers to observe discipline, and not to pitch their demands too high. As the chairman of the central trade union organisation later recalled: 'union officials were threatened, even attacked, if their tactics were not in line with the workers' own ideas . . . the central organisations were forced to follow, and the net result was that illegality became recognised as the law.'[28]

Although faced with the collapse of authority like the rest of the empire, Finland did at least have its own institutions and laws, a truly democratic parliament, and a well-defined territory. This could not be said of the nascent Baltic states, where, moreover, the political and social struggle being waged in the Soviets and on the streets tended to confuse or confound efforts to establish a distinctive national presence. The German occupation, which by the end of February 1918 had extended to the remainder of Livland and Estland, and the activities of residual old elites, especially the Baltic Germans, were additional complications.

The idea of national self-determination emerged slowly, and was often expressed in confusing and convoluted terms, an indication of the uncertainties of the times. The rather negative attitude of the provisional government towards the national aspirations of the non-Russian peoples provoked sharp criticism, but the idea of a democratic Russian federation nevertheless remained attractive to many Estonian, Latvian and Lithuanian socialists. The Finnish social democrats, on the other hand, adopted a noticeably more hostile attitude towards any

28. Lumivuokko J 1919 *Laillinen ammattiyhdistysliike vaiko vallankumous?* Stockholm, p. 24.

idea of a future federation, and were chided by other socialists for abandoning the cause of the revolution. Lenin, who did favour Finland's case for self-determination on the grounds that this would hasten the socialist revolution there, nevertheless urged the Finnish social democrats to drop their 'petty bourgeois' notion of international guarantees. National self-determination for the Finnish socialists was closely linked to democratic aims, as the enabling act pushed through the *Eduskunta* in July 1917 clearly demonstrates.

The continuing uncertainties of the situation – a war which no peace initiative seemed capable of stopping, social unrest which was threatening to get out of control – provided a powerful impetus towards national independence. Although the non-Bolshevik left in Estonia remained loyal to the notion of autonomy within a federal Russia, they joined with the liberals on 7 September in agreeing that the *Maapäev* should act as an Estonian national institution, and they consented to the decision to appoint delegates to represent the country's interests abroad. At a further session in the beginning of October, the majority approved a resolution declaring the *Maapäev* to be the legal representative of the Estonian people, and authorising the drafting of a statute to be presented to a future Estonian constituent assembly. Although the delegates were clearly exceeding the remit allowed them by the provisional government, they stopped short of independence: Estonia was to enjoy autonomy within a federal Russia.

The news of the Bolshevik coup was debated by a group of leading politicians in Reval on 8 November. Their main conclusion was that some sort of independent form of government ought to be established in Estonia until democracy returned in Russia. This was taken up in a dramatic twenty-five minute meeting of the *Maapäev* some three weeks later. Before the Bolsheviks finally broke up the session, the majority voted for the *Maapäev* to be declared the sole bearer of supreme authority in Estonia (thus directly challenging the claims of the Bolsheviks) and authorised its leaders to exercise that authority when the assembly was not in session.[29]

In what remained of Latvian territory after the German conquest of Riga, the executive committee of the Soviets, *Iskolat*, was in effective control. The Latvian Bolsheviks and the Latvian rifle regiments played an important part in the preparations for the seizure of power in Petrograd, being assigned the task of occupying important railway centres and preventing army units loyal to the Kerensky government from reaching the capital. Latvian rifle regiments occupied the

29. Arens 1978, pp. 24–30. Laaman 1964, pp. 131–67.

strategically important centres of Wenden, Wolmar and Walk, and were requested by Lenin for the defence of Petrograd. The commissar of the Latvian rifle regiments became chairman of the executive committee of the Soviet of the Twelfth Army, which also passed under Bolshevik control. The second congress of Latvian Soviets at the end of 1917 vested supreme power in the Soviets and elected a new executive committee, headed by Fricis Rozinš-Āzis. It was to exercise power only briefly, having to flee before the rapid German advance in mid-February 1918; but Latvians were to play a major role in the new Soviet Russia, in government, the Red army and the Cheka.

The Bolshevik seizure of power in the late autumn of 1917 brought to an end an interim phase of the revolution, one in which issues were raised rather than resolved.[30] The initial euphoria and optimism of March and April soon faded as neither the provisional government nor the Petrograd Soviet were able to persuade Russia's allies to enter into peace negotiations. The failure of the brief Russian counteroffensive in July and the remorseless advance of the Germans across the Düna in August sent a wave of panic through the capital, and the hasty closure of many of the factories, throwing thousands out of work, further contributed to the unpopularity of the government. Addressing the *Maapäev* on 7 September 1917, after the fall of Riga, Jaan Tõnisson declared that Russia was no longer capable of resisting the German attack. Threatened by German occupation, the Baltic area had now become an international issue. Tõnisson believed the time right to press for the creation of a Baltic buffer state, 'a union of thirty million people' stretching from Lithuania to Finland and Sweden. His proposal was coolly received, but by identifying the international dimension of the Baltic area, he was at the same time lifting it out of the maelstrom of revolution which threatened to plunge the region into chaos. The great powers in 1917 were hardly in any position to intervene, and the immediate fate of the western borderlands was to lie within the hands of the German High Command; but in 'internationalising' the Baltic question, Tõnisson and others who were quietly seeking to influence politicians and pressure groups supportive of the 'New Europe' in the democracies of the West were banking on a future peace settlement in which the rights of nations to self-determination would be high on the agenda.

30. On the importance of the Baltic region for the October revolution, see Saul N 1973 Lenin's decision to seize power: the influence of events in Finland *Soviet Studies* **24**: 492–505. Ezergailis A 1983 *The Latvian impact on the Bolshevik revolution* East European Monographs **144**, Boulder, Colorado, pp. 169–246.

PART TWO

Nations and States

CHAPTER NINE

The New Order

RUSSIA, GERMANY AND THE EASTERN BALTIC

The Bolshevik seizure of power in Petrograd on 6–7 November 1917 was the signal for action elsewhere. The government commissar for Estonia, Jaan Poska, was obliged to surrender his powers to the Bolshevik Viktor Kingisepp, acting in the name of the Estonian military revolutionary committee, and all other representatives of the provisional government were ordered to hand over their powers and functions to the executive committees of the local Soviets. The Latvian Bolsheviks had been closely involved in the preparations for the uprising, which gave them a further opportunity to consolidate the authority which they had managed to establish in the region during the summer. The exercise of power was by no means easy. The Soviets encountered a good deal of resistance from the civil service, especially in Estonia, and had to cope with a disintegrating economy. The confiscated estates were often badly run down, and the decision to manage rather than partition them, though later criticised by Soviet historians, was probably rather academic at a time of general crisis, and had hardly begun to take shape before the rapid advance of the Germans in February 1918 brought to an end the first brief period of Soviet rule in the Baltic.[1]

1. For typical Soviet interpretations, see Siilivask K et al 1977, 1982 *Revolutsioon, kodusõda ja välisriikide interventsioon Eestis (1917–1920)*, 2 vols Tallinn, vol. 1, pp. 303–39, and Mints I (ed.) 1988 *Inostrannaya voennaya interventsiya v Pribaltike 1917–1920gg*. Moscow, pp. 19–35. There is a brief account of the Bolshevik period in: Raun T 1987 *Estonia and the Estonians*, Stanford, pp. 102–4, and a more detailed one for Latvia in: Ezergailis A 1983 *The Latvian impact on the Bolshevik revolution* East European Monogaphs **144**, Boulder, Colorado, pp. 119–66.

In Finland, further removed from the front line and with its own administrative and legislative structure, the October revolution did not impel the left towards Soviet power. Although the Red guards were actively deployed and exercised de facto control in much of southern Finland during the general strike in mid-November, the socialists remained wedded to what one of their number was later to call 'the parliamentary mirage'.[2] The non-socialist parties were able to use their overall parliamentary majority on 26 November to vote in a bourgeois government headed by a redoubtable opponent of russification, Pehr Svinhufvud. The socialist leadership was excluded from discussions on how best to declare Finland's independence, and widely condemned for condoning outrages and acts of violence during the strike week. They were also under fire from the Red guards for seeming to abandon the struggle by calling off the strike. On 6 December 1917, the bourgeois majority in the *Eduskunta* voted approval of the government's moves to achieve Finland's independence. The socialists favoured negotiated agreement with Russia as the means of becoming an independent republic, and their proposal was vindicated when the Svinhufvud government was finally persuaded by other states that recognition would not be forthcoming until such an arrangement had been made. At the end of 1917, Svinhufvud travelled to Petrograd, where he met Lenin and secured formal acknowledgment of Finland's independence. Lenin and Trotsky had earlier made it clear to the Finnish socialists who had sounded out the attitude of the Soviet government that they were more interested in revolution. The Finns 'thought it possible that conditions would drive the workers into revolution and social democracy could hardly be a bystander', a cautious circumlocution which was hardly calculated to impress the Bolshevik leaders.[3]

In the event, the Finnish socialists were driven into attempting a seizure of power at the end of January. The Svinhufvud government's refusal to have anything to do with the socialists weakened the chances

2. Kuusinen O 1918 *Suomen vallankumouksesta. Itsekritiikkiä*, Pietari, p. 4. Kuusinen's 'self-criticism', which was translated into several languages, including English, is a masterly example of speedy conversion, though it should also be said that, unlike many of his erstwhile social democratic colleagues, Kuusinen did not rush headlong into left-wing communism, and he may indeed have influenced Lenin's thinking on this question in 1920.

3. Report of the meeting between a Finnish socialist delegation and leaders of the Soviet government, 9 December 1917, Finnish Labour Archives, file 329(471)5:328 '1917'. Upton A 1980 *The Finnish revolution 1917–1918*, Minneapolis, Minnesota, pp. 180–202 for details of the recognition of Finnish independence by Russia.

of compromise, and undermined the position of the moderates within the Social Democratic Party. The decision to create an armed force out of elements commonly perceived by the working class as hostile towards them, endorsed by the non-socialist parliamentary majority on 12 January, effectively destroyed the last hope of avoiding an armed confrontation. Over the next fortnight, the socialist leadership gradually edged towards an alignment with the Red guards, already skirmishing with the White forces. The government busily sought aid from Germany and authorised the former imperial Russian army General C. G. E. Mannerheim to take command of the Whites. As the Whites moved into action on the night of 27–28 January, disarming Russian garrisons in southern Ostrobothnia, the Red seizure of power was initiated in Helsinki (Helsingfors). Members of the government had managed to leave the capital beforehand, and established themselves in Vaasa (Vasa).

The Finnish civil war lasted for three months. The Whites were better organised and led, and their objective was straightforward – the defeat of rebellion and the restoration of order. The landing of a German expeditionary force on the southern coast in April hastened the end, though General Mannerheim had achieved a major victory several days earlier with the storming of the city of Tampere (Tammerfors). The Red forces fought bravely, especially in the closing stages, but lacked even the basics of a proper military command. Russian officers provided the expertise, but their efforts were blunted by the incompetence of the general staff of the Red guards and the hesitancy of the political leadership. The Russian troops still remaining in Finland showed little enthusiasm for the Red cause, and it was only on the Karelian front that their contribution was at all significant.

The Red government of People's Commissars (*Kansanvaltuuskunta*) bore little ideological resemblance to that set up by Lenin and his comrades in Petrograd. Their main justification for the seizure of power was the preservation of democracy from black bourgeois reaction. The one major decree issued by the government, suspending the tenurial obligations of leasehold farmers and cottars, had no significance other than as a gesture, since the final working out of its ultimate provisions was dependant upon the outcome of the war. Whereas the Estonian and Latvian Bolsheviks proposed the nationalisation of the land, the Finnish socialists would have permitted former leaseholders to buy their farms. Attempts by the more radical minority to push through socialist measures such as the nationalisation of industry came to nothing; in the words of one of their number, the social democrats appeared to regard the civil war as an unfortunate episode which had to be endured without doing anything to hinder the development of bourgeois democracy.[4]

The Reds' seizure of power in Helsinki occurred at a crucial moment in the peace negotiations between Russia and Germany at Brest-Litovsk. Momentarily, it seemed as if the spark of revolution in Russia had ignited fires elsewhere. Germany was in the grip of a massive strike wave, and discontent echoed throughout the Habsburg lands. The unrest failed to shake the imperial authorities; above all, the German High Command remained firmly in control of the situation. When Trotsky withdrew from the peace talks in February, the Germans resumed their military operations, penetrating deep into the Ukraine and occupying the remainder of the Baltic provinces. Soviet Russia was compelled to sign what Lenin termed a 'Tilsit peace' (a not entirely accurate allusion to Alexander's meeting with Napoleon in 1807) in order to preserve the revolution. Russia relinquished its claims to Poland, Lithuania and Kurland, and agreed to withdraw all troops from the remaining Baltic provinces, Finland, parts of the Caucasus and the Ukraine. Livland and Estland were to be occupied by a German security force until order had been established by proper national institutions.

At the first plenary session of the peace talks in Brest-Litovsk, the Russian side had submitted a six-point programme as a basis for discussions. In highlighting the unrestricted rights of peoples to national self-determination, the Bolsheviks clearly hoped to embarrass their opponents. However, national self-determination proved to be a double-edged weapon, since the Central Powers made it their business to ensure that the desire for separation from Russia was articulated by those peoples under their control. The diplomats and politicians sought to do this by subtle binding agreements; the military preferred rather more direct methods. Tired of the endless debates around the peace table, General Hoffmann of the High Command reminded the conference at the end of December that it was Germany, not Russia, that stood victorious in the field. Russia allowed less self-determination than did Germany, the general continued, and he referred to the

4. 'Aukusti' (Letonmäki L), Suomen sosialidemokratia ja vallankumous. *Kumous* (Petrograd), 17, 24.5.1918. Upton 1980, pp. 388–95. Kirby D (ed.) 1975 *Finland and Russia 1808–1920*, London pp. 222ff., for a selection of documents illustrating attitudes and positions during the civil war. The fear of a reactionary bourgeois regime was deep-rooted, as extracts from workers' meetings testify. The view expressed by the moderate Karl Wiik at a May Day demonstration in 1919 that 'a right-wing dictatorship in Finland was crushed by the American tanks on the meadows of northern France in the autumn of 1918' was not untypical. Wiik collection, Finnish National Archives, file 1.

expressed desire for independence of the *Landesrat* in Kurland, the city magistracy of Riga and the Lithuanian *Taryba*. The first two were Baltic German institutions, whilst the *Taryba* was under heavy pressure to bind Lithuania as closely as possible to the German Reich. The Lithuanians, unable to secure German consent to their request to attend the peace negotiations, and at odds with the heavy-handed German military administration, struggled in vain to release themselves from the obligation attached to the *Taryba*'s declaration of 11 December, that an independent Lithuania would seek a firm and permanent alliance with Germany. The German government refused to countenance a more defiant declaration of independence issued by the *Taryba* in mid-February, and the Lithuanians were obliged to return to the terms of the December declaration in order to secure German recognition of independence on 23 March 1918.[5]

The Lithuanians had their supporters in the Reich, most notably the Centre Party politician Matthias Erzberger. The German military authorities had no wish to strengthen a future Poland, and although less than enthusiastic about a future Lithuanian state, they did not side with Polish politicians in order to counter what they suspected were the 'Great Lithuanian' plans of Erzberger and his allies. The Reich government preferred to keep the Lithuanians on a tight rein, refusing to accept the assumption of the title of 'state council' by the *Taryba*, or its election in July 1918 of Duke Wilhelm von Urach as King Mindaugas II, and relations with Germany remained poor throughout the summer. Nevertheless, the *Taryba* was widely regarded as a German tool in the Entente countries, a label which proved difficult to remove after the collapse of the Central Powers obliged the would-be new states of the Baltic to look elsewhere for recognition and support.

Under the constraints of military occupation, the Lithuanians had little room for manoeuvre. The German occupation of the former Baltic provinces was welcomed as a deliverance by the Baltic Germans, who proved willing accomplices in the Reich's annexationist designs. A carefully selected united provincial assembly (*Landesrat*), consisting of thirty-five Germans, thirteen Estonians and ten Latvians, met in Riga on 12 April and unanimously passed a resolution asking the Kaiser to place Estland and Livland under his personal protection and to secure their final separation from Russia (this was eventually achieved in a supplementary treaty between Germany and Russia at the end of

5. Linde G 1965 *Die deutsche Politik in Litauen im ersten Weltkrieg*, Wiesbaden. Senn A 1959 *The emergence of modern Lithuania*, New York, pp. 25–33.

August 1918). The assembly also expressed the wish for the united Baltic provinces to be linked to the Reich through personal union with the Kingdom of Prussia. Neither this wish, nor other plans for uniting the Baltic provinces under another German prince, were to bear fruition.[6] In other respects, the German occupation of the Baltic provinces was as harsh as it had been in Lithuania. In addition to the economic hardships endured by the local population, the occupying forces sought to strengthen the German presence by inducements to would-be colonists. Latvian and Estonian political organisations suffered repression and persecution, and the Baltic Germans attempted to restore their pre-revolutionary institutions, such as the rural police.

The net effect of these measures was probably to strengthen the resolve of the Estonians and Latvians to seek their own salvation. Of the two, the Estonians were the more united and purposeful. At the beginning of 1918, the committee of elders appointed by the *Maapäev* took steps to ensure continued activity in the event of its suppression by delegating representatives to the major powers, and by setting up a three-man committee with full decision-making powers. On 24 February 1918, as the Bolsheviks were beating a hasty retreat before the advancing Germans, the committee of elders declared Estonia to be an independent and democratic republic within its historical and ethnographic borders. A provisional government headed by Konstantin Päts was also set up. Although these measures reaped little reward in 1918, other than expressions of sympathy from the French and British governments, they served to legitimise the Estonians' case for independence and to establish a base for future activities.

The strength of Bolshevism and the disruptions brought about by the war had tended to weaken efforts to consolidate forces and promote the cause of Latvian independence. In addition, the treaty of Brest-Litovsk had split ethnic Latvian territory in three, with Russia surrendering claims to Kurland but not to Livland (which was under German occupation) nor to Latgale (which was part of Vitebsk province). At the instigation of the Latvian refugee committee in Petrograd, an assembly of delegates from a wide variety of groups had been convened at the town of Walk (Valga/Valka) on the Estonian-Latvian frontier at the end of November 1917. Declaring itself to be

6. On Baltic German politics in 1918 see the contribution of Arved von Taube in: Hehn J von, Rimscha H von, Weiss H, (eds) 1977 *Von der baltischen Provinzen zu den baltischen Staaten 1918–1920*, Marburg, pp. 70–166, and Volkmann H-E 1970 *Der deutsche Baltikumpolitik zwischen Brest-Litovsk und Compiègne* Ostmitteleuropa in Vergangenheit und Gegenwart **13**, Cologne.

the provisional national council, the meeting proclaimed the regions of Vidzeme (southern Livland), Kurzeme (Kurland) and Latgale as the autonomous state of Latvia. Two months later, a second meeting of the provisional national council came out for an independent democratic republic. The democratic bloc, a loose coalition of left-wing forces operating semi-legally in occupied Latvian territory, still favoured federation, but gradually came over to the idea of a neutral, republican state.[7]

Undoubtedly, the experience of German occupation and a desire to escape out of the turmoils of war and revolution strengthened the case for independent statehood, although the need for security also obliged politicians to consider other alternatives. International guarantees of neutrality were much favoured by the left; conservatives tended to look more towards the benevolent protection of major powers – Germany before its collapse, or Great Britain during the brief period when Royal Navy vessels steamed in the eastern Baltic. The idea of Scandinavian federation or a Finnish-Estonian union was taken up by various Estonian leaders during the course of 1917–18. The possibility of forming a Lithuanian-Latvian state was raised at the meeting of Latvian representatives in Walk, though this Lithuanian proposal was coolly received. Marshal Piłsudski's dream of a federation which would include Lithuania, Belorussia and possibly the Ukraine was not a new idea: it had been endorsed by Polish radicals in the 1863 uprising, was taken up by Polish socialists in the 1880s, and had struck a resonant chord with Lithuanian socialists a decade or so later. In the fraught atmosphere of 1918–19, however, it was unacceptable to nationalist Poles and Lithuanians alike. In the turmoil which followed the collapse of imperial Germany, it was the national state which emerged as the only political alternative. Those elements which did not fit had to accommodate themselves as best they could, which in the eastern Baltic could mean not only ethnic minorities, but also those of a different political persuasion.

In the autumn of 1918, aware of impending military defeat, the German generals withdrew to the sidelines and allowed the politicians to take responsibility. A new Reich government headed by Prince Max von Baden was formed, drawn from the parties which had sponsored the peace resolution in the *Reichstag* the previous summer. The grip of the military authorities in the occupied territories was

7. On the Latvian provisional national council, see the contribution of Uldis Gērmanis in: Sprudzs A and Rusis A (eds) 1968 *Res Baltica*, Leyden, pp. 66–71.

loosened. The *Taryba* proclaimed a provisional constitution on 2 November, and assumed powers of government. It also attempted to broaden its base of support by co-opting six Belorussians and three Jews; both minorities were given a ministry without portfolio in the government formed on 11 November by Augustinas Voldemaras. The federalist-minded Poles were far less willing to cooperate, and the Lithuanians were deaf to the blandishments of the Polish government set up by Marshal Józef Piłsudski in November 1918. Piłsudski's great rival, Roman Dmowski, favoured the more brutal option of annexation, a course of action which probably had wider support in Poland than the idea of federation.[8]

The situation in Vilna (Vilnius/Wilno) at the end of 1918 was chaotic. Key figures of the Voldemaras government slipped out of the city and went abroad to negotiate loans and seek diplomatic or military assistance, leaving the nascent Lithuanian state effectively leaderless. The communists tried ineffectively and not very enthusiastically to establish a workers' and peasants' government, with which the city Soviet was in constant conflict (the Soviet also quarrelled with the German soldiers' council). Polish legionnaires roamed the streets, and the air was full of rumours of a coup. On 2 January 1919, the remnants of the Lithuanian government left the city, leaving a note for the Poles stating that in any further talks, recognition of Vilna as the capital of an independent Lithuanian state was a *sine qua non.* The Poles thereupon took over the city and dispersed the Soviet after a pitched battle. Within a couple of days they had withdrawn, together with the German troops, before the advance of the Red Army.

Further north, the Baltic German diehards stoutly resisted any attempts to dissolve their proposed united state in the dying days of military occupation by Imperial Germany. Heinrich von Stryk, on behalf of the united *Landesrat* and the nobility of the provinces, fulminated against 'crypto-Bolsheviks' such as the Progressive member of the *Reichstag*, Gerhart von Schultze-Gaevernitz and the Baltic German liberal Paul Schiemann, who were daring to meddle in the internal affairs of the provinces. Paul Schiemann for his part blamed the failure of Germany's *Ostpolitik* on an excessive reliance on national power rather than on political influence; in urging the new German government to support the national revendications of the Estonians

8. Dziewanowski M 1950 Piłsudski's foreign policy, 1919–1921 *Journal of Central European Affairs* **10**: 113–28, 270–87. Ciencala A, Komarnicki T 1984 *From Versailles to Locarno*, Lawrence, Kansas, pp. 120ff. Senn 1959, pp. 49ff.

and Latvians, he was anticipating the new course which Germany was to follow during the 1920s.[9]

The confusion which followed the signing of the armistice and the outbreak of revolution in Germany tended to offer more comfort for the diehards and German proponents of *Machtpolitik* than it did for progressives. The aristocratic conservatives dominated the Baltic German national committee, set up in November 1918. Heinrich von Styrk continued his activities in Stockholm, from where he tried unsuccessfully to persuade the British government to establish some kind of temporary protectorate over the Baltic provinces. A better opportunity for those wishing to retain German hegemony in the eastern Baltic was offered by article twelve of the armistice, which required German troops to remain for the time being on former Russian territory. Troop units stationed in Estonia displayed little enthusiasm for staying on to fight the advancing Red Army, and their withdrawal diminished hopes of exercising German influence in that area. Latvian territory, with its much larger number of Baltic German landowners and a less well-organised national force capable of resisting the returning Bolsheviks, offered more promising ground.

Advocacy of German hegemony in the eastern Baltic was not confined to right-wing conservatives. One of the most ardent supporters of *Deutschtum* was the trade unionist leader, August Winnig, named plenipotentiary of the German Reich in the Baltic lands on 15 November. The Latvian provisional government headed by Kārlis Ulmanis, leader of the Peasant League, rested on a fragile political basis, and its authority was further weakened by the agreement it made with Winnig on 29 December, which offered Latvian citizenship to all foreign (i.e. German) volunteers who served at least four weeks in the fight against the advancing Bolshevik forces. The moderate socialists resigned in protest from the people's council established on 17 November to proclaim independence, and with several companies of the nascent Latvian armed forces in a state of mutiny, the government was in no state to offer much resistance to the advancing troops of the independent Soviet republic of Latvia (proclaimed in Moscow on 14 December), supported by the Russian Soviet government.[10]

9. Paul Schiemann's views are summarised by von Taube in: Hehn 1977, p. 158. On German policy towards the independent Baltic states, see Hiden J 1987 *The Baltic states and Weimar* ***Ostpolitik***, Cambridge.

10. The validity of the 29 December agreement has been much contested. See the contribution by Hans-Erich Volkmann in Hehn 1977, pp. 386–7.

THE REPERCUSSIONS OF WAR AND REVOLUTION

Estonian resistance to the Bolshevik advance was stiffer and more wholehearted than that of the Latvians, many of whom welcomed the return of a Soviet regime. The Bolsheviks had secured a much higher share of the vote in unoccupied Latvia than in Estonia in the elections to the all-Russian constituent assembly at the end of November 1917 (72 per cent as against 40 per cent). Bolshevism in Estonia tended to be strongest in the industrial centres and cities of the north, where there was also a large Russian population; in the south, it was markedly less successful. Socialism had struck deep roots in the Latvian countryside, and there was a large cadre of party activists willing and able to take up the work of reconstituting a Soviet state in 1919. Neither the Estonian nor the Lithuanian communist parties could draw upon such assistance. The Lithuanian communists evinced little enthusiasm for the task of creating a national Soviet state, opting for fusion with Belorussia in February 1919. Estonia had briefly experienced Soviet power in the winter of 1917–18, and Estonians had a chance to express their opinion at the ballot box in elections to the Estonian constituent assembly at the end of January. Although the electoral process was halted on 28 January by the proclamation of a state of siege, the results obtained gave the Bolsheviks 37 per cent, the Labour Party 29.8 per cent, and the Democratic Bloc 23 per cent. The Labour Party was particularly successful in winning support from the small farmers because it advocated the partition of large landed estates, and in the northern counties of Viru and Harju, the vote for the Bolsheviks declined significantly in comparison with that recorded in the November elections.[11]

The falling-off in support for the Bolsheviks has been attributed to their rather dogmatic policies on the land question. The Latvian communist leader Pēteris Stučka admitted at the end of March 1919 that 'the peasant looks upon the communist as his enemy who intends to take the land from him'. The Bolsheviks came under severe attack from landless workers' meetings in Estonia and were forced to temper their plans for retaining state control of the confiscated estates, whilst in Lithuania, peasants favouring partition started to take over the organs of Soviet power and to run them in their own fashion. Farm

11. Siilivask 1977, vol. 1, pp. 300–2, 324. Raun 1987, p. 104.

workers in Red-controlled parts of Finland were also reluctant to take over and run abandoned farms at the behest of the government.[12] It is, however, possible that peasants were antagonised far more by clumsy requisitioning policies and heavy-handed or coercive tactics employed by local Soviets and committees. In 1917, the Bolsheviks had undoubtedly amassed support as a party of opposition, promising an end to the war, bread and land. In 1918 and again in 1919, the Bolsheviks in power were shown to be as exploitative and ruthless as all the previous rulers the peasant had had to endure.

In the upheavals of war and revolution, numerous atrocities were committed. In Finland, where the judiciary refused to work under the Red government, revolutionary courts attempted with some success to practise socialist morality in upholding bourgeois property values. They were, however, unable to keep under control the more vicious elements of the Red guard. Bloodthirsty psychopaths such as Heikki Kaljunen, the twenty-five year old Red guard commander on the Karelian front who was personally responsible for at least a dozen murders, were exceptional, but their deeds were sufficient to damn the defeated Reds for decades as a bloodthirsty gang of ruffians incited by the malevolent Russian Bolsheviks. Members of the Baltic German community and clergymen in particular are cited by Baltic German historians as prominent victims of the Red terror in Estonia and Latvia. Supporters of the Red regime were likewise identified as victims by communist writers; Viktor Kingisepp, for example, claimed 2,000 were killed in the White terror which followed the collapse of the Estonian Workers' Commune. Allied representatives in Riga after that city had been retaken by anti-Bolshevik forces at the end of May 1919 spoke of a veritable reign of terror, which exceeded that of the Reds. The acts of violence perpetrated in the Baltic lands have yet to be fully investigated in the manner of Jaakko Paavolainen's painstaking analysis of the Red and White terror in Finland. Writing of the 1,649 victims of the Red terror, Paavolainen noted that most were killed in circumstances in which the victim's social status was of little consequence. Farmers constituted over one-third of the victims, but the next largest single group was composed of workers and crofters, few of whom can with any certainty be definitely identified as 'White'. In contrast, the overwhelming majority of the 8,380 victims

12. Stučka's comment is cited by Walter Hanchett in his study of the communists and the Latvian countryside in: Sprudzs and Rusis 1968, p. 89. Siilivask 1977, vol. 1, pp. 321–2. Upton 1980, p. 363.

of the White terror during and after the civil war were from the working class.[13]

Notions of Soviet power were conspicuously absent in Red Finland, and were not very evident either in Finnish left socialist circles during the early 1920s. In other European countries, the term was much bandied about, though the Soviets which were set up bore little resemblance to those of Russia. The rash of enthusiasm for Soviets which broke out in Norway soon faded. Although the Norwegian Labour Party endorsed Soviet power in its 1918 programme and later affiliated to the Communist International, the differences between Leninist communism, as spelled out in the twenty-one conditions of admission to the Comintern, and the rather starry-eyed idealism of the Scandinavian left (which Lenin had earlier subjected to withering criticism), were soon revealed.[14]

During the troubled spring of 1917, there had been much talk of Soviets and Red guards in Sweden, but it was the moderate Hjalmar Branting rather than the left socialists and syndicalists who controlled and led the labour movement. The Social Democratic Party managed to maintain its 86 seats in the Second Chamber elections of 1917 (the left socialists succeeding in winning 11) and entered into coalition with the liberals under the premiership of Nils Edén. In government, however, the socialists were vulnerable to criticism for their handling of Sweden's position with regard to the Finnish civil war and for their seeming failure to alleviate the food shortages which had prompted the unrest in the spring of 1917. The Left Socialist Party seized the opportunity of the collapse of the German empire to issue a manifesto calling amongst other things for a socialist Soviet republic, the abolition of the First Chamber, and a national constituent assembly; the workers were urged to be ready to resort to a general strike to secure victory.

Reports of the unreliability of the troops and rumours of impending revolutionary action may have frightened the king and right-wing circles into quiescence, and persuaded the government to

13. Upton 1980, pp. 369–84, on the revolutionary courts and the Red terror. Paavolainen J 1966 *Poliittiset väkivaltaisuudet Suomessa 1918* (2 vols) Helsinki: vol. 1, pp. 183ff. (on the Red terror), vol. 2, p. 209ff. (on the White terror). Siilivask 1982, vol. 2, p. 263. On the terror in Latvia, see the chapter on the Niedra affair by Hans von Rimscha in: Hehn 1977, pp. 296, 304–5.

14. Lenin was scathing in his criticism of the small-state mentality of the Norwegian left in a 1917 article dealing with anti-militarism, and printed in *Die Jugend-Internationale*, nos. 9 & 10. On the flirtation of the Norwegian Labour Party with the notion of Soviet power, see Langfeldt K 1966 *Det direkte demokrati: rådsrepublikk eller parlamentarisme?* Oslo.

embark upon the path of constitutional reform; but the threat of a red revolution in Sweden was grossly overblown. A significant section of the leadership of the Left Socialist Party had reservations about the contents of the manifesto. The disparate forces of the left were unlikely to be able to mount a powerful, united workers' action without trade union support. Furthermore, the Social Democratic Party was quick to take up the challenge, organising demonstrations and petitions to the government demanding constitutional reform. The possibility of right-wing resistance to constitutional reform had been sensibly diminished by the king and Edén, in talks with conservative leaders; what was at issue in mid-November was the degree of reform. A number of influential social democrats, including the future party leader Per Albin Hansson, demanded radical change: a republican constitution, abolition of the first chamber, the ending of compulsory military service, disarmament, the eight-hour working day and the nationalisation of a number of industries. In the end, however, the party's leaders in government persuaded their colleagues to confine their demands to universal and equal suffrage in local as well as national elections. The refusal of the trade unions to heed the call for a general strike, and the endorsement of the social democratic programme by the influential Stockholm workers' commune on 14 November put paid to any hopes of revolutionary action from the left, though the more radical alternative of a republican constitution and socialist measures continued to act as a spur to the moderates. The objections of the right-wing parties to the abolition of the taxed-based franchise in local elections were gradually whittled down; the intransigents were carefully isolated, and the more moderate leaders were prepared to accept government modifications. A warning by the trade union leader Herman Lindqvist that he was having great difficulties in resisting pressure for a general strike also served to hasten compromise (the *Riksdag* prudently bought in supplies of candles in case its sessions were plunged into darkness).

The series of reforms passed by the 1919 and 1921 sessions of the *Riksdag* gave the vote to all men and women over the age of twenty-three, with the exception of undischarged bankrupts, those under guardianship, or in permanent receipt of poor relief. Although the First Chamber was still elected indirectly, it ceased to be the preserve of the wealthier property-owning classes or the instrument of conservatism upon which the right (including the king) could rely. Royal power was further curtailed by allowing both chambers henceforth to choose their own Speakers, and the county assemblies (*Landsting*) to appoint their own leaders. The king, greatly alarmed by the collapse of monarchy in Germany, and having already conceded the principle of governmental responsibility to parliament, was not prepared to give unconditional support to the right. Without such backing, and with little comfort emanating from the army authorities, even the more intransigent conservatives realised that they were fighting a losing battle. Sweden was unlikely to be plunged into revolution and civil war by the extreme left, but a refusal to compromise on reform of the franchise might well have placed republicanism at the forefront of the agenda. In the jittery atmosphere of late 1918, as the spectre of red revolution seemed to glow again in Europe, the conservative establishment in Sweden opted for moderation guaranteed by Branting's continued leadership of the Social Democratic Party rather than an uncertain future.[15]

The change of system introduced in Denmark in 1901 marked the end of an era of conservative rule resting upon the support of the king. Within a decade, a radical government enjoying the tacit support of the socialists was in office, a coalition which assumed more concrete form during the second Zahle ministry of 1913–20. The constitutional changes of 1915 abolished property qualifications for membership of the *Landsting*, and the king's power to appoint members (though the chamber was to choose a quarter of its own members). The system of indirect election was retained, but the vote was given to men and women over thirty-five, without preferential treatment for the wealthy. The voting age for the *Folketing* was reduced to twenty-five. The adoption in 1915 of a new title (*Det konservative Folkeparti*) and programme by leaders of the old Right was symptomatic of the shift away from the diehard intransigence of the Estrup era to a more pragmatic acceptance of the parliamentary system.

Economic and social unrest in the immediate postwar months placed great strains on the Zahle government. The resolution of the Slesvig territorial settlement also introduced a further element of tension into Danish politics. The moderate position adopted by the government, which feared the consequences of a settlement which might bring too many Germans under Danish rule, was initially supported by the other major parties. In accordance with the programme adopted on 12 October 1918 by the North Slesvig electoral association, the Danish government favoured the holding of a

15. On the events of 1917–18, see the contribution by Carl Göran Andræ in Koblik S 1973 *Från fattigdom till överflöd*, Stockholm, pp. 213–34, and the chapters by Gunnar Gerdner and Göran Nilsson in Hadenius S (ed.) 1966 *Kring demokratins genombrott i Sverige*, Stockholm, pp. 90–135.

plebiscite in one single bloc of territory where it was believed the great majority would opt for Denmark. The demarcation line was to run north of the town of Flensburg, which had a substantial German-speaking majority. In opposition to this moderate position were the members of the Danevirke movement, who looked to the Allies to back their demands for a frontier bounded in the south by an internationalised Kiel canal zone, and a committee which sought to extend the area of the plebiscite to Flensburg and Central Slesvig. The Danish government officially asked the Versailles peace conference to take up the matter in February 1919, but they had to contend with effective lobbying (surreptitiously supported by the French) by representatives of the Danevirke movement. The announcement on 7 May that there was to be a third plebiscite zone, stretching as far south as the river Eider, was a victory for the lobbyists, but a shock for the Danish government, which momentarily considered resigning. The North Slesvig electoral association was also split on the issue, and the hitherto unchallenged leader of the Danish minority in Slesvig, H. P. Hanssen, came under severe pressure for his support for the moderate line. The government managed to survive and secure the backing of the *Rigsdag* in persuading the Allies to abandon the idea of a third zone, but it lived in constant danger of being upstaged by those who wished to secure more than the area of the first zone, which voted three-to-one in favour of Denmark on 10 February 1920.

On 14 March, voting took place in the second zone of Central Slesvig. Here, only 20 per cent voted in favour of Denmark. The British government accepted this as conclusive, but the French sought to spin out discussion in the commission supervising the plebiscites, in the hope that a change of government in Denmark might bring about a change of policy. On 29 March, King Christian X, believing that the *Folketing* no longer fully corresponded with the will of the people, dismissed the government and appointed a caretaker administration which issued a statement endorsing the king's 'constitutional right to seek clarity'. Behind the king's action, according to *Radikale Venstre*, were elements seeking to change the hitherto moderate Danish policy on Slesvig and to press for the annexation of Flensburg. For its part, the labour movement reacted promptly and sharply, denouncing the king's action as a coup and threatening a general strike if it were not immediately rescinded and the *Rigsdag* recalled to discuss the electoral law. Facing a lockout by the employers after the breakdown of talks on 27 March, the general council of the trade unions voted on 31 March for a general strike a week later in protest at the king's action. The social democratic parliamentary group on 30 March committed itself to campaigning at the elections for a republic, a unicameral legislature and a democratic constitution, as well as fundamental social reforms along socialist lines. There now followed a hectic few days of talks and deal-making designed to take the heat out of the Easter crisis. On 4 April, the king appointed another caretaker government, which would agree to accept a new electoral law and to hold new elections as soon as possible. The unions dropped their strike call, and the employers withdrew their threat of a lockout. In the *Folketing* elections at the end of April, *Venstre* (+ 4 seats) and the conservatives (+6) fared rather better than the social democrats (+3), whilst the radicals lost almost half of their mandate. A *Venstre* government supported by the conservatives was appointed in May and held office for the next four years.[16]

The causes of the Easter crisis have been much debated. The minister of the interior in the Zahle government, Ove Rode, believed the *Venstre* leader J. C. Christensen exploited the government's troubles over the Slesvig question in order to bring about its downfall and new elections according to the existing system, which favoured *Venstre* with its largely rural constituency. The historian Tage Kaarsted believes Christensen was more influenced by those lobbying for Flensburg's annexation, and attributes a considerable role to extraparliamentary circles. Bent Jensen lays more emphasis on business rivalries and Denmark's relationship to Russia. A key role was played by H. N. Andersen, the managing director of the *Østasiatisk Kompagni* and intimate adviser to the king. Andersen was accused by his rivals of seeking the dismissal of the Zahle government in order to break off negotiations with Soviet Russia which might have saved the pre-1917 investments of the *Transatlantisk Kompagni*.[17]

The crisis brought to the surface many of the tensions and cross-currents in Danish public life; but set against the much grimmer political scene in Germany, Russia or the new countries of eastern

16. On the Slesvig question, see: Fink T 1978 *Da Sønderjylland blev delt 1918–1920*, 2 vols. Tønder, and Kaarsted T 1974 *Storbritannien og Danmark 1914–1920*, Odense, pp. 143–72. The relevant documents concerning the Easter crisis are printed in: Jensen B 1979 *Påskekrise og Ruslandsforhandlinger*, Copenhagen, pp. 34–8.

17. The interpretations of the Easter crisis are outlined and illustrated in Jensen 1979 *passim*, and the same author's 1978 article, Påskekrise og Ruslandspolitik. En mytes tilblivelse, vækst og forfald *Historisk Tidsskrift* **78**: 53–86. The complexities of Danish business dealings with Russia, and the efforts of Harald Plum and his associates firstly to overthrow the Bolsheviks and then to use the Russian cooperative movement for reconstruction purposes are dealt with in Jensen B 1979 *Danmark og det russiske spørgsmål 1917–1924* Jysk Selskab for Historie **34**, Aarhus.

Europe, it appears a relatively modest and easily managed affair. In the Scandinavian countries, the scope for compromise was always that much greater. There was a lack of powerful landed elites; the military had neither the prestige nor the position it enjoyed in imperial Germany, for example; furthermore, the right lacked confidence. In comparison with central and eastern Europe, the left in Scandinavia was strongly entrenched and more confident. The alliance of intelligentsia and peasant-farmers which had constituted the traditional left had more than held its own during the latter half of the nineteenth century: it was *Højre*, not *Venstre*, which almost disappeared from the benches of the *Folketing* in 1901, and which had to reconstitute itself as a Conservative People's Party in 1915, and it was the right which had to beat a steady retreat in Sweden during the first two decades of the century. Social democracy had begun to overtake the traditional left, but the two were still able to work together. A fully functioning system of laws and institutions over which no one social class exercised predominance ensured informal compromise and formal agreement between the various pressure groups and parties. The lack of a reform-minded party resting on popular support helped further the isolation of the Finnish Social Democratic Party before 1917, and the bitter legacy of the civil war hindered the development of such political alignments during the 1920s; but in essence, the Finnish party political system rested upon not dissimilar foundations.

The events of 1918–20 in Germany were far more dramatic than in the Scandinavian kingdoms, and the irreconcilable, confrontational elements far more powerful. The socialists into whose hands the direction of affairs passed in November faced enormous difficulties – the continued Allied blockade, severe domestic unrest, the necessity of making an unpalatable peace – for which they were temperamentally and politically ill-prepared. The agenda was set by tough-minded right-wingers such as Gustav Noske rather than the hesitant centre-left leadership of the Independent Social Democratic Party, which had broken away from the SPD in 1917, and high on their list of priorities was the maintenance of order. This had been Noske's prime aim in helping set up the soldiers' and sailors' council in Kiel at the outbreak of the revolution, and he was to earn the undying hatred of the left for his zealous and often brutal methods of regaining control. The secret agreement reached between the social democratic leader of the new government of People's Commissars, Friedrich Ebert, and the army High Command on 10 November gave the army a crucial role; big business also received assurances from a weak government anxious not to lose complete control.

The failure of the socialists to push back the old order was nowhere more evident than in rural Pomerania, where the Social Democratic Party received overwhelming support in the elections to the Prussian and national constituent assemblies in January 1919. Pomerania was dominated by large estates and a well-organised landowning class, which made sure their workers remained strictly under their control and surveillance. Anxious not to disrupt vital supplies, the new government trod cautiously in its dealings with the big estate-owners, promising that their estates would not be touched as long as they agreed to recognise the farmworkers' unions. This the farmers were loath to do, and they colluded openly with the military in provoking strikes in order to give the local commander an opportunity to declare a state of siege and wrest control from the workers' council in Stettin and the socialist *Oberpräsident*. The wages and working conditions settlement imposed on the farmers in September 1919 by the socialist minister Otto Braun was rescinded in January 1920, but the farmers were in any event prepared to get round it by recruiting disbanded Iron Division soldiers and billeting them on their estates as workers. The workers in the port of Stettin and the surrounding countryside responded well to the appeal of the Bauer government to strike and resist the right-wing Kapp putsch in March 1920, disarming landowners and confiscating arms dumps. The restored government, however, did little to reward such loyalty. No action was taken against the farmers' chief organisation, which continued to receive weapons from the army, ostensibly to protect its members against marauding farm workers. Membership of the farmworkers' union collapsed in a region badly hit by unemployment and the loss to Poland of territories vital to the region's economy. The social democrats' electoral support also plummeted from 331,523 votes in 1919 to 169,579 in 1925.[18]

INDEPENDENCE

The signing of the armistice at Compiègne between the Allied powers and Germany on 11 November 1918 did not mean the end of a German military presence in the Baltic, nor indeed did it signify the ending of hostilities in the region. The Soviet government repudiated the treaty of Brest-Litovsk two days later, and within a fortnight,

18. Kohler E 1976 Revolutionary Pomerania 1919–20; a study in majority socialist agrarian policy and civil-military relations *Central European History* **9**: 250–93.

Bolshevik forces were moving westward. Opposing them were not only the hastily-recruited troops of the nascent border states, but also a bewildering variety of extraneous forces, each with its own objectives, whilst the victorious wartime allies hovered in the background.

Faced with the necessities of peace-making – in effect, the total reshaping of Europe – in a highly volatile and changing political atmosphere, weary and internally divided by the strains of four years of war, the politicians and officials of Britain and France were in all likelihood less certain of their long-term objectives in the Baltic area than historians have sometimes supposed. The creation of a band of small new states which might serve to weaken the links between Germany and Russia, and fence in both powers, was superficially attractive, but the more prescient foresaw grave dangers in such a development. Neither the American nor the French government showed much enthusiasm for recognising the independence of the Baltic states, and although certain British politicians such as the foreign secretary A. J. Balfour evinced sympathy and support, there was an underlying belief in official circles that these states were too weak economically and too vulnerable politically to survive for long as independent entities.[19]

Policy, such as it was, tended to be formulated according to circumstance. British naval forces, for example, were primarily drawn into the Baltic in the winter of 1918–19 in order to ensure the blockade of Germany and to secure the passage of the Danish Straits, and as a response to the alarming news of the Bolshevik advance in the east. As the Scandinavian governments proved unwilling to comply with British requests for military assistance to hold the line against the threatened Bolshevik advance, it was deemed advisable to retain German troops in the Baltic area for the time being. Notwithstanding Admiralty reluctance, the imperial war cabinet agreed on 20 November 1918 to send a squadron to the Baltic. Commanded by Rear-Admiral Edwyn Alexander-Sinclair, the four cruisers, nine destroyers and seven minesweepers were order to proceed to Liepāja (Libau) and Tallinn (Reval) 'to show the British flag and support

19. The most judicious and well-balanced study of British policy in the Baltic area is: Hinkkanen-Lievonen M-L 1984 *British trade and enterprise in the Baltic states 1919–1925* Studia Historica **14**, Helsinki, pp. 48–86. Hovi O 1980 *The Baltic area in British foreign policy, 1918–1921* Studia Historica **11**, Helsinki, is altogether too schematic in its approach. On France's policy, see: Hovi K 1975 *Cordon sanitaire or barrière de l'est? The emergence of a new French eastern European alliance policy 1917–1919* Turun yliopiston julkaisuja **135**, Turku.

British policy as circumstances dictate'.[20] Having lost one cruiser, blown up by a German mine off the island of Saaremaa (Ösel), Alexander-Sinclair arrived in Tallinn on 12 December. The hard-pressed Estonians urged the British to stay and even to assume the role of temporary occupation force. Such assistance was not forthcoming, though British weapons and ammunition augmented the supplies given by the Finnish government, and Alexander-Sinclair's ships also shelled the coastal road behind the Bolshevik lines, cutting their supply route. Over 3,000 Finnish volunteers were shipped across the Gulf of Finland to join Estonian and Baltic German forces in a counterattack at the beginning of January. The Bolshevik forces, which had reached within thirty miles of Tallinn, were driven back rapidly and expelled from Estonian territory by the end of February.

The situation in Latvia was more serious, for the Ulmanis government had had to abandon the capital to the Red forces and flee to Liepāja. Here it had to contend with the Germans, determined to build up a power base in Kurzeme/Kurland. Count Rüdiger von der Goltz, who had commanded the German force sent to assist the Finnish Whites in 1918, was appointed in February 1919 by the Kolberg-based army High Command (North) to take charge of German forces, including the volunteer detachments and also the Baltic-German *Landeswehr*, on the borders of East Prussia. Von der Goltz conceived his mission not only in terms of protecting East Prussia against the Bolsheviks, but also to strengthen the German presence in the Baltic. He was openly unsympathetic to the Latvian government, which had good reason to mistrust him, for he was included in the plans of the arch-intriguer Heinrich von Stryk for the overthrow of the Ulmanis government and the creation of a Baltic German-dominated coalition. Two months after these plans had been uncovered by the Latvian police, a detachment of the *Baltische Landeswehr* stormed the government building in Liepāja and overthrew the Ulmanis government. Although the action was not sanctioned by von der Goltz, he was by no means displeased with the demise of a government which, as the German representative to Latvia claimed in a report to the foreign ministry, had sought to erect a barrier between Russia and Germany.[21] A new government headed by Andrievs

20. Bennett G 1964 *Cowan's war. The story of British naval operations in the Baltic 1918–1920*, London, p. 34 and *passim.* for details of operations. Hovi O 1980, pp. 71–6, 82–109 also considers the wider ramifications of the presence of British ships in the Baltic.

21. Details in Hehn 1977, pp. 187–203, 256–64, 390–2, 394–5. Bennett 1964, pp. 91–5.

Niedra, a conservative opponent of Ulmanis, and including four (later six) Latvians and three Baltic Germans, was eventually formed. Although the Allied powers expostulated and threatened, they could do little as long as they needed German troops to hold the line against Bolshevism. The Niedra government thus remained in office, though virtually a puppet of the German forces.

During the spring of 1919, the Bolshevik forces had been pushed back by the various forces under von der Goltz' overall command, and on 22 May, Riga itself was stormed and taken. The fact that all senior positions of authority in the recaptured city were occupied by Germans underlined the impotence of the Niedra government. Acting in defiance of instructions, von der Goltz decided to authorise a further advance to secure the territory of the Latvian state. This inevitably brought the *Landeswehr* forces face-to-face with Estonian and Latvian units to the north, and the confrontation ended in defeat for the *Landeswehr* in a four-day battle around Cēcis (Wenden).

It was hardly coincidental that the battle was fought as the German government was agonising over signing the peace terms presented by the Allies. The principal enemy of von der Goltz was the British. In sanctioning the action against forces loyal to the Ulmanis government, he was not only striking a blow against British influence in the area, but also hoping to cause a last-minute upset at the delicate final stage of the Versailles peace treaty. The twentieth-century battle of Wenden was thus as much a turning-point as had been the defeat inflicted on the Muscovite forces by a Swedish-Polish army in 1578.[22] Defeated in battle, the Germans were in no position to contest the terms of the armistice imposed by the Allied representatives, and were obliged to evacuate Riga. The Ulmanis government was restored, with two Baltic Germans added on the insistence of the Allies. The *Landeswehr* was also reformed and made accountable to the government. Although German forces still remained in the Baltic, they were no longer a major factor.

In the eyes of the German military, it was now the British who were seeking to build up their influence in the Baltic. A new naval

22. See in particular the chapter by Hans von Rimscha in Hehn 1977, pp. 306–17, and von der Goltz's own memoirs, *Meine sendung in Finnland und im Baltikum* (Leipzig, 1920), revised in 1936 as *Als politischer General im Osten*. Hiden 1987, pp. 16–26 provides a succinct overview of German policy during this period. Rauch G von 1974 *The Baltic states. The years of independence 1917–1940*, London, pp. 59–66 is somewhat coy about the motives of von der Goltz and the *Landeswehr* leaders. On the earlier battle of Wenden, see Kirby D 1990 *Northern Europe in the Early Modern Period*, London, p. 118.

force commanded by Rear-Admiral Walter Cowan had been sent to replace Alexander-Sinclair's squadron, and had provided shelter for members of the overthrown Ulmanis government; but it lacked clear instructions, as the frequent complaints of the admiralty to the foreign office made plain. The decision of the Allies to send diplomatic and military missions to the Baltic in May 1919 eased Cowan's task, but, in common with the other military men called upon to operate in an area where political decision-making taxed even the most experienced politician, he was generally out of his depth, and his most useful contribution was in naval operations against Kronstadt.

The Baltic was, of course, but one small part of the massively complicated Russian question, over which the Allies never reached a consistent and unanimously agreed policy. In the case of Britain, there were deep fissures within the coalition cabinet between the advocates of intervention in Russia such as Winston Churchill and pragmatic moderates such as the foreign secretary, Balfour, and the prime minister, Lloyd George. Having failed to arrive at some sort of negotiated settlement of the Russian question at the beginning of the year, Lloyd George was obliged in mid-April 1919 to give way to pressure from the interventionists for more effective assistance to be given to the White Russian forces, who were beginning to have some success against the Red Army. On the Baltic front, the Bolsheviks had been driven out of Latvia and Estonia, and in May-June, a joint Estonian-Russian force occupied territory to the south-west of Petrograd. Further north, the British-commanded forces under General Sir Charles Maynard had made considerable advances down the Murmansk railway, and it was hoped to achieve a link-up with the White Russians on the eastern front commanded by Admiral Kolchak.

Maynard's forces had clashed earlier with Finnish detachments which had occupied the area around the town of Uhtua in March 1918. In spite of the efforts of the Finns to foster a movement in East Karelia favourable to union with Finland, the majority of the population of this vast and sparsely-inhabited region remained indifferent or even hostile to the activities of their self-styled fellow-kinsmen. Maynard was able to recruit over 1,000 East Karelians, and 800 refugees from the civil war in Finland into two separate 'legions', and suitably reinforced, pushed the Finns out of Uhtua and back across the border in September 1918. Nothing discouraged by this setback and the failure of another cross-border expedition in February, Finnish volunteers advanced in April 1919 along the northern shores of lake Ladoga and occupied the town of Olonets. This action had the tacit support of their government, but Finnish claims to East Karelia were in the last resort dependent on decisions taken in Paris. The Finnish government had been disappointed in its hopes of German support for these claims during the summer of 1918. A change of political leadership and direction was now put into effect in order to satisfy the victorious Allies of Finland's willingness to abandon its pro-German orientation.[23] Recognition of Finland's *de jure* independence was accorded by the council of foreign ministers on 3 May 1919, but Finland was urged to accept the decisions of the peace conference regarding its frontiers. The persistent refusal of the White Russians unequivocally to concede independence to Finland (which they claimed could only be done by a future all-Russian national assembly) and the reluctance of the British to give their full backing to plans for Finnish involvement in an assault on Petrograd further lessened the chances of Finland acquiring control of all or part of East Karelia.[24]

The most ardent advocate of Finnish intervention on the White Russian side was General Mannerheim, whose pro-Entente credentials had helped him secure the post of regent in place of the pro-German Svinhufvud at the end of 1918. Mannerheim's intrigues with the White Russians and with activist cliques in Finland, which were intended to install a political regime more favourable to Finland's participation in the assault on Petrograd, were effectively destroyed by Kolchak's refusal to recognise Finland's independence. The victory of the republican liberal K. J. Ståhlberg over General Mannerheim on 25 July 1919, in the first presidential election under the new constitution, did not end the activities of those seeking greater Finnish involvement in the anti-Bolshevik campaign, but it was a significant setback. Although Soviet peace overtures were rejected by a majority of the *Eduskunta* in October, as the long-delayed attack on Petrograd launched by General Yudenich seemed to be within an ace of success, the Finnish government refused to join in.[25]

The Estonians, from whose territory the assault was launched, were even more reluctant to become tied to the White Russian cause. The Estonian delegation to the Paris peace conference had been unable to shift the Allies from the position that 'no satisfactory or final settlement of the status of the Baltic states could be secured without the consent

23. Kirby D 1979 *Finland in the twentieth century*, London, pp. 52ff. provides a brief overview; see also Jääskeläinen M 1965 *Die ostkarelische Frage*, Helsinki.

24. Jääskeläinen 1965, pp. 56–84, 145–9, 155–221.

25. Polvinen T 1971 *Venäjän vallankumous ja Suomi 1917–1920*, 2 vols. Helsinki, vol. 2, pp. 128–221. Kirby 1979, pp. 52–61. Ahti M 1987 *Salaliiton ääriviivat. Oikeistoradikalismi ja hyökkäävä idänpolitiikka 1918–1919*, Helsinki, contains much detail of Mannerheim's role in right-wing politics.

of the Russian government, whenever a government was set up in Russia which could be recognised by the Allied powers'.[26] There was considerable support for a negotiated peace with Soviet Russia amongst the socialists and radicals who dominated the constituent assembly elected in April 1919, and the government formed in May by Otto Strandmann resolved to secure peace at the earliest suitable moment. The British military and diplomatic representatives strove to hold the border states within the anti-Bolshevik camp, but the inability of the Paris peace conference or the White Russians to offer any positive inducement in the form of recognition of their independence meant that their willingness to join in the crusade against Red Petrograd was conditional at best. The Bolshevik threat was no longer as serious as it had been at the beginning of 1919, and there were good reasons for the Baltic governments to take seriously the Soviet offers of peace negotiations, not least the pressing need to restore vital economic links to the Russian hinterland. Far more threatening in the summer of 1919 was the continued presence of sizeable units of German and Russian troops, whose loyalty and disposition towards the Baltic governments was highly unpredictable. Von der Goltz had been able to sidestep the Allies by allowing the troops under his command to enrol under the banner of Colonel P. M. Bermondt-Avalov's Russian Western Army, ostensibly to fight against Bolshevism. Denied transit rights by the Latvian government, Bermondt unleashed his troops against Riga on 8 October. Backed by Cowan's ships and Estonian armoured units, the Latvian forces were able to stabilise the line and to take the offensive in November 1919, driving Bermondt's troops out of the city and ultimately, across the frontier.[27]

The Lithuanians also suffered from the attentions of Bermondt's unruly forces, but were even more alarmed at the prospect of Polish troops being brought in to help drive them out. Polish troops had driven the Bolsheviks out of Vilna at Easter, and although marshal Piłsudski declared that military occupation was in no way to prejudice the future political disposition of the region, a civilian government for the 'Eastern Territories' had already been organised. The Lithuanian *Taryba* and government in Kaunas (Kovno) spurned Piłsudski's offers of

26. Record of a conversation between the British foreign secretary Balfour and the Estonian delegation on 12 June 1919, in: *Documents on British Foreign Policy 1919–1939* First Series, London 1949, vol. 3, p. 378. Laaman E 1964 *Eesti iseseisvuse sünd,* Stockholm, pp. 503–514, for details of the delegation's activities in Paris.

27. Hehn 1977, pp. 30–9, 367–9. Bennett 1964, pp. 172–80.

federation, and were well aware that a far more frankly annexationist tendency commanded a majority in the Polish constituent national assembly. On the other hand, they made little headway in Paris, where they were still suspected of being under German influence, an aspersion which the Poles were not slow to exploit. By the late summer of 1919, however, the British government was beginning to adopt a more sympathetic attitude towards the Lithuanians. In September, Lithuania joined the other Baltic states in being accorded *de facto* recognition by Britain, an indication that the country was no longer considered to be under German domination. Britain may also have wished to strengthen the Lithuanians against the demands of a French-backed Poland at a time when relations were tense following the uncovering of a plot to set up a pro-Polish government in Kaunas.

In spite of the preparations for a major offensive against Petrograd and warnings (mostly from the French) of the dangers of seeking an accommodation with the Bolsheviks, the border states could hardly have been unaware of the increasing desire of the Allies to disengage from the continuing conflict in Russia. On 24 September 1919, the British war cabinet resolved to cease providing war materials to the Baltic states and to refrain from expressing any opinion on the impending peace negotiations between these states and Russia, a decision which was conveyed to the British representative in Tallinn. This was a victory for Lloyd George over the interventionist wing of his government, and a clear signal to the Estonian government that its efforts to secure a negotiated peace with Russia would not jeopardise its status in British eyes at least. Yudenich's forces were defeated outside Petrograd at the end of October, and driven back into Estonian-held territory, where they were disarmed and interned. Unable to persuade their neighbours to abide by earlier agreements to enter into joint peace negotiations with Russia, and with the Red Army menacing Narva, the Estonians went it alone. The Soviet side sought by military action to reinforce its claims to the territories around Narva (which contained significant deposits of oil shale), but was obliged to conclude an armistice agreement, and to reach final accord on peace terms at Tartu (Dorpat) on 2 February 1920. Russia recognised the independence of the new state and renounced all territorial claims, giving Estonia the Petseri district and a strip of land on the eastern bank of the river Narova, both of which were occupied by Estonian troops at the time of the armistice. Each side achieved a degree of security, in that they both undertook not to permit foreign armies to establish bases, nor to allow foreign political organisations to operate, on their territories.

The territories over which Estonia laid claim had been cleared of Bolshevik troops in the spring of 1919. Red Army units were, however, still operating along the river Düna/Dvina, where there was the additional complication of Polish military and political ambitions.[28] Cooperation between Latvian and Polish forces in January 1920 cleared Latgale of Bolshevik troops, but aroused the fears of the Lithuanians. The prospect of further Polish-Latvian cooperation was punctured by Moscow's agreement to an armistice with Latvia on 1 February 1920, and the peace negotiations with the remaining border states also effectively deprived Poland of potential allies in the war against Russia which broke out in the spring of 1920. The terms of the peace treaty concluded between the Russian Socialist Federative Soviet Republic (RSFSR) and Latvia in Riga on 1 August 1920 were relatively favourable to the latter, whose claims to Latgale were conceded. The RSFSR also recognised Lithuania's claim to the Vilna region in the peace treaty concluded in Moscow on 12 July, though this was clearly an inducement to persuade the Lithuanians either to join forces with the advancing Red Army or to allow Russian troops unhindered transit to the front (the Lithuanians opted for the latter alternative, and joint control over the Vilna region).

Had the Red Army not suffered defeat at the hands of the Poles in late August, the Vilna region might once again have slipped into the hands of the Lithuanian communists, who were busily preparing a new revolution. Less than a week after its advance into Poland had been halted by the 'miracle on the Vistula', the retreating Red Army handed Vilna over to Lithuanian control. There now followed six weeks of intense negotiations supervised by the League of Nations and its military control commission as Polish and Lithuanian forces jostled for possession of disputed territory. Neither side was willing to accept the provisional demarcation line drawn up by the peace conference in December 1919. The ceasefire agreement imposed by the military control commission on 7 October, which tacitly left the Vilna region in Lithuanian hands, was denounced by General Lucjan Żeligowski, who occupied the city two days later. Officially proclaimed a rebel by the Polish government, though he had acted with the tacit support and encouragement of Piłsudski, Żeligowski announced the formation of the state of Central Lithuania, of which he was to be the head. The Polish *Sejm*, dominated by annexationists, demanded the incorporation

28. See: Dziewanowski M 1969 *Joseph Pilsudski. A European federalist 1918–1922*, Stanford, and Hovi K 1984 *Interessensphären im Baltikum. Finnland im Rahmen der Ostpolitik Polens 1919–1922* Studia Historica **13**, Helsinki.

of Vilna; Piłsudski still hoped for some form of federation, a solution which was also attractive to the League of Nations. Neither Poland nor Lithuania could afford to antagonise the Western powers, but the League failed to come up with a solution acceptable to both sides. The Vilna question remained unresolved, one of the many territorial issues which divided nations and added to the general atmosphere of political instability.

The main issue at stake in the Finnish-Russian peace negotiations was the future of East Karelia. The failure of the Finns to persuade either the Allies or the local inhabitants to go along with their annexationist designs was compounded by the lack of success of the military expeditions launched across the frontier in 1919. The fate of the provisional government set up in Uhtua in February 1919 was sealed by the withdrawal of Allied forces from northern Russia in the autumn of that year. In the spring of 1920, the government was forced to flee to Finland. A Karelian workers' commune, in which exiled Finnish Reds held all the high offices, came into being as the Red Army extinguished the last remnants of resistance. The Finnish negotiators at the peace talks held in Tartu were unable to wrest any significant concessions from the Russians, other than in the north, where an old claim to Petsamo and access to the Arctic was conceded. The existence of what amounted to a Red Finnish state in Karelia merely added fuel to what was already an emotive issue in nationalist circles in Finland, who tended to regard the peace treaty eventually concluded at Tartu on 14 October 1920 as a betrayal of Finnish interests.

The signing of peace between Poland and Russia in March 1921 formally concluded the process of establishing relations between the RSFSR and the former western borderlands of the Russian empire. It remained to be seen how durable that relationship would prove to be. Of the five new republics, Poland was by far the largest in terms of population, and Finland the least afflicted by the depredations of war. The northernmost republic also had the advantage of long-established and fully functioning institutions, which could be accommodated with reasonable ease into the constitution of 1919; the other four had to devise an institutional and constitutional order, in circumstances which were hardly propitious for such a task. The Finnish constitution-makers, mindful of the socialists' penchant for an all-powerful legislature, ensured that there would be a strong executive president; the Baltic states and Poland plumped for the French model of a weak executive, and paid the price. The demise of democracy in eastern Europe cannot, however, be attributed solely to the failings of the constitutional systems set up in the early days of independence. Democracy survived in Finland because it rested upon fairly secure foundations: a tradition of participation and involvement in public life by a literate population, a high degree of social and national homogenity and consensus (the trauma of civil war notwithstanding), and above all, a relatively buoyant economy. Suomi/Finland was by no means predestined to become a 'pacific, neutral, Scandinavian-type democracy' had it not been for the tragic accident of the civil war; but in many important respects, it bore a closer resemblance to its western neighbours than to its southern cousins in the lands between.[29]

Finland occasionally and Poland frequently caused western European policy-makers a great deal of annoyance and frustration; but their viability as independent states was seldom questioned. The same could not be said for the three Baltic states, Eesti, Latvija and Lietuva. Sympathetic observers such as the British commissioner to the Baltic, Sir Stephen Tallents, felt compelled to admit that some sort of union with a future Russia was the inevitable fate of these small states; even after the Allied Supreme Council had granted *de jure* recognition to Estonia and Latvia on 26 January 1921, doubts continued to be expressed. The British government made it clear in mid-1921 that it was not in a position to promise assistance to the Baltic states should they be subjected to attack from Soviet Russia. Britain played no active part in the formulation of strategic policies in the eastern Baltic, other than to offer advice to Finland, which seems to have been regarded as a key element in the preservation of the stability of the eastern Baltic, and to oppose the French policy of trying to build alliances to contain Germany and/or Russia.[30]

In German military circles, the Baltic states were often regarded as unnecessary obstacles placed in the path of the once dominant states of the region. The prospect of a Polish-dominated and French-backed coalition of forces emerging in the eastern Baltic alarmed the generals and the politicians, though the latter sought to counter this by a policy of active friendship towards the Baltic states, using trade as a means of drawing them into the German orbit. The signing of the Rapallo

29. Upton 1980, pp. 534–5.

30. Kirby D 1974 A great opportunity lost? Aspects of British commercial policy toward the Baltic states 1920–1924 *Journal of Baltic Studies* **5**: 364. Hinkkanen-Lievonen 1984, pp. 90–2. French and British aims in the region are discussed by Hovi K 1984 *Alliance de revers. Stabilization of France's alliance policies in East Central Europe, 1919–1921,* Turku, and Patrick Salmon (British security interests in Scandinavia and the Baltic 1918–1939) in Hiden J and Loit A, (eds) 1988 *The Baltic in international relations between the two world wars* Studia Baltica Stockholmiensia **3**, Stockholm, pp. 113–36.

agreement with Soviet Russia in April 1922 was a triumph for German diplomacy. It also coincided with the final collapse of Polish attempts to create a Baltic bloc. The political accord signed by the foreign ministers of Poland, Latvia, Estonia and Finland in Warsaw on 17 March 1922 was little more than a mutual agreement to observe benevolent neutrality in the event of one of the signatories falling the victim of unprovoked aggression. The refusal of the Finnish *Eduskunta* to ratify even this modest agreement also signified an unwillingness to be associated with Polish military designs. The Latvians were also wary of close involvement with Poland, whom they suspected of harbouring designs on Latgale, which had once been a part of the Polish-Lithuanian Commonwealth; only the Estonians were anxious for closer ties with Warsaw. Significantly, the Baltic states did not join Poland in signing the Allied protest at the Rapallo agreement, and they hastened to consolidate their trading links with Germany during the succeeding months.[31]

The attitude of Soviet Russia towards its western neighbours is less easy to evaluate. The loss of a sizeable and strategically vital chunk of territory was a shock which no amount of brave rhetoric about the rights of national self-determination could disguise. Moreover, Lenin tended to see self-determination from a revolutionary, proletarian perspective, as he made clear in his conversation with the Finnish socialists shortly before acceding to the request of the bourgeois P. E. Svinhufvud for recognition of Finland's independence. The revolutionary flame on the borders of Russia flickered and was snuffed out in 1919; attempts to relight the candle were speedily stamped on by the authorities. The signing of the peace treaty with Estonia in February 1920 was a breakthrough for Soviet Russia, as Lenin quickly acknowledged; but only insofar as it was the first sign that the system of encirclement maintained by the interventionist powers was beginning to break up. The hoped-for revival of trade between Russia and the West failed to materialise, and the border states did not become Russia's window to Europe. The business of these states in the 1920s was oriented towards western markets, not Russia. Former connections withered; only a mutual ideological hostility remained. Increasingly isolated and morbidly aware of their pariah status, it was easy for Russian leaders to conjure up visions of malevolent British

31. Hovi K 1984 (*Interessensphären...*), pp. 151–63. Rodgers H 1975 *Search for security. A study in Baltic diplomacy, 1920–1934,* Hamden, Conn., pp. 14–24. Hiden and Loit 1988, pp. 25–42 (chapter by H. Arumäe on the Baltic bloc), 145–56 (chapter by Hiden on Germany and the Baltic states).

imperialists pulling the strings of the weak border states, and to interpret the slightest move of the border states towards cooperation as directed against the RSFSR. Such suspicions were replicated on the other side of the border, most noticeably in Finland; and although there were periods in which a slight improvement in relations was evident, they were rarely cordial and never good. Even during the 1920s, when Russia and Germany maintained a low profile on the international stage, the lands between were never entirely free to determine or evolve a more suitable security policy; their own internal disagreements and jealousies made cooperation unlikely, and offered their big neighbours excellent opportunities to play one off against another. When the skies began to darken in the thirties, the chances of the border states being able to withstand pressure from Russia or Germany (or both) grew perceptibly dimmer.

Independence, like leaving home, is an affirmation of self-conscious maturity; but it is by no means an easy step to take. The border states which achieved independence between 1917 and 1920 did so as a result of the collapse of empires rather than of their own volition. After the national state had finally been established and recognised, independence was usually hailed as the culmination of a long process of conscious striving to fulfil the nation's destiny; but that says more about the need to consolidate and unite the people around a set of values and symbols than it reflects the actual reality. Not even for Poles, supremely conscious of their own recent history, was the reforging of a national state an act which could be performed without assistance and a certain amount of good fortune. Neither Finland nor the Baltic states stepped fully-fledged and confident on to the stage of sovereign nationhood. During the spring and summer of 1917, the Finnish socialists made most of the running, edging from restored autonomy towards the internal parliamentary sovereignty of the abortive July law, endorsing national independence as their ultimate goal but stopping short of out-and-out conflict with the Russian provisional government on this issue. The pro-independence faction in the non-socialist camp, initially rather small, grew in influence during the autumn, partly as a response to the perceived disintegration of law and order in the country. Finland's independence was closely tied to this issue, as the non-socialist government formed by P. E. Svinhufvud on 26 November 1917 made clear. The collapse of the provisional government, which had claimed the right to exercise the prerogatives of the former ruler until the all-Russian constituent assembly could finally resolve the relationship, provided the necessary constitutional-legal argument for breaking free; the fearful prospect of renewed Red disorder and terror was a powerful incentive to act; and Germany, which had trained Finnish volunteers eager to fight for their country's cause, was seen as a potential source of salvation in the fight for independence. The declaration of independence on 6 December 1917 was a cause for reflection rather than rejoicing. Writing at the beginning of 1918, the liberal Zachris Castrén wondered whether or not independence was merely a twist of fate, a piece of good luck which had just happened to come Finland's way. The writer Volter Kilpi doubted whether the Finns as a nation were mature enough for freedom and independence. The tragic experience of civil war produced an even greater wave of self-doubt and gloomy analyses of the failings of the nation.[32]

The steps towards independence were even more hesitant south of the Gulf of Finland. The session of the *Maapäev* which debated the future of Estonia in September 1917 revealed a clear preference for some sort of union or federation, rather than outright independence. It was the prospect of falling victim to Germany's annexationist aims that obliged the Estonians to think far more seriously about independence, as the socialist Mihkel Martna observed in January 1918.[33] Forced underground by the Bolsheviks and then by the German military occupation, the committee of elders of the *Maapäev* had to rely very much upon the activities of its various representatives abroad. As we have seen, a wide range of options were considered, ranging from the establishment of a temporary British protectorate to union with Finland. The Latvians and Lithuanians had to contend with the machinations of the various armed forces and the intrigues of their commanders long after the armistice had been declared on the western front. The arrogance of the German military in occupied territory during 1917–18 and the continued unreliability of condottieri such as von der Goltz and Bermondt-Avalov were a powerful impetus towards national independence as the only solution; but a number of complex issues still remained. In the Latvian case, independence was also about political self-definition, an issue by no means resolved with the final expulsion of the Bolsheviks and the liquidation of the Latvian Soviet republic. Nationhood for the Lithuanians was also a territorial question, with ethnic overtones which tended to mask the relatively

32. The reflections of Castrén and Kilpi were published in the monthly *Valvoja* in January 1918. The intense debate about the causes and consequences of the civil war is analysed by: Kunnas M-L 1976 *Kansalaissodan kirjalliset rintamat* Suomen Kirjallisuuden Seuran toimituksia **320**, Helsinki.

33. Laaman 1964, p. 202. Zetterberg S 1977 *Suomi ja Viro 1917–1919* Historiallisia Tutkimuksia **102**, Helsinki, pp. 49–62.

low level of national consciousness in the disputed areas. The same might also be said about the East Karelian question, though it never assumed the monumental dimensions for Finland that Vilna did for the Lithuanians. There were also, beneath the surface, separatist currents such as that on the Åland islands and amongst the Swedish-speaking minority on the Finnish mainland, or elements which were regarded as potentially disloyal or untrustworthy, such as the Baltic Germans in Latvia. The large Jewish communities in many of the towns of Latvia, Lithuania and Poland constituted yet another distinctive element, both in their relationship with the nation-state and the *goyim* community and also in terms of their own religious and political differences.

In dealing with Germany, the peacemakers at Versailles, particularly the French, tended to set aside the yardstick of national self-determination. The Danish government wisely preferred not to have a substantial minority of discontented Germans foisted upon them, much to the surprise and annoyance of the French. The claims of the German minority of West Prussia and Posen were set aside in the interests of resurrecting the Polish state, and Danzig – which the commission on Polish Affairs wished to give to Poland – became a free state, largely as a result of Lloyd George's insistence. The Memel district was also detached from Germany and placed under French military control; before the apparatus of a free state could be fully devised, however, the district was occupied by Lithuanian troops in 1923. Both Memel and Danzig were to remain high on the agenda of German revisionism, potential trouble spots to be exploited by an aggressive and expansionist Germany under Hitler. The greatest loser of territory in the Baltic area was not Germany, but Russia, and it was unlikely that the new regime would rest easily as long as it perceived itself threatened or exposed in the west. The actions and demands of Hitler occupied the headlines in the late 1930s. Stalin's foreign policy aims were far less vociferously publicised, and attracted relatively little attention in the world media, but there was little comfort to be gleaned by the borderland states from the pronouncements which did emanate, directly or indirectly, from the Soviet leader. As the fragile structure of the new order of international relations, epitomised by the League of Nations, began to collapse, the new countries of eastern Europe became the objects of an increasingly deadly game of territorial revision, in which the two former great powers in the region ultimately colluded, to devastating effect, in 1939.

CHAPTER TEN

The Impact of Change, c.1870–1940

At the commencement of the nineteenth century, the northern periphery of Europe could fairly be classified as a 'backward' economic region. Farming methods were often primitive, as were the implements used. The manufacturing sector was small-scale, weakly organised and hampered by restrictions. Neither seemed capable of absorbing the growing pool of excess labour and thereby overcoming the problems of under-employment, poverty and destitution. Although these problems were by no means resolved by the end of the century, the overall perspective was nevertheless very different. The economies of the northern European countries had shown themselves capable of adaptation and of expansion, albeit at differing tempos and in a diversity of ways. 'Industrialisation' pure and simple is not the most helpful of words with which to describe this process of change, and indeed, there are good reasons to be wary of too much application of general theories of economic growth. Far from being endowed with the advantages of the latecomer, backward economies before the First World War seem to have had few special advantages for the exploitation of strategies of industrialisation other than those based on already existing internal developments. Industrial growth in Sweden was thus in the first instance brought about by the increased and more effective exploitation of natural resources of iron ore and timber for the export market by a workforce which was literate and capable of absorbing and using new skills.[1] In the case of the Baltic provinces,

1. O'Brien P 1986 Do we have a typology for the study of European industrialisation in the nineteenth century? *Journal of European Economic History* **15**: 291–333. Hildebrand K 1978 Labour and capital in the Scandinavian countries in the

industrialisation must initially be considered within the overall context of the Russian empire, and after 1918, almost as an inherited problem for the new countries, unable to sustain the type of large-scale enterprises founded during the final decades of tsarist rule. Insofar as it is possible to speak of typologies of economic development, then the Baltic states ultimately opted for the 'Danish model' of intensive medium-sized agriculture, producing animal products for export, rather than a 'Swedish model' of the kind outlined above.

The 'national' approach to economic development, however, tends to obscure regional differences. As it is very much predicted on 'growth', it also conceals the unevenness of development, and the fact that large areas remained on the periphery. As the momentum of economic development gathered pace, these regions often became increasingly marginalised, their natural resources exploited in the interests of the manufacturing sector or export industry, the more able and energetic of their inhabitants moving elsewhere in search of work or business opportunities, leaving behind the old, the infirm and the less able. Seen from this perspective, the advances towards prosperity made over the last hundred or so years in the name of economic progress have more often than not weakened or destroyed the fragile ecosystems of the marginal land. What the Swedish ethnographer Åke Campbell characterised in the 1930s as a 'ruined landscape', in which ruthless exploitation of the forests or other natural resources completely overwhelms and transforms the way of life of the local community, is part of the price paid for progress and material wellbeing.[2]

PEASANT INTO FARMER? THE FARMING ECONOMY

The transformation of the Scandinavian countries from an impoverished periphery into prosperous states whose inhabitants enjoy

---

nineteenth and twentieth centuries *The Cambridge Economic History of Europe*, Cambridge, vol. 7 pp. 590–628. Jörberg L 1976 The Nordic countries, 1850–1914 *The Fontana Economic History of Europe*, Glasgow, vol. 4:2 pp. 375–485.

2. Campbell Å 1936 *Kulturlandskapet*, Stockholm. It is, however, worth noting that areas which have in the past been ruthlessly exploited for their resources may become tourist attractions in our own time, though this, too, may lead to a further form of exploitation. On this subject, see the interesting essay by Katriina Petrisalo on tourism and local culture in: Ingold T (ed.) 1988 *The social implications of agrarian change in northern and eastern Finland* Transactions of the Finnish Anthropological Society **21**, Helsinki, pp. 63–75.

an enviably high standard of living is nonetheless a remarkable achievement. Whether or not the three small Baltic states were beginning to follow the 'Scandinavian road' before the way was abruptly closed by the war and their incorporation into the Soviet Union is by no means easy to answer, for although there is a large secondary literature on the economic history of the Scandinavian countries, the situation with regard to the Baltic states is less satisfactory, and much of what has been written is rather tendentious in tone.[3] The necessity of strengthening a sense of nationhood through agrarian reforms and – in the case of Estonia and Latvia – of dismantling or abandoning much of the industrial base built up since the 1880s indicates at the very least that an abrupt change of direction took place. There was also an inherent suspicion of big industry, foreign capital and an urban proletariat, as the following extract from the Latvian press indicates:

> If we consider that the main policy of our country is to uplift a healthy peasantry and to avoid the growth of a factory proletariat, we realise that it does not lie in the interest of Latvia to extend big industry, but rather only to facilitate such branches as are necessary for local requirements.[4]

The economic and social policies pursued by the governments of these states also differed in significant respects from the general Scandinavian norm. These were in part a legacy from imperial Russia, in part necessitated by the specific circumstances in which the newly-independent states found themselves. On the other hand, the producers' cooperatives and the marketing of agricultural produce owed not a little to the Scandinavian example, and the achievements of Denmark – also a small and largely farming nation – tended to set a benchmark and act as an inspiration for all three countries.

3. There is much good material to be found in the *Scandinavian Economic History Review*, founded in 1928. Useful studies in English include: Jörberg L 1961 *Growth and fluctuations of Swedish industry, 1869–1912*, Stockholm; Dahmén E 1970 *Entrepreneurial activity and the development of Swedish industry 1919–1939*, Homewood, Ill.; Singleton F 1986 *The economy of Finland in the twentieth century*, Bradford. There is a fairly comprehensive survey of the economy of independent Estonia in: Kaur U 1962 *Wirtschaftsstruktur und Wirtschaftspolitik des Freistaates Estland 1918–1940* Commentationes Balticae **VIII/IX:3**, Bonn, and a very detailed volume in Latvian by: Aizsilnieks A 1968 *Latvijas saimniecības vēsture 1914–1945*, Stockholm.

4. Cited in a consular report from Riga, 29 January 1923: FO 371: 9269, file N 288/288/59, Public Record Office, London. See also consul Lowdon's report of February 1922, which painted a gloomy picture of the prospects of reviving manufacturing industries in Latvia. FO 371:8066, file N1480/891/59.

The success of Danish farming depended on a number of things. The land reforms carried out from the 1780s onwards created an appropriate structure, with farms well-suited in size to cope with the new technology, and a class of freeholding farmers willing to invest and improve. During the course of the nineteenth century, the farmers created and supported a network of associations and institutions dedicated to the promotion of agriculture. The Agricultural Society (*Landhusholdningsselskabet*), founded in 1769, continued to play a key role in the propagation of new ideas and the carrying out of research, and it was involved in the organisation of farmers' associations, which by 1914 had almost 100,000 members. The cooperative movement of the 1880s was closely linked to the political agitation against the undemocratic policies of the Estrup ministry, and drew upon the Grundtvigian traditions of the people's high schools (in which many of the farmers themselves had been educated), though the main impetus was the farmers' desire for greater independence. By 1890, roughly one-third of all milk producers delivered to a cooperative dairy; two decades later, there were over 1,000 cooperative dairies, as against 255 private and 90 estate dairies. The dairy chimney was in many respects the symbol of a new world, in which farming was 'no longer a way of life, but had become a business'.[5] The invention and development of the centrifugal separator in the 1870s gave a major boost to the dairying industry, for it yielded up to 30 per cent more butter than the old methods of cooling. The research laboratory run by N. J. Fjord in the 1880s pioneered investigations into the quality and nutritive value of milk, butter and animal feedstuffs. Quality control was ensured by the adoption of the *lurmærk* symbol by the Danish dairies' butter stamp association in 1900 and by subsequent legislation designed to uphold national standards. These and other improvements led to substantial increases in yields. In comparison with the average standards of the early 1860s, a fully-grown cow on the outbreak of the First World War weighed half as much again and yielded well over twice the amount of milk. Exported agricultural produce quadrupled in value between 1876 and 1914, and made up 85–90 per cent of the total value of Danish exports during this period.

The key element in this transformation was, of course, the shift from cereals to animal products. Danish farmers who benefited from cheap imported grain and feedstuffs whilst selling their bacon, eggs and butter at high prices to British markets in the years before the war (and who were able to reap even greater profits during the early years

5. Bjørn C (ed.) 1988 *Det danske landbrugs historie 1810–1914*, Odense, p. 195.

of the war, when Germans drove up to the farm gate to buy up supplies) remained stout free-traders long after their counterparts in other countries had rallied behind the banner of protectionism. The veritable explosion of productivity on the farm in the 1880s was not only decisive for Denmark's economy for the next half-century; it also shaped attitudes and beliefs, to the extent that one historian has argued that they remained virtually unchallenged until the middle of this century.[6]

The shift from arable farming to animal husbandry in northern Europe tended to benefit the small and medium-sized farmer in several ways. He was far less affected than the large arable farmer by the fall in grain prices, and was able to feed his workforce, his family and his animals more cheaply as a result. By switching to dairying, which employed a large number of low-paid female workers, he could further reduce his labour costs. The disastrous crop failures and the famines of the 1860s also brought home the fact that animal husbandry was a less hazardous venture than arable farming in northern climes. The significant increases in yields and output that occurred throughout northern Europe in the decades before 1914 was conditioned by a complex set of circumstances, of which the slow process of land reform and the greater rationalisation of landholdings was perhaps the most important. Significant changes in practices and attitudes had already taken place before the 1880s. Peasant farmers had been able to discover lucrative markets for their cash crops – Swedish farmers sold oats to feed London's horses, farmers in the Baltic provinces grew flax or sold bullocks fattened on the draff from distillation to the abattoirs of St Petersburg. The greater availability of credit, the opening up of communications and hence of new marketing opportunities, and the growing range of information and advice for the farmer, all played a part. In Sweden and Finland the demand for timber by the wood-processing industries, now freed from legal restrictions and able to exploit to the full all available energy resources, had a major impact upon the countryside. Felling, carting and floating the timber created employment. Farmers earned extra income from the sale of their timber stands (though it has been argued in the case of Finland at least that this income had less impact upon the farm economy than had

6. Clausen H 1973 *Hvor lange varede den 19. århundrede kulturellt?* Det lærde Selskabs publikationer, Ny serie **1**, Århus, p. 3. The parting advice uttered in 1930 by the redoubtable farmers' leader P. P. Pinstrup to the Jutland farmers' association of which he had long been chairman, to polish their boots and stand firm as they had done in the 1880s, was not untypical of the kind of attitude fostered during the breakthrough of Danish farming into world markets.

hitherto been assumed).[7] And by reaching into the remotest parts of the hinterland in the quest for supplies, the timber industry helped break down the barriers of isolation and brought not only new goods and commodities, but also the cash economy.

These changes did not occur overnight, nor did they directly transform the peasant into a farmer. A large proportion of the landholdings were too small to sustain a family, and extra income had to be sought, from seasonal forestry work, fishing, carting or the sale of homemade goods. Small farmers did not necessarily rush to buy up-to-date or even second-hand equipment, when the job could be done more cheaply with manual labour. Machines were not always suitable; the *Revalsche Zeitung* complained in 1860 that manufacturers seemed unaware of the difficult conditions in which their machines had to work, and opined that they were constructed 'as if they were intended to be used by some lady in her boudoir'.[8] Innovative practices, such as marling or the use of artificial fertilisers, tended to percolate down from the big farms, and were more likely to be imitated in regions where such examples were common, such as southern Finland, than where they were not, as in the north-east. Those who sought to promote innovations also encountered mental or moral objections, for instance, that machinery made people lazy. Farmhands had more reason than most to raise objections. Dairies and separators were the subject of protest songs, not least because the farm labourers ended up with skimmed milk instead of the full-cream milk they had been used to:

Lapuan osuusmeijeri on kirkonkylähän siiretty
kurnaalimaidon voimalla ne lapualaaset sivistyy...

Kun trengit lakkaa syömästä, niin vyö on viäla väljällä
palvelusväki saa työtä teherä aivan suurella näljällä

The Lapua co-op dairy has come to the village
with skimmed milk they're civilising the Lapuans...

7. Peltonen M 1992 *Talolliset ja torpparit. Vuosisadan vaihteen maatalouskysymys Suomessa* Historiallisia Tutkimuksia **164**, Helsinki, pp. 190–9. Peltonen does, however, admit that the inflow of income may have helped lower levels of indebtedness.

8. Kahk J 1990 The mechanization of agriculture in Estonia from 1860 to 1880 *Journal of Baltic Studies* **21**: 336. Kahk argues that the spread of the new technology in agriculture was limited by the imperfections of the machinery available, and that it was not until the 1870s that large-scale farming was beginning to forge ahead, thanks to rationalised work practices and the new technology.

When the hinds finish eating,
their belts are still loose
the farmhands must labour half-famished [9]

The vast majority of landholdings in northern Europe *were* small. Three-quarters of Finnish farms in 1910 were of less than ten hectares in size, and half were smaller than five hectares, the minimum size of a holding on which a man might support a family, according to the 1900 Finnish Senate commission's report. The situation was somewhat similar in Sweden and Norway. In Denmark, with its rather different method of measuring land according to its potential, there was a particularly marked growth at the end of the nineteenth century in small farms (1–4 tdr. htk.), and in the number of cottars, or smallholders (*Husmænd*: from around 140,000 in 1860 to over 212,000 in 1905), whilst there was a concomitant decline in the numbers of large and medium-sized farms. Various attempts were made to provide smallholdings for the landless: bona fide and respectable farmhands were, for example, afforded the opportunity of buying a plot of land with the assistance of a cheap state loan, and almost 7,000 such smallholdings were created between 1900 and 1913, mostly in Jutland. On the whole, however, it was the established smallholders themselves who secured the greatest changes, through their credit unions and parcellisation associations.

A survey conducted in 1907 of 269,000 Danish properties, over half of them less than five hectares in size, revealed that most farms possessed modern ploughs, harrows and rollers, but only one in three had a threshing machine (generally horse-powered), and only one in five a seed drill. On the smallholdings of Jutland, broadcasting seed by hand was the normal practice, and machinery of any sort was rare. By 1923, something like half the farms in Denmark were equipped with seed drills, mowers and threshing machines; thirteen years later, three-quarters owned threshing machines, and electrically-powered equipment was used by over one-third. As the above figures show, the fully-mechanised farm was still something of an exception even in Denmark. In the north-eastern corner of the Baltic region, machines were even rarer, both on the land and in the forest. Iron ploughs had virtually displaced the old wooden ones, but were often unsuitable for the terrain. In much of Kurland, according to a Prussian agricultural expert writing during the First World War, the locally-designed

9. This song, and a useful analysis of the patterns of innovation in Finnish agriculture, is in: Anttila V 1974 *Talonpojasta tuottajaksi*, Helsinki, pp. 186–93.

harrow (*Federzahnegge*) had become a universal implement, used to plough in the stubble, to prepare the ground for planting, and even for planting itself. He attributed the deficiencies of arable farming in Kurland to poor drainage, imperfect or inadequate equipment and the lack of skilled operators, unsatisfactory or delayed preparation of the soil and inadequate manuring. In comparison with East Prussia, yields per hectare were considerably lower for all grain crops, in spite of the relative similarity of soil and climate. Ten years later, a Latvian economist admitted that agricultural methods were still very primitive, and that yields could be considerably improved by better drainage and improved fertilisation.[10]

Further north, the mattock and iron bar were for many the most essential tools; the piles of stones and shallow open drains still to be seen in the small fields of eastern and central Finland are a silent and melancholy testimony to the efforts of those who undertook the back-breaking task of bringing marginal land under cultivation. In spite of the wholesale switch to dairy farming from the 1880s onwards and improvements in stock-rearing and the cultivation of forage crops, milk yields lagged significantly behind those of the dairy herds of Denmark or the North German plain. Only a small number of farmers in Finland or Sweden owned more than ten milch cows, and a far smaller proportion than in Denmark or Holland were members of a dairy cooperative.[11]

The second major wave of land reforms which occurred in the newly-independent states after the First World War tilted the balance even more strongly in favour of the small farmer. Tenant farmers in Finland were given the opportunity to redeem their farms on favourable terms, and by 1930, almost 90 per cent of all rented farms and plots had been purchased by the tenants. Further measures designed to promote new settlement and the cultivation of marginal land increased the cultivated land area by over a quarter between 1920 and 1940, and created over 25,000 new farms. The vast majority of these holdings were small, catering mainly for the family's own needs; the opportunity to earn extra income in the forests was often vital,

10. Marquart B 1916, 1917 *Die landwirtschaftlichen Verhältnisse Kurlands*, 2 vols Berlin. The situation was even worse in Lithuania, where crop yields per hectare were half as high as in East Prussia. Bokalders J (ed.) 1928 *The Latvian economist*, Riga, p. 100.

11. See the table in Peltonen 1992, p. 237, and the English-language summary, pp. 406–14, which makes the point that the Finnish farming economy was far from commercialised at the beginning of this century. For the development of dairy farming in Finland between the 1870 and 1914, see: Vihola T 1991 *Leipäviljasta lypsykarjaan* Historiallisia Tutkimuksia **159**, Helsinki.

especially on the northern and north-eastern margins of the country.

The land reforms undertaken in the three Baltic states were rather more sweeping, involving the wholescale redistribution of land taken from the minority of large landowners. In addition to the obvious desire for a more equitable pattern of land distribution, which might produce a more stable social order, the decision-makers in these new states were also moved by nationalistic and political considerations. The majority of the large land owners belonged to the old elites – German in Latvia and Estonia, Polish or Russian in Lithuania – and several had openly sided with those who had sought to subvert the independence of the new states. Such people could expect little sympathy, and in most cases forfeited their lands without compensation. Others who had remained neutral or even loyally supported the new order in the troubled years of 1918–20 sought to advance a moderate programme of reform which would have left them with some of their estates intact, but their efforts met with little success. The Estonian constituent assembly rejected not only the proposals of the Baltic German delegates, but also of the Estonian moderates, and voted on 10 October 1919 for a law expropriating virtually all the landed estates in the country over a period of two years. The level of compensation finally agreed to in 1926 represented only a tiny fraction of the real value of the estates, and was largely paid in the form of state debentures. The Latvian reforms, initiated a year later, allowed landed estate owners the right to keep up to fifty hectares of land, with the appropriate amount of stock and equipment, but the *Saeima* voted in 1924 not to pay compensation for the land expropriated, which totalled some 3.7 million hectares, The Lithuanian reforms treated the big landowners more leniently, eventually allowing them to keep 150 hectares and paying a small measure of compensation.

The reforms were justified on various grounds. The possession of so much land (58 per cent of all cultivated land in Estonia, 48 per cent in Latvia, around 40 per cent in Lithuania) by a small elite traditionally perceived as the enemy and oppressor of the people was deemed politically dangerous and socially unwise, in view of the great numbers of landless workers, who it was feared might be tempted towards communism by the propaganda of the eastern neighbour. A strong 'peasantist' ethos, which sought to create a nation of small farmers imbued with patriotic zeal and impervious to the siren songs of deracinated Reds and the demoralised proletariat of the big factories, pervaded much of the debate on land reform, sometimes to the detriment of agriculture as a whole. Many of the farms created after 1920 were too small to be viable concerns, and the state was obliged to step in with low-interest loans and long-term credits to enable farmers to buy necessary equipment and construct buildings. The Depression of the early 1930s hit farming particularly badly, and compelled governments to adopt radical measures and policies to protect a sector of the economy which directly or indirectly provided a livelihood for a substantial part of the population, even if it was well behind industry in terms of output and productivity per worker.

Nevertheless, measured simply in terms of its own output and yields over the period, the record of the farming economies of the Baltic and Scandinavian countries during the interwar years was impressive. Great efforts were made in the Baltic states to improve standards and quality control, through producers' cooperatives and central export agencies, and the volume of dairy and meat products exported grew steadily during the latter half of the 1930s. Land reform in Lithuania also meant the break-up of the old peasant communes and the creation of independent farmsteads (as was also the case in the Petseri district of Estonia and Latgale in eastern Latvia), and there were numerous problems in the first post-reform years. By the mid-1920s, however, animal products had begun to replace timber and flax as the main export commodities, and by 1935, Lithuania had increased sevenfold the volume of its butter exports, overtaking Estonia in the process. Finnish farmers were remarkably successful in achieving high levels of self-sufficiency in cereal production, and in growing new high-yielding strains of wheat, whilst the quality and quantity of dairy products increased substantially, adding to the volume of exports westwards.

The numbers of the landless were diminishing but had by no means disappeared; their working and living conditions were often wretched, though many poor smallholder families scratching a miserable marginal existence fared no better. A flight from the land had already begun in the eastern territories of the German empire before 1914, as thousands moved westward in search of better-paid jobs. Danish and southern Swedish farmers also began to experience problems in finding workers, and numbers of seasonal labourers from Galicia were brought in to harvest the root crops. Although the number of independent farms in Denmark actually rose over the interwar period, the rural population as a whole declined, both as a proportion of the whole (from 32 to 25 per cent) and in absolute terms (from around one million in 1921 to 964,000 in 1940).

Seen purely in economic terms, the traditional self-sufficient peasant household was by the 1930s a thing of the past, even if its supposed values and ideals were not infrequently trotted out by politicians on the stump or nationalist image-makers. What did survive was a strong sense of attachment to the land, to the farmstead as a family concern. It was the loss of this connection which made the bankruptcies and compulsory auctions of the period of the Depression so tragic, and which undoubtedly inspired many farmers to fight back in locally-organised 'crisis movements'. The Depression profoundly shook the confidence of many farmers in their own organisations, their governments and their own ability to survive. Those who came through found themselves in a world in which cost-accounting, mechanisation and marketing were even more crucial elements than they had been before. Much of rural northern Europe still retained distinctive elements of peasant farming life (nicely captured by J. Hampden Jackson in his 1938 book on Finland) and continued to do so right into the 1960s; but the tide had definitely turned. The area under cultivation in Denmark, for example, reached a peak in the late 1930s, when over three-quarters of the total land area of the country was under cultivation. By 1986, the amount of farmed land was less than it had been in 1915, and the number of farms had fallen from over 200,000 in the 1930s to fewer than 87,000. *Mutatis mutandis*, the same has occurred in the other Scandinavian countries (demographic as well as economic developments in the Baltic states since 1940 have been rather different, though there too, far fewer work the land than did in the 1930s).

INNOVATION, INVENTION AND ADAPTATION

In contrast to the countries or regions which industrialised early, northern Europe never developed huge conurbations of cheap working-class housing interspersed with smoking mill chimneys, pot banks or angry blast foundries. There were large factories, certainly, and the Baltic provinces and St Petersburg region were amongst the most industrialised parts of the Russian empire. The Kreenholm mill outside Narva, founded in 1857, laid claim to be the largest cotton-finishing concern in Europe, and in Riga, Tallinn and St Petersburg there were several factories or shipyards which had workforces numbering several thousand. St Petersburg and Riga could truly be described as big industrial cities by 1914. Riga had become the major port of the empire, and its fifth largest city. It was the leading world exporter of timber, most of which went to to Great Britain, the city's principal trading partner. In 1913, there were 372 factories in Riga, employing over 87,000 workers and with an annual turnover of 220 million roubles, to which the rubber, engineering, chemical and textile industries were the principal contributors. St Petersburg's industrial workforce expanded significantly in the years immediately before the war, and massively during the war years; there was also a sizeable increase in the workforce in Tallinn and elsewhere, where industries supplying the war effort were put into full production.

The industrial spurt which occurred during the last decades of tsarist rule did not, however, establish a pattern of development for the inheritor states on the Baltic littoral. The number of manufacturing concerns in Latvia employing over fifty workers fell from 329 in 1910 to 112 in 1921, whilst the total industrial workforce shrank to one-third of the 1910 level. The loss of the Russian market and the failure of efforts to revive the transit trade in the early 1920s meant that firms such as the Provodnik rubber works or the Russo-Baltic Shipbuilding Company, which had before the war given employment to thousands, either had to shut down completely or continue production on a much reduced scale.[12]

Industrial production did recover, though not on the same scale or tempo as in the immediate prewar years; and the types of industrial enterprise developed during the twenties and thirties were more suited to the resources and marketing possibilities of small, primarily agrarian states on the eastern fringe of the capitalist world. Almost three-quarters of the industrial workforce of Estonia was engaged in production for the domestic market in 1932, and policy after the slump tended to be predicated on self-sufficiency and increasing domestic production levels. Whereas foreign investment was primarily directed towards export industries, the state concentrated on building up the domestic infrastructure, investing substantially in quarrying, electricity and gas. Particularly noteworthy was the rapid development of a chemical industry based on the extraction of oil shale from the extensive deposits on the northern Estonian coast. Lithuania was able to build up its food-processing industry, which by 1939 was responsible for almost half the value of industrial output, and was a significant contributor to the country's exports. Latvia, the most heavily industrialised region of the pre-revolutionary Baltic provinces, succeeded gradually in rebuilding an industrial sector, and was beginning to experience real growth in output during the last years of

12. Romas I 1934 *Die wirtschaftliche Struktur der baltischen Staaten und die Idee einer Zollunion*, Klaipėda, pp. 75–8. On the fading of dreams of a Russian Eldorado, see: Hinkkanen-Lievonen M-L 1984 *British trade and enterprise in the Baltic states 1918–1925* Studia Historica **14**, Helsinki, pp. 113–40.

the 1930s. Like its neighbours, however, its principal exports were agricultural products.

The Baltic provinces had been in the vanguard of Russia's industrial spurt; East and West Prussia were definitely on the backward periphery of the rapidly industrialising German empire. Between 1871 and 1933, there was an annual net migration loss of several thousand from East Prussia, rising to a peak of over 20,000 a year in the 1890s. Entrepreneurs – the vast majority small artisans or businessmen – were handicapped by a lack of capital for investment, and often found that the most able workers moved west after training, in search of better wages and opportunities. Harbour improvements and the building of a canal to Pillau increased Königsberg's attractiveness as a port for the export of Russian grain, which flowed in great quantities through the port after the resolution of the Russo-German tariff war in 1894; but there were signs of a decline in the port's trade before 1914. The volume of trade to Memel, on the other hand, increased significantly, and considerable amounts of Russian timber were shipped out of the port, which together with the surrounding region was separated from Germany in 1919, and eventually seized by the Lithuanians in 1923. In West Prussia, an ambitious programme of industrialisation was mounted in the 1890s to combat migration, though many of the enterprises later folded. The days of Danzig's glory as a port had long since departed; in 1914, it ranked only thirteenth in the Baltic in terms of tonnage and incoming ships. Poor communications with the hinterland made it unattractive to Russian grain or timber exporters. The free state of Danzig established by the peace settlement was highly vulnerable to Polish pressure, and although the volume of trade through the port in the 1920s rose substantially, it was mostly controlled by the Poles. The free state city was unable to support itself economically, and came to depend more and more on German subsidies.

Whereas the pattern of industrial development along the southern shores of the Baltic can best be described as uneven, Sweden and Finland found themselves on a growth curve which was to take them to post-1945 affluence. Finland was still predominantly an agrarian country in the 1930s, and did not experience real industrial expansion until after the Second World War, though growth rates in its major export industries during the interwar years were sizeable. Sweden was already a net exporter of capital before the First World War. Over a third of the industrial workforce was employed in export industries, producing high-quality goods, often of Swedish invention or development, such as milking equipment, steam turbines, telephones, armaments and electrical machinery. Between 1870 and 1914, the annual growth rate of industrial production was 4.4 per cent; there was a ninefold increase in gross investment, and in investment in machinery. Between 1895 and 1913, the volume of exports doubled, whilst their value increased by 160 per cent. Growth continued during the interwar years – the volume of industrial production in the boom years of 1925–29 grew by 35 per cent, more than that of the United States or any western European countries – but a greater proportion of output was consumed at home.

Living standards in Sweden improved markedly during the interwar years. Swedish factory workers were amongst the best paid in Europe, their real incomes increasing by 50 per cent between 1913 and 1939. The agreement concluded in 1938 between representatives of labour and industry at Saltsjöbaden was widely regarded as a model for industrial relations. After the industrial unrest of the early thirties, a pattern of peaceful settlement of disputes through negotiation and arbitration was established. The so-called September agreement concluded between employers and the unions in 1899 had also laid down the foundations for a mutual bargaining system of labour relations in Denmark. In this respect, Finland lagged a long way behind. The civil war had left a bitter legacy of hostility and suspicion towards workers' organisations, which were in any case weakened by the power struggles of communists and socialists, and employers preferred to rely on lockouts and strikebreakers rather than negotiations. The lower wage levels in Finland and the reactionary attitudes of certain influential employers occasionally prompted hostile comment in Sweden, where it was feared that the Finnish timber or paper exporters would be able to undercut prices.[13]

The exploitation of the vast forests which cover much of the land area of Sweden and Finland was a common and key element to industrial growth in both countries. By the beginning of the 1870s, ten times as much sawn timber was being exported from Sweden as forty years previously, and it had become the country's leading export commodity. Sweden accounted for a quarter of all sawn timber exports in the world in 1880, though by the first decade of the twentieth century, it was being overtaken by Russia (in which Swedish timber firms invested heavily), and sawn timber was also being overhauled as Sweden's principal export commodity by pulp and paper. During the 1920s, Finland emerged as the world's greatest

13. As during the 1927 Finnish dockworkers' strike. Mansner M 1981 *Työnantajaklubista Keskusliitoksi*, Jyväskylä, pp. 367ff.

exporter of sawn and planed softwoods. The largest single employer of industrial labour before the war, with 31,347 workers out of a total workforce of 102,751 in 1912, and responsible for a quarter of all industrial production in the country, the timber industry declined in relative importance during the thirties, when pulp and paper emerged as Finland's major industry, accounting for 40 per cent of the total value of exports in 1935–37.

The massive upsurge in the volume of timber-based exports was in the first instance a response to the insatiable demand for building and construction materials in countries such as Great Britain. The lifting of restrictions on the establishment of sawmills and the volume of production, which had been intended to preserve timber stands for the needs of the iron industry, improvements in the transport network, and the lowering and eventual abolition of import duties by Britain between 1842 and 1866 were necessary preconditions for the rise of a modern timber-processing industry in Sweden. Much more was required, however, to sustain and develop a successful native industry, to rationalise, diversify and where necessary cope with the worst fluctuations in world markets (which, for example, gravely hampered the attempts of the Latvian and Lithuanian governments in the 1920s to promote the cultivation and sale of flax). The first phase of development in the 1850s and 1860s was financed largely by Swedish merchant houses (railway construction in Sweden was largely financed by foreign loans raised by the state, which freed domestic savings for industrial and commercial investments). Sweden has been termed an 'impoverished sophisticate', an economically poor country with an advanced range of financial and other institutions, which enabled commercial banks to take over the role of principal financiers of industry from the 1870s. The Swedish economic historian Lennart Jörberg is less inclined to stress the 'backward' nature of the Swedish economy, and attributes the rapid expansion of the 1870s to the country's ability to satisfy foreign demand for a limited range of goods, supported by an agricultural transformation which enabled farmers to contribute to the export drive as well as feed the country's population, a good education system and improved communications, the revival and rationalisation of the iron industry and the abolition of restrictive legislation.[14]

14. Sandberg L 1978 Banking and economic growth in Sweden before World War I *Journal of Economic History* **38**: 650–80. Lundström R (ed.) 1966 *Kring industrialismens genombrott i Sverige* Stockholm, pp. 13–47, for Jörberg's summary.

Timber-processing was not only susceptible to the vagaries of world markets, but also to competition and the finite nature of supplies. By the end of the nineteenth century, Russian competition and the growing scarcity of accessible timber were beginning to bite into marginal costs, and profits fell. From the 1880s, Swedish farmers began agitating for curbs on the sales of forested land, and restrictions began to be imposed on the rights of clearance. In 1906, legislation forbade companies from buying up forested land in most of Norrland and Kopparberg provinces, and by 1925, this ban had been extended to virtually the whole of Sweden. The ban came hard on the heels of a massive wave of emigration caused by land shortage, and one of the strongest arguments in its favour was the preservation of land for the farming peasantry. There was also a wish, common to all the Scandinavian countries, to keep out foreign investors who might buy up land through the timber firms. The counter-argument, that the companies might in fact be more likely to manage the woods properly, and, if denied access, would be forced into devious deals in order to secure supplies, won little support. The purchasing by the timber companies of forested land at low prices during the war years caused a similar outcry in Finland. In both instances, the emotional appeal of the family farm and the peasant inheritance, rather than the medium- to long-term business strategies of the timber companies, carried more political weight.

The technology which carried through the initial phase of expansion was basically that of the previous century, the fine-bladed multiple saw, harnessed to a more efficient form of energy. The further expansion of the timber-processing industry compelled technological innovation. The ability of the Swedes, and indeed the other northern peoples, to adapt and utilise the new technology, and themselves to innovate, was crucial. In the half-century before the outbreak of world war, there was a veritable explosion of creativity and invention, which made the reputation of Swedish industry. Some of the innovating entrepreneurs were quick to learn the essentials of the new technological advances. The self-taught son of a small farmer, L. M. Ericsson, began repairing Bell telephone sets in 1877. Within a year, Ericsson was selling his own telephone apparatuses; by the end of the 1880s, the Bell company had been effectively driven out of the Swedish market; and by 1914, the Ericsson firm was exporting throughout Europe and had acquired a major share of the Russian market. Men such as Jonas Wenström and Gustaf de Laval not only invented new processes; they were also actively involved in the production and marketing of their products. Wenström, the inventor of the three-phase electrical motor, founded the firm of Asea in 1891; Laval, to whose credit can be ascribed the turbo-generator and the centrifugal separator, worked with John Bernström in Ab Separator. Both firms rapidly became major concerns with global trading connections.

Finland produced far fewer indigenous inventions, but was highly receptive to new ideas and quick to adapt in key areas, such as electrification or the chemical pulp-processing industry. If anything more impoverished than Sweden in the early nineteenth century, Finland was nevertheless blessed with some of the features of a developed institutional infrastructure, a literate populace and an intelligentsia that was receptive to new ideas, a relatively free and open society and a modest reserve of accrued capital which was to be put to effective use in the promotion of industrial enterprise. In comparison with its eastern neighbour, into which vast sums of foreign investments were poured, Finland attracted relatively little money from abroad. In terms of results, the Grand Duchy performed rather better than the Russian empire as a whole, with growth rates between 1870 and 1914 amongst the highest in Europe.[15] Comparisons between relatively small, compact and socially homogenous Scandinavian countries and the huge, sprawling land mass of Russia are hard to make, and probably rather pointless; but the relative absence in Russia of circumstances in which an indigenous entrepreneurial spirit could flourish is striking.

THE ROLE OF THE STATE

The social problems which arose during the long drawn-out transition from a predominantly agrarian to a modern, urbanised society caused much heated debate in their time. For much of the nineteenth century, the state remained very much on the sidelines; social welfare was deemed primarily to be the concern of the individual or the local community. By the outbreak of war in 1914, however, the state was

15. On Finland see in particular: Myllyntaus T 1990 *The gatecrashing apprentice. Industrialising Finland as an adopter of new technology* Communications of the Institute of Economic and Social History, University of Helsinki **24**, Helsinki; Myllyntaus T 1991 *Electrifying Finland. The transfer of a new technology into a late industrialising economy*, Basingstoke. On Sweden, Samuelsson K 1968 *From great power to welfare state*, London, pp. 185–202; Kuuse J 1977 Foreign trade and the breakthrough of the engineering industry in Sweden 1890–1920 *Scandinavian Economic History Review* **25**: 1–36.

becoming actively involved in an ever increasing number of areas, from road-building to the provision of old-age pensions, and was being urged to do so by an array of would-be policy makers and publicists across the political spectrum. Protectionism and the promotion of industry should be accompanied by measures to protect workers, argued the association National Work (*Det nationale Arbejde*) set up by Danish industrialists in 1888. Julius Wulff, a leading figure in the campaign to 'Buy Danish' in the 1890s, claimed that free trade was divisive and even unpatriotic, since it made certain sections of the population more dependent on overseas markets than they were upon their fellow-Danes. The rising star of Swedish neo-conservatism in the 1890s, Rudolf Kjellén, supported regulated labour relations, social insurance and an active home-ownership policy. The more stridently nationalist Adrian Molin wanted the state to take over land to provide farms for the landless, and to take over natural resources to prevent them falling into the hands of Swedish or foreign speculators. 'What we need', he told the committee on emigration set up by the *Riksdag*, 'is an effective *democratic* reform policy with a sober, businesslike disposition, and with *conservative* respect for those values that deserve to be conserved.'[16]

Social issues were thoroughly investigated by government commissions, statistics were assiduously collected, regulations and orders governing all aspects of life were issued. Prewar efforts to establish a ministry for social affairs in Sweden were frustrated by the opponents of progress and excessive bureaucracy, though they were unable to stop the inauguration of a central office for social affairs (*Socialstyrelsen*) in 1913. Departments for agriculture (1900) and trade, industry and seafaring (1905) were also set up as part of the general programme of reorganising the Swedish state structure in order to enable the country to compete more effectively in world markets. Pressure from the farmers' lobby in Denmark also brought reforms and the establishment of a separate ministry of agriculture.

After the bitter years of constitutional conflict during Estrup's ministry, Denmark entered upon a period of reform at the beginning of the twentieth century. Old-age pensions, sickness and unemployment benefits, the last paid out of state-assisted trade union funds,

16. Cited by Arne Ruth in his essay on the mythology of modern Sweden in: Graubard S (ed.) 1986 *Norden: the passion for equality*, Oslo, p. 270. See also the chapter by Hans Kryger Larsen in Feldbæk O (ed.) 1992 *Dansk identitetshistorie*, Copenhagen, vol. 3, pp. 468–511 and Kilander S 1991 *Den nya staten och den gamla. En studie i ideologisk förandring* Studia Historica Upsaliensis **164**, Uppsala, pp. 92–7.

were introduced, and the voluntary poor relief system was converted into one funded by the state and local authorities. Considerable advances were also made in the field of industrial relations, with a mediator appointed by the minister of the interior conducting negotiations between the parties where there were evident clashes of interest. Sweden established an arbitration mechanism in 1906, and embarked on a series of social welfare reforms in the years immediately before the outbreak of war. The Russian empire lagged a long way behind Germany and the Scandinavian countries in this respect; those afflicted by ill-health, or who suffered an industrial injury, or who managed to survive until old age had to rely almost exclusively on private charity or, if they were lucky, the meagre funds of voluntary sickness benefit societies or trade unions. The law on sickness insurance of 1912 was a significant improvement, but its main attraction to contemporaries and later historians was the fact that it allowed a modicum of worker participation in the running of the funds. Finland was also noticeably behind developments elsewhere in Europe, and did not produce its first effective legislation on old-age pensions until 1937 (state-sponsored sickness insurance was not introduced until 1963).

Worries about the consequences of mass emigration in the decades before the First World War gave way to concerns about declining birth rates in the interwar years. The Danish progressive K. K. Steincke railed against 'one-child egoists' in his book *Fremtidens forsøgelsevæsen* (The welfare system of the future, 1920) and proposed fiscal measures such as imposing tax penalties on bachelors to persuade people to have more children. In Sweden, which by the 1930s had one of the lowest birth rates in the world, the spectre of a 'dying nation' was raised by Folke Borg, whilst Alva and Gunnar Myrdal spoke of a demographic 'crisis'. The 1938 tax reforms, which were intended to favour families producing children, were a partial response to this perceived crisis.

The powers of the state were greatly augmented during the war years, though in common with most other European countries, many of the regulatory bodies and provisions were dismantled with the return of peace. The efforts of governments to regulate food supplies and prices were rarely popular; workers' organisations complained of the high cost of living and food shortages, farmers were aggrieved by controls. Danish arable farmers were angered by the imposed obligation to deliver grain at specified prices, whilst their colleagues in dairying and pig-breeding reacted strongly to the attempts of the new food council to direct grain to the human consumer, and not to animals. The food committees set up in Finland were rendered virtually powerless by the diminution of imports, on which the country was dependent, and by the political struggles set in train by the revolution. The threat of mass strike action and civil unrest hung in the air throughout northern Europe, though the seizure of power by the Bolsheviks and the abortive Finnish revolution exercised a powerful influence in favour of moderation upon the labour leadership in Sweden and Denmark.

There was never much likelihood that Hjalmar Branting or Thorvald Stauning would give the signal for the revolution. Both men entered government before the war's end, and were to form ministries of their own during the interwar years. Branting – who died in 1925 – was less successful as a minister, but Stauning remained head of the Danish government from 1929 until his death in 1942. Social democracy became the major political force in Scandinavia during the thirties. There has been much discussion of the part played by ideology in the policies adopted and followed by the governments of Stauning and Per Albin Hansson, or of Johan Nygaardsvold, who headed a Labour Party government in Norway between 1935 and 1940. It has been suggested, for example, that Swedish social democrats were influenced by the ideas of J. M. Keynes, although one of the leading figures of the party at the time, Ernst Wigforss, later denied this. Ideological influences of any sort were played down by the Swedish political commentator, Herbert Tingsten, who maintained that the party was operating within long-established welfare traditions in its approach to mass unemployment; others have drawn attention to the works of contemporary Swedish economists such as Bertel Ohlin, or the general evolution of social democratic thinking on welfare problems.[17]

High levels of unemployment during the 1920s, and the patent inability of non-socialist governments to offer any long-term solution to the problem, may well have prepared the social democrats for bolder measures such as deficit budgets, but they were often as cautious and orthodox as their liberal or conservative opponents. Stauning's finance minister C. V. Bramsnæs was a rigid adherent of the overvalued *krone* and proud of his carefully balanced budgets. The

17. There is a useful discussion of this in *Kriser och krispolitik i Norden under mellankrigstiden* Nordiska historikermötet i Uppsala 1974, Mötesrapport, Uppsala 1974, pp. 60–5, 86–90. The notion that the welfare state was created as a result of working-class pressure led by the social democrats is vigorously challenged in: Baldwin P 1989 The Scandinavian origins of the social interpretation of the welfare state *Comparative Studies in Society and History* **31**: 3–24.

Swedish social democrat Gustav Möller warned his colleagues in government and trade union leaders in January 1933 that 'if the state continues a policy of excessive borrowing over a period of years, that will mean the withdrawal from the private capital market of significant sums and that will affect private enterprise and limit its opportunities to create employment'.[18] Alleviating the distress of unemployment, rather than the promotion of stated objectives such as the taking the means of production into public ownership, was the principal political endeavour of the social democrats during the interwar years. In this, as in other respects, their record was rather less impressive than progressive contemporaries, anxious to discern any ray of light in the gloom, believed.

In common with the rest of Europe, the Scandinavian countries were experiencing economic difficulties before they were hit by the Depression. Denmark's foreign trade, heavily dependent on agricultural produce, was especially vulnerable to falling world prices, and was not helped by the insistence of successive governments upon maintaining an overvalued currency. A tight rein was kept on government expenditure. The first Stauning government failed in the autumn of 1926 to reach agreement with the radicals over a series of modest proposals designed to relieve unemployment – which was running at 20 per cent – and resigned after losing seats in the *Folketing* elections. The minority *Venstre* government which then took office pushed through a retrenchment package which lowered civil servants' salaries, cut invalidity benefits, closed down two-thirds of the labour exchanges and drastically reduced the scale and scope of relief for the unemployed.

When the second Stauning government took office in 1929, the economic outlook seemed brighter. Real wages were rising, unemployment had fallen from the record levels of 1927 to around 16 per cent, and the fact that prices of imports were falling more sharply than those of exports relieved the pressure on the *krone*. By the beginning of 1930, however, the crisis was upon Denmark. The prices of bacon and dairy produce began to tumble, to the point where it was rumoured that farmers were using butter rather than the more expensive axle-grease for their carts. The Danes were reluctant to abandon the principles of free trade which had served them so well for decades, but the measures taken by their main trading partners left them with no alternative. Germany withdrew in 1929 the favourable terms of trade hitherto enjoyed by Danish livestock exporters; France

18. Cited in *Kriser och krispolitik*, p. 64.

slapped a 100 per cent increased tariff on Danish butter imports in 1930; Belgium and Holland imposed quotas on imports early in 1932. Britain's sudden departure from the gold standard in September 1931 forced Denmark to follow the example of other northern European governments and suspend convertibility. Tighter exchange and credit controls were introduced, as well as import regulations. The exchange control centre, *Valutacentralen*, created as a temporary measure early in 1932, became a vital instrument of government trade policy. Britain's drift towards Imperial preference and the imposition of quotas on bacon imports obliged the Danes to reduce production, and to establish weekly quotas for each abattoir. The trade agreement made in 1933 contained provisions designed to improve Britain's balance of trade with Denmark, which agreed to buy its salt, saltpetre and bacon wrappers from Britain and to purchase up to 80 per cent of its coal and coke requirements there.[19]

The response of all governments to the slump in world trade was to put up the protective shutters. Swedish millers were obliged to blend a certain proportion of domestic with foreign grain, and a duty imposed on all marketed milk helped subsidise loss-making Swedish butter exports. The imposition of restrictions on egg imports turned Finland from a net importer to exporter within a year; producers were also offered export premiums and other inducements, financed by duties on margarine and artificial fertilisers and revenue from the sale of alcohol, now legally permitted after a referendum had narrowly voted in favour of ending prohibition. The Estonian government operated a subsidy policy for its bacon exporters funded by creaming off a levy when bacon prices were high, and similar controls were also applied to other vital export commodities to offset the vagaries of price fluctuation. Here, as in Germany and the other Baltic states, there were distinctly autarkic tendencies in the policies adopted.

Farmers, often burdened with debt and faced with a catastrophic fall in prices for their produce, were particularly hard hit by the Depression. In spite of the efforts of their organisations and government assistance in the form of credits, export premiums and the

19. Similar bilateral treaties were concluded with other northern European states, as part of a general policy of improving Britain's trading position in the area. See the contributions by Merja-Liisa Hinkkanen and by Patrick Salmon in: Recker M-L (ed.) 1986 *Von der Konkurrenz zur Rivalität. Das britisch-deutsche Verhältnis in den Ländern der europäischen Peripherie 1919–1939*, Stuttgart, pp. 15–49, 101–41, Hiden J and Salmon P 1991 *The Baltic nations and Europe* London, pp. 89–92 and Seymour S 1982 *Anglo-Danish relations and Germany 1933–1945* Odense University Studies in History and Social Sciences **78**, Odense, pp. 47–8.

rescheduling of debts, many went to the wall. In central and northern Finland and Sweden, the situation was made worse by the drastic fall in stumpage earnings and the loss of work opportunities as the timber firms sharply reduced production. Where there had previously been work for 20,000 men in the forests of northern Finland, there was only enough for 7,000 at most in the winter of 1929–30, according to one Finnish trade union organiser. A bad harvest and high prices compounded the misery. Many faced the prospect of hunger and destitution if no aid were forthcoming; on the Russian frontier, groups of workers and small farmers were planning to apply for a group passport to seek work in the Karelian forests.[20] Throughout the worst years of the Depression, there were numerous local protest movements, often sparked off by bailiffs trying to distrain possessions, or by the sheer number of compulsory auctions. Farmers occasionally resorted to direct action, and in general, adopted a more aggressively 'trade-unionist' approach in their dealings with the authorities. Their actions attracted considerable publicity, but the movements were usually short-lived, and rarely had any direct impact, although some of the ideas advanced by, for example, the Danish protest movement *Landbrugernes Sammenslutning*, were taken up by the established organisations.[21]

Angry and emotional protest meetings, blockades of milk deliveries, and demands for state assistance were some of the immediate responses to the crisis. In the long run, greater rationalisation of the kind advocated by Jens Warming, who claimed that by losing up to 8 per cent of its workforce and modernising its methods and techniques, Danish farming could greatly improve productivity levels, was the only solution; but this was a political as well as a socioeconomic impossibility in the early 1930s. Industry, however, was better able to pursue such objectives, and ultimately to forge ahead as the most dynamic sector of the national economy. The crisis compelled many firms to rationalise and modernise in order to be able to compete more effectively. More attention was paid to costing and accounting, marketing, distribution and sales. Labour costs were trimmed by shedding manpower, reducing working hours and cutting wages. Manufacturers came together to establish quotas and cartels. An international agreement on reducing output of sulphite pulp was reached in

20. The situation in northern Finland is described in a report by A. Rytkönen, file 331.88(471)(063), Finnish Labour Archives, Helsinki.

21. The political implications of these protest movements will be considered in the next chapter. For recent literature, see: Brogaard P 1969 *Landbrugernes Sammenslutning*, Aarhus; Lackman M 1985 *Taistelu talonpojasta*, Oulu.

1930; Finnish, Norwegian and Swedish wood-pulp producers were less successful in their agreement, which was threatened by Norwegian exporters outside the cartel. The attempts of the timber industry to limit production also ran into difficulties, partly from Russian competition, though a quota agreement was concluded in 1935 within the framework of the European Timber Exporters Convention.

The measures taken between 1931 and 1934 to combat the Depression gave the state an even greater and certainly a more permanent directive role than had been the case during the war years. How innovative or radical such measures were, and what effect they had upon the overall pattern of economic or social development, is another matter. Most of the major decisions taken were in response to events, such as the effective devaluation of currencies following Britain's departure from the gold standard in 1931, or the devising of schemes to combat unemployment. In Scandinavia, they were also invariably the result of compromise and negotiation. The agreement reached in January 1933 at the home of the Prime Minister Stauning in Kanslergade was described by one of the participants as a bit of a broth, which he doubted would be palatable to all. It was concocted in response to a variety of pressures. The farming lobby had united to demand lower interest rates, tax cuts and tighter price controls on the services offered by the liberal professions. Above all, they demanded a devaluation of the *krone* to maintain their competitiveness in world markets. Devaluation was opposed by Bramsnæs, the minister of finance, and by P. Munch, the foreign minister, who warned of the dangers of upsetting the talks on a trade agreement with Britain if too radical a devaluation was carried through. Neither man was present at the final session of the Kanslergade talks, which settled upon a 10 per cent devaluation. The *Venstre* delegates agreed to abstain when Stauning presented a bill designed to prevent a threatened lockout. In addition, the Kanslergade agreement produced a whole package of reforms. Controls on pig production benefited the small farmer, whilst the large farmer was protected by import duties on grain. This, and a duty on domestic sales of butter were paid into special accounts, which were meant to buy beef for the needy or provide subsidies for small farms which bought in grain. The bank rate was cut to 2.5 per cent, and a range of incentives was provided to stimulate the construction industry. Social welfare legislation was streamlined in a series of laws piloted through the *Rigsdag* by K. K. Steincke in 1933. The law on national insurance built largely on existing schemes covering sickness, old age and disablement. Employers were henceforth to be obliged to provide insurance for their workers against accident or injury. The law on public assistance replaced the 1891 poor law (although over the years a number of categories had been removed from the jurisdiction of this law and allowed relief as of right). The managers of unemployment funds were allowed to build up contingency reserves, largely subsidised by the state, to cope with the long-term out-of-work.

In Sweden, C. G. Ekman's liberal minority government began to run into difficulties in 1932. The death of five demonstrators in Ådalen, shot by soldiers called in to maintain order during an industrial conflict, increased tensions during a period of considerable industrial unrest. The crash of Ivar Kreuger's vast financial empire in the spring of 1932 ruined thousands and eventually brought down Ekman's government after it was revealed that the prime minister had accepted sizeable gifts from the financier.[22] The Swedish social democrats had put forward a programme designed to create employment and stimulate purchasing power, but they were by no means ready to abandon free-trade principles, which they continued to uphold during the elections to the Second Chamber in 1932. In the minority social democratic government formed by P. A. Hansson, however, the advocates of compromise with the farming interests won the day. As in Denmark, the threat of losing vital export markets persuaded the farming lobby to do a deal with the representatives of labour; in return for guaranteed prices, subsidies and regulations, they would support measures to combat unemployment. The deal arrived at by the social democrats and the Farmers' Party in 1933 laid the basis for further cooperation – which was not the case in Denmark – and the Swedish policy of public works programmes also differed from the Danish approach, which was to concentrate on providing financial and material assistance. In fact, the much-vaunted public works projects recruited far fewer jobless than did the long-established system of relief work. The government left the unions to administer unemployment insurance on a voluntary basis, and its social welfare measures amounted to little more than a readjustment of existing legislation. Spending on social welfare and health services, which had totalled 283 million *kronor* in 1926, more than doubled to 593 million in 1939, but as a percentage of the national income, public expenditure in these areas remained fairly constant throughout the 1930s. In 1938, the government declared a halt to social reforms. The practical consequences of what had already been placed on the statute book,

22. Kreuger's convoluted dealings are dealt with by: Gäfvert B 1979 *Kreuger, riksbanken och regeringen*, Stockholm.

concludes Bo Gustafsson, were not sufficient to justify the description of the thirties as a period of breakthrough in social policy.[23]

The achievements of Swedish and Danish social democracy may have been rather less than contemporary progressives, anxious for any ray of light amidst the gloom, were prepared to believe. They did, nevertheless, offer a modicum of security, and above all, a degree of self-respect for those compelled to seek assistance. The levels of public assistance for the jobless were considerably lower in Finland and the Baltic states, where governments continued to cut back on expenditure. In none of these countries was organised labour able to have the kind of impact upon policy that the trade unions had in Scandinavia; indeed, the very existence of the unions and the parties of the left was threatened in the political crisis which affected the eastern Baltic lands. Confrontation, rather than compromise, a legacy of revolution and social division, made it unlikely that the Scandinavian path would be followed here.

23. *Kriser och krispolitik*, pp. 115–20. Gustafsson in fact suggests that it was the twenties, rather than the thirties, which marked a real breakthrough as the consequences of the social legislation of the first two decades of the century made themselves felt.

CHAPTER ELEVEN

The Interwar Years

CONSTITUTIONS, GOVERNMENT AND POLITICS IN THE NEW STATES

The collapse of the Russian and German empires and the ensuing revolutionary upheavals dramatically affected the whole of northern Europe, and the repercussions of these events are still being felt today. Even the Scandinavian kingdoms with their well-established institutions and traditions were shaken by constitutional and political crises. Closer to the epicentre of revolution, the impact of change was far more profound. The new states of the Baltic had not only to define and establish international recognition of their territorial boundaries, but also to create constitutional and institutional frameworks. This was an especially daunting and difficult task for states which lacked clearly-defined historical precedents or viable existing institutions upon which to build. Finland was especially fortunate in having the latter, whilst a resurrected Poland could draw spiritual and emotional sustenance from past memories of the historic *rzeczpospolita.* For the Lithuanians, the lost city of Vilnius (Vilna) was a symbol of their glorious pagan medieval past, but in all other respects, the problems facing the delegates to the constituent assembly which convened in Kaunas in the summer of 1920 were not dissimilar to those encountered by their Estonian and Latvian counterparts. Lacking practical political experience, fired by nationalist and ultra-democratic sentiments, and with no acceptable local institutions which might form the basis for a new constitution, the members of these assemblies looked to the democratic republics of western Europe for inspiration.

All three eventually settled for a constitutional system in which power resided effectively with a directly-elected single-chamber parliament, elected by universal and equal adult franchise based on proportional representation and direct and secret ballots. The Latvian *Saeima* and the Lithuanian *Seimas* elected a president of the republic, whose executive powers were strictly circumscribed. The Estonians preferred to follow the example of the Swiss Confederation and have no separate head of state; instead, the prime minister, or 'senior statesman' (*Riigivanem*), carried out the largely ceremonial functions of representing his country on official occasions. All three constitutions had provisions for popular initiatives and referenda; in the case of Estonia, this was to have dramatic political repercussions.

Governments in the new states were invariably coalitions of relatively short duration. The government of M. Sleževičius which was overthrown in a coup at the end of 1926 was the sixth since the proclamation of the provisional constitution of Lithuania in June 1920. Latvia had fourteen governments in as many years before the establishment of authoritarian rule in 1934. The average life of an Estonian government was less than nine months; by the early 1930s, coalitions were lucky if they survived for five months. Most broke up as a result of disagreements between the parties of the coalition. Although four of the ten men who occupied the post of *Riigivanem* between 1919 and 1934 did so more than once, almost half of those holding ministerial office were not invited to do so a second time. There was a larger cohort of politicians with ministerial experience in Finland, but here too, governments in the 1920s rarely lasted for more than a year. Ironically, the longest government of the entire interwar period, which survived from December 1932 until October 1936, was a minority coalition dependent upon the support of two other non-socialist parties.[1]

Parties claiming to represent the interests of peasant-farmers occupied a central position in the new states of the Baltic. The Finnish Agrarian Union (*Maalaisliitto*) was the largest non-socialist party in the *Eduskunta*, and was rarely absent from government. The main farmers' parties in Estonia and Latvia, although less successful in attracting and maintaining support at the polls, were also central pillars of government, supplying ten of the twenty prime ministers in Estonia and fourteen of the nineteen in Latvia between 1918 and 1934. These

1. For further details, see: Graham M 1928 *The new governments of Eastern Europe*, Princeton, NJ; Mägi A 1967 *Das Staatsleben Estlands während seiner Selbständigkeit*, Stockholm; Kirby D 1979 *Finland in the twentieth century*, London, pp. 75ff., 212ff.

agrarian parties all drew their main support from the more prosperous sections of the farming community, rather than the poor smallholders or landless labourers. For those belonging to minority communities in Estonia and Latvia, there were also farmers' parties; the Swedish-speaking farmers, mechanics, professors and bankers in Finland usually voted for the Swedish People's Party. Agrarian interests in Lithuania were principally represented within the Christian Democratic Party, which dominated the first three parliaments elected under the 1922 constitution and provided the political leadership of the new republic until 1926. In Estonia and Latvia, the interests of the small farmers who had come into possession of their land largely thanks to the agrarian reforms were represented by separate settlers' parties. Small farmers in Finland organised themselves as a pressure group, but there was no smallholders' party as such. In all three countries, left-wing parties also attracted support from the poorer elements of the rural population.

The dominant role of the farmers' parties reflected not only the strongly agrarian character of the countries in question, but also the fact that they represented or epitomised popular nationalist sentiment in a way that none of the parties influenced by the nationalist intellectuals of an earlier generation could match. The Nationalist Party in Lithuania failed even to win a single seat in the constituent assembly elections of 1920, in spite of the fact that it was led by some of the most prominent leaders of the years in which the country gained its independence. Jaan Tõnisson's People's Party was unable to sustain the level of support it won in the Estonian constituent assembly elections of 1919, when it secured 20 per cent of the vote and twenty-five seats; indeed, it lagged behind the moderate Labour Party, with which it merged in 1932 to form the National Centre. A similar merger of centre-liberal parties had taken place ten years earlier in Latvia; the Democratic Centre failed to make much headway at the polls, though it did have some influence on public opinion through the columns of Latvia's largest daily newspaper, *Jaunākās Ziņas*. The Finnish nationalist movement had split into two wings before independence, and a further realignment took place in 1918, with the conservatives forming the National Coalition and the liberals a National Progressive Party. Electoral support for the National Coalition waned in the thirties as a result of competition from the ultra-right People's Patriotic Movement, but over the decades, the party regularly managed to secure around 15–20 per cent of the 200 seats in the *Eduskunta*. The Progressive Party fared less well, falling from a peak of twenty-six seats in the 1919 elections to six in 1939.

In spite of their failure to win seats, the parties and politicians of the centre continued to play an important role in government in Estonia and Finland. Tõnisson held the office of *Riigivanem* three times, and remained a formidable figure on the political scene even after the establishment of an authoritarian regime in 1934. The Progressives T. M. Kivimäki (1932–36) and A. K. Cajander (1937–39) headed coalition governments in Finland at a time when their party's support at the polls was dwindling rapidly. The constitutional expert K. J. Ståhlberg was elected the country's first president in 1919, and another Progressive, Risto Ryti, was to hold that office during the war.

The Finnish Social Democratic Party recovered quickly from the débâcle of civil war, winning eighty seats in the elections of March 1919 to form once more the largest parliamentary group in the *Eduskunta.* There was, however, mounting dissatisfaction with the party leadership, which was accused of abandoning the class-conscious principles of former years and of not fighting hard enough for the release of those still in jail for their part in the uprising. In the winter of 1919–20, almost a third of the party's members and branches left to form the Socialist Workers' Party. This party owed more to a home-brewed mix of class animosity and radical puritanism than it did to the efforts of the Communist Party, which had been founded in Moscow in August 1918.[2] The exiled Finnish Reds who constituted that party were to have mixed fortunes. One, Otto Ville Kuusinen, was to rise high in the ranks of the international and Soviet communist hierarchy and survived to an honoured old age. Some were entrusted with the task of building Soviet power in Karelia, where they created a kind of substitute Red Finland until the suspicions of Stalin cast them down. They, like many others, perished in the purges of the late 1930s.[3]

Success in elections for the social democrats was rarely translated into government office. The Finnish Social Democratic Party retained the largest bloc of seats in parliament even after losing up to a third of its members and seats to the Socialist Workers' Party in the early 1920s; but with the exception of Väinö Tanner's one-year single-party

2. Kirby D 1988 New wine in old vessels? The Finnish Socialist Workers' Party, 1919–1923 *Slavonic and East European Review* **66**, pp. 426–55. The party drew its support from skilled workers in the engineering, construction and shipbuilding industries, but also from the impoverished small farmers and workers of northern and eastern Finland.

3. On the Finnish Communist Party, see: Hodgson J 1967 *Communism in Finland. A history and an interpretation*, Princeton, NJ; Upton A 1973 *Communism in Scandinavia and Finland. Politics of opportunity*, New York.

ministry in 1927, the party remained outside government until 1937. Socialist participation in government in the three Baltic states was slight, even though they did not have to contend with the level of suspicion and hostility that dogged the Finnish social democrats.

In none of the new states of the Baltic were communist parties allowed to operate freely, and the activities of their front organisations were under constant police surveillance. All twenty-seven members of the parliamentary group and most of the leaders of the Finnish Socialist Workers' Party were arrested in 1923, and the party was declared illegal. The attempted coup staged by the communists in Tallinn on 1 December 1924 was the culminating point of a year of rumoured uprisings, mass arrests and trials by military courts, though the operation may well have been guided by Grigoriy Zinoviev, the chairman of the Communist International.[4] The harsh repression of the insurrection crippled the communist movement in Estonia. The left in Finland was able to recover from the blows dealt by the police in 1923, only to be smashed in a wave of populist agitation triggered off by a communist youth demonstration held at the end of 1929 in the town of Lapua, right in the heartland of 'White' Finland.

The potential of the communist left to disrupt or subvert the existing order was probably far less than those in power affected to believe. The communists were moderately successful in penetrating and capturing control of a number of trade unions, but at the cost of further weakening an already feeble structure. The social democrats, particularly in Finland and Latvia, were able successfully to beat off challenges from the communist left for leadership of the labour movement, and retained the loyalty of the majority of the working class.[5] Harassed by the police and employers, the communists were by the early 1930s reduced to small groups of embattled and often very despondent activists, having to cope with sudden shifts of policy emanating from an exiled leadership which was itself often divided and confused about which line to follow. The police were not always the most dangerous enemies of the party. The Latvian Communist Party, which claimed 2,000 members in 1934, paid the price for 'sectarianism' (i.e., willingness to make common cause with left-wing

4. Rauch G von 1974 *The Baltic states 1917–1940*, London, pp. 111–17. Neuberg A 1970 *Armed insurrection*, London pp. 61–80.

5. In comparison with the Scandinavian countries, the trade-union movement in Finland and the Baltic states was much the weaker party in industrial relations. There is a useful overview by Aleksander Loit in: Hiden J and Loit A 1986 *The Baltic in international relations between the two world wars* Studia Baltica Stockholmiensia **3**, Stockholm, pp. 335–74.

socialists), and was decimated by the purges and expulsions of 1937–38. Like the Estonian Communist Party, whose membership also dropped below 200, its organisational hierarchy was broken up and the links with the Communist International were severed (probably deliberately; Stalin preferred his own henchmen). The most fortunate party members were those who survived by virtue of being incarcerated in the jails of the 'fascist' regimes of Konstantin Päts or Kārlis Ulmanis; their less fortunate comrades perished before the firing squads or in the labour camps of Stalin's Russia.[6]

The spectre of communism was frequently conjured up by employers' organisations as a means of combating trade-union demands. A strikebreaking organisation financed by Finnish bankers and industrialists was deployed with considerable success during the 1920s. It had close links with the police and the paramilitary *Suojeluskunta*, and a number of its leaders were to play a central role in the Lapua movement. The wave of righteous anti-communism unleashed by the ill-fated attempt by the young communists to stage a demonstration in Lapua was in fact carefully orchestrated by right-wing groups. The widely-publicised acts of violence against communists and their sympathisers and the bombastic behaviour of the self-styled peasant leaders of the movement encountered little opposition outside the ranks of the left. The government banned the publication of communist newspapers and prepared measures to outlaw all communist activities. It also resigned in order to make way for a ministry more acceptable to the Lapua movement, whose leaders, however, refused at the last minute the two posts offered them by the prime minister-designate, P. E. Svinhufvud. In order to obtain the necessary majority to push through the anti-communist legislation, new elections were decreed for October 1930. The elections were held amidst mounting violence and acts of lawlessness, including the kidnapping of the former president of the republic, K. J. Ståhlberg – an action which was to prove costly to the Lapua movement. The government obtained a narrow two-thirds majority necessary to push through the anti-communist laws, and although the situation remained

6. Details of party membership and of the impact of the purges were first published in: *Ocherki istorii kommunnisticheskoy partii Estonii*, Tallinn, 1963, vol. 2, pp. 343f. and: *Ocherki istorii kommunisticheskoy partii Latvii*, Riga, 1963, vol. 2, p. 365f. The depressed spirits of party members were hardly likely to be lifted by the frequent criticisms levelled at them from Moscow. The Finnish Communist Youth League, for example, was accused by the exiled leadership of inactivity, isolation from the working classes and of living in a world of their own in the early 1930s. *Suomen Kommunistinen Nuorisoliitto 1925–1935*, microfilm reel 16, *Kansanarkisto* (People's Archives, Helsinki).

tense for another eighteen months, the political establishment gradually distanced itself from the excesses of Lapua. Svinhufvud was narrowly elected president in 1931 after the commander of the *Suojeluskunta* had warned the leader of the Agrarian Union bloc in the electoral college that he could not guarantee to maintain order if Ståhlberg were elected. In the face of a rather confused attempt by the Lapua movement and elements of the *Suojeluskunta* to dictate a change of government, the new president stood firm; but the instigators of the Mäntsälä 'revolt' were treated with remarkable lenience, and Svinhufvud himself was present at a meeting convened a mere three weeks after the Mäntsälä episode to discuss the continuation of Lapua's aims by legal means.

The Lapua movement was at bottom little more than a crude form of anti-communism, which served the interests of a diverse group of politicians and employers anxious to smash the trade unions. The People's Patriotic Movement (IKL) which was founded in April 1932 in the spirit of Lapua was in fact rather different, drawing its leadership and active supporters from the ranks of the educated, and much of its initial inspiration from the student activism of the previous decade, when the Academic Karelia Society had set the tone of university politics.[7]

An even more spectacularly successful mass movement emerged in Estonia at the onset of the Depression. The League of Veterans of the War of Liberation, known by their abbreviated title of *Vapsid*, was founded in July 1929 as a patriotic pressure group representing the interests of war veterans. At its first congress in January 1930, there were demands for a political campaign against Marxism and party corruption, and within two years, the movement was challenging the established political parties with its own proposals for constitutional change. After two proposals for reform submitted to referendum by the main political parties had been defeated, the *Vapsid* managed to win a huge majority for their proposals in a third referendum in October 1933. The proposed new constitution would have drastically curtailed the size and powers of the *Riigikogu*, and allowed for the election by popular vote of a president for a five-year term. The authority of the president would have been extensive, including the right to appoint and dismiss governments, issue decrees, dissolve the

7. The Academic Karelia Society was an elite male student organisation dedicated to promoting the ideals of Finnish nationalism; it was overtly anti-Russian. For a brief discussion of the Academic Karelia Society and the Lapua movement, see; Kirby 1979, pp. 66–7, 83–92. The IKL is the subject of study for Uola M 1982 *Sinimusta veljeskunta. IKL 1932–1944*, Helsinki. See also Djupsund G, Karvonen L 1984 *Fascismen i Finland: högerextremistens förankring hos väljarkåren 1929–1939* Meddelanden från Stiftelsens för Åbo Akademis Forskningsinstitut **94**, Åbo.

fifty-member parliament and where necessary, declare a state of emergency.

During the summer of 1933, the economic and political crisis had deepened. The 35 per cent devaluation of the Estonian *kroon* carried out in June by the Tõnisson government was deeply unpopular. In August, a national state of emergency was introduced, and a number of organisations, including those of the League, were forced to close. However, immediately after the results of the October referendum became known, Tõnisson lifted the state of emergency and resigned, to be succeeded by a formally non-party transition government headed by the veteran leader of the Farmers' Party, Konstantin Päts. The breakup of the Agrarian Union (a short-lived fusion of the Farmers' and Settlers' Parties) in the summer of 1933 had weakened Päts' position, and he seems to have sought an alignment with the League, whose proposals for constitutional reform he supported. In office once more, however, he came to an understanding with the socialists to put up a common front against the League, which had taken on a more centralised and hierarchical structure and was preparing to contest the 1934 elections.

In the local elections in mid-January 1934, the League took over 40 per cent of the vote in the towns. Its candidate for the forthcoming presidential elections under the new constitution (which came into force on 24 January), the rather lacklustre General Andres Larka, appeared to be well ahead of his nearest rival, General Johan Laidoner. On 12 March, five weeks before the presidential elections were due to be held, Päts, in his capacity of acting chief executive, proclaimed a six-month state of emergency. Laidoner was appointed commander-in-chief with special powers to maintain law and order, the League was disbanded on the grounds that it was a threat to state security, and over 800 of its leaders and supporters were detained. Having secured parliament's assent to his measures, Päts postponed indefinitely the forthcoming presidential and parliamentary elections, dissolved parliament and ruled by decree. A planned coup in December 1935 by supporters of the League (who were armed and equipped by Finnish sympathisers) failed to materialise. Artur Sirk, the young and charismatic leader of the movement, died in exile two years later.[8]

8. Rauch 1974, pp. 146–51, 156–7. Parming T 1975 *The collapse of liberal democracy and the rise of authoritarianism in Estonia*, London/Beverly Hills, pp. 39–46. Isberg A 1988 *Med demokratin som insats. Politisk-konstitutionellt maktspel i 1930-talets Estland* Studia Baltica Stockholmiensia **4**, Stockholm, pp. 29–63. Marandi R 1991 *Must-valge lipu all* Studia Baltica Stockholmiensia **6**, Stockholm, is the most detailed study of the League of Veterans to date. Kasekemp A 1993 The Estonia Veterans' League: a fascist

Two months after the declaration of a state of emergency in Estonia, the Latvian prime minister Kārlis Ulmanis followed suit, claiming as his justification the threat of civil war as a result of internal political tensions. With the acquiescence of the president of the republic, parliament was suspended and party political life brought to a halt. When the term of office of president Kviesis came to an end in 1936, Ulmanis succeeded him, combining the offices of head of state and prime minister. Parliamentary democracy had come to an abrupt end eight years earlier in Lithuania, when a group of army officers had occupied the parliament building and forced the Populist-Social Democratic coalition government to resign. The coup was backed by the right-wing Nationalist Party and some of the Christian Democrats, and after some initial confusion, a new government headed by Augustinas Voldemaras was appointed by President Grinius. Having secured a promise from Voldemaras to maintain the 1922 constitution, Grinius resigned to make way for Antanas Smetona, who was elected president by a rump session of the *Seimas*, the Populist and Social Democratic members boycotting the meeting. The alliance of the nationalist *Tautininkai* and the Christian Democrats soon broke up. When a majority of the *Seimas* supported a motion of no-confidence in the government in April 1927, parliament was dissolved. The constitution issued by Smetona a year later greatly augmented presidential powers and relegated parliament to obscurity. In 1929, the president asked Voldemaras to resign, and when he refused, had him arrested and placed under police surveillance in provincial exile. The paramilitary Iron Wolf organisation that Voldemaras had attempted to build up as a personal fief was taken over and finally disbanded by Smetona, and attempts to stage a coup in favour of the fallen leader came to nothing – imprisoned in 1934 and released four years later on condition that he went into exile in France, the brilliant but unstable Voldemaras unwisely returned to Lithuania in 1940, and died in a Soviet labour camp.

The personal dictatorships established in the three Baltic states bear some resemblance to each other in certain respects. All three men – Päts, Ulmanis, Smetona – had played a leading role in the winning of their country's independence. This parallel may also be extended to Marshal Piłsudski, whose May 1926 coup offered a model for the Lithuanian army officers, and even to General Mannerheim, the great

movement? *Journal of Baltic Studies* **24**: 263–8, seeks to locate the *Vapsid* in the ideological spectrum. I am indebted to Mr Kasekemp for his useful comments and criticisms of this section.

White hope of Finnish right-wing conspirators, whom the republic eventually rewarded with the title of field-marshal (in 1933), commander-in-chief of the Finnish army during the war, and who ended his active career as president of the republic at a crucial moment in Finland's history.[9] Smetona and Voldemaras were rather more evidently 'outside' the system, since the electorate had consistently refused to give its support to their Nationalist Party, than were Ulmanis and Päts, both experienced in parliamentary politics. Both men came out for a fundamental revision of the constitution in the early 1930s, though neither was able to win the necessary backing for their proposals. There is, moreover, evidence to suggest that their political stars were waning. Päts had been disowned by large sections of the short-lived Agrarian Union, and he came a long way behind General Laidoner in the run-up to the 1934 presidential election. Ulmanis had only just managed to scrape into parliament in the 1931 elections, in which his Farmers' League secured 12 per cent of the vote. Like Päts, he was careful to ensure the tacit support of the army for his coup. General Jānis Balodis, who was also leader of the paramilitary defence force, the *Aizsargi*, and minister of defence in the Ulmanis government, was closely involved in the coup. Both generals Laidoner and Balodis occupied central positions in the authoritarian regimes established by Päts and Ulmanis after 1934. There was little opposition to the coups, which had the silent consent of other political groupings, such as the Christian democrats in Lithuania, the progressives led by Margers Skujenieks in Latvia, and the socialists in Estonia. All three leaders took care to ensure the elimination of potential threats from the extreme right, banning or emasculating movements such as the *Vapsid* in Estonia and the *Pērkonkrusts* (Thunder Cross) in Latvia. They eschewed the Hitler model of leadership in favour of a more modest projection of themselves as fathers of the nation. Of an older generation than the *Führer*, they had all grown to maturity during an intense period of national awakening, in which they had played a central part; their ideological world was based on a sentimental and idealised image of a sturdy, patriotic and patriarchal peasantry, a far cry from the dreams of racist power and conquest which inspired Hitler.

9. The careers and achievements of Päts, Ulmanis and Smetona are currently the subject of much investigation and debate in the Baltic states. On Mannerheim's role in interwar polititcs, see: Ahti M 1990 *Kaappaus? Suojeluskuntaselkkaus 1921, fascismin aave 1927, Mäntsälän kapina 1932*, Helsinki. Jägerskiöld S 1986 *Mannerheim: marshal of Finland*, London, presents the marshal in a rather more favourable light.

Moderate in comparison with Nazi Germany or Soviet Russia, the authoritarian regimes of the Baltic states generated little popular enthusiasm, and all three were beginning to show signs of weakness by the end of the decade. Lithuania came nearest to becoming a one-party state, but the foundations of the Smetona regime and the *Tautininkai* were severely undermined in March 1938, when Lithuania was forced to accept a Polish ultimatum demanding restoration of diplomatic relations. A substantial majority of the voters in a referendum held in February 1936 endorsed the proposal for the convention of a national assembly to draft a new constitution for Estonia. The elections were closely supervised by the regime, and turnout at the polls was low. The new constitution, which came into force at the beginning of 1938, created a parliament of two chambers, one of which was to be popularly elected, the other nominated by the president and an assortment of administrative and professional bodies. In common with a number of other authoritarian leaders, Päts was influenced by the corporatist ideas much discussed in Germany during the 1920s; the example of Mussolini's Italy was less significant. Governments were to be appointed by the president, but were also to be accountable to parliament. The president, elected for a six-year term, retained the right of veto over legislation and the power to issue decrees, and he could dismiss a government which no longer enjoyed the confidence of parliament or he could dissolve the latter and order new elections. The first parliament of the new dispensation met in April 1938, and together with representatives of local government, elected Päts president of the republic. The creation of the Fatherland Front, intended to unite the nation, did little to stifle political opposition, which found its natural centre in the university town of Tartu, and whose leader was the president's long-standing rival, Jaan Tõnisson.

The main base of support for the regime in Estonia, as in the other Baltic states, lay in the countryside; and whilst a contemporary judgement that 'the farmers had every reason to be satisfied with Päts' government' may not be entirely accurate, there is little evidence so far of significant discontent either.[10] Herein lies one reason for the failure of the more dynamic alternatives, such as the *Pērkonkrusts* or the *Vapsid*, neither of which succeeded in winning significant rural support. The League of Veterans, which was by far the more serious

10. Jackson J Hampden 1941 *Estonia*, London, p. 209. Isberg 1988, p. 111 observes that the dictatorial nature of the so-called 'silent era' became more sharply defined after the introduction of the new constitution.

contender for power, undoubtedly owed much of its success to the fact that it managed to articulate popular resentment of the system. As soon as the League converted itself to a political party with a programme, and entered the electoral arena, it lost much of that aura. Its leader, Artur Sirk, explicitly rejected the fascist label, claiming that the League would abide by the will of the people. The *Vapsid* were less influenced by Nazi ideology than members of the *Pērkonkrusts*, but their rhetoric was unmistakably anti-democratic, and their staged demonstrations, mass rallies, and adoption of many of the flashier trappings of fascism, from the hierarchical structure of the organisation down to the paramilitary uniforms, bore the implicit threat of violence rather than reasoned persuasion.

Why did parliamentary democracy survive in Finland, but not in the Baltic states? There were, after all, many superficial similarities; distinctly anti-democratic paramilitary organisations, vociferous and potentially violent 'anti-system' movements, and a dangerous diminution of the centre ground upon which government coalitions had largely rested. Enthusiasm for authoritarian systems was widespread amongst the younger generation of intellectuals and students, for whom the national interest occupied a higher place than liberal-democratic cosmopolitanism. The social democrats were constantly on the defensive, fighting the communists for the support of the working class and fending off harassment from the police and right-wing thugs. Although in many ways the staunchest supporters of democracy, they were never in a position from which they could oversee and guide its fortunes. There were also distinctly anti-democratic elements within the mainstream right-wing parties, and rather few out-and-out defenders of the parliamentary democratic system established in the early years of independence. In that sense, parliamentary democracy died by default in the three Baltic states, but it might well have had few mourners outside the social democratic camp had it perished in Finland.

The survival of the democratic system in Finland undoubtedly owes much to the fact that it rested upon much stronger foundations than in any of the other new states of eastern Europe. Not only did the newly independent country have a full range of functioning institutions, it also had a historic constitutionalist tradition deeply embedded in the national consciousness. P. E. Svinhufvud, whose commitment to democratic principles during the Lapua period was perhaps less than whole-hearted, was nevertheless firmly associated in the public mind with the defence of Finland's constitutional liberties against the tsarist oppressors. To have suspended or otherwise interfered with the 1919 constitution would have gravely damaged that image, but there was never any need for Svinhufvud or his political associates to do so, once the presidency had been secured in 1931.

In Finland, the post-civil war constitutional system was never seriously threatened by the forces of the communist left. The Lapua movement, with its violence against the person and its crude demands, was a bludgeon to crack a nut already effectively contained by the police and the employers' organisations; but its rowdyism also threatened to disturb the body politic in ways unacceptable to the establishment. The leadership of the movement disintegrated amidst a cloud of scandals and a haze of alcoholism. Its putative successor, the IKL, was little more than a refuge for russophobes, anti-socialists and admirers of fascism. Working within and with the system it affected to despise, it was never a serious threat to the Finnish body politic. In the Baltic states, the constitutional system established in the early years of independence was subverted from within by established national leaders acting in collusion with senior military figures and politicians. Challenges from outside the system were speedily extinguished; the utter failure of the attempts to stage a coup in Kaunas in 1934 and in Tallinn in 1935 demonstrated the effectiveness with which Smetona and Päts had managed to stifle potential opposition on the radical right. More moderate opponents enjoyed some leeway, but they too were affected by the failings of the ultra-democratic system set aside by the new regimes and constrained by the fact that Päts, Smetona and Ulmanis had seized the high ground of nationalism, so that criticism could always be construed as being unpatriotic.[11]

IN THE SHADOW OF THE NAZIS

The circumstances in which a Nazi dictatorship was established in Germany are very different from those which obtained in the small, sparsely populated and predominantly agrarian states of north-eastern Europe. The success of the Nazis in capturing and mobilising the vote

11. There are some interesting points of comparison made in: Alapuro R 1988 *State and revolution in Finland*, Berkeley and Los Angeles, pp. 255–9. See also the contributions on the three Baltic states by Hellmuth Weiss, Jürgen von Hehn and Thomas Remeikis in: Gollwitzer H (ed.), 1977 *Europäische Bauernparteien im 20. Jahrhundert*, Stuttgart, pp. 207–70.

of large sections of the rural population of northern Germany is, however, striking in the light of the failure of anti-system parties to win the mass support of the peasantry in northern Europe. The experience of the Prussian province of Schleswig-Holstein provides an interesting point of contrast with what happened north of the border in Danish Jutland. The province was a stronghold of left-wing liberalism and social democracy before 1914, yet over half of the votes cast here in July 1932 went to Nazi party candidates. It has been argued that left-wing liberalism during the closing decades of the nineteenth century attracted small farmers hostile to the conservative big landowners, as well as small businessmen and artisans who were alienated by the National Liberal/Conservative big business lobby. Farmers dependent on imported fodder crops and favourable export markets for their livestock were, for example, strong free-traders, and bitter opponents of the protectionist lobby of the big arable farmers. Self-interest and particularism, rather than a belief in democratic and liberal values, determined their stance. To this extent, they stood on similar ground to their counterparts in Jutland; but the Danish farmers had also been strongly influenced by Grundtvigian and free church ideals, and had become firmly integrated into the political system during the course of the nineteenth century. *Venstre* and its more radical progeny represented a sturdy form of peasant democracy in a way which the city-based *Fortschrittler* and their Democratic Party successors in the Weimar republic could never emulate.

The Democratic Party initially fared well in the elections to the constituent assembly in 1919, winning 27 per cent of the vote in Schleswig-Holstein, but went into rapid decline thereafter. Farmers' confidence in the ability of successive coalition governments to offer them some protection from falling prices and mounting debts was constantly undermined. The inflation of 1923 wiped out previous debts, but having already sold their harvests, farmers had to resort to short-term borrowing to be able to pay the high prices for imported goods such as fertilisers or machinery. As a result, the level of indebtedness amongst farmers in Schleswig-Holstein was higher than before the war, and considerably higher than the average for the Reich as a whole.

Frustrated by the inability of their organisations to come together to push energetically for relief measures, the hard-pressed farmers began to organise themselves. Many of their demands concerning the revision of the treaty of Versailles and the reparations issue or the need for Germany to become less dependent on imports had long been articulated by the various right-wing associations which had taken root in the province. The rural people's movement (*Landvolksbewegung*) was not entirely spontaneous, since leaders of the Farmers' Union and Land League were involved; but neither organisation was able to control or direct the agitation, whose epicentre was on the west coast. The vigorous reactions of the authorities to campaigns of non-payment of taxes and the prevention of bailiffs carrying out the orders of the courts forced the movement on to the defensive. A series of bomb attacks against official buildings resulted in the arrest of leading figures, and divided the movement. Its overall lack of organisational structure made it an easy target for infiltrators. The Nazis were comparative latecomers to the area, and did not begin to make much headway until 1929. By the end of the year, the party had 10,400 members in the province, where its principal base was in the geestlands of Dithmarschen. A year later, membership had risen to 14,000, and the party was beginning to expand into the marshlands, eastern Holstein and around the Danish-German border. Its members were also infiltrating and capturing existing farmers' organisations. Although certain of the leaders of the *Landvolksbewegung* continued to enjoy massive personal support, they no longer had a movement to lead.[12]

The success of the Nazis has been attributed to their ability to identify and build upon frustrations and grievances, and to fuse these with a *völkisch* vision of German greatness. In rural areas of Schleswig-Holstein, they recruited sizeable numbers of young people, particularly the sons of farmers, and they undoubtedly benefited from the earlier activities of anti-democratic and racist organisations, which had helped create a favourable climate of opinion as well as a potential membership. In the larger industrial cities such as Kiel, where the communists and social democrats continued to play a dominant role, they had less success. In a small town such as Eutin, the pre-1933 Nazi Party membership was predominantly middle-class, though there was a not insignificant proletarian element, mostly of the skilled working class. Leadership of the party, however, remained in the hands of the traditional elite.[13]

12. Stoltenberg G 1962 *Politische Strömungen im schleswig-holsteinischen Landvolk 1918–1933*, Düsseldorf. Hopp P 1975 Bodenkampf und Bauernbewegung *Zeitschrift der Gesellschaft für Schleswig-holsteinische Geschichte* **100**: 217–320.

13. Stokes L 1978 The social composition of the Nazi Party in Eutin, 1925–1932 *International Review of Social History* **23**: 1–32. Rietzler R 1982 "*Kampf in der Nordmark*". *Das Aufkommen des Nationalsozialismus in Schleswig-Holstein (1919–1928)* Studien zur Wirtschafts- und Sozialgeschichte Schleswig-Holsteins **4** Neumünster.

Amongst the hard-pressed farmers of Denmark, there also developed a protest movement which at its peak could claim some 100,000 members. *Landbrugernes Sammenslutning* in its actions much resembled the *Landvolkbewegeung*, and indeed other self-help protest movements which sought to prevent goods and chattels being distrained or demonstrated en masse at compulsory farm auctions. The sheer size of the movement – which could claim to represent half the farmers in Denmark – compelled the main farming organisations and the political parties to take note of its demands; but the swell of discontent it represented never spilled over into extremist politics. The movement spawned the Free People's Party in 1934 (renamed the Farmers' Party in 1939). This party was essentially devoted to defending the interests of the small farmer against his perceived enemies, such as the taxman, the trades unions, bureaucracy and the urban consumer. Those with a penchant for Nazism were likely to find a more congenial home in the ranks of the Danish National Socialist Party, founded in the 1920s by an ex-cavalry officer and taken over in 1933 by a veterinary from southern Jutland, Fritz Clausen. The Danish Nazis were split by rivalries and petty jealousies, and never had more than 5,000 members before the outbreak of war. Although there was a degree of cooperation between the Nazis and the Farmers' Party, neither made great inroads amongst the electorate.

In Sweden, the extreme right was even more fragmented and marginal. A far more serious challenge to the constitutional state was posed here, as in Denmark, by elements within the ranks of the conservatives, though in neither case did these succeed in capturing control of the party. The Swedish Right (*Höger*) and a section of the Farmers' Party were unhappy with the constitutional changes brought about in 1917–18, though they were less hostile to organised labour than their counterparts in Finland and Norway. Danish conservatives had adapted more readily to the pre-war constitutional changes, though the party's youth wing was heavily influenced by anti-democratic ideas in the 1930s, and had to be called to order by the party chairman, Christmas Møller.

Ulf Lindström has argued that it was the ability of the political system to adapt and to make concessions when necessary, thus denying any leeway to right-wing radical discontent, which kept Scandinavia free of any serious fascist threat.[14] It might also be said that the level of

14. Lindström U 1985 *Fascism in Scandinavia*, Stockholm. There are also chapters on the various Scandinavian fascist movements in: Ugelvik Larsen S, Hagtvet B and Myklebust J 1980 *Who were the fascists: social roots of European fascism*, Oslo.

consensus and political stability was much higher in Sweden, Denmark and Norway than was the case in Germany, and the potential sources of discontent upon which a mass political movement could feed far fewer. Anti-semitism, which was a potent political weapon in central Europe, had little relevance in Scandinavia; in Sweden, for instance, its use proved to be divisive of the very ranks it was supposed to unite. There were few other easily identifiable scapegoats to blame, and little reason for large sections of the populace to feel alienated socially or politically. Above all, democracy was rather more than the prescriptions of a written constitution; it was to be found in workers' clubs, temperance halls, free church assemblies, local council chambers, and in the everyday attitudes and presumptions of the people. Such experiences and attitudes were by no means absent along the southern and eastern shores of the Baltic either, but here, they lacked the solid foundation of consensual national tradition and sociopolitical continuity. The establishment of a Nazi dictatorship in Germany served if anything to strengthen the commitment to consensual democracy of the principal political parties and national organisations of the Scandinavian countries. Thorvald Stauning's famous offer of a nightcap to the still-divided negotiators ('*Vi kan vel drikke et glas til afsked?*'), which saved the Kanslergade talks in January 1933 was something more than Danish conviviality; it was a subtle reminder of the need to agree, at a time when hopes of compromise elsewhere in Europe were being thrown aside.

TERRITORIAL AND MINORITY QUESTIONS

As a result of war, revolution and the peace treaties, the inhabitants of the lands gradually acquired by the Russian and Prussian states since 1772 found themselves having to adapt to new territorial configurations. Large numbers, and not just the more obvious linguistic or religious minorities, found it difficult to adapt to the confines of the new national states. Those who had sided with the Reds in Finland or the Bolsheviks in Estonia and Latvia found it difficult to identify with a 'bourgeois' state whose representatives kept them under tight surveillance. Others, such as the hapless worker Pate Teikka of Pentti Haanpää's 1931 novel, *Noitaympyrä*, joined the thousands who crossed illegally into the Soviet Union during the hungry thirties in search of work.[15] In remote and isolated frontier regions, hostility towards and suspicion of the outside world was sometimes channelled into political protest; communism found many adherents amongst the poor farmers and labourers of northern Sweden and Finland, for example.[16]

Poor or sometimes non-existent communications, a lack of educational and occupational opportunities and the absence of elites who could act as a conduit for the transmission of national values to these remote regions were some of the perceived deficiencies which the authorities sought to remedy during the 1920s. The eastern frontiers of Estonia and Latvia were also economically backward, remote regions inhabited by a mixture of peoples. Latgale, with over half a million inhabitants – Jews, White Russians, Poles, Catholic Lettgallians with their own dialect – posed particular problems for the new Latvian state. Latgale, annexed by Russia in the first partition of Poland in 1772, had never come under Baltic German administration. Neither had the Estonian province of Petseri, which had formerly been part of the Pskov *guberniya.* The Orthodox *setu* people, who spoke their own dialect, were regarded as russified backward cousins by the Estonians, though they had little close contact with the more numerous Russian population of the region. Energetic educational and school-building programmes were set in motion here, and settlement encouraged, in order to build up a proper sense of national identity.[17]

There were also significant non-Russian minorities, such as the Karelians and Ingrians, on the north-western borders of Soviet Russia. Initially, the communists encouraged education in the vernacular languages. The options available for Finnish-speaking Ingrians to acquire a higher education in their own language increased considerably, for example. There was also a wide range of

15. Kostiainen A 1987 *Loikkarit. Suuren lamakauden laiton siirtolaisuus Neuvostoliittoon*, Helsinki, pp. 57–64, estimates that some 15,000 Finns may have illegally crossed into the Soviet Union during the interwar period, and that the numbers of such illegal migrants from all European countries during the Depression may have been as high as 30,000.

16. A Swedish travel-writer of the early 1920s believed that: 'Bolshevism in Härjedalen is much the same type of backwoods Bolshevism, that flourishes in Karelia and along the Murmansk coast, in the wildernesses of Finland and on the shores of the White Sea in Norway; it is nothing more than an instinctive revolt against an all too depressing and gloomy natural environment, it is the confused and desperate revolt of the wild against society': three decades later, a political scientist noted of the inhabitants of the northern regions of Sweden that 'their sense of national alienation could not have been greater had they constituted a coloured minority'. Böök F. 1924 *Resa i Sverige*, Stockholm p. 156. Rydenfelt S 1954 *Kommunismen i Sverige*, Lund, p. 329.

17. Raun T 1991 The Petseri region in the republic of Estonia *Jahrbücher für Geschichte Osteuropas* **39**: 514–32. Ant J 1990 *Eesti 1920*, Tallinn, pp. 60–6.

Finnish-language publications and cultural activities in Soviet Russia, though these were now directed by exiled Finnish communists and were intended to inculcate new values. Church activities were allowed to continue, though lack of money and a shortage of Lutheran clergy to minister to the Ingrians were a severe handicap. All changed in the 1930s, with the introduction of collectivisation. The Finnish-speaking population of a vulnerable frontier area also bore the brunt of Stalin's paranoic suspicion. Of the 137,569 Ingrians living in the vicinity of Leningrad during the mid-1920s, it is estimated that over 50,000 were forcibly evacuated or exiled into the vast Soviet hinterland during the 1930s. Many more were driven from their homes by the war.[18]

In the mid-thirties, minorities constituted a quarter of the population of Latvia, rather less in Estonia (around 10 per cent) and Lithuania (just over 15 per cent). Minority rights were guaranteed in the Estonian and Latvian constitutions, and both countries granted wide-reaching autonomy in cultural and educational affairs. This was especially important for the Germans and Jews, who did not live in compact communities, as did the small Swedish minority on the offshore islands of Estonia or the Russian fishermen and farmers on the eastern frontiers. Five national minorities in Latvia – Russians, Poles, Jews, White Russians and Germans – set up their own educational administrations with official approval during the 1920s. Estonia went one step further in 1925, granting all national groups of more than 3,000 persons the right to constitute themselves as public corporations with their own cultural institutions. This highly-acclaimed act remained in force, though several of its provisions were violated by the Päts regime. The rights of the minorities in Latvia came under fire even before the 1934 coup, and the Ulmanis regime continued the policy of latvianisation. Both states effectively ended educational autonomy by placing minority schools under the direct control and supervision of the ministry of education; and both introduced language laws curbing the public use of German placenames.[19]

The situation in Lithuania was rather different. The country's 150,000 Jews still had to endure petty everyday anti-semitism and discrimination – there were hardly any senior Jewish army officers, judges or civil servants, for example – but they were allowed a

18. For details of the fate of the Ingrians, see: Nevalainen P and Sihvo H 1991 *Inkeri. Historia, kansa, kulttuuri* Suomalaisen Kirjallisuuden Seuran toimituksia **547**, Helsinki, pp. 234–318.

19. Aun K 1953 The cultural autonomy of national minorities in Estonia *Yearbook of the Estonian Learned Society in America* **1 (1951–53)**: 26–41. Rauch 1974, pp. 135–45.

reasonable degree of autonomy and full civil rights. The Zionist leadership in Vilna had adopted a pro-Lithuanian stance in 1918, and two of their number had joined the provisional government at the end of the year. Although the rights of the Jewish minority in independent Lithuania were gradually circumscribed – the ministry of Jewish affairs, for instance, was abolished in 1924 – the country was by common consent 'a paradise in comparison to Vilna Lithuania', which remained under Polish control.[20] The Polish minority, almost certainly much larger than the 3 per cent of the official 1923 census, bore the brunt of outraged Lithuanian nationalism, especially after the seizure of Vilna by Polish troops in 1920. Although a large proportion of the big landowners were Polish, there were many thousands more *tutejszy*, impoverished frontiersmen whose identification with Polishness owed more to local loyalties than it did to anything else. Rural areas were less affected by communal strife than the towns and cities. Hundreds of Poles were arrested in August 1919 after the discovery of a plot to overthrow the government in Kaunas and replace it with one favourable to union with Poland. Polish deputies in the constituent assembly were physically assaulted after the prime minister had read out their complaint to the League of Nations of discrimination, and they later withdrew in protest from the assembly. Youth gangs fought on the streets of Kaunas, church congregations rioted in protest at what they felt to be over-generous educational provision for the Polish minority, and a constant stream of complaints flowed from both sides to the League of Nations.[21]

By comparison, the Swedish-speaking minority in Finland fared much better. Unlike the Baltic Germans, they had never constituted an oppressive land-owning elite – a majority were in fact small farmers and fishermen in the southern province of Nyland/Uusimaa, on the offshore southern islands and along the Ostrobothnian coast. The replacement of the four-estate Diet by the unicameral *Eduskunta* in 1906 destroyed the principal bastions of the old aristocratic and

20. This was the verdict of Yaakov Vygodski, one of the two Zionists who joined the Lithuanian government in 1918, quoted in: Mendelsohn E 1981 *Zionism in Poland. The formative years, 1915–1926*, New Haven and London, p. 104. On the vexed question of Lithuanian attitude towards and treatment of Jews, see: Lieven A 1993 *The Baltic revolution. Estonia, Latvia, Lithuania and the path to independence*, New Haven and London, pp. 139–58.

21. Krivickas V 1975 The Polish minority in Lithuania, 1918–1926 *Slavonic and East European Review* **53**: 78–91. Senn A 1964 On the state of Central Lithuania *Jahrbücher für Geschichte Osteuropas* **12**: 366–74. Lieven 1993, pp. 158–73. Czesław Miłosz has portrayed the life of the Polish-speaking borderers, most notably in his novel *The Issa valley* (1974) and his essay collection, *Beginning with my streets* (1992).

burgher elites. The creation in 1906 of the Swedish People's Party (SFP) was a tacit and intelligent acceptance of their new status as a linguistic minority whose only home was Finland. Numbering around 343,000, or just over 10 per cent of the population, in 1930, this minority regularly returned 20–25 members of the SFP to the *Eduskunta* during the interwar years. There was an easily-stifled campaign in 1918–19 for some kind of regional autonomy, and a more serious separatist movement on the wholly Swedish-speaking Åland islands; there was also much agitation in Finnish nationalist circles during the 1930s for a one-language state; but in neither instance was the position of the minority within the state of Finland seriously threatened. The idea of regional autonomy for the Swedish-speaking minority was dismissed as a dangerous illusion by Rabbe Wrede, a leading member of that community in 1919. In Wrede's view 'we are bound to this Finnish Finland and its wellbeing is our wellbeing, its misfortunes and ruin our misfortunes and ruin'. This was a bond tacitly acknowledged on both sides of the language divide, one sufficiently strong to ensure that the rights of the minority in an officially bilingual state have been respected to the present day.[22]

The more diverse national minorities of the three Baltic states were too disunited, and too much distrusted by the autochthonous majority to have played any effective or constructive role in nation-building. The Russian minorities were especially multi-layered, ranging from the descendants of the Old Believers who had fled from Russia in the seventeenth century to White army officers. The richness and creativity of Russian cultural life in the Baltic states during the interwar years was not, however, given the kind of underpinning at a national level that the SFP was able to provide for Finnish-Swedish culture. Although Russians constituted the largest minority in Latvia (10.6 per cent of the total population in 1935), they were hopelessly divided and returned fewer members of parliament than the numerically smaller but more united German community. Like the Jews, the Baltic Germans were predominantly town-dwellers; 61 per cent of the German community in Latvia lived in Riga, according to the 1935 census, whilst 40 per cent of the German community in Estonia lived in Tallinn. The Latvian Jewish community, which had

22. *Svenska Finlands Folkting, 19–28 maj 1919*, Helsingfors 1919, p. 173. Sundberg J 1985 *Svenskhetens Dilemma i Finland: Finlandssvenskarnas samling och splittring under 1900-talet* Bidrag till kännedom av Finlands natur och folk **133**, Helsingfors, and: Allardt E, Starck C 1981 *Vähemmistö ja kieli*, Porvoo, offer contrasting views of the development of the Swedish-speaking minority in this century.

been greatly expanded by refugees and repatriates from Soviet Russia, was slightly larger than the Baltic German minority, which had shrunk considerably as a consequence of the war and migration to Germany. It was, however, far more divided politically, culturally and spiritually. The Jewish educational administration had to make provision for teaching in Hebrew, Yiddish, German and Russian in the schools under its auspices, for instance, and five parties, ranging from the orthodox anti-Zionist *Agudas yisroel* to the socialist *Bund*, contested the 1928 elections. The fragmentation of the Jewish minority echoed a broader disunity amongst Latvia's diverse nationalities, after a promising beginning in 1920, when a committee of the minorities, with its own office of information, had been established.[23]

In spite of its vitality and the range of its activities – from the revisionist youth group *Betar*, founded in Riga, to the *aliyah*, which took thousands of east European Jews to Palestine – Zionism failed to win over large sections of the Jewish population.[24] Of all the minorities, the Jews alone had no external state which might offer fraternal assistance or exercise pressure in support of their rights. Polish and German minorities were far more fortunate in that they could look to neighbouring (and much bigger) states for support and assistance. This in turn boded ill for hopes of peaceful coexistence or even assimilation of these minorities into the host nation. Liberal Baltic Germans such as Paul Schiemann, who pleaded the case for loyal and constructive support of the newly independent states, were always fighting an uphill struggle against native resentment and a supercilious elitism which ultimately looked to Germany for salvation.

The policy of successive German governments in the 1920s had been broadly in line with Schiemann's aspirations. Baltic German educational and cultural activities, of which the Herder Institute in Riga was the showpiece, were supported by private foundations and official bodies of the German government, a laudable endeavour in itself but tending to preserve elitist and even racist pretensions amongst

23. On the political activities of the minorities in the Baltic states, see the contribution by Michael Garleff in: Vardys V and Misiunas R (eds) 1978 *The Baltic states in peace and war 1917–1945*, University Park, Pa. and London, pp. 81–94 and Rauch 1974, pp. 135–45. There is a brief survey of the cultural activities of the Russian minority in: Pachmuss T 1985 Russian culture in the Baltic states and Finland 1920–1940 *Journal of Baltic Studies* **16**: 383–402.

24. Mendelsohn 1981, pp. 336–7 concludes, however, that in Poland at least it was more in tune with Jewish thinking than the socialist Bund, the orthodox societies, the communists or the anti-socialist, anti-Zionist *Folkistn*. The Zionists of Poland were initially successful in helping establish a minorities' bloc in the *Sejm*, but this soon fragmented.

a still intensely conservative and exclusivist community.[25] A range of reactionary or romantic notions fashionable in the Reich found fertile ground amongst the Baltic Germans during the 1920s. Deprived of their privileges, losing control of cherished monuments of their former glory such as churches, cathedrals, fraternity lodges and clubs, which were gradually taken over by the Estonian and Latvian states, losing many of their young people through migration or intermarriage, this community topheavy with elderly men and women (almost a third were aged over 50 in 1934–35) entered upon a desperate search for a revival. Bands of young men left the city in summer to foster fraternal links with the remaining settlers brought into Kurland from Volhynia after the 1905 revolution. The *Baltische Brüderschaft*, a secret society formed in 1921 by Baltic emigrants to Germany, embraced Christian-conservative views of a 'renewed' German community. Respected community leaders filled the columns of the still-extensive Baltic German press with sententious articles. The younger generation was more attracted to Nazism, though it did not have the same degree of success amongst the Baltic Germans as it did in the former Reich cities of Danzig or Memel. The Baltic German Party in Estonia was briefly captured by the Nazis in 1933. After the local Nazi leader Viktor von zur Mühlen had expressed his support for the *Vapsid*, the government arrested a number of leaders of his movement and closed down the German club; this prompted the Baltic-German establishment to reassert itself and force von zur Mühlen and his associates to withdraw. By the late 1930s, more openly Nazi sympathisers were beginning to capture key positions, but the leadership of the Baltic German community in the two Baltic states remained essentially in the hands of the establishment right up until the final curtain was rung down on seven hundred years of settlement in 1939–40.

MEMEL, DANZIG AND THE COMING OF WAR

In the chaotic winter of 1918–19, fighting had broken out between Polish troops and the *Heimatschutz* units set up by the local German

25. Hiden J 1987 *The Baltic states and Weimar Ostpolitik*, Cambridge, pp. 36–61, 171–97, argues that trade considerations played a vital role in determining Germany's attitude. For a detailed study of the politics of the Baltic German minority, see: Garleff M 1976 *Deutschbaltische Politik zwischen den Weltkriegen*, Bonn.

population of Posen and West Prussia. Skirmishing continued until February 1919, when the armistice commission drew a demarcation line through the area. Attempts to set up a separate east German state which might serve to prevent the eastern regions falling into Polish hands came to nothing. The German High Command refused to sanction an offensive against Poland in the summer of 1919, and the plan collapsed amidst much mutual recrimination. The peace treaty gave Posen and much of West Prussia to Poland, and decreed that plebiscites be held in the Marienwerder and Allenstein districts. German East Prussia was left marooned, cut off from the rest of the Reich by the Polish corridor, an area of some 16,000 square kilometres stretching from the river Notec in the south to the Baltic Sea. The population of the western territories taken by Poland was a mixture of Poles, Germans, Cashubians and Jews. By the winter of 1921–22, the German element had been drastically reduced. Something like 700,000 of the 1.1 million German inhabitants of West Prussia and Posen left for the Reich, driven out by discriminatory measures, the weakening of the Polish currency, and the general lack of prospects in a region which had been colonised as a matter of policy, but from which hundreds of thousands had already departed during the years of empire. Those who remained were subject to trade discriminations and boycotts; the large landowners of Pomerelia were particularly hard hit by the Polish land reform of 1925, which sought to break up the large estates. The Reich government for its part provided substantial funds to support the educational and cultural activities of the beleaguered German minority in Poland. Breaches of the minority rights agreement signed by Poland were brought before the League of Nations by the Reich government, for whom the Germans in Poland were an integral part of the general policy of revising the terms of the Versailles peace treaty.[26]

The real or imagined grievances of the German minority in western Poland was an issue ripe for exploitation by a regime more aggressive in its revisionism than that epitomised by Gustav Stresemann's adroit diplomacy of the 1920s; but it was the city-state of Danzig which more readily captured the headlines and provided the slogans for Nazi revisionism. Unlike the Polish corridor, Danzig had an overwhelmingly German population. The peacemakers at Versailles had made Danzig a free city under the protection of the League of

26. Broszat M 1963 *Zweihundert Jahre deutsche Polenpolitik*, Munich, pp. 154–64, 175–81. Schultze H 1970 Der Oststaat-plan 1919 *Vierteljahrshefte für Zeitgeschichte* **18**: 123–63.

Nations. Its sovereignty was circumscribed in that Poland was in overall charge of its foreign affairs, owned most of the railways and had its own munitions depot and a small garrison on the Westerplatte peninsula. From the start, the free state ran into difficulties, and had to be bailed out by Germany. Agreements concluded in 1920 ensured that the city would be supplied with foodstuffs and other vital commodities at subsidised rates. Orders were placed with Danzig firms by government agencies. The *Reichsbank* advanced hefty loans to the hard-pressed administration, which was almost entirely in the hands of Reich Germans, who worked there on extended and fully guaranteed 'leave'. Although the volume of trade through the port increased substantially, most of the trade was in Polish coal, and Danzigers themselves controlled very little of the commerce. Poland employed a range of economic sanctions in the early thirties to demonstrate its economic grip over the city, which also faced stiff competition from the new Polish port of Gdynia. By the end of 1932, 20 per cent of the workforce was unemployed, adding an even heavier burden to the already straitened finances of the city. Massive sums of money had to be pumped in from the Reich, as part of the policy of sustaining German outposts until such time as Germany could press her revisionist claims.[27]

The rising tide of Nazism in Germany alarmed Marshal Piłsudski, who seized the opportunity offered by the conclusion of a Soviet-Polish non-aggression pact in 1932 to adopt a belligerent posture on Poland's western borders. Troops were massed on the frontier and a battleship cruised off Danzig. This, however, only served to strengthen Hitler's cause, for the military in East Prussia strongly opposed Chancellor Brüning's ban on the SA, claiming it was an essential element in the defence of the border. Piłsudski sounded out France about the possibility of a preventive war against Germany. In March 1933, the Westerplatte garrison was strengthened, in breach of existing agreements. Under League pressure, Piłsudski was forced to withdraw the reinforcements; the French appeared unwilling to be drawn into a war; and Hitler, much to everyone's surprise, adopted a friendly attitude towards Poland. The Nazi *Gauleiter* in Danzig, Albert Forster, was ordered to curb anti-Polish demonstrations, and Hermann Rauschning, the new head of the Senate following the Nazi electoral victory in April 1933, was encouraged to negotiate with the Poles.

27. Kimmich C 1968 *The free city. Danzig and German foreign policy 1919–1934*, New York and London. Tighe C 1990 *Gdańsk. National identity in the German-Polish borderlands*, London, pp. 87–106.

The agreement between Poland and Danzig signed in August 1933 guaranteed the rights of the Polish minority in the free state, with Poland undertaking to ship a specified quantity of goods through Danzig and to lift discriminatory customs duties. Neither this agreement nor the Polish-German non-aggression treaty concluded in 1934 met with the approval of the German foreign office, which felt that ten years of hard work had been sacrificed, and it was not much to the taste of Danzig's citizens either. The Reich was no longer able to provide sufficient credits to keep the economy above water. In 1935, the Senate carried out a hurried 57.5 per cent devaluation and imposed currency and exchange controls, to which the Poles promptly responded by insisting that duty on goods destined for Poland should be paid in *złotys* in Gdynia, effectively bringing the port of Danzig to a halt. Prices rose sharply, and a wages freeze only added to the atmosphere of panic and despair; at one stage, the city's rulers even contemplated the introduction of the Polish *złoty* to restore some measure of economic stability. The situation was only saved by Göring's personal intervention, but Danzig's economy and finances remained in a waterlogged condition.

The once-flourishing port of Memel was also badly affected by the changes wrought by the war, and the loss of the vital Russian timber trade. Separated from East Prussia and placed under Allied control pending the final decision on whether or not to cede the area to Lithuania, the 2,565 square kilometres of the Memel (Klaipėda) district had been occupied in January 1923 by Lithuanian forces, taking advantage of French preoccupation with the Ruhr crisis. Having registered a formal protest, the conference of ambassadors in Paris agreed to approve the transfer of the area to Lithuania, on condition that it be given autonomous status and that Poland be guaranteed free harbour and transit rights. The Lithuanians refused to accept the latter condition, but the convention agreed to in 1924 set up a provincial assembly in which both German and Lithuanian languages had equal validity, and laid down other autonomous rights for the Memellanders. The Lithuanian government was to appoint the president of the provincial government, who was to enjoy the confidence of the assembly (*Landtag/Seimelis*). Although the united front of the three main German parties won 27 of the 29 seats in the first elections to the assembly in October 1925, the government sought to impose a Lithuanian as president. This state of affairs continued throughout the early years of the Smetona dictatorship; the Lithuanians were unable to break the German grip over the *Landtag*, but the government in Kaunas sought to impose its own candidate as head of the administration. The one president they were constrained by external pressure to accept, Otto Böttcher, was forced to resign after little more than a year.

In neither Danzig nor Memel did the Nazis make much progress before 1930. Hermann Göring had to intervene in a bitter dispute which threatened to wreck the party in Danzig. In Memel, two Nazi-influenced parties emerged, the Christian Socialist Workers' Community of Pastor von Sass and the Socialist People's Community of Dr Neumann. Both fell foul of the Lithuanian authorities, alarmed by the Polish-German non-aggression pact, and were banned under the provisions of the February 1934 law protecting the security of the state. Although the Reich consul-general claimed that both parties could count on the support of 60 per cent of the German population, no more than 5 per cent were party members. The failure of the *Gauleiter* of East Prussia to end the conflict between the two movements and enforce Nazi party discipline would also suggest that the Reich NSDAP exercised rather little influence in Memelland.

In the case of Danzig, the situation was saved by the youthful, energetic but unscrupulous Albert Forster, sent to the free state in October 1930. Forster managed to increase party membership to 9,519 in December 1932, and in the May 1933 elections to the *Volkstag*, the NSDAP received just over half the votes cast and an absolute majority of the seats. Part of this success was undoubtedly due to the defection from the German nationalist camp of Hermann Rauschning, the respected spokesman of the farmers of the Grosses Werder region of the free state. It was Rauschning who formed the first Nazi-led Senate in coalition with the Centre party. He was, however, soon driven out of office and into exile and opposition to Hitler by the hard-boiled Forster, who was also busily engaged in eliminating other forms of opposition with the aid of a law granting emergency powers 'for the relief of the distress of the people and state', passed in June 1933. The League of Nations, distracted by international crises, paid little heed to the efforts of its High Commissioner Sean Lester to take steps against the nazification of Danzig. By 1938, virtually all the parties and groups in some way opposed to the Nazis had been eliminated.[28]

What was happening in Danzig and Memel during the 1930s was a microcosmic reflection of the intolerance, petty persecution and general viciousness characteristic of much of central and eastern Europe. Many managed to avoid unpleasantness by conforming and

28. Tighe 1990, pp. 107–28. Levine H 1973 *Hitler's free city. A history of the Nazi party in Danzig, 1925–1939*, Chicago. Plieg E-A 1962 *Das Memelland 1920–1939* Marburger Ostforschungen **19**, Würzburg.

keeping quiet; others sought security or advancement by putting on the right uniform, joining the party in power, or denouncing those deemed threatening to state security. But for those who did not conform, either willingly or because of their race, nationality, religion, physical or mental disability, life was not so pleasant. The level of harassment varied, from the everyday annoyance of the Memellanders whose letters were not delivered because they were not addressed in the Lithuanian language or the obligation imposed upon non-Latvians to give their names Latvian spelling on official documents, to the closure of churches, clubs, institutions and organisations and the use of physical violence. Those who were persecuted rarely stood together, often because they were divided by personal animosities or jealousies or because they were uncertain which strategy to adopt.

Those who persecuted were all too rarely criticised by outsiders. On the whole, the Protestant churches of Scandinavia remained silent over the persecution of the Jews and other victims of the Nazis, and their governments were less than sympathetic to the influx of refugees. They were also not immune to the arguments of the eugenicists and propagandists of 'racial hygiene'. A law providing for sterilisation of the mentally feeble was passed by the Danish *Rigsdag* in 1934, and the prohibition of marriage between mentally and psychologically ill people was extended in 1938 to cover psychopaths, alcoholics, epileptics and the mentally retarded. Similar measures were introduced or considered in other Nordic countries.[29]

Intolerance, repression and persecution fostered an atmosphere of suspicion and fear, much as the propaganda employed in the service of the party, nation or state distorted reality and created illusory or imaginary worlds. The men who led Europe into war for the second time within a generation were more purposeful and malevolent than the warmakers of 1914; those whom they led were as blinded and bemused as their parents had been, in spite of the brave hopes of the postwar world. It is perhaps too easy to blame the evident failings of democratic systems, of the League of Nations, of disarmament conferences and international courts of arbitration, or to take refuge in the standard undergraduate explanation, that the peoples of Europe really longed for 'strong' leadership to solve their problems. There was rather a failure of leadership in many crucial instances; an unwillingness to provide and enforce civil rights for all within the

29. Hansen S, Henriksen I 1980 *Sociale brydninger 1914–1939* Dansk socialhistorie vol. 6, Copenhagen, p. 220. Hatje A-K 1974 *Befolkningsfrågan och välfärden. Debatten om familjepolitik och nativitetsökning under 1930- och 1940-talen*, Stockholm, pp. 173–87.

state's territories, a reluctance to accept and work within imposed limits, a lack of determination to unite and fight for these policies, and against those which discriminated or jeopardised the general peace. There was a marked predisposition towards bellicosity of language and appearance. Marshal Piłsudski may have called Voldemaras' bluff in December 1927 when he interrupted the Lithuanian prime minister's speech at a session of the League of Nations in Geneva with the words: 'There's only one thing I want to know; do you want war or peace?', but this did not solve the Polish-Lithuanian dispute. The ultimatum delivered by Poland to Lithuania in March 1938 may have restored diplomatic relations, but did nothing to bring about amity or cooperation between the two countries.[30] The instability and tension which was caused by the dispute over Vilna and a score of other unresolved conflicts offered fertile ground for the ruthless great powers of Germany and Russia, each in its own way dedicated to the wholescale revision of peace treaties and a redrawing of the map of eastern Europe.

In the crisis which welled up into a general conflagration in 1938–39, Memel and Danzig were destined briefly to occupy a central position. The inhabitants of both cities had been allowed little say as to their future in 1919. The efforts of local patriots to do the best they could for their city, to seek accommodation wherever possible with their new neighbours, were of little avail. Rather like the local patriots of an earlier age in the duchies of Slesvig and Holstein, they were swept away in the strong currents of rival nationalisms. For the nationalist zealot, erecting (or defacing) statues symbolising the national struggle was more important than preserving or studying the many diverse strands that constituted the people and their heritage: the distortion or falsification of archaeological and ethnographical evidence for racialist ends more overriding than the truth. Both Germany and Poland invested a great deal of money and resources into academic and scholarly research and publications to support their national revendications.[31] Both also spent a great deal more money on arming for war, whilst at the same time weakening the last remaining safeguards of collective security. In signing the non-aggression pact with Germany, Poland lost the confidence of France; more disastrously, it gave the Poles the false notion that they could play the

30. Rauch 1974, p. 105. Senn A. 1961 The Polish-Lithuanian war scare, 1927 *Journal of Central European Affairs* **21**: 267–84.

31. On this, see especially Burleigh M 1988 *Germany turns eastwards. A study of* Ostforschung *in the Third Reich*, Cambridge. Tighe 1990, pp. 255–88. Jussila O 1983 *Venäläinen Suomi*, Helsinki. Rauch 1974, p. 184.

part of a third force in eastern Europe, and encouraged them to declare that they were no longer prepared to carry out their obligations under the minorities protection treaty. Since Germany had left the League, Poland no longer felt constrained by its sanctions. This in turn seriously weakened the position and authority of the League's High Commissioner in Danzig.

As German troops massed on the borders of Austria in March 1938, a Polish soldier was killed in an incident on the Lithuanian frontier. Warsaw learnt of this incident at the same time as German troops began marching into Austria, and the Polish government seized the occasion to settle its dispute with Lithuania. Amidst a wave of anti-Lithuanian demonstrations and banner headlines demanding action, the government ordered troops to the frontier and on 17 March, delivered a 48-hour ultimatum to Kaunas, demanding the restoration of normal diplomatic relations. Receiving no comfort or support from the Western powers or from the Soviet Union, the Lithuanians had no option but to accept this ultimatum. There were anti-government demonstrations in Kaunas, where it was widely believed that the ultimatum was but the prelude to an *Anschluss* of Lithuania by Poland, and President Smetona was obliged to change the cabinet.[32]

Had the Lithuanians rejected the ultimatum, they would also have had to face a German as well as a Polish attack, for Hitler had ordered the army command on 18 March to occupy the Memel region and a much larger area extending to Šiauliai in central Lithuania. The Baltic area was, according to the Führer, second only to the Sudetenland in Germany's list of objectives. In October, only a few weeks after the Munich agreement, Hitler ordered the army to be ready to move into what remained of Czechoslovakia and the Memel area. In an effort to satisfy Germany, the Lithuanian government lifted the state of emergency in Memel. This was greeted with torchlit demonstrations in the streets of Memel and demands for a return to the Reich. Dr Neumann, released from jail in March, refused to negotiate with the Lithuanian government, and took his instructions directly from Berlin. In the December 1938 elections to the *Landtag*, his Memel German list won 87 per cent of the vote. The new government took over

32. On the Polish-Lithuanian crisis and its consequences, see: Pagel J 1992 *Polen und die Sowjetunion 1938–39* Quellen und Studien zur Geschichte des östlichen Europa **34**, Stuttgart; Sabaliūnas L 1972 *Lithuania in crisis. Nationalism to communism, 1939–1940*, Bloomington. More generally, Myllyniemi S 1977 *Baltian kriisi 1938–1941*, Helsinki, pp. 21–2 (German version *Die baltische Krise 1938–1941*, Stuttgart, 1979).

'with the aim of leading our homeland to a happier future founded on the national socialist world-view'; the Lithuanian government, reshuffled for a second time in December, uttered not a word of protest. Measures were taken to restore German as the language of administration; the Lithuanian security police were ordered back to Kaunas, and the local police were issued with green, white and red Memel cockades to replace the Lithuanian yellow, green and red. On 20 March 1939, the Lithuanian foreign minister, hurrying back from Rome to be ready to deal with German actions following upon the occupation of the remainder of the Czech lands, had a meeting with his German counterpart in Berlin. Ribbentrop threatened military occupation of the Memel area if it were not restored immediately to Germany. Neither Britain nor France was willing to act on Lithuania's behalf, and no offer of assistance was forthcoming from Moscow. The treaty handing over the Memel district to the German Reich was concluded on 22 March, and signed the following day, as Hitler in his flagship *Deutschland* sailed into the harbour of Memel to welcome the district back into the Reich.[33]

The loss of Memel, coming hard on the heels of the climbdown in the face of the Polish ultimatum, dealt a hard blow to the prestige and credibility of the Smetona regime, though the Lithuanians were also relieved that their country had not suffered the same fate as Bohemia and Moravia, and become a German protectorate. For the world at large, the event was overshadowed by the growing possibility of conflict between Germany and Poland over Danzig and the Corridor. Ribbentrop had raised the issue of the return of Danzig and extra-territorial rail and road links through the Corridor in talks with the Polish ambassador to Berlin in October 1938; these demands were presented personally by Hitler to the Polish foreign minister on 5 January 1939, and repeated by Ribbentrop immediately after the annexation of Memel. Plans were already afoot for an occupation of Danzig by units of the armed forces stationed in East Prussia. On 11 April, orders were issued by Hitler, detailing contingency plans to destroy Poland should that country change its policy towards Germany. This document ('Plan White') also intimated that 'in the course of further developments it may become necessary to occupy the Baltic states up to the border of the former Kurland and to incorporate them in the Reich'. Although this sentence was removed two days later by the German High Command, the whole tone of the

33. Plieg 1962, pp. 203–11. Myllyniemi 1977, pp. 24–8. Rauch 1974, pp. 197–9. Sabaliūnas L 1972, pp. 113–24.

document was a mockery of the non-aggression provisions of the German-Lithuanian treaty signed less than a month earlier, and the offers of similar agreements made at the end of April to Estonia and Latvia.[34] Alarmed by the threatening noises emanating from the Soviet Union, and increasingly worried that Britain and France would conclude an agreement with Moscow which would deliver them to the protective care of the Red Army, the governments of the three Baltic states were to face their greatest danger divided and ultimately alone as the summer of 1939 drew on.

34. *Documents on German Foreign Policy* Series D *1936–1941* Vol. 6, London 1956, pp. 224–8.

CHAPTER TWELVE

The Tragic Decade, 1939–1950

WAR IN THE NORTH, 1939–1940

Hitler's demands for a resolution in Germany's favour of the Danzig question finally disabused the Polish foreign minister Józef Beck of any remaining hopes of reaching a reasonable compromise with the Führer. Beck now turned to the western powers, and on 6 April 1939, the preparation of a treaty of alliance between Britain and Poland was announced. The British guarantee of aid to Poland in the event of German aggression was intended more as a warning to Hitler than as a serious military commitment, as the cataclysmic events of September 1939 starkly revealed. It also destroyed any last faint hopes of bringing the Soviet Union into an eastern European collective security system to counter potential German aggression. The guarantee fuelled Russian suspicions of a malevolent western plot to unleash Hitler against the Soviet Union. Deeply suspicious of the Polish government, and disinclined to believe in the ability or inclination of the Baltic states and Finland to resist German pressure for their territory to be used as a base for an assault on the Soviet Union, Stalin appears to have decided in the spring of 1939 to pursue two options: alliance with the western powers or an accommodation with Germany. In the end, it was the German option which proved by far the more attractive. Whereas the British and French negotiators seemed only to cavil during the long and wearisome negotiations in Moscow throughout the summer, the Germans were swift to agree to a brutal territorial carve-up of north-eastern Europe. At one p.m. on 23 August 1939, the German foreign minister Joachim von Ribbentrop landed in Moscow after an early morning flight from Königsberg. Twelve hours later, he was signing the non-aggression pact and the infamous secret protocol. So eager had the Germans been for such an agreement that they abandoned their original claim to the territories of the former duchy of Kurland; at eleven p.m., the Führer agreed to assign the whole of Latvia to the Soviet sphere of influence.[1]

In terms of its impact upon the political map of northern Europe, the Nazi-Soviet pact of 1939 bears comparison with the Treaty of Tilsit and the Peace of Brest-Litovsk. For millions of contemporaries, and for future generations living in the lands directly affected by the territorial partitions of the secret and additional secret protocols, its consequences were profound. Without the pact, Hitler would hardly have dared launch his attack on Poland nine days later, thereby unleashing an avalanche of war and destruction that was to end only after he himself lay dead in the smouldering ruins of Berlin. Without the pact, Stalin would not have been able to extend Soviet influence so easily into eastern Europe and, more importantly, would not subsequently have been able to parade before his new allies the morally objectionable but politically essential excuse of 'legitimate' security interests.[2]

The German attack on Poland began during the night of 31 August–1 September. In Danzig, the Polish garrison stationed on the Westerplatte was fired on by the battleship *Schleswig-Holstein.* German troops occupied key locations in the town and overcame the brief but gallant resistance of the armed postal workers in the Polish post office; the few survivors were later executed as agents provocateurs. The Westerplatte garrison surrendered on 5 September; the Polish forces in Gdynia and on the Hel peninsula, cut off and hopelessly outnumbered, fought on for another fortnight as the Germans overran most of western Poland. On 17 September, Soviet forces moved into eastern Poland. Two days later, Red Army units occupied Vilna. This triggered off a second round of negotiations; on 25 September, the German ambassador to Moscow transmitted to Berlin a Soviet

1. On the tripartite negotiations and the origins of the Nazi-Soviet pact, see: Watt D 1989 *How war came. The immediate origins of the Second War 1938–1939*, London, pp. 361–84, 430–61. On the authenticity of the secret protocol, see: König H 1989 Das deutschsowjetische Vertragswerk von 1939 – eine Faksimile-Dokumentation *Zeitschrift für Gegenwartsfragen des Ostens* **39**: 413–58. Oberländer E (ed.) 1989 *Hitler-Stalin Pakt 1939. Das Ende Ostmitteleuropas?* Frankfurt. Crowe D 1993 *The Baltic states and the great powers: foreign relations 1938–1940,* Boulder, Colorado.

2. On this, see my chapter on the Baltic question in Anglo-Soviet relations, 1941–2 in: Vardys V and Misiunas R 1978 *The Baltic states in peace and war 1917–1945,* University Park, Pa. and London, pp. 159–72.

proposal that 'if we consented, the Soviet Union would immediately take up the solution of the problem of the Baltic countries in accordance with the protocol of 23 August and expect in this matter the unstinting support of the German government. Stalin expressly indicated Estonia, Latvia and Lithuania, but did not mention Finland'.[3]

The process of bullying the Baltic states into agreeing to non-aggression pacts which would allow thousands of Soviet troops to occupy bases on their territory had in fact already begun. The Estonian foreign minister had been subjected to relentless pressure to sign such an agreement the previous night; on the afternoon of 26 September, the Estonians decided to bow to the inevitable and to try and soften the terms offered. Instead, they had to face new demands. Using as an excuse the reported sinking of a Soviet vessel by an unidentified submarine, Molotov insisted on the right to station 35,000 troops on Estonian soil for the duration of the war. After much wrangling, at which Stalin was the kindly foil to Molotov's hard-man act, the Soviet side agreed to lower the figure to 25,000, and to locate their naval base outside the Estonian capital. Similar agreements were concluded with Latvia and Lithuania in the early days of October. All three countries were assured that the Soviet Union would respect their sovereignty and form of government. Stalin half-jokingly promised the Lithuanian foreign minister Juozas Urbšys that Russian troops would help put down any communist insurrection in his country, should one occur, and reportedly told the Latvian foreign minister: 'There are no communists outside of Russia. What you have in Latvia are Trotskists [*sic*]; if they cause you trouble, shoot them.'[4]

The occupation of Vilna clearly gave Stalin an advantage in the subsequent redefinition of spheres of influence. For the first two weeks of war, the German foreign office had encouraged the Lithuanians to believe that Germany would support their claims to Vilna: there were even hints that Lithuania should abandon its neutrality and seize the region. On 16 September, the tune abruptly changed, and the German foreign office now complained of 'false information' being circulated

3. Ambassador Schulenburg to Berlin, 25 September 1939: *Documents on German Foreign Policy (DGFP) Series D 1936–1941* vol. 8, London 1954, p. 130.

4. As reported by the British minister to Kaunas, 19 April 1940: FO 419/35, *Public Record Office,* London. For full documentation of these discussions, see *Report of the Select Committee to investigate communist aggression and the forced incorporation of the Baltic states into the USSR. (Third interim report)* House of Representatives. 83rd Congress. Second Session. Washington, 1954, pp. 216–26, 312–17, 389–90, 428–31. Arumäe H 1989 *Molotovi-Ribbentropi paktist baaside lepinguni,* Tallinn, Urbšys J 1989 Lithuania and the Soviet Union 1939–40 *Lituanus* **35**: 36–40.

in hostile countries that Germany had exerted pressure on Lithuania to attack Vilna. Had the Lithuanian government abandoned its neutrality and occupied Vilna during the first week or so of the war, the Soviet Union would have been placed in a quandary, for such an action would have been perfectly compatible with the secret agreement ('the interest of Lithuania in the Vilna territory is recognised by both parties') and yet would have fuelled Stalin's suspicions of aggressive and malevolent German intentions.

It is worth noting the existence in the German foreign office archives of a draft defence treaty (dated 20 September) which would have placed Lithuania under the protection of the Reich. On 25 September, the very day when Stalin upped his demands for a solution of the Baltic question, Hitler sent a directive to the supreme commander of the German armed forces, ordering him to maintain sufficient forces in East Prussia in readiness for a speedy occupation of Lithuania. Three days later, however, the German foreign minister Joachim von Ribbentrop agreed in Moscow to an additional secret protocol which assigned Lithuania to the Soviet sphere of interest. Although Ribbentrop was clearly anxious to avoid any friction creeping into a relationship which he had done so much to achieve, it is nonetheless hard to believe that the German foreign minister travelled to Moscow simply to negotiate away eastern Poland and Lithuania in return for the Suwałki strip. The German claim to this strip of territory caused Ribbentrop no little embarrassment, as Molotov was able to use this in the talks with the Lithuanian delegation on 3 October to contrast the great generosity of the Soviet Union in returning Vilna to the Lithuanians with the meanness of the Germans. To save themselves further embarrassment, the Germans had to inform the Lithuanian government on 5 October that they did not regard the question of frontier revision as urgent.[5]

On the evidence available, it would seem that the Germans offered no hope of assistance to Estonia or Latvia, and that ruling circles in Estonia at least appeared to have resigned themselves to accepting some sort of Soviet protection before Selter's visit to Moscow.[6] It is

5. For the relevant documents, see: *DGFP*, vol. 7, p. 450, 467: vol. 8, pp. 38–9, 54–6, 62–3, 75, 83–4, 112, 135, 159–61. Seidl A (ed.) 1949 *Die Beziehungen zwischen Deutschland und der Sowjetunion 1939–1941,* Tübingen, pp. 120–39. The Germans eventually renounced their claims to the Suwałki strip in return for 7.5 million dollars, paid in gold and non-ferrous metals by the new Soviet masters of Lithuania. Sužiedelis S 1989 The Molotov-Ribbentrop pact and the Baltic states *Lituanus* **35**: 8–46.

6. This is the conclusion reached by Ilmjärv M 1993 *Nõukogude Liidu ja Saksamaa vahel. Balti riigid ja Soome 1934–1940,* Tallinn, p. 70.

tempting to speculate whether a less crushingly negative German response to Estonian soundings at the end of August might not have stiffened the resolve of the Estonian government to hold out for a better deal from the Soviet Union a month later. This in turn might have given Ribbentrop a much better bargaining hand over Lithuania and the Polish frontier; at the very least, it would have thrown the Soviet side on to the defensive. It would certainly have increased Soviet suspicions of German bad faith, and this leads one to suppose that the Germans – or Ribbentrop – deemed this to be an unwarrantable risk at the time. One can also conclude, albeit with the benefit of hindsight, that this was a miscalculation, that it might have made better sense for Ribbentrop to have tested the extent to which Stalin and Molotov were willing to give way in order to uphold the non-aggression pact.

The government-controlled press in all three Baltic states professed satisfaction with the pacts, which, in the words of Professor Ants Piip, the new Estonian foreign minister, allowed the nation to enjoy complete liberty and independence plus the benefits of peace, thanks to a cordial and trustworthy relationship with their great eastern neighbour. In private, opinion varied. Gratified at the restoration of Vilna/Vilnius to Lithuanian rule, foreign minister Urbšys was initially inclined to view the future optimistically. Piip's predecessor Kaarel Selter and his Latvian counterpart Vilhelms Munters were more pessimistic; neither man was able to foresee how long his country would be able to retain its independence. A mood of despondency sapped the already weakened morale of government ministers. High-ranking officials in Estonia, for example, aware of their own impotence, seemed to have pinned their hopes on being rescued by Germany.[7]

Given their inability to coordinate defence plans and strategy during the years of peace, the three Baltic states had little option but to agree

7. See for example Selter's comment on 26 September: 'the stronger Germany is in the East, the better it will be for us'. Arumäe 1989, p. 144, and the report of the German minister on 29 September that 'informed persons . . . regard Germany as the only power which by its weight saved the country from Soviet Russian pressure and which is alone capable of giving this protection in the future as well': *DGFP*, vol. 8, pp. 174–5. According to the Estonian scholar Magnus Ilmjärv, Berlin continued to hint to the Estonians that Germany's economic interests would help keep the Soviet Union in check, and that the Soviet bases in the Baltic states would only be a temporary phenomenon (personal communication to the author, March 1993). On reactions in the Baltic states, see Ilmjärv M 1993 Veel Balti liidu moodustamisest ja Eesti välispoliitilisest orientatsioonist *Looming* **8**: 1107–19, and Myllyniemi S 1977 *Baltian kriisi 1938–1941*, Helsinki, pp. 75–86.

to the Soviet demands in the hopes that this would buy them enough time in which circumstances might change for the better.[8] The Finns found themselves in a rather better negotiating position when their turn came in mid-October. In the first instance, the Soviet Union had already served notice of its demands in the spring of 1938, as Finland was contemplating joint action with Sweden for the defence of the Åland islands. Nothing had come of this initiative, and the Soviet terms presented to the Finnish negotiators in October 1939 were a good deal tougher. They were nevertheless presented in a reasonably cordial atmosphere, and the Finns were also treated more as equal negotiating partners than as contemptible weaklings to be bullied into submission. The room for compromise on either side proved, however, to be extremely limited. By mid-November, the talks in Moscow had broken down; the Finnish government refused to accept the establishment of bases in the Gulf of Finland or a readjustment of the frontier in the Karelian isthmus, which the Soviet side adamantly demanded as vital elements in their security system. After a short period of silence, the Soviet press launched a concerted campaign of attack against the 'imperialist lackeys' of the Finnish government. On 30 November, using a stage-managed border incident as a pretext, Red Army units began crossing the frontier. The next day, a puppet government headed by the veteran exile and senior official of the Comintern, Otto Ville Kuusinen, was set up in the border town of Terijoki. On 2 December, a mutual assistance treaty between this government and the USSR was concluded, giving the Soviet Union all it had demanded in the autumn negotiations in return for the unification of the western regions of Soviet Karelia with a future People's Republic of Finland.[9]

8. On the security policies of the Baltic states, see: Vardys and Misiunas 1978, pp. 97–135, Hiden J and Salmon P 1991 *The Baltic nations and Europe* London, pp. 59–106; Hiden J and Lane T (eds) 1991 *The Baltic and the origins of the Second World War,* Cambridge; Ilmjärv M 1992 Balti liidu loomine, tegevuse ja pankrot *Looming* **9**: 1249–60.

9. Details of the negotiations in: Upton A 1974 *Finland 1939–1940,* London, pp. 26–46; Nissen H (ed.) 1983 *Scandinavia during the Second World War,* Oslo and Minneapolis, pp. 62–5. The events of the November-December 1939 have recently been the subject of much re-evaluation, especially on the Soviet side, and there are some interesting contributions in: Vihavainen T (ed.) 1991 Talvisota, *Venäjä ja Suomi* Historiallinen Arkisto **95**, Helsinki, pp. 89–315. Jussila O 1985 *Terijoen hallitus 1939–1940,* Helsinki, argues that the Kuusinen government was not hastily improvised, but part of Stalin's strategy towards Finland, which, had it been successful, would have created the first of the people's republics; in other words, Finland would not have been annexed to the Soviet Union, like the Baltic states.

The war which ensued, fought in the bitter cold of a northern winter, assumed epic proportions in the columns of the world's press, starved of news from the major war front. The advance of the Red Army was halted and thousands of ill-equipped Soviet troops killed or captured by the white-clad Finnish soldiers; by the end of December, the invasion had ground to a halt. Stalin's response to this setback was to replace his commanders, and send in reinforcements. Gradually, the superior and concentrated firepower deployed on the Karelian isthmus in the early weeks of 1940 wore down the Finnish resistance. The situation was saved by a combination of circumstances, not least the readiness of Stalin to abandon his puppets in Terijoki at the end of January and open up negotiations in Stockholm with representatives of the true Finnish government. His motives for doing so are almost as unclear as his intentions towards Finland in autumn 1939. Stormclouds in Asia and Europe undoubtedly encouraged him to settle quickly a war which had proved a costly mistake. The threatened intervention of France and Britain on Finland's behalf (although the plans for intervention were really intended to deprive Germany of Swedish iron ore) may also have persuaded Stalin to negotiate a peace settlement. The Finnish government, well aware that military defeat was only a matter of time and not convinced by Allied promises of aid, finally agreed to talk peace on 5 March 1940. As the Allied powers continued to urge the Finns to issue the appeal for aid which would allow them to land troops in northern Europe – and as Hitler was setting the timetable for a German invasion of Norway – peace was signed in Moscow on 13 March.[10]

Within three months of the signing of that peace, the situation in northern Europe had dramatically changed. On 9 April, German troops occupied Denmark after minimum resistance and invaded Norway, where fighting lasted another two months. In May, the German armed forces launched their attack westward, driving through Belgium and Northern France to the Channel ports. Hitler's *Blitzkrieg* in the west gave Stalin the opportunity to consolidate his grip on the hapless Baltic states. The first in line this time was Lithuania. Complaints were lodged on 25 May that two Russian soldiers had

10. On the campaigns of the Winter War, see: Tillotson H 1993 *Finland at peace and war 1918–1993*, Wilby, pp. 121–75. On Allied plans for intervention: Nevakivi J 1976 *The appeal that was never made*, London, and Nissen 1983, pp. 71–84. The diplomatic manoeuvres of the war are also dealt with by Upton 1974 and Jakobson M 1961 *The diplomacy of the Winter War*, Cambridge, Mass. See also the special issue of *Revue internationale d'histoire militaire* **62** (1985): entitled: *Aspects of security: the case of independent Finland*.

been kidnapped. Attempts by the Lithuanian government to comply with Soviet demands proved of no avail; on 15 June, an ultimatum calling for the creation of a government capable of fulfilling the terms of the 1939 treaty and the admission of more Red Army units was handed to Juozas Urbšys in Moscow. The protests of the Lithuanian foreign minister, in his own words, were 'like peas thrown against the wall'. Molotov was adamant. Whatever the reply, 'the army will march into Lithuania tomorrow.'[11] President Smetona having transferred temporary authority to prime minister Merkys and removed himself to Germany, the remaining members of the government bowed to Moscow's demands, as did the governments of Estonia and Latvia after receiving similar notes on 16 June. To reinforce the message, sizeable contingents of troops and armoured vehicles were sent into the three countries, arriving in Riga even before Stalin's emissary Andrey Vyshinsky. The task of these high-ranking emissaries (V. G. Dekanozov in Kaunas, Andrey Zhdanov in Tallinn) was to supervise the formation of popular front-type governments and to oversee the stage management of popular 'revolutions'. Elections were hurriedly arranged and held in July, after all likely sources of opposition had been stifled by arrests, deportations and much chicanery, and the docile assemblies duly elected voted on 21–22 July to apply for admission to the USSR, a request granted by the Supreme Soviet at the beginning of August.[12]

The patent inability of the League of Nations and collective security to stop aggression had caused the northern European states, one by one, to abandon their commitment to article 16 of the League Covenant and to turn to neutrality as the best form of protection. The Scandinavian kingdoms had managed to survive as neutral states throughout the First World War, and clearly hoped to be able to do so again. This time, only Sweden escaped direct involvement, though its neutrality was seriously compromised by the arrangements made with Germany in summer 1941 for the transit of troops from Norway to Finland.[13] Scandinavia was drawn into the war for economic and strategic reasons; Germany wished to forestall any Allied moves to cut off iron-ore supplies and sought to secure the Norwegian coastline for

11. Urbšys 1989, p. 62. *Third Interim Report* 1954, pp. 321–37. Myllyniemi 1977, pp. 136–40.

12. On the events of June-July 1940, see: Myllyniemi 1977, pp. 138–57, and more recently, Hyytiä O 1992 *Viron Kohtalontie 1933 . . . 1939 . . . 1940*, Helsinki. *1940 god v Estonii*, Tallinn, 1989, contains a wide range of documentary material.

13. Nissen 1983, pp. 98–181. Carlgren W 1977 *Swedish foreign policy during the Second World War*, London. Sweden had also been accommodating to German demands for increased deliveries of iron ore in the summer of 1940.

its naval operations in the Atlantic. The attack on northern Norway was regarded as a foolhardy venture by many German officers, and the secret opposition to Hitler hoped that it would prove his undoing; the occupation of Denmark also puzzled contemporaries, since it seemed to bring no advantage to Germany. Hitler did not seek the kind of political solution favoured by Stalin, preferring initially to seek the cooperation of existing authorities. The withdrawal into exile of the king and government made this difficult in Norway, where a *Reichskommissar* was installed on 24 April 1940; in Denmark, on the other hand, the government remained in office and pursued a policy of cooperation with the Germans until 1943.

WAR IN THE EAST, 1941–1945

In contrast to the Führer's wild dreams of global domination, Stalin set himself the more attainable goal of extending the security zone of the Soviet state. The staging of the 'revolutionary' charades in the Baltic states was necessary to justify the *raison d'être* of the Soviet state, and to reaffirm the ideological legitimacy of the 1917 revolution. The disintegration of the old political order and the generally demoralised state of the populace made the task of Stalin's henchmen that much easier. There were many who hoped for something better, or who believed that some vestiges of independence would remain.[14] The brief period of Soviet rule, before German troops overran the Baltic countries, did nothing to strengthen such hopes. As Molotov bluntly told Vincas Krėvė–Mickevičius, a liberal who had taken the post of foreign minister in the new Lithuanian government: 'Your Lithuania along with the other Baltic nations, including Finland, will have to join the glorious family of the Soviet Union. Therefore you should begin now to initiate your people into the Soviet system, which in the future shall reign everywhere, throughout all Europe.'[15] The new

14. Kalnins B 1950 *De baltiska staternas frihetskamp*, Stockholm, pp. 227–8; Sabaliūnas L 1972 *Lithuania in crisis 1939–1940*, Bloomington, Ill., pp. 185–201. Left-wing Jews were particularly prominent in their support for the new order, and pro-communist organisations campaigned actively in the 1940 elections: Levin D 1975 The Jews and the Sovietisation of Latvia, 1940–1941 *Soviet Jewish Affairs* **5**: 39–56; Levin D 1980 The Jews and the election campaigns in Lithuania, 1940–41 *Soviet Jewish Affairs* **10**: 39–51.

15. *Third Interim Report* 1954, p. 342. The minister, who tried to resign from the government on his return home, told the British minister on 5 July that: 'the incorporation of Lithuania in the USSR in the immediate future had been decided upon'. FO 371/24761, *Public Record Office* London.

citizens of the Soviet Union, faced with an overall deterioration in living standards and having to cope with a weekly barrage of new orders and instructions designed to accommodate them to the Soviet system, were rather less enthusiastic. 'The feelings of the Estonian people', reported an official from the British embassy in Moscow, who visited Tallinn in September 1940, 'are at present a mixture of apathetic resignation to their fate, forlorn hope for an ultimate delivery by Great Britain or Germany, fear of the OGPU, contempt for their conquerors, and bitter regret that they did not, like the Finns, make a bid for freedom.'[16]

The Germans launched their attack on the Soviet Union in the early hours of 22 June, 1941, on a front stretching from the Baltic to the Black Sea. Within three days, the Red Army had been driven out of most of Lithuania; Riga fell to the Germans on 1 July; only in northern Estonia and on the offshore islands, which were held until the autumn, was there any noticeable resistance to the German advance. Barely a week before the German attack, thousands had been rounded up and deported to Russia in what seems to have been a carefully prepared operation aimed specifically at key social and economic groups such as large landowners, army officers or high-ranking civil servants. The deportations disrupted the activities of the nationalist resistance movement in Lithuania. Nevertheless, the Lithuanian Activist Front moved into action on the day of the invasion, and within two days, a provisional government had been set up in Kaunas. This government was, however, cold-shouldered by the Germans as soon as it became apparent that it was not willing to abandon its aim of restoring the independence of Lithuania. Lithuanian partisans were disarmed, martial law was imposed, and the provisional government dissolved in early August. The more cautious attempts of the Estonians to persuade the Germans to accept a modified restoration of sovereignty were equally in vain: a memorandum submitted by the last prime minister before the Soviet takeover, asking for an Estonian

16. Memorandum by J. W. Russell, Sept. 1940: Both Russell and Preston, the departing minister to Kaunas, commented on food shortages and high prices. Preston also discounted the rumour that Stalin had been so impressed by the cooperatives of the Baltic states that he was contemplating retaining the system as a model to be copied. He believed Stalin could not accept the implicit loss of prestige, nor could he allow history to repeat itself and risk a Decembrist revolt by troops infected with liberal ideas: 'The Soviet government will adopt the simple method of removing temptation from their soldiers' eyes by reducing the new victim countries to the same slum level as Russia itself.' FO 371/24762 *Public Record Office* London.

government and army, was ignored.[17]

The three Baltic countries and Belorussia were placed under the administrative control of Hinrich Lohse, *Reichskommissar* for the *Ostland*, with a *Generalkommissar* in each of the four territories. Native administrations headed by compliant tools of the occupying power were also set up. Lohse had to contend with rival organisations and claimants of power in the *Ostland*, such as the SS and the Baltic German Alfred Rosenberg, Reich minister for the occupied eastern territories. Both shared the long-term goal of the wholesale expulsion of the indigenous populations and massive German colonisation of territories to be annexed to the Reich. The war against the Soviet Union had overriding priority, however, which meant that such grandiose plans were never put into practice. Instead, the Germans ruthlessly exploited all available resources, conscripting and directing labour to the Reich, setting up military units, and taking over enterprises expropriated by the Soviet regime. Their racial arrogance precluded any serious attempt to win the confidence and support of the indigenous population. Deportations, death and exile had decimated the political and cultural leadership, and although some steps were taken in 1944 to create national resistance councils and provisional governments, these were steamrollered by the armies and virtually ignored by the western Allied powers.

The German attack on the Soviet Union was undoubtedly seen by many in the Baltic states as a deliverance; but it also gave some an opportunity to vent their spleen against the Jewish population. One of the worst massacres occurred in Kaunas, where over 30,000 Jews lived, but there were pogroms in other Lithuanian and Latvian towns. Traditional anti-semitism was fuelled by resentment against supposed Jewish treachery and collaboration with the hated Soviet regime. It is certainly true that Jews during the Soviet period did gain access to jobs in the public domain to which they had hitherto been denied entry; it is equally true that Jewish entrepreneurs and all who did not or could not accommodate to the new order suffered in equal measure with the rest of the population. In Lithuania, there were Jewish ministers in the government and a substantial number in certain departments, such as the ministry of commerce and the prosecutor's office. This, however, owed more to the lack of qualified Lithuanians than to any

17. Myllyniemi S 1973 *Die Neuordnung der baltischen Länder, 1941–1944* Historiallisia Tutkimuksia **90**, Helsinki. Misiunas R and Taagepera R 1983 *The Baltic states: Years of dependence 1940–1980*, London, pp. 44–58. Budreckis A 1968 *The Lithuanian national revolt of 1941*, Boston.

enlightened policy by the new regime.[18] In the run-up to the 1940 elections, the communists made the elimination of anti-semitism a major issue. Jewish communal leaders were given assurances that their activities would be allowed to continue; and although there was hostility towards the right-wing *Agudas Yisroel*, secular Zionist organisations were generally left alone. As soon as the elections were over, however, the dissolution of non-communist organisations began, and leaders of the Jewish community such as Mordecai Dubin, the head of *Agudas Yisroel* in Latvia, and David Varhaftig, the leader of the revisionist *Betar* youth movement, were arrested. A number of officially suppressed Zionist organisations continued to operate, collecting and coordinating information on Jewish culture and about Palestine; Vilna, whose prewar Jewish population of 50,000 was swollen by up to 30,000 refugees, became a major centre of Zionist activity. Many of these activists were picked up and deported to Siberia in June 1941. Accurate figures are hard to establish; what is beyond doubt is that much of the leadership was removed, leaving the remaining community – already weakened by the dissolution of many of its traditional organisations, and caught up in the increasingly difficult business of getting by – defenceless and leaderless in the face of rising chaos as the German armies advanced.[19]

The peoples of the Baltic countries were caught helplessly in the crossfire as war erupted on the eastern front; the Finns, having preserved their independence, now found themselves fighting alongside Germany in what they called the 'Continuation War'. In many ways, the experience of the Winter War had served to draw the nation together and to help heal old wounds. If the spirit of unanimity

18. In May 1941, for example, the Lithuanian communist party central committee resolved, with regard to the ministry of commerce, 'to take urgent steps to purge the administration of alien elements, and to promote new cadres from among the workers'. Levin D 1980 The Jews in the Soviet Lithuanian establishment, 1940–41 *Soviet Jewish Affairs* **10**, p. 24. When the Lithuanian communist party was legalised in 1940, Jews constituted at least a third of the membership. In January 1941, this had fallen to 15 per cent, although five of the 21-member central committee were Jewish.

19. In addition to the articles by Dov Levin (cited above), see also: Gordon F 1990 *Latvians and Jews between Germany and Russia*, Stockholm. In contrast to Gordon's rather sympathetic portrayal of the Latvians, a survivor of the Kaunas ghetto, Avraham Tory, has little good to say about the Lithuanians. Tory A 1990 *Surviving the Holocaust*, Cambridge, Mass. Of the large, bustling and vibrant prewar Jewish communities of Riga, Kaunas and Vilna, few survived and little remained by the end of 1944. The Jews of Denmark were more fortunate; warned in advance via a member of the staff of the German plenipotentiary Werner von Best that the order for their deportation was imminent, over 7,000 managed to escape, hidden and helped across to Sweden. Fewer than 500 were rounded up and sent to Theresienstadt concentration camp.

and reconciliation was perhaps less wholehearted than is commonly believed, survival of the ordeal did much to strengthen the ties of national identity.[20] The losses sustained in the fighting (25,000 killed, 45,000 wounded) and the surrender to the Soviet Union of the Karelian isthmus, including the town of Viipuri, were a severe blow. In addition to returning to a peacetime footing in a world at war, the Finns had to accommodate over 400,000 refugees from the ceded territories. This and the other onerous burdens of reconstruction were tackled with much resolve and determination. The disturbing turn of events in Scandinavia and the Baltic states, however, meant that Finland's security remained a top priority. Moscow had torpedoed any plans for a Nordic defence union at the end of the Winter War, and viewed with suspicion the prospect of Swedish-Finnish collaboration over the defence of the Åland islands. At the end of June 1940, the Soviet Union presented a series of demands, including the demilitarisation of the islands and transit rights for troop-trains to the leased base at Hanko. The timing of these demands, accompanied by cries from the left-wing Finnish-Soviet Peace and Friendship Society for a new government capable of forging close and cordial relations with the USSR, was particularly worrying, coming as the last vestiges of independence were being snuffed out in the Baltic states. Hitler's victory speech to the *Reichstag* on 19 July seemed to rule out any hopes of German support for Finland; the Führer appeared to be as committed as ever to the Nazi-Soviet pact.

The Finns had good reason to fear the intentions of the Soviet Union in summer 1940, though it would appear that Moscow was trying to force the Finns to accede to its security demands, and was not planning a Baltic-style takeover. Unbeknown to the Finns and the equally anxious Swedes, Hitler had already set in motion the first moves which were to lead to war with Russia a year later. In August, a transit agreement allowing passage for German troops through Finland to northern Norway was concluded amidst much secrecy. This agreement was greeted with relief by Finnish army officers as a sign that Hitler was now moving away from cold neutrality and would bring Finland into the German orbit. From December 1940, when the plan to destroy Soviet Russia was authorised by Hitler, the contacts between the German and Finnish military increased significantly, although details of the Barbarossa plan were never revealed to the

20. A critical look at aspects of the Winter War is offered by the various contributors to: *Tuntematon talvisota* Helsingin yliopiston poliittisen historian laitos, Helsinki 1989.

Finns. Plans for closer cooperation between Sweden and Finland under consideration in Stockholm and Helsinki were given short shrift both in Berlin and in Moscow, thereby reducing Finland's options still further. The more conciliatory attitude adopted by the Soviet Union in the spring of 1941 was too late; Finland's course was already being steered parallel to that of Germany. High-level military discussions took place in Germany and Finland between 25 May and 5 June 1941. The inner circle within the Finnish government and the commander-in-chief, Marshal Mannerheim, were prepared to go along with German suggestions for the mobilisation of Finnish forces and to allow large numbers of German troops to move through northern Finland in preparation for their attack towards Murmansk, but they would not initiate hostilities, nor would they allow the Germans to do so from Finnish territory. Should these conditions not be realised, Germany undertook to guarantee Finland's independence and to support the demand for the restoration of the 1939 frontiers in the event of diplomatic pressure from the Soviet Union.[21]

Informed of the date of the attack a bare three days earlier, and embarrassed by Hitler's statement on the outbreak of hostilities that the Germans were operating in alliance (*im Bunde*) with the Finns, the Finnish government hastened to proclaim that Finland was not at war, in spite of the mobilisation of the armed forces which had been taking place over the previous days and the mining of Soviet coastal waters which began immediately after hostilities commenced. German bombers from East Prussia landed on Finnish airfields after attacking Leningrad, and there were other clear indications that Finnish neutrality was less than absolute. The Soviet Union retaliated with a series of air attacks on Finnish towns on 25 June, thereby allowing the government to claim Finland was obliged to renew its defensive struggle. Finland's fight was now, however, linked to the anti-Bolshevik crusade launched by Germany.

The Finnish armed forces in the summer of 1941 were better equipped, thanks mainly to the Germans, larger and better prepared for war than had been the case in 1939. The offensive launched in July advanced rapidly into Karelia, on a front depleted of troops drawn off to stem the main German advance further south. By the end of August, the old frontiers had been regained. This success was achieved at the cost of straining the nation's resources to the uttermost. Well

21. Upton A 1964 *Finland in crisis 1940–1941*, London. Carlgren 1977, pp. 73–113. Nissen (ed.) 1983, pp. 139–81. For a recent overview of the 'interim peace' see Hietänen S (ed.) 1989 *Kansakunta sodassa,* 3 vols, Helsinki, vol. 1, pp. 264–90.

aware of this, Mannerheim refused to accede to Hitler's request to commit his forces to the siege of Leningrad, though he did order an advance into East Karelia, in anticipation of meeting up with the Germans on the river Svir'. The Germans were never able to reach that rendezvous; further north, on the Lapland front, their offensive also ran into difficulties. The Swedish government, which had been pressured into concessions in June, refused at the end of July to permit the transit of an Alpine division, which subsequently arrived too late at the front to be effective. Finnish forces fighting on the German flank also made slow progress, and an attack intended to cut the vital railway line to Murmansk was halted, partly as a response to fears of Allied reactions.

Finnish casualties during the autumn offensive were high, and the country as a whole underwent a severe crisis in the winter of 1941–42 as supplies dwindled to alarmingly low levels. The initial euphoria as lost territories were regained was replaced by a mood of uncertainty and confusion, not helped by the government's failure to define clearly and unambiguously Finland's war aims. Mannerheim's refusal to join in the siege of Leningrad or to overcommit his troops against the Murmansk railway was intended to demonstrate the separate nature of Finland's war, though he also had sound military and logistic reasons on his side. It was not easy for the Western Allies to accept the 'separate war' argument; although the Americans kept open diplomatic channels until the summer of 1944, the British government was persuaded by Stalin to declare war on Finland at the end of 1941. The Finns weakened their case for fighting a purely defensive war against Soviet aggression by their evident collusion with the Germans, and by their occupation of East Karelia. This was justified to the Allies as a security measure; but as early as February 1941, president Ryti had given his blessing to scholarly investigations designed to show that East Karelia 'belonged' ethnologically and economically to Finland, an argument which influential nationalist organisations such as the Academic Karelia Society had been promoting for years.

Plans for the administration of the East Karelia region were drawn up in July 1941, and a meeting at Vuokkiniemi on 20 July, ostensibly to indicate the wish of the Karelian people to be united with Finland, was stage-managed by the Finnish army HQ's intelligence section. Of the population that remained in East Karelia, only half were Finnish-Karelian, and their response to efforts to inculcate Finnish values through elementary education or conversion to Lutheranism was lukewarm. The Russian population was subjected to discriminatory measures; low rates of pay for compulsory labour, and inadequate rations. By the beginning of 1942, 24,000 Russians had been placed in internment camps. Malnutrition and disease contributed in 1942 to the alarmingly high death rate in the camps, and obliged the authorities, worried about the bad image this was creating abroad, to begin releasing internees. There was some partisan activity, largely organised from unoccupied territory; but in general, the population remained passive and unresponsive to the propaganda battle waged by both sides.

The plight of the Ingrians was even more poignant, caught as they were in the midst of the battlefield around the besieged city of Leningrad. It is thought that half of those trapped with the other civilians in the city of Leningrad and the Oranienbaum enclave perished during the siege, and most of the rest were evacuated to Siberia. The Finnish government was initially unwilling to accept German plans to evacuate the Ingrians who remained behind their lines, and over 6,000 perished of cold and hunger during the first winter of the war. Relief supplies were organised in spring 1942 at the request of the Finnish government, and some evacuation to Estonia took place. By October 1943, as the German grip on Leningrad was broken, full-scale evacuation of the region was under way. In all, 63,000 were shipped to Finland, where they were first placed in quarantine camps and then sent to work on farms throughout the southern half of the country. In spite of the professions of ethnic solidarity which had for years been emblazoned on the banners of nationalist organisations, these refugees were offered little prospect of permanent residence in Finland, much less citizenship or land. The armistice agreement signed by Finland in September 1944 demanded the return of all Soviet citizens who had been interned or forcibly taken to Finland, but it would appear that the Soviet side accepted that the Ingrians had come to Finland of their own free will. Nonetheless, considerable pressure was brought to bear by Soviet officials, who persuaded an additional 10,000 to join the 40,000 who had already expressed the wish to return. In all, some 55,000 went back; a few thousand fled to Sweden, and 3,748 remained in Finland. Those who returned were not allowed back to their native villages, but were settled elsewhere in central Russia.[22]

22. On the Finnish occupation of East Karelia, see: Laine A 1982 *Suur-Suomen kahdet kasvot. Itä-Karjalan siviiliväestön asema suomalaisessa miehityshallinnossa,* Helsinki, and Kulomaa J 1989 *Äänislinna. Petroskoin suomalaismiehityksen vuodet 1941–1944* Historiallisia Tutkimuksia **148**, Helsinki. On the fate of the Ingrians, Nevalainen P and Sihvo H 1991 *Inkeri*, Helsinki, pp. 267–99.

The case of the Ingrians is one of the more distressing episodes of 'ethnic cleansing'. The Baltic Germans appeared to be rather more fortunate in that they were favoured with the Führer's protection, and returned to the bosom of the fatherland their ancestors had left centuries before. In fact, the *Umsiedlung* of 1939–41 destroyed a historic community and offered very little; the resettlement of the Baltic Germans in Warthegau, the territory carved out of the western provinces of the former Polish state, was not a success. The non-German population of these conquered territories were subjected to the whole gamut of Nazi racialist policies; deportation, forced labour, and for hundreds of thousands, a miserable death in the concentration camps. The occupiers were not even able to carry out their brutal policies with any consistency; the exigencies of the war situation tended to override everything else, which meant the shelving and ultimate abandonment of plans for resettlement. Like robber barons jealously guarding their fiefs, the administrators of the occupied and incorporated territories interpreted directives as they thought fit. Albert Forster, the *Gauleiter* of Danzig and West Prussia, was, for example, notoriously lax in his application of the strict criteria for the classification of ethnic Germans devised by his erstwhile rival, the *Gauleiter* of Posen and the Warthegau, and endorsed by Himmler. He was moved less by any generosity towards the Poles and Kashubians (whom he believed could be easily germanised) than by hatred of outside interference. Similarly, Forster was reluctant to accept settlers or to employ local ethnic Germans in the administration of West Prussia, preferring to appoint his Nazi party cronies from Danzig.[23]

The average German resident of Danzig or Königsberg was rarely confronted directly with the evil and inhumane treatment meted out by the Nazis and their minions during the years of occupation, though it cannot be doubted that most had some inkling of what went on behind the barbed wire of the Stutthof camp, or were aware of people disappearing, and of the evident malnourishment of the gangs of Polish or Ukrainian labourers on their streets. In the terrible winter of 1944–45, they were brought face to face with the disaster into which the Führer – who had been welcomed on the streets of Danzig by huge, flag-waving crowds a mere five years earlier – had led them. As

23. Levine H 1969 Local authority and the SS state: the conflict over population policy in Danzig-West Prussia, 1939–1945 *Central European Affairs* **2**: 331–55. Tighe 1990, pp. 154–77. Boszat M 1963 *Zweihundert Jahre deutsche Polenpolitik*, Munich, pp. 213–42. On the removal of the Baltic Germans: Hehn J von 1982 *Die Umsiedlung der baltischen Deutschen* Marburger Ostforschungen **40**, Marturg.

the Red Army advanced on Berlin, pillaging and raping without mercy, huge numbers of refugees choked the roads, adding still further to the millions of displaced persons scattered across the entire continent.

The sheer volume of numbers of those who perished or suffered frightful deprivations as a result of war and occupation is so overwhelming as to make any attempt at description or enumeration futile. It must, however, be said that although thousands of Nazi war criminals have been brought to book, and thousands more investigated, tried, imprisoned and in some cases shot for acts of collaboration in the countries occupied by the Germans, the crimes against humanity committed by Stalin's henchmen, often against the most loyal communists or the most innocuous sections of the Soviet population, have gone almost entirely unpunished.

THE END OF THE WAR IN NORTHERN EUROPE

As the fortunes of war swung decisively against Germany in 1943, the inner circle of ministers who were largely responsible for Finland's war effort began to look for ways to detach their country from its partner-in-arms. Although the Soviet Union let it be known that it would respect Finland's continued independence, Stalin was not prepared to abandon the territorial gains made in 1940, and all efforts to get talks started soon ran into the sand. The Red Army offensive towards Narva in January 1944 left the Finnish forces on the Karelian isthmus dangerously exposed; the air raids on Helsinki and other southern Finnish towns a month later underlined the perilous position Finland was now in. With Mannerheim urging the government to negotiate, and with the discreet encouragement of the Swedish government, Paasikivi went once more to Moscow, only to learn that the Russians had increased their demands. These terms were rejected, though the Finnish government indicated its willingness to continue peace talks. These activities could not be concealed from the Germans, who were already irritated by criticisms of their actions in the Finnish press. In April 1944, grain deliveries to Finland were suspended and the export of all but the most essential armaments was discontinued, and not resumed until three days after the Red Army launched its offensive on the Karelian isthmus.

By the end of June, the Finnish army had been driven back behind Viipuri, and the order had been given to withdraw troops from East

Karelia to form a reserve defence. The Soviet government called upon the Finns to surrender; Ribbentrop, who flew to Helsinki on 22 June, offered to ensure further supplies of vitally-needed arms and equipment in return for a politically binding treaty. After much agonising, president Ryti managed to satisfy Ribbentrop with a personal undertaking that Finland would not negotiate a separate peace. This gave Finland a much-needed breathing space, and also a way out; with the threat of imminent disaster averted, Ryti resigned to make way for the *Eduskunta* to elect Mannerheim as president. Mannerheim informed the Germans that he did not consider himself bound by the agreement made by his predecessor, and established contact with the Soviet government via Sweden. The terms of the armistice agreed to by the *Eduskunta* on 19 September were severe. In addition to the restoration of the 1940 frontier and the surrender of the Petsamo region on the Arctic coast, Finland had to disarm and expel the German forces still in the country, and agree to pay a hefty reparations bill within six years. The Soviet Union also secured a fifty-year lease on a naval base at Porkkala, just to the west of Helsinki. Finland nevertheless avoided occupation by Soviet troops, and was able to fulfil the most urgent military requirements of the armistice without undue difficulty. The Germans had drawn up contingency plans in the spring of 1944 to hold only those areas deemed strategically important – northern Lapland, the Åland islands and Suursaari in the Gulf of Finland – in the event of Finland withdrawing from the war. These plans were put into operation in September 1944. The Germans attempted to storm the island of Suursaari on 15 September, but were repulsed by Finnish forces. This precipitate action helped ease the transition from co-belligerency to hostilities, though the Finnish armed forces in Lapland played a tacitly agreed series of 'autumn manoeuvres' with the retreating Germans before fighting broke out. It was not until April 1945 that the last German forces were pushed out of Finnish Lapland.[24]

Finland was heavily dependent on German deliveries of food and weapons, as the crisis of summer 1944 revealed, but it was by no means an obedient satellite. The Germans did little to prevent Mannerheim withdrawing his country from the war; the minister to Helsinki had quickly disabused Ribbentrop of any notion of trying to stage a pro-German coup; the leadership and the men were simply lacking. With the political leadership of Germany in disarray as the

24. On the last stages of the war, see: Polvinen T 1986 *Between East and West: Finland in international politics, 1944–1947*, Minneapolis.

bastions of 'Fortress Europe' began to crumble (Hitler himself was badly shaken by the attempt on his life on 20 July), the army chiefs preferred to withdraw their troops for the defence of Germany rather than risk them in a futile attempt to force Finland to remain in the war.

The Finnish 'peace opposition' which emerged in 1943 helped keep open lines of communication with the Western Allies via Sweden, but in the end, it was to the aged commander-in-chief, Marshal Mannerheim that the *Eduskunta* turned for salvation. Mannerheim was not an adept politician, and he was slow to recognise the need for change. In November 1944, he was persuaded to turn to the veteran conservative J. K. Paasikivi to form the third government under his presidency, and after much argument, Paasikivi managed to force Mannerheim to agree to communist representation in the government. With the exception of Mannerheim, who resigned the presidency in 1946 for health reasons (and who feared that the Soviet Union might demand that proceedings be taken against him as well as those accused of war guilt), the Finnish wartime leadership did not survive Finland's defeat. The most prominent, including ex-President Ryti and the social democratic leader Väinö Tanner, were tried and sentenced to terms of imprisonment by Finnish courts under the war-guilt clause of the armistice; others were advised by Paasikivi (prime minister from November 1944, president from March 1946) to withdraw from public life. A number of organisations deemed to be fascistic or anti-Soviet, such as the paramilitary *Suojeluskunta*, the Academic Karelia Society and the Patriotic People's Front (IKL), were banned; the Communist Party was legalised, political prisoners and internees released and surviving exiles (but not Otto Ville Kuusinen) allowed to return from the Soviet Union.

The effects of this scene-shifting on the political stage were less dramatic than contemporaries believed, and certainly less profound than the changes wrought in eastern Europe. The emergence of the communists from the underground, their initial electoral success under the banner of the Finnish People's Democratic Union (SKDL) and their participation in government did not break the mould of political continuity. The social democrats managed to prevent a communist takeover of their party, and fought a successful anti-communist campaign within the trade union movement. The communist leadership showed itself to be rather inept on a number of occasions, and the party itself appears to have been regarded as very much a second line of attack should president Paasikivi fail to satisfy Soviet demands. On the whole, Paasikivi succeeded remarkably well, though

Finland was probably rather less important in Stalin's overall calculations than the Finns themselves liked to believe.[25]

For neutral Sweden and occupied Denmark, 1943 also marked a turning-point. The government of Per Albin Hansson, reconstructed in December 1939 to include representatives of all the major parties, terminated the transit arrangements with Germany in the summer of 1943. This eased relations with the Allies, although Sweden continued to come under pressure to reduce the volume of its exports to Germany of vital commodities such as ball-bearings and iron ore. Sweden was increasingly called upon to provide assistance to its neighbours, acting as intermediary in the Soviet-Finnish war, providing training facilities for Danish and Norwegian police units, arranging the exchange and repatriation of prisoners, taking in refugees from east and west. The coalition government was often overly cautious, and the Swedes were harshly criticised for not doing enough, or for putting profits from exports before principles. Within Sweden itself, there was general consensus on the necessity of neutrality, but the cost of maintaining the country's defences and the many restrictions placed on civil liberties, in addition to the general niggles of coping with rationing and shortages, placed great strains upon this unanimity.

'Balancing on a tightrope', the phrase used by Wilhelm Carlgren to describe Swedish policy towards Germany, could equally well be applied to the Danish government's efforts to minimise the degree of German control during the first three years of the occupation.[26] The position adopted by the reconstituted national government in its reply to the German note of 9 April 1940 was a curious mixture of acceptance of the facts and refusal to abandon sovereignty; hence, relations with Germany were to be conducted as far as possible via the Danish foreign office, and Danish neutrality, though violated, was still to be upheld. The *ad hoc* nature of this 'policy of negotiation' enabled the Danish government to obtain some protection for its citizens – a Danish state prosecutor, and not the German police and military courts, was to investigate all suspected acts of sabotage, for example –

25. Kirby D 1979 *Finland in the twentieth century*, London, pp. 129–69.

26. Carlgren 1977, p. 125 and *passim* for details of Sweden's negotiations with the belligerents. Articles outlining some of the research undertaken in the 'Sweden during the Second World War' project are to be found in the January issue of: *Revue d'histoire de la deuxième guerre mondiale* **109** (1978). See also: Hägglöf G 1960 A test of neutrality; Sweden in the Second World War *International Affairs* **36**: 153–67. For German policies towards occupied Denmark, see: Nissen (ed.) 1983, pp. 111–15, 119–26. Thomsen E 1971 *Deutsche Besatzungspolitik in Dänemark 1940–1945* Düsseldorf.

but considerable concessions had to be made. Dissatisfaction with the composition of the government, and fears of continued Nazi-inspired unrest on the streets, brought the four major *Rigsdag* parties together in June 1940 to create a liaison committee, and led to the formation of a new coalition. Stauning remained prime minister, but Erik Scavenius, who had held the post of foreign minister during the First World War, was recalled to replace Peter Munch. Unlike his predecessor, Scavenius favoured much greater accommodation with the Germans; and it was he, rather than the depressed and sick Thorvald Stauning, who effectively determined policy. Scavenius replaced the socialist Vilhelm Buhl as prime minister in November 1942, after Christian X's terse telegram response to Hitler's birthday greetings had sparked off a crisis. Werner von Best of the SS replaced the former minister to Copenhagen as German plenipotentiary, but he too maintained the policy of cooperation in preference to working with the Danish Nazis, who managed to secure no more than 43,000 votes (2.1 per cent of the total) in the national elections held in March 1943.

The margin for cooperation was, however, steadily shrinking as resistance to the occupation grew. The communists had begun underground activities as soon as the party leadership was arrested in June 1941; the activities of communist saboteurs were nevertheless not popular with the population at large, and provoked the prime minister to broadcast in September 1942 a denunciation of such actions as against the interests of the fatherland. There were more surreptitious forms of resistance, such as the work of Danish intelligence officers in supplying information about German defences to the British, and the printing and distribution of illegal pamphlets and newspapers. The flight to London in May 1942 of the conservative leader Christmas Møller, who had been forced out of government for his anti-German utterances, helped establish the credibility of the Danish opposition in Allied circles. His radio broadcasts offered encouragement to the resistance movement, although his call for active sabotage in October 1942 was not fully accepted until the winter of 1943–44.

The acts of sabotage carried out by the SOE and the Danish resistance were far more effective in 1943 than in the previous year, culminating in the blowing up of the minelayer *Linz* in the Odense shipyards and the destruction of the Forum exhibition hall in Copenhagen. The industrial unrest which had simmered throughout the summer erupted in August in a series of uncoordinated local strikes across the country. The strikes were largely protests against German actions – countermeasures against sabotage in Esbjerg, the sentencing to death of a member of the resistance in Aalborg – and were led by local communists. They were opposed by the trade union and social democratic leadership and the government, which strove in vain to restore order. On 29 August, after the government had refused to accept Best's ultimatum for the introduction of a state of emergency and the death penalty for strikers and saboteurs, martial law was declared by General von Hanneken, commander of the German forces in Denmark, who assumed executive power and ordered the disarming and internment of the Danish armed forces. Efforts by the Germans to find a new government to replace that which had resigned proved fruitless; instead, the policy of negotiation was continued by an administration of civil servants, the permanent heads of ministries.[27]

In September 1943, the Freedom Council was set up to coordinate the activities of the resistance. It embraced a wide range of political beliefs, and defined its aims as the restoration of democracy and just punishment for all who had violated the rule of law or who had profited from the occupation. It operated without the sanction of the major political parties, whose role was now curtailed with the demise of the coalition government. With the further erosion of lawful order following the mass arrests of the police in September 1944, and more than a little alert to the possibility of a communist seizure of power, the politicians and the leaders of the Freedom Council entered into discussions, which lasted until the eve of liberation. The government formed in May 1945 contained nine members of the Council, with all four main resistance groups represented; but it was headed by Vilhelm Buhl, Stauning's successor as leader of the Social Democratic Party and as wartime prime minister in 1942, and included ten politicians from the four main parties. In general, the public preferred to stick with the familiar rather than venture into new political pastures. Although the communists did well in the October 1945 elections, largely at the expense of the social democrats, they were unable to retain this popularity, losing half of their eighteen seats in the 1947 elections. The communists had campaigned for a united party from 1943, seeking to isolate the compromised social democratic leadership and win rank-and-file support. The social democrats responded with a radical programme for peacetime, closer cooperation with the Freedom Council, and by using the communists' declared commitment to democracy as a weapon against attempts to take over the Social Democratic Party from within. None of the wartime

27. On the events of August 1943, see: Nissen (ed.) 1983, pp. 222–38. Kirchoff H 1979 *Augustoprøret 1943*, 3 vols, Copenhagen.

resistance leaders made much impact in peacetime politics. Christmas Møller, an embittered man at odds with his own party, angered Danish farmers and his colleagues in government by concluding a highly disadvantageous trade treaty with Britain. The resultant fall in the export price of bacon, butter and eggs obliged the government to increase subsidies to farmers to maintain their guaranteed prices, and probably helped boost the vote for *Venstre* in the October 1945 elections. Once the public had satisfied its need to settle with collaborators – 34,000 were taken in and interned by the resistance forces during May 1945, 13,000 were tried, mostly receiving light sentences, and 46 were executed by firing squad after the *Rigsdag* had bowed to the demand of the Freedom Council for the restoration of the death penalty – it turned to more mundane matters and away from the often rather vaguely formulated ideals of the wartime resistance. Almost 3,000 of the German minority in Denmark were sentenced for acts of collaboration, and although the Danish state continued to support the educational and cultural institutions of the minority, the wartime experience left deep scars. The pro-Danish movement which suddenly blossomed in Schleswig-Holstein in the immediate postwar years received some support in Denmark, but calls for a new referendum failed to move either the British occupation authorities or the Danish *Rigsdag*.[28] A declaration respecting the rights of the Danish minority was issued in 1949 by the Schleswig-Holstein *Landtag*, and steps were taken to reduce the numbers of those claiming Danish connections – not without concern being expressed north of the border, where fewer than 10,000 Germans could elect a member to the *Rigsdag* in 1953, whilst 42,000 voters for the Danish list south of the border failed to elect a single representative to the *Landtag*.

DIVISION

With the collapse of Germany, the entire Baltic world fell under the dominance of the power which had for centuries struggled to maintain a presence on the eastern fringes. Russian troops drove relentlessly

28. For conflicting views on this issue, see: Jürgensen K 1986 Die britische Südschleswig-Politik nach dem zweiten Weltkrieg *Zeitschrift für Gesellschaft für Schleswig-Holsteinische Geschichte* **111**: 185–205, and the reply of J. P. Noack in the same journal, vol. **112** (1987): pp. 267–82.

westward, flooding acros the north German plain to the outskirts of Lübeck, moving into northern Norway, and liberating the Danish island of Bornholm. Soviet rule was being re-established in Estonia, Latvia and Lithuania, against a desperate guerrilla resistance which lasted into the 1950s. The Soviet Union dominated the Allied Control Commission in Finland, where it maintained a military base until 1955. It wrangled with the Norwegian government over the sovereignty of the Svalbard islands in the Arctic, and with the Swedish government over the delineation of territorial waters. The Swedes also came under pressure to return refugees who had fled from the Baltic countries at the end of the war.

The options open to the Nordic countries in the atmosphere and tension of the immediate postwar years were few. The need for an effective defence force and a sound security policy after the sobering experiences of invasion and occupation was generally recognised, but there was also a reluctance to become involved in the plans for a Western military alliance, which began to take shape in 1947. Relations between the Western powers and the Soviet Union had deteriorated rapidly throughout that year, culminating in the final collapse of the foreign ministers' conference in December. At the secret meeting held in the autumn to launch the new communist international organisation, Cominform, Andrey Zhdanov spoke of the world dividing into two mutually hostile camps. Throughout eastern Europe, the communists were tightening their grip on government. On the northern periphery, there was much unease and concern about Soviet intentions. The final withdrawal of the Allied Control Commission from Finland after the peace treaty signed in Paris came into force in September 1947 did not remove the threat of further Soviet demands. On 8 July, the vice-chairman of the Allied Control Commission, General G. M. Savonenkov, had told the Finnish prime minister that Moscow expected that Finland would not attend the conference convened in Paris to discuss the Marshall plan for European economic recovery, and the Finnish government had reluctantly bowed to this pressure. Six months later, Savonenkov presented his credentials as the new Soviet ambassador to Finland, and sought an audience in the near future with the Finnish president. Rumours that Moscow intended to conclude a military pact with Finland had been circulating for some time in the West, and President Paasikivi himself well knew what the topic of the requested meeting would be. Savonenkov's pressing invitation for the septuagenarian president to travel to Moscow for talks seemed to Paasikivi analogous to the tactics used by Hitler towards President Hacha of

Czechoslovakia in 1939.[29] The idea of a military pact between Finland and the Soviet Union had in fact been discussed by Zhdanov, Mannerheim and Paasikivi in 1945, and Mannerheim had sketched out a draft of such an agreement. Stalin and Zhdanov had alluded on subsequent occasions to the desirability of a Finnish initiative on this matter; but Stalin's letter proposing talks on a mutual assistance treaty, received on 23 February 1948 by President Paasikivi, caused considerable unease. It was feared that Finland was about to be drawn completely into the Soviet sphere of influence, like Bulgaria, Rumania and Hungary, with whom the Soviet Union had recently concluded mutual assistance treaties. Increased communist agitation following visits to Moscow by the party leaders seemed to suggest that Finland might also be going the way of Czechoslovakia, where the communists had recently overthrown the government and assumed power.

The treaty of friendship, cooperation and mutual assistance which was signed in Moscow on 6 April 1948 followed the general principles publicly adumbrated by President Paasikivi in February: Finland would join forces with the Soviet Union in resisting any armed aggression against the latter via Finnish territory. The treaty provided for consultations between the two contracting parties if the threat of an armed attack 'by Germany or any states allied with the aforementioned' against Finland or the Soviet Union via Finnish territory were established.[30] On the whole, the Finnish delegation had good reason to be relieved and pleased with the way things had gone. In subsequent years, the treaty acquired quasi-canonical status in Finnish political life; all the major political parties subscribed to its maintenance, and few queried its usefulness or validity until the mid-1980s. In April 1948, however, the relief felt that Finland had escaped relatively lightly was overcast by persistent rumours of an impending communist coup. Nothing came of these rumours, which were sufficiently serious for the president and army commander to take security precautions. In reality, the Finnish communists were far weaker than their opponents. Smarting under the criticism of their Soviet mentors, and divided over strategy and tactics, they suffered a further blow with the successful completion of the treaty negotiations, on which they had hoped to rouse the masses against the obstructive

29. Blomstedt Y and Klinge M (eds) 1985 *J.K. Paasikiven päiväkirjat 1944–1956*, Porvoo-Helsinki, p. 544.

30. For the text of the 1948 treaty, see Kirby 1979, pp. 226–8. On Soviet-Finnish relations generally, see: Allison R 1985 *Finland's relations with the Soviet Union 1944–1984*, London; Maude G 1976 *The Finnish dilemma. Neutrality in the shadow of power*, London.

forces of reaction. The Finnish social democrats showed themselves far more adept at fighting back than their colleagues in eastern Europe, and there is good reason to believe that the rumours of a coup were fed, if not caused, by the Social Democratic Party leadership. In the July 1948 elections, the communist-led People's Democratic Union (SKDL) lost eleven seats, whilst the other two partners of the 'Big Three' government (the Agrarian Union and the Social Democratic Party), as well as the conservatives, registered gains. Initial attempts to maintain the coalition came to nothing, and a socialist minority government was appointed.[31]

The Prague coup, Stalin's note to Finland and rumours that Norway was about to receive a similar offer of alliance impelled the Scandinavian countries towards the creation of a joint security policy, though it also strengthened the faction in the Norwegian government that sought a strong alignment with the Western powers. In May 1948, the Swedish foreign minister Östen Undén proposed a Scandinavian defence union independent of outside powers, thereby launching a series of discussions between representatives of the three states. The alternative of Scandinavian military cooperation was seriously considered at the highest level in 1948–49, but ultimately proved unrealisable. As had been the case nearly a century before, when there had been a prospect of Scandinavian military cooperation over the Slesvig-Holstein question, national interests prevailed over notions of Nordic solidarity. The Norwegians appeared to have been playing a double game of carrying on negotiations for a defence agreement with their neighbours whilst at the same time making sure of Western support. The Swedes assumed that the other two states would raise their defence preparedness to Swedish levels; the Danes and Norwegians argued that to accomplish this would necessitate foreign assistance and hence alignment with the Western powers. The Swedes for their part were unwilling to jeopardise their neutrality, which had stood them in good stead during the war, by entering into an arrangement which might tie them to a Western military alliance. The socialist-radical coalition in Denmark sought to bridge the gap between the Norwegians and Swedes, but faced mounting criticism at home, where the liberals and conservatives favoured alignment with

31. The events of spring 1948 are considered in detail by Jussila O 1990 *Suomen tie 1944–1948*, Porvoo-Helsinki, pp. 176–252. Beyer-Thoma H 1989 *Vasemmisto ja vaaran vuodet*, Helsinki, pp. 237–97 (an edited version of the author's doctoral thesis; *Kommunisten und Sozialdemokraten in Finnland 1944–1948* Veröffentlichungen der Osteuropa-Instituts, Munich).

the Western defence alliance. On the whole, the Western powers remained sceptical about the defensive capabilities of the Scandinavian countries, much as the Russians had doubted the ability of their western neighbours to defend their neutrality in the thirties. The British ambassador to Norway, for example, feared that a Nordic defence union dominated by Sweden might easily succumb to pressure and close the Sound to Western shipping, whilst the permanent under-secretary at the foreign office Sir Orme Sargent bluntly told the Swedish ambassador that the value of such a defence alliance was 0+0+0=0.

By the time the joint defence committee set up in September 1948 presented its final report, the differences between the three negotiating states had hardened. The Swedes made it clear that they would not abandon their neutrality, and would refuse to join a Scandinavian alliance if either Norway or Denmark joined the proposed North Atlantic military alliance. The Norwegians were seriously considering such a step; Halvard Lange, the Norwegian foreign minister, visited Washington in February 1949 to ascertain the terms for entry into the Atlantic pact. The Danish ambassador reported that the Americans assumed plans for a Scandinavian defence union were now dead, and that unless the Atlantic powers were sure of Greenland's security, they were unlikely to be sympathetic or to provide assistance to Denmark. After a last-minute attempt to secure a bilateral defence agreement with Sweden had come to nothing, the Danish prime minister, Hans Hedtoft, recommended adherence to the North Atlantic Treaty, and talks with this in mind were held in Washington. The radicals maintained their opposition to the treaty, but not to the point of overthrowing the government of which they were a partner, and Denmark joined Norway in entering the North Atlantic alliance, in the spring of 1949. Both countries insisted on a proviso that foreign bases would not be permitted on their territory, and there was a residual left-wing opposition to membership of NATO throughout the decades of the Cold War.[32]

The death and destruction wrought in northern Europe during the 1940s was without parallel in the history of the region. Ancient cities such as Lübeck and Rostock were ravaged by Allied air attacks, or reduced to rubble by the advancing Red Army, such too was the fate

32. There is a general survey of Nordic security policies during this period in: Nissen (ed.) 1983, pp. 324–82. See also Einhorn E 1975 The reluctant ally: Danish security policy 1945–49 *Journal of Contemporary History* **10**: 493–512; Lundestad G 1980 *America, Scandinavia and the Cold War, 1945–1949*, Oslo.

of Königsberg and Danzig. Considerable damage was caused in the last months of war, often in remote areas. The retreating German troops laid waste to much of northern Finland; Russian planes bombed the island of Bornholm in May 1945, after the German garrison commander refused to surrender to the Red Army; and there was much devastation in Kurland, where the German forces continued their resistance until the very end of the war. Material losses caused by the fighting, inflicted by the policies of occupying forces, or as a consequence of territorial settlements, were severe and hard to overcome. Some 86,000 Finns were killed and a further 57,000 were permanently injured or crippled by the war; nearly half a million refugees from the ceded or leased territories, plus a further 100,000 inhabitants of Lapland whose homes were destroyed by the Germans had to be found accommodation and work in the winter of 1944–45. By the terms of the peace, Finland lost around 13 per cent of its national wealth to Russia, including 22 per cent of the timber needed by the wood-processing industries, over three million hectares of forest and 17 per cent of the national railway network. The Baltic lands, which had suffered the ravages of war so often in the past, were badly afflicted. The oil-shale industry developed with considerable success in Estonia, for example, was in ruins, as were many of the country's roads, bridges, houses and factory plants. Agricultural production was down to half its prewar level. The demographic consequences of occupation and war were severe: it has been calculated that Lithuania lost 15 per cent of its population between 1939 and 1945, Estonia 25 per cent and Latvia as much as 30 per cent.[33]

The territorial map of north-eastern Europe was also altered. Estonia lost 5 per cent of its prewar territory (the right bank of the Narva river plus much of the Petseri district) and Latvia 2 per cent (part of the Abrene district) to the Russian SSR, though the Klaipėda (Memel) district reverted to Lithuania. Further to the west, the territorial adjustments were of a far greater magnitude. East Prussia was split between Poland and the Soviet Union, which took the city of Königsberg (and renamed it Kaliningrad) with its hinterland; Poland's Baltic frontier was shifted westward, to embrace the city of Stettin (Szczecin) at the mouth of the river Oder. The Germans who still remained in these so-called Recovered Territories were expelled, and the area resettled by Poles. The expulsion of several million Germans from Polish territory between 1945 and the 1960s completed, in a

33. Misiunas and Taagepera 1983, pp. 274–5. These estimates are, as the authors remark, educated guesses.

brutally ironic fashion, the work begun by Hitler in 1939 with the evacuation of the Baltic Germans – the eradication of a centuries-old presence east of the Oder. The wholescale murder of the Jewish population of eastern Europe (around a quarter of a million were killed in the Baltic states alone) virtually eradicated another ancient community, whose memory succeeding generations of communist functionaries have done little to preserve.

The denizens of Sweden were spared these horrors, and the sufferings of the Danes were light in comparison to those experienced elsewhere in occupied Europe. They remained, moreover, on the western side of the iron curtain which was descending across Europe from Lübeck on the Baltic to Trieste on the Adriatic. Finland, after three winters of quasi-occupation by the Allied Control Commission and the fraught spring of 1948 when it appeared that the iron curtain might stretch northwards to the Tornio river, remained on the outer edge, an oddity with its own special relationship to Moscow, but a fully-functioning western-style democracy nonetheless. The new orthodoxy of good relations with the Soviet Union preached by President Paasikivi and more forcefully by his successor, Urho Kekkonen, did something to raise the Finns' awareness of their eastern neighbour (as a trading partner and a source of cheap vodka as well as a nuclear superpower); but until the reopening of the tourist traffic route to Tallinn in the mid-sixties, the Baltic states all but faded from the consciousness of their northern neighbours.[34]

34. The Swedish-Estonian journalist Andres Küng was one of the first to draw attention to this, with the publication of his *Estland – en studie i imperialism* (1971) and *Vad händer i Baltikum?* (1973). See: Küng A 1980 *A dream of freedom: four decades of national survival versus Russian imperialism in Estonia, Latvia and Lithuania*, Cardiff.

CHAPTER THIRTEEN

Affluence and Welfare: the Nordic States since the War

One of the beliefs that helped sustain the peoples of the three Baltic states reincorporated into the Soviet Union at the end of the Second World War was that they had enjoyed a prewar living standard comparable to that of the Finns (and by implication, might also have joined the ranks of the affluent welfare states, had they not been dragged into the mire of Soviet Communism). A wide-ranging economic survey initiated by the Swedish foreign ministry in the early 1990s acknowledged some similarities, but also indicated significant differences. A higher proportion of the working population of Finland in 1939 had been engaged in industry and construction than in any of the Baltic states, for example, and there had been striking differences between Finland and Lithuania, which had had lower agricultural output, rates of literacy, and life expectancy and where a far smaller proportion of the population had owned consumer goods such as cars and telephones. Whilst the precise nature of the comparison between prewar Finland and the Baltic states may be disputed, there can be little doubt that the gap in living standards has widened greatly since the war. The authors are careful to point out the difficulties of measuring comparative standards of living on the basis of Soviet statistics. Significantly, they tend to confine themselves to the Soviet Union and eastern European countries when they do make comparisons. They suggest, for example, that in terms of real income, Latvians in 1989 were probably better off than Poles, but some way behind Czechs and East Germans. Wages and living conditions generally were better than the Soviet average in what Russians referred to as 'our West': it is only when comparisons are made with Western

European standards that the extent of the gap (and the grimness of life in the USSR) is revealed. Life expectancy in Estonia was higher than in Finland before the war, but now lags behind, and has remained constant for the past three decades. Infant mortality rates, though only half the Soviet average, are twice as high as for the Scandinavian countries, as is the proportion of deaths by accident and unnatural causes. Denizens of the Baltic Soviet republics also had to cope with cramped and poor quality living accommodation, grossly inadequate services, shoddy goods (when available), whilst being constantly reminded by the state-controlled media of the blessings and benefits of life in the Soviet Union.[1]

With their many links to the West (relatives in emigration, the opening up of the tourist trade, even the opportunity to watch Finnish television in northern Estonia) and their consciousness of recent national independence, the indigenous peoples of the Baltic republics were undoubtedly less susceptible to such propaganda than those who had experienced Soviet rule from its inception. At the very least, they were better able to maintain an alternative vision of life as it might be, even if awareness of the superior comforts of their Finnish or Swedish neighbours could induce feelings of inferiority or even despair. Although the restoration of independence in 1991 exposed the citizens of the Baltic republics to a number of unpleasant truths about the forces which shape the free market, in circumstances hardly propitious for venturing forth into that bustling forum, it was in many ways a vindication of the determination to hang on to hopes of an alternative future rather than succumb to the pressures to conform to the ideal of *homo sovieticus*. At the time of writing, it is far too early to predict what may be the outcome, though there are grounds for cautious optimism. The final chapters of this book are inevitably shaped by the events of 1988–91 which shattered the Soviet empire. These events not only restored independence to the Baltic states, but also had a momentous impact on their Nordic neighbours, already considering the pros and cons of closer ties with the European Union. After decades of division and avoidance of issues, the problems of the Baltic region (and notions of a common Baltic identity) are now being seriously debated. A new vision of the North is being propounded, not as a periphery of Europe, but as a region with highly developed

1. Arkadie B and Karlsson M (eds) 1992 *Economic survey of the Baltic states*, pp. 51–2, 70, 95, 113. *World War II and Soviet occupation in Estonia: a damages report*, Tallinn, 1991, pp. 70–5, offers some revealing comparisons between Estonia and Finland.

national economies, a valuable cultural and natural heritage, and an internationally unparalleled social and intellectual infrastructure.[2]

The final two chapters of this book cannot hope to cover in any detail the events of the past fifty years, which have been more than adequately dealt with by a wide array of political and social scientists, as well as a few historians. Instead, I shall endeavour to bring together some of the themes which have run through the volume – the transformation of rural society and how this has affected cultural values; the evolution of ideas of identity; the relationship of citizen and state; and finally, the position and role of small states in Europe. My perspective will remain essentially 'Nordic', which not only reflects my own more specialist area of knowledge and linguistic expertise, but also, it has to be said, the much greater degree of scholarly investigation, particularly in the social sciences, which has taken place in Scandinavia and Finland in comparison with the three former Soviet republics. This perspective may be partially justified by the wish of the Baltic states to be in some degree identified with their Nordic neighbours, though it should be evident from the preceding pages that the differences between the Baltic and Nordic states far outweigh the similarities. Finally, the relative absence of any kind of Soviet or Russian perspective should not be taken to imply that it is unimportant. Whatever state eventually emerges from the ruined heartland of the Soviet empire will clearly have an immense influence and part to play. Russians, whether resident in the new republics, inhabitants of St Petersburg, the largest city in the Baltic region, or settlers in former East Prussia (now an isolated enclave of Russia), are as much part of the Baltic mosaic as Finns, Latvians or the Poles who have settled in the former German territories and the former free city of Danzig (Gdańsk).[3]

2. Björn Engholm, the then minister-president of Schleswig-Holstein, was an early and prominent advocate of Baltic regional cooperation; see his statement in: *Nordisk Kontakt Tema: Östersjön* (1992), pp. 4–5. An earlier number of this magazine, published by the Nordic Council, also took up the theme of Baltic cooperation: *Nordisk Kontakt* **12** (1990).

3. Russians and Poles, it can be argued, constitute nations which are not primarily 'Baltic' or 'northern European', and it is on these grounds that I have left their national history to others to tell. For similar reasons, I feel that the history of Leningrad/St Petersburg is intimately tied up with that of the Soviet/Russian state, and I have tended to confine consideration of that city to points at which it impinges upon the history of the surrounding Baltic lands. Russian and Polish minorities, as presently defined, are another matter; their history remains largely to be written, though there is much useful material, as well as some strongly-argued views, in: Lieven A 1993 *The Baltic revolution*, New Haven, Conn. and London, pp. 158–213.

This chapter will focus primarily on the affluent welfare states which emerged in postwar Scandinavia and Finland and will attempt to assess the consequences of the changes which have taken place since the 1930s; the effects of four decades of Soviet dominance in the eastern Baltic and the experience of the Baltic peoples will then be considered.

RECOVERY AND RESURGENCE 1945–1960

The Nordic countries experienced the war years in very different ways, and had to cope with their own specific problems at the onset of peace – collaborators and profiteers in Norway and Denmark, the 400,000 refugees from the lost territories who had to be resettled in Finland – as well as the more general difficulties of adjustment. The atmosphere in the immediate postwar years was tense. There were heated and often bitter debates over the running of the economy and the retention of wartime controls and regulations. There was unrest in the workplace – Denmark and Finland in particular were afflicted by a rash of protest wildcat strikes – and a good deal of street-corner belligerency to worry the bourgeoisie, already harassed by inflation and the decline in real earnings. The advent of more prosperous times in the 1950s smoothed away some of the sharper edges of strife. There began to emerge an image of consensus and willingness of all to work within defined and accepted parameters to achieve social or economic aims – in short, the 'Nordic model' of the social scientists and other image-makers.

The *fons et origo* of this model was Sweden. The only Nordic country to come through the war with its neutrality intact, Sweden also had the advantage of a well-developed industrial sector which ensured a steady growth rate in per capita GDP and provided the wealth which was to help finance the extensive welfare system developed since 1945. Although by no means unaffected by the war, which had meant additional spending on defence, reductions in trade, rationing and higher taxes, the country nevertheless emerged in rather better shape than its neighbours to tackle the problems of postwar reconstruction. The steady accumulation of national wealth had transformed it from an impoverished agrarian land into a modestly prosperous country. With prosperity, it has been argued, came a new image: Sweden as a 'modern' state, hailed by progressive outsiders such as the American Marquis Childs or socialist refugees of the

International group in wartime Stockholm as the model for the future.[4] Swedish social democrats enthusiastically took up the cause of modernity. *Morgonbris*, the party's journal for women, was in the forefront of the campaign in the 1930s for light, airy functionalist housing, furniture and fittings. The eminent social thinker Alva Myrdal advocated rationalisation, cooperation and organisation as the way ahead. *Woman's two roles* (1957), the English-language title of the book she co-authored with Viola Klein, was based on the premise of technological progress yielding ever-expanding work opportunities for women, whose continued tasks as house-keepers would be made simpler by household appliances manufactured by Electrolux or Husqvarna.

As the party of government from 1933 to 1976, the social democrats were in a powerful position to realise their proclaimed desire for Sweden to become a 'strong society' (the term used by the postwar prime minister, Tage Erlander; his predecessor Per Albin Hansson had spoken of a 'people's home' (*folkhemmet*) in the late 1920s to describe the social democratic vision of security and solidarity). Security (*trygghet*) was the underlying theme of much of the party's thinking and policies. It underpinned the socialists' 1944 programme for the postwar years, which looked for full employment, expansion of the social welfare network, greater business efficiency and more democracy in the workplace. 'The future goal of the Social Democratic Party must be to create a livelihood and economic security for the people of Sweden', was how Rickard Lindström summed up the party's policy in December 1944. 'Nebulous ideas about the miracles resulting from state intervention', i.e. nationalisation, were definitely not on the agenda.[5]

The record of the social democratic government of the immediate postwar years was rather less impressive than its ambitions. Instead of the anticipated depression predicted by the party's chief adviser on

4. See the contribution by J. Nilsson in: Linde-Laursen A and Nilsson J 1991 *Nationella identiteter i Norden – ett fullbordat faktum?*, Eskilstuna, pp. 59–99, and the chapter by A. Ruth in: Graubard S (ed.) 1986 *Norden – the passion for equality*, Oslo, pp. 240–82. On the *Internationale-Gruppe*, whose members included the future German and Austrian chancellors, Willy Brandt and Bruno Kreisky, see: Misgeld K 1976 *Die 'Internationale Gruppe demokratischer Sozialisten' in Stockholm, 1942–1945*, Uppsala. The book by Marquis Childs, *Sweden: the middle way*, New Haven, Conn., 1935, was primarily intended to show Americans that New Deal interventionism was no threat; but it helped create an image of Sweden as the quintessential modern state, refined (and maligned) in many subsequent publications.

5. Editorial in the social democratic newspaper *Morgon-Tidningen*, cited by: Lewin L 1988 *Ideology and strategy. A century of Swedish politics*, Cambridge, pp. 170–1.

social policy, Gunnar Myrdal, Sweden was caught up in an inflation spiral and faced pressures on its foreign currency reserve as the balance of payments tilted heavily into the red. Instead of forward planning, the government was obliged to take a series of *ad hoc* measures to protect the currency; the maintenance of controls and regulations provided the opposition with a welcome opportunity to accuse the social democrats of economic incompetence. In spite of these attacks, the social democrats managed to retain their position as the leading party in the 1948 *Riksdag* elections; together with the communists (who lost heavily in the elections), they held 87 of the 150 seats in the First Chamber and 120 of the 230 seats in the Second Chamber. The red-green alliance with the Farmers' Party was reconstituted in 1951, but from 1957 until 1976, the social democrats ruled alone, backed by a left-wing majority in both houses and in the new unicameral *Riksdag* elected in 1970.

Renewed economic growth in the 1950s allowed for the fairly rapid abandonment of most of the controls and regulations. In a period of full employment and rising standards of living, the tense atmosphere of political confrontation that had characterised the 1948 election campaign was dissipated. The social democrats continued to explore ways of bolstering the security of the Swedish people, most notably by developing an active labour market policy to tackle structural unemployment. As self-proclaimed guardians of the welfare state, they also sought to extend and deepen the system of benefits. A fully comprehensive national pensions scheme was introduced in 1946; child allowances in 1947; health care and housing were more contentious issues, but reforms were introduced during the fifties. There was further acrimonious debate at the end of the decade over the social democrats' proposed compulsory superannuation scheme, which was ultimately carried by a narrow margin in the Second Chamber; the main losers of the argument appear to have been the non-socialist parties, where cracks and divisions occurred at crucial moments.[6]

Sweden's Scandinavian neighbours were both under German occupation from the spring of 1940 to the spring of 1945. Of the two, Denmark fared rather better in a number of respects than did Norway, and much better than other parts of Europe occupied by the Nazis. Danish farmers were able to make up for the shortfalls and losses suffered as a result of the drying-up of imports; the centre for exchange control, *Valutacentralen,* had sensibly purchased large stocks of

6. Lewin 1988, pp. 204–37. Baldwin P 1990 *The politics of social solidarity. Class bases of the European welfare state 1875–1975*, Cambridge, pp. 212–23.

necessities at the beginning of the war; and the fact that a Danish administration continued to function for much of the Occupation helped ensure that a good proportion of what was produced remained within the country. The worst-affected sections of the community were poor working-class families, who could not afford expensive necessities such as fuel, but those living on fixed incomes also felt the pinch, and all wage-earners suffered a loss in real earnings. Efforts were made to maintain and even extend the social security system established in the 1930s; expenditure on maternity benefits, for example, quintupled, and the school meals service was considerably expanded. The fabric of the system was, however, stretched to its limits, and conservative critics of the social reforms introduced by K. Steincke in the 1930s, now with a voice in the national coalition government, attempted to cut back on provisions. Legislation passed in 1942 introduced compulsory work cards, and obliged those in receipt of unemployment benefit to take work offered by the communal authorities as long as the hourly rate of pay met the level of benefit entitlement (this was largely in response to farmers' complaints of having to support the costs of paying dole to the urban unemployed when there was work to be had in the countryside).

In Finland, the wartime experience was decisive in reshaping attitudes towards social welfare provision. The underlying assumption, that poverty was an individual failing, could no longer stand up in a situation where those who suffered were often the dependants of those on active service. Several voluntary organisations sprang up during the Winter War, and these were to play a major role in keeping up morale and the will to fight on. The sharp decline in the numbers receiving assistance under the provisions of the poor law (which cared for some 200,000 during the worst period of the Depression) or in institutions would seem to suggest that the assistance offered by voluntary welfare organisations such as *Suomen Huolto* or *Aseveliliitto* more than took up the slack. The need to provide for the 30,000 war widows and the 50,000 orphans, as well as those disabled in the fighting also gave a powerful impetus towards the extension of a state-sponsored welfare system in Finland.

For Denmark and Finland, the 1950s was a difficult decade of change and adaptation. In spite of a steady rise in industrial output, an excessively large share of the working population was still engaged in farming, which had low rates of productivity relative to industry. Denmark's position was, if anything, more difficult than that of Finland, where farmers produced largely for the domestic market, their other assets – forests and labour – helping to sustain the principal element of Finland's export trade, the timber-processing industries. Denmark had no equivalent raw material that could be converted into an export commodity. Danish agriculture produced only a small and dwindling proportion of the GDP, but still dominated the country's export trade. During the early 1950s, Denmark suffered from a chronic balance of payments problem, which government sought to counter by curbs on domestic consumption and currency restrictions. The way out of the problem was to borrow in order to cover the deficit and to finance expanded industrial production, a policy pursued from the late fifties. The effect was dramatic. Growth rates, which at an average of 2.5 per cent a year had been much lower than those of Norway or Sweden, now rose to 4 per cent. The structure of Danish industry underwent major change, with a significant shift away from the capital to the provinces. The new light industries were run on highly rational lines, usually with the enthusiastic collaboration of the unions, which acknowledged that high productivity generated wealth and created work, especially for white-collar employees.

Finland's economic transformation followed a somewhat different pattern, in part occasioned by the special circumstances created by the war. The burden of war reparations to the Soviet Union imposed great strains on an already stretched economy, particularly in the first years after the war, when foreign credits were not easy to obtain; on the other hand, the Soviet insistence on being recompensed with ships and machinery boosted the Finnish metal and engineeering industries and laid the basis for future expansion. The subsequent development of bilateral Soviet-Finnish trade was also beneficial to certain labour-intensive industries which found a ready (and grateful) market in the Soviet Union for their garments and shoes. Finland's principal earner of foreign currency, however, remained the timber-processing industries, which accounted for 80 per cent of all exports in the early 1950s. The forest helped Finland on the road to recovery in the late 1940s; it also provided seasonal employment for large numbers of rural workers – a source of earnings which began to diminish rapidly as mechanisation took over from man and horsepower. Finland has had a persistent problem of rural overpopulation, exacerbated by the resettlement of large numbers of refugees on small farms created by the postwar land acquisition legislation. The principal beneficiary of this pool of surplus labour in the 1950s and 1960s was Sweden; in all, it has been estimated that some 300,000 Finns moved across the Gulf of Bothnia to seek work during this period.

Out of the wartime experience also grew a new style of industrial relations in Finland, more akin to the Scandinavian pattern of national collective bargaining. Over time, the annual round of negotiations has been greatly extended in all the Nordic countries, to cover such things as social and incomes policy, and has given rise to comment about the 'corporatist' nature of the system. Here, as in many other areas of policy-making, prosperity and full employment have tended to make the way easier for consensus and agreement. During the 1950s, this was far less the case, as workers, farmers and industrialists chafed at the restraints imposed by government and fought over the too meagre dividends of the national income. The abolition of wage and price controls in Finland at the end of 1955 pushed the cost of living index above the threshhold which had been artificially maintained by government, and led to the unions staging a general strike and the farmers withholding their dairy produce. There was also considerable industrial unrest in Denmark, after workers rejected the deal arrived at by the national arbitrator and imposed by law for a two-year period.

In spite of the resurgence of the labour movement in Finland during the immediate postwar years, the left did not achieve the degree of political dominance here that it did in the Scandinavian countries. This was in no small measure due to the divisions on the left in Finland, where not only was there a large Communist Party, left in the political wilderness after 1948, but also differences within the Social Democratic Party, which culminated in a split in 1957. These divisions also affected the trade unions and other workers' organisations, which were in any event less well established in public life than their Scandinavian counterparts. The principal party of government in Finland remained the Agrarian Union, though coalitions were the norm, and non-party governments of senior civil servants not infrequent. In contrast to the other Nordic countries, Finland has a powerful head of state, who plays an active role in government. Urho Kekkonen, president from 1956 until his resignation on grounds of ill-health in 1981, was a supreme example of this. It would not be an exaggeration to say that he had a far more decisive say in the formation of government than did the electorate, or that he was prepared to use his self-appointed role as the chief architect of the postwar Soviet-Finnish relationship to exclude from office individuals or parties deemed to be unacceptable.[7]

Social democracy was indisputably the dominant political force in postwar Scandinavia, though in terms of voter support and occupancy

7. Häikiö M 1991 *Suomen lähihistoria*, Helsinki, p. 37ff. On postwar politics in Finland in general, see: Arter D 1987 *Politics and policy making in Finland*, London/New York.

of governmental office, somewhat less so in Denmark and Norway than in Sweden. The length of the period in which the social democrats were in charge of government here – a virtually unbroken run from 1933 to 1976 – has lent credence to the notion that they are not only the guardians but also the begetters of the Swedish welfare state. In fact, the foundations of modern welfare in Sweden were laid down whilst the Social Democratic Party was yet in its infancy. It was the farming interest which played a major part in deflecting Sweden away from the Bismarckian model of state social insurance for one particular section of the community to the provision of benefits (largely financed through taxation) for all. It has been claimed that this was in fact no more than the outcome of the farmers' long-standing conflict with the urban middle classes and the bureaucracy over taxation and other burdens, and their anxiety not to be excluded from the benefits, which they believed should be financed by all. The universality and apparent solidarity of the social welfare reforms enacted in postwar Sweden are also attributed more to wishes of the middle classes and their political representatives to benefit from the state's largesse than to the redistributionalist principles of social democracy. Though not without its merits – particularly in questioning assumptions about the motives and aims of the politicians who helped formulate the legislation – this line of argument tends to underestimate the underlying desire for security which is probably the main cement of solidarity.[8]

CONSOLIDATION 1960–1973

The sixties were a decade of unprecedented economic growth throughout northern Europe. The ascendancy of industry over

8. Baldwin P 1990, pp. 83–94, 112, 134–46. For a critique of Baldwin's arguments, see: Olsson S 1989 Working-class power and the 1946 pension reform in Sweden *International Review of Social History* **34**: 287–308. Baldwin also neglects other features, such as labour market policy, which have played an important part in the development of the welfare state. See: Einhorn E and Logue J 1989 *Modern welfare states. Politics and policies in social democratic Scandinavia*, New York, pp. 131–45. Critical, but essentially pro-welfare state, are the views advanced by one of the leading post-war Swedish conservatives: Hecksher G 1984 *The welfare state and beyond. Success and problems in Scandinavia*, Minneapolis, and by a Marxist social scientist, Göran Therborn, in: Therborn G et al. 1987 *Lycksalighetens halvö. Den svenska välfärdsmodellen och Europa*, Stockholm, pp. 13–44, and in: Pfaller A, Gough I and Therborn G 1991 *Can the welfare state compete?* London, pp. 229–70.

agriculture as the major employer of productive labour was emphatically confirmed. By the 1970s, fewer than one in ten of the active working population was engaged or employed in farming in Denmark and Sweden; a decade later, the Finnish farm workforce had shrunk to the same proportions – from nearly half to less than a tenth of the working population in less than forty years. The range of industrial production became more varied, as new industries began to carve a niche for themselves on domestic and foreign markets, alongside the traditional and established firms. The timber and paper industries continued to dominate the Finnish export trade, for example, but their share of the market fell from 68.8 per cent in 1960 to 54.3 per cent in 1971. Over the same period, the Finnish metal industry's share of exports rose from 15 to 23.5 per cent, whilst other industries accounted for 15.6 per cent of the export trade in 1971, as against a mere 4.5 per cent a decade earlier.[9]

During the 1960s, Danish industry finally ended farming's dominance of the country's export trade. Membership of the European Free Trading Association (EFTA) had opened up new markets for Danish industry, but offered relatively few new opportunities for Danish farmers. In the fifties, mechanisation and rationalisation had been seen as the way forward for agriculture. In the sixties, the emphasis was upon rationalisation of landholdings; almost 60,000 farms 'disappeared' during the decade. By 1975, fewer than one-third of Danish farms were of less than ten hectares, compared to half in 1937. The process of rationalisation was aided by the provision of cheap credits and the easing of legal restrictions; but farming was no longer the flagship of the Danish export industry. By the end of the sixties, one-third of the farmers' income was coming from subsidies.

The impressive growth rates achieved by Danish industry during this period – at 5 per cent per annum, they exceeded those of Sweden and Norway – were more than enough to compensate for the decline of agriculture. After the austere, cramped postwar years of low growth and high unemployment, prosperity was a pleasant prospect. For the social democrats, it also offered new opportunities, as the party's leader and prime minister Viggo Kampmann put in it 1960:

> Now we're on the way up. The automatic rise in incomes means that taxes will pour in. We will know how to seize this historical opportunity.

9. *Suomen tilastollinen vuosikirja/Statistical Yearbook of Finland* New Series, **68**, 1972 Helsinki, 1973, p. 140. There were significant increases in the volume and value of exports of ships, machinery, iron and steel, electrical goods, textiles and furniture.

> This money will not be paid back in the form of tax reliefs, but will be used to provide the population with the things the majority want. We will build universities and institutes of learning. We will build social institutions. We will support the arts. We will raise standards in every area.[10]

There was indeed considerable expansion of the public sector, where the number of employees more than doubled between 1960 and 1972. Not all of the ideals expounded by Kampmann were welcomed by the public at large, especially the growing tax burden. The state art fund established in 1964 provoked a populist protest movement. The social democratic-dominated governments of this period were also criticised by a small number on the left for their seeming devotion to the promotion of materialist objectives. Their housing policies also seemed less than successful in tackling needs. In 1966, tenants were given the opportunity to buy their flats or houses, but this only served to encourage speculation, such as the subdivision of older properties into small flats. Four years later, this was amended to exclude pre-1960 buildings. Government efforts to underwrite cheap housing also proved to be inadequate, and housing shortages continued to be a problem, especially in the capital.

Education in particular received considerable attention in Denmark, where the amount of the national income devoted to schooling rose from 2.4 per cent in 1952 to 7.5 per cent in 1974. The 1958 school reform established a unitary system of basic education. In larger schools, children in their fifth year of schooling were to be streamed according to their abilities, interests and parents' wishes. A social democratic amendment allowed parents and/or local authorities to opt out of this provision, and this option was most frequently used in succeeding years. The 1975 act acknowledged this by delaying streaming until at least the eighth year of study. To cope with increasing student numbers – from around 9,000 in 1960–61 to 35,000 a decade later – new universities were opened in Odense, Roskilde and Ålborg. Efforts were also made to provide new and different training opportunities alongside traditional apprenticeship schemes, though with limited success – between a quarter and a third of Danish children still leave school with no formal qualifications.

Education has also received high priority in the other Nordic countries, accounting for around 15 per cent of total public expenditure. All have gone over to a nine-year comprehensive school

10. Cited in: Haue H et al. 1980 *Det nye Danmark 1890–1975*, Copenhagen, p. 278.

system, but there are wide variations in the form and pattern of secondary education. New-style teaching methods, curriculum changes and measures to extend participation in the administration and direction of schools and universities have proved controversial. The appointment by the minister of education of three external rectors to control the administration of the radical new university of Roskilde in the mid-seventies was one of the more spectacular occurrences in a series of battles between the self-styled democratic forces and their perceived enemies of the old guard, a conflict which has more often than not ended in stalemate rather than resolution.

The overall expansion of education and the strong emphasis upon the acquisition of skills was a vital prerequisite for economic growth, but opinion is divided on how far the equalisation of opportunities through the education system has in fact fostered substantial social mobility. As in other affluent Western European states, it is the children of the middle classes, rather than of the working class, who seem to take greater advantage of the system. There is thus still a heavy preponderance of children of middle-class background in the higher ranks of the civil service and in the professions. It is these people, the lawyers, architects, senior administrators and managers who constitute the new elite. There is a considerable gulf between them and those at the lower end of the white-collar spectrum, whose job security and social status have been eroded by modern technology and market forces.

The economic expansion of the sixties and seventies dramatically increased the percentage of women in the workforce. By 1960, most of the formal restrictions on a woman's right to work, irrespective of marital status, had already been abolished. Women had the vote, equal rights of access to higher education and most sectors of public employment; the principle of equal pay for equal work had been conceded; women had long since ceased to be legally subordinate, and had full rights over the disposal of their property and income. Nevertheless, the traditional images and role-models still dominated. Marriage was frequently made more financially attractive for men than for women; in 1956, for example, newly-married Danish men were granted a large chunk of tax relief if their wives gave up work within three months of marriage. The often marked differences between men and women in performance levels and completion rates in higher education would suggest that women were under-achievers – perhaps resigned to the fact that men secured the best jobs, or content to play out a civilising function devised for them by nationalist-minded public men in the preceding century.

The rising numbers of women workers did not lead to a concomitant increase in the number of women in top positions. A mere 2 per cent of the women members of the Finnish association of professional economists were in top jobs, and only 8 per cent were in middle management, according to a survey conducted in 1975; the corresponding figures for their male counterparts were 37 and 39 per cent. Four-fifths of female office workers in Denmark were employed in a lowly subordinate capacity; less than a fifth made it to the upper echelons. Women have begun to make inroads into male-dominated occupations, but they still tend to dominate the 'caring' professions, where average earnings are perceptibly lower than in male-dominated middle-class professions.

The rapid expansion of the social services and healthcare sector was very much a precondition for and a consequence of so many women coming on to the job market in the sixties and seventies.[11] The provision of child care has been a major issue in all the Nordic countries, where the proportion of working women with young children has grown from a small minority in the early fifties to an overwhelming majority by the 1980s. The parties of the left have favoured the creation of day care facilities to enable the mother to go to work; the parties of the right have preferred tax credits, whilst those with sizeable rural constituencies have favoured home-care arrangements and financial support for women who stay at home (often as farmers' wives). At the other end of the age spectrum, a great deal of attention has also been paid to the needs of the infirm and elderly; here again, the memories and examples of a rural past may have had some bearing on the nature and outcome of discussions.[12] The modern welfare state has, however, come a long way from the debates of the early twentieth century, and it is women, more than any other single group, that have sustained its growth. It is perhaps no accident that, as the welfare state has come under threat, women have entered politics in a big way in all the Scandinavian countries.

The sixties were dominated politically by the left. The Danish social democrats ruled in coalition with the radicals or as a minority from 1953 to 1968. Electorally, the four main parties in Denmark seemed to be well entrenched, though *Venstre* began to suffer from the decline of the rural population, whilst there was a breakthrough on the left by

11. A conclusion reached by Berg A, Frost L and Olsen A, (eds) 1986 *Kvindfolk*, Copenhagen, vol. 2, p. 116.

12. On this subject, see the essay by Zitomersky J 1987 Ecology, class or culture? Explaining family residence and support of the elderly in the Swedish agrarian past *Scandinavian Journal of History* **12**: 117–60.

the Socialist People's Party (*Socialistiske folkeparti, SFP*) founded by Aksel Larsen and a number of other ex-communists in the late fifties. In the 1966 *Folketing* elections, the two parties of the left secured an absolute majority of seats. Negotiations between the social democrats and the SFP with a view to forming a coalition government came to nothing, though the SFP informally supported a number of fiscal reforms launched by Jens Otto Krag's minority cabinet. The devaluation of the *krone* in 1967 split the SFP, however, and the social democratic government resigned shortly afterwards after losing a vote over freezing supplementary payments. In the ensuing elections, the non-socialist parties secured an overall majority, and formed a government. This break in the run of successive social democrat-dominated governments was not however extended, and Jens Otto Krag returned to office once more in 1971.

Left-centre coalitions, which included the communists until 1971, became the norm in Finland after 1966. The foundations of the modern Finnish welfare state were nonetheless laid by the two centre-right governments which held office between 1962 and 1966. New occupational pensions schemes were introduced from 1962 onwards, and a universal sickness insurance scheme was launched in 1964. The pivotal party in Finnish political life has continued to be the Agrarian Union, which followed the example of its Swedish counterpart and became a Centre Party in 1965, seeking to win the votes of the new urban middle classes. In this endeavour it has proved markedly less successful, a circumstance which may be ascribed to the fact that the Swedish Centre, as a party of opposition until 1976, has had more freedom to manoeuvre and to project a new image than has the Finnish party, which as a party of government has had to defend the farming interest against the urban consumer and industrial lobbies of the socialists and conservatives.[13]

The Finnish Centre Party nevertheless continued to play a key role in government throughout the seventies, and managed to maintain a reasonable level of support at the polls. By contrast, the Swedish Centre Party's brief experience of government in the mid-seventies was not a particularly happy one, and the subsequent slump in the party's electoral fortunes would seem to point up the perils of becoming an 'issues', rather than an 'interest' party.

13. An argument advanced in: Elder N, Thomas A and Arter D 1988 rev. edn *The consensual democracies? The government and politics of the Scandinavian states*, Oxford, pp. 69–76.

In Sweden, the unbroken run of Social Democratic Party dominance continued unabated until Thorbjörn Fälldin of the Centre Party formed his first coalition in 1976. The debate over the superannuation scheme in the late fifties had revealed serious differences amongst the non-socialist parties. The Liberal People's Party was soon reconciled to the new system, which proved beneficial to many white-collar workers, but the conservatives remained opposed. Defeat in the 1960 elections led to a re-evaluation and a distinct moderation of their stance on the welfare state by the conservatives under their new leader Gunnar Hecksher. Hecksher's efforts to bring together the non-socialist parties into an effective coalition ran into difficulties at national level, though there were several local alliances. He himself was jettisoned as leader of the party in 1965; four years later, after a poor showing at the polls, the party abandoned its distinctly old-fashioned and forbidding title of Right (*Höger*) for the more persuasive Moderate Coalition Party (*Moderata Samlingsparti*).

In 1968, the social democrats had succeeded in reversing a decline in their support, winning half the votes cast and 125 seats in the second chamber elections. The high turnout (89.3 per cent) of voters was in some ways an endorsement of continuity in an uncertain world (the election was held only a month after the reformist Dubček government in Prague was brought down by Soviet intervention). Social democracy, rather than the divided opposition parties, was perceived as the upholder of order and stability, and the guarantor of continued prosperity and well-being. Representatives of business and labour met regularly to discuss and thrash out economic and even social policy with the government: the 'spirit of Harpsund' symbolised this smooth cooperation.[14] With a membership of almost a million (most of whom were affiliated to the party through the union branches), a broad array of intellectual luminaries, and a confidence built up over decades of governing the country, Swedish social democracy seemed set to continue as *the* party of government for years to come.

14. Lewin 1988, pp. 204–5. Harpsund was the official country residence of the Swedish prime minister, and it was here that many of the meetings were held under Tage Erlander's premiership (1957–69). See also: Castles F 1975 Swedish social democracy: the conditions of success *Political Quarterly* **46**: 171–85.

THE OIL CRISIS AND AFTER

The Swedish social democrats' triumph at the polls in 1968 was to remain, however, the high peak of their achievement. The constitutional reform finally agreed to in 1967, which replaced the two chambers of the *Riksdag* with one house of 350 members, placed a question-mark against the continuation of social democratic rule. The traditional base of party support, the working-class, was shrinking – only 26.3 per cent of the economically active population was employed in the mining and manufacturing sector in 1980, as against 34.8 per cent twenty years earlier – and in spite of the fact that the party had sought to broaden its appeal since the days of Hjalmar Branting and had made inroads into the middle classes, it was still heavily reliant on the blue-collar vote. In common with the other social democratic parties of northern Europe, it had the difficult task of appealing to a new generation of voters, no longer bound by the same loyalties or traditions as their parents; and it also had to contend with a new set of problems, many of which challenged the comfortable assumptions of progress and continued economic growth which the party had adopted.[15]

In the event, the party fared rather better at the polls in the 1970s and 1980s than its counterparts elsewhere in Scandinavia. In the first elections to the new unicameral *Riksdag* in 1970, the social democrats won 163 seats, and were able to continue in office with the tacit support of the reformed Communist Party. The elections of 1973 were held a few days after the death of King Gustav VI and in the wake of a dramatic bank robbery-cum-siege in Stockholm. Turnout was at an all-time high of 90 per cent, and the outcome was a tie, with the parties of the left and right each holding 175 seats. The government of Olof Palme survived by compromise and negotiation, but the social democrats fell back slightly in the 1976 elections (to avoid future ties, the number of seats had been reduced to 349), and went into opposition for the first time in over forty years.

The Centre Party had succeeded in becoming the principal opposition party in the late 1960s, attracting votes from a wide range of people alienated or frustrated by the cosy relationship of big

15. Elder et al. 1988, pp. 76ff. Einhorn and Logue 1989, pp. 92ff. The Swedish social democrats had in fact recognised the need to maintain the initiative, and had instituted a thorough scrutiny of the welfare system in the mid-sixties, concluding that more attention needed to be paid to the disadvantaged – the unemployed, the elderly and the infirm.

business and unions, an all-embracing and centralist bureaucracy and a rather smug belief in continued growth and progress – workers in small firms outside the main zones of industry, small businessmen struggling against the onset of recession, clerical workers and younger voters concerned with ecological and environmental issues.[16] Thousands were drawn to the Centre Party by the high-profile campaign against nuclear power launched in 1973–74 by its leader Thorbjörn Fälldin; but Fälldin's personal commitment to phasing out nuclear power in Sweden placed great strains on the non-socialist coalition government which took office under his premiership in 1976.

The oil crisis triggered by the Arab-Israeli war of 1973 and the subsequent economic recession provided an added dimension to the debate over energy. Buffeted by economic problems, the four non-socialist governments between 1976 and 1982 tried to prop up major industries by pouring in massive sums for structural rationalisation, and strove successfully to keep down levels of unemployment; the price they paid was high inflation, a huge addition to the national debt, and the dashing of hopes for tax cuts. It was, however, the nuclear energy question which destroyed the precarious unity of the three-party coalition which took office in 1976. The Centre Party was forced by its partners to compromise its position on nuclear power from the outset. There was no mention in the government's policy declaration of phasing out nuclear power or even of halting the ongoing programme of construction of the reactors unanimously agreed to by parliament in 1971; instead, permission to fuel up would be conditional upon the state power board being able to satisfy stringent safety and waste disposal regulations. This uneasy compromise was tested in 1978, when permission was sought to charge up two new reactors. After months of procrastination, permission was withheld pending further test drilling to see if the stipulations on waste disposal in the bedrock could be met. This was widely interpreted as a further 'betrayal' by Fälldin of his binding commitment to phase out nuclear power, but the subsequent public disagreements between the coalition parties extinguished the last traces of consensus. The government resigned in October 1978, and was replaced by a minority liberal government.

16. Särlvik B 1970 Voting behaviour in shifting 'election winds' *Scandinavian Political Studies* **5**: 241–83. Elder N, Gooderham R 1978 The Centre Parties of Norway and Sweden *Government and Opposition* **13**: 218–35. The Centre Party's share of the vote and of the seats in the *Riksdag* elections of 1970, 1973 and 1976 were: 19.9 per cent (71): 25.1 per cent (90): 24.1 per cent (86).

The nuclear accident at Three Mile Island, Pennsylvania, in March 1979 did what the Centre Party had failed to do – it caused the other major parties substantially to shift their position. The social democrats came out in favour of a referendum on the issue, with the decision on fuelling to be postponed until the outcome was known. The result of the referendum was hard to decipher. The Centre Party-Communist Left proposal to phase out all reactors within ten years won 38.6 per cent of the vote; but over half of those voting favoured the two other proposals which envisaged phasing out the nuclear reactors after their economical and technical lifespan had expired. The *Riksdag* eventually approved the commissioning of twelve nuclear reactors, which were to be shut down successively, the last one no later than the year 2010.[17]

The nuclear issue sharply divided the parties in Sweden, but it did not lead to fragmentation; indeed, by taking up the anti-nuclear cause, the Centre Party may well have helped preserve the basic four-party system by attracting thousands of potential protest voters. This system survived the upsets of recession and fissiparous bourgeois government. The Social Democratic Party – which returned to office in 1982 – continued to capture 43–45 per cent of the vote and 150–160 seats, with the Communist Left managing to scrape over the 4 per cent threshold with 17–20 seats. Support for the individual parties within the non-socialist bloc tended to fluctuate quite considerably, though the overall vote remained fairly constant. The Centre Party fell back from the high peak of success in the early seventies to the nadir of 12.4 per cent of the vote in 1985, almost the reverse of the conservatives' fortunes. In 1982, the Liberal People's Party bore the brunt of the electorate's displeasure even more than the Centre Party, but three years later, it had managed a spectacular recovery, increasing its share of the vote from a mere 6 per cent (21 seats) to 14.2 per cent (51 seats).

Unlike its Nordic neighbours, Sweden's political system was relatively untroubled by protest parties until the late 1980s. The Christian Democratic Union, founded in 1964 on the wave of a protest against the proposal to reduce the amount of religious instruction in secondary schools, failed to break through the 4 per cent barrier. The sundry groupings on the extreme left were even less popular with the electorate. In 1988, the Environment Party did manage to break through the barrier, winning 20 seats; but the conclusion made at the time, that this breakthrough was unlikely to be permanent because of the highly volatile nature of the Green vote and

17. The nuclear power issue is extensively analysed in Lewin 1988, pp. 238–73.

the largely elitist nature of the 'alternative Green dimension', appears to have been justified by subsequent electoral setbacks.[18]

The electoral breakthrough achieved in the 1991 *Riksdag* elections by the Christian Democrats (27 seats) and the populist anti-tax New Democracy (24 seats) occurred almost twenty years after right-wing protest parties had disturbed the political order in Finland, Norway and Denmark. The success of these parties owed a good deal to the personal charisma of their leaders, who were able – at least temporarily – to tap a rich vein of discontent. The ex-Agrarian Veikko Vennamo was able not only to draw upon a large personal following amongst the Karelian settlers, but also to rally the 'forgotten people' of the towns as well as the countryside to his Rural Party. As an outspoken opponent of President Kekkonen, Vennamo attracted considerable support in the 1968 presidential elections, and his party won 10 per cent of the vote and 18 seats in the 1970 *Eduskunta* elections. In Norway, an exhausting referendum on entry into the European Economic Community split the liberal and labour parties in 1972. The Norwegian Labour Party's electoral support had been declining since the early sixties; the split in the party proved not to be as serious as that within the ranks of the liberals, who disappeared from the political scene in 1985, but it marked the beginning of a period of short-lived and unstable minority governments, and of electoral success for the radical left as well as the anti-tax protest party led by Anders Lange, which secured 5 per cent of the vote in 1973.

The breakup of the established party political order was most spectacular, however, in Denmark. The four main parties had for decades secured the lion's share of the votes, and still managed to take 84 per cent in the 1971 elections. Two years later, that share had dropped to 58.4 per cent, and the second largest group in the *Folketing* was the anti-tax Progress Party led by the flamboyant lawyer Mogens Glistrup. Another new party, the Centre Democrats, led by a former social democrat, Erhard Jakobsen, also fared well. The Christian People's Party, founded in 1970 by citizens outraged by the liberal abortion and pornography laws enacted by a conservative minister of justice, secured 7 seats, whilst the communists and the Justice Party (which draws upon the single tax philosophy of the American economist Henry George) both re-entered the *Folketing* after several years' absence.

18. Bennulf M, Holmberg S 1990 The Green breakthrough in Sweden *Scandinavian Political Studies* **13**: 165–84.

The reasons for this dramatic upsetting of the old order – which has since managed to some degree to reassert itself, though a plethora of parties still crowd the benches of the *Folketing* – are varied. The elections of 1973 were held as the economy was beginning to falter. The non-socialist coalition government of Hilmar Baunsgaard (1968–71) had been unable to tackle the rising burden of taxation or to reduce public expenditure. Baunsgaard's endeavours to secure a Nordic Common Market (Nordek) had been frustrated by the stop-go tactics of the Finns, but the EEC had been more receptive of Denmark's third application for membership. Unlike the Norwegians, the Danes voted 'yes' in their referendum, albeit by a narrow margin. The campaign in both countries was divisive, and anti-EEC parties benefited from the backlash in the subsequent national elections.[19]

The collapse of the old four-party system coincided with the downturn in the economy following the oil crisis of 1973–74. Danish industry suffered severe setbacks, and many firms went to the wall, especially in the highly vulnerable construction industry. Recovery in the late 1970s was not accompanied by any significant fall in the rate of unemployment, which hovered around the 11 per cent level in 1977. Industry emerged from the recession leaner and fitter, more efficent but also needing fewer workers; the industrial workforce of 370,000 in 1977 was 50,000 fewer than in 1970. Sweden, and to a lesser extent Finland, managed to ride out the recession more successfully. In both countries, extensive retraining programmes were set up to deal with the problem of structural unemployment. Finland's bilateral trading relationship with the Soviet Union also helped safeguard jobs in labour-intensive industries such as construction and furniture-making.

By the mid-seventies, it was clear to all that the era of full employment and rapidly rising living standards was over. Many of the component elements of the 'Nordic model' seemed to be coming unstuck. The battalions of labour and industry which had cooperated so smoothly now began to bicker as the pace of economic growth faltered, inflation and unemployment rose, and the necessity of cutting public spending grew more urgent. Suddenly, there were populist movements protesting against the high levels of taxation, against joining the EEC, against the permissive society, against immigrants.

19. On the Nordek negotiations and the Danish referendum, see: Arter D 1993 *The politics of European integration in the twentieth century*, Aldershot, pp. 153–8, 163–8. Wiklund C 1970 The zig-zag course of the Nordek negotiations *Scandinavian Political Studies* **5**: 307–36. Petersen N, Elklit J 1973 Denmark enters the European Community *Scandinavian Political Studies* **8**: 200–9.

The margins for consensus now seemed to be wearing exceedingly thin, even in prosperous Sweden, as the harassed second coalition government headed by Thorbjörn Fälldin discovered in 1979. In the spring of 1980, Sweden experienced its worst labour conflict since the general strike of 1909: never mind that Sweden continued to remain, after Switzerland, the country with the least number of days lost for work stoppages – in the eyes of the world, it seemed as if the bubble had finally burst.[20]

Sweden is often portrayed as a country burdened with high taxes and a top-heavy bureaucracy administering welfare programmes which the country is increasingly unable to afford: and indeed, with taxes constituting around 52 per cent of GDP, and almost one in five of the labour force employed in the public social services sector, Sweden in the late 1980s topped the tables of OECD countries. But, in spite of a number of well-publicised cases of tax-oppressed personalities and the emergence of an anti-tax movement in the late 1980s, a remarkable degree of consensus on the necessity of maintaining the welfare state has prevailed. The highly-organised trade union movement is strongly committed to social welfare policies, which are an integral part of the bargaining process with the equally well-organised employers' federations, in which the state is also far more than an interested observer. There has also been relatively little opposition to the welfare state as a concept, or even to some of its principal provisions, from the non-socialist parties, which are in any event often divided over specific issues.[21]

In many respects, the welfare state has served an integrative purpose, affording new career and work opportunities, especially for women, and providing a network of social security for all. The welfare states created in the other Nordic countries may differ in the manner

20. On industrial relations in Scandinavia, see: Einhorn and Logue 1989, pp. 228–60, and the contributions by Nils Elvander, Walter Korpi and Bjørn Gustavsen in: Allardt E et al. 1981 *Nordic democracy*, Copenhagen, pp. 279–358. For an upbeat assessment of Sweden's economy in the late 1980s, see the chapter by Göran Therborn in: Pfaller A, Gough I and Therborn G 1991 *Can the welfare state compete?* London, pp. 229–70. Nannestad P 1991 *Danish design or British disease? Danish economic crisis policy in comparative perspective*, Aarhus, argues that the policies pursued by the governments of five countries (Austria, Denmark, Germany, Sweden and the United Kingdom) during the period 1973–79 were crucial in determining economic performance.

21. The different approaches towards the provision of child-care allowances, for instance, has been charted by: Hinnfors J 1991 *Familjepolitik. Samhällsförändringar och partistrategier 1970–1990* Göteborg Studies in Politics **26**, Göteborg. The costs of the welfare state are considered by, amongst others, S Olsson in: Friedman R, Gilbert N, Sherer M (eds) 1987 *Modern welfare states. A comparative view of trends and prospects*, Brighton, pp. 44–82.

in which they are financed or administered, but in broad terms it can be said that they all developed during an era of growth and increasing prosperity, and have been internationally lauded as worthy of emulation. Being in the spotlight of international attention may have blinded Danes or Swedes to some of the failings of their system; to the outside observer, Scandinavian pronouncements on this issue often have more than a touch of consensual smugness. But what many of the non-Scandinavian critics of the Nordic welfare systems fail to appreciate is the degree of attachment to them as a logical and vital extension of participatory democracy, of social integration and economic emancipation. It is this which has helped sustain a general determination to maintain and defend the welfare state, even though it is widely recognised that the systems established in the mid-twentieth century are in urgent need of reform and renewal.[22]

THE RESONANCES OF CHANGE

The decline in the number of Europeans earning a livelihood from the land has been particularly marked since the end of the Second World War. On the northern periphery, where the land has been not only the prime source of sustenance, but also the key element of social, cultural and political identity, this change is especially significant. Indeed, the rapid transformation which has occurred in the last fifty years may with some justification be dubbed a quiet revolution.

The pace and manner of change has varied over time and from country to country, but the underlying reasons have been the same. In order to survive, Scandinavian farmers have had to adopt new strategies of organisation, in the market place and the antechambers of parliament as well as on the farm. Given the relatively unfavourable circumstances in which they work – harsh climate, poor soils, short growing season, and so forth – they have succeeded remarkably well in raising output and productivity levels. Swedish farmers managed, for example, to harvest in 1973 double the tonnage of grain their forefathers had in 1900, in spite of the fact that the amount of land under crop cultivation had shrunk from 3.5 million to just under 3 million hectares. Milk production in Finland remained fairly constant between 1960 and 1980, although the size of the dairy herd

22. See, for example, the contributions by politicians and academics to the debate in *Nordisk Kontakt Tema: Välfärd-arbete* **3**/1993.

diminished from over one million in 1963 to under 700,000 in 1982. Danish farmers have continued to maintain the high yields and standards of production in dairying and pig-rearing already laid down in earlier decades, and their fields in the 1990s produce a far greater volume of crops than forty years previously, even though the total area under cultivation is now less than it was at the beginning of the century.

The fruits of this drive for greater productivity have been bitter-sweet. Farmers today in all the Nordic countries are more efficient and enjoy a much higher standard of living than their equivalents of fifty years ago; but they are far fewer in number, far more reliant on technology (including the computerised farm office), and in certain respects more isolated from the rest of society than were their predecessors. Farming has also become an occupation with a high proportion of middle-aged and elderly practitioners. The average age of those running Denmark's 41,600 full-time farms in 1988, for example, was 48; part-timers, who looked after 44,700 farms, were on average even older – 55. Most of the country's farms were run without hired labour, though in Denmark, as in the other Scandinavian countries, the state pays relief workers to take over temporarily and give the farmer a break. It is often difficult to find a partner willing to share the burdens of running a farm, especially in the more isolated areas. The level of recompense is not always satisfactory; whereas the average income of civil servants in Denmark increased by 79,300 *kroner* between 1950 and 1974, and that of workers in industry by 56,870 *kroner*, farmers' average income rose by only 44,100 *kroner*. Small farmers in particular were earning considerably less than they would have by working in a factory – one of the reasons for the massive flight from the land in the 1960s, when 60,000 farms were sold up, and over 100,000 left the agricultural labour force.

The movement out of farming and away from the countryside has had an impact in all rural communities, but it is the remote and isolated areas, far from the job-creating centres of population, which have probably suffered the most. Small farmers and their families have shown great resourcefulness and adaptability to changing circumstances. Their greatest worry tends to be the gradual erosion of the infrastructure – the closure of schools, the village shop or post office, the departure of friends and relatives and the decay of social and cultural activities. In a country such as Finland, where a massive amount of effort and energy was channelled into farming in the period of reconstruction from the end of the war to the mid-fifties, the decay of rural life is particularly poignant. For many, the abandoned buildings and small fields rapidly reverting to nature symbolise a bitter end to youthful hopes and aspirations fostered and encouraged by a national ethos which no longer has much relevance to a post-industrial, urban society.[23]

Farming and the land have historically occupied a central position in Nordic politics and in the shaping of national ideology. The farming interest has been ably represented at the national level, by political parties as well as by a variety of farm producers' organisations. It has played a crucial role in determining important constitutional issues, in defining the provisions and scope of social reforms, and in shaping defence policy. Indeed, given the diverse and often clashing interests of those who farm the land, it might be argued that the farmers' parties have wisely preferred to engage in 'high politics' rather than become enmeshed in farming matters pure and simple. In Denmark and Finland in particular, the land has tended to be equated with 'national' values. Industry was long held to be 'unDanish', for example, and influential figures such as the Danish agronomist R. Kampp continued to preach the virtues and necessity of small farms well into the fifties, as hundreds of smallholders were selling up and leaving for better-rewarded jobs in town.[24]

Farming now provides a living for only a small fraction of the population. Urban values and lifestyles are pushing out the last remnants of a genuinely rural culture, and the weavers of commercial fantasy are busily engaged in the reconstruction of an idyllic rural past for a growing number of city-dwellers who have little or no personal contact with or recollection of the farm or the countryside. There is much speculation about, and many ambitious plans for future rural development; but it is clear that the dynamic force no longer emanates from the farming population itself, as was the case a hundred years ago, when farmers responded vigorously to new challenges and helped carry forward the fortunes of the nation.

23. On this subject, see the essays in: Ingold T. (ed.) 1988 *The social implications of agrarian change in northern and eastern Finland* Transactions of the Finnish Anthropological Society **21**, Helsinki, and: Abrahams R 1991 *A place of their own. Family farming in eastern Finland* Cambridge Studies in Social and Cultural Anthropology **81**, Cambridge. 2.8 million hectares of land was redistributed in Finland as a result of postwar legislation, twice as much as in the last land reform period of the 1920s. In Lapland province alone, 3,500 new farms were created, and some 12,000 hectares of new land was brought under cultivation, mostly as tiny smallholdings.

24. See the chapter by Hans Kryger Larsen in: Feldbæk O 1992 *Dansk identitetshistorie* Copenhagen, vol. 3, pp. 468–511, and Hansen S, Henriksen I 1980 *Velfærdsstaten 1940–1978* Dansk socialhistorie vol. 7, Copenhagen, pp. 137ff.

A study carried out in the early sixties by the sociologist Antti Eskola revealed a high degree of congruence in the attitudes and views of Finnish town and country dwellers, but concluded that this link could be weakened by rural decay and an inability or unwillingness of the town dweller to keep up those ties. The British anthropologist Ray Abrahams came to similar conclusions almost thirty years later.[25] The resilience and adaptability of the Northern farmer, honed over centuries, has without doubt shaped and helped sustain the pragmatism and sober realism which characterises much of public life. The farmers of the Scandinavian countries have responded well to the severe challenges they have faced since the 1870s. They have managed to maintain a high political profile, influencing the outcome of numerous issues from defence to social welfare. But they have had to pay a price for becoming more productive and efficient, and they may well be facing the stiffest challenge yet as the pressures increase for freer world trade and domestic subsidies and protective measures are phased out or abolished. Increasingly, Scandinavian governments are treating farming as much as a social question as a branch of the national economy, encouraging farmers to take their land out of cultivation, or to sell up, whilst ensuring that a reasonable network of social and health services are maintained. The sizeable number of part-time farmers would seem to indicate a deeply passionate commitment to the land, but it also suggests that farming as a full-time occupation is seen by many as too unprofitable and too lonely.

The flight from the land has also brought regional differences into sharper focus. During the 1950s, there was much talk of '*det skæve Danmark*', a country whose regional imbalances had to be corrected: hence the attempts to locate government offices in areas of high local unemployment, and the 1958 regional development act, which was designed to lure industry to such areas. In the 1960s, the Finnish geographer Ilmari Hustich wrote of the 'three faces' of Finland, a prosperous southern region in which half the country's population lived and enjoyed the highest standards of living, a transitional central region, and an underdeveloped northern and north-eastern quarter. Regional policy has also attempted to bring new forms of employment to these northern regions, but has not succeeded in stemming the outflow of population to the rich south or to Sweden. Much of the industry which has been set up in regions of high unemployment has proved very vulnerable to recession. It is in marginal areas such as parts

25. Eskola E 1965 *Maalaiset ja kaupunkilaiset*. Helsinki, pp. 163–82. Abrahams 1991, pp. 168–70.

of Jutland, or the north of Norway, Sweden and Finland, where protest parties (and religious revivalism) have often made the deepest inroads.

The comparatively placid waters of Scandinavian politics have been disturbed in recent decades by the emergence of protest parties and movements on left and right; but the system has accommodated them remarkably well. In the case of Finland, where political developments during the first three decades of independence were rather different, and certainly less consensual, the Communist Party was gradually integrated into the political and social fabric after 1944. The radical student generation of the sixties in Finland tended to gravitate towards rigid orthodoxy rather than Trotskyite deviancy – a rather belated *rencontre* with the 'people' by the youthful intelligentsia.[26] The radical left elsewhere in Scandinavia was more diverse and more lively, perhaps because they did not live under the burden of having to conform with a rather dogmatic policy of friendship towards the Soviet Union, but also because there were new causes to be championed – squatters' rights, feminism, third-world liberation movements, and in Norway and Denmark, opposition to NATO and the EEC.

Protest has rarely degenerated into violence, though in recent years, there have been worrying signs of physical hostility towards immigrants, and Sweden also experienced the trauma of Olof Palme's murder on the streets of Stockholm in 1986. The perceptible downturn in turnout at elections has been seen as evidence of a growing disillusionment with politics and politicians; and in the rather fraught circumstances of the early 1990s, with unemployment sharply rising and many of the provisions of the welfare state now under threat, there are few grounds for optimism that the halcyon days of the sixties will return.

The rapid economic and social transformation of the Nordic countries has virtually eliminated many of the less romantic features of life in the past – the gross overcrowding, the sub-standard housing, and the sheer isolation of country life. Northern Europeans today are incomparably better housed, nourished and cared for than their forebears; they have not only the leisure, but also the wherewithal to enjoy it. Life in the modern world also brings its problems – loneliness, the breakdown of relationships, alcoholism, drug abuse,

26. For a discussion of this, see the contribution by Risto Alapuro in: Engman M and Kirby D 1989 *Finland. People – nation – state*, London, pp. 160–5.

homelessness – none of which are unique to Scandinavia, but all of which are exhaustively studied, investigated and discussed.

In many respects, the Nordic countries with their relatively small, scattered populations remain isolated from the rest of Europe, not least in their own estimation. There has always been a strong undercurrent of resistance to closer ties with Europe, whether it be in the form of a defence alliance or economic and political union. Neither Denmark's nor Norway's membership of NATO has been entirely trouble-free; the echoes of the 1972 referenda on Common Market membership still reverberate in both countries – most notably, in the Danish case, with the rejection of the Maastricht treaty in the June 1992 referendum (a verdict narrowly reversed a year later).[27] There are certainly traces in Scandinavian neutralism of a desire to remain aloof and uninvolved; but there has also been an activism which has at times caused irritation elsewhere – the pro-Vietnamese stance of the Swedish social democratic government under Olof Palme, the espousal of a number of third-world causes, or the active involvement in United Nations peace-keeping forces. There has also developed a high degree of regional cooperation. The Nordic Council has extended the range and scope of its activities over the years, and its work has been closely studied by the governments of the Baltic states. Other forums for cross-national debate have also emerged; the Scandinavian trades unions have met regularly for the best part of a century, for example, whilst the far northern regions have come together since the war to discuss common problems. A wide range of cultural initiatives have been launched, ranging from student exchange programmes to Nordic centres and institutes.[28]

There are limits to such cooperation, as we have seen. The hopes of the Scandinavists were not fulfilled by their respective governments, and national interests have tended to prevail at other crucial moments, such as the later 1940s. Recent initiatives towards membership of the European Community taken by governments have not always been endorsed wholeheartedly by their peoples. The seemingly placid waters of national unity have also been ruffled on occasion. The Nordic countries have perhaps been fortunate in that their minorities are small, relatively modest in their demands, and – like the 'awakened' Christians of an earlier epoch – willing to reach accommodation and to remain within the broad national framework. The most significant

27. On the Maastricht treaty, and opinion in the Nordic countries about membership of the European Union, see Arter 1993, pp. 189–236.

28. On the Nordic cooperation, see: Allardt et al. 1981, pp. 653–742. Elder et al. 1988, pp. 194–215.

minorities have been island peoples. Denmark has conceded full independence to Iceland, and a large measure of self-government to the Færoes and to Greenland. The Swedish-speaking Åland islanders have enjoyed a measure of autonomy since the early 1920s. The numerically much larger Swedish-speaking minority on the Finnish mainland have their language and cultural rights guaranteed in the constitution. The position of the minorities on either side of the Danish-German border has considerably improved since the joint declaration made in 1955 by the West German chancellor, Konrad Adenauer, and the Danish prime minister H. C. Hansen. The small and scattered Same (Lapp) people of the far north are faced with rather different problems of adaptation and survival, but have had a far more sympathetic response from the authorities in the past two decades. Considerable efforts have also been expended towards providing the basic means of integration – such as intensive language-teaching – for exogenous minorities, who have sought refuge or work in the Nordic countries; but it has to be said that the host nations have often been less than willing to recognise or accept the presence of racially very different peoples.

In the eyes of the rest of the world, the Nordic countries have become models of stability – consensual democracies, prototypes of modern society, their public administration, industrial relations, education and social welfare provisions exciting admiration.[29] The images of poverty and remoteness which prevailed throughout the nineteenth century have long since been replaced by visions of modernity – in architecture, furniture and fashion design, glassware and ceramics – prosperity and a generous welfare provision. Such stereotypes of course conceal as much as they reveal, but in one important respect, they reflect what has been a central objective of Nordic societies this century – the search for security. This has been, by and large, a common endeavour, by as much as for the *folk*. It has strengthened notions of equality, certainly, though it has also resulted in a high degree of conformity.[30] It might, however, be argued that

29. Marquis Childs can fairly claim to have led the way in presenting the Nordic countries in this favourable light: in 1980, he published a reappraisal of Sweden, forty-three years on, entitled *Sweden, the middle way on trial*, New Haven, Conn., which made the management of the economy the touchstone of success. Other favourable outsiders' reports include: Connery D 1966 *The Scandinavians*, New York; Parent J 1970 *Le modèle suédois*; Paris; Tomasson R 1970 *Sweden: prototype of a modern society*, New York. Sweden has attracted the lion's share of comment, and also criticism, as in Roland Huntford's 1971 *The new totalitarians*, London.

30. See the arguments put forward by H. F. Dahl in: Graubard (ed.) 1986, pp. 97–111.

small peripheral states have rather narrow margins for diversity and dissent in any event; when these limits are exceeded, the cost may be a heavy one.

The collapse of the Soviet empire poses new questions for the Nordic countries bordering the Baltic, not least how to cope with the potential ecological disaster zone which stretches from Murmansk to Mecklenburg. Disintegration in eastern Europe occurred as the western half of the continent was contemplating further steps towards European union. The Nordic countries are aware of the economic imperatives which urge them to follow, but at the same time, they are wary of being relegated to a mere appendage of the Brussels-Strasbourg-Frankfurt triangle, and they are acutely conscious of the possibility of being engulfed in the chaos and disaster which threatens to erupt on their eastern borders. As the twentieth century draws to its close, the Baltic world may be rather more of a regional reality than it has been for many decades; but it is also one overclouded with doubts and uncertainties.

CHAPTER FOURTEEN

A Baltic Renascence?

STALIN AND AFTER

The return of the Red Army to the Baltic states in 1944 brought little relief or joy to the war-weary populace. Thousands fled across the sea to Sweden or ended up in displaced persons' camps in postwar Germany; hundreds more took to the woods, living in rudimentary concealed bunkers and fighting a bitter and protracted guerrilla campaign against the militia and army units.[1] The political police (MVD) carried out a major screening operation, singling out 'war criminals' and 'enemies of the people' for transportation to the Soviet hinterland. An even more massive wave of deportations took place in 1949, in conjunction with the collectivisation programme; according to one estimate, the three Baltic countries lost about 3 per cent of their native populations during the last ten days of March 1949 alone.[2]

The re-establishment of Soviet rule appears to have been as confused as the imposition of communism elsewhere in eastern Europe. Dedicated and experienced party members were few on the

1. Misiunas R, Taagepera R 1993 *The Baltic states. Years of Dependence 1940–1990*, London, p. 90. On this period, see the essay by Vardys in: Vardys V 1965 *Lithuania under the Soviets. Portrait of a nation 1940–1965*, New York, pp. 85–110. Taagepera R 1979 Soviet documentation on the Estonian pro-independence guerrilla movement, 1945–1952 *Journal of Baltic Studies* **10**; 91–106. Laar M 1992 *War in the woods. Estonia's struggle for survival 1946–1956*, Washington.

2. Misiunas and Taagepera 1993, p. 99. Lithuania suffered in particular, with up to a quarter of a million people deported between 1947 and 1949. See Senn A 1990 *Lithuania awakening*, Berkeley and Los Angeles, pp. 40–5, for the beginnings of the debate over deportations amongst Lithuanian historians in 1988.

ground – only the Latvian party could claim more than 10,000 members at the beginning of 1946, of whom around half were non-Latvian (the Estonian and Lithuanian parties were also heavily weighted by non-native members). Enrolment of native cadres into the party remained sluggish into the fifties – which may have owed as much to prudence as to principles. Targeted by the partisans in the immediate postwar years, the native communists were also increasingly relegated to the sidelines by Soviet-educated personnel. In 1950, the Estonian communists were accused by the Politburo of the Communist Party of the Soviet Union (CPSU) of harbouring a bourgeois nationalist group, and a number of leading native communists including the first secretary Nikolai Karotamm and several ministers were purged. By 1951, the top posts within the party were all held by Russians or Russian-born Estonians such as the first secretary Ivan Käbin. Nothing quite as dramatic occurred in the other two republics, though the Central Committee of CPSU kept a careful watch via its subsidiary bodies and agents.

The lack of dedicated and competent personnel, as well as the dogged resistance of the partisans, meant that the reimposition of Soviet rule in the countryside took time and encountered a number of difficulties on the way. Agriculture had been badly affected during the war years. According to Soviet estimates, the area of land under cultivation in the Baltic republics shrank by between a quarter and a third, and the harvest in 1944 was only half the size of average pre-war yields. Livestock losses were high. The labour force had been savagely reduced. For these reasons, the Soviet authorities may have preferred not to antagonise the remaining farmers still further. Obligatory quotas were relatively light, allowing farmers to sell the bulk of their produce on the free market, and producers' cooperatives were encouraged. By 1947, recovery was well under way, though harvest yields and the numbers of livestock were still below pre-1939 levels.

The land reforms inaugurated in 1940 had established thirty hectares as the maximum size for an individual farm. The excess land was expropriated and made available for redistribution to the landless or smallholders, in plots no larger than ten hectares (or twelve ha. in the case of Lithuania). The sequestration of land belonging to those deemed collaborators or traitors (i.e., those who had fled to the West) in 1944–45 considerably augmented the state land funds. The process of redistribution in the postwar years was sluggish. The experience of recent years, and the prospect of intimidation or attack by the 'forest brothers', made many potential applicants cautious. A certain proportion of the confiscated lands went to the 'socialist sector' (state farms, machine tractor stations and machine-horse lending stations). These were intended as showpieces of large-scale mechanised farming as well as providers of traction power for the small farmers, but were greatly hampered by their lack of tractors or other equipment.

Collectivisation of agriculture, the hallmark of Stalinism, was not an immediate priority in the Baltic republics. The new order went to some lengths in 1940 to dispel fears of such measures being implemented, and although articles extolling the benefits of collective farms began appearing in the press in 1941, only a handful were actually started during the first period of Soviet rule. The process was resumed after the war, but there was no rush to join, in spite of inducements such as the lighter tax burdens and lower delivery quotas for produce imposed upon collective farms. Towards the end of 1947, a new phase began. The virtues of collectivisation were heavily publicised, whilst swingeing income tax increases were used to undermine the private farming sector. The most prosperous farmers were especially singled out for attack, though ironically, it was often these 'kulaks' who were most eager to enter collectives in order to escape the crippling burden of taxation. The initial drive towards collectivisation was not a success, though the percentage of farms collectivised did begin to rise significantly in the first quarter of 1949. All this changed dramatically in March, as a massive wave of deportations drove those who remained into the collective farms. The proportion of farms collectivised in Latvia jumped from just over one-tenth on 12 March to more than half by 9 April, and had reached 93 per cent by the end of the year. In areas still troubled by guerrilla activity, especially in Lithuania, the rate was slower, but in general, the final process of collectivisation throughout the Baltic was extremely rapid.[3]

The collectivisation of agriculture finally destroyed any lingering illusions that the Baltic peoples might still have had concerning their status within the Soviet Union. There is little evidence to date to suggest that the Soviet rulers were having second thoughts; their caution during the immediate postwar years was dictated by the need to stabilise the situation in the countryside and to restore agriculture to something like normal. Collectivisation as such was a social and

3. On the land reforms of the 1940s, and collectivisation in the Baltic republics, see Misiunas and Taagepera 1993, pp. 34–6, 94–107. Hanchett W 1968 The Communists and the Latvian countryside 1919–1949 *Res Baltica* edited by A. Sprudzs and A. Rusis, Leyden, pp. 88–116. Zundė P 1962 *Die Landwirtschaft Sowjetlitauens*, Marburg.

economic disaster, in the short term at least; but pragmatic economic considerations mattered far less than the political imperatives of Soviet rule. The destruction of the landowning peasantry was more than the final phase of class struggle, as Soviet propaganda portrayed the events of 1949; it was also intended to obliterate the social, economic and ideological foundations upon which the prewar independent republics had rested.

The history and culture of the Baltic peoples were also subjected to redefinition according to Stalinist criteria. Russian hegemony and leadership were constantly emphasised: the image of a wise and kindly Stalin advising adulatory representatives of the various peoples of the Soviet Union was conveyed in thousands of posters, newspaper articles, sycophantic poems, novels and paintings. Artists and writers who deviated from the principles of socialist realism were pilloried as decadent bourgeois nationalists and forced either to recant or to be silent. The history of the recent past was rewritten. In the initial version of events, the working peoples of the Baltic states had spontaneously risen up and cast off the yoke of fascist dictatorship in the summer of 1940, and had eagerly sought admission to the family of Soviet socialist nations. Later versions had to take account of the official Soviet response to the publication in the West of documents revealing the extent of Nazi-Soviet collusion. This response justified the Soviet presence in the Baltic states as a necessary and vital defence measure against aggression, but said nothing about the revolutionary achievements of the Baltic peoples.[4]

The compulsive need to justify and sanctify every twist and turn of Soviet policy, and endlessly to laud the deeds and genius of comrade Stalin, trapped thousands in a web of lies and falsehoods. The anguished cry of the sculptor in Daina Avotiņa's 1970 novel *Nenogaliniet stirnu* (Don't kill the dove): – 'Spiritually I have nothing left to live for . . . I have become entangled and confused by all sorts of clichés . . . I have ploughed myself under, I have buried myself, I have suffocated myself' – is a mournful epitaph for all whose artistic

4. See the chapter on Soviet historiography and the Baltic states by Romuald Misiunas in: Vardys V, Misiunas R 1978 *The Baltic states in peace and war 1917–1945*, University Park, Penn., pp. 173–96, which deals largely with Lithuania. The re-evaluation of recent Lithuanian history which erupted in the late 1980s is ably chronicled in: Senn A 1990, pp. 25–33, 47–54. See also Krapauskas V 1992 Marxism and nationalism in Soviet Lithuanian historiography *Journal of Baltic Studies* **23**: 239–60.

creativity was ruined, or whose moral and intellectual values were compromised and distorted under Stalinism.[5]

The damage done by the cult of personality was openly admitted in the late fifties, after Nikita Khrushchev's famous denunciation of the crimes of Stalin at the twentieth party congress of the CPSU in 1956. During the 'thaw' which followed, the rigid guidelines on literature and art laid down in 1946 were relaxed. The works of a number of writers who had made their reputation before 1940 were reissued, and some who had survived but had found disfavour with the regime were once more permitted to publish. Aspects of Soviet life came in for criticism, and writers also began to venture into highly sensitive areas of the recent past. The returned Latvian deportee Harijs Heislers caused a sensation with the publication of his autobiographical poem *Nepabeigtā dziesma* (Unfinished song, 1956), which depicted life in an Arctic labour camp, and the deportations of 1941 were the backdrop of the novel *Maa ja rahvas* (The land and the people, 1956) by the Estonian writer, Rudolf Sirge. The younger generation also produced its angry young men, such as the Latvian Visvaldis Eglons-Lāms, whose 1960 novel *Kāpj dūmu stabi* (Smoke is rising), a grim and realistic portrayal of working-class life in Riga, provoked official ire.

Officialdom was ever vigilant, and began to crack down in the wake of Khrushchev's 1957 speech on art and literature, in which he stressed adherence to the guiding role of the party. In Lithuania, there was something akin to a mini-purge of those deemed to have been negligent in this regard, such as the Lithuanian minister of culture and the rector of the university of Vilnius. The premiere of an opera based on the rebellion of 1863 was also cancelled. The mass demonstrations and strikes in Poland and the Hungarian uprising of 1956 undoubtedly made the Soviet hierarchy nervous about repercussions in the Baltic republics, and may explain why Antanas Sniečkus, the first secretary of the Lithuanian Communist Party, took pre-emptive steps in order to forestall interference by Moscow in his personal fiefdom.[6]

5. Ekmanis R 1978 *Latvian literature under the Soviets 1940–1975*, Belmont, Mass., p. 316. For a general overview of literary and cultural developments in the Baltic republics during the Soviet period, see Misiunas and Taagepera 1993, pp. 115–24 151–83, 241–50. Translations of poems, short stories and extracts of novels have appeared over the years in the émigré journal *Lituanus*; the *Journal of Baltic Studies* has also published articles on Soviet Baltic literature and culture generally.

6. Misiunas and Taagepera 1993, p. 156. Vardys V (ed.) 1965 *Lithuania under the Soviets. Portrait of a nation 1940–1965*, New York, pp. 207–8 (chapter on literature and the arts by Jonas Grinius). There had been student riots in Vilnius at the time of the Hungarian uprising. As a further indication of the anxiety caused in ruling circles by the events of 1956, mention may be made of a lengthy article published in the party

In the event, it was Latvia which bore the brunt of a new onslaught against 'bourgeois nationalism' in 1959. The purge of much of the native leadership, which had begun to take control of the party in the late fifties, was a sharp reminder that moves towards greater autonomy would not be tolerated in Moscow, though personal rivalries within the party leadership may also have played a part. Interestingly, the reason given for the dismissal of the deputy chairman of the council of ministers, Eduards Berklāvs, was that he had favoured developing industries which used local raw materials and labour, and which would satisfy Latvian consumer demands before those of the Soviet Union as a whole – policies advocated in a general critique of economic planning made three years earlier by the chairman of the council of ministers of the Estonian SSR, Aleksei Müürisepp. The purges halted the gradual process of 'nativisation' of the leadership, and Latvia was to remain under the tight grip of Moscow loyalists like Arvīds Pelše, party first secretary from 1959 to 1966, when he was elevated to the politburo of the CPSU central committee, and Augusts Voss, his successor to the post.[7]

In Estonia and Lithuania, the long-serving party first secretaries Ivan Käbin (1950–78) and Antanas Sniečkus (1936–74) managed to maintain and even to promote an element of nativist autonomy. The percentage of Estonian members of the party slowly rose, and by 1971, over 80 per cent of the members of the Communist Party Central Committee and the council of ministers were Estonian. Although a number of these were 'Yestonians' – Russian-born like Aleksei Müürisepp and Ivan Käbin, often with an imperfect or non-existent knowledge of the language – they were far less zealous in following the dictates of Moscow than their counterparts in Riga. The Estonian leadership in the sixties was able to make criticisms and even to take initiatives which would have been unthinkable in Latvia. Estonia also became a kind of testing-ground for innovations in administration and management. A regular shipping line between Helsinki and Tallinn was opened in 1965, and Finnish-built hotels in the Estonian capital

newspaper *Cīņa* in September 1957 by the Latvian novelist Andrejs Upīts, one of the most faithful watchdogs of the established order, accusing Polish and Hungarian writers of attacking the USSR and socialist realism, and hailing the suppression of the Hungarian uprising.

7. Misiunas and Taagepera 1993, pp. 140–6. It has also been suggested that Latvian opposition to the implied weakening of the status of Latvian-language teaching in Russian-language schools in the republic (according to an opt-out provision incorporated in the 1958–9 education reforms) was instrumental in forcing Berklāvs' dismissal: Bilinsky Y 1962 The education laws of 1958–59 and nationality policy *Soviet Studies* **14**: 146–7.

helped cater for the needs of the steady stream of tourists. Estonians were also able to watch Finnish television programmes, and to read in translation a wide selection of Western literature. For the less fortunate citizens of the Soviet hinterland, Estonia was indeed '*nash zapad*' (our West).[8]

The party in Lithuania was adroitly managed by Sniečkus, and remained largely in Lithuanian hands. Sniečkus was outspokenly loyal towards Moscow, and he made it plain that separatist or autonomist tendencies would be resisted. Lithuania, however, was less subjected to centralist economic pressures than the more industrialised northern Baltic republics, and did not have to contend with the levels of immigration which in the seventies and eighties threatened to overwhelm the indigenous populations of Estonia and Latvia.

ACCOMMODATION AND DISSENT

Lithuania had long been the most rural of the three Baltic states, and remained so during the first two decades of Soviet rule. Over the next two decades, however, it began to catch up with its more urbanised and industrialised northern neighbours. By 1979, the rural population of Lithuania had shrunk from 61 per cent of the total for the republic in 1959 to 39 per cent. The proportion of the labour force engaged in agriculture also declined rapidly, reaching the same level as Latvia – 24 per cent – by the late sixties.

For the large numbers who left the land, the 'pull' factor of increased work opportunities (especially for women) was probably decisive. Farm work was generally regarded as physically demanding and tiring, and farms often had difficulties in recruiting or retaining qualified, skilled personnel. Those who remained on the land in the three Baltic republics faced a rather different set of problems to those encountered by their equivalents in Scandinavia, where the prosperity generated by industrial expansion and trade and the comprehensive infrastructure of services provided by the welfare state did much to cover the disparities of income levels. The large numbers of elderly people living in the countryside (as early as 1970, almost one-quarter of the rural population of Lithuania were old-age pensioners) often experienced great difficulties in coping on low pensions, and they did

8. For in-depth analysis of a number of facets of Soviet Estonia, see: Parming T and Järvesoo E 1978 *A case study of a Soviet republic. The Estonian SSR*, Boulder, Colorado.

not have access to the kind of social care and health provisions of their counterparts in Finland, Denmark or Sweden. In spite of considerable improvements in living conditions since the grim postwar years, much of the housing stock and many of the basic amenities such as a piped water supply or even tarred roads were lacking. Drunkenness was acknowledged to be a serious problem in the countryside. In the year 1989, for example, collective farmworkers in Estonia spent on alcohol an average 352 roubles, compared with 200 roubles for all other occupational groups. The rate of alcohol-related deaths and accidents remained high, but until the anti-drink campaign launched in the eighties, little was done to change attitudes or habits.[9]

The development of postwar agriculture in the Baltic has in certain respects followed the broad pattern of other northern European countries, but it has also been far more affected by the actions of the state. The destruction caused by the war, and even more, by the forced deportations and collectivisation was further compounded by the rigid procurement policies of the Stalinist regime, so that agricultural output (and living conditions on the land) fell below prewar levels. The situation began gradually to change for the better after Stalin's death. By the mid-sixties, rural incomes had appreciably risen, and members of collective (*kolkhoz*) or state (*sovkhoz*) farms with a private plot of land were able to earn a good deal more than the average wages of urban workers. The departure of thousands from the land – as many as 100,000 between 1960 and 1965 in Lithuania, for example – coincided with considerable improvements in productivity and output. The prices paid by the state for produce delivered by the farms were increased significantly, and more capital and resources were allocated to agriculture; state farms in the Baltic adopted the principles of self-management without government subsidies at the end of the sixties, and many were able to provide a wide range of up-to-date services and facilities, including comfortable modern homes. Collective and state farms also trod a path which would have been familiar to the large estate-owners of previous centuries, developing their own processing plants and light industries. By 1972, a mere five years after farm industry was declared legal, auxiliary industry accounted for 14 per cent of Estonia's total agricultural production, and there were numerous examples of enterprising and wealthy collectives, of which

9. On the problems of rural life, see: Mačiuika B 1976 Contemporary social problems in the collectivized Lithuanian countryside *Lituanus* **22**: 5–27. Simpura J and Tigerstedt C (eds) 1992 *Social problems around the Baltic sea*, Helsinki, pp. 23–68.

the Kirov fishing *kolkhoz*, on the outskirts of Tallinn, was the most famous.[10]

Impressive though these achievements were, especially in comparison with the general pattern of agricultural development in the Soviet Union, farming standards in the Baltic still lagged behind those of the Scandinavian countries. With an average annual milk yield of 4,103 litres per cow in 1987, Estonia led the field in the Soviet Union (where the overall average milk yield was a mere 2,682 litres per cow), but was way behind Finland (5,461 litres per cow in 1979), for example. Harvest yields followed the same pattern: high in comparison with the rest of the Soviet Union, but mediocre by Western standards. The economic survey conducted by a team of experts engaged by the Sweden ministry of foreign affairs in 1991 identified a number of reasons for poor performance, including inadequate and ineffective equipment and machinery, bad management practices, poor social as well as economic infrastructures, and the negative attitude of the farmworkers themselves: but it also attributed the better-than-Soviet-average levels of production and productivity to a greater range of incentives, a degree of local autonomy and enlightened farm management, and the survival of the prewar peasant spirit.[11]

Agriculture's share of national income at the beginning of the 1990s was relatively high in all three Baltic republics (though price restructuring in favour of agriculture in the 1980s distorted the proportions), and the ideological and emotional values attached to farming and the land were still strong: but at a time when there is a large question-mark against the future of farming in northern Europe as a whole, the prospects for post-collective agriculture in the Baltic states cannot be rosy. The restoration of the private farm is, however, as much to do with cultural and national values as it is with productivity.[12] Very large numbers of town-dwellers in all three Baltic republics are from the countryside: a 1978 survey of the origins of

10. Misiunas and Taagepera 1993, pp. 189–92, 230–3. Järvesoo E 1974 Private enterprise in Soviet Estonian agriculture *Journal of Baltic Studies* **5**: 169–87. Arkadie B van and Karlsson M 1992 *Economic survey of the Baltic states*, London, pp. 275–94.

11. Arkadie and Karlsson 1992, pp. 275–8.

12. In 1989, agriculture and forestry provided between 25–30 per cent of the national income in all three republics, and gave employment or an income to substantial numbers of people, both within the collective-state sector and on private farms. Well over 300,000 people in Lithuania claimed that farming was either a secondary or major source of income in the census of 1989, for example. Arkadie and Karlsson 1992, pp. 226–7, 280–7. There is a well-balanced assessment of the post-Soviet situation in Lieven A 1993 *The Baltic revolution*, New Haven, Conn., and London, pp. 347–55.

factory workers in Estonia, for example, found that one-third of those working in Tallinn, one-half in medium-sized Estonian towns, and two-thirds in small towns had come from the land. The uncertain future of many factories and other places of urban employment and the many unpleasant features of urban life – overcrowding, rising crime rates, the stress and strain of everyday life – are often a strong inducement to return to the old family farmsteads, now being rescued and restored.

There is a further dimension, which in some ways is a reaffirmation of the strongly rural character of Baltic identity, and that is the frequently expressed mistrust of or hostility to the 'alien' ethnic or cultural character of the city, particularly in Estonia and Latvia. In comparison with the other two Baltic republics, Lithuania was fortunate in having a large pool of native-born rural labour (and a significantly higher birth rate) for industrial expansion, and a fairly constant ratio between the Lithuanian and non-Lithuanian population (around 4:1) was maintained throughout the sixties and seventies. There has been considerable expansion of the towns and cities of Lithuania, but in their ethnic composition, they are probably more 'Lithuanian' than they were before the war, when there were sizeable Jewish and Polish communities (this is certainly the case with the capital Vilnius, where Lithuanian speakers probably constituted one-fifth of the population on the eve of war and now make up over half of the 592,000 inhabitants).

In Latvia and Estonia, on the other hand, the balance between the autochthonous inhabitants and the non-native population has changed significantly, especially in the larger cities. In 1959, Estonians made up three-quarters of the population of the republic; thirty years later, that had dropped to 61.5 per cent, with Russians making up 30.3 per cent. The 1989 census showed that Russians made up a large majority of the population in the towns of north-eastern Estonia, built to accommodate workers recruited to mine and process the oil-shale deposits, and in nearby Narva. Estonians were also slightly outnumbered by non-Estonians in the capital, Tallinn. In neighbouring Latvia, the Russian share of the population was even higher – 34 per cent – and the Latvians had fallen from 62 per cent in 1959 to 52 per cent thirty years later. Riga had always had a high proportion of non-Latvian inhabitants, though Latvians had made up a clear majority of the city's population on the eve of war. By the sixties, this was no longer the case, and by 1989, Russian-speakers constituted 60 per cent of the city's population, as against a mere 36 per cent with Latvian as their mother tongue. Russian speakers also made up the majority of the population in Latvia's other major cities.

The greatest single cause for the shifting ethnic balance was immigration on a major scale, though there was always an outflow of migrants almost as great as the inflow. By 1980, there were more than ninety departures from Estonia for every hundred arrivals to the republic; ten years later, the net outflow was beginning to exceed the inflow of migrants. Although there is little evidence of a deliberate policy of russification through the direction of labour, the mixing of peoples within the Soviet Union as a whole was seen as a welcome development, as for instance, by the then head of the KGB, Yuri Andropov, in a speech made in 1977. Migration statistics for the late seventies showed an intensification of movement in all republics, though with higher than average figures for Estonia, Latvia and Lithuania, which also recorded the highest levels in the percentage of persons moving permanent residence at least once.

Immigrants were drawn to the Baltic republics primarily to meet the demand for labour in the new industrial complexes being built. By the late 1960s, demand had begun to outstrip supply, and recruitment campaigns had to be mounted by enterprises desperate for workers. Inducements such as the offer of housing caused resentment amongst the indigenous population, to whom such precious benefits were denied. The immigrants themselves, drawn from a wide variety of regional, social, linguistic and occupational backgrounds and frequently moving on in search of a new or better job, did not easily cohere. In this respect, the actual danger of wholescale russification in Estonia and Latvia was a good deal less than the shifting demographic balance might have suggested, especially as control of the local administration was still largely in the hands of native cadres.

On the other hand, the immigrants remained largely outside the host community, where they were regarded with a mixture of contempt and hostility, fuelled by resentments over housing allocation and the inability or unwillingness of immigrants serving the public to speak the local language. For the local non-Russian population, having to negotiate in Russian with shop assistants, taxi-drivers, paramedics, policemen and the grim guardians of hotel and restaurant entrances was not only a daily irritant; it was also a constant reminder of their loss of national sovereignty.

The local leadership occasionally voiced its unease about the unrestrained inflow of migrants, especially in the more liberal atmosphere of the 1980s; but even during the Brezhnev era, local managers and planners had preferred increased labour efficiency rather than employing more workers in order to meet production targets.

This brought them into conflict with the central sectoral ministries, which had resumed responsibility for the bulk of industrial production in 1965, after a brief period of devolved regional control. At the end of the 1980s, for example, less than 10 per cent of industrial output in Estonia was under local control; the rest was produced by enterprises either fully or partially under orders from Moscow. Industries were also heavily dependent on imports of raw materials, components and energy from other parts of the Soviet Union.[13]

The rapid industrialisation which occurred during the third quarter of this century in the three Baltic republics created problems which a cumbersome and corrupt centralised bureaucracy tried in vain to remedy with outmoded and inefficient methods. The 1980s were a disastrous decade in terms of economic performance; the stagnation of the later years of the Brezhnev era turned into decline, as output levels plummeted. Overmanned, poorly managed, reliant on outmoded equipment and technology and a major cause of environmental pollution, the massive industrial complexes thrown up in the sixties and early seventies were to cause even more of a headache for the new rulers of the Baltic states in the 1990s than had the legacy of wartime industrial expansion for their predecessors of the 1920s.

Industrialisation has caused many problems, and may indeed have helped destroy the old political order; but it has also brought undeniable benefits to the peoples of the Baltic republics. Living standards rose appreciably, and more rapidly in the three republics than in the rest of the Soviet Union. A much wider range of consumer goods, many of them manufactured in the region, became available. Greater prosperity coincided with a sunnier political and cultural climate after the grim, overcast postwar years, helped revive the self-confidence of the Baltic peoples, and allowed them an opportunity to come to terms with their situation. By the early sixties, a growing number, especially younger people, were willing to work within the system, either in pursuit of a career, or for more idealistic motives. Economic growth provided the opportunities; education the means; but both threatened to weaken or undermine the national distinctiveness of the Baltic peoples, by virtue of their integrative and assimilationist tendencies.

Soviet education policy did not seek to impose Russian as the medium of instruction, as had occurred in tsarist days, but it had fixed ideological objectives which permeated all subjects. Immense effort and

13. Misiunas and Taagepera 1993, pp. 183–9, 227–30. Arkadie and Karlsson 1992, pp. 44–51, 69–73, 95–102.

resources were channelled into the promotion and inculcation of Soviet ideas and values, through the party educational structure as well as in the schools and institutions of higher education. In Latvia alone, the party employed in 1975 25,000 trained propagandists, 20,000 political information specialists and 18,000 assigned agitators, and a total of 525,000 people, one-fifth of the entire population of the republic, were enrolled in party schools.[14] How successful these efforts were is hard to determine. It is unlikely that Marxism-Leninism as such made much impact, but the more day-to-day aspects of Soviet life and achievements undoubtedly did shape attitudes in the goldfish-bowl environment which existed, in much the same way as work habits and life-styles were affected. The community of fate (*Schicksalsgemeinschaft*, a term coined by the Austrian Marxist Otto Bauer at the beginning of the century) which the Baltic peoples shared with other citizens of the Soviet Union for almost half a century has left a legacy more durable than the ideology which was supposed to guide and direct it – and also more dangerous. Decades of Soviet education and propaganda have not persuaded the Baltic peoples that they entered that community voluntarily, but they have nevertheless been deeply influenced by that experience, and coming to terms with that fact has been and will continue to be a painful process.

By contrast, the Russian language appears to have had little impact upon the non-Russian indigenous population. Linguists and writers have vigilantly protected the native languages from the intrusion of Russianisms. The annual output of original and translated literature in the indigenous languages is impressive. Levels of bilingualism are highest in Latvia, with its large Russian-speaking population; but even here, Latvian language and culture have more than held their own against encroachment. In neighbouring Estonia, there were few indications that the two major linguistic communities were coming together. The rate of intermarriage remained low, whilst levels of bilingualism amongst Estonians and amongst Russians in the republic declined in the seventies, and were well behind comparable rates in the other two Baltic republics.[15]

14. Figures quoted by Christopher Doersam in: Allworth E (ed.) 1977 *Nationality group survival in multi-ethnic states. Shifting support patterns in the Soviet Baltic region*, New York, p. 156.

15. In addition to the chapter on sovietisation, culture and religion by Christopher Doersam in Allworth 1977, pp. 148–93, see also: Hilkes P 1987 The Estonian SSR as an example of Soviet school reform in the 1980s *Journal of Baltic Studies* **18**: 349–66. Kriendler I 1988 Baltic area languages and the Soviet Union: a sociolinguistic perspective *Journal of Baltic Studies* **19**: 5–20.

During the relatively prosperous and untroubled sixties, accommodation within the Soviet system became something of a guiding principle for the younger generation, aware that the past their parents talked about was unlikely to return, conscious of the need to make a career, and reasonably confident that their national identity would at least be respected, maybe even allowed to develop more freely.[16] This mood of cautious optimism turned sour during the long years of stagnation and decline, presided over by Leonid Ilyich Brezhnev. This was partly a reflection of a general atmosphere of disenchantment within the Soviet Union as a whole, but local issues – in particular, the perceived threat to national identity posed by the uncontrolled influx of immigrants and the Great Russian undertones of offical policy – sharpened the focus considerably. There emerged a small, courageous hard core of dissidents in all three Baltic republics, but as in Russia, they remained largely isolated from the community at large, honoured more in the Western media than in their homeland.[17] The Catholic church in Lithuania proved to be a persistent thorn in the flesh of the authorities, and a rallying-point for the nationalist aspirations of the people; the religious congegations of Estonia and Latvia (where there is also a sizeable Catholic minority) were far more quiescent and conformist, with the exception of a few Lutheran pastors in Estonia and the small Baptist communities.[18] Anti-Soviet feelings occasionally erupted into violence, most notably in the riots which followed the self-immolation of a Lithuanian student in a Kaunas park in 1972: but by and large, the resentments were stored up, allowed only the occasional outlet in chalked messages or mutterings about the behaviour of the immigrants.

LIVING WITH THE BEAR

In the winter of 1917–18, imperial Germany had triumphed in the east against a disintegrating Russian state wracked by revolution.

16. This is the theme of Rein Taagepera's essay on nationalism, collaborationism and new-leftism: Parming and Järvesoo E 1978, pp. 75–103.

17. See, for example, the section on dissent, and the accompanying footnotes, in Misiunas and Taagepera 1993, pp. 250–71. Lieven 1993, pp. 103–8 makes some interesting observations on the present position of the dissidents.

18. For a recent overview, see: Vardys V 1987 The role of the churches in the maintenance of regional and national identity in the Baltic republics *Journal of Baltic Studies* **18**: 287–300.

Twenty-seven years later, the tables were turned with a vengeance. When the Allied commanders received the German surrender on Lüneburg Heath in May 1945, it was in the knowledge that a vast swathe of territory lying eastward was under Red Army control, and that Generalissimo Stalin was unlikely to relinquish his grip on what had been acquired by force of arms. 'Around the whole of Russian-dominated territory, we may expect that the Soviet government will erect a sort of political Chinese wall', was the chillingly accurate prediction of Paul Winterton, the wartime Moscow correspondent of the *Daily Telegraph*: 'Russia will expect complete non-interference by foreign countries with affairs on her side of the wall.'[19]

Paul Winterton had visited Tallinn shortly after the Red Army had reoccupied most of Estonia, and recorded his impressions in print. He acknowledged the justice of the Baltic peoples' desire for independence, but it was Russia's perceived need for security which clearly was uppermost in his mind; the best he could hope for was some degree of autonomy under Soviet rule for the Baltic states. In this, he did not differ greatly from the views of the wartime leaders of Britain or the United States.[20] Although neither country recognised the *de jure* incorporation of the Baltic states into the Soviet Union, they offered little encouragement to the governments in exile. Much was achieved by the émigré communities by way of cultural activities; but they had always an uphill battle in trying to keep alive in their host countries the memory of their distinct and sovereign nationhood. The term 'Soviet' became synonymous with 'Russian' to the great American or British public. The us-and-them attitudes fostered by the Cold War simply did not allow for other distinctions to be made. That the Soviet Union was a complex and potentially explosive mixture of nationalities was little understood by the public at large in the Western world. Newsworthy stories of protest or dissidence amongst the Baltic peoples were relatively few – partly no doubt because Western correspondents were largely confined to Moscow – and the specifically national/ethnic dimensions were rarely treated in a balanced or informative fashion. As a result, the already feeble perception of the

19. Winterton was speaking at Chatham House, London, in July 1945. Winterton P 1946 The aims of the USSR in Europe *International Affairs* **1**: 19.

20. Winterton P 1945 *Report on Russia*, London, pp. 84–90. On British and American wartime policies towards the Baltic states, see my chapter in: Vardys V and Misiunas R 1978 *The Baltic states in peace and war 1917–1945*, University Park, Penn., and London, pp. 159–72: Kochavi A 1991 Britain, the Soviet Union and the question of the Baltic states in 1943 *Journal of Baltic Studies* **22**; 173–82.

Baltic peoples in the West faded still more behind the frontiers of the Soviet empire.

The boundaries of that empire were even unwittingly moved westward on occasion, much to the chagrin and annoyance of the Finns, who found their country appearing behind the 'Iron Curtain' in maps printed in German newspapers, and otherwise consigned to the tender mercies of Moscow. Such errors and misconceptions continued to occur in spite of vigorous and sustained efforts to promote an image of Finland as a neutral Nordic democracy which was acting as a bridge-builder between east and west. Finland did not fit easily into the bipolarised world of NATO and the Warsaw Pact. It was patently not neutral in the classic Swiss manner, since it had specified military obligations in the event of attack by Germany or its allies on Finland or on the Soviet Union via Finnish territory, according to article one of the 1948 mutual assistance treaty. The concept of *active* neutrality developed in the sixties by President Urho Kekkonen and his advisers was intended to lessen the risk of conflict in the northern European area, and hence to make the prospect of Finland having to abide by article one less likely: in other words, it was entirely consonant with Finland's own national interests. This was not always grasped by Western politicians or commentators, for whom Finland was hampered at least by its treaty obligations, and at worst, was subservient to Moscow's wishes.[21]

The 1948 treaty faced its first major test during the late fifties. The most evident cause was the admission into NATO of a rearmed West German state, and the prospect of a challenge to Soviet military and naval strength in northern Europe, but the actions of the Soviet leadership had internal political consequences in Finland. In 1958, Moscow showed its displeasure at what it perceived to be an anti-Soviet trend in Finnish politics by not replacing an ambassador to Helsinki and suspending trade talks. This 'night-frost' crisis was brought to an end only after the Agrarian Union withdrew from the socialist-led coalition government, causing its collapse in January 1959. Three years later, as the two sides in the Cold War confronted one another over the Berlin wall and the missiles being sent to Cuba, a more dramatic step was taken when the Soviet government, adducing the growing military strength of West Germany and the crisis over Berlin as constituting a threat, proposed consultations in accordance

21. There is an extensive literature in English on Finnish foreign policy. The *Yearbook of Finnish Foreign Policy*, published since 1973, offers useful insights into Finnish thinking (not all of it official) and good bibliographical references.

with article two of the 1948 treaty.[22] As in the earlier 'night-frost' crisis, President Kekkonen resorted to personal discussions with the Soviet leader Nikita Khrushchev. Khrushchev agreed to postpone consultations, which Kekkonen argued would only increase tension in Scandinavia, and expressed the wish that Finland should henceforth act as a kind of watchdog in northern Europe and the Baltic, alerting the Soviet government as and when necessary. The anti-Kekkonen electoral alliance broke up that same day, and Kekkonen was able to secure a comfortable victory in the presidential elections held a few weeks later.

By virtue of his much-publicised personal diplomacy, the president's prestige was boosted, and the correctness of his policy of good relations with the Soviet Union reaffirmed. The losers were those perceived to be hostile to such a policy, like the social democrats, thrown into the political wilderness after the collapse of the government in January 1959. When the social democrats returned to office seven years later, they stood foursquare behind the Paasikivi-Kekkonen line of good relations with the Soviet Union – a necessity which gradually became an orthodox doctrine to which all parties seeking office had to subscribe.

Finland undeniably obtained a number of advantages from this policy. By satisfying the basic security concerns of their eastern neighbour, the Finns were able to develop and extend vital trade links with their major Western markets, and to play an active part in the process of detente during the early seventies, when Helsinki hosted the European Security Conference and strategic arms limitation talks. After the 1961 note crisis, the Finns were able to avoid further moves towards more intimate military arrangements with the Soviet Union. The Finnish armed forces never carried out exercises predicated on dealing with the eventuality of article one being invoked, and the request made by the Soviet defence minister in 1978 for joint exercises was politely but firmly turned down. The Soviet Union also returned the Porkkala base in 1955, and signed a fifty-year lease in 1962, allowing Finland to reconstruct and bring back into use the Saimaa canal which linked the eastern hinterland to the now Russian port of Vyborg (Viipuri). Bilateral trade agreements and joint projects which were arrived at under the broad auspices of the 1948 treaty also helped provide much-needed employment for Finns, and eased the balance of payments situation.

22. 'The High Contracting Parties shall confer with each other if it is established that the threat of an armed attack as described in Article One is present.'

For the Soviet side, the treaty provided a reasonable degree of security and protection on the northern flank (though the development of a new generation of strategic missiles in the 1970s posed questions which were never adequately resolved). Dissidents and political refugees found no safe haven in Finland, unlike their predecessors at the turn of the century. The extensive trading links with Finland offered a window of opportunity to the West, and Soviet foreign trade associations sought to cash in on Finnish technical expertise by pushing for more joint projects in Third World countries. To the non-aligned world, Finland could be held up as a shining example of a 'peace-loving' country that was willing to work in harmony with the Soviet Union (a relationship that also had its attractions for certain countries of the Warsaw Pact).[23]

The price paid by Finland for the policies pursued for nearly three decades by President Urho Kekkonen and his advisers was a high one, as Finns themselves now recognise.[24] Self-censorship, a rather egregious subservience and a willingness to work and if necessary intrigue with Russian officials may be characteristics inherited from the tsarist era as much as they are the unpleasant consequences of the former president's love of power; but they distorted the party political system, ruined the careers of many promising people who refused to toe the line, created a bad impression abroad, and probably weakened the credibility of Finland's claim to neutrality. It may be the case that Kekkonen's foreign policy helped strengthen the Finns' own confidence in their country's future; but in many respects, that confidence rested upon insecure foundations.[25] In spite of continued loud professions of friendship, the motives and actions of the Soviet Union did little to inspire trust. The various proposals for a nuclear-free zone in northern Europe which were advanced by the Soviet Union and by Finland alarmed rather than won over the other

23. On trade between Finland and the Soviet Union, see: Möttölä K, Bykov O and Korolev I, (eds) 1983 *Finnish-Soviet economic relations*, London. Some interesting parallels between the tsarist and the Soviet periods are drawn by Risto Penttilä in his contribution to *YYA-Suomi*, Helsinki 1993, pp. 47–57, though he fails to make the contrast between the ease with which revolutionaries such as Trotsky and Lenin could slip into and stay in tsarist Finland (and receive support from Finnish sympathisers) and the zealous efforts of the authorities of independent Finland to keep out not only dissidents, but also their publications.

24. For example, Penttilä 1993, p. 48 (although he believes that the damage was slight in the end). For a detailed account of this period, Vihavainen T 1991 *Kansakunta rähmällään: suomettumisen lyhyt historia*, Helsinki.

25. Kirby D 1979 *Finland in the twentieth century* London, p. 208, citing opinion polls carried out between 1964 and 1974.

Nordic countries; Sweden was constantly troubled by Soviet violations of its air space and territorial waters; and the near-catastrophe at the Chernobyl nuclear reactor in 1986 highlighted the threat to the environment posed by the decaying superpower. Far from being a 'sea of peace' – a favourite Soviet slogan of the seventies – the Baltic threatened to become an ecological disaster, choked with untreated sewage, industrial effluent and the seepage of uncontrolled and unrecorded waste-dumping.

The collapse of the Soviet Union in 1991 finally nullified the 1948 treaty, although the Finnish government had effectively declared it redundant a year before, after Moscow agreed to the reunification of the two Germanies. Its inadequacies had come under increasingly critical scrutiny during the more open era of Mauno Koivisto's first period of office as president (1982–88), though the government had always been careful to ensure the limits were not overstepped, and had maintained an ultra-cautious line on events in the Soviet Union right up until the end, refusing, for example, to join the other Nordic countries in an explicit condemnation of the attempted coup of August 1991.

Compliance with, rather than resistance to what were taken to be the legitimate demands of Russian state interest had been the hallmark of conservative Finnish nationalism, from the elder statesman J. V. Snellman to the elder statesman J. K. Paasikivi. Finnish nationalists rarely envied the Poles their rebelliousness, which seemed to lead only to destruction and ruin.[26] The survival of Finland as an independent democracy, whilst Poland was reshaped territorially and politically at Stalin's command, seemed to vindicate the Finns' caution; and yet, Stalin and his successors found it rather easier to slip a halter over the quiescent Finnish horse than to saddle the Polish cow. The Finnish nag might have kicked had the Russians used the whip or spurs, and the Polish cow might have become more tranquil had it been allowed to roam freely in greener pastures. But the fact is that Finland was a relatively marginal area outside the communist bloc in which a range of remote controls could be deployed, whilst Poland was a large, populous and strategically important country over which Stalin had decreed the communists should rule.

The Polish government, and to some extent the Polish people, were moreover kept in check out of fear of German revanchism: the

26. See for example the sentiments expressed by Snellman in 1863 and Yrjö Koskinen in 1901, in: Kirby D (ed.) 1975 *Finland and Russia 1808–1920*, London, pp. 50, 88.

new Poland had, after all, acquired former German territories in the north and west in compensation for territorial losses in the east. The recognition of the Odra-Nysa (Oder-Neisse) frontier by West Germany in 1970 reduced that anxiety, and undermined the government's ability to whip up such fears to strengthen its own position. The riots and strikes which broke out in protest at the raising of food prices shortly after the signing of the treaty were a clear warning that, no longer haunted by the German bogey, the Polish people were no longer going to put up with abysmal living standards.

In the disturbances of 1971, a prominent part was played by industrial workers in the so-called Recovered Territories of north-western Poland – Edward Gierek, the new first secretary of the communist United Workers' Party (PZPR), felt constrained to listen to the demands of the striking shipyard workers in Szczecin, for example – and it was the Baltic shipyards, especially the Lenin yard in Gdańsk, that gave birth to the workers' movement which eventually toppled the regime. The transformation of the resettled north-west territories into a major industrial base of the new Poland had been one of the greatest achievements of the communist government: but the impressive statistics of industrial production and housing units completed could not hide the deficiencies of the system. Corrupt officials, food shortages and declining living standards gave the lie to the increasingly desperate claims of the PZPR to represent the workers' interests. Former political prisoners released from Soviet jails in the amnesty of 1956 and resettled in the Gdańsk region by the government helped sustain a spirit of resistance and resentment. The Roman Catholic church, much boosted by the visit of the Polish-born Pope John Paul II in 1979, gave invaluable moral and spiritual support. Dissidents provided intellectual leadership to the Committee for the Defence of Workers, set up in 1976, and organised secret study classes through the Society for Academic Courses. But it was in the end the workers on the streets and in the shipyards and factories of the Baltic coast who were the driving force, compelling General Jaruzelski first to impose martial law in 1981, and then to negotiate with the leaders of the *Solidarność* movement in the winter of 1988–89. These negotiations marked the end of one-party rule in Poland, and the first significant breach in the wall which had separated eastern Europe from the rest of the continent since the late 1940s.

Within little more than a year of these talks, Poland had a coalition government headed by a non-communist, after *Solidarność* candidates swept the board in the June 1989 elections for the Senate and the 35 per cent of the seats of the *Sejm*. The East German government, under fire not only from its own people but also from the reformist Soviet leader Mikhail Gorbachev, finally collapsed with the Berlin wall, at the end of 1989. Across eastern Europe, the old order disintegrated rapidly, leaving a legacy of economic chaos, environmental pollution, and bad habits developed over four decades or more – a legacy which has proved more insidiously durable than the euphoria and enthusiasm of the crowds which hastened the demise of communist rule.

For East Germans, the problems of adapting to the free-market economy and all that implies were doubly difficult, for unlike the Poles or Czechs, they no longer had a state of their own after 1990, but were compelled to follow the pace set by West German decision-makers. The demise of the German Democratic Republic removed the cap-stone of the Soviet security system, and probably helped precipitate the final collapse of the Soviet Union itself. For the Baltic region, the consequences were portentous, as politicians and commentators were not slow to realise.

THE END OF EMPIRE

When the new CPSU general secretary, Mikhail Gorbachev, launched his campaign of reform in the mid-eighties, few would have dared predict that within less than seven years, the entire Soviet empire would have collapsed. Notwithstanding the massive economic problems, an ossified and largely incompetent administrative structure, deep-seated social malaise and political lethargy, it was widely believed that the new party secretary could somehow make the empire adapt to a rapidly changing world. As it turned out, that optimism was misplaced, not to say misguided. The reasons for the demise of the Soviet Union are many, and will doubtless be hotly debated for years to come. One thing, however, is fairly plain: a system which had hitherto relied on coercion and conscription was always likely to run into difficulties once it opened up the tempting possibility of consultation and consent, especially as its coercive agencies refused to fade gracefully into the background.

As it became apparent that the new leadership had neither a clear notion of the direction in which it wished to proceed, nor the confidence necessary to embark upon such a path, the indigenous peoples of the Baltic republics, whose own self-confidence had grown enormously in the atmosphere of openness (*glasnost'*) proclaimed by the CPSU general secretary, came to realise that their moment had come. Unlike the other non-Russian nationalities of the Soviet Union, they were able to rally round a crucial moral and political issue – the manner in which they had become part of the Union. The campaign to publish the secret protocols of the 1939 Molotov-Ribbentrop pact, and to have them condemned as illegal and invalid, was one of the earliest and most successful of the actions launched in the Baltic republics in the late 1980s. The Soviet authorities were obliged to admit the existence of documents they had hitherto refused to acknowledge. The Congress of People's Deputies condemned the agreements as illegal and invalid in December 1989, thereby undermining the increasingly implausible claims of the leadership that the Baltic peoples had nevertheless freely and voluntarily entered into the Union in 1940.[27]

Environmental issues also stimulated protest actions. A successful campaign was waged in Latvia in the autumn of 1986 to stop the construction of a massive hydro-electric power station; plans to expand open-cast phosphorite mining in north-east Estonia were postponed after public protests; and the secrecy surrounding plans for expanding the Ignalina nuclear power station in Lithuania provoked an outcry which compelled the authorities to suspend construction of the third Chernobyl-style reactor in 1988. The announcement on 2 June 1988 of plans for major expansion of the chemical industry in Lithuania, coinciding with the decision of the Central Committee of the Communist Party to ignore the mood of reform by nominating old-style bureaucrats for the forthcoming 19th party conference in Moscow, helped launch the Lithuanian popular front, *Sąjūdis*.[28] Worries about pollution and ecological damage were, however, only one aspect of the environmental protest movement. Beneath these anxieties lay another fear, of a further wave of immigrants which would tilt the fragile ethnic balance even more in favour of the non-indigenous population. Green issues rose up the political agenda throughout Europe in the seventies and eighties, but they tended to remain isolated and specific (for example, the nuclear power debate in Sweden, or the controversy over the proposal to bridge the Sound between Sweden and Denmark) and lacked any deeper sustaining

27. Gerner K, Hedlund S 1993 *The Baltic states and the end of the Soviet empire*, London, pp. 62–8. The first demonstrations commemorating the signing of the pact had been held in August 1987 in Vilnius, Riga and Tallinn. A riveting on-the-spot account of the way in which the pact was publicly debated in Lithuania in August 1988 can be found in Senn 1990, pp. 116–35.

28. Gerner and Hedlund 1993, pp. 70–3, 83–6, 91. Senn 1990, pp. 55–73. Misiunas and Taagepera 1993, pp. 303–7.

force. In the Baltic republics, they went to the very heart of national existence.

The initial two years of intense political activity (1987–89) saw the initiative pass almost entirely out of the hands of the established Communist Party leadership to the popular fronts. Nevertheless, a number of reform proposals, such as the Estonian plan for economic self-management published in September 1987, did emanate from the ranks of the disintegrating party, and a significant number of ex-communist reformists were subsequently to play leading roles in the crucial two years in which independence was once more regained (1989–91).

During the early months of 1988, the pace was set in Estonia. Having apparently sanctioned in April the formation of a popular front in support of reform, the old-style party first secretary Karl Vaino then attempted to clamp down in the time-honoured fashion, by appealing to Moscow for military support. In mid-June, having lost the backing of the reformists at home and in Moscow, he was ousted from office, and replaced by Vaino Väljas. Väljas identified the party with the reform movement, which formally constituted itself as the Estonian Popular Front (*Eestimaa rahvarinne*) in October. A number of symbolically significant changes, such as official recognition of the blue-black-white flag of the independent republic, and the adoption of Estonian as the official language of state, were made, but the most controversial move was the declaration of sovereignty made by the Estonian Supreme Soviet on 16 November 1988, giving the republic the right to veto all-Union legislation. This was declared unconstitutional by the Presidium of the Supreme Soviet of the USSR ten days later, but reaffirmed in December by the Estonian Supreme Soviet.

The old guard communist leadership had managed to ride out the summer storms in Latvia and Lithuania, but their position was fatally undermined by the public rebukes delivered by Aleksandr Yaklovlev, sent by Gorbachev to Riga and Vilnius in August 1988 on a fact-finding mission. The hardline Latvian first secretary Boris Pugo (he was subsequently appointed Soviet minister of the interior at the end of 1990, and was involved in the plot to overthrow Gorbachev eight months later) was replaced in September, and his counterpart in Lithuania a month later. The major institutional link between Moscow and the republics was thus effectively destroyed; and the popular fronts which Gorbachev hoped would support and advance his programme of reconstruction were beginning to push forward demands which were designed to weaken the connection with Moscow still further.

The Estonian plan for economic self-management was taken up and developed by economists of all three republics, and formed the basis of the programmes for republican sovereignty taken up by the Supreme Soviets of Estonia and Lithuania in November 1988. The new party first secretary, Algirdas Brazauskas, managed to persuade the Lithuanian Supreme Soviet to refrain from following the Estonian example; but his was a pyrrhic victory. The initiative now passed to *Sąjūdis*, which issued a declaration on 20 November, refusing to recognise laws which restricted Lithuania's independence. With the election of the musicologist Vytautas Landsbergis as the movement's first president, *Sąjūdis* embarked on a confrontational course which was to place Lithuania in the forefront of the struggle for independence in the Baltic region.

The developments in Estonia and Lithuania were viewed with increasing alarm in Moscow. Aleksandr Yakovlev, who had backed *Sąjūdis* during his visit to Vilnius in August, complained at the end of October that the ideas of 'performers and musicians and people of this sort' were 'out of touch with reality', and there were other warning notes sounded in the Moscow press.[29] In all three Baltic republics, pro-Soviet movements were organised during the course of 1988–89. In Estonia and Latvia, these 'international' fronts drew their support almost entirely from the Russian population. In Lithuania, the 'Unity' organisation brought together Russians and Poles, the latter attracted by the demand for autonomous regions for ethnic minorities. In all three republics, the communist parties divided into 'national' and 'pro-Soviet' factions in 1990; for the most part, the split followed ethnic lines.

In spite of their considerable nuisance value to the harassed Soviet leadership in the growing conflict between Moscow and the republics, these 'Intermovements' proved to be largely ineffective. Stage-managed strikes caused little disruption, with the possible exception of the August 1989 strike in Estonia, and were supported by only a small minority of workers. Bereft of strong and decisive guidance from above, the local leadership offered little inspiration to their followers. The most successful were those who managed to distance themselves from a corrupt communist past and to project themselves as capable of defending minority interests.[30]

At the beginning of 1989, an alliance of communist reformists and moderates in the popular front movements was still in control, but was

29. Yakovlev's interview, published in the *New York Times* on 28 October 1988, is summarised in Senn 1990, p. 238.

30. On the weaknesses of the Intermovements, see: Lieven 1993, pp. 188–201; Gerner and Hedlund 1993, pp. 107–14.

under pressure from those who favoured bolder moves towards full independence. The strategy taken up by the national independence movements in Estonia and Latvia of bypassing the institutions of the Soviet era, and electing citizens' congresses to deliberate over the future of the republic, was less than successful in its final outcome but it succeeded in drawing the popular front movements away from the idea of republican sovereignty within the Soviet Union towards full endorsement of national independence. The issue of citizenship was of less significance in Lithuania. Here, the high profile adopted by *Sąjūdis* in 1989–90 effectively cast into the shade earlier rivals such as the Freedom League, which had made the running in 1988. In the March 1989 elections to the Soviet Congress of People's Deputies, *Sąjūdis* candidates swept the board, winning 36 of the 42 seats allotted. Popular Front candidates, who included prominent Communist Party reformists, won 27 of the 35 seats in Estonia, whilst three-quarters of those elected in Latvia were reformists.

Encouraged by these victories, and anxious not to allow the initiative to pass to the more outspoken nationalists, the popular front movements began to prepare for the eventual restoration of independence. An assembly of delegates from all three fronts met in Tallinn in May 1989 to coordinate plans. A clear desire for a radical redefinition of identity was contained in the assembly's expressed wish for national sovereignty for the Baltic republics within a neutral and demilitarised Baltic-Scandinavian region. As an Estonian official of the Soviet ministry of justice observed, the three countries were now aiming for complete separation from the Soviet Union.[31] The concessions made on economic self-management (which several central ministries in Moscow subsequently attempted to sabotage) were no longer enough to satisfy the peoples of the Baltic republics. On 23 August 1989, the fiftieth anniversary of the signing of the Nazi-Soviet pact, an estimated two million people linked arms in a human chain from Tallinn to Vilnius to demand the restoration of independence – an impressive and poignant demonstration of the popular mood.

In the elections to the Supreme Soviets (or as they were now called, Supreme Councils) held in each of the three republics in February-March 1990, candidates supporting independence triumphed. On 11 March, the *Sąjūdis*-dominated Supreme Council voted for the restoration of Lithuania as an independent state, using as justification the denunciation of the Nazi-Soviet pact by the Congress of People's

31. Gerner and Hedlund 1993, p. 120. Dreifelds J 1989 Latvian national rebirth *Problems of Communism* **38**: 87.

Deputies of the USSR on 24 December 1989. The Estonians and Latvians were more circumspect, preferring to opt for an indeterminate transition period in which to achieve their stated objective of restored independence. Led by the slight and unprepossessing figure of Vytautas Landsbergis, the *Sąjūdis* president and chairman of the new Supreme Council, the Lithuanians stood up to months of harassment and pressure, which culminated in the seizure by Soviet troops of the press and television centres in Vilnius in January 1991. This action appears to have been part of a plan to capitalise upon a sudden government crisis; but neither this bloody clash, nor other attacks and provocations in the three Baltic republics, could shatter the resolve and steely determination of the nationalist-minded majority.

The size of the majority was revealed in the referenda on independence organised by the Supreme Councils of the three Baltic republics in advance of an all-Union referendum on the preservation of a renewed Soviet Union, decreed for mid-March by the Supreme Soviet in Moscow. On a high turnout in all three republics, 90 per cent said 'yes' to independence in Lithuania, 78 per cent in Estonia and 74 per cent in Latvia. Far fewer turned out to vote for the preservation of the Union in the Moscow-sponsored referendum, which seems to have been confined mainly to Russian-dominated districts and workplaces and to military personnel stationed in the republics. The evidence of the two sets of polls would seem to suggest that, whilst not insignificant numbers of the non-native population favoured or did not oppose Baltic independence, there was a substantial majority that did.[32]

The end of the Soviet Union came with dramatic suddenness in August 1991. The nationalist governments of the three Baltic republics had already secured a valuable ally in Boris Yeltsin, elected president of the Russian (RSFSR) republic in June, During the January 1991 crisis in Vilnius, Yeltsin, at that time chairman of the RSFSR Supreme Soviet, had flown to Tallinn, where he joined the leaders of the Baltic republics in appealing to the United Nations to intervene. Yeltsin also issued a personal appeal to Russian troops stationed in the Baltic republics not to use arms against civilians. This intervention did not prevent further acts of aggression, mostly committed by the feared 'Black Beret' troops of the ministry of the interior, but it was a significant boost to the hard-pressed governments in their struggle against the Kremlin, and it probably lessened the chances of any large-scale mobilisation of local Russian support for a coup in the

32. Gerner and Hedlund 1993, pp. 155–7.

Baltic republics. The triumph of Boris Yeltsin in Moscow, after the ill-managed attempt to oust Mikhail Gorbachev collapsed on 21 August, was also a victory for the three Baltic states. Estonia and Latvia now joined Lithuania, and proclaimed their independence, which was speedily recognised by Russia (24 August), the Soviet Union (6 September) and the international community. By the end of the year, all three had been admitted to the United Nations and a number of other international bodies.

Many problems remained to be dealt with. Reconstructing the economy will take many years, though all three states managed to effect currency reform without plunging into the choppy waters of hyperinflation, and they have begun to attract investment and to find new markets for their exports. The mood of nationalist euphoria which was so essential during the critical years of 1988–91 has faded, as politicians squabble over policies and the people tire of promises. The popular fronts began to disintegrate even before independence was finally regained. Many of the leading figures of the period 1989–1991 faded from the limelight or suffered electoral defeat, as did Vytautas Landsbergis and his supporters in the 1992 parliamentary elections in Lithuania, in which the victory went to the reformed communists, led by Algirdas Brazauskas. In Estonia and Latvia, on the other hand, voters tended to favour the parties of the centre-right in the parliamentary elections held in 1992–93.

The continued presence of large numbers of Soviet military units in particular posed a serious threat, not least as the new leaders in Russia began to talk ominously of the necessity of protecting Russian security interests and the Russian minorities in the 'near abroad'. Lithuania was the first of the three Baltic countries to be completely free of the troops of the former Soviet armed forces, though it still has to contend with a Russian territorial enclave – the Kaliningrad region – on its western border. In marked contrast to other areas of the former Soviet Union, the Baltic states have not witnessed violent inter-ethnic conflict. Opinion-poll surveys carried out in Estonia during the early 1990s would seem to suggest that the level of outright hostility towards the new states is relatively low, outside the predominantly Russian-speaking enclave on the north-eastern border, and that a large number see their future as citizens and as a recognised minority in the republic of Estonia.[33] This may be an unnecessarily optimistic conclusion, belied by the heavy support for the ultranationalist Liberal

33. Kirch A, Kirch M and Tuisk T 1993 Russians in the Baltic states: to be or not to be, *Journal of Baltic Studies* **24**: 173–88.

Democratic Party amongst those voting in the Baltic states in the December 1993 Russian parliamentary elections: but it should also be noted that in Estonia, for example, only 25 per cent of those entitled to vote did so. The decisions taken by the Estonian and Latvian Supreme Councils in the autumn of 1991 to restrict automatic citizenship to those who had held it before 1940 and their descendants has been much criticised elsewhere, not least in Russia. The issue of citizenship and guarantees for minority rights is a contentious one, especially since the minorities in question are large (and in many Latvian cities, a majority of the population) and imbued with attitudes inimical to the aspirations of the now-dominant indigenous peoples. For many, especially recent immigrants who came to the Baltic to find a better life for themselves and their families, the future has become far less certain, as the heavy industrial base shrinks, and their economic privileges disappear.[34] Some have already left the Baltic states, but most cannot and do not wish to do so. The exogenous peoples are more diverse and lacking in traditions than was the Baltic German community, and for this reason, it might be argued, they are more likely in the long run to accept a guaranteed and defined minority status, which could also give them a common identity. This search for a new identity would certainly be helped by measures which would encourage them to feel they had a positive role to play in the new republics; this would, however, necessitate a degree of goodwill and disinterested support from the Russian state that has so far been conspicuously absent. The successful integration of the minorities, in other words, is not simply an acid test for the Baltic peoples and their governments: it is conditional upon a host of other variables, such as the political stability and economic prosperity of Russia, which are beyond the control of the Baltic states themselves.[35]

34. A survey carried out in Riga in May 1992 found that Russian speakers had a more positive image of the past and were more pessimistic about the future than were Latvian speakers. Worries about economic well-being and the future tended to rank above concern about ethnic problems in the survey conducted amongst the Russian population in a variety of locations in Estonia during 1992–93. For discussion of these findings, see the special issue on public opinion in the Baltic states of: *Journal of Baltic Studies* **24/2** (1993).

35. There has been no shortage of advice from outside observers: see, for example, the conclusion by the former head of the CSCE mission to Estonia, Klaus Törnudd, that Estonia would be a multinational state in future, and his recommendations as to how that could be achieved (Virosta tulee monien kansallisuuksien maa *Savon Sanomat* 2 Jan. 1994). Anatol Lieven concludes that unless the Russians in the Baltic learn to live without empire, and the Baltic peoples learn to live with the Russians, the Baltic states themselves will remain 'a debatable territory'. Lieven 1993, pp. 374–84.

The independence of the Baltic states came about in the aftermath of the First World War as the result of an empire disintegrating. This is not to decry the actions and activities of those who sought to create sovereign national states; but they were caught up in the raging torrent of war and revolution with very few navigational aids to assist them, and they could not be certain that the craft they were attempting to steer was one in which all the people wished to voyage. The situation in 1988–91 was rather different. The fact that the reformists in the ruling Communist Party were able to oust the old guard leadership, and were willing to align themselves with the national cause espoused by the popular front movements was crucial, for this provided vital and experienced local leadership in the struggle with Moscow. This time, there was a memory of the past and a burning resentment at the way in which that memory had been distorted and falsified by those who upheld the legitimacy of Soviet rule. This time, the indigenous peoples of Estonia, Latvia and Lithuania were solidly united in fighting for their independence. They were resilient and remarkably self-confident in their resistance to threats and pressure from Moscow and they demonstrated their courage and determination on the streets, in meetings and rallies and in confrontations with the armed forces. This determination was spurred on by a belief that this might well be the last chance to resurrect the national state created during the interwar years.

It is difficult for the outsider to grasp the emotional and psychological importance of this reassertion of identity by small nations, just as it is easy for the neutral observer to point out the evident differences between the present independent Baltic states and their predecessors of half-a-century ago. It is one of the ironies of history that, just as the western half of the European continent is busying itself with the process of economic and political integration, the eastern half is in the grip of resurgent nationalism after the collapse of what turned out to be a wholly false, coercive integrating force. The established capitalist democracies of northern Europe, busily seeking to find their place in the European Union, are also acutely aware of the dangers on their back doorstep. That is one of the reasons why the Nordic countries have been extremely active in the eastern Baltic region, not only providing funding for educational, commercial and environmental purposes, but also adopting an unusually high profile in declaring their interest in the stability of the region. Sweden's special role in the Baltic region has been stressed by the conservative Swedish government of Carl Bildt, who has publicly queried the usefulness of neutrality in the event of conflict in the vicinity of Sweden.[36] The Finnish concept of neutrality has also come under scrutiny, and the possibility of joining NATO raised. The Baltic states have far fewer misgivings about membership of NATO, and have signed up as members of the 'Partnership for Peace' scheme. They too are actively seeking to become involved in a wide variety of cooperative international and regional organisations, partly as a profile-raising exercise, but also to further their own ambitions for integration into a wider Europe.

On the outer edge stands the rickety Confederation of Independent States, whose prospects at this present time seem distinctly poor. Within the still-vast Russian state, there are signs of regional vigour and assertiveness, which may thwart attempts to revive authoritarian centralist rule from Moscow. The opening up of the frontier between Finland and Karelia and the numerous commercial and other contacts which have been established over a relatively brief period suggest that at the very least it would be difficult to return to the stiflingly hermetic days of the past. In former autonomous republics of the Soviet Union like Karelia, with its diverse ethnic mix, a process of defining identity not dissimilar to that experienced by its western neighbours in an earlier epoch may also be taking place.[37] This will inevitably be a long drawn-out and painful process in which neighbours to the south and west will no doubt interfere, as on previous occasions; but it may well be the only way to deal with the intractable problem of a state in which social and national forces have always been distorted or suppressed in the interests of the ruling power.

The period in which the icebound waters of the Baltic begin to break up is always dangerous. We are living through such a period at the present moment, and there are many who look back with longing to the winter which is now over. The melting of the ice has revealed a terrible mess of environmental pollution and economic chaos, carefully concealed by Soviet leaders and studiously ignored for

36. The Swedish prime minister's speeches at the end of 1993, and the rather subtle redefinition of Swedish security policy, are analysed by Bo Huldt in *Nordisk Kontakt* **1** (1994): 4–6.

37. The ethnic composition of Karelia ranges from Vepsians and Karelians who have lived there for centuries to Finns who came there from the United States during the Depression and postwar Belorussian immigrants, some of whom have moved there to escape the consequences of the nuclear fallout in the Chernobyl region. The Kaliningrad *oblast*, carved out of East Prussia by the USSR in 1945, is another melting-pot of immigrants seeking some sort of identity. On this region, see Misiunas and Taagepera 1993, pp. 336–49, and Smith R 1993 The Kaliningrad region: civic and ethnic models of nationalism *Journal of Baltic Studies* **24**: 233–46.

decades by their Scandinavian counterparts in the interests of preserving the Baltic region from conflict. It has released the peoples of the former Soviet empire from a social-cultural milieu which they may have detested but which shaped their lives, and the subsequent shock of discovering the differences has been great – on both sides of the Baltic Sea. The peoples of the Nordic countries have to contend with their own problems, not least record levels of unemployment, and they view with misgiving some of the less desirable consequences of the disintegration of the Soviet Union – growing poverty and the rising crime rate – which threaten to spill over their borders. These are indeed tense and hazardous times, but there are optimistic signs amidst the uncertainties. Western European countries have responded positively to the restoration of independence of the three Baltic states, and there are small but encouraging indications of economic renewal in the area. Relations with Moscow have deteriorated, but there are still considerable formal and informal connections between the Baltic republics and other parts of the former Soviet Union. Above all, there is a general determination on both sides of the Baltic to forge a new and distinctive regional identity with which to enter the new millenium.

Select Bibliography

This list is primarily confined to works in English, though important studies in other languages are also included. Useful guides to further reading include Volumes 31 (Finland), 80 (Sweden), 83 (Denmark) and 161 (the Baltic States) in the World Bibliographical Series, published by Clio Press, Oxford.

GENERAL

Allardt E *et al.* (eds) 1981 *Nordic democracy. Ideas, issues and institutions in politics, economy, education, social and cultural affairs of Denmark, Finland, Iceland, Norway and Sweden,* Copenhagen

Arter D 1993 *The politics of European integration in the twentieth century*, Aldershot

Derry T 1973 *A History of Modern Norway 1814–1872*, Oxford

Derry T 1979 *A History of Scandinavia*, London

Engman M, Kirby D (eds) 1989 *Finland. People – nation – state*, London

Hiden J and Salmon P 1991 *The Baltic nations and Europe: Estonia, Latvia and Lithuania in the twentieth century*, London

Hovde B 1943 *The Scandinavian countries 1720–1865* 2 vols, Ithaca, NY

Kirby D 1979 *Finland in the twentieth century*, London

Koblik S (ed) 1975 *Sweden's development from poverty to affluence, 1750–1970*, Minneapolis

Lindhardt P 1983 *Kirchengeschichte Skandinaviens*, Göttingen

Raun T 1987 *Estonia and the Estonians*, Stanford

Scott F 1977 *Sweden: the nation's history*, Minneapolis, Minnesota
Tighe C 1990 *Gdańsk. National identity in the German-Polish borderlands*, London

1772–1914

Barton A 1986 *Scandinavia in the revolutionary era 1760–1815*, Minneapolis
Berdahl R 1988 *The politics of the Prussian nobility. The development of a conservative ideology 1770–1848*, Princeton, NJ
Ezergailis A, Pistohlkors G von, (eds) 1982 *Die baltischen Provinzen Russlands zwischen den Revolutionen von 1905 und 1917* Quellen und Studien zur Baltischen Geschichte **4**, Cologne
Feldbæk O 1980 *Denmark and the armed neutrality 1800–1801. Small-power policy in a world war* Institut for Økonomisk Historie Publikation no.**16**, Copenhagen
Garve H 1978 *Konfession und Nationalität. Ein Beitrag zum Verhältnis von Kirche und Gesellschaft in Livland im 19. Jahrhundert* Wissenchaftliche Beiträge zur Geschichte und Landskunde Ostmitteleuropas **110**, Marburg
Haltzel M 1977 *Der Abbau der deutschen ständischen Selbstverwaltung in den Ostseeprovinzen Russlands 1855–1905* Marburger Ostforschungen **37**, Marburg
Hroch M 1984 *Social preconditions of national revival in Europe*, Cambridge
Kirby D (ed.) 1975 *Finland and Russia 1808–1920: From autonomy to independence. A selection of documents*, London
Koselleck R 1967 *Preussen zwischen Reform und Revolution*, Stuttgart
Lindberg F 1958 *Scandinavia in great power politics 1905–1908*, Stockholm
Lindgren R 1959 *Norway-Sweden. Union, disunion and Scandinavian integration*, Princeton, NJ
Loit A (ed.) 1985 *National movements in the Baltic countries during the nineteenth century* Studia Baltica Stockholmiensia **2**, Stockholm
Loit A (ed.) 1900 *The Baltic countries 1900–1914* Studia Baltica Stockholmiensia **5: 1**, Stockholm
Luntinen P 1975 *The Baltic question 1903–1908* Suomalaisen tiedeakatemian toimituksia B 195, Helsinki
Mitchison R (ed.) 1980 *The roots of nationalism. Studies in Northern Europe*, Edinburgh
Paasivirta J 1981 *Finland and Europe. The period of autonomy and the international crises 1808–1914*, London

Philipp G 1974 *Die Wirksamkeit der Herrnhuter Brüdergemeinde unter den Esten und Letten zur Zeit der Bauernbefreiung*, Cologne

Pistohlkors G von 1978 *Ritterschaftliche Reformpolitik zwischen Russifizierung und Revolution* Göttinger Bausteine zur Geschichtswissenschaft **48**, Göttingen

Sabaliūnas L 1990 *Lithuanian social democracy in perspective 1893–1914*, Durham/London

Sandiford K 1975 *Great Britain and the Schleswig-Holstein question 1848–1864: A study in diplomacy, politics and public opinion*, Toronto

Scholz F 1990 *Die Literaturen des Baltikums. Ihre Entstehung und Entwicklung* Abhandlungen der Rheinisch-Westfälischen Akademie der Wissenschaften **80**, Opladen

Steefel L 1932 *The Schleswig-Holstein question*, Harvard

Thaden E (ed.) 1981 *Russification in the Baltic provinces and Finland, 1855–1914*, Princeton, NJ

Thaden E 1984 *Russia's western borderlands, 1710–1870*, Princeton, NJ

Thaden E (guest co-editor) and others 1984 *Finland and the Baltic provinces in the Russian empire* (Special issue of the *Journal of Baltic Studies* vol. **15: 2/3**)

Tommila P 1962 *La Finlande dans la politique européenne en 1809–1815* Studia Historica **3**, Helsinki

Verney D 1957 *Parliamentary reform in Sweden 1866–1921*, Oxford

Zawadzki W 1993 *A man of honour. Adam Czartoryski as a statesman of Russia and Poland 1795–1831*, Oxford

WAR AND REVOLUTION, 1914–1920

Alapuro R 1988 *State and revolution in Finland*, Los Angeles

Ezergailis A 1974 The 1917 revolution in Latvia *East European Monographs* **8**, Boulder, Colorado

Ezergailis A 1983 The Latvian impact on the Bolshevik revolution *East European Monographs* **144**, Boulder, Colorado

Hehn J von, Rimscha H von, Weiss H (eds) 1977 *Von der baltischen Provinzen zu den baltischen Staaten 1918–1920*, Marburg

Koblik S 1972 *Sweden, the neutral victor*, Stockholm

Linde G 1965 *Die deutsche Politik in Litauen im ersten Weltkrieg*, Wiesbaden

Upton A 1980 *The Finnish revolution 1917–1918*, Minneapolis, Minnesota

THE NEW STATES OF NORTH-EASTERN EUROPE, 1918–1923

Graham M 1928 *The new governments of Eastern Europe*, Princeton, NJ

Hinkkanen-Lievonen M-L 1984 *British trade and enterprise in the Baltic states 1919–1925* Studia Historica **14**, Helsinki

Hovi O 1980 *The Baltic area in British foreign policy, 1918–1921* Studia Historica **11**, Helsinki

Hovi K 1975 *Cordon sanitaire or barrière de l'est? The emergence of a new French eastern European alliance policy 1917–1919* Turun yliopiston Julkaisuja **135**, Turku

Jääskeläinen M 1965 *Die ostkarelische Frage*, Helsinki

Page S 1959, reprint 1970 *The formation of the Baltic States*, Cambridge, Mass.

Senn A 1959 *The emergence of modern Lithuania*, New York

THE INTERWAR YEARS

Hiden J 1987 *The Baltic states and Weimar Ostpolitik*, Cambridge

Hiden J and Loit A (eds) 1988 *The Baltic in international relations between the two world wars* Studia Baltica Stockholmiensia **3**, Stockholm

Hodgson J 1967 *Communism in Finland. A history and an interpretation*, Princeton N.J.

Kimmich C 1968 *The free city. Danzig and German foreign policy 1919–1934*, New York and London

Levine H 1973 *Hitler's free city. A history of the Nazi party in Danzig, 1925–1939*, Chicago

Lindström U 1985 *Fascism in Scandinavia*, Stockholm

Mägi A 1967 *Das Staatsleben Estlands während seiner Selbständigkeit*, Stockholm

Paasivirta J 1988 *Finland and Europe. The early years of independence 1917–1939* Studia Historica **29**, Helsinki

Pagel J 1992 *Polen und die Sowjetunion 1938–39* Quellen und Studien zur Geschichte des östlichen Europa **34**, Stuttgart

Parming T 1975 *The collapse of liberal democracy and the rise of authoritarianism in Estonia*, London/Beverly Hills

Plieg E-A 1962 *Das Memelland 1920–1939* Marburger Ostforschungen **19**, Würzburg

Rauch G von 1974 *The Baltic States. The years of independence 1917–1940*, London

Rodgers H 1975 *Search for security. A study in Baltic diplomacy, 1920–1934*, Hamden, Conn.

Seymour S 1982 *Anglo-Danish relations and Germany 1933–1945*, Odense University Studies in History and Social Sciences **78**, Odense

Vardys V and Misiunas R (eds) 1978 *The Baltic states in peace and war 1917–1945*, University Park, Penn.

Upton A (ed.) 1973 *Communism in Scandinavia and Finland. Politics of opportunity*, New York

THE SECOND WORLD WAR

Budreckis A 1968 *The Lithuanian national revolt of 1941*, Boston

Carlgren W 1977 *Swedish foreign policy during the Second World War*, London

Crowe D 1993 *The Baltic states and the great powers: foreign relations 1938–1940*, Boulder, Colorado.

Hiden J, Lane T (eds) 1992 *The Baltic and the outbreak of the Second World War*, Cambridge

Jakobson M 1961 *The diplomacy of the Winter War*, Cambridge, Mass.

Myllyniemi S 1973 *Die Neuordnung der baltischen Länder, 1941–1944*, Historiallisia Tutkimuksia **90**, Helsinki

Myllyniemi S 1979 *Die baltische Krise 1938–1941*, Stuttgart

Nevakivi J 1976 *The appeal that was never made*, London

Nissen H (ed.) 1983 *Scandinavia during the Second World War*, Oslo and Minneapolis

Polvinen T 1986 *Between East and West: Finland in international politics, 1944–1947*, Minneapolis

Sabaliūnas L 1972 *Lithuania in crisis. Nationalism to communism, 1939–1940*, Bloomington, Ill.

Tory A 1990 *Surviving the Holocaust*, Cambridge, Mass.

Upton A 1974 *Finland 1939–1940*, London

Upton A 1964 *Finland in crisis 1940–1941*, London

1945–1988

Allison R 1985 *Finland's relations with the Soviet Union 1944–1984*, London

Allworth E (ed.) 1977 *Nationality group survival in multi-ethnic states. Shifting support patterns in the Soviet Baltic region*, New York

Arter D 1987 *Politics and policy making in Finland*, London/New York

Baldwin P 1990 *The politics of social solidarity. Class bases of the European welfare state 1875–1975*, Cambridge

Castles F 1978 *The social democratic image of society: a study of the achievements and origins of Scandinavian social democracy in comparative perspective*, London

Einhorn E and Logue J 1989 *Modern welfare states. Politics and policies in social democratic Scandinavia*, New York

Ekmanis R 1978 *Latvian literature under the Soviets 1940–1975*, Belmont, Mass.

Elder N. Thomas A and Arter D 1988 (rev. ed.) *The consensual democracies? The government and politics of the Scandinavian states*, Oxford

Hecksher G 1984 *The welfare state and beyond. Success and problems in Scandinavia*, Minneapolis

Küng A 1980 *A dream of freedom: four decades of national survival versus Russian imperialism in Estonia, Latvia and Lithuania*, Cardiff

Laar M 1992 *War in the woods. Estonia's struggle for survival 1946–1956*, Washington

Lewin L 1988 *Ideology and strategy. A century of Swedish politics*, Cambridge

Loeber A, Vardys V, Kitching L (eds) 1991 *Regional identity under Soviet rule: the case of the Baltic states*, Hackettstown, NY

Lundestad G 1980 *America, Scandinavia and the Cold War, 1945–1949*, Oslo

Maude G 1976 *The Finnish dilemma. Neutrality in the shadow of power*, London

Misiunas R and Taagepera R 1983 *The Baltic states: Years of dependence 1940–1980*, London (revised and updated edition, 1993 *The Baltic states. Years of dependence 1940–1990*, London)

Nannestad P 1991 *Danish design or British disease? Danish economic crisis policy in comparative perspective*, Aarhus

Parming T and Järvesoo E 1978 *A case study of a Soviet republic. The Estonian SSR*, Boulder, Colorado

Vardys V (ed.) 1965 *Lithuania under the Soviets. Portrait of a nation 1940–1965*, New York

Westin A (ed.) 1989 *Comprehensive security for the Baltic. An environmental approach*, London

THE END OF THE SOVIET EMPIRE, 1988–1993

Clemens W 1991 *Baltic independence and Russian empire*, London

Gerner K, Hedlund S 1993 *The Baltic states and the end of the Soviet empire*, London

Lieven A 1993 *The Baltic revolution. Estonia, Latvia, Lithuania and the path to independence*, New Haven, Conn. and London

Senn A 1990 *Lithuania awakening*, Berkeley and Los Angeles
Trapans J (ed.) 1991 *Toward independence: the Baltic popular movements*, Boulder, Colorado

ECONOMIC AND SOCIAL HISTORY

Abrahams R 1991 A place of their own. Family farming in eastern Finland *Cambridge Studies in Social and Cultural Anthropology* **81**, Cambridge
Arkadie B and Karlsson M (eds) 1992 *Economic survey of the Baltic states*, London
Dahmén E 1970 *Entrepreneurial activity and the development of Swedish industry 1919–1939*, Homewood, Ill.
Graubard S (ed.) 1986 *Norden: the passion for equality*, Oslo
Henriksson A 1983 The tsar's most loyal Germans. The Riga German community: social change and the nationality question 1855–1905 *East European Monographs* **131**, Boulder, Colorado
Ingold T (ed.) 1988 *The social implications of agrarian change in northern and eastern Finland* Transactions of the Finnish Anthropological Society **21**, Helsinki
Jörberg L 1961 *Growth and fluctuations of Swedish industry, 1869–1912*, Stockholm
Kahk J 1969 *Die Krise der feudalen Landwirtschaft in Estland*, Tallinn
Montgomery A 1939 *The rise of modern industry in Sweden*, Stockholm
Myllyntaus T 1990 *The gatecrashing apprentice. Industrialising Finland as an adopter of new technology* Communications of the Institute of Economic and Social History, University of Helsinki **24**, Helsinki
Nelson M 1988 *Bitter bread. The famine in Norrbotten 1867–1868* Studia Historica Upsaliensia **153**, Uppsala
Samuelsson K 1968 *From great power to welfare state*, London
Schissler H 1978 *Preussische Agrargesellschaft im Wandel* Kritische Studien zur Geschichtswissenschaft **33**, Göttingen
Simpura J and Tigerstedt C (eds) 1992 *Social problems around the Baltic sea*, Helsinki
Singleton F 1986 *The economy of Finland in the twentieth century*, Bradford
Åkerman S et al. (eds) 1978 *Chance and change. Social and economic studies in historical demography in the Baltic area*, Odense

Maps

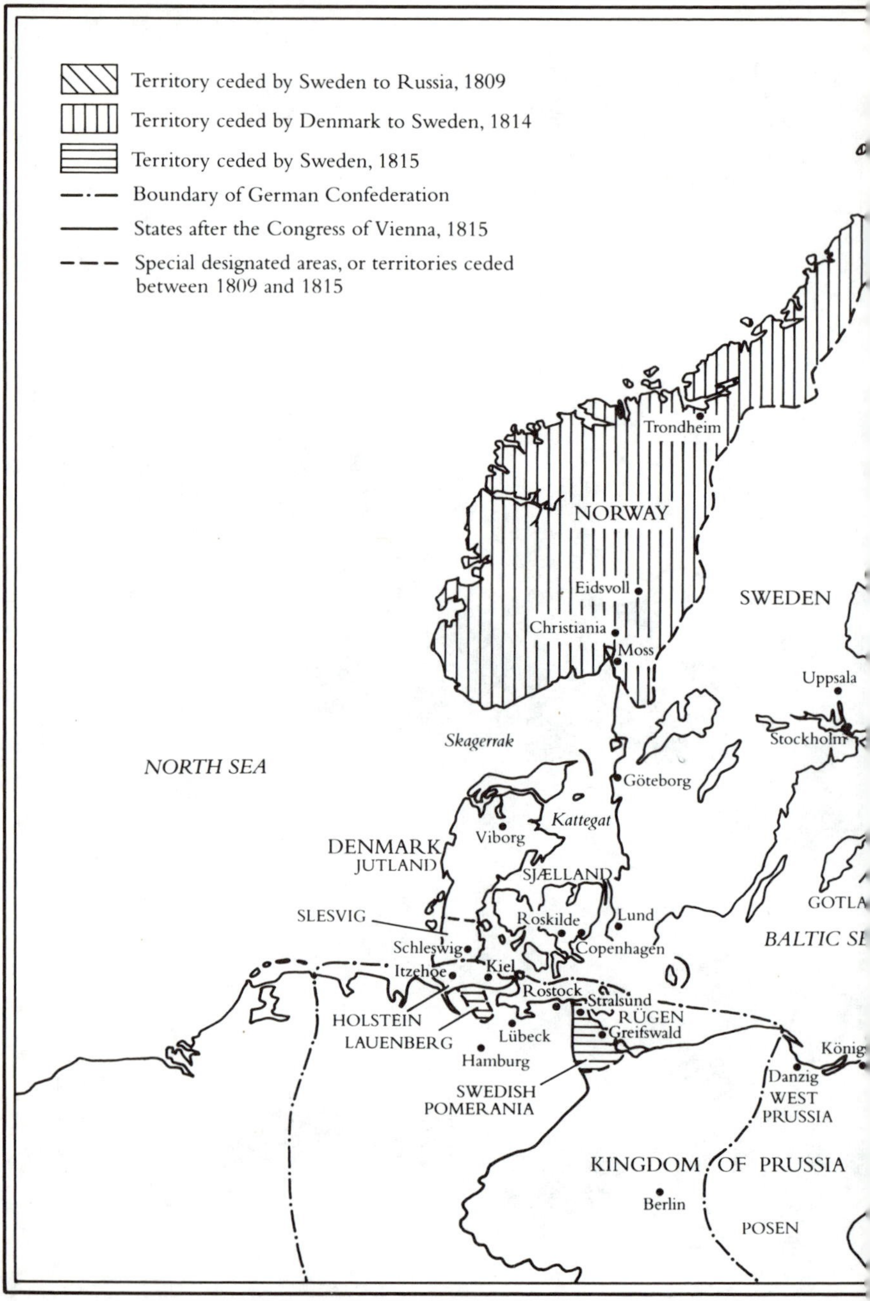

1. Northern Europe in 1815

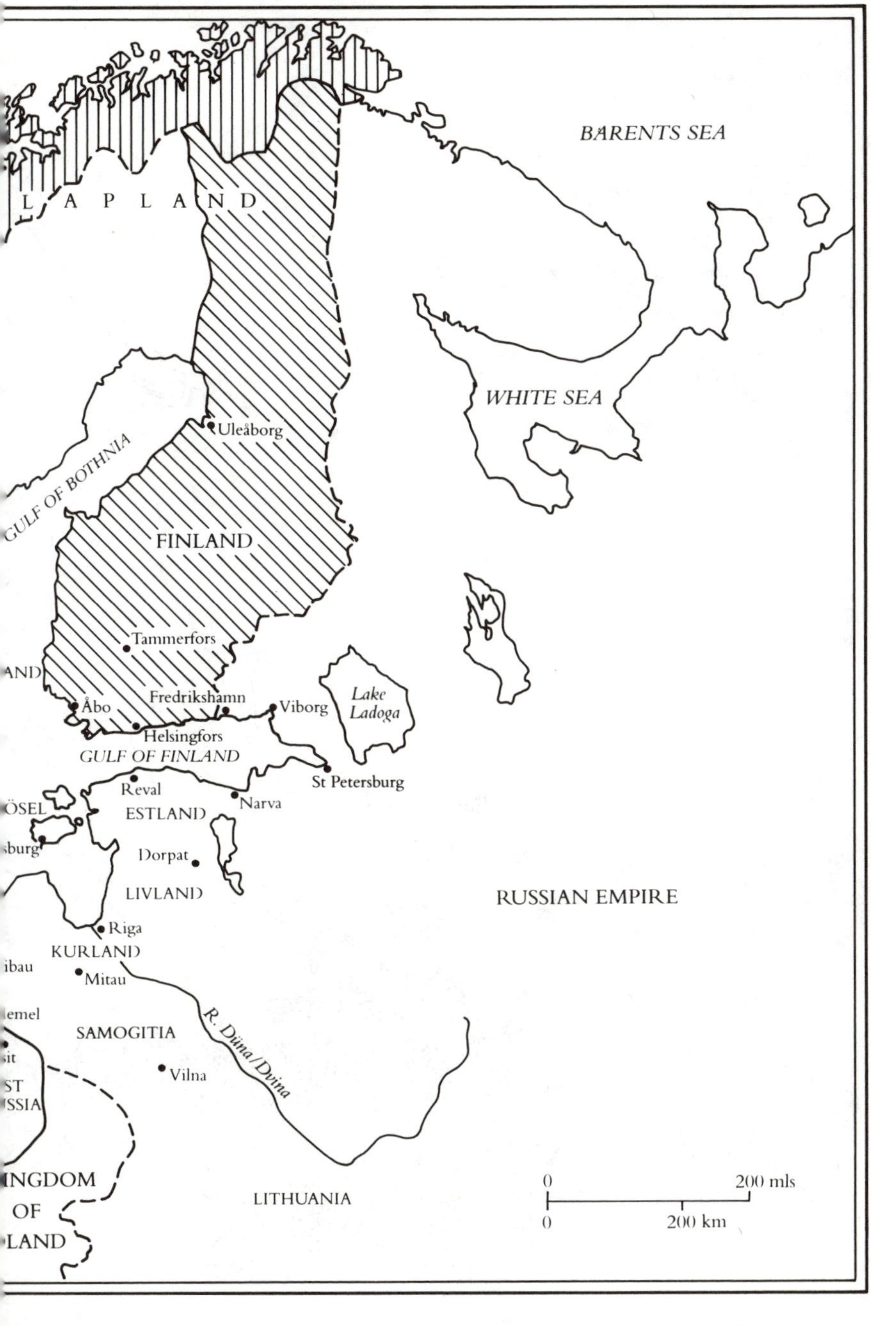
BARENTS SEA
L A P L A N D
WHITE SEA
Uleåborg
GULF OF BOTHNIA
FINLAND
Tammerfors
AND
Åbo
Fredrikshamn
Viborg
Lake Ladoga
Helsingfors
GULF OF FINLAND
St Petersburg
Reval
ÖSEL
ESTLAND
Narva
sburg
Dorpat
LIVLAND
RUSSIAN EMPIRE
Riga
KURLAND
ibau
Mitau
emel
SAMOGITIA
R. Düna/Dvina
it
Vilna
ST
SSIA
INGDOM
OF
LAND
LITHUANIA
0
200 mls
0
200 km

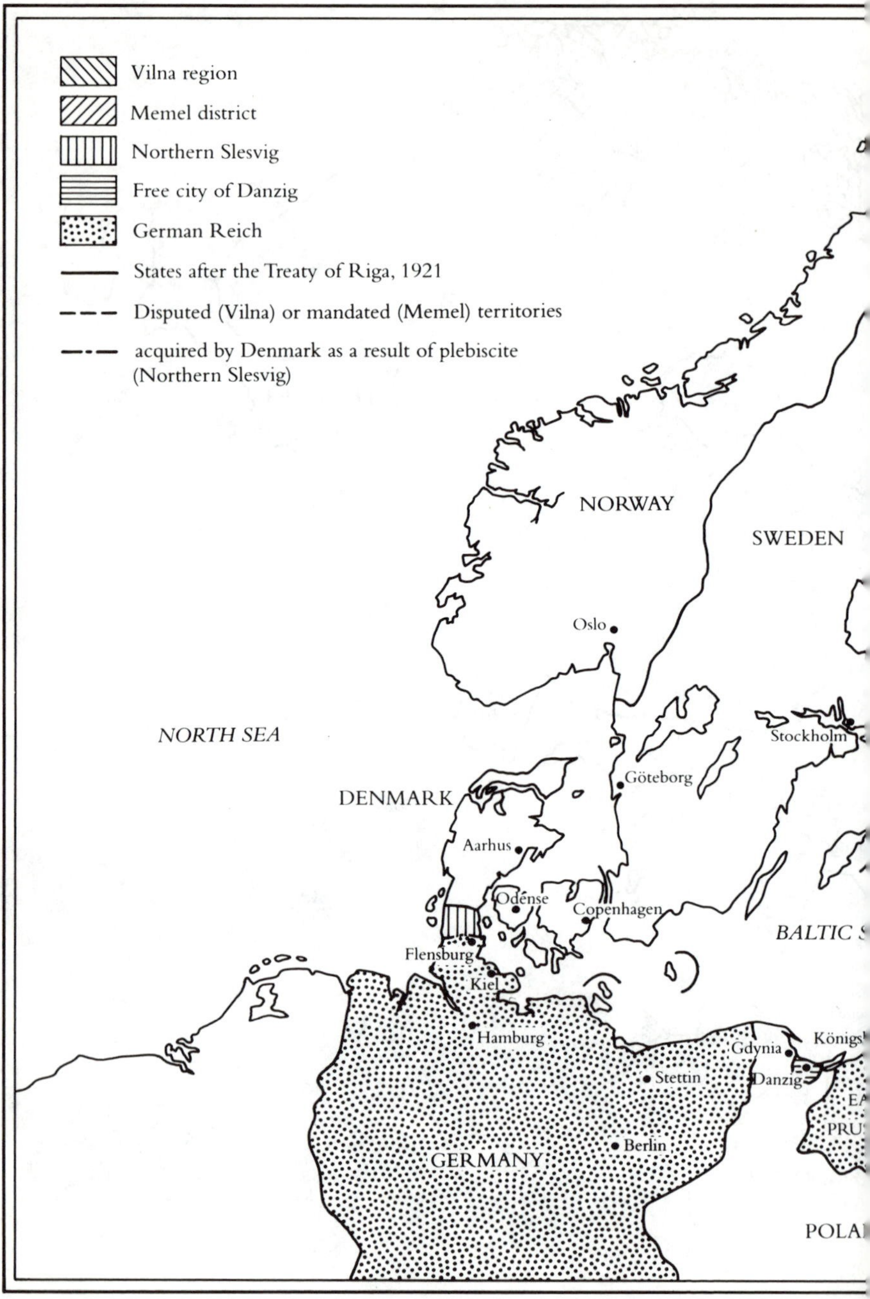

2. Northern Europe in 1921

L A P L A N D
BOTHNIA
OF
svall
Vaasa
FINLAND
Tampere
Turku
AND
Helsinki
Viipuri
Terijoki
GULF OF FINLAND
Petrograd
Lake Ladoga
Lake Onega
Uhtua
EAST KARELIA
WHITE SEA
Tallinn
Narva
R. Narva
ESTONIA
Lake Peipsi
Pärnu
Tartu
Pskov
PETSERI
Riga
LATVIA
ntspils
R. Daugava / Dvina
LATGALE
emel
LITHUANIA
Kaunas
Vilna
sit
Warsaw
RUSSIA
0
200 mls
0
200 km

3. Northern Europe in 1950

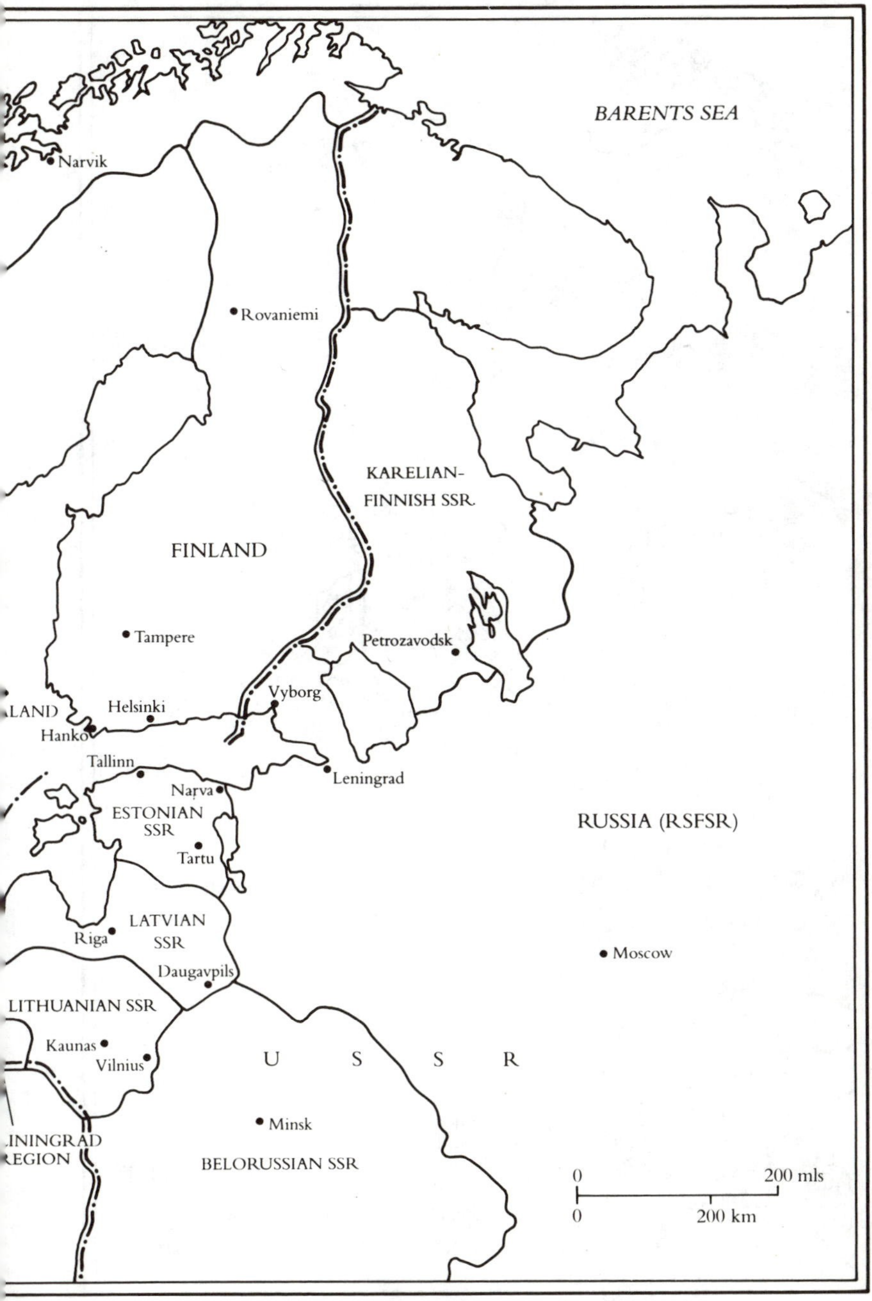
BARENTS SEA
Narvik
Rovaniemi
KARELIAN-
FINNISH SSR.
FINLAND
Tampere
Petrozavodsk
Vyborg
LAND
Helsinki
Hanko
Tallinn
Leningrad
Narva
ESTONIAN
SSR
RUSSIA (RSFSR)
Tartu
LATVIAN
SSR
Riga
Moscow
Daugavpils
LITHUANIAN SSR
Kaunas
Vilnius
U S S R
Minsk
ININGRAD
REGION
BELORUSSIAN SSR
0
200 mls
0
200 km

0
200 mls
0
200 km
Murmansk
L A P L A N D
KOLA
PENINSULA
Murmansk railway
Vuokkiniemi
KARELIAN-
FINNISH SSR
(EAST
KARELIA)
FINLAND
Lake Onega
ÅLAND
ISLANDS
Saimaa
Canal
Lake
Ladoga
R. Svir
Helsinki
Viipuri
Karelian
Isthmus
Suursaari
Terijoki
GULF OF FINLAND
Leningrad
INGRIA
Tallinn
Narva
ESTONIA
Tartu
Ventspils
Petseri
RUSSIA (RSFSR)
Riga
LATVIA
Augspils
Dangavpils
Klaipeda
LITHUANIA
Kaunas
(to RSFSR)
EAST
PRUSSIA
(to
Poland)
Vilnius (Vilna)
Suwałki
1938 borders
Post-1945 borders
Lithuania's gains in 1939 and 1940
Estonia's and Latvia's losses in 1945
Finnish losses to USSR, 1944
Porkkala base, leased to USSR

4. The Eastern Baltic, 1938–1947

Glossary of Recurrent Terms and Abbreviations

Amtmand (Danish): governor of a local administrative unit, similar to an English county.

Bauerngemeinde (German): self-governing peasant communities established in the wake of emancipation from serfdom in the Baltic provinces during the reign of Alexander I.

CPSU: Communist Party of the Soviet Union.

Duma (Russian): Imperial Russian parliament, 1906–17.

Eduskunta (Finnish): unicameral Finnish national parliament, constituted in 1906.

Folketing (Danish): see *Rigsdag*.

guberniya (Russian): province of the Russian empire.

Helstat (Danish): territories under the rule of the king of Denmark, including Norway (until 1814) and the duchies of Slesvig and Holstein (until 1864).

Højre (Danish): the Right, or conservative group in the *Rigsdag*.

indelningsverk (Swedish): system of military apportionment perfected during the reign of Karl XI, abandoned in the latter half of the nineteenth century.

Iskolat (Russian): executive committee of the Latvian soviet, 1917–18.

Kreistage (German): district, or county assemblies in Prussia.

Landesrat (German): provincial council set up in Kurland during the German occupation in the First World War.

Landesprivilegien (German): rights and privileges accorded to the Baltic German nobility by the rulers of Russia upon the incorporation of the provinces into the Russian empire in the eighteenth century.

Landrat, -räte (German): councillor, adviser to the ruler in the Baltic provinces; leader of local administration in Prussia.

Landschaften (German): credit institutions for the Prussian landed gentry.

Landtag (German): diet, or parliament, in the north German duchies and Baltic provinces.

Landsting (Danish): see *Rigsdag*.

Lantdag (Swedish: the four-chamber diet of the Grand Duchy of Finland.

Maapäev (Estonian): the diet established for Estonia during the 1917 revolution.

Riddarhus (Swedish): house of the nobility in the four-estate Swedish *Riksdag*, which was replaced in 1866 by a two-chamber parliament.

Rigsdag (Danish): the Danish national parliament: bicameral (*Landsting* and *Folketing*), 1849–1953; since 1953, the *Folketing* has functioned as the sole chamber of parliament.

Rigsforsamling (Danish): the Danish national constituent assembly of 1848–1849.

Riigikogu (Estonian): unicameral parliament of Estonia, constituted in 1920.

Riigivanem (Estonia): prime minister and head of state of the republic of Estonia under the 1920 constitution.

Riksdag (Swedish): national parliament of Sweden: bicameral from 1866 to 1971.

Riksråd(et) (Swedish): council of the realm, government.

Ritterschaft(en) (German): privileged corporation of nobility in the north German lands and Baltic provinces.

rzeczpospolita (Polish): the Polish-Lithuanian commonwealth.

Saeima (Latvian): unicameral parliament of Latvia, constituted in 1922.

Seimas (Lithuanian): unicameral parliament of Lithuania, constituted in 1922.

Sejm (Polish): Diet of the Polish-Lithuanian commonwealth, unicameral parliament of Poland, constituted in 1921.

sockennämnder (Swedish): parish councils, established in Sweden in 1843.

Sogneforstandskaber (Danish): rural councils, created in 1841.

Stand, Stände; adj. *ständisch(e)* (German): estate(s); corporate mentality or viewpoint.

Statsråd(et) (Swedish): council of state, government; councillor of state.

stattholder (Norwegian): viceroy, or king's representative in Norway during the first years of the union with Sweden.

Stavnsbaand (Danish): system established in the eighteenth century to prevent peasants of military age leaving their home district without their lord's permission; abolished in the 1780s.

Storting (Norwegian): national parliament of Norway, constituted in 1814.

Stænderforsamlinger (Danish): the four provincial estates (Jutland, the islands, Slesvig and Holstein) convened on the order of the king of Denmark in the 1830s and 1840s.

Suojeluskunta (Finnish): paramilitary units, set up in 1917–18 and banned by the terms of the armistice with the USSR and its allies in 1944.

szlachta (Polish): petty nobility of the Polish-Lithuanian commonwealth.

Taryba (Lithuanian): Lithuanian national council, 1917–22.

Venstre (Danish): the Left, or liberal party in the *Rigsdag*.

Verfassung (des Landes) (German): fundamental laws, or constitution, conceded or confirmed by the ruler of a historic land, such as Pomerania or Mecklenburg.

zemstvo (Russian): regional and provincial assemblies, created for European Russia (but not Finland and the Baltic provinces) in 1864.

Index

(Currently-used placenames are given in parentheses)